LOUISVILLE HIGH SCHOOL
FOOTBALL
1913-2023

A NOTE TO ALL WHO PLAYED

Being a former high school player at Saint Aloysius (Vicksburg) in the mid-1980s, I understand that the following account contains numerous inaccuracies. Even when the right players are identified for their accomplishments (depending on which source you trust), other names will be omitted or misspelled. Most who fought to give the glory to the one with the newspaper ink aren't mentioned at all.

All efforts were undertaken to get it right. Player rosters are perhaps the most frustrating part of the project. Even yearbooks fail to mention every person who donned the jersey, put in the practices, and more. If you missed a team picture, for example, it could be that your name was lost forever. Efforts were high to garner old programs so that those mentioned would get their rightful acknowledgement. However, even that, while nearly impossible over this many years, may be missing certain individuals.

This is especially true of the early years. It was common that many young men enrolled in a football program would be late additions or leave school at a moment's notice. A great number of students did not graduate. Once a job opportunity arose, many would drop out of school to begin working and building their life and families.

In the case of managers, that part is missing. It was rare that those who gave their time and talents to help the squad gained any notoriety. I found many, but to leave out the others would not be right. The same could be said, though in a lesser degree, to the assistant coaches, cheerleaders and mascots.

As for statistics, well … that is for entertainment purposes only. If you compared reports from two sources, it is doubtful that you would find the same numbers. Add in another source such as The Clarion-Ledger (Jackson, MS) and it gets even more confusing.

Please understand that the best efforts were invested to get it as accurate as possible. Regardless, this is for you. It is my sincere hope that it brings back fond memories, helps to create more conversation and comradery among you and your brothers about your time together, and reinforces the tradition of Louisville Football. Anyone is welcome to add to this project and continue it for future years. The same for criticism. As an aside, I know there will be typos in this book. It is a one-man project, so my apologies if it does not come out to be as perfect as I hope!

ACKNOWLEDGEMENTS

Perhaps the most amazing thing I discovered during this years-long project is the unmatched love that so many have for this football program. Everyone with whom I spoke was more than anxious to assist in providing as much information as they had to ensure that the football story was saved and told.

The staff of the Mississippi Department of Archives and History played a vital role in this venture. It is a vast undertaking to try to find every mention of Wildcat football in other newspapers so that a complete picture can develop. I have been blessed to get to know all of those fine folks and have gained new friends along the way. To name just one person is not fair. They know who they are.

Finally, this book would be impossible were it not for the fine people at The Winston County Journal. Had it not been for their commitment to reporting on Wildcat football, almost every bit of the history would not exist aside from the memories of those who played. Starting in its infancy, that institution recorded the activities of your team for almost every contest. There are few newspapers who can claim that honor, and it is important that any who love the Wildcats share with them your deepest gratitude.

For all of the young men who left high school halls to fight, and sometimes die, on foreign soil for a cause that they believed in, your service is still appreciated.

To all who put on the Cat jersey to represent your school in every year, share your love with those who came before and those who will come afterwards. In the end, you are all part of one amazing "fraternity".

And, as always, my thanks to Lee, Haley, Ty, Matt, Hayden, and Rhett.

"Louisville turns out boys that just don't know when they are defeated".

The Winston County Journal; *October 30, 1953*

"This town expects these kids to go out there and have a winning team and the kids know it. And these kids have grown up used to winning. They will go out there on Friday nights and try to win the best they can".

Tony Stanford
August 30, 1995; The Winston County Journal

1913–1919

1913

It could very well be that the team actually began play in 1913, though no notations of the squad nor outcomes are found. This year is inserted as informational.

1914 (0-1)

There is nothing found about the early beginning of the season. Only a lone game notation is found thus far. The Wildcats could very well have had other pop-up contests as the sport began to take root.

GAME 1:   LOUISVILLE (UNKNOWN) @ ACKERMAN (UNKNOWN)
            LOUISVILLE 6 ACKERMAN 72
            November 6, 1914

The only comment on the game comes from the Choctaw Plain Dealer. *"The Ackerman boys and the Louisville boys played a football game here Friday afternoon which resulted 72-6 in favor of Ackerman. This was a very fine game. Both sides played well"*.

1915 (4-1)

The Winston County Journal said on October 1, *"The boys are enthusiastic over football. We hope their classroom enthusiasm will keep pace with it"*. A later report from the month noted the mentors as Coach Ross and Reverend Stephens.

GAME 1:   LOUISVILLE (0-0) vs ACKERMAN (UNREPORTED)
            LOUISVILLE 7 ACKERMAN 6
            October 14, 1915

Apparently, the Winston County boys grew a bit in experience as the paper called this a *"snappy game"*. A very early move to within six yards of the goal finally crossed. In the 3rd quarter, Ackerman found paydirt with *"the old pig skin"* by *"hard line plunging and a spectacular end run by the Ackerman full. At this point there arose a squabble and a certain decision of the referee which was contrary to the rules of football. The Ackerman coach refused to play more and the game closed somewhat abruptly. The score stood 7-6 in favor of the Louisville team"*.

GAME 2:   LOUISVILLE (1-0) @ PHILADELPHIA (0-0)
            LOUISVILLE 19 PHILADELPHIA 6
            October 22, 1915

The Neshoba County Democrat posted the day before the 3pm kickoff, *"Remember the big football game Friday afternoon between our school and the Louisville team. Louisville has a fine team and the game will be worth seeing"*. The same paper said after, *"The Louisville team was heavier and their experience gave them the advance somewhat. We have some good material and believe the boys will give a good account of themselves before the season is over"*.
The Winston County Journal said on the 29th, *"Our boys made big gains by forward passes, which the Philadelphia boys were unable to break up. Features of the game were an 85-yard touchdown in the first quarter by (Robert) Butler, terrific line plunges by (Calvin) Newsom, and the play of linemen Wilson, (Baby) Hight and Liddell. Arnett played good ball for Philadelphia"*.
Worth noting is that the Philadelphia paper called this the Cats' fourth contest of the season. Since no reports of games are found prior to the Ackerman contest of the previous week, if actually occurring, they are omitted. It presumably marked the first Philly game in their history.

GAME 3:   LOUISVILLE (2-0) @ ACKERMAN (UNREPORTED)
            LOUISVILLE 13 AKERMAN 18
            October 29, 1915

Prior to the contest, many business owners of Louisville *"gave the football team their uniforms, which they appreciate very much"*.

There was much to be proud of in the Louisville eleven. There were several backfield runs of 15 or 25 yards at a clip. Team Captain Newsom had one of the scores. *"The local team showed the real fighting spirit when they held Ackerman on the 2-yard line for four downs. The ball went over and the boys sturdily carried it back up the field. Although the locals out-played the Ackerman boys on straight football, they were not able to knock down the long forward passes to the end, which made all three touchdowns for Ackerman"*.

Despite the loss, the local paper said the team *"played a good game. The local boys fought bravely and had the Ackerman boys outclassed. But by Ackerman's left pulling out to the sidelines 'hiding' near the subs, he was able to complete three forward passes which resulted in touchdowns. The local boys plunged through the line for first down several times"*.

GAME 4:   LOUISVILLE (2-1) vs PHILADELPHIA (UNREPORTED)
                      LOUISVILLE 19 PHILADELPHIA 6
                      November 5, 1915

The rematch against Philadelphia went scoreless in Louisville for the first half. Philly picked up an early 3rd quarter fumble by Patty and returned it for a touchdown. *"All of the pep was taken out of the visiting team and it was somewhat one-sided during the remainder of the game. The game ended with the ball in the possession (of Louisville) who were carrying it down the field when time was up"*.

Credited for their play was Reynolds, Atkins, "Baby" Hight, and Newsom. Their paper noted that Philly was hampered by the absence of Dewitt DeWeese, described as one of their best players. The JV team made their initial appearance on November 12th against Ackerman. The paper noted that they *"hope they will win it"*.

GAME 5:   LOUISVILLE (3-1) vs WEST POINT (UNREPORTED)
                      LOUISVILLE 39 WEST POINT 0
                      November 19, 1915

It was reported that West Point could *"have the championship of East Central Mississippi"* win a win. When over, the <u>Winston County Journal</u> said, *"The crack football team of West Point came down … to wipe up the Louisville High School team in a warm up game but were greatly disappointed"*.

Numerous reports claimed that Louisville was scheduled to play French Camp on Thanksgiving Day. Nothing was found thereafter.

1916 (8-1)

<u>The Winston County Journal</u> reported on September 29th that the leader of the team would be Coach Cleave Jones. Jones was a Tulane graduate and taught both English and history at the school. His approach was to run the same schemes developed *"and introduced by the aggressive Tulane tactics which have been used with fine effect in all games thus far played"*.

They practiced at the Fairgrounds in the evenings with two teams scrimmaging. *"Everything points to an exceedingly successful season. The entire squad is in good condition, willing and is a bunch of hustlers. The majority of last year's team are back in school and with the new material, it should be easy to fill in the gaps in the rank"*.

GAME 1:   LOUISVILLE (0-0) vs MACON (UNREPORTED)
                      LOUISVILLE 79 MACON 7
                      October 6, 1916

After the defense held over and over at the Fairgrounds, Louisville wasted no time. Their first early tally came on an Atkinson 20-yard reception while the next quickly followed on an Earhart *"cross tackle play"*. Macon then intercepted an Atkinson pass for a

60-yard pick six but it was all Louisville afterwards. The defense held Macon to just two first downs in the contest. It may very well be the most points a Wildcat team ever posted.

GAME 2:   LOUISVILLE (1-0) @ NOXAPATER (UNREPORTED)
                        LOUISVILLE 31 NOXAPATER 0
                        October 13, 1916

The Noxapater squad was heavier, but *"the Louisville boys had the advantage of experience and skill and repeatedly threw their heavier opponents back for losses. Atkinson's pass opened scoring and he did the same later. Then, Parker scored from a blocked punt. Patty went over from center and Butler followed with a 'skin tackle' play"*.
The home team once recovered a fumble and got as far as the Cat 2. The defense held.

GAME 3:   LOUISVILLE (2-0) vs ACKERMAN (UNREPORTED)
                        LOUISVILLE 65 ACKERMAN 0
                        October 20, 1916

The team that defeated Louisville 72-6 back in 1914 came to the Fairgrounds *"boasting of her prowess. This is the first game in which the strength of Louisville's team will be really tested"*.
It was payback time after at least three meetings. The Winston County Journal said, *"It was simply a walkaway for Louisville in which the local boys were able to show that their pretentions to a championship team are by no means a myth. The heavy, swift backs mowed down whatever opposed it and the line surged over their antagonists like a wave"*.
Louisville marched 70 yards on their first drive for a score. Two tallies came after Parker blocked a pair of punts to lead to touchdowns.

GAME 4:   LOUISVILLE (3-0) @ FRENCH CAMP (UNREPORTED)
                        LOUISVILLE 64 FRENCH CAMP 0
                        October 27, 1916

French Camp was reportedly coming back from a resounding 44-0 loss at DeKalb against Scooba Agricultural School. The Neshoba Democrat said, *"our boys will redeem their defeat by Scooba if they can conquer Louisville"*.
Despite a first half *"marred by the beefing of French Camp's team and the unsportsmanlike actions of those in authority"*, Louisville was not to be denied. Wilson was first to paydirt after a long 35-yarder and eventual dive over left tackle to take it 6-0. Newsom was next from 15 yards. Wilson was last in the final frame with just thirty seconds remaining. In all, Newsome had 10 TDs while Earhart had three and Wilson two more. If reports are in context, the JV also beat Columbus 49-0 during this week.

GAME 5:   LOUISVILLE (4-0) @ FRANKLIN ACADEMY (UNREPORTED)
                        LOUISVILLE 49 FRANKLIN ACADEMY 0
                        November 3, 1916

A scant report from The Winston County Journal refers to a whipping of (potentially) Franklin Academy the following week. *"With all the teams they have played, they encountered no trouble in scoring at will"*. The JV may have won against Aberdeen this week as well.

GAME 6:   LOUISVILLE (5-0) @ PHILADELPHIA (UNREPORTED)
                        LOUISVILLE 6 PHILADELPHIA 0
                        November 10, 1916

It was now widely reported that Louisville had thus far outscored opponents 239-7 in just four contests. That report was printed before the previous game to make it even more impressive afterwards. Philly was led by Professor O.E. Vancleave. The school had a reported 100 students and more expected before sessions began.
The scant report from the 10th noted a slim 6-0 win over Philadelphia. A later report from the 17th said only, *"The teams were evenly matched as is shown by the close score of 6-0 in favor of Louisville. These two teams will meet again this season and perhaps*

(Philly) can have better luck". <u>The Neshoba Democrat</u> called it *"evenly matched as shown by the close score..."*.

GAME 7:   LOUISVILLE (6-0) @ ACKERMAN (UNREPORTED)
                            LOUISVILLE 21 ACKERMAN 6
                            November 17, 1916

The only notation aside from the outcome was a cryptic phrase by <u>The Winston County Journal</u> on November 24th. *"While the locals came out victorious as usual, the game was evidently rotten and should not be mentioned any more than possible"*.

GAME 8:   LOUISVILLE (7-0) vs PHILADELPHIA (UNREPORTED)
                            LOUISVILLE 20 PHILADELPHIA 0
                            November 24, 1916

The visitors arrived in Louisville *"fully expecting to carry away the laurels of the game here. It required only a few minutes, however, for the home team to convince the visitors that they were utterly outclassed"*. After Louisville held the 20-0 lead leading to the final frame, Philadelphia requested the remainder to be *"called off"*.

GAME 9:   LOUISVILLE (8-0) @ MERIDIAN (UNREPORTED)
                            LOUISVILLE 11 MERIDIAN 26
                            November 24, 1916

If Louisville wanted to be undefeated and continue their amazing streak of scoring versus opponents, it would have to go through Meridian. It was something that all lobbied to see since earlier in the season. Now it was time to play against Coach Cameron and his Wildcat team.

A report afterward by <u>The Winston County Journal</u> called the team *"crippled"* and added, *"The local boys really and truly deserved to win and probably would have won but the (Meridian) Wildcats took advantage of the crippled team and with fast aerial tosses and fast sprinting made it more like handball rather than football"*.

An early run by Meridian's Shoemaker at the Fairgrounds went to the 20-yard line and they crossed later (presumably by McWIlliams) and added the PAT. Meridian added another touchdown before Patty could do the same in the 2nd quarter and added the PAT. One report said, *"Meridian's touchdown came as the result of a PENALTY enforced by the referee, over the protests of the umpire and both coaches. Another Meridian touchdown was scored by an end 'hiding out' on the side line and receiving a forward pass"*. Earhart added a 38-yard drop kick in the second half.

McWilliams (2), Pigot and Culpepper were credited with scores and McWilliams a PAT. For Louisville, Patty had both touchdowns and Earhart a PAT.

Miss Linfield, a teacher at Louisville, *"entertained the members of the football team the night before Thanksgiving while they were between trains on their way to Meridian. The affair proved one of real enjoyment to those who were so fortunate as to be present. Dainty refreshments were served"*.

Newsom and other graduates immediately enlisted to serve in the armed forces. Originally, West Point was to be an opponent but did not apparently materialize.

1917 (2-0)

There most certainly had to be more games played that those found for the years of 1917 and 1918. Despite the war that was in the final years, it must be assumed that those remaining young men in the school played more than just the following. Anyone is welcome to add or criticize the following:

GAME 1:   LOUISVILLE (0-0) vs/@ MASHULAVILLE (UNREPORTED)
                            LOUISVILLE 25 MASHULAVILLE 0
                            October 12, 1917

One online report notes a game against Mashulaville on October 12 resulting in a Louisville shutout.

GAME 2: LOUISVILLE (0-0) @ NOXAPATER (UNREPORTED)
LOUISVILLE 6 NOXAPATER 0
November 9, 1917

A report from The Winston County Journal says that the Winston County kids picked up the win due to *"timely gains of Prisock, Wilson, Gully, Bennett and Parker. Metts, Craig and Wilson played better ball on the defense. The entire Louisville team played good football both on offense and defense"*

After a scoreless half, Louisville held Noxapater to a punt. Craig recovered the fumbled attempt at the 10-yard line. Two plays later, Louisville found paydirt for the only tally of the evening. A Thanksgiving Day game was reportedly scheduled at home against Franklin County, but if it occurred, no paper mentioned the outcome.

1918 (1-1)

GAME 1: LOUISVILLE (0-0) @/vs LEE HIGH (UNREPORTED)
LOUISVILLE 19 LEE HIGH 0
December 12, 1918

One report from the East Mississippi Times on the following day noted the win by the Louisville team. Nothing else from any source found was noted.

GAME 2: LOUISVILLE (1-0) @ LAUREL (UNREPORTED)
LOUISVILLE 0 LAUREL 25
December 25, 1918

Only from an account the following year do we know that Louisville lost their only game at Laurel. That comes from the November 21, 1919 Winston County Journal.

1919 (4-1)

The season was originally thought to begin on October 18th (Ackerman) and 24th (French Camp). However, they must have not occurred as both were reported as having contests against other squads. That was strange as The Winston County Journal reported on the 24th that the two would meet at the Fairgrounds that same day.

Winston County A&M, in their inaugural season of football, also reported on October 10th a potential game with Louisville on the 18th. However, that did not apparently materialize until later in the season.

GAME 1: LOUISVILLE (0-0) vs MERIDIAN (UNREPORTED)
LOUISVILLE 12 MERIDIAN 14
October 31, 1919

Noxapater played a school called Winston County A&M (or Winston County AHS) the previous week and ended the contest with a 6-6 tie. Historical reports put the two schools as the same, so the confusion is obvious. Now the coaching trio of Bottoms, Bruce Stribling and Jones were bringing their team to the Fairgrounds to meet Louisville. This comes from The Neshoba Democrat on October 30th.

Apparently, the game was moved up a week and Louisville now welcomed a strong Meridian club. *"Meridian(s) team, notwithstanding its long and careful coaching … found in the Louisville team the strongest contestants of the year"*. In the end, it came down to a pair of missed extra points that spoiled the opener.

"From the first whistle to the last minute, the game was replete with sensational and thrilling plays. There has never been a more interesting football game played in Louisville".

GAME 2: LOUISVILLE (0-1) @ NOXAPATER (UNREPORTED)
LOUISVILLE 6 WINSTON COUNTY 0
November 7, 1919

The Jackson Daily News said, *"The features of the game were the brilliant end runs of the Louisville team, the consistent gains through the line of Oldham, the splendid 30-yard end run of Hinze and the superb defensive work of Young and Woods, all in the (Noxapater) aggregation"*.

GAME 3:   LOUISVILLE (1-1) vs LAUREL (UNREPORTED)
                             LOUISVILLE 25 LAUREL 0
                             November 14, 1919

Along with the final score, The Jackson Daily News called it *"the greatest game ever played on the Louisville grounds. The Laurel team could do nothing with the Louisville line and when they resorted to forward passes and end runs, the strong defensive work of the Louisville team made the visitors lose ground repeatedly"*.

If the score is accurate, it exactly matched the outcome of Christmas Day in 1918; a game in which they lost

GAME 4:   LOUISVILLE (2-1) @ PHILADELPHIA (UNREPORTED)
                             LOUISVILLE 7 PHILADELPHIA 6
                             November 21, 1919

One recap noted that Philadelphia was *"outweighed but not outclassed in the brand of ball put up by them"*. They went on to say, *"had there been a few more minutes of play the way our boys were going, the result would no doubt have been different"*.

The Neshoba Democrat may have been referring to a tremendous scuffle that happened during the contest. *"Some little friction came up over the game which it is claimed came near resulting in a free for all fight and is evidence sufficient that these teams should not meet again"*.

GAME 5:   LOUISVILLE (3-1) vs NOXAPATER (UNREPORTED)
                             LOUISVILLE 24 NOXAPATER 0
                             November 27, 1919

Only a lone sentence from the November 11th Winston County Journal gives us the final score. *"It was a fast game from the start and the Noxapater boys played good ball but the LHS was too much for them"*.

Big plans were in place for a December 5th finale against Canton High. *"Canton has not been defeated this season and you may expect a fast game this evening"*. Conflicting reports emerged. One report noted that Canton did not play due to widespread illness while another noted that they could not find any opponents and, therefore, claimed themselves champions.

1920–1929

1920 (9-0)   State Champions

No early reports have been found relative to the 1920 team or prospects. If written, it must have been optimistic as the team accomplished a great feat in just their early years of the program. An article during the season (and a follow up on September 7, 1961) notes the leader as Coach E. Bryan Smith.

GAME 1:   LOUISVILLE (0-0) @ MERIDIAN (UNREPORTED)
                     LOUISVILLE 60 MERIDIAN 0
                     October 15, 1920

A notation from the Oct 25, 1995 Winston County Journal gives the date and score of the blowout win over Meridian. The Meridian paper gave no mention.

GAME 2:   LOUISVILLE (1-0) vs STARKVILLE (UNREPORTED)
                     LOUISVILLE WIN STARKVILLE LOSS
                     October 29, 1920

An online notation leads us to believe that Louisville met nearby Starkville at the end of October. Since they were later noted as defeating all opponents, this was a victory.

GAME 3:   LOUISVILLE (2-0) vs PHILADELPHIA (UNREPORTED)
                     LOUISVILLE 13 PHILADELPHIA 6
                     November 7, 1920

The same online report notes a Louisville win over Philadelphia 13-6. However, their date conflicts with the Kilmichael contest fully documented the following week. Furthermore, the same online site lists two games for Philadelphia that day.

GAME 4:   LOUISVILLE (3-0) vs KILMICHAEL (UNREPORTED)
                     LOUISVILLE 48 KILMICHAEL 0
                     November 12, 1920

The Winston County Journal notes the "*landslide*" game and score but focuses on the upcoming tilt against traditional power Tupelo.

GAME 5:   LOUISVILLE (4-0) vs TUPELO (AT LEAST ONE LOSS)
                     LOUISVILLE 20 TUPELO 7
                     November 19, 1920

The day of the game, The Winston County Journal noted, "*This afternoon may give our boys all they can handle. The game is with Tupelo, said to be a crack team*". During the day of the contest, The Big Southern Minstrel team gave "*an entertainment at the schoolhouse for the benefit of the Athletic Association*".
When over, the local paper called it "*the greatest football game ever played in our city*". Nearly all businesses closed and the town emptied to watch the contest. There was even a parade featuring the players dressed as clowns and more.
"*For a time, it looked as though the team was well matched, but soon the local boys got on to the trick plays which the Tupelo boys showed good training in and it was easy to see the Louisville team was the stronger*".
Bob Clark had the only touchdown of the opening frame "*when he broke through the Tupelo line and recovered a fumble behind the goal line*". David Boswell blocked a punt in the 2nd quarter with Boyd McMillin and Albert Metts recovering. Vic Metts and John Hopkins did the carries until Metts crossed for the third touchdown in the final frame. Tupelo had their only score in the 2nd quarter.
Though the players were "*fair and square*", there was a fistfight among a couple of spectators "*but it did not amount to much*".

GAME 6:   LOUISVILLE (5-0) @ ACKERMAN (UNREPORTED)
                     LOUISVILLE 26 ACKERMAN 0
                     November 25, 1920

One online report points to a 26-0 win at Ackerman on Thanksgiving Day. No other details are found.

GAME 7:   LOUISVILLE (6-0) @ LEE HIGH (UNDEFEATED)
                        LOUISVILLE 26 LEE HIGH 0
                        December 4, 1920

This would be the biggest game, perhaps, in Louisville's relatively short football program. The opponents from Columbus were also undefeated and both were looking to claim the State Championship. The contest was held in Starkville at the A&M (Mississippi State) field but conditions were brutal. The Winston County Journal said, *"heavy rain during the morning left the field in a slippery and muddy condition and rendered open play almost impossible".*

After a scoreless opening frame, Louisville struck twice *"mainly through the efforts of (Vic) Metts and Hopkins … who gained repeatedly through the right side of the Columbus line".* Metts recorded both touchdowns; the last from ten yards. They added another in the 3rd quarter on a 50-yard dash by Hopkins. The last came after a blocked punt recovered for a touchdown.

They added after it was over, *"Today's victory gives the Louisville team the state high school football championship as they have met and defeated the best high school team of the state".*

There were apparently other winning games against Derma and Noxapater during the campaign, but no notation from any source has provided insight.

1921 (2-2)

Once again, there were no reports on the team as they began their attempts to defend their State Championship.

GAME 1:   LOUISVILLE (0-0) vs MERIDIAN (UNREPORTED)
                        LOUISVILLE 44 MERIDIAN 0
                        October 7, 1921

Aside from those involved in the overwhelming win, The Winston County Journal noted little else aside from the following. *"From the very start there was little doubt as to what the outcome would be as the home boys had their lighter opponents outclassed in every stage of the game".*

James Davis recorded the first tally, followed by Vic Metts from a yard, Jim Earhart from two yards and Davis from three yards. The bench cleared for Louisville but the scoring continued. Of Meridian, the paper said, *"(the) Meridian boys showed the same fight from start to finish and too much cannot be said of their conduct on the field and off".*

GAME 2:   LOUISVILLE (1-0) @ LAUREL (UNREPORTED)
                        LOUISVILLE 10 LAUREL 13
                        October 14, 1921

Though the long string of victories finally expired, it was *"hard fight from start to finish".* The Winston County Journal said, *"a break on a forward pass caused the defeat".* Joe Hull had the first tally from 60 yards and Earhart converted within the first 10 minutes.

In the 2nd quarter, Hull added a 30-yard FG to push the lead. However, Laurel came right back before halftime with a 40-yard McAmis scoring dash and McKee kick. In the 3rd quarter, Earhart's passed to Travis Wilson who *"failed to turn in time to take the pass. The ball hit him on the back and rebounded into the arms of a Laurel lineman (Martin) who carried over for their second".*

GAME 3:   LOUISVILLE (1-1) @ NOXAPATER (UNREPORTED)
                        LOUISVILLE 7 NOXAPATER 0
                        October 21, 1921

During the *"hard fought game"*, Noxapater (also called Winston County AHS) threatened twice to score in the opening frame but were turned back by *"beautiful defensive work"*. In the 3rd quarter, Metts picked off a Winston pass and took it the necessary 30 yards. Earhart's kick was true.

That evening, a *"sumptuous banquet"* was held in the Reed Hotel. *"The evening was thoroughly enjoyed by the guests, and thanks were tendered the host and hostess for the good time on this occasion"*.

GAME 4:   LOUISVILLE (2-1) vs ACKERMAN (UNREPORTED)
                               UNREPORTED
                               October 28, 1921

The Ackerman boys were coming to Louisville fresh off a 21-0 win over Pheba. While publicized in October 28th by the (Ackerman) <u>Choctaw Plain Dealer</u>, no final report is found.

GAME 5:   LOUISVILLE (2-1) @ TUPELO (5-0)
                               LOUISVILLE 14 TUPELO 35
                               November 11, 1921

The Armistice Game featured a *"special car secured for that night carrying all who may wish to go at a very reduced price"* to Tupelo. In the end, it appeared to be a rough ending for the Louisville team. *"The game was a hard-fought battle, but the Tupelo boys got the run on Louisville and secured their revenge from last year's defeat"*.

Most assuredly there are more games that went unreported for this team.

1922 (3-4-1)

Like other seasons, little was reported on the team before the first game. The squad consisted of almost all new players, according to <u>The Winston County Journal</u>. However, many veterans returned. One online report notes the coach as Steve Blair.

GAME 1:   LOUISVILLE (0-0) vs FRENCH CAMP (UNREPORTED)
                               LOUISVILLE 12 FRENCH CAMP 19
                               September 29, 1922

Louisville struck first after holding FCA on their first possession. Irie "Biscuit" Wilson took their punt at midfield and brought it back to the 30-yard line. Numerous runs by the backfield resulted in an off-tackle Wilson tally. Hull's kick was unsuccessful and the quarter ended 6-0.

A fumble at midfield in the 2nd quarter led to French Camp's initial touchdown and they soon followed that with another to make halftime 12-6. Louisville went to the air in the last quarter and found paydirt with just 5:00 remaining. However, a long pass to near the stripe led one play later to FCA's winning score.

GAME 2:   LOUISVILLE (0-1) vs STARKVILLE (UNREPORTED)
                               LOUISVILLE 54 STARKVILLE 0
                               October 13, 1922

Macon was penciled in as the opponent for the week, but an outbreak of diphtheria forced a cancellation of the contest. Therefore, the team took the extra week to prepare for their 3:00pm game against Starkville.

Two of the scores came on 4th quarter kick returns. Wilson was first from 85 yards while McGee did the same from 65 yards. Three other touchdowns came on Patty passes. In all, Logan led scorers with three, Wilson and Wood each had a pair and Earhart and McGee each recorded one.

GAME 3:   LOUISVILLE (1-1) @ FRENCH CAMP (UNREPORTED)
                               LOUISVILLE L FRENCH CAMP W
                               October 20, 1922

The Choctaw Plain Dealer said the rematch "promised to be a battle royal". Strangely, there is no report of the details or outcome. An online note points to a second Louisville loss.

GAME 4:   LOUISVILLE (1-2) vs MACON HIGH (UNREPORTED)
                        LOUISVILLE W MACON HIGH L
                        October 27, 1922

The Winston County Journal said, "This game promises to be one hard fought affair. The Macon boys are ranked among the best in Northeast Mississippi, having played together for the past three years".

While no final score is reported, it must have been a solid night of production. Hull had four place kicks and a deep kick. Wilson took a kickoff 70 yards in the 2nd quarter for another kick return touchdown. For his feat, the owners of M.C.s Café gave the team a "big feed" as they promised to do if Louisville pulled off the accomplished kick return.

GAME 5:   LOUISVILLE (2-2) vs PHEBA (UNREPORTED)
                        LOUISVILLE 20 PHEBA 6
                        November 3, 1922

The team headed to Starkville to meet "the Freshies of A&M College". Online reports referred to them as Pheba and showed a 20-6 Wildcat victory.

GAME 6:   LOUISVILLE (3-2) vs TUPELO (UNREPORTED)
                        LOUISVILLE 0 TUPELO 19
                        November 10, 1922

There was a lot of excitement in Winston County for the rubber game against formidable Tupelo. Local business owners even closed stores from 2:30 to 4:00 in order to allow everyone to attend. Additionally, new grandstands were completed for this contest.

It was not the outcome hoped for by the spectators. Early in the game, a bad punt snap gave the visitors the ball at their 20. They scored a few plays later. The remaining Tupelo points came in the second half. Wood, Wilson, Clark, Dempsey and Joe Hull were complimented for outstanding play.

GAME 7:   LOUISVILLE (3-3) vs PHILADELPHIA (UNREPORTED)
                        LOUISVILLE 0 PHILADELPHIA 0
                        November 17, 1922

In Philadelphia, the school actually moved Friday classes to Saturday in order to allow students to make the trip to Louisville. If reports are accurate, Philly had never defeated the Wildcats on the gridiron.

The best chance for a score came in the 1st quarter. Team captain Logan nearly crossed the stripe but was tackled at the 1-yard line from where he fumbled it away. Wood nearly saved things in the final frame on a 60-yard punt return but the last defender tackled him at the 20-yard line.

The Neshoba County Democrat called it "the cleanest game of the season".

GAME 8:   LOUISVILLE (3-3-1) @ ACKERMAN (5-0)
                        LOUISVILLE 3 ACKERMAN 14
                        November 24, 1922

The familiar Ackerman team was the next, and probably last, contest. Ironically, papers from neither town reported on the game specifics. Only a notation in The Choctaw Plain Dealer from December 22nd shows the score. Ackerman ended the year undefeated and their paper proclaimed them State Champions.

Louisville High was anxious to play one last time on Thanksgiving and issued an invitation to any interested teams. Apparently, there were no takers.

1923 (5-1-1)

Prospects were high for the squad as a number of returners were back at LHS. The leader of this year's squad is noted as Coach E. Bryan Smith. That seems to be confirmed in a 1974 article with surviving players.

GAME 1:   LOUISVILLE (0-0) vs BROOKSVILLE (UNREPORTED)
LOUISVILLE 39 BROOKSVILLE 0
September 28, 1923

At least one player was out for the contest as Kenneth Wood, a veteran, broke his thumb during a scrimmage practice. Despite such a lopsided victory, Smith was somewhat unpleased. *"The game ... brought out weaknesses that are to be corrected before the team appears (against Ackerman). Coach Smith is busy developing some interference, which the team was without ... and he promises to have the squad looking like a different team..."*

GAME 2:   LOUISVILLE (1-0) vs ACKERMAN (UNREPORTED)
LOUISVILLE 34 ACKERMAN 0
October 5, 1923

The promised *"walloping"* of the visitors came to fruition. Biscuit Wilson *"stood head and shoulders above anything when it came to broken field running"* having taken a pair of carries over 50 yards. Each time, he ran *"through the entire Ackerman team"*.

Marshall Legan had a 3rd quarter touchdown run of 35 yards and added a 45-yard pick-six. Louisville led in first downs 19-2.

GAME 3:   LOUISVILLE (2-0) vs NOXAPATER (UNREPORTED)
LOUISVILLE 0 NOXAPATER 13
October 12, 1923

This matchup with the Winston Aggies promised to be *"one of the real treats of the football season"*. In at least five other occasions, the Noxapater team left the field in defeat. The tide turned on this Friday.

It took only four plays in the first five minutes for Noxapater to take the lead on a running touchdown. They soon added their second and last tally. Louisville had chances but lost them on a fumble at the 1-yard line and a failed pass to an open receiver.

GAME 4:   LOUISVILLE (2-1) vs PHILADELPHIA (UNREPORTED)
LOUISVILLE 0 PHILADELPHIA 0
October 26, 1923

A report from October 19 noted the upcoming opponent to be Macon. That was apparently scrapped for the Philadelphia squad that tied the Cats in a scoreless contest in 1922. It would be eerily similar this season.

The Winston County Journal said the tie came despite Louisville stopping their opponents at the 1-yard line and gaining more yardage. The Neshoba County Democrat noted that Louisville got only as far as the Philly 4 but *"at no time was the goal in danger"*. That paper claimed that Philadelphia had 'twice as many first downs to their credit and fought like Trojans but could not score".

Numerous Cats received praise for their play: Wood, Wilson, McMillin and Roger Parkes in particular.

GAME 5:   LOUISVILLE (2-1-1) vs FRENCH CAMP (UNREPORTED)
LOUISVILLE 13 FRENCH CAMP 0
November 2, 1923

In 1922, French Camp beat the Wildcats not once, but twice. Now they were set to meet again in Louisville. *"The home team went in with a rush that soon carried two touchdowns over in the first quarter and from then on it was a defensive game by the home boys"*.

GAME 6:   LOUISVILLE (3-1-1) vs LONGVIEW (UNREPORTED)
                       LOUISVILLE 19 LONGVIEW 0
                       November 9, 1923

As soon as the victory against French Camp was secured, the Cats underwent *"a hard week of practice getting ready for the heavy Aggies from Longview"*. Only a final score came on December 19th in a season recap. The date is also a mystery but was probably the Friday following the French Camp tilt.

GAME 7:   LOUISVILLE (4-1-1) vs LEE HIGH (UNREPORTED)
                       LOUISVILLE 13 LEE HIGH 0
                       November 23, 1923

Indications point to a week of rest before the final game of the season against Lee High of Columbus. The two played at least twice before (1918 and 1920) with the Cats coming out victorious in both.

Louisville had the initial kickoff return and marched the ball all the way toward the stripe. Legan had the honors and J.T. Earhart the extra point. They added a 60-yard scoring drive capped by Earhart's touchdown.

Injuries were numerous for the Wildcats. Pat Parker broke a collarbone and was lost for the remainder of the year. Parkes suffered a badly bruised nose and Wood a broken thumb and twisted ankle.

There was an attempt after the earlier Philadelphia tie to get a rematch on either Thanksgiving Day or December 7. Philly had only two losses thus far (Noxapater and Columbus). It appears that it never came to fruition.

M.C.'s Café hosted a banquet for the football team around mid-December. J.T. Earhart *"was elected to lead the team for another season and great are the predictions for a winning team"*.

1924 (10-1)   STATE CHAMPIONSHIP RUNNER-UP

For what was to be such a successful year, it is unfortunate that no early mentions were recorded of the team. The team was apparently led by Steve Bailey.

GAME 1:   LOUISVILLE (0-0) @/vs EUPORA (UNREPORTED)
                       LOUISVILLE 48 EUPORA 0
                       September 26, 1924

Only an end-of-season recap from The Clarion-Ledger notes the 48-0 shellacking of Eupora. No paper found to date lists the details of the event.

GAME 2:   LOUISVILLE (1-0) vs PHILADELPHIA (UNREPORTED)
                       LOUISVILLE 24 PHILADELPHIA 0
                       October 3, 1924

After consecutive seasons with scoreless ties, many fans circled this game before the season kicked off. Which of these two would come out victorious in the rubber game? Or, would it be yet another tie?

Only The Neshoba County Democrat notes any meaningful insight. *"This is usually a hard-fought game, but the Louisville boys got the run on the home team this time and the boys could not offset the gains made by Louisville early in the game. The game was played on a wet gridiron"*.

GAME 3:   LOUISVILLE (2-0) vs LONGVIEW (UNREPORTED)
                       LOUISVILLE 53 LONGVIEW 0
                       October 10, 1924

As noted above, only the final score remains.

GAME 4:   LOUISVILLE (3-0) @ FRENCH CAMP (UNDEFEATED)
                                      LOUISVILLE 12 FRENCH CAMP 0
                                      October 17, 1924

The Winston County Journal's only notation said that Louisville "*went up against the French Camp Academy giants, who have not been scored against this season in football, and laid them low, making a score of 12-0*". This marked the fourth consecutive game in which the defense held opponents off the scoreboard.

GAME 5:   LOUISVILLE (4-0) @ LAUREL (UNREPORTED)
                                      LOUISVILLE 19 LAUREL 6
                                      October 24, 1924

Louisville faced Laurel at least twice before but were just 1-2 against them. However, despite the trip to Laurel, this edition of Wildcat football seemed just the group to change that record.

The Winston County Journal said, "*By outplaying and out rushing Laurel at every stage of the game, Louisville carried the pigskin three times between the goal posts ... to defeat them in their own backyard*".

Just seconds into the contest, Biscuit Wilson took the ball 80 yards to paydirt around right end. Aided by penalties, Laurel evened things by the end of the quarter via a 3-yard Louis Gates plunge. The Cats added another before the half as Wilson "*got away*" and he added the PAT. Patty added the last Cat touchdown in the final frame.

Laurel moved to the half-yard line late but the defense held. Louisville led in first downs 19-6.

GAME 6:   LOUISVILLE (5-0) @ NOXAPATER (UNREPORTED)
                                      LOUISVILLE 12 NOXAPATER 6
                                      October 31, 1924

Only the score, aside from the year-end report, came from The Winston County Journal the following Friday.

GAME 7:   LOUISVILLE (6-0) vs WEIR (UNREPORTED)
                                      LOUISVILLE 25 WEIR 6
                                      November 7, 1924

It was called "*a hotly contested game ... on Armistice Day*". "Biscuit" Wilson's running was a highlight as the Cats played without Walter Patty and Spiva Richardson. Weir's only tally came with just forty seconds remaining on a "*completed forward pass and a 40-yard run*".

GAME 8:   LOUISVILLE (7-0) @/vs EUPORA (UNREPORTED)
                                      LOUISVILLE 53 EUPORA 6
                                      November 14, 1924

The end-of-year recap notes the rematch during the season but lists the game results in an apparently non-consecutive manner. Since we know that Tippah AHS was next and that Greenville was the first playoff game, it must have been on this date. Like the first match, no details are found.

GAME 9:   LOUISVILLE (8-0) vs TIPPAH AHS (UNREPORTED)
                                      LOUISVILLE 18 TIPPAH AHS 7
                                    November 21, 1924

The contest was held at A&M College in Starkville to decide the Northeast Mississippi Championship. Originally, the competitor was noted to be New Albany. However, other more reliable reports indicate it to be Tippah AHS out of Chalybeate, Mississippi.

It took only a few minutes of play before Tippah had their first touchdown "*after an aerial attack placed the ball in scoring position. After the Aggie fullback carried it over, they added the extra point by a perfect drop kick*". Louisville made it 7-6 in the next quarter on a Wilson carry.

Soon after, J.P. Fulton *"broke through the Aggie line for a sprint of 30 yards, one man standing between him and a touchdown"*. Thanks to a *"fake play"*, Wilson eventually *"slipped over the right side of the line for our second touchdown"*. He ended the game in the final stanza with a long pick-six.

GAME 10:   LOUISVILLE (9-0) vs/@ GREENVILLE (UNREPORTED)
                LOUISVILLE 14 GREENVILLE 7
                November 28, 1924

This next playoff step was important to make it official later as State Champions. Unfortunately, only end of year recaps show this tight and crucial encounter.

GAME 11:   LOUISVILLE (10-0) vs HATTIESBURG (10-0)
                LOUISVILLE 14 HATTIESBURG 20
                December 5, 1924: STATE CHAMPIONSHIP; LAUREL, MS

It was now time for the Wildcats, champions of the North, to face South champion Hattiesburg. The Cats, along with hundreds of fans, arrived in Laurel on December 4th around *"noon aboard a special train of 12 coaches"*. The opponent was no pushover; undefeated with impressive victories under their belt.
Hattiesburg pushed out with a pair of opening frame scores. The first was a 40-yard toss from Walker to Conn. Their next touchdown also came with a pass. Louisville responded in the 2nd quarter with an unsuccessful drive to the 1-yard line. However, Wilson got the Cats going in the 3rd quarter with a running touchdown and the first of his two extra-point kicks.
The exciting final frame started with an 80-yard Wilson dash to paydirt. *"Wilson squirmed and dashed his way down the field through the entire Tiger combine"*. As the contest concluded, *"the ball was pushed over by Batten after which they kicked goal"*. That gave the Tigers the championship.
Hattiesburg was dominate in the air while Louisville relied on the ground attack. *"Louisville made one contested touchdown which the referee ruled out"*.

1925 (0-5)

Nothing in found in pre-season reports of the upcoming campaign for the Winston County squad.

GAME 1:   LOUISVILLE (0-1) vs ACKERMAN (UNREPORTED)
                LOUISVILLE 12 ACKERMAN 20
                October 2, 1925

The Choctaw Plain Dealer notes on October 9 that their team beat Louisville 20-12. *"Those who saw the game pronounced it lively and interesting from beginning to end. Despite that the Ackerman team averaged ten pounds lighter than the Louisville team, the home boys out played the Louisville eleven at practically every turn of the contest"*.

GAME 2:   LOUISVILLE (0-2) @ MERIDIAN (UNREPORTED)
                LOUISVILLE 6 MERIDIAN 7
                October 9, 1925

The big event in Meridian was to be not only the football game, but also the Ringling Brothers Show. A special train ran from Louisville to allow attendees the opportunity to take in either or both. Only the final score remains.

GAME 3:   LOUISVILLE (0-3) vs/@ NOXAPATER (UNREPORTED)
                LOUISVILLE 0 NOXAPATER 12
                UNKNOWN

The November 26 paper from Philadelphia notes the Noxapater win.

GAME 4:   LOUISVILLE (0-4) vs/@ PHILADELPHIA (UNREPORTED)
                     LOUISVILLE 0 PHILADELPHIA 8
                     UNKNOWN

The November 26 paper from Philadelphia notes the Tornado win.

The Starkville Daily News announced on November 13 that the Yellow Jackets were to meet Louisville on the road the next week. That would have been on November 20. However, the December 4 edition notes that the Jackets did not play the Cats.

GAME 5:   LOUISVILLE (0-4) @ LAUREL (UNREPORTED)
                     LOUISVILLE 6 LAUREL 20
                     November 26, 1925

Despite a dismal season thus far, The Laurel Daily Leader believed the Wildcats *"a strong team and one that will put up a stiff fight for the Laurel pig-skinners"*.

The visitors made the round trip to the Fairgrounds for the Thanksgiving Day tilt on the F.M. and N. railroad. Despite numerous fumbles from both sides, it was called *"the most hotly contested seen on the local field this year"*. Halftime stood scoreless, but the Golden Tornado struck early in the 3rd on a 50-yard march ending on a 10-yard Weems pass to Howard Jackson. Weems then burst through in the same frame from two yards and added the PAT.

Wilson tightened it a bit in the quarter from three yards for what would be the lone Cat touchdown. Bill Anderson garnered the last tally in the finale from ten yards and Weems' PAT iced the affair.

The Clarion-Ledger pronounced both Walker and Wilson as Honorable Mention All-State players.

1926 (3-2)

No reports from the local paper note pre-season prospects for the Cats.

GAME 1:   LOUISVILLE (0-0) @ EUPORA (UNREPORTED)
                     LOUISVILLE 27 EUPORA 0
                     October 8, 1926

A report from the previous week's edition of The Winston County Journal notes that Louisville would meet Weir on the Cat home field on October 1st. If played, it was unreported. Now they were in Eupora to take on the Aggies.

The Wildcats *"showed real power in downing the Aggies by outplaying them in every feature of the game"*. Louisville scored on their first possession via J.P. Fulton's 15-yarder over right tackle and Fair converted the extra point. James Turner had the next on a 15-yard run to make halftime 14-0.

Fair took the opening kick thereafter 65 yards to paydirt for another six points. Fulton recorded the last on a 40-yard pick-six.

GAME 2:   LOUISVILLE (1-0) @ ACKERMAN (UNREPORTED)
                     LOUISVILLE 0 ACKERMAN 13
                     October 15, 1926

The Choctaw Plain Dealer gives us the only notation of activity by noting W.C. Hight, editor of The Winston County Journal, attended the contest but *"returned sadly disappointed"*.

GAME 3:   LOUISVILLE (1-1) @ MERIDIAN (UNREPORTED)
                     LOUISVILLE 0 MERIDIAN 7
                     October 22, 1926

The entire contest came down to late in the final frame when a Louisville punt *"went straight up and the ball bounced back to the 14-yard line"* where Meridian took it another two yards. Hart eventually crossed from ten yards and McElroy converted the PAT.

The Cats had almost no time to mount a response. Meridian led with two interceptions while the Cats had just one.

GAME 4:   LOUISVILLE (1-2) @ NOXAPATER (UNREPORTED)
                                UNKNOWN
                                October 28, 1926

No notation is found of the final result.

GAME 5:   LOUISVILLE (1-2) vs PHILADELPHIA (UNREPORTED)
                                LOUISVILLE 12 PHILADELPHIA 7
                                November 5, 1926

The Neshoba Democrat gives a full recap of the Wildcat win in Winston County. The first quarter was nothing short of a game of fumbles on both sides but remained scoreless. Philly took the lead with a strong 2nd quarter drive with Black crossing from a yard and Bill Richardson adding the extra point to keep halftime 7-0.

Fair opened the 3rd quarter with a *"sneak pass"* to Dempsey for the tally but the PAT failed. Now in the final frame more fumbles occurred. Fulton hit May *"laying out for the touchdown"* but again the conversion failed. Fulton ended any threat of a comeback with an interception late in the contest.

"The Tornado worked like a machine in the whole game and made 12 first downs while Louisville only made three first downs".

GAME 6:   LOUISVILLE (2-2) vs MASHULAVILLE (UNREPORTED)
                                LOUISVILLE 13 MASHULAVILLE 0
                                November 11, 1926

Another team from Noxapater was on the schedule for the Wildcats. The lone notation called it *"a hard-fought game throughout"*.

GAME 7:   LOUISVILLE (3-2) vs FRENCH CAMP (UNREPORTED)
                                LOUISVILLE
                                November 19, 1926

Though scheduled, no notation occurs.

GAME 8:   LOUISVILLE (3-2) @ LAUREL (UNREPORTED)
                                LOUISVILLE
                                November 25, 1926

As with above, no notation is found.

1927 (0-3)

Unfortunately, there was nothing printed about the 1927 squad found to date. This particular season seems one of the most unreported of the Wildcat history.

GAME 1:   LOUISVILLE (0-0) vs SHUQUALAK (UNREPORTED)
                                LOUISVILLE L SHUQUALAK W
                                UNKNOWN

Only by a report from The Winston County Journal of October 5, 1928 do we know that the teams played. *"Shuqualak invaded our territory last season and carried victory back home with them"*.

GAME 2:   LOUISVILLE (0-1) @ MERIDIAN (UNREPORTED)
                                LOUISVILLE 0 MERIDIAN 45
                                October 7, 1927

The Meridian recap notes that their version of Wildcats *"swarmed over and around the Louisville High eleven"* moving *"like a well-oiled machine"*. Two tallies came in the 1st quarter on a Buddy Hart pass to Broadfoot, Hart run for the extra point, and a Danner run. Hart added another in the next frame from 28 yards while Danner knotted the next before halftime. Hart's kick made it 26-0.

Their last 19 points came in the 3rd quarter on a pair of 40-yard Hart escapes and another Danner run. One PAT was successful. In the finale, "Coach Young sent in every man on the field". Temple recorded a Meridian interception

GAME 3:   LOUISVILLE (0-3) @ PHILADELPHIA (6-0)
                 LOUISVILLE 0 PHILADELPHIA 73
                 November 3, 1927

In the face of what The Neshoba County Democrat called a "disastrous season", things got even worse. The Tornado scored on their first possession via a Black run around right and a Richardson PAT.

The opening quarter ended 25-0 after a Black 28-yarder and Billingsley passes to Richardson and Hampton for other tallies. That score held through halftime thanks to a Billingsley interception and numerous punts. Black added scoring runs of 40 yards and one yard while Billingsley escaped from 60 yards to end the 3rd quarter 44-0.

A Cat fumble set up a 5-yard Black tally, Billingsley ran in from 20 yards and then hit Hampton from 30 yards. The same two hooked up for the final touchdown from 15 yards for the devastating defeat.

Certainly, there must have been games against teams like Mashulaville, Longview and others but no details or reports are found thus far.

1928 (0-2-1)

Coach Sheffield had numerous games scheduled prior to the season that either did not come to fruition, or were noted incorrectly. Two accounts had Philadelphia meeting Louisville on October 26th. Another had the "Choctaw Aggies" (Noxapater) meeting the Wildcats on September 28th. The schedules may have been altered due to a "late opening of the school" that had the team with only two weeks of practice by October 5th.

That same report by The Winston County Journal noted, "About 25 boys have been out for practice these two weeks and are showing up well as a whole". The paper reported on August 24 that Sheffield announced first practices on September 10.

GAME 1:   LOUISVILLE (0-0) @ MERIDIAN (UNREPORTED)
                 LOUISVILLE 6 MERIDIAN 7
                 October 5, 1928

The Wildcats were originally scheduled to play Shuqualak on this day. Only by the same report of October 5th do we know of the scheduled encounter and the game of 1927. However, it seems to have changed to a tilt against Meridian.

The home team scored first in the opening frame on a Henry Earl Dement TD run from close and a "Greek" Hart PAT. Louisville killed a Meridian drive in the next frame with an interception. Now in the finale, Walker Wilson drove across the stripe from short yardage but the home team blocked the extra point attempt to seal the win.

GAME 2:   LOUISVILLE (0-1) vs NOXAPATER (2-0)
                 LOUISVILLE 0 NOXAPATER 24
                 October 12, 1928

The Winston County Aggies opened their season with a 7-6 win over Jasper County. They took on the Wildcats in Louisville and won their third game before heading to Philadelphia.

GAME 3:   LOUISVILLE (0-2) vs ACKERMAN (UNREPORTED)
                 LOUISVILLE 6 ACKERMAN 6
                 October 19, 1928

A report from The Greenwood Commonwealth noted a 6-6 tie with Ackerman. No details are provided in paper from either town.

GAME 4:   LOUISVILLE (0-2-1) vs PHILADELPHIA (UNREPORTED)
                 UNKNOWN
                 October 26, 1928

Multiple reports for months had this contest scheduled. Nevertheless, neither The Winston County Journal nor The Neshoba Democrat provide any clue as to the outcome. One online source notes that the Tornado played and defeated Noxapater on this particular day.

It is possible that the Wildcats faced Newton this season, but no report has survived to date.

1929 (6-1)

The local paper was now fully behind reporting on the team and their early progress. On September 13th, they noted, "A number of people have asked what is causing such a cloud of dust and flying grass over the Louisville athletic field every afternoon now. Well, it is 35-40 Wildcats fighting and scratching for a pennant position on the 1929 football team that is to boil from Louisville".

Coach Roy Sheffield, player at Mississippi College from 1921-1924, was pleased with the progress thus far. He was "putting the Cats through some rapid and strenuous practices and they are coming through in splendid form".

GAME 1:   LOUISVILLE (0-0) vs LONGVIEW (UNREPORTED)
                 LOUISVILLE 27 LONGVIEW 0
                 September 27, 1929

According to school reports, Louisville fumbles caused a slow start to the game. The students continued their "yells and songs" to encourage the boys to a victory.

Omer Melton had the first tally by "blocking a punt, grabbing the ball and stepping across the goal line". Oliver Clark apparently made that possible with a big block. The remainder of the scoring credits are unreported.

GAME 2:   LOUISVILLE (1-0) vs SHUQUALAK (UNREPORTED)
                 LOUISVILLE 49 SHUQUALAK 0
                 October 4, 1929

Displaying all of the "speed and strength" with the "brilliance of a highly polished jewel, the (Cats) displayed plenty of class to a large delegation of spectators". The score was high enough such that reserves had plenty of time to be acclimated to playing. No specific scoring details are found.

GAME 3:   LOUISVILLE (2-0) vs/@ NOXAPATER (UNREPORTED)
                 LOUISVILLE 18 NOXAPATER 12
                 October 11, 1929

A previous report noted that Cunningham, "shifty halfback will be very unlikely or not able to play Friday as he has been sick in bed for several days and is in a very weakened condition".

One report calls this a 24-0 Cat win. However, The Winston County Journal reported the following week as a Cat win 18-12. Noxapater was first to score but the Cats evened it quickly 6-6. That score remained through halftime. Noxubee's Ming took the opening kickoff 80 yards to paydirt "with Wildcats after him like policemen after a robber".

Louisville responded with a 30-yard Oliver Clark pass to B. Melton to make things 12-12. In the final stanza, Clark "bucked the line for the last touchdown". Thanks for their effort; the team was invited to a "wiener roast" with marshmallows that evening. "The team responded very heartily notwithstanding the fact that they were very tired after the strenuous game."

GAME 4: LOUISVILLE (3-0) @ PHILADELPHIA (UNDEFEATED)
LOUISVILLE 7 PHILADELPHIA 0
October 18, 1929

The Rotary Club had the team to a feast on Wednesday of game week. Team captain Ned Peters *"assured them that victory would be theirs if real fighting would win it"*. It would not be an easy assignment as the Tornado were carrying a three-year undefeated record.

"The game was hard-fought with Louisville holding the edge throughout, threatening on several occasions when the ball was carried to the Philadelphia one-yard line". The first half was dotted by turnovers on both sides. Hamill (Philly) and Clark (Louisville) each recorded interceptions.

In the 3rd quarter, the Cats got all they needed. It began when Parker *"rushed through the line, blocked the punt and recovered it at the 10-yard line"*. From there, Clark tossed the touchdown. Four reports note four different recipients of the aerial: B. Melton, Metts, Parks and Peters. Clark then *"bucked the line"* for the extra point.

GAME 5: LOUISVILLE (4-0) vs BROOKSVILLE (UNREPORTED)
LOUISVILLE 64 BROOKSVILLE 0
October 25, 1929

There was an apparent schedule shakeup this week. The Union Appeal noted on October 24th that the Union Yellow Jackets were set to play Louisville on this Friday. However, The Winston County Journal recaps a 64-0 defeat of Brooksville.

GAME 6: LOUISVILLE (5-0) vs ACKERMAN (UNREPORTED)
LOUISVILLE 20 ACKERMAN 7
November 8, 1929

The heavy Forest Bearcats were to be the team's next opponent in Scott County. However, an unusually heavy rain made roads impossible. The two agreed to play on the Wednesday before Thanksgiving. It never materialized.

An off-week allowed the Cats to prep for long-time rival Ackerman. Called *"a hard game"*, Louisville scored just seven minutes into the contest when *"Metts bust the line open and stepped into the promised land"*. The extra point was good. Both found paydirt in the 2nd quarter. Louisville crossed by *"line play"* while Ackerman pulled in a pick-six to make halftime 13-7.

Clark recorded the final tally in the last quarter and Louisville sat at the 1-yard line as the final whistle sounded. *"Both teams played good, straight football; Louisville being victorious because of a hard-driving backfield and a charging line"*.

GAME 7: LOUISVILLE (6-0) vs KOSCIUSKO (UNDEFEATED)
LOUISVILLE 0 KOSCIUSKO 27
November 28, 1929

Once again, a promised tilt went nowhere. The Neshoba County Democrat proclaimed an October 14 rematch with Philadelphia and Louisville *"to determine the winner of the regional championship"*. This was the result of association officials pitting regional winners against one another. If it happened, it was unreported by either paper.

Regardless, Louisville was reported as undefeated when it met the Big Black champions for the first inter-district game for state title playoffs. Their record of victories over strong opponents was impressive. When game day arrived, the home field was covered in snow. Therefore, the game was postponed until Thanksgiving.

It was to be yet another late defeat by an undefeated Wildcat squad. Jordan had the first touchdown on a 45-yard dash. At least one other score could have come from Smythe, described as their *"All State Halfback"*.

The 32 team members assembled at Budd's Café on December 6th for their banquet. This was given *"by the city business men to express their appreciation for the fine spirit and effort shown by the members"*. Letter winners included Peters, Clark, Cunningham, Boyd, Harlan, McCool, Smith, Metts, B. Melton, Omer Melton, Hill, Parker, Ward McMillan and team manager Walker.

1930–1939

1930 (6-1-2)

First practices began on September 1st; a week before school started. The team practiced every afternoon and climaxed each with half hour scrimmages. Unfortunately, the head coach went unreported.

GAME 1:   LOUISVILLE (0-0) vs LONGVIEW (UNREPORTED)
                                    LOUISVILLE 21 LONGVIEW 6
                                    September 26, 1930

The Oktibbeha AHS squad under Coach Davis was the first opponent of the season for the Wildcats. Unfortunately, only an online report gives us the 21-6 victory and that is referred to as against "Progress".

GAME 2:   LOUISVILLE (1-0) vs MASHULAVILLE (UNREPORTED)
                                    LOUISVILLE 7 MASHULAVILLE 0
                                    October 3, 1930

The next tilt found the Noxubee County Aggies on the schedule. It proved to be a tight contest as the lone score in the *"hard fought game"* came from B. Melton. He also annexed the extra point. Melton, John Smythe and Guy Hill were complimented for outstanding play.

GAME 3:   LOUISVILLE (2-0) vs KILMICHAEL (3-0)
                                    LOUISVILLE 7 KILMICHAEL 0
                                    October 10, 1930

This week would perhaps prove the toughest of the year. Kilmichael, led by former player Vic Metts, was destroying competition thus far. In games against Sallis, Bennett Academy, and Yazoo, they stood 107-0 in scores.

The single touchdown came in the last minute of play. Kilmichael's punt was blocked near the 4-yard line from where Maurice Mullendore snagged the ball and *"raced over the line. The PAT was perfect. The Wildcat team as a whole starred, playing witty football. Their opponents outweighed them about ten pounds to the man"*.

GAME 4:   LOUISVILLE (3-0) @ NOXAPATER (UNREPORTED)
                                    LOUISVILLE 13 NOXAPATER 6
                                  October 16, 1930

It was a rare Thursday tilt against nearby rival Noxapater, alternately called the Winston County Aggies. John Metts gave the Cats the early 6-0 lead on his *"line buck"*. Noxapater's Varnardo grabbed a 2nd quarter fumble and raced the field for a responding touchdown.

Now in the final frame, McMillan raced to just short of the stripe. From there Mullendore crossed and Melton notched the PAT. There was a missed FG opportunity for Louisville in the 3rd quarter.

GAME 5:   LOUISVILLE (4-0) vs PHILADELPHIA (UNDEFEATED)
                                  LOUISVILLE 12 PHILADELPHIA 12
                                  October 24, 1930

The game promised *"to be the best game of the season, both teams being undefeated and a keen rivalry existing between the two schools"*. Over 1,000 spectators came for the competitive event.

Louisville crossed twice in the opening frame for the 12-0 lead. The initial score came after a Philadelphia fumble allowed Melton an eventual touchdown reception. The next was also via the air to Mullendore. However, Philly countered in the second and final quarters. The initial score came on a Kyser pass to Moss while the last came on a short Moss run. Ward had not only a blocked punt, but also a blocked place kick.

GAME 6:   LOUISVILLE (4-0-1) vs PONTOTOC (UNREPORTED)
                                 LOUISVILLE 6 PONTOTOC 6
                                 October 31, 1930

Once again, Louisville struck early on *"a chilly field"* with a touchdown pass and failed extra point. *"At the start of the game, it appeared as though the Wildcats would be the victors because they were making large gains through the line and around the end..."* Pontotoc evened it for the Cats' second consecutive tie in the last quarter.

GAME 7:   LOUISVILLE (4-0-2) @ PHILADELPHIA (UNREPORTED)
                                 LOUISVILLE 12 PHILADELPHIA 6
                                 November 6, 1930

The two played on *"neutral ground"* in Noxapater for the East Central Regional Championship with *"a record crowd"* in attendance from both towns.

Lamont Cunningham opened the contest with a 25-yard reverse for the touchdown and 6-0 lead. That score held until the 3rd quarter when Melton recovered a Kyzar fumble at the Philly 2. Mullendore crossed the line from a half yard two plays later for the Cats' final points. Redd cut into the lead in the final stanza after his blocked punt went into the end zone for a touchdown. Their PAT failed, much as they did for the Wildcats.

GAME 8:   LOUISVILLE (5-0-2) vs QUITMAN (UNREPORTED)
                                 LOUISVILLE 13 QUITMAN 0
                                 November 14, 1930

The game in Meridian was initially set for November 11th but had to be postponed until the 13th due to bad roads.

At Greer Field, Ned Peters claimed responsibility for the initial tally in the 2nd quarter when he took a Panther punt all the way to their 9-yard line and eventually crossed from six yards. A blocked punt in the 3rd quarter and a 15-yard Quitman penalty *"for slugging"* put Louisville at the 10-yard line. From there, Albert McMillin did the job and Melton dropped kicked the extra point.

The muddy conditions made fumbles numerous and the players *"were indistinguishable"* after a few minutes.

GAME 9:   LOUISVILLE (6-0-2) vs FOREST (7-0)
                                 LOUISVILLE 7 FOREST 14
                                 November 21, 1930: UNION, MS

The race for a state championship was at-hand and against another undefeated team, and again on a muddy field. Though slim on the scoreboard, The Clarion-Ledger said, *"A powerful line attack that netted 20 first downs during the game proved too much for the Louisville Wildcats and the Bear Cats took their eighth-straight victory..."*

Though stopped at the Louisville 20 on their first march, Forest drove 60 yards on their next possession and crossed on a 10-yard Anderson run around the left. His PAT put it 7-0. The Wildcats responded quickly on Peters' 43-yard gallop to paydirt and his PAT. The News Register called it a *"fluke"* and said *"McClanahan tackled the runner (and the whistle blew but) the runner kept going without interference and the referee called it a touchdown"*.

In the 3rd quarter, both threatened with drives to their opponents' goal, but neither could turn them into points. After blocking a FG attempt, Forest marched 90 yards for the game-winner. They had a chance to increase the lead in the final minutes but fumbled at the Louisville 10-yard line.

Forest was 2-10 passing but held Louisville to 0-7. The defense also held the Wildcats to just two first downs while their offense put up 20.

In appreciation for a wonderful season, the Louisville businessmen hosted the team with a banquet at The Post Office Café followed by *"a picture show"*.

1931 (6-3)

While nothing is noted preseason about the team, one online report notes that this was the first year for Coach Harold Webb as Wildcat mentor.

GAME 1:   LOUISVILLE (0-0) @ STURGIS (UNREPORTED)
                          LOUISVILLE 34 STURGIS 0
                          September 25, 1931

        Only a September 26th report from The Greenwood Commonwealth provides the
final score.

GAME 2:   LOUISVILLE (1-0) @/vs VARDAMAN (UNREPORTED)
                          LOUISVILLE 34 VARDAMAN 14
                          October 2, 1931

        Only an October 3rd report from The Greenwood Commonwealth provides the
final score.

GAME 3:   LOUISVILLE (2-0) vs MASHULAVILLE (UNREPORTED)
                          LOUISVILLE 26 MASHULAVILLE 0
                          October 9, 1931

        The Winston County Journal said, "The Louisville Wildcats defeated the
Mashulaville Aggies last Friday afternoon …. The Wildcats, being outweighed by the
opponents, played masterful football, outsmarting the Aggies with numerous trick plays.
The perfect coordination of the line and the superb teamwork of the backfield accounted for
the victory".
        The Clarion-Ledger added, "Notwithstanding the fact that the Mashulaville boys
outweighed the local boys by an average of ten pounds, the entire game was played in
Mashulaville territory; the visitors never having a chance to score".

GAME 4:   LOUISVILLE (3-0) @ MERIDIAN (2-1)
                          LOUISVILLE 6 MERIDIAN 12
                          October 16, 1931

        Coaches Jim Baxter and Thad Vann of Meridian were coming off a humbling 14-
12 loss to Laurel. Now they had to entertain an undefeated Louisville squad in a game that
promised to be hard fought.
        The opening Big Black Conference Meridian drive moved as far as the Cat 15 but
fizzled. Halftime saw both teams scoreless though it seemed Meridian had more potential
with seven first downs compared to Louisville's one. Things looked brighter in the 3rd
quarter when Ward blocked a punt deep in their territory. Bob Parker did the honors
around off-tackle to make it 6-0.
        The home team, attacking via sweeping runs around the end, finally found the
end zone twice in the final parts of the 4th quarter to seal the win. Both came via Louis
Sutherland runs of a yard and two yards. Parker had to be taken out "on account of an
injured leg" and therefore hampered Louisville chances. Meridian led in first downs 15-5.

GAME 5:   LOUISVILLE (3-1) vs/@ LEE HIGH (UNREPORTED)
                          LOUISVILLE 20 LEE HIGH 0
                          October 23, 1931

        The team was "somewhat crippled up" after the Meridian contest, but all were
somewhat minor. It did not stop the Cats who "gained through the opponent line at will".
        Roy Ward blocked a Lee punt early in the game and recovered for the first score.
Peters added the extra point. Ward then pulled in a long pass for the score and Guy Hill
threw for the PAT. They finally began a long drive for the finale. Peters "carried the ball
across on a very deceptive off-tackle play". Second string players manned the second half.

GAME 6:   LOUISVILLE (4-1) vs/@ PHILADELPHIA (UNREPORTED)
                          LOUISVILLE 0 PHILADELPHIA 47
                          October 30, 1931

        Injuries must have been worse than reported or worsened by the previous
contest as at least three varsity members were unavailable. "The Cats, it seemed, could not
get to clicking as in previous games. Philadelphia had a strong and hard-fighting team but it

was believed by most that the score would have been quite different had the Louisville eleven been in good condition".

The scoring barrage began early with a Moss touchdown from inside 10 yards and a Moss 4-yard plunge and PAT reception from Bowie made it 20-0. Moss added another score from 12 yards and DeWeese nailed his first of two extra points. In the second half, a Cat fumble led to Black's 4-yarder. Moore later crossed as did Bowie from two yards. The Tornado won the battle of first downs 21-4.

GAME 7:   LOUISVILLE (4-2) vs NOXAPATER (UNREPORTED)
                        LOUISVILLE 26 NOXAPATER 6
                        November 11, 1931

The Wildcats were originally set to play Kilmichael this week. However, the injury situation did not bode well for the upcoming contest with rival Noxapater. Therefore, Herbert Webb decided to cancel the contest and rest for the Winston County Aggies.

Peters opened in splendid fashion with an 85-yard kickoff return for a touchdown to make it 6-0. *"Noxapater came back with blood in their eyes"* and marched for the response. Back came the Cats with Roy Ward *"completing a 30-yard pass in the end zone"*. With the PAT, it was 13-6 at halftime.

Parker had the next in the 3rd quarter and, again, the extra point was true. He then picked off a Noxapater throw for a 65-yard pick-six. *"During the last of the fourth period, the varsity men were withdrawn one by one and the 'Kittens' were given a chance to show their stuff"*.

GAME 8:   LOUISVILLE (5-2) vs LONGVIEW (UNREPORTED)
                        LOUISVILLE 21 LONGVIEW 0
                        November 24, 1931

Though playing a heavier team, the Cats were able to cross the stripe three times in the contest. Peters, McMillan and Guy Hill all recorded scores with all three extra points successful.

GAME 9:   LOUISVILLE (6-2) vs ACKERMAN (UNREPORTED)
                        LOUISVILLE 0 ACKERMAN 12
                        December 5, 1931

The Wildcats decided on a postseason game in order for them (and their opponents) to raise money for player sweaters. Though some may not count this as a regular season game, it is recorded here. There is an argument either way.

The high school section of The Winston County Journal noted the season wrapped with a 6-2 record and this game a surprise for fans. The Clarion-Ledger said it was a *"post season game arranged ... due to the fact that the two teams had failed to meet this season and satisfy the friendly spirit of rivalry which always exists"*. The Jackson paper called the contest *"hard and fast"*. It is counted here for historical purposes.

Rambler touchdowns came in the second and third quarters; the first via the air and the last on the ground. *"The Wildcats played outstanding football but were too light to gain much through the heavy Ackerman line"*.

An All-State Prep School list by Starkville's Morris Cohen, Jr. included Morris Lynch as Honorable Mention.

1932 (8-1)

Harold Webb and assistant Nick Duncan were *"real pleased with the squad and feel confident they will put out another winning team"*. That thought came as the boys opened practices in early September. They had *"only one or two positions left vacant by last year's graduation (and) there will be plenty of fight for these vacancies"*.

After a week of practices, he noted that the team was *"rounding into shape"* and indicated *"strength in the varsity as well as scrub material"*. They would mold their team around *"speed and shifty formations"* due to the *"absence of weight"*. A week later, the team scrimmaged with a mixed squad of varsity and scrubs to prepare for the opener against Bruce High.

GAME 1: LOUISVILLE (0-0) vs BRUCE HIGH (UNREPORTED)
LOUISVILLE 44 BRUCE HIGH 0
September 23, 1932

A report from The Winston County Journal noted the opener to be against Atalla AHS. That apparently changed quickly as Bruce was now the opponent. *"The Bruce team was clearly outclassed by the Wildcats but at time put up stubborn opposition"*.

While fumbles stalled opening quarter Cat scores, they quickly made up for it with four touchdowns before halftime to make it 26-0. The second string came in for the 3rd quarter and held Bruce but were unable to score. The varsity came back in the final frame and scored three more times.

GAME 2: LOUISVILLE (1-0) vs McADAMS (UNREPORTED)
LOUISVILLE 14 McADAMS 0
September 30, 1932

Things began quickly with a Lamont Cunningham run while Albert McMillin did the same in the 2nd quarter. *"Although the Wildcats have a light team, excellent playing was witnessed from the very start of the game. McAdams was able to invade the Wildcats territory only twice but the Wildcats held them on downs"*.

GAME 3: LOUISVILLE (2-0) vs ACKERMAN (1-0)
LOUISVILLE 19 ACKERMAN 0
October 7, 1932

Coach Mills' Ramblers did a wonderful job in the first half defensively and kept intermission scoreless. The Clarion Ledger said, *"At the beginning of the second half, the Wildcats got loose and led the visitors for a real scrap, scoring three touchdown and making one extra point"*. Touchdowns may have come from either McMillin, Cunningham or Lynch.

GAME 4: LOUISVILLE (3-0) vs WEIR (UNREPORTED)
LOUISVILLE 33 WEIR 0
October 14, 1932

Ned Peters, called *"Galloping Ghost"*, scored all of the touchdowns except one by Henry McGraw. *"Although the Wilson team (Weir) fought a brave battle, they had to give way to the fiercer Wildcats"*. On the Thursday after the game, Bob Parker moved to Texas. In his place was a fullback named David Wilson.

GAME 5: LOUISVILLE (4-0) vs KOSCIUSKO (UNREPORTED)
LOUISVILLE 7 KOSCIUSKO 6
October 21, 1932

The Clarion Ledger noted that the Cats had *"long been an outstanding contender in north Mississippi"* and expected this to be *"a good scrap"*. The kids from Kosciusko were going thru injury issues and thought, *"the odds are shifted in favor of the Louisville clan"*.

The Whippets from the Big Black Conference were one of the ranking teams in east Mississippi after winning the 1931 championship. They had the initial score in the 3rd quarter *"when a back broke through off tackle"*. Louisville responded in the finale on a close Ned Peters pass to Ennis Catledge. The decisive PAT was true by Peters.

GAME 6: LOUISVILLE (5-0) vs UNION (1-1-2)
LOUISVILLE 32 UNION 0
October 28, 1932

Prospects at the beginning of the season were high under Coach J.E.R. Saunders. Though *"light"*, they were out to *"prove themselves to be dangerous foes even against overwhelming odds"*.

The only notation from The Winston County Journal said, *"Louisville's running attack was too much for Union, and the Louisville line was far too strong for opponents to gain any ground. The second string went in during the last quarter and they were also too strong for Union"*.

GAME 7:   LOUISVILLE (6-0) vs/@ NOXAPATER (UNREPORTED)
LOUISVILLE 13 NOXAPATER 0
November 4, 1932

The weeks leading up to the contest came with disappointing news. Louisville requested membership in the Big Black Conference but it *"was not acted upon due to incomplete information on that school's standing at present with the East Central region"*.

The Cats had passing touchdowns in both the 2nd and 3rd quarters. Both came on Peters throws to Catledge. *"The Wildcats' goal was in danger only one time during the game when Noxapater, late in the fourth quarter, advanced the ball to the Cat 35 by a series of passes"*.

GAME 8:   LOUISVILLE (7-0) vs PHILADELPHIA (UNREPORTED)
LOUISVILLE 0 PHILADEPHIA 13
November 11, 1932

Playing conditions were described as *"muddy"*. The visitors gained touchdowns in the first and second quarters. Strangely, one notation stated that the loss was *"more than likely caused by the loss of five first string players"*.

That may have been the result of ineligibility. The Clarion Ledger said on the 29th that the Cats *"used three ineligible men against Kosciusko"*. That caused the game to be discounted in standings. While assistant coach Nick Duncan did not discount the ineligibility, he strongly argued the point that it should not throw out victories based on existing accepted rules.

As for the game, Philly gained their first touchdown eight minutes in on Moore's 8-yard effort. Their last came on a 76-yard drive via a Bowie score and the Bowie PAT pass to Brantley.

GAME 9:   LOUISVILLE (7-1) vs KILMICHAEL (7-1)
LOUISVILLE 26 KILMICHAEL 6
December 2, 1932

Called the last of the season, this contest would benefit letterman sweaters. A report from The Clarion Ledger indicated that Louisville was to travel to Calhoun City to take on their version of Wildcats on November 18th. The game did not evolve.

Halftime ended in a 6-6 deadlock as *"the first half was a hard fought one"*. In the second half, Wilson, Chapman and Carr each crossed the goal line.

There was another contest just for fun as former players took on the 1932 team. The younger kids pulled out the surprise victory 19-13.

1933 (6-3-1)

Herbert Webb and assistant Nick Duncan were back to continue solid Wildcat programs. *"There is a wealth of big, fast, shifty, but green, material on the squad"*.

GAME 1:   LOUISVILLE (0-0) vs/@ UNION (UNREPORTED)
LOUISVILLE 27 UNION 0
September 29, 1933

The lone report of the outcome comes from far later on November 3rd by The Winston County Journal in a season overview.

GAME 2:   LOUISVILLE (1-0) vs KILMICHAEL (UNREPORTED)
LOUISVILLE 20 KILMICHAEL 7
October 7, 1933

Louisville had seemingly little trouble with the Montgomery County team historically and that continued on this Friday. Coach Vic Metts' heavy squad *"came with the intention of taking a terrible revenge on the local team for a defeat last year and when the game started, it looked as if they would make good on their threat"*.

Kilmichael scored in the opening frame but Louisville responded with a touchdown in the second quarter and two more in the third quarter

GAME 3:   LOUISVILLE (2-0) vs/@ NOXAPATER (UNREPORTED)
                      LOUISVILLE 26 NOXAPATER 7
                      October 13, 1933

The Winston County Journal reported on game day that Meridian was a Saturday opponent for the big community event. It apparently never materialized. Unfortunately, this game also went mainly without mention. The Greenwood Commonwealth reported the 26-7 finale while the local paper later called it 27-0. The first score reported is noted here.

GAME 4:   LOUISVILLE (3-0) @ KOSCIUSKO (4-0)
                      LOUISVILLE 6 KOSCIUSKO 34
                      October 20, 1933

The one defeat incurred by the Whippets in 1932 came at the hands of Louisville. The Clarion Ledger noted that they were *"hard at work in preparation"* for the rematch. *"The locals are out to get revenge this year"*. Coach Davis was missing a few starters but had 13 lettermen back for the Kosciusko roster.

In the end, it would not be close. Robert Hardison hit Land for a 60-yard tally on the very first possession while Ralph Gober broke away on a 57-yard tally. They added three more touchdowns in the 3rd quarter before Louisville avoided the shutout in the *"last few minutes"* on a 50-yard Ennis Catledge reception against the second team.

GAME 5:   LOUISVILLE (3-1) vs/@ DERMA (UNREPORTED)
                      LOUISVILLE 6 DERMA 6
                      October 27, 1933

Only by a notation from The Winston County Journal on November 3rd do we know that Louisville tied Derma, a first-time opponent, this week.

GAME 6:   LOUISVILLE (3-1-1) @ MACON (UNREPORTED)
                      LOUISVILLE 26 MACON 0
                      November 3, 1933

The Macon Beacon described the game as *"a thorough licking"*. The only thing we know about the contest is that Edward McCool was responsible for all but one touchdown and even blocked a punt causing the remainder. *"He started passing when the game commenced and did not quit until late in the game when he was removed to give someone else a chance. Most of them were completed. The Macon secondary could not seem to be able to do much with them, although they were using five men to stop him"*.

GAME 7:   LOUISVILLE (4-1-1) @ ACKERMAN (6-1)
                      LOUISVILLE 0 ACKERMAN 7
                      November 11, 1933

The Choctaw Plain Dealer said of the upcoming contest, *"Ackerman and Louisville have been rivals so long that the memory of so many runneth to the contrary. Both teams would rather win this game than any other on the schedule"*. In the end, the same paper called it *"the best played on the local field in many years"*.

Archie Moss put Ackerman up early on a 6-yard run and converted PAT. The Cats relied on the passing game but did not complete any and even threw interceptions. They got as far as the 10-yard line in the 3rd quarter and inside that mark in the finale before failing. *"Excitement and interest was so high that considerable time was lost clearing the field of spectators. Both teams used their full quota of timeouts. This was necessary because of the terrifically hard hitting"*.

GAME 8:   LOUISVILLE (4-2-1) vs/@ PHILADELPHIA (UNREPORTED)
                      LOUISVILLE 26 PHILADELPHIA 13
                      November 28, 1933

A report from the September 27th Clarion Ledger reported that Louisville was to host McAdams on November 17. Apparently, it did not come to fruition. Meanwhile, Philly also lost to Ackerman by a touchdown. *"This game is the one counted on to turn a hard season into a success"*. Only a December 8th notation from The Winston County Journal provides the result.

GAME 9:   LOUISVILLE (5-2-1) @ NEWTON (6-2-1)
                            LOUISVILLE 6 NEWTON 7
                            December 8, 1933

Newton was no slouch in the competition for the East Central regional championship contest. The Clarion Ledger gave Louisville *"the slight edge"* despite only two losses by Newton. Those were 7-0 to Meridian and 6-0 to Forest. Nevertheless, their local paper said Newton was *"expecting to give the visiting team a good licking"*.

The home team had at least five scoring opportunities close to the Cat goal but each time were repelled. Louisville had the initial tally on a 2-yard McCool dive. Newton's Lawson blocked the crucial extra point attempt. That put halftime 6-0.

As the game was :15 from conclusion, and after a long Newton march, Baker drove in from inside the 1-yard line to tie the game. The PAT gave them the win. First downs (13-6) went to Newton. Hill had a fumble recovery and Roger Ward an interception. ,

GAME 10:   LOUISVILLE (5-3-1) vs LEE HIGH (UNREPORTED)
                            LOUISVILLE 7 LEE HIGH 6
                            January 1, 1934: MAGNOLIA BOWL; COLUMBUS, MS

The very first Magnolia Bowl was held in Columbus before an estimated 4000 fans and, not surprisingly, the Cats were to face the local Lee High School team. However, Lee was co-champs of the Little Ten Conference while the Cats were having a down year compared to previous seasons.

Lee High had their score in the first half via Dodson's 24-yard run but could not convert the pivotal extra point. With only 4:00 remaining, *"The Louisville passing attack clicked and the victors scored, converted and the game was over"*. That came on a 45-yard McCool strike to Catledge. Brantley *"calmly booted the winning point"*.

The business leaders of Louisville once again hosted a banquet for the team on January 2nd at the Post Office Café. Mr. Allen, called the team manager, served a six-course menu. Mr. Z.A. Brantley served as Master of Ceremonies. Again, the boys were treated to a movie at The Louisville Theater.

1934 (1-5-1)

No preseason recap of the team was recorded by the local paper. The names of coaches were found nowhere.

GAME 1:   LOUISVILLE (0-0) vs WEIR (0-1)
                            LOUISVILLE 20 WEIR 0
                            September 28, 1934

The Winston County Journal said that the Cats would *"get an idea of the prospects for the year"* though not *"expecting a stiff battle"*. Weir was coming off an opening week loss to Kosciusko.

Only The Clarion Ledger provides the short recap. *"Weir lost a hard-fought game … Friday afternoon. Weir showed bits of flashy work. It was a clean game and showed much improvement as far as Weir was concerned over their game with Kosciusko last week"*.

GAME 2:   LOUISVILLE (1-0) @ HATTIESBURG (2-0)
                            LOUISVILLE 20 HATTIESBURG 53
                            October 5, 1934

One report from The Clarion Ledger seemed to indicate that former Wildcat coach Roy Sheffield was now in Hattiesburg. Both he and Coach Don Wilmoth *"were far from satisfied with … a landslide over Quitman 33-0"* the week before. The same paper picked Hattiesburg 21-13. *"Taking the place of Forest High on this date, Louisville will give 'em lots to think about before the sixty minutes expire"*.

The Hattiesburg paper called it *"an orgy of scoring with the boys from Jungleland grabbing the king's share. The visiting team was unable to punch through the first or second team of the Tigers but took to the air in the third period against a conglomeration of third and fourth stringers and scored three touchdowns"*.

Kent Massengale had the first just 2:00 into the game from nine yards. Bradley *"pounded through the line for the extra point"*. Bobby Edmonson had the next a few minutes later and Massengale added the PAT. Howard Miller added a 16-yarder and Massengale the extra point. The two did the same later to make it 28-0.

Irvin Rippy then crossed from 12 yards and later from 22 yards. Massengale's fumble recovery set up his later tally and "Deety" McAulay added the PAT. Other tallies came from the teamwork of Edmonson and Massengale while Massengale hit Edmonson for another. Rippy had their last. Freeman Lightsey, V. Reaves and Odie Woodward *"showed up best on the line"* for the Cats.

The Clarion Ledger said, *"Louisville was badly outclassed and second and third string players played much of the game for Hattiesburg"*. The Hub City team was now 112-26 in scoring for three games.

GAME 3: LOUISVILLE (1-1) @ NEWTON (3-0)
LOUISVILLE 0 NEWTON 21
October 12, 1934

The Clarion Ledger picked it a 7-7 tie. *"And each should be satisfied"*. That was not to be as the Cats *"yielded to the onslaught of the locals"*. Newton led first downs 11-2 while Louisville completed only three out of ten passes. *"Tiger backs, behind a fast-charging line, gained at will"*. The Winston County Journal inaccurately called this one 19-7 in favor of Newton.

GAME 4: LOUISVILLE (1-2) @ FOREST (2-1)
LOUISVILLE 0 FOREST 13
October 19, 1934

The two faced one-another in 1930 with Forest walking away victorious 14-7. This one was similar in nature. Forest made a drive to the 10-yard line early but was stopped. Before the end of the quarter, Eugene King burst through from four yards and then added the PAT. Just before halftime, and after a drive had gone to the 5-yard line unsuccessfully, Andrew Webb blocked a Louisville punt and "Dynamite" Weems recovered in the end zone for the last point.

Forest got to the 10-yard line in the 3rd quarter but was again repelled. Louisville answered with a march to the Cat 4 but also could not penetrate. *"Seales, Jones and Stevens were outstanding in the Forest backfield and Lott, Weems and Webb played the best game in the line with Webb starring with many tackles in Louisville's backfield"*. First downs (18-10) went to Forest. Passing (1-5-2) for Forest was matched with 3-14-3 by Louisville.

GAME 5: LOUISVILLE (1-3) @ KOSCIUSKO (UNREPORTED)
LOUISVILLE 0 KOSCIUSKO 0
October 26, 1934

Little offense and strong defense led to the Whippets' second tie of the season. The Cats came within a foot of scoring on a long pass from Mills to Ward *"but the officials ruled that the receiver had been stopped before the crossed the marker a foot short of the touchdown"*. Efforts thereafter proved fruitless.

First downs were even (8-8). Louisville was 7 of 14 in the air.

GAME 6: LOUISVILLE (1-3-1) @ NOXAPATER (UNREPORTED)
LOUISVILLE 6 NOXAPATER 7
November 2, 1934

Only a season recap from the November 9 Winton County Journal provides the final score.

GAME 7:   LOUISVILLE (1-4-1) vs ACKERMAN (UNREPORTED)
               LOUISVILLE 6 ACKERMAN 12
               November 9, 1934

The local paper said the game *"promises to be a well-matched game as both teams are just hitting their stride"*. Their November 16 recap of scores gives the final.

GAME 8:   LOUISVILLE (1-5-1) vs DeKALB (UNREPORTED)
               UNKNOWN
               November 16, 1934

No reports to date provide the outcome.

GAME 9:   LOUISVILLE (1-5-1) vs PHILADELPHIA (UNREPORTED)
               UNKNOWN
               November 29, 1934

No reports to date provide the outcome.

1935 (4-4-1)

The outlook was apparently not positive as The Winston County Journal said, *"The local team is especially desirous of getting off to a winning start although the odds are against them"*.

GAME 1:   LOUISVILLE (0-0) vs CONEHATTA (UNREPORTED)
               LOUISVILLE 13 CONEHATTA 0
               October 4, 1935

Expectations were low as Conehatta returned numerous players with most outweighing the Cats. In the end, however, it was Louisville with the unrelenting pressure. They *"got going early … and kept the ball in enemy territory practically all the way"*.
The first score came in the 3rd quarter when James Mills took the kick 80 yards to paydirt and Castle converted. The last came in the final frame on a Phil Cunningham toss to Woodrow Hollingsworth.

GAME 2:   LOUISVILLE (1-0) @ MACON (UNREPORTED)
               LOUISVILLE L MACON W
               October 11, 1935

Only a report from the October 25th Winston County Journal provides the result. The loss came only by a touchdown.

GAME 3:   LOUISVILLE (1-1) @ NOXAPATER (UNREPORTED)
               LOUISVILLE 0 NOXAPATER 6
               October 18, 1935

Only a report from the October 25th Winston County Journal provides the result. Similar to the Macon contest, the loss came only by a touchdown.

GAME 4:   LOUISVILLE (1-2) vs WEIR (4-0-1)
               LOUISVILLE 6 WEIR 0
               October 25, 1935

Though Louisville had yet to lose to Weir in their history of meetings, this one would be different. The Cats had at least three players sick but were hoping a couple would recuperate in time to suit up for the squad.
The name of the Louisville scorer is not found, but one report called the plays of the game *"four consecutive"* defensive stands from the 1-yard line.

GAME 5:   LOUISVILLE (2-2) vs HICKORY (UNREPORTED)
                       LOUISVILLE 20 HICKORY 0
                       November 1, 1935

The team was in good shape for the upcoming tilt with the exception of
Cunningham, now sidelined with pneumonia. Still, the team had *"plenty of confidence"*.
        Louisville started early on a 55-yard Travis Castle touchdown run. Also adding
tallies were Mills and Hollingsworth. After their last touchdown in the 2nd quarter, reserves
took the field.

GAME 6:   LOUISVILLE (3-2) @ UNION (UNREPORTED)
                       LOUISVILLE 2 UNION 7
                       November 8, 1935

Union, a team that lost a couple of consecutive games to Louisville in recent
years, was back on the schedule. Coaches Childress and Saunders thought the Yellow
Jackets faced *"the toughest assignment in years and (were) developing a team that bids fair
to make Union football history"*.
        The Cats were hoping to turn the trend of losing road games this night in Union.
The home team put up their lone touchdown in the opening quarter on Wilson Fulton's run
and his extra point. The only Louisville score came on a 2nd quarter safety.

GAME 7:   LOUISVILLE (3-3) vs CARTHAGE (UNREPORTED)
                       LOUISVILLE 0 CARTHAGE 6
                       November 11, 1935

Apparently, coaches were unimpressed with the efforts and execution from the
previous game. Practices focused on improvement during the week.
        Like with that one, the opponent opened early with their lone score. That came
on an 80-yard march capped by a 4-yard Wallace rush. *"The Louisville team constantly
threatened to score but when in the shadows of its own goal posts, the Carthage line held
like a stone wall"*. A Hall (or Baker) reception late got as far as the 8-yard line to no avail.

GAME 8:   LOUISVILLE (3-4) @ LAKE (UNDEFEATED)
                       LOUISVILLE 0 LAKE 0
                       November 22, 1935

The *"dope"* favored the home-standing Lake squad under Coach C.C.
McClenahan as the Cats were without McAlilly and Smith. Only by a 1936 notation for their
rematch did we learn the outcome to be scoreless.

GAME 9:   LOUISVILLE (3-4-1) vs ACKERMAN (UNREPORTED)
                       LOUISVILLE 6 ACKERMAN 0
                       November 27, 1935: HOMECOMING

On a muddy field with rain continuing to pour, the Wildcats moved early to the
six-inch line but fumbled it away quickly to Ackerman. However, Mills soon took a punt 50
yards to the end zone for the only score.
        Though ending the season 4-4-1, the paper was complimentary due to *"the small
size and inexperience of the players (and) injuries..."*

1936 (8-2)

All signs pointed to a successful season as Coach W.E. Strange's Wildcats lost
only a pair of starters from 1935 to graduation. However, they had lost others to transfer.
Just as the season started, the Cats saw the return of *"several promising new men and the
return of three veterans"*.

GAME 1:   LOUISVILLE (0-0) vs CONEHATTA (UNREPORTED)
                       LOUISVILLE 32 CONEHATTA 0
                       September 25, 1936

The Winston County Journal noted that Conehatta was "*reported to have the strongest team in its history and has been practicing since the school opened early in August*". After the game, the paper said, "*The local team showed real strength at times on running plays but appeared weak on passing*".

Travis Castle opened with a first-play 40-yard dash and crossed three plays later to make it 6-0. They added three more Travis running scores before halftime. The last score came in the second half on David McCool's 40-yard punt return.

GAME 2:   LOUISVILLE (1-0) @ UNION (UNREPORTED)
                       LOUISVILLE 0 UNION 7
                       October 2, 1936

The lone tally came in the second half when Bill Cannon partially blocked a Cat punt. Wilson Fulton grabbed the loose ball and ran to the 1-yard line. On the next play, he dove across and annexed the extra point. The Winston County Journal said, "*the team showed great defensive power but was very weak in teamwork and team spirit. No alibi is offered for the defeat*".

GAME 3:   LOUISVILLE (1-1) vs ACKERMAN (UNREPORTED)
                       LOUISVILLE 0 ACKERMAN 6
                       October 9, 1936

Ackerman was ready for the local annual matchup. "*It's no secret that they had rather beat Louisville than any other team in the state. Regardless of the outcome, it will be a good game and football fans are in for a treat*".

The only notation notes that Louisville had a late chance for the win while sitting at the Ackerman 5. However, an errant pass was intercepted and taken back 95 yards for the shocking win.

GAME 4:   LOUISVILLE (1-2) vs/@ MACON (UNREPORTED)
                       LOUISVILLE 39 MACON 0
                       October 16, 1936

Numerous Wildcats were out with injuries for this contest and Odis Woodward left the team under doctors' orders. Nevertheless, practices continued with emphasis on blocking and tackling.

The final score comes from the December 10th Clarion-Ledger.

GAME 5:   LOUISVILLE (2-2) vs PHILADELPHIA (3-1)
                       LOUISVILLE 7 PHILADELPHIA 6
                       October 23, 1936

The Winston County Journal called it "*one of the most thrilling football games ever played between the teams*". The Wildcats took an early lead for their only points courtesy of Orville Castle's 14-yard run through the middle. He also added the PAT kick. Midway through the 2nd quarter, Philly garnered their only points via the air but could not added the extra point.

GAME 6:   LOUISVILLE (3-2) vs LAKE (UNREPORTED)
                       LOUISVILLE 7 LAKE 0
                       October 30, 1936

Unlike the previous week, coaches were significantly disappointed in Cat efforts for this tilt. Strange called it "*The poorest exhibition of blocking, tackling and fight I've ever seen a Louisville team offer. We must show a far better brand of football next Friday if we hope to avenge the 6-0 defeat handed us by Carthage last year*".

The final score comes from the December 10th Clarion-Ledger.

GAME 7:   LOUISVILLE (4-2) vs CARTHAGE (UNREPORTED)
                       LOUISVILLE 38 CARTHAGE 6
                       November 6, 1936

The contest started with a quick Louisville touchdown while Carthage came right with a Harmon Hendrix buck to tie it. The Cats ended with a 12-6 halftime lead and pulled away for the final points. One touchdown came on an 86-yard Cunningham kickoff return.

GAME 8:   LOUISVILLE (5-2) vs NOXAPATER (UNREPORTED)
                           LOUISVILLE 19 NOXAPATER 0
                           November 14, 1936

David McCool took an early Noxapater punt 50 yards to paydirt for the initial tally. Midway through the next quarter, Orville Castle *"hit left tackle, cut back to the right, shook off three tacklers and scored standing up"* from 42 yards away.

The final score came in the last frame after an intercepted pass. Odis Woodward, now apparently back on the team, added the extra point. Henry Wood recorded three interceptions.

GAME 9:   LOUISVILLE (6-2) vs/@ OKOLONA (UNREPORTED)
                           LOUISVILLE 27 OKOLONA 0
                           November 21, 1936

Strange put out a request for opponents to fill an open date. Apparently, Okolona stepped in to provide the competition. The final score comes from the December 10th Clarion-Ledger.

GAME 10:   LOUISVILLE (7-2) vs WEST POINT (UNREPORTED)
                           LOUISVILLE 6 WEST POINT 0
                           December 2, 1936

In a scant Clarion-Ledger report, the difference in the hard-fought battle came in the 3rd quarter when McCool hit Jimmie Woodward for the touchdown.

The end of year banquet, with feature speaker F.L. Fair, Sr., saw 18 letters presented to standout players. Travis Castle and Jimmie Woodward were named co-captains. After the feast, the Louisville Theater treated the team to a movie.

1937 (8-1-1)

The Cats had new lights, bleachers and a fence for the field. It also featured the last year for Strange as mentor. Assisting as coach was Cohen "Money" Jenkins. Practices began just before the start of September with a crew of new faces to replace those graduating or out of eligibility. Before the opener, Henry Woods had to leave the squad on doctors' orders while coaches were not pleased with performances thus far.

GAME 1:   LOUISVILLE (0-0) vs STARKVILLE (1-0)
                           LOUISVILLE 6 STARKVILLE 0
                           September 24, 1937

The first opponent of the season was nearby Starkville High. Around 1,000 fans were on hand to watch the defensive battle. Louisville pulled out the win in the 3rd quarter when Phil Cunningham *"got loose for a 50-yard sprint"*. The Winston County Journal called it a 65-yard dash.

GAME 2:   LOUISVILLE (1-0) vs QUITMAN (UNREPORTED)
                           LOUISVILLE 14 QUITMAN 0
                           October 1, 1937

Orville Lee Castle was the hero in the second game of the season. He scored twice, the first in the opening quarter on an 80-yard dash. His next came in the 3rd quarter from 20 yards. Cunningham missed the contest due to a back injury. The Cat defense never let Quitman inside the 20-yard line.

GAME 3:   LOUISVILLE (2-0) @ KOSCIUSKO (UNREPORTED)
               LOUISVILLE 0 KOSCIUSKO 0
               October 8, 1937

Louisville was predicted to drop a Whippet team *"by at least two touchdowns"*. The previous week, Kosciusko recorded a tie. That would be similar this week. The best opportunity for Louisville came as the half ended at the Whippet 10. Kosciusko got as far as the Cat 5 in the 3rd quarter but fumbled.

GAME 4:   LOUISVILLE (2-0-1) vs ACKERMAN (2-0-1)
               LOUISVILLE 18 ACKERMAN 6
               October 13, 1937

Up next was the team that tied Kosciusko the week before their tilt with the Cats. Coach Sanders drilled his Ackerman team in hard practices in preparation in order to *"do everything he can to upset the Louisville aggregation"*.

The only report came from The Clarion-Ledger. *"The results of the game Friday did not surprise Coach Sanders as he knew he was up against a heavier and more experienced team. He is not complaining about the results and was happy to get our without any injuries to his first-string men"*.

GAME 5:   LOUISVILLE (3-0-1) @ PHILADELPHIA (4-0-1)
               LOUISVILLE 0 PHILADELPHIA 31
               October 25, 1937

Philly ran roughshod over the visiting Cats with scores in each quarter. *"(The) most spectacular play of the game was the 50-yard run Parks made when he retrieved a fumble and raced for a touchdown"*. The Winston County Journal called the performance one that the Cats *"folded like a well-known accordion"*. They added that the coaches were *"very disappointed with the blocking, tackling, fight and team spirit"*.

GAME 6:   LOUISVILLE (3-1-1) @ ABERDEEN (3-1)
               LOUISVILLE 26 ABERDEEN 6
               October 29, 1937

Homer Lee Horton opened the game on the Cats' first possession with a tally while Junior Batte raced 70 yards on a 3rd quarter punt return touchdown. In the last frame, Orville Castle added the next while the finale came via an interception. Aberdeen finally hit the board on a connection between Jones and either R.L. Cooper or Commander.

The Aberdeen paper noted the Aberdeen defenses *"shot to pieces by Louisville's heavy line and heavier backs. All the boys knew that they had been beaten by a good ball club"*. Aberdeen was 4-12-3 in passing.

The Clarion-Ledger noted on November 11th that Coach Strange was looking for opponents to fill open dates. Additionally, the Noxapater tilt sat on the schedule for November 11th, but was moved due to inclement weather to a later date.

GAME 7:   LOUISVILLE (4-1-1) vs WEST POINT (2-?)
               LOUISVILLE 6 WEST POINT 0
               November 5, 1937

The West Point Leader showed the Cadets' 6-0 loss to the Cats via *"a hard-fought gridiron battle"*. The lone Louisville touchdown came in the 3rd quarter from two yards. Louisville led in first downs 7-5.

GAME 8:   LOUISVILLE (5-1-1) vs OKOLONA (5-3-1)
               LOUISVILLE 40 OKOLONA 0
               November 19, 1937

This one got out of hand quickly as Louisville scored twice in the opening minute. First was a 70-yard kickoff return by Junior Batte. Then Graham Hill recovered a fumble at the 18-yard line and Castle roamed to paydirt. Early in the 3rd, Castle added a 50-yard run. Before the quarter was done, Horton intercepted and Cunningham got in from 30 yards.

Early the final frame, Allen Pugh recorded a 65-yard pick-six. Okolona got to the Cat 2 late but could not make it count.

GAME 9:　　　　　　　LOUISVILLE (6-1-1) vs@ BROOKSVILLE (ONE LOSS)
　　　　　　　　　　　LOUISVILLE 28 BROOKSVILLE 0
　　　　　　　　　　　November 26, 1937

Originally, Louisville was to play Tupelo but that game was cancelled and Brooksville stepped in. Things got going with a midfield pick by Cunningham. One play later, Castle ran in. He then threw a touchdown to Cunningham. Hill had the next in the 2nd quarter from 30 yards around the left. They added a safety in the final frame and Orville Castle ran in from 10 yards after a Richard Castle 40-yard escape. Brooksville had one good threat in the 3rd quarter that made it to the Cat 4.

GAME 10:　　　　　　LOUISVILLE (7-1-1) vs NOXAPATER (UNREPORTED)
　　　　　　　　　　　LOUISVILLE 13 NOXAPATER 0
　　　　　　　　　　　December 3, 1937

The tough season-ender sat scoreless until the final 4:00 when Castle hit Norton from 30 yards. Castle also added a plunge for the last score of the season.

The Winston County Journal noted that there was to be one last game on December 3 against Philadelphia. It was *"called off"* for unknown reasons and would *"possibly be had later"*. No reports of that even happening can be found.

1938 (7-3-1)

Cohen "Money" Jenkins was back but now head coach along with assistant coach Jackson. The Winston County Journal noted that the Wildcats went to camp for ten days while coaches were *"working with them hard since school opened"*.

GAME 1:　　　　　　　LOUISVILLE (0-0) vs ACKERMAN (UNREPORTED)
　　　　　　　　　　　LOUISVILLE 18 ACKERMAN 0
　　　　　　　　　　　September 16, 1938

Despite the services of several starters, Louisville opened the 1938 season with a touchdown just two minutes into play in front of an estimated 1,600 fans. *"Although weak in their passing attack, the Wildcats excelled in running plays and defense. Although strong in spirit, the Ackerman squad lacked the material and were outclassed from the opening"*.

GAME 2:　　　　　　　LOUISVILLE (1-0) @ TUPELO (1-0)
　　　　　　　　　　　LOUISVILLE 7 TUPELO 33
　　　　　　　　　　　September 23, 1938

The Cats faced the Tupelo team at least three years previously (1920-1922) and pulled out one victory versus a pair of defeats. The Winston County Journal thought it an uphill road battle despite strong morale due to the fact that *"Tupelo has one of the best and heaviest teams in the state"*.
　　　　Tupelo gained all of their points in the first half of play. *"By the end of the first quarter, the Wildcats seemed to realize what they were up against and began to show much more enthusiasm"*. Three scores came in the opening frame and two more before halftime. Fain, Bryant and Daniel crossed with two Bryant kicks. McElroy scored both tallies afterward while Lewis added an extra point.
　　　　The only Cat tally came when Orville Castle garnered a 60-yard pick-six. Said Jenkins, *"If we had scrapped, it would have been a better ball game"*.

GAME 3:　　　　　　　LOUISVILLE (1-1) vs EUPORA (0-2)
　　　　　　　　　　　LOUISVILLE 46 EUPORA 0
　　　　　　　　　　　September 30, 1938

The game looked to be a tough one early with an impressive passing start by Eupora. However, it would not last long. Orville Castle and Richard Castle each had a pair of touchdowns. Floyd Wells, E.T. Bartlett and Joe McCullough each added lone tallies.

Regardless of the outcome, the local paper praised the opponent. *"Eupora has a very nice team and we are sure they are going to do big things later on"*.

GAME 4: LOUISVILLE (2-1) @ LEE HIGH (UNREPORTED)
LOUISVILLE 6 LEE HIGH 14
October 7, 1938

A large contingent followed the team to Columbus to see a game called *"one of the best of the season and was hard-fought from start to finish"*. Floyd Wells had the first Cat tally on a 4-yard run.

GAME 5: LOUISVILLE (2-2) vs ABERDEEN (UNREPORTED)
LOUISVILLE 47 ABERDEEN 6
October 14, 1938

The Clarion-Ledger said, *"The Wildcats out-blocked, outran and out-passed the Monroe County team throughout the game with the visiting eleven scoring when the locals made a bad pass in the 2nd quarter"*.

Despite four starters out for injuries, the Cats scored 20 points in the opening frame, 14 more before halftime, six more in the 3rd quarter and finally seven points in the end. Aberdeen's only score came after a bad snap caused a fumble across the stripe.

GAME 6: LOUISVILLE (3-2) @ PHILADELPHIA (UNREPORTED)
LOUISVILLE 13 PHILADELPHIA 6
October 21, 1938

Apparently, the outcome was not indicative of how much the Cats dominated the contest. Orville Castle opened with a 65-yard score that came back on a penalty. Another from 40 yards was also returned. McCullough dashed 50 yards in the opening frame to set up a 15-yard Horton tally *"standing up"*. In the 3rd quarter, Orville Castle took a punt 90 yards to paydirt for their last.

GAME7: LOUISVILLE (4-2) vs NOXAPATER (UNREPORTED)
LOUISVILLE 44 NOXAPATER 6
October 28, 1938

Noxapater threw a scare into Cat supporters just three minutes into the game when they recovered a fumble and Webb rushed in two plays later. McCullough then ran 53 yards to paydirt for his first of three scores. Orville Castle added another in the 2nd quarter, Richard Castle in the 3rd quarter and, finally, Graham Hill in the final stanza.

GAME 8: LOUISVILLE (5-2) vs NEWTON (UNREPORTED)
LOUISVILLE 7 NEWTON 7
November 4, 1938

This began a three-game road schedule for the Tigers. The Newton Record called their team underdogs due to comparative scores against Philadelphia as the rationale. Aside from that, they thought the teams *"about even in weight with Louisville possibly having a small edge because of a heavier line"*.

The Winston County Journal added, *"the coaches have been working hard with the boys and if the team shows the same defense against Newton that they demonstrated... Newton is in for a hard afternoon"*.

Injuries and sickness plagued the Wildcats this week as numerous players were incapacitated for practices. Newton had their lone score in the 2nd quarter on a Gordy pass to Daniels and Gordy's conversion pass to L. Robinson (or Freeman). Louisville picked up a fumble at the Tiger 20 near the end of the game and Orville Castle eventually carried it over for the score. He also added the game-tying extra point.

"The local boys show little form in the game and the blocking and tackling was far below par. In fact, the team played as an over-confident team that would not try to pull itself together".

GAME 9:   LOUISVILLE (5-2-1) @ McCOMB (UNREPORTED)
                           LOUISVILLE 6 McCOMB 33
                           November 11, 1938

        In McComb, Coach Charles Moore was *"teaching his boys several new tricks to pull"* in the upcoming game with the Cats. Moore was expecting a battle, calling Louisville *"about the toughest Tiger opponent on the home field to date"*. To make matters worse, his squad was crippled after a tough fight with Crystal Springs the previous week.
        The home team scored first with just 3:00 remaining in the opening quarter on Elmer Felder's 20-yard strike to Purser Newman to make it 6-0. In the next quarter, Bill Pope reversed to the Cat 2 and Felder found paydirt after. Newman's kick made it 13-0. Louisville punched back before halftime when Orville Castle hit McCullough for 54 yards and McCullough plunging in from there.
        Felder added another tally in the 3rd quarter from inside 19 yards and Newman converted. A Pope pickoff in the last frame led where he later galloped 50 yards to the end zone. Finally, Felder got in from 13 yards and Newman finished scoring with the kick.

GAME 10:   LOUISVILLE (5-3-1) vs KOSCIUSKO (UNREPORTED)
                           LOUISVILLE 20 KOSCIUSKO 0
                           November 18, 1938

        The Wildcats showed *"the best defense of the year"* as they held Kosy without a first down *"on a soggy field"*. Richard Castle scored from 60 yards just two plays into the game. The last scores came in the finale with Hill accounting for both. One came via his 55-yard dash.

GAME 11:   LOUISVILLE (6-3-1) vs QUITMAN (UNREPORTED)
                           LOUISVILLE 27 QUITMAN 0
                           November 23, 1938

        Despite freezing temperatures, a large crowd came for the wrap up of the 1938 season. Orville Castle *"proved a powerhouse throughout the game with his passing, running and defensive work"*. He notched a pair of touchdowns and converted three of four attempts. McCullough and Hill accounted for the other two scores.
        Quitman *"showed stubborn resistance"* and *"threw a scare in the Wildcat's ranks"* by marching to the Cat 3 in the second half.

        Tupelo ended as winners of The Little Ten conference with an 8-0 record and giving up only 20 points on the year. One of those came against Louisville. Kosciusko's coach M.B. Holmes created an All-Opponent squad for the year that gave the Whippets their toughest competition. That included E.T. Bartlett and Orville Castle.

1939 (11-1)

        Cohen Jenkins began training his Wildcats toward the end of August *"with one of the heaviest schedules in the history of the school"*. They scheduled scrimmages against Tupelo on September 1 and Magnolia on September 8 to prepare. Cohen lamented the loss of his graduate players but also noted the difficulty of the coming schedule.
        Unbeknownst to the Cats, this would be the last season for Coach Jenkins to lead the Louisville squad. The ending would be somewhat poetic.

GAME 1:   LOUISVILLE (0-0) vs CORINTH (0-0)
                           LOUISVILLE 19 CORINTH 6
                           September 15, 1939

        The Winston County Journal noted that they believed the Cats to be prepared and *"ready to go"* against Coach Cecil Myers' Corinth team. Against the first-time opponent, Floyd Wells hit the end zone in the opening frame and Richard Castle via a Wells lateral soon did the same. Castle also recorded another in the final frame from 10 yards. *"As a whole, the locals played well doing excellent blocking. The visitors showed good passing and stiffened up and played outstanding ball in the second half"*.

The game came with a cost as Denton "Dink" Chapman broke a collar bone "*in the last few minutes of play*".

GAME 2:   LOUISVILLE (1-0) vs ACKERMAN (UNREPORTED)
                 LOUISVILLE W ACKERMAN L
                 September 22, 1939

The game would come without not only Chapman, but also Coach Jenkins. Apparently, he "*suffered an acute attack of appendicitis and was rushed to the hospital on the Wednesday of game week*". Ackerman was described a "*large, husky and experienced*" with only one lost player from the previous season.

A report from the article on the Natchez contest the following week noted this contest as a Cat victory.

GAME 3:   LOUISVILLE (2-0) vs NATCHEZ (1-0)
                 LOUISVILLE 32 NATCHEZ 0
                 September 29, 1939

Coaches Truitt and Goussett practiced their blue and white team in hard, daily scrimmages to prepare for the trip to Louisville. In their previous game against Meadville, they "*ran up a large score*" with a 44-6 victory.

In front of a "*record crowd*", Floyd Wells pulled in a 50-yard scoring pass early to set the tone. Richard Castle dashed on two long runs for a pair of tallies while Joe McCullough and H.C. Earhart added the last pair. Graham Hill converted two extra points. One touchdown came on a 40-yard pick-six while another came via a fumble.

Coach Truitt noted, "*We are glad we played Louisville. They had a wonderful high school team and played a differed class of football to what we accustomed. Louisville is the kind of team we want to keep on the schedule and plan to have them here in 1940*". The visitors were entertained in a Louisville home "*and commented highly on the spirit of friendliness and hospitality shown them*".

After the game, Jenkins, his wife and another couple went to Baton Rouge for the LSU-Tennessee football game.

GAME 4:   LOUISVILLE (3-0) vs UNION (2-0-1)
                 LOUISVILLE 19 UNION 0
                 October 6, 1939

Coaches Childress and Smith called their team "*young and inexperienced*" and efforted to get the fundamentals down before their next contest. Nevertheless, The Union Appeal reports show them to be 2-0-1 entering the contest.

That paper also tells us "*It was a hard-fought game throughout with both teams doing their best*". The Cats' first score came in the second period on Hill's 40-yard dash to make halftime 6-0. McCullough added a 1-yarder and Hill converted. The final tally came on Richard Castle's 30-yard dash. Louisville led in first downs 11-8. Union lost only two more games this year on the way to a 7-2-1 season.

GAME 5:   LOUISVILLE (4-0) @ LAUREL (4-0)
                 LOUISVILLE 7 LAUREL 38
                 October 13, 1939

Regardless of the outcome of this tilt, Laurel still stood atop the Big Eight conference since Louisville was not in the mix. It was definitely a tough fight for the undefeated Cats despite being 2-3 against them from 1918 to 1925. The Enterprise Journal in McComb picked it 20-7 in favor of the Tornados.

To the surprise of many, the contest sat tied 7-7 at halftime. Laurel was first on a Lidell Howard punt block with Joe Connolly racing 19 yards to paydirt. Before halftime, McCullough ran for six yards before handing to Howard Clark for the remainder of the 39 yards. Laurel took over from there as Harold Pearcy found the end one three times (43, 18 and 5 yards) while Ray Woodward added a few more.

GAME 6:   LOUISVILLE (4-1) vs PHILADELPHIA (UNREPORTED)
                 LOUISVILLE 27 PHILADELPHIA 0
                 October 20, 1939

The local paper called it *"hard-fought (but) never in doubt"*. The first half ended 6-0. In the next half, Castle took the kickoff 90 yards to the 9-yard line and Wells ran in standing up. Castle then ran in from 41 yards and Clark Horton added the next. The Neshoba County Democrat reported the final as 26-0.

GAME 7:   LOUISVILLE (5-1) @ YAZOO CITY (UNREPORTED)
                                LOUISVILLE 46 YAZOO CITY 6
                                October 27, 1939

Despite tackling called *"the poorest of the season"*, the Cats moved to 5-1 on the year. Four plays into the game, Castle scored his first of four touchdowns from long distance. Hill added his first of four extra points. After Yazoo City cut it to 7-6 when Wilburn charged across in the opening frame, Louisville took over.

An Indian fumble at their 7-yard line soon turned into a Hill touchdown while Earhart did the same before halftime to make it 20-6. He added the next from 18 yards to start the 3rd quarter after a partially blocked punt. Castle's long punt return set up a McGaugh dash afterwards while Hill grabbed an interception. Wilburn turned that into a 36-yard escape for another tally. Harris tallied the last for the Cats to end scoring.

Louisville was 4-4-1 for 125 yards in the air and a total of 253 yards. *"Coach Jenkins was much pleased with some of the young men in this game"*.

GAME 8:   LOUISVILLE (6-1) vs NOXAPATER (UNREPORTED)
                                LOUISVILLE 32 NOXAPATER 12
                                November 3, 1939

After two missed contests due to injuries, McCullough and Chapman were finally back in uniform. *"The local squad clearly outclassed the opposing team, although the game Noxapater squad, led by Webb, put up a brave and interesting fight"*.

Webb started with a 50-yard run and eventual touchdown to start for Noxapater. McCullough opened Cat scoring with a touchdown while Earhart and Richard Castle added two more before halftime. Boots Jay got one in the 3rd quarter and Clarence Castle did the same in the finale. Hill and Dan Harris added extra points. Webb had the first Noxapater score in the opening frame while Covington did the same in the last.

GAME 9:   LOUISVILLE (7-1) @ KOSCIUSKO (ONE LOSS)
                                LOUISVILLE 14 KOSCIUSKO 7
                                November 10, 1939

The Kosciusko paper called the contest *"a good game, hard-fought throughout"*. They added, *"Without a doubt, Louisville had the best team seen here this year"*. Injuries kept a majority of Whippet starters off of the field. *"Although the local boys put up a gallant fight, the superior weight and reserve power of the visitors finally showed up in the results"*.

GAME 10:   LOUISVILLE (8-1) @ NEWTON (8-0)
                                LOUISVILLE 19 NEWTON 6
                                November 16, 1939

The Clarion-Ledger called these two teams *"the two leading teams in the state"*. The game was moved up a day at Byrd Field *"at the request of the coaches and students of other school in this second ... so that they can see the game"*. There was good reason as the opponents for Newton included Meridian and Hattiesburg; both teams falling to the Tigers.

Only Clarion-Ledger reports note the final. The November 18 edition gives the score while the article on the 19th is in praise of the group. *"Hats off to Cohen Jenkins and his scrappy little Louisville High team once again! Without a man as heavy as 170 pounds, the scrapping little boys from up in Winston, well-coached and smartly trained, took the measure of undefeated Newton High"*.

GAME 11:   LOUISVILLE (9-1) vs STARKVILLE (UNREPORTED)
                                LOUISVILLE 6 STARKVILLE 0
                                November 24, 1939

The Starkville Daily News called it the *"hardest-fought game of the year"* for the locals. The lone tally came via Long's 38-yard dash.

GAME 12:   LOUISVILLE (10-1) @ CLARKSDALE (UNREPORTED)
                                  LOUISVILLE 13 CLARKSDALE 12
                                  December 5, 1939

Although Louisville was to end the season before Thanksgiving, they had one last contest to play. It came against a Coahoma County team and perhaps for good reason.

The Sun Herald (Biloxi) said, *"Clarksdale closed by losing to a fast Louisville High squad 13-12. A line buck by Castle and a long pass to Wells gave the visitors two touchdowns in the second period and Hill kicked one extra point. Clarksdale scored on (Conerly) passes to Taylor and (a Taylor pass to) Tarzi but failed to make either extra point".*

The Greenwood Commonwealth noted the win and, more importantly, that Jenkins would now take the reins of the team in Clarksdale. *"Of course, the Clarksdale school didn't hire Jenkins after last night's game, but that victory certainly gives him an impressive start".*

The Clarion-Ledger reported later, *"He has accomplished wonders at Louisville this fall with a light squad but gives all the credit to the boys. Jenkins told us the other day that his team was 'the fighin'est bunch of boys I've even seen".*

The team banquet was held around December 13 at Warrior's Café with numerous short speeches. Guest speakers included Weens Baskin, assistant coach at Ole Miss, and Bill Schneller, captain of the Rebel team. The Cats were later named East Central Region champions.

1940-1949

1940 (6-4-2)

The Cats entered their third week of practice by September 9th well before the August 25th opening of school. The new mentor, ex Tupelo coach Elzie Hinze, and assistant Haskell Jackson had to replace a number of departed senior starters.

"Many of the hopefuls are new men as the majority of the men on the 1939 team were lost through graduation and the Louisville squad will rise or fall this season on the play of newcomers slated to take over starting assignments..."

The team started with a 10-day football camp at Rock Bottom in Macon where the coach called them *"all in good shape"*. An early scrimmage game showed promise as the Cats beat Tupelo, called *"one of the strongest Big Eight teams"*, 7-0. The lone tally came on a Castle 40-yard run. Tupelo picked off a Cat throw but could not pass the 2-yard line.

GAME 1:   LOUISVILLE (0-0) vs ETHEL (0-0)
           LOUISVILLE 67 ETHEL 0
           September 13, 1940

It's was an overwhelming start for Louisville against Ethel's Coach Cy Butts. Scoring started within minutes *"and continued wildly throughout the game"*. The only other notation was, *"Louisville displayed exceptionally good form for an initial game and substituted freely using practically all men against the light, scrapping Ethel squad"*.

GAME 2:   LOUISVILLE (1-0) vs ACKERMAN (UNREPORTED)
           LOUISVILLE 33 ACKERMAN 0
           September 20, 1940

The Cats were again out-weighed, but it did not matter. An early Jack Bray pick taken 85 yards set up Richard Castle's touchdown plunge. Dan Harris ran in for the extra point. That lead grew to 27-0 at halftime courtesy of another Castle run and two more by Harris. Fred Hudson had the last tally.

"The game showed up several weak spots in the Louisville defense which will have to be ironed out before the journey to Union Friday for the third game of the season".

GAME 3:   LOUISVILLE (2-0) @ UNION (2-0)
           LOUISVILLE 7 UNION 7
           September 26, 1940

Union, though replacing a number of veterans, outscored opponents 52-0 thus far. The contest was originally set for Friday but moved to Thursday to allow more to come.

Two initial deep Louisville drives went for naught on a fumble and loss of downs. In the 3rd quarter, a George Worthen pass to Rob Lewis gave them the touchdown and the conversion made it 7-0. Late in the game, the Cats drove to the 4-yard line and then ran over right end for the tally. The conversion tied the game. The game ended with Louisville at the Union 35.

The tie was made worse by a leg injury to Richard Castle; now out indefinitely.

GAME 4:   LOUISVILLE (2-0-1) vs NOXAPATER (UNREPORTED)
           LOUISVILLE 27 NOXAPATER 6
           October 4, 1940

"Hopefully outclassed from the start of the game, the Noxapater squad nevertheless fought gamely. Louisville's defense and offense proved too much for them". No other game specifics are found.

GAME 5:   LOUISVILLE (3-0-1) @ MERIDIAN (UNREPORTED)
           LOUISVILLE 0 MERIDIAN 59
           October 11, 1940

This road trip brought the Wildcats back to earth as Meridian completely thumped the visitors. Meridian scores came on *"long runs and passes"*. Eleven players shared in the embarrassment with eight scoring touchdowns and three others extra points.

The only score of the first came on Hardy Henry's 30-yarder from R.C. Britt. Jay Jackson kicked the PAT. The blue and white added 33 more in the 2nd quarter. First was a Forrest Page lateral to Kenneth Strange and Bill Thornton kick. Britt ran from 50 more, Henry for 15 yards (Thornton PAT), Dan Gentry ran in from 13 yards, Johnson interception leading to his 48-yard pass to Culpepper (Pete Piggott kick) and 60-yard Page escape.

Johnson picked it off again in the 3rd quarter to no avail but he later ran 30 yards to paydirt. The last came after Williamson blocked a punt and Piggott found paydirt.

GAME 6:   LOUISVILLE (3-1-1) @ PHILADELPHIA (FOUR GAMES)
                         LOUISVILLE 6 PHILADELPHIA 7
                         October 18, 1940

Like Louisville, the home team under coach Luther Hollingsworth was also coming off a loss. This came at the hands of Newton. However, Richard Castle appeared to be back for the Cats and could increase the odds as the visitors would be *"in there scrapping all the way"*.

Harris put the Wildcats ahead before halftime from the one-foot line and after a *"long pass from Castle to Wells"*. Philly took the lead when Sony Jones dashed 62 yards to paydirt and then added the crucial extra point. The Tornado has a pair of scores called back in addition to a James Hardy 40-yard run and an M. Jones interception.

GAME 7:   LOUISVILLE (3-2-1) @ YAZOO CITY (UNREPORTED)
                         LOUISVILLE 27 YAZOO CITY 7
                         October 25, 1940

The Yazoo Semi-Weekly says that the Cats won *"a one-sided game"*. Harris had the first on a run and extra point. Wallace Romedy recovered a blocked punt in the 2nd quarter and Harris against converted. Minutes later, Howard Clark ran in for the third score.

Minutes later, Harris hit Wells for another and Wells again converted. The lone Indian score on a 55-yard Rainwater dash.

GAME 8:   LOUISVILLE (4-2-1) vs NEWTON (UNDEFEATED)
                         LOUISVILLE 0 NEWTON 0
                         November 1, 1940

Called *"a record crowd"* and *"one of the largest ever to witness a ball game in this section"*, it ended as the second tie of the season for the Wildcats. The Winston County Journal noted that *"Both teams displayed unbelievable determination and grit, never allowing the other to reach paydirt..."*.

Both were still in search of the end zone as the game expired. The paper said the Cats may have won *"had (she) not been halted by the clock"*. The local Newton paper noted that the field was so muddy that even open-field runners lost their footing and slipped.

GAME 9:   LOUISVILLE (4-2-2) vs SALLIS (6-2)
                         LOUISVILLE 33 SALLIS 7
                         November 8, 1940

Coach Robert Jelks had 27 candidates for spots at the beginning of the season, including seven lettermen. By kickoff, they apparently suffered losses only to Greenwood and Kosciusko; both by large margins.

Clarence Castle opened the game with a score while Richard Castle did likewise. Harris annexed both extra points. Sallis hit the board in the 2nd quarter on a Kuykendall throw to Allen. Kuykendall ran around the end for the PAT to make halftime 14-7. Their local paper gives credit to Newton Allen via his 50-yard escape.

In the 3rd quarter, Harris got in up the middle while Howard Clark did the same. Again, Harris added a PAT. The final score came in the last period when Nathan Hudson recorded a pick-six.

GAME 10:   LOUISVILLE (5-2-2) vs QUITMAN (UNREPORTED)
                         LOUISVILLE 33 QUITMAN 0
                         November 15, 1940

On a bitterly cold evening, the game ended up being a competition of reserves. *"Louisville substituted freely using practically all reserves and the Quitman team played many substitutions"*. The Cats put up points each of the four quarters.

GAME 11:   LOUISVILLE (6-2-2) @ STARKVILLE (9-0-1)
                           LOUISVILLE 0 STARKVILLE 26
                           November 20, 1940

This was to be a Wednesday night event against the visiting Yellow Jackets from nearby Starkville. The Oktibbeha County team sat undefeated and outscored opponents 246-14. Over 5,000 *"enthusiastic fans"* watched the Jackets play *"a smart, heads-up game all the way"*.

Joe Ed Robinson found Hindu Reynolds from 10 yards at the beginning of the 3rd quarter while Robinson added the next from the same distance in the final frame. Robinson dove in from two yards while Bill Bell recorded a 30-yard pick-six to seal it.

GAME 12:   LOUISVILLE (6-3-2) vs KOSCIUSKO (7-2)
                           LOUISVILLE 0 KOSCIUSKO 7
                           November 29, 1940

Coach Walter Scales brought his strong Whippet team to Winston County in an attempt to get revenge on the 14-7 defeat the previous year. The Clarion-Ledger said, *"the Whippets are confident they will offset the setback suffered last year"*.

Another cold game was on hand but in front of *"a record crowd"* to wrap the 1940 season. Just before the halftime whistle, Kosciusko tallied the only points of the game. *"Although the Wildcats made numerous threats, the strong Whippets never allowed them to reach paydirt and the teams battled through the third and fourth quarters with neither side scoring"*.

1941 (8-3)

Elzie Hinze and assistant Haskell Jackson were back with a team of 37 candidates but without many key players lost due to graduation. *"An ample supply of newcomers along with last year's reserves make prospects encouraging"*. The squad did show potential in a preseason scrimmage by defeating Clarksdale 7-6.

In that pre-season tilt, Clarksdale hit the board first on a Kersterton run around right. Early in the final frame, Dan Harris found paydirt and Fred Hudson added the winning extra point.

GAME 1:   LOUISVILLE (0-0) vs NOXAPATER (UNREPORTED)
                           LOUISVILLE 33 NOXAPATER 0
                           September 12, 1941

The Cats scored twice in the opening frame via end runs. Scores in the game came from Pete Castle, Hughes, Harris, Bob Clark and Jones. Harris added a pair of extra points while Gene Yarbrough had the last. Louisville led in first downs 11-4 and went 2-5 in the air.

GAME 2:   LOUISVILLE (1-0) vs ACKERMAN (UNREPORTED)
                           LOUISVILLE 35 ACKERMAN 0
                           September 19, 1941

"The crack Ackerman team put up a good fight but were outplayed by the locals throughout the game". Fred Hudson had the opening score around left end and Harris made his first of three extra-point kicks. Johnson had the next around the left while Hudson Harris nailed the kick.

Johnson added the next on the ground and Hudson hit Jack Bray for the PAT. In the 2nd quarter, Pete Castle found paydirt from 65 yards away (Harris PAT). Hudson added another via a 65-yard pick-six in the final stanza. Louisville led first downs (13-2). The Cats were 2-5 passing while Ackerman was 3-15-4.

GAME 3:   LOUISVILLE (2-0) @ LEE HIGH (0-1-1))
                          LOUISVILLE 6 LEE HIGH 0
                          September 26, 1941

Lee High dropped a 13-0 game to Memphis Tech before tying traditionally tough Laurel 6-6. The Columbus team *"threatened to score only once and an intercepted pass ended that rally"*.

Bill Johnson (or Pete Castle) had the lone score on a final frame 45-yard dash around the left. Louisville won in first downs 18-2 and held Lee within their own 30-yard line the entire first half of the game. Unfortunately, Dan Harris broke his collarbone and was out for the foreseeable future.

Louisville dominated first downs 19-3. They had over 400 offensive yards while holding Lee High to just 24 rushing yards.

GAME 4:   LOUISVILLE (3-0) @ GRENADA (UNREPORTED)
                          LOUISVILLE 26 GRENADA 0
                          October 3, 1941

Louisville and Coach Hinze went *"through strenuous workouts"* to prepare for the Grenada Maroons under Coach Hathorn.

The Wildcats hit the board in the 2nd quarter on a run around the right end. Hudson picked off a later Grenada pass and Bill Johnson tallied on a run. In the 3rd quarter, Hudson hit Herrington for a 60-yard tally. Hill grabbed a 60-yard pick-six to wrap it up. The Clarion Ledger said Louisville won this one 27-0.

GAME 5:   LOUISVILLE (4-0) vs UNION (UNREPORTED)
                          LOUISVILLE 18 UNION 0
                          October 9, 1941

One report from The Clarion-Ledger shows the game moved back a day to Thursday the 9th. This marked the first conference game of the season and only Newton, Philadelphia and Kosciusko stood in the way of another conference title. It would come without Harris and Hudson due to injuries sustained in previous tilts.

Another *"record crowd"* saw *"a good defensive game with Johnson showing up best"*. Gene Yarbrough finally crossed the stripe for the Cats in the 2nd quarter from close range. Castle did it again in the 3rd quarter and Yarbrough added his second in the finale. The Union Appeal noted, *"Louisville's team says we have one of the cleanest teams they have played. They also say that we have the best team they have played this season"*.

GAME 6:   LOUISVILLE (5-0) @ KOSCIUSKO (3-2)
                          LOUISVILLE 0 KOSCIUSKO 26
                          October 17, 1941

The Cats were undefeated and had not allowed a score while the home Whippets were just a game over .500. It did not matter in the end as Kosciusko scored three times on the ground and another in the air.

After an early exchange of fumbles, Biggs drove in from three yards for the first tally. In the 2nd quarter, and despite an earlier Moore pickoff for the Whippets, Biggs hit Woodward for a 29-yard touchdown and Moore made it 13-0. Now in the 4th quarter, Bradford raced 37 yards to paydirt and Moore converted. The dagger came on a 6-yard Biggs dive.

The best Wildcat threat came in the final frame *"when the Winston countians had eight downs to advance five yards to the goal. Kosciusko held the first time and took over on downs and then fumbled and gave the ball back.... Again, they failed"*.

GAME 7:   LOUISVILLE (5-1) vs PHILADELPHIA (?-1)
                          LOUISVILLE 7 PHILADELPHIA 6
                          October 24, 1941

The Clarion-Ledger called the crowd as estimated around 4,000 fans of both schools. Louisville had the only score in the opening quarter by Max Herrington on a short Hudson toss to end a long drive. That came from a partially blocked punt. Yarbrough added the PAT. Philly had a chance in the last frame on a Clayton Blount tally but Yarbrough blocked the extra point.

Louisville led first downs 11-7 and went 3-5 passing compared to Philly's 2-7.

GAME 8:   LOUISVILLE (6-1) @ NEWTON (ONE LOSS)
                                    LOUISVILLE 0 NEWTON 21
                                    October 31, 1941

Coach E.L. Morgan called his opponent *"probably the toughest gridiron adversary his men are likely to meet"*. Their only loss came at the hands of Philadelphia 13-6. The Clarion-Ledger called it a *"battle of the little giants"*. In Newton, they expected an overflow crowd of 5,000 or more and installed another 3,500 seats. Rain ruined the planned event for Friday and the game was moved, therefore, to Monday.

The tough battle came down to just two minutes of the 3rd quarter at Byrd Field. First, Toby Majure hit Dick Dean. Next, Red Robinson took a punt 75 yards to paydirt and, finally, Dean hit Charles Parker from 30 yards. All extra points were successful.

GAME 9:   LOUISVILLE (6-2) vs WINONA (UNREPORTED)
                                    LOUISVILLE 12 WINONA 0
                                    November 7, 1941

Only by a Clarion-Ledger note and Winston County Journal season recap do we know that the Cats won over Winona 12-0.

GAME 10:   LOUISVILLE (7-2) vs QUITMAN (UNREPORTED)
                                    LOUISVILLE 12 QUITMAN 0
                                    November 11, 1941

Due to the big Armistice Day events in Louisville, the game moved from Friday to Tuesday; giving the Cats a pair of games in five days. The festivities included parades, speeches, bands and much more before the 2:00pm kickoff.

In the 2nd quarter, Hudson hit Bray for a touchdown. The last touchdown came in the final quarter when Castle *"plunged over left guard"*. The PAT for both were blocked.

GAME 11:   LOUISVILLE (8-2) vs STARKVILLE (UNDEFEATED)
                                    LOUISVILLE 0 STARKVILLE 13
                                    November 27, 1941

When Lions Bowl Chairman E.W. Cook stated that the winner of Newton and Hazlehurst would be one team in the Lions Bowl, there was also considerable interest in the winner of the Starkville vs Louisville game as the opponent.

"Because of the steady downpour of rain here Thanksgiving Day, the football game between Louisville and Starkville set for that day was shifted to next Thursday afternoon". That put the Cats with 16 days of rust and rest.

"Keen rivalry exists between the two teams and the local Wildcats are expecting heavy competition from the powerful Starkville eleven. Although the Wildcats boast a splendid record, having lost only two games to date, their record is lacking against the Yellow Jackets' more perfect record".

The Cats moved into Jacket territory at least three times but each were driven back before crossing the stripe. Reynolds hit Bryan (Howard PAT) for the first tally and they added another from midfield on a Reynolds pass to Bishop in the 3rd quarter. *"Starkville could not gain over the Wildcat line and had to take to the air for both tallies. Louisville allowed Starkville only 6 first downs while they rolled up 8"*.

In a short recap of the Lion's Bowl commentary, the outcome put Starkville in the Bowl. They won 24 consecutive games over two seasons.

Louisville was scheduled to finish the season against West Point on November 28. If played, it was never reported from any source and likely never occurred.

1942 (5-5-1)

Only a short notation exists that Coach Elzie Hinze, now in his third year, worked the team hard with drills and scrimmages to prepare for the upcoming season.

GAME 1:   LOUISVILLE (0-0) @/vs NOXAPATER (UNREPORTED)
        LOUISVILLE 30 NOXAPATER 6
        September 11, 1942

Only a September 25 notation on the schedule thus far gives us info that Louisville opened the 1942 season with a win over Noxapater.

GAME 2:   LOUISVILLE (1-0) @ VICKSBURG (0-0)
        LOUISVILLE 6 VICKSBURG 13
        September 18, 1942

The next tilt of the season took the Wildcats to Warren County to meet the tough Vicksburg Greenies. It would not be as easy as it appeared as the green and white won only by a lone touchdown.

Billy Shirley had a 1-yard dive in the opening frame and Alton Joseph converted. Later in the quarter, a Christmas interception set up a 27-yard Nicholson scoring run. Louisville added their points later when the Cats blocked a punt and Jim Warner fell on it in the end zone.

GAME 3:   LOUISVILLE (1-1) vs LEE HIGH (1-0-1)
        LOUISVILLE 0 LEE HIGH 13
        September 25, 1942

The defeat was not the only loss as Max Herrington injured an ankle against Vicksburg and would not be playing against Lee High. Nevertheless, Lee High Coach Willie Saunders was not expecting great things for the 1942 edition of General football. Since the War effort took much of the talent, as it did for everyone, he expected a break-even season.

The lone report from The Clarion-Ledger said, "Louisville made a good showing … despite the fact she lost to Columbus due principally to a badly crippled team with a number of first stringers out of the game". According to The Winston County Journal, Lee hit the board after a Cat fumble led to a 7-yard Ellis touchdown and the Jordan PAT connected. Before halftime, Lee recorded a 55-yard B. Wray pick-six or the finale.

Lee led in first downs 10-7 while the Cats attempted nine passes with a pair of those intercepted.

GAME 4:   LOUISVILLE (1-2) vs GRENADA (UNREPORTED)
        LOUISVILLE 12 GRENADA 7
        October 2, 1942

The good news for this contest was that many of the injured starters sidelined for so long would be back in uniform for the home game. "The Cats emerged from their game in good shape…".

The visitors hit the board for the only tally of the opening half when a Cat fumble picked up by Turnipseed picked it up and ran 85 yards across the stripe. In the next half, Hudson hit Carter from 30 yards and then lateralled to Jack Warner to the 5-yard line. Max Herrington crossed in the final frame to even it. Hill then picked off a Grenada aerial and took the ball 55 yards to paydirt.

Louisville led first downs 12-7 and went 1-4 passing. They also led in total yards 155-103. The Cats lost both fumbles in the game.

GAME 5:   LOUISVILLE (2-2) vs UNION (UNDEFEATED)
        LOUISVILLE 33 UNION 0
        October 9, 1942

The Union squad had yet to give up a score this season. Meanwhile, Hinze "will probably have his full strength to throw into battle this week". It marked the first conference game for Louisville.

The visitors "never seriously threatened Louisville's goal during the entire game". Herrington got things going early with a scoring run and extra point. Warner had the next on a 20-yard dash down the sideline to make it 14-0 at halftime. Herrington added the next in the 3rd quarter via the ground and added the PAT.

Buck Clark had the following score from 13 yards while Bill Johnson finished things with his 6-yarder. Louisville led first downs 19-5 and passing 74-24. Total yardage went to the Cats 375-64.

GAME 6:   LOUISVILLE (3-2) vs KOSCKUSKO (UNREPORTED)
                               LOUISVILLE 20 KOSCIUSKO 12
                               October 16, 1942

The Clarion-Ledger said, "The teams, old rivals, are expected to present a wonderful game and no doubt will draw a record crowd of fans. This will be the Wildcat's second conference game and Kosciusko is expected to give Louisville keen competition".

Kosciusko struck first on a 45-yard Colston pass to Jackson to make it 6-0. They then picked off an errant Cat throw but the defense held. In the 2nd quarter, Fred Hudson found Carter from 10 yards to tie the game. As halftime approached, the Whippets regained the 12-6 lead on a 5-yard Colston plunge.

Max Herrington not only tied it again on his run but also added the extra point. For Kosciusko, it was a double whammy as their team captain Stonestreet broke his leg. Now in the final frame, Jones ran from midfield to the 5-yard line. Hudson finally got across and then hit Carter for the PAT. Hudson then picked off a late pass to seal it. This marked the second conference win for Louisville.

GAME 7:   LOUISVILLE (4-2) vs PHILADELPHIA (UNREPORTED)
                               LOUISVILLE 7 PHILADELPHIA 14
                               October 23, 1942

Louisville had a pair of open dates on the calendar and Philadelphia agreed to jump in to one spot despite the fact that they played again later in the season.

Between four and five thousand were on hand as Philly took the opening drive 75 yards, scored and annexed the PAT via a Blount throw to Bassett. Hudson hit Richard Boykin on the first play of the 2nd quarter who "ran for the touchdown". Herrington "smashed over for the extra point". The Cats then moved to the 1-yard line but threw an interception.

The visitors wrapped it up in the 3rd quarter via a Blount scamper. The Blount pass to Bassett for the extra point was successful.

GAME 8:   LOUISVILLE (4-3) vs NEWTON (UNREPORTED)
                               LOUISVILLE 0 NEWTON 0
                               October 30, 1942

The Wildcats were working hard to avenge the 21-0 loss to the Tigers in 1941. The Clarion-Ledger said that they "feel they will be in just as good condition as the Tigers when they arrive..."

The closest Louisville came to scoring in the first half was a Jones pickoff taken 40 yards "almost getting loose for a marker". Newton got to the Cat 2 in the final frame but the defense held. After a Boykin interception, Herrington got as far as the Newton 7 on a run but the clock expired. Newton was 10-26 in the air.

GAME :9   LOUISVILLE (4-3-1) vs ACKERMAN (UNREPORTED)
                               LOUISVILLE 27 ACKERMAN 6
                               November 13, 1942

Ackerman was one of the longest running rivals in Cat history with at least 24 games since 1914. Louisville was on a five-game win streak and expecting to keep the streak going at least one more year.

The home team scored in each of the first three quarters, and nearly did it on their first possession before Hudson fumbled at the 1-yard line. On the next, however, J.W. Carter got over for the score and Hudson ran for the extra point. They added a pair more in the 2nd quarter. Herrington had the first with a Hudson pass to Lee accounting for the point. Then, Clark got across and Hudson ran it in to put halftime 21-0.

Within ten seconds of the opening second half, Ackerman misjudged the kick and Carter raced 65 yards to recover for the touchdown. With just fifteen seconds remaining,

Ackerman avoided the shutout on a 25-yard pass. Louisville led in first downs (18-8), rushing (290-85) and passing (100-55).

GAME 10:   LOUISVILLE (5-3-1) @ STARKVILLE (8-0)
                              LOUISVILLE 12 STARKVILLE 14
                              November 20, 1942

Powerful Starkville was considered by all as the favorite due to their stellar record of 35 consecutive wins over the last four years. This also marked the departure of Jim Warner to serve *"in Uncle Sam's Services to do some real fighting"*.

The Yellow Jackets recorded both scores in the opening quarter. The first came after an interception taken 60 yards to the Cat 6. "Chicken" Howard soon took it across and added the kick. They then went to the air from four yards for their next and converted. Louisville retaliated in the 2nd quarter via Hudson's pass to Carter to make it 14-6.

In the final frame, the two Cats hooked up again to make it 14-12. Herrington had a chance to win late on a reception *"when Starkville determined not to lose her record raced down the field to stop him. From indications, if the game had continued for two more minutes, Starkville would have suffered their first licking in 36 games as Louisville outplayed them in everything except the extra points"*.

The Cats led first downs (12-7) and rushing (250-184).

GAME 11:   LOUISVILLE (5-4-1) @ PHILADELPHIA (UNREPORTED)
                              LOUISVILLE 13 PHILADELPHIA 32
                              November 27, 1942

Horrible news came on game day with the announcement that Harold Majure, former Cat football player in the late 1920s and early 1930s, died in a plane crash *"somewhere in New Guinea"* in the service of his country.

The first period ended with Louisville ahead 6-0 thanks to a short Hudson run. Philly came back in the next on Hardy's 1-yard effort to tie it. Before halftime, they added another to make it 12-6. The first play of the 3rd quarter saw a passing touchdown for the home team and it was 18-6. While Louisville got as far as the Philly 6, they would not go further.

Philadelphia, however, *"broke loose for another marker, giving them a 24-6 lead"*. In the 4th quarter, Hudson dove in from a yard and then hit Carter for the extra point. With under a minute remaining, the Tornado added their last on a 15-yard pass and extra point kick. The Cats led in first downs (19-16) and threw for 160 yards.

1943 (7-4)

Coach Elzie Hinze had been practicing his team for a month by game day. Two open dates on the first and twenty second of October were still yet filled.

GAME 1:   LOUISVILLE (0-0) vs NOXAPATER (0-0)
                              LOUISVILLE 47 NOXAPATER 0
                              September 10, 1943

Noxapater, a longtime rival of the Wildcats, *"boasts one of her strongest teams in years"*. As such, and with it being the first game of 1943, *"a record crowd is expected... Noxapater promises Louisville plenty of competition"*. The Winston County Journal added that Noxapater was *"expected to give Louisville its best game in years"*.

Completely different from expectations, the Cats dominated from start to finish. James Faulkner led scorers with 24 points while the defense held strong. James Coleman hit Faulkner in the opening frame for an 18-yard TD while Faulkner drove in from two yards to make it 20-0. In the 3rd quarter, both Faulkner (20-yard pass) and Coleman (1-yard dive) found paydirt. In the finale, Smith crossed as did Bobby Parkes from 38 yards.

The Cats dominated first downs (13-0), rushing (267 to -25) and were 8-6-1 in the passing game.

GAME 2:   LOUISVILLE (1-0) vs NEWTON (UNREPORTED)
                              LOUISVILLE 19 NEWTON 7
                              September 17, 1943

This contest was back-and-forth for years. It was time to see what the 1943 edition held for both. Three of the five games since 1938 were ties.

Newton dotted the board first after a bad punt led to Strickland's 15-yarder and Payne's pass to Phillips put them up 7-0. Bruce Holman countered on their next drive with a 56-yard pick-six *"picking up great interference"* to make it 7-6. An ensuring Newton fumble put the Cats at the Newton 45. Grady Langley soon dashed 35 yards for the score with just eight minutes gone in the game. Louisville got to the Newton 7 just as halftime came.

In the finale, Coleman plunged over from within a yard and Langley's *"drop kick"* put them ahead for the last tally. Newton *"desperately took to the air"* and got to the Cat 18 before the game ended. The Cats led in first downs (9-5) and rushing (180-63).

GAME 3:   LOUISVILLE (2-0) @ LEE HIGH (1-1)
                    LOUISVILLE 0 LEE HIGH 6
                    September 24, 1943

The agonizing loss came 5:00 into the game when Hubert Holmes *"raced forty yards for a touchdown"*. To make it worse, the defense held but an offside penalty gave the first down to enable the scoring drive. Lee High *"had to make a goal line stand in the last period to keep Louisville out of paydirt"*. Louisville led in first downs ((12-6) but Lee held the ground (122-99).

GAME 4:   LOUISVILLE (2-1) vs FRENCH CAMP (UNREPORTED)
                    LOUISVILLE 6 FRENCH CAMP 0
                    October 1, 1943

It was probably since the mid-1920s that the two teams faced one another on the gridiron. It was tighter than most expected. Both threatened with drives to the one-foot line in the 2nd quarter. Louisville lost their opportunity via a fumble just a foot short.

However, the Cats drove 84 yards in the 3rd quarter with Coleman *"going over for the Wildcats to ring up the lone marker of the game"* from two yards. French Camp threatened late with *"two layout passes"* but both were incomplete. Louisville led in first downs (15-6) and rushing (192-70).

GAME 5:   LOUISVILLE (3-1) @/vs KOSCIUSKO (UNREPORTED)
                    LOUISVILLE 6 KOSCIUSKO 32
                    October 8, 1943

Previously unreported by other sources, the Wildcats filled their open date with Kosciusko. It did not fare well for the Cats.

Colston started with a fake run and 6-yard toss to Womble for Kosy to make it 6-0. An offside penalty gave them another PAT try which made it 7-0. Kosy then added a 60-yard escape and PAT to make it 14-0 after a frame. An interception stopped the next Cat drive and the Whippets turned it into a 3-yard tally to put halftime 20-0. Louisville's only score came in the 3rd quarter on an 85-yard drive ending with Coleman's 15-yarder to Gregory.

Colston picked off a Cat pass in the finale and took the necessary 40 yards and then added another after. Louisville led in first down (13-11) but *"she could not stop the long pass completions which netted several touchdowns"*.

GAME 6:   LOUISVILLE (3-2) @ PHILADELPHIA (3-?)
                    LOUISVILLE 6 PHILADELPHIA 27
                    October 15, 1943

Philadelphia also lost to Kosciusko, and esteemed writer Billy Ray said, *"the two teams are considered about equal in strength and it should be a bang-up game"*. This was despite the fact that both Faulkner and Dempsey *"were unable to play"*.

Partridge closed the first Philly (or Barefoot from 34 yards) drive with his 9-yard running touchdown. They converted the extra point to make it 7-6. Louisville responded in the next frame via Faulkner's 1-yard plunge. *"A heavy wind prevented Langley's dropkick from going between the goals, thus giving Philadelphia a 7-6 lead at the half"*. The Tornado began pressing the Cats in the second half *"to weaken the small but fighting Louisville squad"*. Cunningham added three more touchdowns before the final whistle.

Philly led in first downs (19-14) and rushing (265-185). Faulkner rushed for 80 yards of the 185.

GAME 7:	LOUISVILLE (3-3) @ NEWTON (UNREPORTED)
	LOUISVILLE 13 NEWTON 12
	October 29, 1943

The Cats started with a drive to the Newton 6 but got no further. Faulkner picked off second pass for a pick-six and Langley converted. Newton answered in the 2nd quarter with a 13-yarder from Payne to Phillips to make it 7-6 but Faulkner then bulldozed in from a yard to make it 13-6 at halftime.

Strickland took the opening kick of the second half 75 yards to the end zone to close the gap. The Newton newspaper claimed it an 80-yarder by Tom Stricklin. *"Both teams battled it out the remaining two quarters but were unable to score"*. Louisville led in first downs 17-7 and picked off three passes.

GAME 8:	LOUISVILLE (4-3) vs KOSCIUSKO (UNREPORTED)
	LOUISVILLE 13 KOSCIUSKO 0
	November 5, 1943

The Clarion-Ledger said, *"Kosciusko's team is considered one of the strongest high school teams in this section of the state and holds victories over Columbus, (Meridian), Philadelphia, Natchez, Carthage and Crystal Springs..."*

Coleman broke a scoreless tie in the finale to avenge the previous loss with a 1-yard dive while Parkes took the last in from nine yards with under 2:00 left in the game. The extra point proved the last. Louisville led in first downs (20-9) and yardage (305-180).

GAME 9:	LOUISVILLE (5-3) vs ACKERMAN (UNREPORTED)
	LOUISVILLE 30 ACKERMAN 7
	November 12, 1943

Coleman was the obvious star in this rivalry game as he *"zig-zagged his way for four touchdowns; two being 20-yard runs"*. Another came from his 1-yard effort while Bobby Donald added a 6-yarder. Ackerman put up their only touchdown in the 3rd quarter on Weaver's 3-yard run. Louisville led in first downs (21-15) and yardage (425-225).

GAME 10:	LOUISVILLE (6-3) vs STARKVILLE (UNREPORTED)
	LOUISVILLE 19 STARKVILLE 6
	November 19, 1943

After three consecutive losses to the Yellow Jackets, it was time to gain revenge. It came on this night in Winston County as Louisville *"proved too much for Starkville"*.

Faulkner and Parkes connect for 41 yards to put the ball at the 14-yard line. Coleman got in from two yards to make it 6-0. The Cats then recovered a fumble at the 40-yard line and soon Coleman went across from 24 yards to make it 12-0. Both Langley kicks were blocked. Bobbit answered with their only score on a 5-yard run. A Parkes fumble kept the half from being greater. In the second half, Faulkner crossed from a yard and then hit Gregory for the PAT. The Cats led in first downs 15-6.

GAME 11:	LOUISVILLE (7-3) @ PHILADELPHIA (9 WINS)
	LOUISVILLE 12 PHILADELPHIA 42
	November 25, 1943

There are conflicting reports about the final. The Clarion-Ledger reported on consecutive days a loss of 48-13 and 42-12. The Winston County Journal broke the tie with the report of the finale. Either way, it was not the way Coach Hinze nor the team wanted to close the 1943 campaign.

Philly put up 21 points in the 2nd quarter, Banks was first taking a Henley lateral from 30 yards and Cumberland converting. Stewart was next on 37-yard reception while Jack Gipson added a 25-yard pick six. Louisville got on the board in the final frame on Warner strike to Langley. The last Cat score came via a 1-yard Faulkner dive.

The Clarion-Ledger said that other tallies came from a Cumberland 6-yarder, another Gipson pick-six, and passes from Cumberland to Blount and Stewart. Louisville led in first downs (12-11) and was 14-28-3 for 172 yards.

The Wildcats were feted at the Parks Colonial Terrace on December 2 with "a very good dinner". Roger Parkes was the Master of Ceremonies. Numerous members of the team made speeches and each were given billfolds as tokens. After, all went to the Strand Theater for a film.

1944 (11-0)

Fifth year Coach Elzie Hines got his Wildcats on the practice field August 14 to prepare for the opening game at home against Noxapater.

GAME 1:   LOUISVILLE (0-0) vs NOXAPATER (0-0)
               LOUISVILLE 41 NOXAPATER 6
               September 14, 1944

The Clarion-Ledger reported that the touchdowns came from James Coleman, Jack Warner, George Smith, Grady Langley, Gregory and Roberts. "The extra points were made by (Bobby) Donald's running who scored two points. (Chester) Herrington and (James) Metts each ran for an extra and Langley kicked for his point".
Noxapater's lone tally came from Hodge in the final frame. Louisville dominated running (440-258) and first downs (20-9). Noxapater went only 1-8 in the air. The line garnered praise for "showing excellent blocking for those plays".

GAME 2:   LOUISVILLE (1-0) @ STARKVILLE (UNREPORTED)
               LOUISVILLE 13 STARKVILLE 7
               September 22, 1944

The Little Ten Conference Yellow Jackets hit the board first in the 2nd quarter on a Green run and the PAT made it 7-0. Langley immediately responded with an 80-yard kickoff return and his PAT tied it. Coleman "crowded over the winning marker" in the 3rd quarter. Louisville reportedly led in first downs 12-0.

GAME 3:   LOUISVILLE (2-0) vs LEE HIGH (3-0)
               LOUISVILLE 13 LEE HIGH 6
               September 29, 1944

The Sun Herald of Biloxi said that it would be "a hard game for the Generals". The Cats struck early on a long Jack Warner strike to George Smith to make it 6-0. Lee drove to the Cat 5 before fumbling the opportunity away. In the 2nd quarter, however, they tied it on a Nimrod Ellis 35-yard run.
Langley put the Wildcats ahead for good on an 80-yard punt return "with the aid of perfect 'man-to-man' blocking". Warner then pulled in the Langley lateral for the PAT. Louisville led in first downs 10-9 (or 9-7) and went 5-8 passing versus 3-6 for Lee High.

GAME 4:   LOUISVILLE (3-0) vs FRENCH CAMP (UNREPORTED)
               LOUISVILLE 39 FRENCH CAMP 6
               October 6, 1944

Coleman crossed on the initial drive to make it 6-0 and Donald soon followed. This time Langley's kick was good. Coleman added two more in the 2nd quarter with an extra point coming via a Warner pass to Gregory. With reserves playing the second half, Herrington add six more points in the 3rd quarter to increase the advantage. Turner avoided the shutout in the finale while Warner answered with a long pass to Smith and Langley kicked the PAT.

GAME 5:   LOUISVILLE (4-0) @ PHILADELPHIA (UNREPORTED)
               LOUISVILLE 35 PHILADELPHIA 0
               October 13, 1944

This was called *"the lightest squad in the history of the school"* for Coach W.C. Hunsmann. He reportedly had only three lettermen back on the team. *"Prospects are pretty gloomy as the entire remainder is inexperienced and light".*

Donald opened with a running touchdown and Langley the point-after. Coleman added the next and Langley the kick. In the 2nd quarter, Langley picked off a Tornado pass and Donald used it later to cross. Langley made it 21-0. In the 3rd quarter, Coleman found paydirt again as did Bobby Parkes. Langley added the first PAT while Warner hit Parkes for the final point.

Louisville led in first downs (18-5) and went 7-12 in the air. Philly was 6-14-2. The home team newspaper had the score and scorers incorrect, but noted, *"The entire Louisville team played bang-up ball. The Wildcats have proved they are the outstanding team in this section".*

GAME 6:   LOUISVILLE (5-0) @ KOSCIUSKO (UNREPORTED)
                           LOUISVILLE 34 KOSCIUSKO 0
                           October 20, 1944

Coleman started the scoring parade with a touchdown and Langley added his first of four extra points. In the same frame, Langley took a punt 85 yards to the end zone. In the 2nd quarter, a Kosy fumble led to Donald's run and he added another before halftime. The last tally came in the 3rd quarter from Coleman. The Clarion-Ledger said, *"Kosciusko never was deep in the Cat territory. The entire Cat team played excellent offense and defense during the whole game".*

GAME 7:   LOUISVILLE (6-0) vs NEWTON (UNREPORTED)
                           LOUISVILLE 18 NEWTON 6
                           October 27, 1944

Roughly 3,000 fans showed up to watch the long-time rivals. *"Both teams played good football all through the tight game".* Gregory had the lone opening half touchdown in the 1st quarter on a Warner throw. Warner hit Smith from 20 yards in the 3rd quarter and the two hooked up again in the finale. Amis dashed in late from three yards for the lone Newton score. Newton gave credit to Thomas.

The Cats led in first downs (14-5) and yardage (304-263). In the air, Louisville was 12-24-3 while Newton was 5-26-4.

GAME 8:   LOUISVILLE (7-0) vs CANTON (UNDEFEATED)
                           LOUISVILLE 14 CANTON 6
                           November 3, 1944

Not only were the Panthers undefeated, they outscored opponents thus far 114-0. *"This week's game with the undefeated Louisville eleven should go far toward establishing an outstanding team in this section of the state".* It would have to come without Coleman, injured in the Newton game.

Louisville opened scoring in the 1st quarter on a 78-yard march with Warner finding Langley from four yards for the first score against Canton this year. Langley converted his first of two extra points. Canton responded with a 62-yard drive ending with Billy Mustin's 22-yard strike to Gober. Scoring was finalized in the next stanza despite a Mustin interception when Warner hit Smith from 25 yards. The remainder was marked by numerous fumbles and interceptions on both sides. Louisville led 16-5 in first downs.

GAME 9:   LOUISVILLE (8-0) @ GREENVILLE (?-1-1)
                           LOUISVILLE 28 GREENVILLE 4
                           November 10, 1944

Talk was already beginning about the December 1st Lions Bowl with Louisville among many noted as potential participants. First, however, was the trip to Greenville to face Coach Rab Rodgers and the home team. They lost only to Clarksdale and had a 6-6 tie against the Jackson Tigers. The local paper called the nucleus of the Cat team *"speed merchants"* and added, *"the Hornets are in for a busy evening".*

Though the Delta Democrat Times stated that *"this game is the first time the Winston County grid crew has appeared on Greenville's schedule"*, forgotten was that Louisville beat them 14-7 back in 1924. Said Rodgers, *"This should be a good game".*

The Cats showed up at Murphy Stadium clad in all white. Though the first quarter was scoreless, Louisville began adding in each following frame. Both threatened in the opening with drives inside the 25-yard line but neither registered. A Roberts (or Triplett) interception taken ten yards to the 23-yard line led to Warner's 17-yard toss to Gregory to the 5-yard line and then Donald ran in from there. Langley made it 7-0.

Greenville added a safety to put halftime just 7-2. In the 3rd quarter, Warner found Smith from 30 yards and Langley put it 14-2. Then they blocked a punt and Coleman found paydirt from a yard. The Hornet's final tally came on a Dan Williams safety. Now 21-4, they blocked another punt and Coleman dove in from a yard. Louisville paced first downs (12-8).

GAME 10:   LOUISVILLE (9-0) vs KOSCIUSKO (UNREPORTED)
                                  LOUISVILLE 32 KOSCIUSKO 0
                                  November 17, 1944

Before this contest occurred, Louisville accepted the bid to play Gulfport in Meridian for the first annual Magnolia Bowl. As for Kosciusko, Coleman notched a pair of opening frame touchdowns; the second from 20 yards. Gregory added another in the next quarter on a 45-yard touchdown via the air from Warner.

In the 3rd quarter, Warner "raced through the line for the fourth Cat touchdown". Gregory had the last in the 4th quarter and Langley booted the extra points. Louisville led in first downs (14-3).

GAME 11:   LOUISVILLE (10-0) vs GULFPORT (7-1)
                                  LOUISVILLE 14 GULFPORT 7
                                  December 1, 1944: THE MAGNOLIA BOWL; Meridian, MS

Originally, the Wildcats were to face Philadelphia in Winston County; a team they already faced in a shut out earlier in the season. "The prompt cancellation was due to the opinion of the school officials that the Louisville squad would be in better condition to meet the Gulfport Commodores, a team of the Big Eight Conference..." The opponents were fine with the logic and Hinze praised them with their "act of sportsmanship (that) will contribute much towards promoting better athletic relations between the two schools".

On the 27th, the Rotary hosted a dinner for the Wildcat football team at the Parks Colonial Terrace. Ole Miss Coach Harry Mehre was the featured speaker. In addition to Coach Hinze, Jack Warner spoke for a bit after being chosen unanimously as the team MVP.

First-time opponent Gulfport lost only to Meridian 13-6 early in the season. The remainder of their schedule, and victories, was not easy. Said numerous sources about the contest at Ray Stadium, "The game is expected to be a free-scoring affair as it will see Louisville's Jack Warner and James Coleman and (Gulfport) back Jimmy Edwards, Nick Pitalo and Edward McCaleb in action tonight".

It was called "freezing weather" in Meridian as Louisville tallied their first touchdown in the second stanza on a 20-yard Langley run and his kick. The touchdown was set up by George Kimbrough's blocked punt. Coach James Landrum's Commodores responded immediately on a Pitalo toss to Alleman. Edwards was true to tie it at halftime. The game was won with just two minutes remaining on Coleman's two-foot plunge and Langley's kick. A late interception killed any threats of a comeback.

1945 (8-4)

After one of the best seasons ever recorded in Louisville, it was going to be an uphill climb for Coach Elzie (Ralph) Hinze. He opened practices minus a number of stars who enlisted in the service but The Winston County Journal added, "May their successors take up the torch and carry on to the same splendid triumph".

By the night of the first game, the paper said, "The team has a big job this year defending our title and they really mean to do it. Our ball club is planning to go places this year. Coach Hinze seems pleased with the boys and expresses his confidence in them".

GAME 1:   LOUISVILLE (0-0) vs ETHEL (0-0)
                                  LOUISVILLE 59 ETHEL 0
                                  September 14, 1945

Unfortunately, Hinze missed the game as he was *"at that time undergoing an operation in the Louisville Hospital"*. *"The boys have been getting plenty of hard practice under the coaching of Mr. Cunningham…"*

Bobby Donald garnered the first of three Cat touchdowns in the opening frame by taking a blocked punt 15 yards to paydirt. Bruce Holman added the PAT. Roy Roberts then added the next while Bobby Braxton recorded the next. Other touchdowns went to Donald from 80 yards, Blue, Metts and Hancock. First downs favored Louisville 6-3.

GAME 2: LOUISVILLE (1-0) @ STARKVILLE (0-0)
LOUISVILLE 0 STARKVILLE 20
September 21, 1945

Though having two straight years of wins against the Oktibbeha County squad, it would be a tough battle since the Yellow Jackets still held three of the last five contests. This proved to be their bounce-back.

The Winston County Journal noted that the Cats *"played a hard game but the Yellow Jackets showed up too well-experienced for our team. The Starkville team has only lost two men since last year"*. Stanley had two Jacket scores while Wright added the last.

Starkville led first downs 9-5. *"Thompson, Weddle, Long, Bell and Kinard were outstanding on the defense for the Starkville line"*.

GAME 3: LOUISVILLE (1-1) @ LEE HIGH (2-1)
LOUISVILLE 0 LEE HIGH 27
September 28, 1945

The Generals opened early with a pair of consecutive blowouts before losing to Laurel the previous week. For this season, Coach Bruce was utilizing a new Notre Dame and Mississippi State formation on the offense.

It must have been successful as Jack Odom ran in from 15 yards for the first touchdown and added another in the 2nd quarter from eight yards. Cliff McDonald (15) and Bobby Jones (5) had the final pair of scores and McDonald notched three PAT kicks.

Lee High led in first downs 13-6, and yardage 363-101 while passing yardage went to Louisville 42-22. The Generals had a pair of interceptions compared to just one by the Cats.

GAME 4: LOUISVILLE (1-2) @/vs FRENCH CAMP
LOUISVILLE 27 FRENCH CAMP 0
October 5, 1945

Conditions were not ideal as it was described as the "Mud Bowl". *"The squad really played a hard and interesting game. Most of the game consisted of fumbles from one team to the other"*. Hinze now returned to lead the squad.

Touchdowns came from Holman, Donald, Chester Herrington, and Roberts. Extra points came from Holman, Donald and Herrington.

GAME 5: LOUISVILLE (2-2) vs KOSCIUSKO (UNREPORTED)
LOUISVILLE 20 KOSCIUSKO 0
October 12, 1945

Herrington started with a pair of touchdowns in the opening frame. Donald added the next on *"a hard center line buck"* and notched two extra points.

GAME 6: LOUISVILLE (3-2) vs PHILADELPHIA (UNREPORTED)
LOUISVILLE 12 PHILADELPHIA 13
October 19, 1945

With the win over Kosciusko, one source thought the Tornado underdogs in this meeting. It was not to be as *"both squads played the entire game in dead earnest"*.

Herrington recorded the initial tally of the game in the second period to make halftime 6-0. Holman added the next in the 3rd quarter to increase the lead. Philly started their comeback as Billy Young hit Dees for a tally and Langston (or Johnson) converted. In the finale, and with just a minute to play, Young hit Greenleaf for the winner. First downs were even 9-9.

GAME 7:   LOUISVILLE (3-3) @ NEWTON (UNREPORTED)
                                   LOUISVILLE 18 NEWTON 0
                                   October 26, 1945

Scoring did not get underway until James Hancock crossed around the left end in the 2nd quarter. Herrington got the next in the 3rd quarter while Donald hit Roberts for the last in the final quarter. Donald and Roberts both recorded interceptions on the evening. Louisville led in first downs 6-3.

GAME 8:   LOUISVILLE (4-3) vs CANTON (6-1)
                                   LOUISVILLE 0 CANTON 13
                                   November 2, 1945

Canton hit the board for their first of two touchdowns in the 3rd quarter when M.A. George flashed a 75-yard pick-six and Farish added the extra point. The second tally came when Ivan Rosamond added a 25-yard pick-six. *"Louisville fought on until the end of the game. Roberts was out most of the game because of an injury during practice"*.

GAME 9:   LOUISVILLE (4-4) vs NOXAPATER (UNREPORTED)
                                   LOUISVILLE 33 NOXAPATER 6
                                   November 9, 1945

It was the second team that played most of the game in the blowout win. Noxapater garnered their only score on a blocked punt taken the distance. "Tater" Doug Coggin added the initial Cat tally while Charlie Blue had the next. John Metts and Holman added 3rd quarter scores as did Herrington on an 83-yard dash. He also added the PAT.
Louisville lost first downs 9-8 perhaps due to four penalties.

GAME 10:   LOUISVILLE (5-4) vs HOUSTON (UNREPORTED)
                                   LOUISVILLE 47 HOUSTON 13
                                   November 16, 1945

Louisville jumped out with 1st quarter touchdowns thanks to two Donald tallies and another by Herrington. The PAT came from a Donald toss to Braxton. Alford put up the Hilltopper's first score before halftime. Roberts added the next in the 3rd quarter and Holman the kick.
Metts then notched the next for the Cats while Alford did the same for Houston. Donald rushed across for another in the finale while Charlie Blue hit James Wood for the extra point.

GAME 11:   LOUISVILLE 6-4) @ PHILADELPHIA (UNREPORTED)
                                   LOUISVILLE 32 PHILADELPHIA 6
                                   November 23, 1945

Philly's Buddy Dees opened the game with a touchdown but it was all they muster. Donald responded quickly with one of his own. In the 2nd quarter, Holman hit Braxton for the lead they would not relinquish.
In the 3rd quarter, Donald ran 70 yards to paydirt and Holman added the kick. Roberts did the same after. In the final frame, Donald picked off a Billy Young pass for the pick-six and Holman was again true. First downs favored the Cats 11-4 despite suffering a deficit in penalties 4-1.

1946 (7-2-2)

Coach Elzie Hinze returned for what would be his seventh and final season as head Wildcat. Practices were underway by mid-August twice a day *"with rugged drills"* and were showing *"great improvement"*.

GAME 1:   LOUISVILLE (0-0) @ STARKVILLE (UNREPORTED)
                                   LOUISVILLE 0 STARKVILLE 19
                                   September 20, 1946

In front of 4,000 fans, Green crossed from 12 yards in the 1st quarter and Frye "*booted the extra point*". He did it again in the 2nd quarter "*off tackle*" after the Jackets' Kilpatrick blocked a Cat punt. Their last came in the final frame on a Green dash.

GAME 2:   LOUISVILLE (0-1) vs LEE HIGH (UNREPORTED)
                                 LOUISVILLE 0 LEE HIGH 12
                                 September 27, 1946

While Coach Sonny Bruce lost a number of key players to graduation and transfer, he still felt as if the Generals could field a solid squad for the 1946 campaign.

The scoreless game changed in the 3rd quarter as Nimrod Ellis runs put the ball at the Cat 18 from where Dick Brewer found James Chrestman for the touchdown. James Reeves added the last in the final frame on a 9-yard carry. Two other General touchdowns came back on penalties. Lee led first downs 9-5 and rushing 259-86.

GAME 3:   LOUISVILLE (0-2) vs COLUMBIA (UNDEFEATED)
                                 LOUISVILLE 2 COLUMBIA 0
                                 October 4, 1946

Columbia, undefeated and yet to give up points, found themselves scoreless at intermission with Louisville. Donald picked off a 1st quarter pass but got only to the 14-yard line. The contest came down to the last :35 when Dempsey "*broke through and blocked a Columbia punt, giving the Cats a close margin of 2-0*".

GAME 4:   LOUISVILLE (1-2) @ KOSCIUSKO (UNREPORTED)
                                 LOUISVILLE 2 KOSCIUSKO 0
                                 October 11, 1946

In a repeat of the previous week, a safety made all the difference. On a "*mud-soaked Whippet gridiron*", Donald Addkison blocked a 3rd quarter Dedeaux punt with the punter recovering in the end zone for the second Cat victory.

The (Kosciusko) Star Herald said, "*Fumbles, intercepted passes, blocked punts and heavy penalties were all included in a hard-fought football game*".

GAME 5:   LOUISVILLE (2-2) vs NEWTON (SIXTH GAME)
                                 LOUISVILLE 27 NEWTON 0
                                 October 18, 1946

Coaches Morgan, Brown and Beatty had a lot of youth "*reporting for practices*" in Newton. The Wildcats took advantage in the opening frame on a 23-yard Donald scamper. The Newton squad drove as far as the Cat 9 before the halftime whistle sounded.

Herrington opened the 3rd quarter with a 1-yard plunge while Dempsey ran in for the PAT. Later in the contest, Fulton picked off a pass and turned it into a 45-yard pick-six. Dale added the point. Another interception return by Donald came back on penalty. In the 4th quarter, Louisville went 95 yards with Donald adding the last 40 yards. Donald and Dempsey hooked up for the extra point.

First downs (15-4) went to Louisville as did rushing (396-86).

GAME 6:   LOUISVILLE (3-2) vs GRENADA (UNREPORTED)
                                 LOUISVILLE 19 GRENADA 0
                                 October 25, 1946

The Bulldogs provided the fourth win of the season for Louisville on a muddy field. In the 3rd quarter, Herrington crossed from five yards. In the finale, John Earhart picked off a pass for the 30-yard pick-six. Then, Charlie Blue raced for a 35-yarder for the last. Louisville led first downs 6-1 and rushing 151-35.

GAME 7:   LOUISVILLE (4-2) vs HAZLEHURST (UNREPORTED)
                                 LOUISVILLE 7 HAZLEHURST 7
                                 November 1, 1946

The Wildcats originally had November 1 as an open date but were able to fill it with the first-time opponents from Hazlehurst. It was called *"one of the most thrilling games ever witnessed on the Louisville gridiron"*.

An early Cat drive got only as far as the 6-yard line. Late in the 3rd quarter, Hazlehurst blocked a Wildcat punt and Jimmy Spitchley later scored from two yards. That play marked the first of the last quarter. His kick made it 7-0. Late in the contest, Bobby Donald found Fulton to put the ball at the Cat 20. After numerous solid runs, Jim Dale *"smashed center"* for the last six yards and Donald hooked up with Fulton for the critical extra point.

GAME 8:   LOUISVILLE (4-2-1) vs NOXAPATER (UNREPORTED)
                LOUISVILLE 33 NOXAPATER 12
                November 8, 1946

Louisville began with a 70-yard march and long 43-yard Blue scoring run. On the first play of the 2nd quarter, Herrington blasted in from a yard. Donald and Dempsey hooked up for the PAT. Noxapater garnered their first of two scores with a 1-yarder in the frame. Fulton picked up where they left off with his 30-yard pick-six.

In the 3rd quarter, Donald hit Dempsey from 30 yards for the touchdown and Donald converted around the end. In the finale, Hensley found Joe Horn from 22 yards for their last. Late in the game, the Cats finished things with a 35-yard connection between Donald and Dempsey.

GAME 9:   LOUISVILLE (5-2-1) @ CANTON (UNREPORTED)
                LOUISVILLE 25 CANTON 7
                November 15, 1946

Things appeared gloomy as the home team scored just two plays into the game when Farish drove in from a yard and Lutz converted. However, it was far from over. Shortly afterwards, Blue escaped from the 13-yard line to make it 7-6. Herrington had the next from 13 yards in the 2nd quarter. Then, Fulton snagged an errant pass to allow Donald a 40-yard strike to Dempsey to make it 16-7. Before the half came, Donald recovered a Canton fumble. Lamar Cockrell got in from 20 yards and Donald rushed in for the PAT.

The second half was a defensive slugfest. Louisville did record a Dale 15-yard touchdown, but it was brought back due to clipping. First downs (12-7) favored Louisville.

GAME 10:   LOUISVILLE (6-2-1) @ PHILADELPHIA (UNREPORTED)
                LOUISVILLE 12 PHILADELPHIA 12
                November 22, 1946

Herrington capped the opening drive of the contest with a 2-yard plunge through the middle to make it 6-0. Young answered for Philly in the frame from six yards to tie it through halftime. Dempsey and Donald hooked up for a 45-yard tally in the 3rd quarter but again the PAT failed.

In the finale, Prince took the ball across the stripe from eight yards but they, too, missed the conversion. The game closed after an 80-yard Donald run put the ball at the 12-yard line. First downs were even (9-9) while Louisville barely held the ground (129-126).

GAME 10:   LOUISVILLE (6-2-2) vs INDIANOLA (10-0)
                LOUISVILLE 13 INDIANOLA 7
                December 6, 1946: LIONS DELTA BOWL; Greenwood, MS

The committee for the fourth annual Lions Delta Bowl in Greenwood decided to invite the Cats over to take on the undefeated Indianola squad. They were formidable having allowed only 19 points on the season.

An overflow crowd was on hand to see the underdog Wildcats against the nearby Indians. A first-drive fumble did no damage and the Cats took the next drive 92 yards to paydirt. The final score came on a fourth down Donald 4-yard strike to Herrington. George Kimbrough added the extra point.

Now in the 4th quarter, Donald and Cockrell hooked up from 15 yards to make it 13-0. Kimbrough's kick was blocked. Indianola chalked their lone score later on Frank Bellipanni's long pass to Pete Wilson *"who battered his way over for a touchdown"*. The extra point pass from Bellipanni to Bobby Webb proved the last.

Indianola controlled first downs (11-8) and yardage (197-116). Louisville was 8-12 passing while the Indians were 15-27.

On New Year's Eve, The Delta Democrat Times reported Hinze to be the new coach in Greenwood; thus, ending a long and successful stretch in Louisville. In the end, he ended up as LHS Superintendent and no longer the mentor for the Wildcats.

1947 (4-5-1)

New head coach James "Obie" Brown began grid drills in mid-August. Brown was previously the coach at Meridian. While he returned 15 lettermen and four starters, the team lost five first-team players of six total.

GAME 1:   LOUISVILLE (0-0) vs EUPORA (0-1)
                 LOUISVILLE 55 EUPORA 0
                 September 19, 1947

Eupora, another Choctaw Conference opponent, was upset 7-6 in their opener with Vardaman. Herrington wasted no time getting the 1947 off on good footing when he took the opening kick 40 yards to the end zone. Sam Fulton took a handoff 45 yards a few plays later while James Dale added one from 75 yards before the frame was over. Dale added one more before halftime from 20 yards.
Fulton gained 56 for a score in the 3rd quarter while Herrington did the same from 30 yards. Fulton added the next from 30 yards and again from 40 yards. Dale then traveled from 46 yards while Jack Dempsey notched the kick. The last came from Dale with a 49-yard effort.
Yardage favored Louisville a whopping 617-43. The September 26 Greenwood Commonwealth said, "Louisville last week ran roughshod over little Eupora 55-0 on their warmup for the season but Coach Obie Brown will probably concentrate on all weak spots developed even in that one-sided affair ".

GAME 2:   LOUISVILLE (1-0) @ GREENWOOD (UNREPORTED)
                 LOUISVILLE 6 GREENWOOD 27
                 September 26, 1947

The Cats headed back to Greenwood; site of the season finale win over Indianola in 1946. Unfortunately, the outcome was significantly different.
An opening quarter Cat punt fumble, their second, was recovered by the Bulldogs at the 5-yard line. Bobby Barrett plunged in from a yard a few plays later and Jimmy Lear converted. Lear added a 2nd quarter touchdown on his 55-yard dash and converted to make it 14-0. To make it worse, the Cats fumbled again four plays later. Another Barrett run put it 20-0. Louisville had the only other score before halftime when Johnny Fulcher dashed 80 yards to set up Jimmy Dale's run.
Greenwood added one last touchdown in the 3rd quarter after yet another fumble at the Dog 5. Lear had the honors from the 2-yard line. The home team led on the ground (194-165). The Wildcats fumbled an amazing five times and lost four of them but surprisingly led first downs 7-3.

GAME 3:   LOUISVILLE (1-1) @ COLUMBIA (UNREPORTED)
                 LOUISVILLE 6 COLUMBIA 14
                 October 3, 1947

Another road trip to a non-conference opponent awaited. This time it was to Columbia Stadium to face another band of Cats under Coaches R.G. Weems and Red Stevenson.
Columbia scored on their opening possession when Pittman reversed into the end zone from 11 yards and Spud Alford converted. The visitors responded in the 3rd quarter on a 1-yard Jimmy Dale dive. A pass for the extra point failed. In the last frame, Charles Berry picked off a pass to set up Gene Dozier's tally and Alford's kick.
Herrington and Dozier (Columbia) also had interceptions. "The statistics gave Columbia a slight edge of eight first downs to seven and few more yards gained by rushing. But, the figures were close all the way".

GAME 4: LOUISVILLE (1-2) vs KOSCIUSKO (3-0)
LOUISVILLE 27 KOSCIUSKO 0
October 10, 1947

The Whippets circled this game in advance with intentions of revenge for the slim 2-0 defeat in 1946. Coach Robert Henderson's team had a strong chance with an unblemished record on the young season.

An opening play fumble by Kosy allowed the Cats to get only as far as the 1-yard line. However, Dale *"crossed the double stripe in the waning moments of the second quarter after having three touchdowns called back by offside penalties"*. Jack Dempsey converted.

Later in the 3rd quarter, Herrington broke away from 55 yards and Dempsey *"again split the uprights"*. Herrington did it again shortly after from eight yards and, again, Dempsey converted. The final score came in the 4th quarter. Dempsey broke through the Kosy line and blocked a punt at the Whippet 17. John Fulcher capped that with the score.

The Clarion-Ledger reported total yardage in favor of Louisville 225-16 while also controlling first downs 11-5.

GAME 5: LOUISVILLE (2-2) @ NEWTON (UNREPORTED)
LOUISVILLE 7 NEWTON 0
October 17, 1947

The Cats now traveled to Newton to face *"a hard-fighting Newton eleven"*. Louisville moved to the Newton 4 in the 2nd quarter only to be stopped. Now late in the game, the Wildcats blocked a punt. Louisville moved to the 1-yard line from where Dale crossed from around end.

Louisville had one more drive to the Newton 2 and John Earhart recorded an interception in the game. The Cats led first downs 13-6 and rushing 208-115.

GAME 6: LOUISVILLE (3-2) @ HAZLEHURST (UNREPORTED)
LOUISVILLE 7 HAZLEHURST 13
October 24, 1947

While The Union Appeal noted that the Cats were to face Starkville, they actually tangled with Hazlehurst on the road. An early Indian fumble was returned later by a Bush interception for Hazlehurst.

The home team drove 70 yards in the 2nd quarter with Jimmy Spitchley recording the last 14 yards to make it 6-0. Dale answered with a 1-yarder before halftime and Dempsey gave them the 7-6 lead. Early in the final frame, Wallace Beech took a Bryan Simmons pitch and escaped for a 74-yard touchdown. Spitchley provided the last point.

One report said, *"An outstanding non-conference battle between two of the strongest teams in the state was staged ... between the Louisville Wildcats and Hazlehurst. Hazlehurst stopped Louisville's winning streak 13-7"*. Two major losses occurred for the Cats on the evening as Bobby Faulkner broke his collar bone and Sam Fulton dislocated his shoulder. Coggin was also knocked unconscious in the game.

GAME 7: LOUISVILLE (3-3) vs STARKVILLE (UNREPORTED)
LOUISVILLE 19 STARKVILLE 21
October 31, 1947

Only an online report shows the loss though the game was mentioned several times in other reports. Ironically, the November 7 Starkville paper notes the game as cancelled due to *"inclement weather"* with the one end of the field *"under about four inches of water from the 30-yard line through the end zone"*.

GAME 8: LOUISVILLE (3-4) @ ACKERMAN (7-0)
LOUISVILLE 0 ACKERMAN 28
November 7, 1947

This edition of Ackerman football was impressive as they had outscored opponents 256-33 thus far. Despite the losing overall record, this tilt meant the Choctaw Conference championship. In the end, The Winston County Journal called it *"too much Draper, Files and Ackerman as a whole"*.

Four plays after an opening Cat fumble, Sonny Draper scampered 15 yards for the first score and Clayton converted. In the 2nd quarter, it was Davis Files ending a 65-yard drive from a yard and Draper with the PAT. In the finale, Files found paydirt from four yards and Garner the extra point. They finished it on O.B. Garner's 80-yard TD to L.E. Hunt and Garner was true.

Ackerman dominated 15-3 (or 11-3) in first downs and 264-37 on the ground. The Lions Bowl committee in Greenwood could have asked the Wildcats to come back to defend their title. However, they *"had some of their grid picks thrown into a spaghetti tangle Friday night when Ackerman whaled the daylights out of Louisville"*.

GAME 9: LOUISVILLE (3-5) vs CANTON (UNREPORTED)
LOUISVILLE 0 CANTON 0
November 14, 1947

While both teams threated, neither could cross the stripe. The Cats moved to the Tiger 37 while Canton marched to the Cat 25 before losing via fumble. Early in the 4th quarter, Canton got to the Cat 4 to no avail. Louisville moved to the 3-yard line as the final whistle sounded. Louisville led in first downs 34-30 and 232-130 rushing.

GAME 10: LOUISVILLE (3-5-1) vs PHILADELPHIA (UNREPORTED)
LOUISVILLE 20 PHILADELPHIA 0
November 21, 1947

The season-ender for both was perhaps the longest-running opponent the Cats faced with games going back to at least 1914.

Herrington finished a 70-yard 2nd quarter march from nine yards and Dempsey connected. In the 3rd, he did it again from 30 yards while Dale picked recorded a 45-yard pick-six in the last quarter. Dempsey added the last extra point of the year. The Wildcats led 309-122 rushing and 15-9 in first downs.

1948 (9-3)

Obie Brown was back for his second stint in Louisville and expectations were positive despite coming off their first losing season since 1934. As practices unfolded, The Winston County Journal thought the team *"steadily improving and shaping up for their initial game"*.

GAME 1: LOUISVILLE (0-0) vs MERIDIAN (0-0)
LOUISVILLE 0 MERIDIAN 19
September 10, 1948

The opener was not an easy one as Meridian visited Winston County to kick off the 1948 campaign. The Enterprise Journal of McComb picked the visitors 33-6 while the local paper predicted it to be a *"thriller diller from the initial kickoff until the game's end"*.

Slight differences exist in reports on the contest. The local paper notes that Jack Norris hit paydirt as the opening quarter ended from 20 yards while a James McCoy ensuing interception made it possible for Sonny Morgan to cross from a foot for the next. With just :19 left in the first half, McCoy grabbed another pick and took it 60-yards to the end zone. Jack Norris added the extra point

Warren Trest suffered a broken ankle in the game and was pronounced out *"for some time"*. Louisville led in first downs 7-6 but lost passing 52-15 and rushing 98-20.

GAME 2: LOUISVILLE (0-1) vs EUPORA (1-1)
LOUISVILLE 33 EUPORA 13
September 17, 1948

The Choctaw Conference opener seemed a sure bet for the Cats. The Clarion-Ledger noted on game day that they *"should enter the win column this week"*. The Cats scored five times in the first half with three conversions. In the second half, *"the Yahoos really dug their cleats in the turf to hold Louisville and they did, allowing Louisville only five first downs in the second half"*.

Carroll got the first Eupora tally on a 55-yard breakaway and Brannon had the last. The conversion was successful to add the final point.

GAME 3:   LOUISVILLE (1-1) vs WINONA (0-0-2)
                               LOUISVILLE 43 WINONA 0
                               October 1, 1948

Requests for an opponent for the open week went out in late August. Apparently, no teams stepped into the void and the Cats had an extra week to prep for Winona.

Scoring went rampant for the Wildcats in each possession but one. Four plays into the game, Rhodes found a fumble on the kickoff and marched 45 yards with Herald Crowson hitting Davis for the first touchdown. Doug Coggins got across form 16 yards for the next, again from 30 yards to end the half. The Cats scored four times in the 3rd quarter as Crowson, Ellis, Davis and Coggins crossed with Harrison adding the lone PAT.

The Cats led on the ground 440 to -7 and first downs 18-2. In the air, Louisville was 10-18 while Winona was 0-6. The win put the Cats up to fourth place in conference standings at 2-0.

GAME 4:   LOUISVILLE (2-1) @ KOSCIUSKO (4-0)
                               LOUISVILLE 0 KOSCIUSKO 31
                               October 8, 1948

As the home-standing Whippets held first place in conference play, this contest would have a lot of bearing on the eventual winner. Kosciusko had been shut out by Louisville for five consecutive years and last won against the Cats in 1941. This year, however, they were Choctaw leaders outscoring opponents 168-12.

The Homecoming crowd watched as Kosy opened scoring in the 2nd quarter with a 55-yard John Irving dash. Soon after, they recovered a fumble at the Cat 28. It took two plays before Irving had his second tally to make halftime 12-0.

Quinton Clegg recovered a 3rd quarter blocked punt for the next and Punk Jones notched the extra point. In the last frame, John Ables connected with W.S. Donald for a touchdown and Jones grabbed a kick fumble and took in across from a yard one play later.

GAME 5:   LOUISVILLE (2-2) vs NEWTON (4-1)
                               LOUISVILLE 12 NEWTON 6
                               October 15, 1948

Coaches Preston Beatty and WR. Lindsley's Newton squad recorded a second-place finish is 1948 after being in the conference only a year. Of their 48-man roster, only four were starters from that season.

While the game sat deadlocked 6-6 at halftime, the Cats came through in the second half on a long drive to snatch the victory.

GAME 6:   LOUISVILLE (3-2) vs FLORA (UNREPORTED)
                               LOUISVILLE 45 FLORA 7
                               October 21, 1948

The contest, along with most other Choctaw Conference games, was moved up to Thursday to allow many to attend the critical Kosciusko and Ackerman struggle. The final score comes from the October 22 Enterprise Journal.

GAME 7:   LOUISVILLE (4-2) @ STARKVILLE (UNREPORTED)
                               LOUISVILLE 21 STARKVILLE 6
                               October 29, 1948

A short recap from the October 31 Clarion-Ledger notes that Starkville held a slim 6-0 halftime lead. The Cats *"got going in the final period"* to defeat *"one of the leading Little Ten Conference teams"*.

While the Yellow Jackets had the only tally of the opening half via George Reed's 30-yard pass to Gene Douglas, Crowson crossed in the 3rd quarter and Harrison put the Cats ahead 7-6. The Jackets picked off a Cat pass later at the 6-yard line to stop a drive. Donald

Addkison added the final two touchdowns in the last frame and Harrison converted. Addkison picked off a late pass before time expired.

Louisville led in first downs 14-2. Both teams suffered interceptions and neither completed a pass. The Wildcats recovered a pair of Jacket fumbles in the victory.

GAME 8: LOUISVILLE (5-2) @ ACKERMAN (7 CONFERENCE WINS)
LOUISVILLE 14 ACKERMAN 7
November 6, 1948

This road tilt was critical as a Cat win threw the conference into a three-way tie. Experts originally believed it was highly likely to occur but a differing opinion was offered after rain cancelled the contest until Saturday.

The Wildcats *"fought with the fury of a jungle beast"* in front of a *"capacity crowd"*. No other game specifics were offered. The Choctaw Plain Dealer noted that *"The Ackerman boys seemingly did their very best. The officials did their work perfectly. But Louisville was something different under the sun"*.

Conference officials now had to make a decision on how best to hold a playoff contest to determine the championship.

GAME 9: LOUISVILLE (6-2) @ CANTON (UNREPORTED)
LOUISVILLE 27 CANTON 7
November 12, 1948

The Tigers were under new leadership in Madison County. Coaches Glynn Cook and Woodrow Marsh had 30 boys as practices began with more expected. Though described as *"lighter"* than past squads, they did have the services of nine lettermen.

Crowson had the initial score from 60 yards with a Harrison PAT while Crowson did it again in the next frame. Again, Harrison was true. Canton found their lone points in the frame via the air. John Davis increased the lead in the 3rd quarter from 22 yards while Crowson put up the last in the final stanza. That came via a Billy Fulton fumble recovery.

GAME 10: LOUISVILLE (7-2) @ PHILADELPHIA (6-2)
LOUISVILLE 25 PHILADELPHIA 13
November 19, 1948

Philadelphia, under direction of coaches Bill Richardson and Jack Cheatham, were long-time opponents of the Wildcats. The Clarion-Ledger said only, *"Clawing from behind, the Louisville Wildcats won a decisive 25-13 win … in a bitterly fought contest in Philly"*.

The Tornado scored first in the opening frame on a 70-yard Oliphant dash and Dorman Pope PAT. Addkison responded a few minutes later from three yards but the blocked PAT kept it in their favor by a point. As the frame ended, Philly again found paydirt on Dees' 57-yarder but the failed PAT kept it 13-6. Crowson added a 30-yarder in the 2nd quarter, one more later, and Addkison ended the half with an interception. Now 19-13 in the final frame, John Davis notched the last score after a Cat fumble recovery.

The game ended with Louisville knocking on the Philly door from five yards. Louisville won first downs (16-8) and rushing (203-150).

GAME 11: LOUISVILLE (8-2) vs KOSCIUSKO (11-1)
LOUISVILLE 6 KOSCIUSKO 0
November 29, 1948

The Choctaw Conference had to draw straws to determine which two teams would open play on November 24th. It came out as an Ackerman and Kosciusko tussle in Louisville. The winner was to meet the Wildcats in Ackerman for the title. The Whippets took the measure of the Indians 12-7 to earn that right.

The lone touchdown came from Crown on the first drive of 80 yards when he went in from 12 yards. *"From there out it was Kosciusko trying to halt the continuous Louisville drives. And stop them they did"*. The Cats led first downs 15-2 against a Kosy team called *"crippled"*.

In 1946, the Cats made their first trip to Greenwood to take on Indianola in the fourth annual Lions Delta Bowl. That ended in an upset 14-7 victory over Indianola. Now they were back to face the District 3 Delta Valley Conference champions. The Eagles had only a single loss on the season; that 21-20 to Leland.

Drew notched the only score of the first half on Travis Parker's 1-yard plunge to cap a 50-yard drive. The Cats came back on the first march of the 3rd quarter and capped it on a 2-yard John Davis run. The extra point by Harrison made it 7-7. Just before the end of the stanza, Parker found Robert Jackson from 13 yards and Henry Mims added his second extra point. Louisville sat at the Eagle 17 as the game ended.

"*The Drew line outplayed the highly touted Wildcat line and smeared many plays in the backfield*". The Cats led in first downs (15-14) and rushing yardage (162-127). Drew held the air (194-124). The Wildcats lost one of two fumbles and had at least one interception.

The All-Choctaw Conference list included Buddy Davis, L. Harrison and Herald Crowson. Crowson, averaging 181 yards per game, also made All-Southern High School.

1949 (8-3)

Obie Brown had twelve letter winners back "*from the crack championship 1948 outfit*". As such, both the Wildcats and Kosciusko were projected clear favorites to face once again for conference bragging rights. Practices began in mid-August with "*very few casualties besides a few pulled muscles and a few sore heads*".

GAME 1:

LOUISVILLE (0-0) vs STARKVILLE (0-0)
LOUISVILLE 33 STARKVILLE 6
September 9, 1949

Starkville was willing to "*throw the book*" against the Cats with 10 lettermen and seven starters from a number two Little Ten Conference team. They were 7-3-1 in that season. In the last 10 against Louisville, they were 7-3.

It was a successful start for the Cats against Coach "Juicy" Scales for the season and the game. Their first drive, behind runs from John Davis and Herald Crowson, ended with a 26-yard James Jones to Donald Addkison pass and Bobby Faulkner PAT. Donald Addkison added his second on an end run and Faulkner added his second PAT.

Early in the 3rd quarter, Crowson drove through the middle from seven yards to make it 21-0. A Davis interception of Wofford led his 45-yard pick-six. Now 27-0, Crowson (or Davis) added a theft of Parker and ran it back 45 yards. Late in the game, the Yellow Jackets avoided shutout on a 1-yard Mosley dive.

Louisville led first downs 11-9 but went just 5-16-2 in the air versus 3-12-3. The Starkville paper gave the Cats air credit for six passes for 119 yards.

GAME 2:

LOUISVILLE (1-0) @ EUPORA (1-0)
LOUISVILLE 39 EUPORA 0
September 16, 1949

The Eagles lost "*only one or two lettermen from their team last year and should be, and are, in good condition to give the Wildcats a hard fight*". Eupora shocked sports experts with a decisive 57-6 victory the previous week over Kilmichael. That win "*indicates that the Eagles will not give up without a mighty struggle*".

The Clarion-Ledger, however, said the Cats were "*growing stronger every week*". On a muddy field before roughly 2,000 fans, the Wildcats stacked three scores in the opening frame. Crowson dashed 51 and 20 yards while Addkison added a 35-yarder. Carmichael was true on one extra point. An Eagle fumble then led to Crowson's next in the 2nd quarter.

Louisville put the game away with scores in each of the last two frames. Davis had the first from 15 yards while Pearson notched the last. The visitors led in first downs 11-3 but were only 1-5 in the air.

GAME 3:   LOUISVILLE (2-0) @ LEE HIGH (UNREPORTED)
                        LOUISVILLE 12 LEE HIGH 27
                        September 23, 1949

        The Big Eight Conference Generals were not a new face for Louisville as they
played one another as early as 1918. Louisville recorded numerous victories over that time,
but not this one. Lee High was coming off a 40-7 shellacking by Laurel.
        The half-ended 6-6. Addkison had the Louisville tally *"going over from the eight"*
while Wade Alexander did the same from 20 yards. Alexander found paydirt in the 3rd
quarter on a 69-yard scamper while Bobby Redwood followed with a 21-yarder. Louisville's
last response came from Crowson from three yards. In the last frame, Alexander recorded
his third touchdown on a 32-yard run. Ken Kennedy went 3-3 in extra-point kicks.
        The Cats led first downs 15-4 while Fulton completed 12 passes for 190 yards.

GAME 4:   LOUISVILLE (2-1) @ WINONA (0-1 CONFERENCE)
                        LOUISVILLE 52 WINONA 0
                        September 30, 1949

        The cupboard was empty for Coach Jack WIndborn as he had only three
lettermen in camp. Therefore, he was *"not optimistic of winning many games this year"*.
Brown ended up *"using substitutes to smother Winona"*. Unfortunately, the article from
The Winston County Journal is illegible but the score is confirmed.

GAME 5:   LOUISVILLE (3-1) vs KOSCIUSKO (UNDEFEATED)
                        LOUISVILLE 6 KOSCIUSKO 27
                        October 7, 1949

        This marquee matchup was *"the top game of the night with the winner being
tagged the team to beat for the conference title"*. A loss would closely resemble 1948 when
the Cats dropped an early game to Kosy before taking the playoff rematch and the Choctaw
crown.
        Over 5,000 fans were on hand as the home Whippets scored in four plays when
Hendrix Brentz crossed to make it 6-0. Crowson immediately punched back with a 61-yard
escape to tie things 6-6. Back came Kosciusko with a 54-yard drive ending on a Horace
Williams carry. Jones' PAT ended the opening frame, and eventually the half, 13-6.
        Louisville had a chance to tie again in the 3rd quarter, but a fumble at the 1-yard
line ended the threat. Later, Brentz picked off a Fulton pass that led to a Punk Jones off-
tackle score and his PAT. As the game neared the end, Earl William Young blocked a Cat
punt and took it the remaining 30 yards. Jones added the PAT.
        Louisville led first downs (10-7) and rushing (268-225). Turnovers ended as the
cause of the defeat.

GAME 6:   LOUISVILLE (3-2) @ NEWTON (UNDEFEATED IN CONFERENCE)
                        LOUISVILLE 19 NEWTON 6
                        October 14, 1949

        Herald Crowson starred in this road tilt as he tallied 1-yard touchdowns in each
quarter before halftime. Faulkner was true on the PAT after the initial touchdown.
Newton's only tally came in the 2nd quarter on a Pepper Thomas 20-yard pass to Frank May
but Carmichael blocked the extra point attempt.
        The final tally came from Crowson from two yards. Louisville led 15-4 in first
downs and 290-144 in yardage.

GAME 7:   LOUISVILLE (4-2) @ MACON (5-2)
                        LOUISVILLE 26 MACON 13
                        October 28, 1949

        Macon thrilled home fans with an opening 60-yard play to put them at the Cat
20. However, the defense held firm. Louisville took the 7-0 lead to the lockers on a 70-yard
march ending with a 1-yard Crowson smash and Carmichael kick.
        The Cats opened the 3rd quarter with a 57-yard march with Crowson doing the
honors from the 3-yard line. Down 13-0, Macon responded on a Ferris carry. The PAT

failed. Back came Louisville with a Crowson 6-yarder and Carmichael kick. Both scored in the finale. Addkison got across for the Cats while Ferris did the same for Macon.

Louisville led 16-10 in first downs (or lost 14-13), and 308-184 (or 269-262) in yardage. As noted, stats varied wildly according to which team reported.

GAME 8: LOUISVILLE (5-2) vs ACKERMAN (UNREPORTED)
LOUISVILLE 39 ACKERMAN 13
November 4, 1949

Turmoil erupted during the week when Kosciusko was deemed to have used an ineligible player as Hendrix Brentz apparently had a residence outside of the territory. The Clarion-Ledger then called the Cats the Choctaw Conference leader as Kosy was to forfeit all games and a perfect record. Now it was time to solidify things with a victory.

The only score of the first half came via an opening quarter 36-yard Crowson sprint and Carmichael kick. It could have been worse as the Cats moved to the Ackerman 1 before being halted. The two opened the second half with a trade of touchdowns. Jackson found Garner from 18 yards. Kitchens put it 7-7.

Louisville responded with three Crowson tallies. One came on a 12-yard pick-six. Addkison added a pair of others; one from midfield. Carmichael connected on two of the scores. The final Indian score came on a 13-yard Jackson strike to Hemphill. The Cats held first downs 13-9 and yardage 322-140.

GAME 9: LOUISVILLE (6-2) vs CANTON (UNREPORTED)
LOUISVILLE 34 CANTON 26
November 11, 1949

Approximately 4,000 fans watched as the Tigers took the opening drive 80 yards where Allen Muirhead recorded the last five yards to make it 6-0. Only minutes later, Crowson found the end zone from 10 yards and Carmichael added the go-ahead kick. The lone score of the next frame came after a Cox interception gave Crowson a 5-yarder. The Cats sat at the 1-yard line as the 13-6 halftime whistle sounded.

Crowson added three more tallies in the second half and Carmichael was true after all three. Ray Pevey added one Canton touchdown from four yards while Muirhead crossed twice (49 and 28 yards). Massey had one extra point. Louisville led in first downs (19-8) and yardage (391-206).

GAME 10: LOUISVILLE (7-2) vs PHILADELPHIA (UNREPORTED)
LOUISVILLE 44 PHILADELPHIA 14
November 18, 1949

The landscape for conference bragging rights changed this week as Kosciusko filed an injunction with the MHSAA to halt the forfeit of games. As such, and since the organization had yet to respond, Kosy held the rights to the crown.

Meanwhile, the Philly team made its way to Winston County to continue the long-time rivalry. Long runs by Addkison and Crowson made way for Crowson's 4-yarder and 6-0 lead. Minutes later, the Tornado took the lead on a Ratcliff 9-yarder to Thomas and Pope PAT.

Back came Louisville in the 2nd quarter on a 1-yard Fulton dive. Then, Addkison "raced 70 yards of broken field" for another. Crowson "got loose on a 46-yard stretch" afterwards and Faulkner added the extra point. Philly added their last on a 30-yard Ratcliff pass to Oliphant and Pope kick.

In the finale, Crowson rushed in from five yards. He then picked off a Ratcliff throw leading to his 30-yard tally a few plays later. Faulkner again connected for the point. Crowson's last came from 40 yards away and Faulkner connected.

GAME 11: LOUISVILLE (8-2) @ MERIDIAN (4-6)
LOUISVILLE 12 MERIDIAN 19
November 24, 1949

This was not the usual Meridian team facing the Cats as they averaged only 154 pounds and were picked seventh in the Big Eight. However, history seemed to favor the other brand of Wildcats and this last tilt proved no exception.

While Crowson had the first points on the board in the 2nd quarter via his 21-yarder, Meridian bounced back with a 21-yard Bobby Robbins run and Elmo Irby PAT. Now 7-6 in the 3rd quarter, Crowson crossed from 13 yards. Charles Russell *"circled left end for 10 yards and touchdown"* afterwards. In the last quarter, Irby found Mickey George from 27 yards to insert the dagger. Meridian paced first downs (14-12) and yardage (293-155).

The Meridian paper called Louisville *"next to Jackson, THE toughest team the Meridian bunch tangled with all year"*.

All-Choctaw Conference awardees including Herald Crowson, Byron Rhodes, Bobby Faulkner, and Sonny Carmichael. Donald Addkison was Honorable Mention. Crowson also made First Team All-State and First Team All-Southern. When over, no Choctaw Conference championship was awarded.

1950–1959

1950 (8-0-1)

Fourth year coach Obie Brown and assistant H.C. Earhart had only 24 players after losing 14 "stalwarts". However, he did have eleven lettermen with which to work. Not long after first practices began mid-August, injuries began piling up. The most important was Billy Fulton, Cat QB, who projected to miss at least a pair of games. Also hampered were Tommy Etheridge and Gerald Herrington. The last two would be back before the lid-lifter.

GAME 1:   LOUISVILLE (0-0) @ STARKVILLE (0-0)
                        LOUISVILLE 6 STARKVILLE 6
                        September 9, 1950

The 30-minute trip up Highway 25 was to occur on Friday. However, rain forced a move to Saturday for this game and many others. The Little Ten Conference Yellow Jackets were *"heavily favored"*. There was a surprise, however, as Fulton was prepared to play.

The field was called *"mud-soaked"* before an estimated 5,000 fans. Fulton hit Charles Crowell and Charles Kugle with 2nd quarter passes to put the ball at the 3-yard line. From there, Faser Triplett crossed the stripe on his second attempt. Now in the 4th quarter, Starkville drove 87 yards and capped it with a 14-yard Bob Kirkpatrick pitch. Kirkpatrick fumbled the critical potential winning point.

Louisville had a chance to still come out victorious but a fumble and interception late at the Jacket 17 ended the threat. Fulton was 11 of 21 for 132 yards. Starkville led first downs (12-6) and rushing (180-34) but the Cats held the air.

GAME 2:   LOUISVILLE (0-0-1) vs EUPORA (1-0)
                        LOUISVILLE 35 EUPORA 18
                        September 15, 1950

Sportswriters thought Louisville best in this one, but warned that Coach Grady McCool's Eagles were *"capable of pulling an upset"*. The Eagles, coming off a 7-4 season, returned 9 lettermen but just one starter (Dean Hall).

The Cats were first on the board in the opening frame after recovering an Eagle fumble at the 30-yard line. Triplett dashed eight yards for the score and Fulton made it 7-0. Eupora came back on the next drive with a 75-yard march capped by a 53-yard Pete Chambliss pass to Ward. The failed PAT kept it 7-6. Another Eagle fumble set up Fulton's 2-yard sneak and his conversion put it 14-6.

In the 2nd quarter, Chambliss dove in from two yards but the conversion failed again. Minutes later, the Wildcats sacked Chambliss for a safety. Triplett then added his second TD from 23 yards and Fulton made it 22-12. They added two more before the end on a 28-yard Fulton pass to Kugle and Triplett's third tally, this from nine yards after another fumble. As time expired, Peeler crossed from two yards to end it.

First downs went to Eupora 15-12 while Louisville held total yards 315-295. <u>The Webster Progress</u> proclaimed, *"This humble writer believes without a doubt that the Eagles are just as powerful as the Wildcats. You just can't beat hard luck"*.

GAME 3:   LOUISVILLE (1-0-1) vs LEE HIGH (UNREPORTED)
                        LOUISVILLE 26 LEE HIGH 7
                        September 22, 1950

Another upset was in the making as the Cats welcomed the Generals to Louisville. When over, The Clarion-Ledger said, *"Obie Brown's Louisville Wildcats kicked over the dope-bucket by upsetting the highly favored Columbus Generals"*. The Big Eight Generals had only four lettermen from a 5-6 season but were *"fast as lightning"*.

While Lee High got inside the Cat 20 twice in the opening frame, neither march ended with points. In the next frame, Fulton snuck in from two yards after his 47-yard dart to Crowell. Up 6-0, Fulton found Kugle to the 1-yard line and Kugle dove over on the next play. Fulton's conversion made halftime 13-0.

Lee High marked their only points in the 3rd quarter on a McPherson 27-yard dash and Ken Kennedy conversion. Fulton went to the air again to get the ball to the 10-yard line. It took Triplett two attempts to reach paydirt. Fulton's conversion made it 20-7. In the final frame. Fulton hit Crowell for a 20-yard score.

In all, Fulton went 16-32 for 176 yards with no interceptions. The Cats held first downs 19-8 and passing 176-5 but lost the ground 140-107.

GAME 4:   LOUISVILLE (2-0-1) @ PHILADELPHIA (1-2)
                      LOUISVILLE 40 PHILADELPHIA 0
                      September 29, 1950

The Tornados had only five letter winners back and Coach Jack Cheatham had to *"depend largely upon freshmen and sophomores. Only two juniors and one senior are on the squad"*. By kickoff, they had beaten only Brooksville 28-0 the previous week.

Philly actually had the first score on a 60-yard Jerry Lott dash, but it came back for clipping. The Cats scored, meanwhile, on their first four possessions. Reports show that Triplett, Crowell, Jack Pearson and John Davis all crossed the stripe. One came from a Fulton pass to Crowell. Fulton was 6-8 for 115 yards and a pair of touchdowns.

GAME 5:   LOUISVILLE (3-0-1) @ ACKERMAN (4-0)
                      LOUISVILLE 21 ACKERMAN 6
                      October 6, 1950

As both teams were undefeated in conference play, this tilt gave the winner a large jump in chances for the Choctaw Conference title. Sportswriters picked Ackerman as the favorite due to the homecoming environs. They also picked them as a favorite for the title pre-season despite going just 5-4-1 the previous campaign.

The home team looked formidable as they moved on their first drive of the game to the 5-yard line from where Karon Covington found paydirt from six yards. The extra point failed. Louisville answered in the next on Triplett's 30-yarder and Fulton made it 7-6 at halftime. Early in the 3rd quarter, Ackerman's Garner fumbled to Crowell at the Indian 10. Davis moved it to the 1-yard line and Triplett again crossed. Fulton put it 14-6.

In the final frame, Fulton and Crowell connected to the 5-yard line and, three plays later, Fulton snuck in and converted. Fulton was 7-15 for 123 yards in the air. First downs (14-11) and total yards (279-132) went to the Cats.

GAME 6:   LOUISVILLE (4-0-1) vs NEWTON (4-1)
                      LOUISVILLE 40 NEWTON 0
                      October 13, 1950

Though their conference record was blemished, the lone Newton loss came to a tough Jackson team. This time, the Cats were *"slightly favored over Prep Beatty's always dangerous Tigers, but the game is expected to be close and hard fought all the way"*.

Louisville opened with a drive nearly the length of the field in seven plays with Triplett adding the last three. Fulton hit Triplett for the conversion. A few minutes later, Davis crossed from a yard and Fulton kicked the PAT. In the 2nd quarter, Triplett crossed from 19 yards. Kugle then picked off a pass and, three plays later, Triplett ran in from eight yards to make halftime 27-0 after a Fulton kick.

Fulton and Kugle opened the 3rd quarter with a long connection and Fulton made it 34-0. Finally, Percy Mac Frazier picked off a pass for a 15-yard pick-six. Billy Herrington ended any comeback hopes with an interception. The Cats dominated first downs (15-6), passing (174-40) and rushing (249-45).

GAME 7:   LOUISVILLE (5-0-1) vs MACON (1-4-1)
                      LOUISVILLE 40 MACON 14
                      October 27, 1950

Many teams, including the Wildcats, enjoyed an open week to rest and heal from the first six contests. Brown did seem to have a tilt with Brooksville for that open date but it did not come to pass due to weather. It seemed a relatively easy week back as Coach Van Brewer had only five letter winners back.

Davis chalked up the opening touchdown just four plays in from 15 yards. Fulton hit Kugle from 36 yards minutes later and two Fulton kicks made it 14-0. Macon hit the board on Larry Morris' 45-yard pick-six and Jimmy Goodwin PAT. Louisville came right back with a Crowell 41-yard run to the 1-yard line from where Fulton hit Triplett for the score.

In the 3rd quarter, Davis crossed from a yard and Fulton hit Crowell from 12 yards. The score was now 33-7. In the last frame, Jack Pearson got in from 11 yards and

Fulton ended Cat scoring. Goodwin had the final score for Macon from seven yards. Fulton went 8-13 for 150 yards passing.

GAME 8:   LOUISVILLE (6-0-1) vs CANTON (4-3; 2-2)
                                     LOUISVILLE 19 CANTON 7
                                     November 10, 1950

Another open week greeted the Cats to prepare for the upcoming Canton matchup. Hopes were high that the Brooksville game could occur but, again, weather prevailed. A win against Coach Mike Campbell's Tigers sealed the Choctaw Conference title but *"overconfidence or an off-night could rue the day for the Wildcats"*.

Louisville jumped out early and held thereafter on a bitter cold evening. Eight plays in to the game, Davis capped a 63-yard drive with his 19-yarder. Fulton made it 7-0. Kugle picked off a Canton toss and they drove 67 yards with Triplett scoring his 13th touchdown on the season from eight yards. The visitors responded with an Allen Muirhead 11-yard escape and Williams' run made it 13-7.

Canton fumbled at the Cat 24 early in the 2nd quarter and Davis made it count from five yards away. Though Louisville fumbled at the Panther 6 to kill a threat, Tommy Etheridge also picked off a wayward Canton pass. In celebration for clinching the title in front of a cold crowd, the team carried Brown off the field.

GAME 9:   LOUISVILLE (7-0-1) @ COLUMBIA (UNREPORTED)
                                     LOUISVILLE 13 COLUMBIA 7
                                   November 17, 1950

The Clarion-Ledger noted that the Wildcats, high from claiming the Choctaw Conference crown, *"ran into gobs of trouble"* in Columbia. The Cats opened with a 20-yard Fulton pass to Crowell but Eagle Day responded from two yards for Columbia and Day tied it 7-7. With just :05 remaining, Fulton hit Kugle from the 35-yard line to seal the nail-biter. Fulton went 14-24 for 174 yards. Louisville led in first downs 14-5 and yardage 307-139.

The fathers of the players hosted an end-of-year chicken and steak dinner after the Canton game at Legion State Park. Boyd McMillin served as Master of Ceremonies. Brown said, *"This was not the heaviest bunch of boys I've ever coached but the most spirited and determined group I've ever dealt with. When they're like that, it's a pleasure to be their coach"*.

Both Billy Fulton and Charles Crowell made the All-Choctaw Conference list. Fulton ended 76-146 for 1,164 yards. Other First Team members included Henry McGee, Jack Whites and Fraser Triplett. Honorable Mentions included John Davis.

The Reflector All-State list included Fulton on their First Team list. Whites and Crowell were Honorable Mentions.

1951 (9-2)

Although H.C. Earhart now held the mentor's whistle, voters still thought the Wildcats prohibitive favorites to repeat as Choctaw Conference winners. That hinged much on the return of Billy Fulton.

The 42 Wildcats on the team endured four weeks of tough practices starting on August 15 *"braving the hot scorching sun in preparation of facing one of their toughest schedules in the school's history"*. Of those reporting for the season, only two were veteran starters with six total lettermen. Coaches Earhart and Walker were pleased thus far and seemed healthy enough to begin games.

On September 11, the team was treated by the Business Men's Club to a speech by Carl Walters, sports editor of The Jackson Daily News.

GAME 1:   LOUISVILLE (0-0) @ EUPORA (1-0)
                                   LOUISVILLE 27 EUPORA 0
                                   September 14, 1951

Eupora opened a week earlier than the Wildcats and walked away with a 26-7 win over Kilmichael. The paper said they looked *"hungry"* with 19 lettermen back.

In the opening frame, Billy Fulton hit Bob Clark for a long touchdown. A Eupora fumble in the next frame set up Dale Bennett's 8-yard scamper and the second of three Fulton extra points. Fulton found "Bird Dog" Talbert for the next touchdown to make it 20-0. Another fumble allowed Bennett a 4-yard tally. In the last quarter, Charles Kugle picked off an Eagle pass to no avail.

Fulton 10-19 for 208 yards. Louisville also rushed for 119 yards while the defense held the Eagles to a total of 95 yards.

GAME 2:   LOUISVILLE (1-0) @ KOSCIUSKO (0-1)
            LOUISVILLE 14 KOSCIUSKO 0
            September 21, 1951

Though already 0-1, there was no giving up in Coach Doug Colston's 30-man squad as they lost to powerful Crystal Springs in the opener. The (Kosciusko) Star-Herald thought the Cats prohibitive favorites, but added, "However, when the Whippets and Wildcats tangle, anything can and usually does happen".

In their first home game since 1949, the only two scores came in the second half. First was a 1-yard Fulton run following a Kugle pickoff in the 3rd quarter followed by Billy Herrington's 5-yarder in the 4th quarter. A blocked punt by Talbert set up the last. Fulton added both extra points. Fulton was 11-21 in the air.

GAME 3:   LOUISVILLE (2-0) vs PICAYUNE (UNREPORTED)
            LOUISVILLE 27 PICAYUNE 0
            September 28, 1951

This week brought a strong south Mississippi powerhouse to Louisville in the form of Picayune. Coaches John Read and Dot Walker were scheming to find a way to stop the strong passing game of Fulton.

Again, it was Fulton leading the charge. He notched a pair of 1-yard scores in the first and second quarters. Bobby Clark had the next touchdown when he "stole the ball on the Picayune 35 and galloped into the end zone". Clark also had the last via his reception from Fulton. Fulton was able to add one extra point.

Kugle was able to add yet another interception on the evening. Fulton went 10-17 for 128 yards and the team rushed for another 129 yards.

GAME 4:   LOUISVILLE (3-0) vs ACKERMAN (0-3)
            LOUISVILLE 47 ACKERMAN 0
            October 5, 1951

The previous week was not good for Ackerman as they dropped a 40-0 decision to league-leading Macon. Since their record stood 0-3 with just three returning players, The Clarion-Ledger believed that Louisville "should win with ease".

As expected, scoring was fast and furious. Fulton found the stripe in the 1st quarter from ten yards and added the PAT. Bennett ran in from 35 yards in the same frame. Other scores came when Wister Allen recorded a 20-yard pick-six. Fulton hit Clark for another. Herrington added scores on a pick-six and a 5-yard run. Clark again snagged a Fulton aerial for a touchdown in the last frame. Every Wildcat saw playing time in the affair.

The Cats led in first downs (11-4), rushing (178-96) and passing (83-6).

GAME 5:   LOUISVILLE (4-0) @ NEWTON (4-1)
            LOUISVILLE 33 NEWTON 7
            October 12, 1951

The Tigers pulled off the amazing the previous week by scoring 20 points in just 14 minutes to come from behind to defeat Columbia 28-27. Nevertheless, writers felt the Cats to be at least two touchdown favorites. The winner remained undefeated in Choctaw Conference play.

"As usual, Louisville's powerful offense was led by passing wizard Billy Fulton who either set up all scores on passes or threw touchdown passes". Herrington drove in from a yard in the opening frame and Fulton converted. Kugle recovered a fumble to lead to a 2nd quarter Clark touchdown to make it 13-0. The last before halftime came via Fulton's 5-yard toss to Kugle. Fulton made halftime 20-0.

Kugle opened the 3rd quarter with a short scoring run and Fulton converted. The Wildcat record of shutouts finally snapped when Pepper Thomas hit Junior Nelson for a deflected touchdown and Thomas converted. Now 27-7 in the final frame, Fulton hit Talbert from two yards to end things. Fulton picked off a late pass to stop a drive.

The Cats led in first downs (17-8), passing (162-40) and rushing (191-94).

GAME 6:   LOUISVILLE (5-0) vs STARKVILLE (3-2)
                        LOUISVILLE 13 STARKVILLE 28
                        October 19, 1951

The week brought Coach W.W. Scales' Little Ten Conference Yellow Jackets to Louisville. Starkville also had a passing phenom as Bob Kirkpatrick accounted for 60 points on the season. In the end, interceptions and fumbles spelled defeat for the Cats.

Fulton's first pass interception by Walker led to Bob Kirkpatrick's 36-yard strike to McElroy and subsequent Walker dive. Later in the frame, McElroy escaped to *"lope the length of the field (80 yards) for the second score"*. Walker followed with a 44-yard dash. Kugle cut into the lead before halftime with a 1-yard plunge after Fulton hit Bennett from 34 yards. It was 21-6.

Walker added their last from 32 yards and Slaughter notched his last of four extra points. In the same 3rd quarter, Fulton passing led to a 2-yard Herrington run. Fulton's conversion marked the last point. This marked the first defeat since the 1949 Meridian game. Ironically, Louisville led in first downs (14-11) and passing (133-36).

GAME 7:   LOUISVILLE (5-1) @ MACON (6-1)
                        LOUISVILLE 25 MACON 13
                        October 26, 1951

While the Starkville loss was deflating, the Wildcats were still undefeated in conference play. In fact, a wave of upsets during the previous week put Louisville in the top spot. Had Macon not lost the previous week, this one would essentially be for the title. *"Both the mighty Macon men and the stalwart Wildcats will be out for blood in this tussle, eager to make up for last week's humiliation"*.

In the opening quarter, Fulton found Talbert and Bennett to set up Kugle's 1-yard dive. Herrington *"charged across"* in the 2nd quarter from four yards but Macon responded with a Larry Morris 10-yarder and Jimmy Goodwin PAT. Now 12-7 in the 3rd quarter, Kugle crashed in from a yard and Fulton connected with Talbert from 28 yards. Fulton converted. The final Macon tally came on a Morris toss to Jack Adams.

The Cats led in first downs (19-10) and rushing (197-58) while Macon held the air attack (236-182).

GAME 8:   LOUISVILLE (6-1) @ CANTON (4-2-2)
                        LOUISVILLE 7 CANTON 14
                        November 9, 1951

A loss by DeKalb, not on the Wildcat schedule for 1951, gave the title to Louisville. Meanwhile the Cats were taking *"a highly beneficial rest"* the week of November 2 and watching for results. DeKalb ended up squeaking by Philadelphia 12-7 to create the possibility of a playoff.

At Ben Roberts Field, Coach Mike Campbell's Panthers *"paid little notice to the passing record of Billy Fulton and proved that without a better running attack, a passing team has little chance against a team with a good pass defense"*. While Louisville held the 7-0 halftime lead on Herrington's 2nd quarter 40-yard pick-six and Fulton extra point run, Canton scored twice in the 3rd quarter to upset the Cats.

Charles Wright got away from defenders for a 63-yard touchdown and his PAT while also taking advantage of a Billy Queen interception to score the other from two yards. Johnny Williams added the extra point. Canton led in first downs (8-7) and rushing (198-106) while Louisville held the air (45-0).

GAME 9:   LOUISVILLE (6-2) vs COLUMBIA (4-4)
                        LOUISVILLE 18 COLUMBIA 6
                        November 16, 1951

Things became a bit fuzzy now and all teams had to await outcomes to see what scenario would unfold. It could still be a Louisville title outright, a playoff with DeKalb, or a three-way tie. Regardless, conference rules *"state that the first and second place teams must meet in a decisive game if they have not played each other during the season".*

Columbia, under the leadership of Coach Bill Hazel, had 28 players featuring nine letter winners. However, one player (Eagle Day) was considered among the best in any conference. Called a *"nip and tuck affair"*, the Cats jumped out first on a 16-yard Jeep Cox dash around the right end set up by a Talbert interception. Back came Columbia in the 2nd quarter with a 10-yard Frank Robertson run.

Louisville had the only two scores of the second half. First, Fulton found Talbert from 18 yards while Kugle had the last on a 22-yard reception.

GAME 10:   LOUISVILLE (7-2) vs PHILADELPHIA (8-2)
                                     LOUISVILLE 20 PHILADELPHIA 0
                                     November 22, 1951

Things continued to get crazy in the conference as Carthage upset DeKalb 12-6. Now, scenarios ranged considerably. A win over Philly pitted the Cats against DeKalb in the championship match. Carthage was declared out of the run due to *"a lower percentage rating"* unless Louisville lost to Philadelphia.

The Cats marched to the 1-yard line in the 2nd quarter before turning it over on downs. However, the Tornado fumbled it right back to Herrington who went across a play later. Fulton converted to make it 7-0. In the 3rd quarter, Kugle plunged in from two yards after numerous Fulton passes. Fulton added the PAT. In the last quarter, another Philly fumble to Paul Sullivan seemed promising. However, Louisville fumbled it back immediately.

Unbelievably, Philadelphia fumbled again and Fulton marched his team to the 27-yard line from where he hit Talbert for the last touchdown. Brister blocked the Fulton kick. The visitors recorded their first conversion of a first down in the final frame. Louisville led in first downs (10-4), passing (150-0) and rushing (99-52).

GAME 11:   LOUISVILLE (8-2) vs DEKALB (9-1)
                                     LOUISVILLE 20 DEKALB 7
                                   November 30, 1951; Ackerman, MS

On paper, Coach Landon Mitchell's DeKalb team seemed favorites in the contest. They stubbed their toe at the end of the season, but still had a better overall record than the Wildcats. Nevertheless, conference records were the only thing that mattered and, therefore, this one was for all of the bragging rights.

Louisville was first on the board in the opening frame when Fulton picked off a Sterling Davis pass. Bennett ran twice and then Fulton hit Clark from 39 yards. Bobby Childress responded for DeKalb on a 14-yarder and a Davis throw to Bernard Rush tied the game 7-7. Long passes and short runs moved to the 1-yard line from where Kugle dove across. Fulton made halftime 14-7.

Now in the final stanza, Clark and Talbert blocked a Davis kick and Talbert recovered at the 11-yard line. Fulton hit Clark from five yards for the final score and, once again, the Wildcats were Choctaw Conference champions. DeKalb got to the 1-yard line late without success.

The Reflector All-State list included Billy Fulton (First Team) as did the All-Southern squad. All-Choctaw included Fulton, Franklin Talbert, Percy Frazier, James Mayo, Raymond McKay and Bobby Yarbrough.

1952 (7-2-2)

Second year Coach H.C. Earhart and assistant Bill Duncan returned nine letter winners from his 1951 Choctaw Conference championship squad. Voters picked them second pre-season in the conference. The stadium now had an *"electric scoreboard, steel bleachers with seating capacity of 2,500, and a cyclone fence".*

GAME 1:   LOUISVILLE (0-0) vs EUPORA (1-0)
                 LOUISVILLE 32 EUPORA 0
                 September 12, 1952

With the departure of Billy Fulton, QB duties now fell to Charles Kugle. In this one, he threw three touchdown passes to Jerome Parker and Joe Hancock. The first came in the opening frame on a 27-yard effort to Parker and Parkers' PAT. In the 2nd quarter, the two hooked up from 19 yards.

Before halftime, Dewitt Crawford raced 95 yards for a touchdown and Parker added the point. In the final frame, Kugle and Parker hooked up from 25 yards while Hancock raced 25 yards for the last. Parker picked off a late pass to end hopes. The Cats led in first downs (11-7), rushing (282-101) and passing (113-0).

GAME 2:   LOUISVILLE (1-0) vs KOSCIUSKO (0-1)
                 LOUISVILLE 33 KOSCIUSKO 7
                 September 19, 1952

The (Kosciusko) Star-Herald thought the local Whippets outplayed Crystal Springs in their opener but still lost 6-0. "The Kosy boys are determined to jump into the win column but will enter the Louisville bout as decided underdogs. The Wildcats are larger and more experienced and are out for their third consecutive football crown".

The renovated Wildcat field now had over 4,000 spectators to welcome their long-time rivals. Henry Boyd grabbed an early fumble recovery at the Cat 43. Great runs led to Herrington digging over from two yards and Parker adding the PAT. Kugle picked off a Kosy pass to put the ball at the Whippet 20 in the 2nd quarter. He later tallied from a yard.

Before halftime and "with scarcely time for one more play", Hancock raced around left end for 25 yards and the score. Bobby Yarbrough grabbed a loose Kosy football in the 3rd quarter and Herrington "smashed the final yard for the score". Parker's "boot went through the posts for the point". With a minute left, Herrington tallied from 25 yards and then added the running PAT. The visitors scored only in the 3rd quarter after a fumble at the Cat 2. Smith carried it over and Williams converted.

The Cats led in first downs (11-3) and yardage (275-72).

GAME 3:   LOUISVILLE (2-0) @ PICAYUNE (UNREPORTED)
                 LOUISVILLE 0 PICAYUNE 13
                 September 26, 1952

The Wildcats were "somewhat battered", facing a powerful Picayune team, and making the trip to southern Mississippi for the encounter. Moreover, Picayune had "a big weight advantage". It was more of a fight that many expected.

The Maroon Tide took a Cat punt to the 27-yard. Two plays later, Jimmy Ross hit Buzzy Grice for the 6-yard tally and Dallas Whitfield notched the PAT. In the 3rd quarter, Whitfield took a punt 74 yards for the finale. Louisville still led in first downs (13-5). They were 8-20 for 94 yards in the air but lost two fumbles. Herrington led rushers with 37 yards.

GAME 4:   LOUISVILLE (2-1) @ ACKERMAN (2-1)
                 LOUISVILLE 19 ACKERMAN 0
                 October 3, 1952

The Indians were coming off a 28-12 win over Macon and described by some as "giant killers of the Choctaw Conference". Coach Dale Davidson had done a remarkable job as he had started "almost from scratch" with just three letter winners on the squad.

In the opening frame, Glenn Watson rushed the Ackerman QB, "knocked the ball from his hands and tackle Long John Kennedy scooped up the free pigskin and galloped across for the six points". Parker added the PAT. Kugle added the next before halftime from five yards up the middle. That, too, was set up by a Kennedy fumble recovery.

Ackerman moved deep into Cat territory twice in the 3rd quarter, but the defense held initially and Yarbrough recovered a fumble on the next march. Kugle added the last in the final frame from 10 yards eluding tacklers on a "keep play". The Indians came within inches of avoiding the shutout before expiration to no avail.

Louisville led first downs (11-6) and rushing (187-78) while Ackerman had the passing attack (92-32).

GAME 5:   LOUISVILLE (3-1) vs NEWTON (3-2)
LOUISVILLE 26 NEWTON 14
October 10, 1952

The Tigers under Coach Prep Beatty would need to *"chalk up a victory over the Louisville gridsters in order to stay in the running and for this reason the game is expected to be a thriller"*. Meanwhile, the Cats now held first place in the Choctaw Conference and needed to add more wins to solidify another title.

The Cats opened scoring in the 1st quarter on a 19-yard Edwards toss to Watson to make it 6-0. Herrington opened the next frame with a 1-yard dive and Parker converted. Back came Newton with a Pepper Thomas pass to Kirby from two yards and Thomas' PAT. Louisville punched back immediately with a 58-yard Kugle strike to Watson. The failed extra point kept it 19-7. Thomas responded with a 1-yarder and PAT to keep the game tight at the half.

Herrington expanded the Cat advantage in the 3rd quarter from two yards. Now in the finale, incomplete passes and penalties kept either from reaching paydirt. Louisville led in first downs (16-10) and the ground (253-47) but Newton had passing (207-98).

GAME 6:   LOUISVILLE (4-1) @ STARKVILLE (UNREPORTED)
LOUISVILLE 26 STARKVILLE 0
October 17, 1952

Originally, the Cats were to enjoy an open week. However, a game was scheduled sometime during the season with Starkville. This proved a chance to pay back the Yellow Jackets for the 28-13 defeat of the previous year.

The visitors jumped out with a first drive touchdown capped by Edwards' 7-yarder and Jack Parker kick. Shortly thereafter, Dewitt Crawford recovered a Jacket fumble and Kugle was able to hit Jerome Parker from 20 yards for the score. Fumbles and interceptions kept the 2nd quarter scoreless.

Louisville opened the 3rd quarter with a long drive and 3-yard Crawford tally. In the last stanza, another fumble set up another Kugle pass to Parker from the last eight yards. Louisville led in first downs 18-3 and rushing (234-55).

GAME 7:   LOUISVILLE (5-1) vs MACON (1-5-1)
LOUISVILLE 26 MACON 0
October 24, 1952

It would be a tough task for Coach Brewer's Tigers to repeat the 8-2 season of 1951 as they had only three lettermen back. Though the Wildcats were prohibitive favorites, The Clarion-Ledger said, *"the Tigers have shown some spirit and will be gunning for the top team with increased vigor"*.

On the opening drive, Kugle crossed from a yard and Parker converted. In the 2nd quarter, Bobby Yarbrough blocked a punt and Henry Boyd took it the 1-yard line. From there. Herrington crossed but fumbled to Boyd for the 13-0 score. In the finale, Kugle ran in from 26 yards, Hancock crossed from seven yards, and Kenneth Addkison added the PAT.

The Cats led in first downs (14-4) and yardage (357-67).

GAME 8:   LOUISVILLE (6-1) @ CRYSTAL SPRINGS (UNREPORTED)
LOUISVILLE 0 CRYSTAL SPRINGS 14
October 31, 1952

Big Crystal under Coach Wendell Webb was supposed to have a tough season ahead with six lettermen and a difficult schedule. As they had just dropped a game to Columbia 13-0, The Clarion-Ledger picked the Cats by 19 points.

This out-of-conference contest did not go as planned. A 2nd quarter Cat fumble at the Tiger 40 led to an eventual 1-yard Jerrell Purvis dive and Elvin Burgenmeyer PAT. As the game ended, Lynfield Beazley rammed in from a yard and Burgenmeyer added the final point. *"The Louisville Wildcats repeatedly threatened but could never quite make the goal line"*. Two drives got to the 4-yard line before dying. The Cats led first downs 12-9.

GAME 9:   LOUISVILLE (6-2) vs CANTON (7-1)
LOUISVILLE 20 CANTON 20
November 7, 1952

This was the biggest game of the season as it could determine the outright champion of the Choctaw Conference. A Canton win gave it to them. A Wildcat victory would send it to percentage margins. This was due largely to a conference committee decision that counted the Crystal Springs loss as a conference loss since they had just removed their team at the beginning of the year.

The Cats moved to the Canton goal line where Billy Queen picked up a fumble and raced 91 yards to paydirt. Junior Harvey made it 7-0. Back came Louisville moments later on a 67-yard touchdown pass from Kugle to Watson. Queen picked off a Cat throw in the 2nd quarter and took it the necessary 56 yards. Harvey's kick made halftime 14-6.

Canton added more in the 3rd quarter on Harvey's 10-yarder to Donald Moore. The PAT failed to keep it 20-6. Kugle tightened it after on a 1-yard sneak and Parker added the kick. After recovering a last quarter fumble, Louisville scored on Kugle's 18-yarder to Jerome Parker. Jack Parker was true on the crucial PAT for the last point. Louisville led in yardage (287-171) and first downs (15-11).

Although a tie, Canton now claimed the coveted conference championship.

GAME 10:   LOUISVILLE (6-2-1) @ CLEVELAND (WINLESS WITH ONE TIE)
                           LOUISVILLE 51 CLEVELAND 0
                           November 14, 1952

The inaugural meeting of the teams appeared to be one-sided even though it was held on Cleveland's home turf. Scoring came in waves and at will. Herrington started with a 5-yard run, Kugle added a 1-yard dive, Kugle and Watson combined for a 62-yarder, Kenny Addkison dashed 77 yards and Crawford ended the half with an 11-yarder.

In the second half, Charles Clark had a 1-yarder and 36-yarder, and Clark hit Pete Smith from 28 yards. Tommy Kirkpatrick had a fumble recovery while Jack Parker and Addkison had extra points.

GAME 11:   LOUISVILLE (7-2-1) @ PHILADELPHIA (7-1)
                           LOUISVILLE 7 PHILADELPHIA 7
                           November 27, 1952

The Tornado under Coach Joe Dollar were no slouch. They were powerful on offense and the defense allowed just 70 points thus far on the year.

Just a few plays into the wet game, Kugle *"took the ball, faked a handoff, then struck out around left end for a 74-yard scoring run"*. Jack Parker added the PAT. On the last play of the half, Charles Banks pulled in a Kugle pass for an 80-yard pick-six. Jerry Lott's kick tied the contest. Louisville repeatedly moved into Philly territory but lost drives on fumbles and downs. Philadelphia made only one move into Cat territory. Louisville, wrapping up the season, led in yardage (297-166).

First Team All-Choctaw honors included Billy Herrington and Marshall Mitchell. Honorable Mentions were Charles Kugle, and Bobby Yarbrough.

1953 (7-4)

While Coach H.C. Earhart and assistant Bill Duncan returned to the Wildcat squad, at least 15 former players graduated. Nevertheless, the cupboard was not all bare in Louisville as 10 letter winners were back along with a host of other talent. Sportswriters thought Louisville had a fine chance of claiming another Choctaw Conference crown.

GAME 1:   LOUISVILLE (0-0) @ EUPORA (1-0)
                           LOUISVILLE 39 EUPORA 6
                           September 11, 1953

The Eagles under Coach Hollis Rutter started season play the previous week with a "romping" over Kilmichael. Graduation brought the loss of seven lettermen but 14 were back. Rutter thought his Eagles *"a great deal heavier and should prove to be a great improvement over last year"*.

It was a quick start as a host of Cats knocked the ball from the QB, Glenn Watson picked it up and galloped 50 yards to paydirt. Later, Charles Clark faked a handoff and ran

19 yards to the end zone. Jack Parker's kick was true. In the 2nd quarter, the Eagles moved as far as an inch from scoring but fumbled. That kept halftime 13-0.

Kenny Addkison pulled a few nifty moves to score early in the 3rd quarter to make it 19-0. Addkison did it again in the 4th quarter from just inches away. It was here that Johnson found a hole in the middle of the Cat defense and ran the kick 74 yards to daylight. Their PAT failed. Pete Smith then got into the books with his 34-yard run and Jack Parker converted. Finally, another Eupora fumble led to an Edwards 6-yarder and Hathorn point.

Louisville led in first downs (16-7), rushing (235-173) and passing (132-0)

GAME 2:   LOUISVILLE (1-0) vs DEKALB (0-1)
                   LOUISVILLE 42 DEKALB 7
                   September 18, 1953

Despite eight lettermen returning. Coach Ray Thornton had *"green"* material and writers were unsure of how they would perform. Their opener was against a strong Aliceville, AL team that *"licked"* them 19-0.

A long first Cat drive ended sadly when Smith fumbled to DeKalb's Bud Brown as he crossed the stripe. Addkison found paydirt, however, on the next march from a yard. Then, Clark and Sullivan hook up from 46 yards to make it 12-0. In the 2nd quarter, Clark did the job from a yard but again the extra point failed. A late fumble kept halftime 18-0.

Louisville added another touchdown in the 3rd quarter on an 11-yard Hathorn dash but the run for the point failed. Edwards followed with a 6-yarder and it was 30-0. In the final frame, Addkison ran in from nine yards. DeKalb followed with their only tally, that a 3-yard Bobby Rose escape and they notched the PAT. The final score came on an Addkison 5-yarder.

GAME 3:   LOUISVILLE (2-0) @ KOSCIUSKO (1-1)
                   LOUISVILLE 6 KOSCIUSKO 7
                   September 25, 1953

Though a definite dark horse for Choctaw honors, the Whippets did have new leadership in Coach Jack "Pop" Warner. Warner was a standout player for the Wildcats in his past. *"The game between these two rivals can always be depended upon to be a good show and this one will be no exception"*.

Before fans could get their seats, Jerry Moore found Quinton Smith for a 60-yard Kosy TD and Charlie Ray Williams converted. They threatened again, but Watson picked off the ball. Twelve plays later, Hancock ended the 67-yard march with a 17-yard run, but Parker's game-tying extra point was blocked. The Cats nearly pulled off the comeback, but fumbled at the 1-yard line with under 3:00 left to play for the heartbreaking defeat.

GAME 4:   LOUISVILLE (2-1) vs ACKERMAN (1-2)
                   LOUISVILLE 18 ACKERMAN 7
                   October 2, 1953

Despite the loss of starters to graduation, Coach Dale Davidson felt his Indians still stood a chance to be better than their 5-5 mark of 1952. This one was called *"wide open all the way with long and spectacular runs stealing the show"*.

After a pair of unsuccessful drives inside the Cat 20, Clark put Louisville on the board with a tricky 71-yard scamper to paydirt. After a Watson fumble recovery, he scored again later on a sneak play. In the second half, a Clark fumble led to Shorty Sallis *"picking up the ball and breaking away into the clear"*. A touchdown-saving tackle by Edwards ended the threat.

In the final frame, and after an Ackerman drive to the 8-yard line, Addkison raced 82 yards to the end zone for the final Cat tally. The Indians avoided the shutout with a 7-yard Ross pass to McClure. Ray found Stricklin for the PAT.

GAME 5:   LOUISVILLE (3-1) @ NEWTON (2-3)
                   LOUISVILLE 27 NEWTON 13
                   October 9, 1953

Coach Prep Beatty was rebuilding completely after the loss of so many letter winners the previous year to graduation. Said The Clarion-Ledger, *"This tilt between two*

Choctaw powerhouses is always one of the hardest fought of the year for both clubs and a win over the opponent is a great help toward a successful season for either team".

Coach Earhart noted during the week that his "team (is) in good shape. The boys look like they are ready". They were as they took the opening drive to paydirt with Charles Clark doing the honors from two yards. Newton promptly fumbled their opening drive to Hathorn and it didn't take long before Addkison rushed in from 21 yards. Parker's second PAT made halftime stand 14-0.

In the 3rd quarter, Addkison added a 2-yard tally to make it 20-0. Newton finally responded in the finale after recovering a Cat fumble in the previous frame. Tommy Williams found Lewis from 25 yards put the kick failed. Edwards then inserted the dagger on an end run of 48 yards and Parker was true. The late Newton score came on a Williams connection to Lewis and a Jimmy Thrash PAT.

GAME 6:   LOUISVILLE (4-1) vs STARKVILLE (4-2)
               LOUISVILLE 18 STARKVILLE 20
               October 16, 1953

This was no easy non-conference game despite playing in Cat confines. "It might be the case of an irresistible force hitting an immovable object", said The Clarion-Ledger.

Louisville got on the board early when Clark found Parker for a 47-yard tally. In the 2nd quarter, Edwards rushed in from two yards. The Yellow Jackets tightened things later on a 1-yard McReynolds plunge and Crigler PAT. Halftime sat 12-7 for the Cats. The visitors took the lead in the 3rd quarter on a Duncan toss to Drane and Crigler made it 14-12. Prior to that, the Cats lost two fumbles while Hancock recorded an interception.

Now with just 3:00 remaining, Clark ran from a yard in for what appeared the winning touchdown. However, Starkville drove 73 yards and tallied on a Duncan pass to McReynolds with just under a minute remaining to snatch the win. "The Louisville boys played exceptionally well, but it seemed that fate was against them as they saw a well-deserved victory slip through their hands in the fading seconds".

GAME 7:   LOUISVILLE (4-2) @ MACON (3-4)
               LOUISVILLE 25 MACON 12
               October 23, 1953

The Wildcats were "working overtime in practice" after the heartbreaking loss. "The Cats are putting forth every effort to see that this does not happen again". Their 4-1 conference record put them behind a couple of teams and they were hoping for losses from both. Their two defeats came by just three points.

In Macon, Coach Van Brewer and his 11 letter winners were a bit less than pre-season expectations. This one would not be better, though there was an upset in the air. In fact, Macon's second drive ended on a James Barnett pitch to Willie Daniel, who flipped to Holley for the 44-yard touchdown. A 2nd quarter Daniels interception allowed Barnett a 1-yard score and halftime 12-0 lead.

The next half was a different story. A first-drive fumble from a yard away did no damage and Edwards found paydirt on the next from the 11-yard line while Addkison added the PAT. As the last frame began, Addkison crossed from four yards to make it 13-12. Then he did it again shortly thereafter from the 2-yard line. Joe Hancock then picked off a Billy Graham pass leading six plays later to Smith's 8-yarder.

Addkison had 10 touchdowns and 61 total points in Choctaw play thus far but still sat in fourth place. Rose in DeKalb already had 16 touchdowns and 106 points.

GAME 8:   LOUISVILLE (5-2) vs CRYSTAL SPRINGS (4-2)
               LOUISVILLE 19 CRYSTAL SPRINGS 0
               October 30, 1953

Those still on the team remembered the 14-0 loss from 1952 that eventually played a big role in denial of their quest for another conference crown. "Reports are that this is the best Crystal Springs team that Coach (Wendell) Webb had had. Louisville (will) have to dig in and play heads-up ball if they expect to take this game. We believe that the Cats will take this game by two touchdowns if the boys really want to win".

An early Tiger fumble to Edwards led shortly afterwards to Addkison's 6-yard score to keep the first half just 6-0. Now in the final quarter, another fumble at the Tiger 15 led to a 9-yard Edwards plunge and Parker kick. Yet another fumble, recovered by Hancock, did no damage.

However, they fumbled it again at their 10-yard line. Clark then hit Parker from five yards for the final score of the evening. Smith grabbed another interception late that came back on penalties by both teams.

GAME 9:   LOUISVILLE (6-2) @ CANTON (5-2)
                           LOUISVILLE 6 CANTON 19
                           November 6, 1953

Writers thought the Panthers were going to be hard to beat. First year Coach Bobby Wilson expected to find good replacements to accompany his ten returners. This contest, in essence, meant the crown. A loss by the Wildcats gave them two conference losses with only a game to go. On Tuesday of game week, The Louisville Business Men's Club hosted the team and coaches.

The game was scoreless until the 2nd quarter when Junior Harvey hit George Pittman from 22 yards. Before halftime, Louisville evened it 6-6 with a 2-yard Addkison run. Turnovers and tough play took the game to the final frame. From here, Canton took over. Pittman escaped from 61 yards for a score and Harvey hit Peterson for the PAT. Billy Halbert then picked off a pass and later crossed from a yard for the finale.

"*This game was played before one of the largest crowds to witness a night ball game in Canton*". Louisville led 16-7 in first downs and 81-73 in passing yardage.

GAME 10:   LOUISVILLE (6-3) vs CLEVELAND (0-8)
                           LOUISVILLE 27 CLEVELAND 0
                           November 13, 1953

This edition of the Delta Valley Conference school was in bad shape as the offense had barely put together any points on the season. Although spirits had to be down as Canton secured their second-straight title, Cleveland was just the medicine needed.

Herky Jordan now took the QB role in this contest to lead the Cats to victory. The initial score came after a Kerr fumble near midfield. A solid drive moved it to the 5-yard scoring run and 6-0 advantage. In the same frame, Jordan hit Hathorn from 20 yards and Parker converted. In the 2nd quarter, Parker grabbed a 27-yard pick-six. Edwards followed with an interception and later 1-yard dive and Parker kick for the final points.

The second half was played to a scoreless draw with numerous substitutes manning positions for valuable experience and playing time. Jordan was admirable in his debut going 9-18 in the air.

GAME 11:   LOUISVILLE (7-3) vs PHILADELPHIA (9-1)
                           LOUISVILLE 0 PHILADELPHIA 45
                           November 26, 1953

Unbelievably, pre-season writers thought Coach Joe Dollar's prospects to be "*not so good*". They lost 11 letter winners with "*no promising material*" to replace them. In reality, this edition of Tornado football ended as one of their better squads.

This Thanksgiving game was one to forget as the Wildcats suffered their worst shutout since the Meridian game in 1940 (59-0). Philly scored in the opening quarter on John Mooney's 1-yarder and a Bobby Burgin kick. In the 2nd quarter, an exchange of fumble was followed by a Tornado interception. They soon made it 13-0 on a 1-yard Mooney dive. Before halftime, W.H. "Duck" Banks broke away from 35 yards and Burgin made it 20-0.

Mooney quickly made it 26-0 on his early 63-yard escape. Kinnard then picked off a Cat throw and Banks passed to Earl Marshall for a 2-yard touchdown. Down 32-0, another interception did no damage. Yet, Philly scored again after a Dewey Partridge pickoff in the last frame on a short Banks run. Others tallies are unreported except for a Keith Eldridge 5-yarder. Philly led 17-4 in first downs and picked off four Cat passes.

The yearbook noted Berlyn Edwards as All-Choctaw.

1954 (5-4-1)

New head coach Hugh Ellis Walker and assistant Harold Ming had a tremendous rebuilding job as only two starters (Joe Hancock and Kenny Addkison) were back. H.C. Earhart was now principal at the junior high. The Wildcats did have a history of finding talented players to fill spots and had a reported all-time record of 34-7 in Choctaw Conference play. Canton (19-11) was a distant second.

The team had a chance to see how they were unfolding in an August 27 jamboree against DeKalb. Conference voters picked Kosciusko as leading favorites for the crown wile Louisville was third behind Canton.

GAME 1:   LOUISVILLE (0-0) vs EUPORA (1-0)
                  LOUISVILLE 13 EUPORA 7
                  September 10, 1954

Originally a *"dark horse"* in conference outcome, some were changing their minds as Eupora romped over Kosciusko the week before. Coach Hollis Rutter had 15 letter winners back from a 6-4 season and would be formidable.

The first score came at the beginning of the 3rd quarter when Addkison took a Herky Jordan handoff 17 yards to paydirt. Charles Ward's kick failed. A later turnover gave the Eagles' Charles Weatherall a 10-yard running touchdown and Gayden Hughes added the go-ahead PAT. The day was saved with 7:00 remaining when Addkison found the end zone on another run. This time, Ward's kick was true.

GAME 2:   LOUISVILLE (1-0) @ GREENWOOD (1-0)
                  LOUISVILLE 13 GREENWOOD 53
                  September 17, 1954

Coach Jim Champion returned six lettermen to Greenwood and, as such, he did not think his Bulldogs to be as strong as 1953. Their opener was a 26-0 thumping of West Tallahatchie. One paper thought they may find Louisville *"troublesome"* but all agreed that the Big Eight team was favored.

It turned out as anything but troublesome. In fact, the first string played only in the initial quarter while the team continued a *"deluge of touchdowns"*. Louisville notched only a pair of Addkison touchdowns on runs of 25 and 18 yards. In all, the Cats fumbled away seven footballs. One report said Greenwood led in first downs (10-7) but Louisville surprisingly held the ground (257-219). Another is more likely with the home team leading both (11-10) and (246-152).

GAME 3:   LOUISVILLE (1-1) vs KOSCIUSKO (2-0)
                  LOUISVILLE 19 KOSCIUSKO 19
                  September 24, 1954

The Greenwood contest hurt more than feelings as at least four Wildcats were injured and would watch from the sidelines. Kosy coach Jack Warner feared *"that (Louisville) will be snapping back with vengeance"*.

In the opening quarter, Whippet QB Larry Therrell ran around the left for the last 25 yards. Back came Ward with a 1-yarder. Ward's PAT put the Cats up 7-6. In the next quarter, Therrell hit Braswell from 20 yards but Jordan hit Phillip Metts from 15 yards. Louisville nearly scored on the last play of the half via Jordan's 50-yard connection with Ward but it ended at the 1-yard line.

Tied 13-13, both teams had one more touchdown in the 3rd quarter. Braswell had Kosy's and Ward for Louisville. Stats, as usual, disagreed somewhat. The Star-Herald (Kosciusko) said the Whippets held the slimmest of margins in yardage (257-253) and first downs (13-12). Jerry Donald had an interception for the Cats.

GAME 4:   LOUISVILLE (1-1-1) @ ACKERMAN (1-2)
                  LOUISVILLE 20 ACKERMAN 14
                  October 1, 1954

Ackerman, slightly worse in record, outweighed the Wildcats 10-15 pounds per player. *"Coaches Walker and Ming say that they just hope that their small team can stand up against the big Ackerman line and not suffer any more casualties"*.

Until there was only 5:00 remaining, it was all Louisville with a 20-0 advantage. Ward (or Addkison) had the first touchdown on an 18-yard run, Hancock notched the next on his 70-yard pitchout from Jordan, and Addkison (or Hancock) sprinted 20 yards for the last. A late on-side kick fumble by Louisville allowed Bowman a 10-yard Ackerman score and another fumble resulted likewise by Bowman. The defense, held, however, to keep the win.

Louisville led on the ground (264-212) while Ackerman led in first downs (10-8).

GAME 5:   LOUISVILLE (2-1-1) @ STARKVILLE (5-1)
                 LOUISVILLE 7 STARKVILLE 20
                 October 15, 1954

An open date was just the medicine needed to get some injured Cats back in good health. It would be needed as Coach Walter "Juicy" Scales' Yellow Jackets were 8-2 the previous season including a 20-18 win over Louisville.

In freezing temperature, Hancock ended a 65-yard drive with his 1-yard plunge and Ward PAT to make it 7-0. A Henry Hudspeth fumble recovery for Louisville immediately afterwards went for naught. In the 2nd quarter, Starkville tied the contest going to the lockers via a Paul Duncan pass to Charlie McReynolds and Slaughter kick.

Now in the final quarter, and with Addkison and Hancock injured, Duncan found the end zone from the right 5-yard line. He also hit McReynolds as the whistle sounded for end things. The Starkville report noted the last as a Duncan run.

Starkville led first downs 11-7. They were 4-8 passing compared to the Cats' 1-5.

GAME 6:   LOUISVILLE (2-2-1) @ MACON (3-4)
                 LOUISVILLE 7 MACON 6
                 October 22, 1954

Despite eight lettermen back, the visitors started winless in three efforts but turned the corner since. Although out of the running for the title, it could improve their final Choctaw position and mark the second-ever win over Louisville (1935). It did not help that injuries abounded in Louisville. Said Walker, *"If we get any more boys hurt, we'll just about have to call off the game"*.

A Cat fumble in the opening frame by Allen Hunter led to a 30-yard drive capped by a Tommy Woodfin dive. Willie Daniel's PAT hit the bar and bounced back. The Cats recovered a 3rd quarter fumble at the Macon 30 leading to a 10-yard Addkison dash. Ward *"iced the game with a perfect placement and we moved out front to stay 7-6"*.

Louisville led rushing (216-134) and first downs (8-4).

GAME 7:   LOUISVILLE (3-2-1) vs NEWTON (1-6)
                 LOUISVILLE 46 NEWTON 0
                 October 29, 1954

Hopes for another Choctaw title were still in their hands, but it would take beating hapless Newton and Canton in order to get the opportunity. This game would be without Coach Walker who was in the hospital due to a short illness.

It was somewhat as expected and scoring came in droves. Ward had the first from 35 yards and added the PAT. In the 2nd quarter, Addkison (6 and 78 yards) and Ward hit paydirt. In the second half, Ward added, Addkison touched twice, and Harold Files got into the books. The Wildcats had 647 in yardage and 20 first downs. Jordan went 8-14 for 99 yards.

The Clarion-Ledger claim Addkison tallies came from 82, 12, 35 and 5 yards. Ward had five extra points.

GAME 8:   LOUISVILLE (4-2-1) vs CANTON (6-1)
                 LOUISVILLE 7 CANTON 0
                 November 5, 1954: HOMECOMING

Homecoming festivities, including parades and honoring of past classes, were underway in Louisville. It would be a tough game and Coach Bobby Wilson's Tiger had a good run of wins against the Cats and had 11 lettermen back. A win in front of alums and fans assured Louisville a shot against Philadelphia for the title.

An early opportunity to score deep in Panther territory ended with a fumble. However, Louisville later got all they needed when Jordan hit Addkison for the 40 yards and lone touchdown. *"Yessir, it was a team victory in the strictest sense of the word. Louisville blockers were as sharp as we've ever seen them and their tackling was a fierce and their namesake".*

GAME 9:   LOUISVILLE (5-2-1) @ YAZOO CITY (8-0)
                     LOUISVILLE 7 YAZOO CITY 43
                     November 12, 1954

Yet another tough out-of-conference foe awaited down in Yazoo County. This time it was the Delta Valley Conference leaders on their turf at Crump Field.

Yazoo City scored quickly on Bubber Trammel's 60-yard punt return and nearly did the same after a James Roberts pick before they fumbled at the 2-yard line. Sidney Fletcher added an 11-yard reception before Addkison found paydirt to make halftime 14-7. It was over after that. Touchdowns came from Trammel (3) and a safety by Howard Fulgham). The Yazoo Herald said YCHS led in first downs 21-6, passing 116-5, and rushing 140-64.

GAME 10:   LOUISVILLE (5-3-1) @ PHILADELPHIA (9-0)
                     LOUISVILLE 7 PHILADELPHIA 25
                     November 25, 1954

The Wildcats got what they wanted but it would not be easy. In fact, this week marked their third game in a row against opponents with a combined 23-1 record. Both teams had two weeks of rest to prep for the Thanksgiving Day affair. *"Philadelphia may have a slight edge in team speed, but Louisville offsets this with a bit of an advantage in the passing department. Both teams feature hard blocking and both have fast backs".*

Just 3:00 in, Jackie Oliphant found Dewey Partridge at the 1-yard line. He took it across shortly after. That 6-0 lead held through halftime. Billy Kilpatrick opened the 3rd quarter added a 5-yarder followed later by a 15-yard Oliphant pass to Partridge and James Spears PAT. Addkison took off from 85 yards to tighten things but it didn't last long before Partridge tallied his third score on a 50-yard reception. Louisville outrushed the Tornado 257-147 while Philly led first downs 13-8 (or 10-3).

All-Choctaw Conference honors included Stanley Hathorn and Kenny Addkison. Honorable Mentions noted Phillip Metts, Doug Sullivan, Charles Ward, Joe Hancock, and Herky Jordan.

1955 (3-7-1)

It was likely that the head coaching job was split this season between second-year man Hugh Walker and newcomer Ken Lawrence. Harold Ming still worked in the assistant role. As many as 40 candidates were practicing in mid-August. Missing were nine key players due to graduation. Nevertheless, the Cats were ironically *"voted the team most likely to win the (Choctaw) conference championship".*

GAME 1:   LOUISVILLE (0-0) @ EUPORA (1-0)
                     LOUISVILLE 13 EUPORA 13
                     September 9, 1955

Eupora had a lot of buzz surrounding Coach Hollis Rutter's Eagle program as serious challengers to the conference crown. Their initial contest ended in a tough 21-0 win over Kosciusko. With only two lettermen graduated, this promised to be a tough opener.

Within the first 4:00, Joe Hancock reversed around the left for 65 yards to paydirt to make it 6-0. With 2:00 left before halftime, Gorge Cummings (or Donald Duncan) ran in from 14 yards and Charles Weatherall added the go-ahead kick. Cummings added the next Eagle touchdown early in the 3rd quarter to make it 13-6.

Late in the final frame, and after a fumble recovery, Billy Smith hit Bubber Hudspeth for 50 yards. Donald Lee Fulton crashed in and Paul Woods tied it with the kick.

Said Walker, "*There were plenty of mistakes made Friday night but Coach Lawrence and I plan to work the squad hard all week in an effort to remedy some of our errors*".
Eupora led in first downs (16-9) and rushing (245-141).

GAME 2:   LOUISVILLE (0-0-1) vs ABERDEEN (1-0)
                   LOUISVILLE 13 ABERDEEN 6
                   September 16, 1955

Another tough 1-0 team was next with Aberdeen, a team last on the Wildcat schedule in 1937 and 1938. Both were Cat victories. The royal blue and white went 6-4 last year under Bert Thompson.

The contest marked a nice bounce-back for the Cats. Numerous fumbles stalled opening drives for both, but Louisville found paydirt before it was over when Billy Smith hit Kenneth Talbert for a 70-yarder. Woods' kick made it 7-0. The Cats threatened before halftime but interceptions for both sides (Jackie Giffin for Louisville) and fumbles stalled drives.

Louisville moved inside the 20-yard line in the 3rd quarter only to come up empty. Another 4th quarter fumble to Snuff Tucker gave Jimmy Walden a QB sneak to close the gap to 7-6. The Wildcats then drove 50 yards with Donald Fulton providing the last six yards. Louisville led in first downs (13-7), rushing (177-12) and the air (70-59). The win came with a loss of Joe Hancock who broke his foot in the 4th quarter and was out indefinitely.

GAME 3:   LOUISVILLE (1-0-1) @ KOSCIUSKO (2-1)
                   LOUISVILLE 0 KOSCIUSKO 33
                   September 23, 1955

Jack "Pop" Warner's Whippets were 1-1-1 against Louisville since his arrival three years before. In Winston County, Hancock's loss was the focus of practices to see who could "*fill (his) potent shoes*". While losing to non-conference Indianola in the opener, Kosciusko was undefeated since in Choctaw play against Union and Newton. That fit as they were predicted second in the conference pre-season.

The early first half appeared to favor Louisville. Fulton actually scored but it came back for holding. A Cat fumble in the 2nd quarter led eventually to Roy Braswell's 10-yard scoring dash and PAT run. Late in the 3rd quarter, Braswell found Larry Therrell for another score and the soon capitalized on another fumble with Braswell's 11-yarder.

Early in the final frame, Braswell ran in for another, Warren Sanders followed it with the PAT and James Cagle capped it with a score. Kosy led in yardage (275-99) and first downs (10-6). In all, the Cats lost six fumbles. Fans, knowing of Hurricane Janet hitting the state, called this one the "*Hurricane Kosy game*".

GAME 4:   LOUISVILLE (1-1-1) vs ACKERMAN (2-1)
                   LOUISVILLE 13 ACKERMAN 7
                   September 30, 1955

More injured joined Hancock as Jackie Giffin (concussion) and Jack Mitchell (pulled ligament) were scheduled to be out. Giffin did come back in this one. Long-time foe Ackerman was led by new coach Prentiss Irving. Said The Clarke County Tribune (Quitman, MS), "*Ackerman is eagerly awaiting their chance to add to their heated rival's troubles*".

An early Indian drive to the Cat 10 stopped but a fumble put them at the 2-yard line. From there, Bright slipped across and Cagle added the kick. "*Some ten minutes and two fumbles later*", the Cats were at the Indian 36. Harold Land eventually crossed from eight yards to make it 7-6.

Talbert picked off one of his two passes on the evening before halftime and ran it back the 16 yards. Woods connected for what would be the final point. The Indians led in first downs (10-6) while Louisville held yardage (111-50). The Cats nearly matched the Kosy game with five lost fumbles while Ackerman threw three picks.

GAME 5:   LOUISVILLE (2-1-1) @ LEE HIGH (1-2)
                   LOUISVILLE 6 LEE HIGH 27
                   October 7, 1955

Though the Columbus team lost at least five meetings between 1918-1933, they held a 6-3 record since that time. This one would be no better on the road for the Cats despite an opponent with a worse record.

Joe Clark "*brought the crowd to its feet*" on the opening kickoff with a 94-yard scoring return, but clipping nullified his effort. After being held, Jerry Donald rushed around and blocked a Generals punt. Nevertheless, the Cats could not advance. Halfway through the 2nd quarter, Tommy McCann (The Clarion-Ledger gives credit to Billy Ray Adams) fought his way "*into our end zone from six yards out with 5:00 left to play in the first half*". A Cross PAT to made halftime 7-0.

A blocked punt in the 3rd quarter at the 2-yard line led immediately to Cross (or Adams) running in from four yards to make it 13-0. A few minutes later, McCann connected for a 60-yard scoring toss and Ray Cross' kick made it 20-0. With 4:00 left, Cross "*rammed through the Louisville defense for their final tally*".

Now just 2:00 on the clock, Wood found Paul Moody who "*in turn uncorked a beautiful left-handed pass down the sideline to Larry Hight who completed the 60-yard play with a dazzling 20-yard run across the last big white line*". Lee led in first downs (19-6) and yardage (300-121). Fumbles were still an issue, but at least there were only three lost.

GAME 6:   LOUISVILLE (2-2-1) vs STARKVILLE (6-0)
                    LOUISVILLE 14 STARKVILLE 48
                    October 14, 1955

This was the last year for Coach "Juicy" Scales as he would assume duties as Oktibbeha County Sheriff soon. Therefore, he was looking to go out on a high note. In Louisville, more injuries and obligations began to wipe out experienced starters.

It took only :40 for the Jackets to score on 10-yard Self run. He did it again shortly after from 29 yards for another. Bobby Neal quickly added the third opening quarter 9-yard touchdown and Kenny Nason added all three extra points. The Cats responded as the frame expired when Stuart Yarbrough rammed through the center for a 60-yard tally and Wood converted.

Hight tightened it even more late in the 2nd quarter with his 2-yarder and Wood made it 21-14. Two plays later, Bobby Neal danced his way 42 yards to paydirt and Nason added the 29-14 PAT. Before halftime, Neal scampered 35 yards in the cold on a pick-six and fans were starting to realize the prognosis. Neal found Eugene Keller for an 80-yard score in the 3rd quarter and Self wrapped it up on the final frame from two yards.

Starkville led first downs (29-24), passing (155-0) and rushing (256-216). Stats are markedly different according to Starkville reports.

GAME 7:   LOUISVILLE (2-3-1) @ MACON (1-6)
                    LOUISVILLE 41 MACON 6
                    October 21, 1955

The maroon and white Tigers, long-time opponents of the Cats, were just 3-5-2 the previous year. Coach R.M. Spaulding's team was not better this season thus far.

Yarbrough opened the contest with his 40-yarder and Wood's PAT. He added his second from five yards a bit later and Wood put it 14-0. That score stayed until halftime despite a late threat by the Cats. On their first drive of the 3rd quarter, Wood got across and added the PAT. B. Skipper tallied the only Macon score afterwards on his 60-yard burst up the middle.

It took 3:00 before Wood recorded the final seven yards of their drive. After reserves took the field, Ralph Frazier found paydirt as did Billy Smith on a 63-yard scamper. The Wildcats led 20-2 in first downs, 33-0 in passing, total yardage (393-104) and recorded a pair of interceptions.

GAME 8:   LOUISVILLE (3-3-1) @ NEWTON (3-5)
                    LOUISVILLE 14 NEWTON 34
                    October 31, 1955

Despite the Cats sitting 12-0-1 against Newton since 1941, The Clarion-Ledger rated this one a "*toss up*". Prep Beatty's Tigers felt they had a strong chance of finally getting over the hump this season. They were correct. The Friday affair was rained out and moved to Monday; Halloween.

Newton dotted the board early on a Giles Bound run to make it 6-0. Early in the 2nd quarter, Jerry Wade added a 15-yarder and Bounds converted. Then, a 45-yard bomb from Milton Thomas to Wade and Bounds kick put the contest 21-0. Milton Thomas added a pair of 3rd quarter touchdowns of 20 and 25 yards with Bounds added both PATs.

Louisville recorded their only points thereafter. First, Joe Clark ran in from ten yards while Fulton grabbed a 70-yard pick-six. The Winston County Journal said it was a Billy Smith with the 84-yard pick-six. First downs (20-7), yardage (274-234) and passing (167-45) favored Newton's Tigers.

GAME 9:   LOUISVILLE (3-4-1) @ CANTON (6-1)
                     LOUISVILLE 7 CANTON 33
                     November 4, 1955

Black and gold Canton, under Bobby Wilson, went 6-2-2 the previous season. A Panther win this night gave them their third Choctaw crown in a row. A Cat loss meant a probable second-to-last place finish in the conference.

Like three of the last four games, Louisville was not in the fight. It did not take long for George Mitchell to race 38 yards to the end zone and Paul Downey to prance 15 yards to paydirt. With extra points, it was a quick 14-0. Before you know it, both Mitchell (1 yard) and Downey added touchdowns to make halftime 27-0. The Cats had no first downs and -2 yards in the half.

Bobby Montgomery added a 4th quarter tally from nine yards to make it 33-0. Louisville's Jack Mitchell blocked a punt later and Elkin "Doc" Hudspeth scooped and scored from the Panther 21.

GAME 10:   LOUISVILLE (3-5-1) vs YAZOO CITY (4-2-1)
                     LOUISVILLE 13 YAZOO CITY 41
                     November 11, 1955: HOMECOMING

Coach Doug Hamley's Indians enjoyed an off-week to prep for the seemingly hapless Wildcats. They went 8-2-1 the previous year but now made the trip to Winston County to face the Cats during Homecoming week. Their previous encounter at Yazoo City was not close at YCHS won going away 43-7. Lynn Cunningham reigned as Queen.

A first-play Indian fumble put the ball at the 30-yard line. Hight "bucked over from their 10-yard line" to make it 6-0. Bee Barrier responded with a 74-yard bolt to paydirt and the PAT made it 7-6. Smith came right back with a 65-yard escape to set up Yarbrough's finishing run through the middle. Wood's PAT made it 13-7.

After that, it was all Yazoo City. Richard Mansfield ran in from two yards, Barrier returned a punt 70 yards and Ken Netherland dove in near the goal. Barrier hit Pugh later from 38 yards and Netherland "plowed over from the 2-yard line". Then Barrier, "who must have been very tired by this time", rushed in for the last. Joe Powell added five extra points.

Yazoo City edged the Cats in first downs (10-6) and demolished passing (162-14). Stats obviously differ by three newspapers.

GAME 11:   LOUISVILLE (3-6-1) vs PHILADELPHIA (7-2)
                     LOUISVILLE 13 PHILADELPHIA 28
                     November 24, 1955

Philly was on the Cat schedule as early as 1915 and played them almost each year since. Billy Jarrell's red and black Tornado held a much better record than that of the Wildcats and the game was simply for Cat pride. As an aside, they went a perfect 10-0 the previous season with a 25-7 win over Louisville.

Louisville "played their best defensive game of the year" this Thanksgiving Day with Paul Moody the outstanding player. He had a pair of fumble recoveries, picked off a pass and led rushers in the second half. The Cats still had two key players out and Coach Walker thought it best to hold them for this one to prep for the following season.

After a 1-yard Billy Kilpatrick score and Jimmy Kilpatrick PAT, Smith came back with an 8-yarder to be behind just one point (7-6). In the 3rd quarter, Jackie Oliphant dove in and later found paydirt from midfield. In the finale, he hit Kilpatrick for the last touchdown. The Cats added their last points of 1955 on a Smith pass to Bubber Hudspeth.

Philly led first downs (15-10) and rushing (203-170). Louisville held passing 102-71. The Cats recovered four fumbles. This marked the worst year since the mid-1930s.

All-Choctaw selections included First Team Jackie Giffin and Honorable Mention Elkin Hudspeth, Larry Hight and Joe Hancock.

1956 (1-10)

The departure of Hugh Ellis Walker now left the whistle solely with Ken Lawrence. First practices began on August 15th. With just five lettermen back after a loss of 16 lettermen, the Wildcats were strongly considered bottom feeders for the upcoming year. The businessmen of the town created the "booster club" and treated the players to a chicken supper at The Rebel Café on September 3rd.

GAME 1:   LOUISVILLE (0-0) vs EUPORA (1-0)
                          LOUISVILLE 6 EUPORA 26
                          September 7, 1956

Since 1924, the Eagles were 0-12-1 against "rival" Louisville. That one tie game came the year before. However, Coach Hollis Rutter's team ranked no less than third in the Choctaw Conference and were coming off a 20-0 "slaughtering" of Kilmichael. Fans in Eupora thought this their best team in many years. The Clarke County Tribune (Quitman) said of Eupora, "spilling Louisville on (their) field will take a great team effort. This one could turn into the best of the night". It did not.

The Winston County Journal called it "a fair licking". The Eagles found paydirt in the 2nd quarter on a Cecil Staggs 9-yarder and added another with about 1:00 left before halftime on George Cummings' 3-yarder to make it 13-0. In the 3rd quarter, Donald Duncan broke away for 22 yards. Louisville drove to the Eagle 4 unsuccessfully, but Torris Ryals found a fumble at the 10-yard line. Ralph Frazier "bounced into the end zone for our only score".

Duncan added his second, this from six yards, with 7:00 remaining to finalize scoring. Stuart Yarbrough rushed for 67 yards and added a 60-yard kick return. Joe Clark picked off a pass in the game and John Mitchell led tacklers. Eupora led first downs (17-9) and rushing (263-166). Passing went to the Cats 16-12.

GAME 2:   LOUISVILLE (0-1) @ ABERDEEN (0-0)
                          LOUISVILLE 14 ABERDEEN 38
                          September 13, 1956

A rare Thursday night affair awaited the traveling Wildcats to face Coach John Tidwell's Aberdeen team they defeated in the only three matches. This time the Bulldogs ranked third in The Little Ten. "Whipping Aberdeen on their field will take a deal of doing and off their performance against Eupora last week, Louisville doesn't figure to be strong enough to turn the trick".

The Cats' only two tallies came from Joe Clark on a 45-yarder and an 8-yarder. Both extra points were successful. Meanwhile, Aberdeen was busy with Robert Gosa with a 22-yard TD reception from Tommy Barrett, Barrett's 5-yard run for another tally (Gosa PAT), and a Frank Halbert run from 22 yards. Then, Jerry Shelton got across and Halbert finished things with a minute left on his 25-yarder. Gosa and Barrett provided the extra points.

Aberdeen won in rushing (265-161), passing (47-36) and first downs (14-7). They picked off a pair of passes and recovered two fumbles.

GAME 3:   LOUISVILLE (0-2) vs KOSCIUSKO (1-1)
                          LOUISVILLE 14 KOSCIUSKO 39
                          September 21, 1956

Despite playing Aberdeen closer than the score showed for three quarters, The Clarke County Tribune said Louisville "may be improved enough to give the Whippets all they can handle. It ought to be a fairly close one and could easily turn into a corker". Their one loss came to Canton 13-0.

It took only two minutes before both Billy Landrum and Warren Sanders found paydirt. Joe Clark responded for the Cats and the conversion was successful. Wood found Billy Rives for another score in the 2nd quarter to tighten things and the conversion ended scoring at the half.

In the second half, the Whippets put up four more touchdowns. Three came from James Cagle on runs of 30, 35 and 9 yards.

GAME 4:   LOUISVILLE (0-3) @ ACKERMAN (1-1-1)
            LOUISVILLE 12 ACKERMAN 13
            September 28, 1956

Though Ackerman had won only once since 1936, they were a solid favorite *"on the basis of play so far this fall"*.

Clark put the Cats up 6-0 early with his 35-yard pick-six. Just seconds before halftime, Clark recorded his second on a 10-yarder to make it 12-0. However, Ackerman had a secret weapon in Billy Bowman. He tallied in both the 3rd and 4th quarters. The critical PAT came via Hunt pass to Fulce. Unfortunately, the paper reported that Clark sustained a season-ending broken foot. It would not help chances to improve.

GAME 5:   LOUISVILLE (0-4) vs LEE HIGH (0-3)
            LOUISVILLE 18 LEE HIGH 33
            October 5, 1956

As both teams were winless, there was a glimmer of hope that the Cats could finally avoid the winless season. Furthermore, the game was in Louisville.

It started as bad as it could get as Harold Land took the opening kick 88 yards to paydirt. It came back for clipping but Billy Ray Adams added two more later, the first from three yards and Ray Cross added the PAT. James Wright then hit Larry Witt from 60 yards for another. Next it was Wright dashing untouched 71 yards on a punt return. Pounders added an 8-yarder and Ken Morgan wrapped up their scoring from two yards.

The only Wildcat points came on a 2nd quarter Wood pass to Rives (10 yards) and a 20-yarder to J.E. Gray in the 4th quarter. With seconds remaining, and after a fumble recovery, Frazier crossed the stripe from the 10-yard line. Louisville won first downs (14-7) and rushing (226-110). Frazier ran for 102 yards in the contest.

Details vary by the local newspaper accounts.

GAME 6:   LOUISVILLE (0-5) @ STARKVILLE (6-0)
            LOUISVILLE 0 STARKVILLE 26
            October 12, 1956

As the Yellow Jackets were nearly invincible for three straight years, there was very little hope of coming home with a win. In fact, Jack Nix's Starkville team was undefeated in 33 consecutive games and finished this year undefeated.

Midway through the opening frame, George Self ran in from five yards to cap a 65-yard march. By halftime, it was 14-0 after Dal Cook squeezed in from two yards. David Parvin managed both kicks. The Cats opened the 3rd quarter with a drive to the 1-yard line but came up empty. The :03 left in the frame, Starkville added a 19-yard Parvin touchdown pass to Mickey McKell to extend the lead. Stillman had the last from two yards.

Louisville held first downs (13-12) while Starkville dominated yardage (275-193). Reports from Starkville had them ahead 17-13 in first downs. Bell had an interception for the Jackets.

GAME 7:   LOUISVILLE (0-6) vs MACON (3-3)
            LOUISVILLE 0 MACON 14
            October 19, 1956: HOMECOMING

The Tigers were coming off a 24-0 shutout of DeKalb and *"drooling over the prospect of winning its first game in history over Louisville"*. Reports actually say that Macon won their only time in 1935.

After a scoreless first half, Macon added touchdowns in each of the next two quarters. The first came after a Bill Lantz pickoff gave Jeffries his 6-yarder. Jeffries added the PAT. Doug Ferris had the last on a 1-yard QB sneak and Jeffries converted. Macon led in first downs (9-5) and yardage (178-158).

GAME 8:   LOUISVILLE (0-7) vs NEWTON (5-2)
            LOUISVILLE 27 NEWTON 12
            October 26, 1956

Not that a winless year was bad enough, but the Cats had lost by a combined 189-64 thus far on the season with no points in the last two games. Writers thought Newton appeared *"to have far too many horses for Louisville"* in this one.

Paul Woodruff recovered a first-play Tiger fumble near midfield in a driving rainstorm. Yarbrough turned that into a 20-yard scoring scamper to make it 6-0. Four minutes later, Wood found Gray *"with a perfect strike"*. Wood faked the kick and ran in to make it 13-0. Woodruff again found a loose football but it ended with a missed FG from the 16-yard line. Bounds cut the lead to 13-6 at halftime via his 2-yard effort.

Yarbrough blocked a 4th quarter Newton punt at the Tiger 26. He later found paydirt on a five-yarder and Wood converted. Back came Newton with Jerry Wade's 95-yard kick return but Ellis Holdiness later nabbed a Tiger fumble. Yarbrough took advantage with an 8-yard score. The Cats led first downs (17-11) and yardage (371-249).

GAME 9:   LOUISVILLE (1-7) vs CANTON (6-0-1)
            LOUISVILLE 7 CANTON 18
            November 2, 1956

The upset over Newton gave hope to Wildcat fans despite the stellar record of the Panthers. When over, The Winston County Journal said, *"For the first time in as long as anyone can remember, the Canton football team whipped Louisville on our own field"*. If reports are accurate, the last time came in 1945.

Bobby Montgomery scored in the opening frame from 14 yards. Louisville tried to respond with a drive to the Panther 8 but could go no further. Snuffy Smith increased the lead in the 2nd quarter with his 6-yard keeper to make halftime 12-0. Montgomery *"broke the Wildcats' back"* with a 70-yard dash to the 2-yard line and then the remainder on the next play.

With 2:00 left, Wood hit Gray from six yards and then added the PAT for the lone Cat tally. Louisville led 15-9 in first downs and 76-0 passing while Canton held the ground (296-165).

GAME 10:   LOUISVILLE (1-8) @ WEST POINT (5-2-2)
            LOUISVILLE 6 WEST POINT 33
            November 16, 1956

These two met in both 1915 and 1936. Each were Wildcat victories. This one would not be nearly the same. It started well as the Wildcats held a 7-0 lead after a quarter thanks to a Wood 34-yard pass to Gray. That lead held through halftime.

West Point got back into the game in the 3rd quarter on a Sandy Sams run. The 6-6 score held until there was just 5:00 remaining. However, WPHS scored three times in 1:50. The first was on a pickoff, the next via the air after recovering an onside kick, and a fumble return. They added their last near the final whistle. The Cats held first downs 12-5.

GAME 11:   LOUISVILLE (1-9) @ PHILADELPHIA (4-3-2)
            LOUISVILLE 7 PHILADELPHIA 26
            November 23, 1956

This game was solely for pride as neither was close to a championship this season. On paper, the Tornado seemed to be the clear favorite.

Philly was in first on Floyd Burt's 6-yard run and PAT, Eddie Johnson tallied from 35 yards, Tom Norton added a 20-yarder (Burt PAT), and Norton closed with his next tally. Turnovers seemed to spell defeat as the 1956 season drew to a close. The Winston County Journal report of the Cat scorer is unreadable. Philly led rushing 384-234 and first downs (10-6), according to the Philadelphia paper.

As a historical side note, one online source notes a 20-0 win over Kilmichael the week before the opener; though no evidence if found. Regardless, injuries and youth led to one of the worst Wildcat seasons in history.

All-Choctaw Conference voters had only Paul Wood and J.E. Gray on the Honorable Mention list.

1957 (8-2)

Second year Coach Ken Lawrence and assistant Fred Morris opened first practices on August 15th with 13 lettermen among the many in attendance. Said Lawrence, *"Our prospects seem good. We have probably the toughest schedule Louisville has had in years and the boys seem in high spirits"*. He addressed Rotary on Sept 4 saying, *"We have the best material we have had since I have been in Louisville. We have a heavy line and mighty good material in the backfield"*.

GAME 1: LOUISVILLE (0-0) @ EUPORA (0-0)
LOUISVILLE 6 EUPORA 19
September 6, 1957

The Eagles had a new coach in Leon Garner but returned a predominate number of players that captured the Choctaw Conference crown in 1956. Said Lawrence, *"We believe we have two advantages over Eupora this year that we did not have last year. One is that Eupora has a new coach and the other is that we hope Eupora will come on the field overconfident"*.

Ralph Frazier capped a first possession drive with his 2-yard keeper to make it an early 6-0 game. Back came the Eagles in the 2nd quarter on a Billy Cook 2-yard run and Boyd Edwards pass to Johnny Gary for the PAT. In the 3rd quarter, Cook rushed in from eight yards while adding another in the final frame from the same yardage.

GAME 2: LOUISVILLE (0-1) vs ABERDEEN (1-0)
LOUISVILLE 12 ABERDEEN 6
September 13, 1957

Aberdeen, picked second in the Little Ten, opened with a win over Bruce. The Bulldogs under John Tidwell were 5-4 the previous year.

The Wildcats again started early when Yarbrough broke off *"a bruising 65-yard dash"* to make it 6-0. That advantage held until the 4th quarter when Jerry Shelton pulled in a 12-yard David Colbert pass to even the game. With less than 5:00 on the clock, Don Hall came into the game at QB and lofted a 12-yarder to Johnny Frank Smith to solidify only their second win since the end of 1955. Louisville led 11-6 in first downs.

GAME 3: LOUISVILLE (1-1) @ KOSCIUSKO (0-2)
LOUISVILLE 18 KOSCIUSKO 7
September 20, 1957

As Coach John Abels' Kosciusko squad just suffered a whipping to Macon 46-0, the Cats entered as *"a slight favorite"* unless the Whippets *"could catch them napping"*. In Louisville, rain was hampering practices and Tucker White was now out for a potential five weeks with a broken hand.

It was not a great first half performance by the Wildcats, but Kosciusko held only a 7-0 halftime lead. That score came in the 2nd quarter by recovering a fumble. Jimmy Fisher hit James Horne from 15 yards and Benny Odom rushed in for the PAT. The Winston County Journal gave extra point credit to Luke Terry.

The second half version was much better. As the 3rd quarter closed, Joe Clark found paydirt from two yards. In the final frame, Clark raced 36 yards for the next tally. With only seconds remaining, Yarbrough dashed 43 yards for the last

GAME 4: LOUISVILLE (2-1) vs ACKERMAN (3-0)
LOUISVILLE 9 ACKERMAN 0
October 4, 1957

A win over the unbeaten Indians strengthened the Cat case for conference bragging rights. It would not be easy as Ackerman featured fine play from All-Choctaw back Billy Bowman. *"Old Man Weather"* prevented play on September 27 and the game moved up a week.

The Winston County Journal praised the brilliant defensive play of the Wildcats as the offense struggled somewhat to get going. Their lone touchdown came in the 2nd quarter on a 39-yard drive capped by Frazier's 2-yard plunge. Clark added the PAT to make halftime 7-0. The last points came in the 3rd quarter when a bad punt snap sailed over Bowman's head and resulted in a safety.

GAME 5:   LOUISVILLE (3-1) vs STARKVILLE (3-2)
                          LOUISVILLE 20 STARKVILLE 14
                          October 18, 1957: HOMECOMING

The victory propelled the Wildcats to number 22 in the Mississippi High School rankings. Originally, the game was to be a home encounter with first-time opponent (Jackson) Provine. However, an outbreak of the Asian flu in Louisville forced a move to October 25. Therefore, it was an off-week for both teams.

Starkville enjoyed three years of amazing football with unbeaten marks. Now, they were back down to Earth with a record similar to Louisville. The Union Appeal said the game "rates about even and should be one of the best played in this region".

A pair of first half Yellow Jacket touchdowns, a 12-yarder by Jack Nix, the other a 1-yarder by John Stillman, and two PATs from Dal Clark (or Larry Bell) put the game 14-0. That held until the 4th quarter when the Wildcats went on a flurry. Larry Aycock picked off a Jacket pass to kill a threat. Clark hit Smith from 30 and 25 yards for tallies while Aycock "romped 30 yards for another". The last came on a 50-yard Smith to Clark pass and Smith conversion.

Louisville led first downs 14-8. Starkville was 4-8-2 in the air again the Cats' 4-7.

GAME 6:   LOUISVILLE (4-1) vs PROVINE (2-3)
                          LOUISVILLE 18 PROVINE 20
                          October 25, 1957

Non-conference (Big Eight) Provine was now back on the calendar. Said Coach L.W. "Tap" Godbold of his Rams, "This is one of those games where we have everything to lose and nothing to gain and Louisville (is the opposite). I'll be satisfied to win by one point. I naturally think we are capable of beating Louisville. In fact, we should beat them, but whether we will or not is another thing".

Provine jumped out early when Charles Underwood capped a 55-yard march with his 35-yard dash. Dale Stuart added the 7-0 PAT. Back came the Cats with Clark's 23-yard pass to Smith to make it 7-6. Provine added a 2nd quarter tally after recovering a Wildcat fumble. Underwood again found paydirt, this time from two yards. In the 3rd quarter, Yarbrough escaped from 43 yards to cut it to 13-12.

In the wild finale, Clark picked up a Ram fumble and raced 43 yards to the end zone for the go-ahead, and seeming game-winning, points. However, with :30 remaining and no timeouts, Provine drove to the Cat 4. As there was just :02 left, it seemed over. However, officials ruled that Louisville called a timeout; something they vehemently denied. Regardless, Underwood found paydirt in those few seconds to steal the win.

The play resulted in arguments and fans swarming the field. The Cats led in first downs (11-8), rushing (295-167) and passing (88-76).

GAME 7:   LOUISVILLE (4-2) @ NEWTON (3-3)
                          LOUISVILLE 41 NEWTON 19
                          November 1, 1957

The disappointing end to the Provine game had no bearing on the race for the Choctaw Conference title. There were still five teams with opportunities, but some would have to suffer upsets for the Cats to jump ahead. For this one, The Clarion-Ledger thought Newton would be "one of (Louisville's) biggest hurdles".

By halftime, it was obvious they were not. Newton, however, jumped out to an early lead after recovering the opening kickoff fumble at the Cat 39. Billy Baucum capped the march with a 1-yarder to make it 6-0. Two plays later, the Wildcats ended up in the end zone when Frazier escaped for 39 yards and Smith converted.

In the 2nd quarter, Yarbrough found gold from 21 yards (Smith conversion) but Newton responded on a 2-yard Vonnie Mack Breland dive. Now 14-12, Yarbrough (19) and Frazier (9) raced past the stripe while Clark hit Smith for the last. Smith was true on all attempts to make it 35-12 at halftime.

While Billy Wayne later got in for Newton from three yards, Smith did the same for Louisville. The final score was secure by the end of the 3rd quarter and reserves took the field for experience.

GAME 8:   LOUISVILLE (5-2) @ CANTON (6-1)
                 LOUISVILLE 19 CANTON 6
                 November 8, 1957

A Canton win put them 6-0 in conference while a loss moved the Wildcats up the ladder. If Louisville wanted to keep fighting for the crown, a win here was critical. Coach Howard Willoughby's black and gold Panthers went 7-1-1 the previous year and were on track to equal or better that mark.

While Yarbrough opened the game a 33-yard dash (Smith conversion), the team "then dropped into a lackadaisical performance for 37 long minutes". Canton moved 70 yards with Joe Turner (or Billy Simpson) finishing from eight yards it to make the game 7-6. It was only in the finale that the Wildcats came back to life. Yarbrough "flashed" 73 yards and "moments later", Aycock did the same from 21 yards.

The Canton report notes first downs in favor of the home team (10-7) while Louisville led rushing (230-146). The Cats were 2-5-2 for 21 yards.

GAME 9:   LOUISVILLE (6-2) @ MACON (5-2-1)
                 LOUISVILLE 21 MACON 0
                 November 15, 1957

The win over Canton moved the Cats to 15th in the state polls. That meant nothing as a loss would end that ranking and their shot at the title. The good news was that both Eupora and Macon suffered defeats the previous week to make it a bit easier. The Tigers led by Coach A.J. Kilpatrick went a break-even 5-5 the previous year.

Yarbrough took a Frazier lateral for 45 yards for the first tally. In the second half, Clark found Johnny Smith and John Crowell for the last touchdowns.

GAME 10:   LOUISVILLE (7-2) vs PHILADELPHIA (2-7)
                 LOUISVILLE 21 PHILADELPHIA 6
                 November 28, 1957

A win here against seemingly hapless Philadelphia gave the Wildcats the title once again. They won in 1948, 1950 and 1951 to go along with other honors and championships. A loss moved Canton and Union into a playoff for the crown. For historical purposes, Louisville was to face West Point on November 22 at Morgan Field. However, the game appears to have been cancelled and no reports of the rationale are found.

A muddy field due to two days of rain forced a defensive battle that left halftime scoreless. In the 3rd quarter, Philly tallied their only points on Eddie Johnson's short run. The Cats responded heartily when Frazier tallied from a yard and the Smith conversion gave them the lead they would not relinquish. In the 4th quarter, Clark got across on a dive and the Smith conversion made it 14-0.

Finally, "in the closing moments of the game", Yarbrough ended the season with a 35-yard run and Smith faithfully converted. The title now belonged once again to Louisville's Wildcats.

On December 12, The Bank of Louisville honored the team with "a festive banquet" at The Rebel Café. Harper Davis served as the guest speaker. In December, awards were announced for the conference. Ken Lawrence was voted Coach of the Year. First team All-Choctaw honorees included John Mitchell, Joe Clark, and Stuart Yarbrough. Honorable Mention went to Neil Hooker.

1958 (9-1-1)

Third-year mentor Ken Lawrence and assistant Fred Morris were picked by voters to finish first in the Choctaw Conference. This was despite the loss of 15 lettermen. Three others were out indefinitely with injuries. One, Howard Ryals, was out for the season with a head injury. Two starters were back for the Wildcats with the remainder "inexperienced personnel for the most part. Team desire and spirit are expected to take up a great portion of the lack of experience".

GAME 1:   LOUISVILLE (0-0) vs EUPORA (0-0)
                     LOUISVILLE 25 EUPORA 0
                     September 5, 1958

Amazingly, after years of domination over the Eagles, the Cats found themselves 0-2-1 in the series over the past three years. The trend stopped on this evening.

Louisville held a slight 6-0 lead at halftime thanks to a 2nd quarter 2-yard plunge by David Wilson. Paul Woodruff added 3rd quarter score on a short run as did Johnny Frank Smith. Woodruff sealed it in the final frame from 32 yards and Wilson had the lone conversion for the Cats.

GAME 2:   LOUISVILLE (1-0) @ ABERDEEN (0-0)
                     LOUISVILLE 20 ABERDEEN 13
                     September 12, 1958

Roughly halfway through the 1957 season, the Aberdeen football season ended after a bit of *"extracurricular activity"*. Deemed one of the more powerful Little Ten teams, they were determined to *"make up for lost time"*.

While Louisville hit the board early on a 32-yard Dickie McGraw toss to Johnny Frank Smith, Aberdeen proceeded to take the lead. Jerry Shelton's 12-yarder tied the game 6-6 while a 2nd quarter pickoff by Buddy Lasky let to another Shelton 11-yard tally and Ronnie Gray pass to Bobby Barrett. That made halftime 13-6 for the home team.

A recovered fumble at the Bulldog 26 allowed McGraw a 15-yard scamper and Smith connected for the 13-13 game-tying point. In the last frame, Billy Watson and Johnny Woodward combined to block kicks. The last set up McGraw's 11-yarder and Smith PAT.

GAME 3:   LOUISVILLE (2-0) @ ACKERMAN (0-3)
                     LOUISVILLE 40 ACKERMAN 0
                     September 26, 1958

The Aberdeen victory moved Louisville to 11th in the Mississippi High School poll. The Wildcats were originally scheduled to meet Kosciusko this evening, but bad weather postponed the game until late November. After a week off, they dropped to 17th prior to traveling to Ackerman.

The Indians were having a tough go this year after losing to Philadelphia, Union and Newton. This meeting would not help. First quarter scores came from Paul Woodruff (31 yards) and Johnny Frank Smith (15 yards). Smith's two kicks made it 14-0. In the next frame, Wilson ran 49 yards to paydirt while Woodruff did the same from 30 yards. Smith's conversion after the last put halftime 27-0.

In the 4th quarter, Woodruff dashed 59 yards and Smith converted. Then, with reserves on the field, Don Hall found the end zone on a 15-yard pass from Jim Davis to mercifully end the evening. The victory moved them to 9th place in polling.

GAME 4:   LOUISVILLE (3-0) vs MACON (3-0-1)
                     LOUISVILLE 28 MACON 6
                     October 3, 1958

If the Cats were to make room in their chase for a second straight title, it would take a win over the Tigers this evening. *"Judging from the records of both teams thus far, the game is rated as a toss-up between two teams battling for top spot in the Choctaw Conference"*. With a pair of Cat touchdowns called back for penalties, it was even worse than the scoreboard showed.

The only score that counted came in the 2nd quarter on a 6-yard Woodruff run and Smith PAT. Freddie Chiles' interception kept halftime 7-0. Louisville opened the 3rd quarter with a 77-yard march ending on a David Wilson 4-yarder and Smith kick. Smith added two more touchdowns in the last frame on runs of 42 and 26 yards. Late in the game, Jimmy Anderson escaped for his 91-yard kick return to avoid the shutout.

GAME 5:   LOUISVILLE (4-0) @ PROVINE (2-2)
                     LOUISVILLE 13 PROVINE 12
                     October 9, 1958

Wildcat fans vividly remembered the ending of the 1957 contest in which Louisville was "robbed" of another victory; albeit non-conference. Now the 7th ranked Cats rolled into Jackson for the rematch. It was to be a rare Thursday night encounter.

The opening Cat drive moved 60 yards ending with Smith's 25-yard bully into paydirt. Provine managed two drives into Wildcat territory before halftime and Louisville did the same to the Provine 8 but all ended unsuccessfully. Down 6-0, Charles Underwood tied it on his 85-yard kickoff return up the middle. Chiles recovered a fumble on the Provine 12 and, early in the final quarter, Wilson *"knifed through left tackle"* from three yards for the tally. Smith's PAT made it 13-6. With just 7:00 remaining, Underwood broke in from 13 yards. *"However, at this point the Wildcats stopped Noble's attempt through right tackle for the extra point"*.

Louisville ran out the last 2:43 on the clock to leave Provine with only one last play. That seemed similar to the previous year. However, it went for naught. The victory moved the Wildcats to fifth in polling.

GAME 6:   LOUISVILLE (5-0) @ STARKVILLE (3-1)
                     LOUISVILLE 26 STARKVILLE 26
                     October 17, 1958

Coach Jack Nix had a Yellow Jacket team called *"one of the strongest clubs in the state of Mississippi"*. Their lone loss came to rival Oxford. Louisville had already handled one non-conference opponent and now they attempted to do the same on another road contest.

The Jackets opened with a 60-yard march ending with a 25-yard John Stillman dash to make it 6-0. The Cats tied it in the frame on a 46-yard drive and McGraw 23-yarder. Woodruff added a 50-yarder in the 2nd quarter as did Smith from 20 yards. Just a minute before halftime, a Jack Nix pass of 63 yards to John Echols paid off and made it 19-12.

Early in the 3rd quarter, a Cat fumble to Stillman deadlocked the game on a 6-yarder. McGraw put Louisville back in front 26-19 with a 2-yard sneak and Smith PAT. Stillman responded for Starkville with a 1-yard dive and his PAT. Starkville recovered an onside kick and moved to the Cat 4. However, the defense held to preserve the tie.

Louisville led 11-10 in first downs. The Cats were 3-6 passing compared to 4-6. In fumbles, Starkville lost two of three while Louisville lost one of two.

GAME 7:   LOUISVILLE (5-0-1) vs NEWTON (5-3)
                     LOUISVILLE 7 NEWTON 13
                     October 31, 1958: HOMECOMING

With four games left, the Wildcats needed only three more wins to secure another crown. Two losses may put Canton and Carthage in the top spot but only if they did not lose in the interim. While Louisville was favored by as much as 13 points in this one according to The Union Appeal, the visitors were not to be taken lightly and *"stronger that they were their last two contests"*.

The rainy and muddy environment forced a low score and plenty of turnovers. The Cats scored on their first drive when McGraw raced in from inside ten yards and Smith made it 7-0. A Newton fumble at the Cat 2 kept halftime 7-0. A 3rd quarter Wildcat fumble led to Billy Baucum's 4th quarter run from four yards. His PAT evened the game.

The kickoff was fumbled by Louisville to put Newton at the 27-yard line. Baucum finally found the stripe from five yards to the go-ahead score. A last-minute opportunity arose on a short punt but another Cat fumble led to their first loss of 1958.

GAME 8:   LOUISVILLE (5-1-1) vs CANTON (6-2)
                     LOUISVILLE 18 CANTON 13
                     November 7, 1958

A win was imperative as a loss created numerous possibilities for three teams to claim the championship. Canton could be no worse than tied for the rights. However, everything rested in the hands of tenth ranked Louisville. The opportunity was unexpected by Tiger coach Willoughby as he said pre-season, *"it's hard to see how we can seriously figure into the pennant chase"*.

David Wilson put it 6-0 early while Jimmy Bolding dove in from a yard to tie it. Billy Simpson's PAT put them ahead 7-6 but Wilson found paydirt as the halftime whistle was about to sound to make it 12-7. Now in the 4th quarter, Johnny Smith added a 66-yard pick-six while Charley Halbert ran in from two yards as the game closed. Canton led in first downs 16-11.

GAME 9:　　　　　　　LOUISVILLE (6-1-1) vs KOSCIUSKO (3-6)
　　　　　　　　　　　LOUISVILLE 33 KOSCIUSKO 0
　　　　　　　　　　　November 20, 1958

　　　　The Whippets were going through *"one of their worst seasons in the history of the school. However, Kosciusko has nothing to lose and everything to gain"* by upending the tenth ranked Wildcats. Coach John Abels expected this with the loss of 10 of 16 lettermen that took away valuable playing experience. *"Looks like a lean year in these parts"*.
　　　　Four first half touchdowns allowed the reserves the second half of play. Three Smith PATs accompanied Woodruff (5 yards), Wilson (24 yards), a 24-yard toss from McGraw to Hall, and Woodruff's 29-yard dash. Late in the game, Smith drove in from 16 yards to finish the game.

GAME 10:　　　　　　LOUISVILLE (7-1-1) @ PHILADELPHIA (4-5-1)
　　　　　　　　　　　LOUISVILLE 20 PHILADELPHIA 0
　　　　　　　　　　　November 27, 1958

　　　　The Thanksgiving Day matchup still held consequences. A win gave them the title. A loss gave it to Macon. A tie forced a playoff between the two teams.
　　　　The Wildcats put it all to rest early on McGraw's 65-yard pass to Smith and a Smith PAT to make halftime 7-0. After a late 3rd quarter interception, Wilson rushed in from five yards and Smith put it 14-0. Finally, McGraw snuck in from a yard to claim Choctaw Conference bragging rights.

GAME 11:　　　　　　LOUISVILLE (8-1-1) vs FOREST HILL (7-3)
　　　　　　　　　　　LOUISVILLE 26 FOREST HILL 20
　　　　　　　　　　　December 5, 1958: DELTA BOWL; Greenwood, MS

　　　　The Wildcats accepted a bid to go to yet another Delta Bowl in Greenwood, MS. This time, they faced the Little Dixie Conference Rebels. As shown by their record, Forest Hill was a good team with victories over some of the stronger Little Dixie foes.
　　　　An early Johnny Woodward pass deflection landed in Woodruff's hands and taken into Forest Hill territory. Smith finished the drive with a 12-yard dash and PAT. The Rebels tied it in the 2nd quarter on a 20-yard Dennis Huffman toss to Tex Duddleston and Gail Davis kick. However, McGraw later found Smith for a 35-yard touchdown and Smith put them back on top 14-7. Just before the halftime break, Davis plunged in from four yards to leave it 14-13.
　　　　McGraw's 3rd quarter dive put the lead back with Louisville. Back came Forest Hill with a 10-yard Davis escape and Duddleston run for the PAT. However, with 1:55 remaining, McGraw hit Smith from 21 yards and the game was over.

　　　　The Louisville Booster Club gave the team a choice of sweaters for their successful season or a trip to the Sugar Bowl. They chose the sweaters. The Bank of Louisville feted the team with a dinner on December 19.
　　　　Ken Lawrence was again named Choctaw Conference Coach of the Year. First Team honors went to Billy Watson, Roy Humphries, Johnny Woodward, Dickie McGraw, and Johnny Frank Smith. Honorable Mentions included Edwin Young, and Freddie Chiles.

1959 (8-1-1)

　　　　The new season brought a new head coach. Fred Morris now held the whistle and assisted by Matthew "Bud" Turner. Although normal graduation of key players took its annual toll, voters picked the Wildcats first in the Choctaw Conference thanks in part to the return of seven returning starters from an 8-1-1 season.

GAME 1:　　　　　　LOUISVILLE (0-0) @ EUPORA (0-0)
　　　　　　　　　　　LOUISVILLE 34 EUPORA 14
　　　　　　　　　　　September 4, 1959

Like Louisville, the Eagles also had a new mentor in James Nichols. Reporters thought Eupora *"considerably improved"* for the upcoming campaign. It was still a tough match for the home team that held just a 2-13-1 all-time record against the Cats. Those two lone wins came after a tie game in 1955.

The first quarter was not impressive for the Cats as Billy Cook put up the Eagles' first tally after an exchange of punts. In the next frame, Louisville scored twice to take a halftime lead they would not relinquish. After a Eupora fumble at the Eagle 20, Tommy Tabor took the pigskin the final seven yards and Harry Shurden converted to tie things. David Wilson then dashed 75 yards to the end zone, and Shurden made it 14-7.

In the 3rd quarter, Paul Woodruff *"made the 80 yards look like a track meet"* for the next touchdown. He did it again from 34 yards *"in record time"* to make it 28-14. That other Eupora touchdown apparently came via Cook's 6-yarder. Mike Forster recovered an Eagle fumble and Dickie McGraw took it the remaining 13 yards. Shurden again was true for the last points.

Louisville led on the ground 296-129 while Eupora had more first downs 9-7.

GAME 2: LOUISVILLE (1-0) vs WEST POINT (0-0)
 LOUISVILLE 33 WEST POINT 6
 September 11, 1959

"Rough and ready" West Point enjoyed an open date to prepare for Louisville and was considered a contender for Little Ten Conference honors. The Cats now lost Howard Ryals due to another head injury and was out for the season. The Clarion Ledger thought, *"it should develop into an interesting game to witness"*.

While details are sketchy relative to specifics, 140-pound Tabor opened with his double reverse. Then, he threw a 21-yard score to Wilson who had recovered an earlier fumble. McGraw was not to be outdone on runs of seven, nine and one yards. Woodruff picked off a Wave throw and raced 30 yards for another. Shurden, who also had a fumble recovery, added a couple of point-after kicks. The lone West Point tally came via a 3rd quarter Jerry Woolridge 37-yard pass to Eddie Dickenson.

Louisville led on the ground 241-148 and first downs 12-11 but lost the air 22-16.

GAME 3: LOUISVILLE (2-0) vs ACKERMAN (0-3)
 LOUISVILLE 41 ACKERMAN 6
 September 25, 1959

An open date despite two practices lost to rain gave the Cats a chance to prepare for perennial foe Ackerman; a stalwart on the Louisville schedule at least 38 times since 1914. The opponent was having a tough time thus far with losses to Philadelphia, Union and Newton. In each of those contests, they scored only a lone touchdown.

Details are not complete in any found material. After a scoreless first quarter, the Cats began scoring to put the game safely away. Wilson tallied twice while Tabor, Woodruff, Jimmy Davis and McGraw also added touchdowns.

GAME 4: LOUISVILLE (3-0) @ MACON (4-0)
 LOUISVILLE 12 MACON 7
 October 2, 1959

This contest was much tighter than any expected. Aside from the obvious 1956 loss, their only other came in 1936. Louisville held victories in the other 13 reported games.

Late in the opening frame, Wilson took a McGraw lateral 60 yards for the initial score. Just before halftime, James Lever ran in from six yards for the Tigers and Jimmy Woodfin gave Macon the 7-6 advantage. In the final frame, McGraw ran in from six yards for the game winning points. *"The victory was, in every sense, a team victory since there was outstanding play on the part of every man on the team"*.

Louisville led in first downs 14-7, rushing 291-138 and passing 46-15.

GAME 5: LOUISVILLE (4-0) @ MERIDIAN (3-0-1)
 LOUISVILLE 0 MERIDIAN 13
 October 9, 1959

The Clarion Ledger predicted the Big Eight team from Meridian to win *"by two or three touchdowns"*. Passes in the final minutes of contests propelled them to their three victories. <u>The Winston County Journal</u> noted that the battle was an *"uphill fight"* and that they would *"count themselves lucky to tie the game or lose by a small margin"*.

In the opening quarter, Jim Birdsong blocked a Cat punt and raced 25 yards for the score. He also added the PAT. A 2nd quarter Pat Tomlinson fumble recovery led to a drive as deep as the Meridian 5 but to no avail. In the final frame, Sonny Fisher capped a 79-yard march with his 1-yard dive and Fisher converted. Meridian led 13-8 in first downs and 238-153 rushing.

GAME 6:   LOUISVILLE (4-1) vs STARKVILLE (5-0)
               LOUISVILLE 7 STARKVILLE 7
               October 16, 1959: HOMECOMING

The familiar opponents were undefeated with wins over New Albany, Oxford, West Point, Aberdeen and Grenada. This game against Little Ten champs Starkville marked the fifth undefeated opponent. *"This should be one of the most exciting games in the long rivalry between the two clubs"*. Halftime presented Carol Cunningham as Queen and former coach and current educator Elzie Hinze a new car.

This closest contest in a long time, played on a rainy field, came down to the last 2:25 when Starkville's Andy Hines took a 59-yard reverse to paydirt and Barry Montgomery converted. What looked like a sure win evaporated when Wilson took the kick 90 yards to the end zone and Shurden added the game-tying PAT. A pickoff ended the Jacket last gasp. It was a *"significant win"* for the Cats as one sportswriter had the Yellow Jackets second in the game.

Starkville did lead in first downs (9-6 or 10-5) and rushing (175-80 or 167-94) but the scoreboard showed it tied. Louisville also lost in fumbles 4-3.

GAME 7:   LOUISVILLE (4-1-1) @ KOSCIUSKO (3-4)
               LOUISVILLE 41 KOSCIUSKO 6
               October 23, 1959

Louisville hit early on a 10-yard McGraw toss to Shurden and then tossed to Wilson for the next. Shurden hit both extra points. Wilson added another from five yards before halftime but Jimmy Davis missed the PAT. Woodruff added another in the 3rd quarter from 70 yards yard and Shurden converted. Later, Tabor got in from 12 yard and Shurden was true.

With second stringers in the game, Louisville marched 80 yards with Sonny White (or George Aycock) adding the last four yards and Davis converting. Kosy added its only tally after on Jack Fenwick's 2-yard dive. The Cats led in first downs 11-5, rushing 306-127, and passing 107-7. Both lost a pair of fumbles while Louisville had the lone interception.

GAME 8:   LOUISVILLE (5-1-1) @ NEWTON (3-5)
               LOUISVILLE 33 NEWTON 7
               October 30, 1959

Familiar foe Newton had only a pair of returning letter winners from their 8-3 team. Their record showed the results of the losses as they attempted to rebuild. Nevertheless, the game was vastly important for the Wildcats as they needed the win to march to another Choctaw Conference title.

Injuries were starting to take their toll on the Cats as Cecil Chiles had a concussion from the Kosciusko tilt and others were nursing injuries that may keep them off the field. McGraw, in a 5-7 passing night, opened with an early 14-yarder to Wilson while Woodruff added an 8-yard dash to the next. Shurden added the PAT. Newton countered when Ray Grissett (or Melvin Payne) hit Sammy Weir from six yards and Buddy Lindsey ran in the PAT.

Now 13-7, McGraw found Tabor from 15 yards and later plunged in from four yards. Shurden was true on the first touchdown. In the finale, Woodruff dashed 55 yards and Wilson ran for the PAT. Woodruff rushed for 155 yards on the night and was acclaimed for his defensive play to keep Newton to just seven points. Shurden and Pat Tomlinson also gained noted as stout defensive players.

GAME 9:   LOUISVILLE (6-1-1) @ CANTON (3-3-1)
               LOUISVILLE 23 CANTON 14
               November 6, 1959

Howard Willoughby probably expected better with 10 letter winners back from a 6-4 squad. With a home tilt against powerful Louisville, it could be a statement game. According to the Clarion Ledger, they lost only one conference game against Philadelphia 21-12. Regardless, Louisville needed the win to claim another title.

In "freezing temperatures" and after a 1st quarter fumble recovery, Canton hit the board on a 33-yard march ending on Jimmy Bolding's 1-yard dive and Jim Grace's PAT. In the same frame, Wilson blocked a punt and Bolding recovered in the end zone for a safety. The Cats marched 40 yards in the 2nd quarter with McGraw gaining the last three yards and Shurden converting. They then went 65 yards and Woodruff did the honors from the last four yards. Shurden was yet again true on the kick.

Before halftime, Canton went 75 yards with Bolding finding Larry Robinson for a 31-yard touchdown. Grace's kick made it 16-14. Early in the finale, Woodruff picked off a pass to set up to set up a McGraw scoring tally to Tabor. Shurden finished scoring with the kick. The Cats led in first downs (16-14) and rushing (250-147) but lost in passing (93-11).

GAME 10:   LOUISVILLE (7-1-1) vs PHILADELPHIA (8-2)
                  LOUISVILLE 27 PHILADELPHIA 20
                  November 13, 1959

The hard work by Louisville set up the game of the year against Bobby Posey's Tornado. The winner claimed the conference crown outright as each would have a conference loss but Philly holding the tiebreaker.

Much of the game recap is illegible, but the contest came down to two crucial plays for Louisville. John Alford had the opening tally for the visitors. Just before the end of the first half, McGraw "snatched a lateral pitch out of the Tornados at midfield and turned on the steam for a beautiful 49-yard scoring play". That, with other scores, put it 20-13.

Jimmy Thompson tied it in the 3rd quarter. McGraw's 2-yard run and Shurden's kick marked the last score of the game to seal the title. In all McGraw had three touchdowns and threw 19 yards for another.

Louisville led in first downs (18-16), rushing (240-182) and passing (19-0).

The Wildcats were under consideration for the Thanksgiving Day initial Broiler Bowl in Forest. That eventually ended as the host Forest team defeated Meadville 31-0. As for All-Choctaw honors, First Team Cats included Henry Shurden, David Wilson, Jimmy Crowson, Mike Forster, and Dickie McGraw. Honorable Mentions went to Sherrill McQuirter and Paul Woodruff. McGraw also earned an All-State nod while Fred Morris earned Coach of the Year in the Choctaw Conference.

Internal awards went to Henry Shurden, Anthony Clark, Paul Woodruff, David Wilson, and Mike Forster.

1960–1969

1960 (4-7)

First practices began on August 15 for Coach Fred Morris and assistant Bud Turner. There were many out to compete which was good news as only five lettermen and 17 former players returned. Many of those lost made up the entire first string from 1959. It did not matter to voters who slotted the Wildcats first in the Choctaw Conference slightly ahead of a strong Macon squad.

As a historical side note, the team now had an actual Wildcat as their mascot.

GAME 1:   LOUISVILLE (0-0) vs EUPORA (0-0)
                       LOUISVILLE 27 EUPORA 6
                       September 2, 1960

The maroon and white Eagles under Coach James Nichols finished the previous campaign 6-3-1. One of those losses came to the Cats 34-14. Like Louisville, they were replacing departing starters and were rebuilding.

The first score came on Jimmy Davis' 20-yard toss to James Humphries. Davis then kicked his first of 3 PATs to make it 7-0 for the Wildcats. Then, Moe Yarbrough ran in from 40 yards. Yarbrough later added a 55-yarder. Finally, Larry Shurden crossed from four yards but the PAT failed. The only Eagle tally came from David Hall's 5-yarder in the last frame.

GAME 2:   LOUISVILLE (1-0) @ WEST POINT (0-0)
                       LOUISVILLE 35 WEST POINT 18
                       September 9, 1960

As with the previous year, the Wildcats took the next week to play out-of-conference West Point. This marked their initial game of the 1960 season.

After an early trade of fumbles, Sonny White put the Cats on the board with a 30-yarder and the first of many Davis PATs. West Point responded on the next drive with a 12-yard Moon Mullins run but the failed kick kept it 7-6. Davis and Dennis Hudson came back with a 30-yard pass connection and Davis put it 14-6. The two did it again on the next drive from 19 yards. D.A. Richardson then picked off a Dickerson pass and took it 40 yards to the 4-yard line. From there Louisville scored but it came back on a penalty to keep intermission 21-6.

The Wildcats overcame a 3rd quarter fumble to allow Hudson a tally. While West Point added another touchdown on an Eddie Dickerson pass to Bulldog Coggins, so did Davis from four yards. West Point ended the contest with their last cross of the stripe on another Dickerson strike to Coggins. The home team led in first downs (12-11) and Louisville amassed over 400 yards of offense.

GAME 3:   LOUISVILLE (2-0) @ ACKERMAN (2-1)
                       LOUISVILLE 40 ACKERMAN 0
                       September 23, 1960

The Winston County Journal said that this contest against Leon Garner's Indians "could be a one-sided affair". That was due largely to the 0-9-1 record in 1959

As the score indicates, touchdowns came early and often. Hudson (3), Yarbrough (6), Therrell Files (4-yard reception), White (3), Shurden (2) after his interception, and Doug Cunningham (4) all got into the record books. Sonny White had an 85-yard dash called back as did Hudson from 46 yards.

GAME 4:   LOUISVILLE (3-0) vs MACON (2-1-1)
                       LOUISVILLE 7 MACON 14
                       September 30, 1960

Coach A.J. Kilpatrick's Tigers, tough the previous year with a 10-1 campaign and Dairy Bowl win, gained pre-season nods to be a Choctaw contender. They returned 11 veterans to make their case strong. Now they needed this game to keep hopes alive.

Macon surprised everyone with an opening onside kick, recovered, and drove for their first touchdown. That came from Joe Baker (or John Morris) with Smitty Henley (or Baker) converting. Henley was just a ninth grader. Louisville responded with an ensuing drive ending on a 10-yard White run and Davis PAT to tie it 7-7. That score held through halftime thanks to a Cat turnover and missed FG.

The finale came in the 3rd quarter when Macon's Baker punched in and converted for the upset. There was another loss in Files due to an unreported injury. Louisville sustained three interceptions and four lost fumbles. The visiting Coach Kilpatrick garnered Coach of the Week for his team win.

GAME 5:　　　　　　　LOUISVILLE (3-1) @ MERIDIAN (1-2)
　　　　　　　　　　　　LOUISVILLE 13 MERIDIAN 33
　　　　　　　　　　　　October 7, 1960

Always tough Meridian was now under .500 to face the opposing Wildcats, but history was on their side along with size and experience. It went as many expected though Jerry Taylor managed a fumble recovery in the opening quarter that went for naught.

Meridian quickly got in from 5-yards from Jerry Greene to make it 6-0. Chiles recovered an onside kick and Davis hit Hudson from 19 yards for the tally to tie it 6-6. Meridian then crossed again on Buster Pool 32-yarder and added the 13-6 kick. Before intermission, Buddy Owen added another from 10 yards to send the teams to the lockers up 19-6.

In the 3rd quarter, Meridian drove 76 yards to paydirt with Don Rigsby gaining from 7 yards, a fumble recovery soon set up a drive 47 yards to paydirt with Pool hitting Don Rigsby and Davis then hit Hudson from nine yards and added the PAT to make the final 33-13. The home team dominated first downs (20-11) and rushing (316-129) but lost the passing game (90-64).

GAME 6:　　　　　　　LOUISVILLE (3-2) @ STARKVILLE (4-0-1)
　　　　　　　　　　　　LOUISVILLE 14 STARKVILLE 26
　　　　　　　　　　　　October 14, 1960

It had been since the disastrous 1956 season that the Cats lost three in a row. However, Starkville was traditionally tough and this was to be no easy contest for their Homecoming. Their lone tie game came the week before against Grenada. Though called "hard-fought", it still turned into another loss.

Early fumbles stopped drives on both sides. However, Davis found paydirt later from two yards and added the kick to take the 7-0 lead. The Yellow Jackets took no time in responding with a long drive and 1-yard Larry Nix touchdown. With a missed PAT, it was 7-6. They soon picked off a pass and George Chesser scored from two yards to make it 12-7. In the second half, Davis hit Hudson from 18 yards and added the go-ahead PAT.

Starkville again came back with a 47-yard Chesser run for the score, and with the Clark PAT, it was 19-14. They took their next drive 80 yards with Chesser scoring to make it 26-14. Louisville got as far as the Jacket 4 before eventually fumbling the opportunity. The Jackets led in first downs (10-8 or 20-12) and yards penalized (65-30). The Cats were 7-12-1 in the air versus the Starkville's 1-4 night.

GAME 7:　　　　　　　LOUISVILLE (3-3) vs KOSCIUSKO (7-0)
　　　　　　　　　　　　LOUISVILLE 13 KOSCIUSKO 14
　　　　　　　　　　　　October 21, 1960: HOMECOMING

The season was starting to slip away. A win kept the Wildcats in contention while a Whippet victory gave them the championship early. The Clarke County Tribune said, "Both teams are capable of victory this Friday night. Game breaks and ability to take advantage could be the deciding victory". This was a much better season for coach Sim Cooley as his Kosy team was just 4-7 in 1959.

A large homecoming crowd attended to see the game and Janet Younger crowned as Queen. The outcome would not be as eventful until just 2:30 remained in the contest. Exchanges of early fumbles and missed opportunities eventually led to a Davis toss to Hudson for the initial tally and Davis converted. Shurden then picked off a pass to lead to a later Davis 1-yard plunge to keep halftime 13-0.

Kosy opened the 3rd quarter with a drive to the Cat 4 but got no further. However, they finally managed a Mike Nelson 3-yard touchdown and his PAT. Now in the final frame, Kosy fumbled to Billy Hull. Louisville fumbled it back but held. Yet another Cat fumble put the Whippets at the Cat 20. Kosciusko drove to the 9-yard line and then Nelson scored and added the PAT.

The Cats led in first downs (12-10) and passing (127-33) while Kosciusko held the ground (141-131). The (Kosciusko) Star Herald featured a pic of Nelson apparently scoring another touchdown, but officials did not agree.

GAME 8:   LOUISVILLE (3-4) vs NEWTON (4-3-1)
                               LOUISVILLE 7 NEWTON 20
                               October 28, 1960

Coach Bill Lindsley already equaled his victory mark of 1959 after a 4-7 season. This would mark improvement for his subsequent year.

An early Newton fumble to Hull and Louisville did no damage but their next to Hull allowed Hudson a 3-yard tally and Davis conversion. Two more lost fumbles also produced no Cat points. The two then traded more fumbles and Newton also picked up an interception before fumbling yet again to Hull. However, the visitors eventually found paydirt with 3:30 remaining before halftime on a Sam Weir run and Melvin Payne PAT and it was 7-7. Yarbrough ended the frame with an interception.

Newton added a tally somewhere in between on a Weir run but the PAT failed. Another Cat fumble in the 3rd quarter did no damage, but Newton eventually managed their last score when Van Lucas "hit paydirt for six" and Weir converted.

GAME 9:   LOUISVILLE (3-5) vs CANTON (1-6)
                               LOUISVILLE 20 CANTON 14
                               November 4, 1960

Things were not good in Canton as Coach Howard Willoughby's black and gold were far behind the 5-4-1 record of 1959. It could have been a bad start as Canton drove within yards of the stripe early but could not cross. The Cats did, however, when Davis found Humphries for the 11-yard touchdown and Davis converted. Canton immediately responded with a Roger Bynum pass to Durwood Robinson and Bynum PAT to tie the game 7-7 at halftime.

Canton went ahead in the 3rd quarter on Pat Grace 2-yarder and Leon Mabry PAT while White did the same for Louisville. A Davis missed PAT left it 14-13. White again scored later and Davis added the last point. The Cats led first downs 12-10 and total yards (220-192).

GAME 10:   LOUISVILLE (4-5) @ PHILADELPHIA (4-4-2)
                               LOUISVILLE 13 PHILADELPHIA 14
                               November 11, 1960

While it did not mean much, a win against Bobby Posey's Tornado would bring the Cats back to .500 on the season. The red and black, worse than 1959 when they went 8-3, were not to be a pushover as they were 4-3 in the past seven meetings against Louisville.

Numerous punt exchanges in the opening quarter eventually ended with 75-yard Jimmy Hardy return to paydirt and his extra point. Davis responded for the Cats from three yards and added the game-tying kick. While Yarbrough quickly recovered a Tornado fumble, Louisville gave it right back the same way. While the Wildcats did have a touchdown before halftime, it came back on a penalty to keep it 7-7 at intermission.

Hard-nosed defense and gang tackling soon gave way to a 3rd quarter Philly James Pair 2-yard touchdown and Hardy PAT to make it 14-7. In the final frame, the Cats fumbled it away but so did the home team to Chiles. Davis soon found the end zone on his 7-yard toss to Hudson. However, the critical PAT was blocked to end hopes of a victory.

GAME 11:   LOUISVILLE (4-6) @ GULFPORT (7-2)
                               LOUISVILLE 14 GULFPORT 40
                               November 18, 1960

While the only past meeting came in 1944 with a Wildcat victory, this would not be an easy game at Joseph W. Milner Stadium. Coach Lindy Callahan had a solid Commodore squad and this marked their last tilt of the year, too. "Louisville has a good football team and our kids know they will have to put forth their best effort if they hope to win". The Sun Herald mistakenly reported Louisville to have a 7-3 record.

Gulfport had their initial tally midway through the 1st quarter on a 12-play drive ending with Loupe Farve's 4-yarder to make it 7-0. They soon blocked a Cat punt and turned it into a Donnie Viator 47-yard scoring run and 14-0 PAT. Davis finally responded with a short run and kick to cut the lead early in the second quarter. The half ended after Gulfport went 11 plays for the 6-yard Farve touchdown and added the PAT.

The first drive of the 3rd quarter ended on a Cat fumble. Gulfport scored again as the last frame began on a 10-yard Sidney Smith run but the kick failed. Louisville began a drive in response, but fumbled again to the Commodores. They eventually crossed two plays later on Butch Palazzo's 14-yarder but again missed the PAT. The Cats struck for their second TD on Davis' 5-yarder to Hudson and his PAT. The home team was not to be denied as they immediately found the stripe from 14 yards on Teddy Roberts' pass to Phil Carriere for their last tally.

Louisville won in first downs (15-14) and passing (203-28) but lost the ground a whopping 241-83.

As for All-Choctaw honors, Cecil Chiles made the First Team while Jimmy Davis was Honorable Mention. The paper also noted Dennis Hudson as a member. Internally, awards went to Larry Shurden, Jimmy Calvin Davis, Freddie White, and Cecil Chiles.

1961 (7-3)

Fred Morris and Bud Turner were back with anticipation of improving on a dismal 4-7 season. "Barring injuries to key players, Louisville has a very good chance to take the conference crown. The team seems to be much improved over last year (and) its attitude good", he said before the season. Morris did have 15 returning letter winners and another 11 returning players with which to work.

Voters in the Choctaw Conference again picked the Wildcats to finish on top with Newton and Kosciusko behind in second and third place.

GAME 1:　　　　　　　LOUISVILLE (0-0) @ EUPORA (0-0)
　　　　　　　　　　　　LOUISVILLE 28 EUPORA 0
　　　　　　　　　　　　September 1, 1961

Pre-season practices hampered a few Wildcats as they prepared for Coach James Nichols' maroon and white, but nothing that seemed drastic. The Webster Progress called the Eagles "small and (would) depend on passing and speed for most of their yardage". To their credit, they did have 11 lettermen back but depth would be of concern.

Louisville scored late in the opening quarter on a 4-yard Sonny White dash and the first of four Jimmy Davis kicks. George Aycock opened the next frame with a 65-yard punt return to paydirt to put halftime 14-0. White added a 3rd quarter run from three yards while Moe Yarbrough dashed 85 yards for the last in the finale. Eupora did make deep advances into Cat territory on numerous occasions.

First downs favored Eupora (12-11) though that could be off a bit (12-8). Cat Players of the Week included Aycock and E.L. Miles.

GAME 2:　　　　　　　LOUISVILLE (1-0) vs STARKVILLE (0-0)
　　　　　　　　　　　　LOUISVILLE 13 STARKVILLE 0
　　　　　　　　　　　　September 8, 1961

These two nearby teams played consecutively since 1940 with other games mixed in, as well. It had not gone well as the Cats were just 2-6-3 in the last eleven games. Once again, Louisville jumped out of conference for their second tilt of the season.

It took just eight plays for the Cats to jump ahead courtesy of a 1-yard Davis plunge and the PAT. A James Humphries fumble recovery produced no points but neither did a later Wildcat fumble and halftime stayed as it was. Two deep 3rd quarter drives ended on downs and a fumble but White later found points on his 15-yard effort. Starkville tried desperately late in the game but fumbled to Bert Thompson at the Cat 10.

Louisville led first downs (19-9), rushing (273-12) and yardage (315-130).

GAME 3:　　　　　　　LOUISVILLE (2-0) @ NEWTON (2-0)
　　　　　　　　　　　　LOUISVILLE 3 NEWTON 7
　　　　　　　　　　　　September 15, 1961

Coach W.R. Lindsley returned 10 seniors in the group of 11 starters including a pair of All-Choctaw linemen. With equal records, reports called them *"rated as the top and among the best in the loop. Both are deep with carryover material from last season. There can be no odds in favor of either side"*.

The first three quarters remained scoreless. Newton had a deep drive to the Cat 3 before fumbling away. Humphries recovered another loose football but to no avail. After more recovered fumbles, Davis hit a FG from the 5-yard line with just 2:30 remaining. However, with under 1:00 to go, Buddy Lindsley found K. Mann all alone in the end zone for the winner.

GAME 4:   LOUISVILLE (2-1) vs ACKERMAN (1-2)
                 LOUISVILLE 42 ACKERMAN 0
                 September 22, 1961

Sam Kendricks' Indians were just 4-6 in 1960 but he did have eight lettermen back. Thus far, the team was not looking any better and this evening would make it worse.

The score was brutal despite White and Yarbrough out with injuries and the reserves playing a big part of the contest. Davis opened with a 17-yarder to Aycock in the 1st quarter. In the next, they did it again from nine yards and Davis added his second PAT to make it 14-0.

In the second half, Bobby Fulcher drove in from the 9-yard line while Aycock added the next from six yards. Again, Davis was true on kicks. Jim Boswell picked off an Indian pass to set up Robert Garrigues' 15-yarder and Davis conversion. Mike Peterson added another score late to end things.

GAME 5:   LOUISVILLE (3-1) @ MACON (5-0)
                 LOUISVILLE 6 MACON 14
                 September 29, 1961

This contest against Coach A.J. Kilpatrick's red and gray Tigers was of utmost importance. If they wanted to stay in contention for the title, a win was essential. The previous year, the Cats lost just 14-7 against an eventual 7-2-1 team. Macon, with one more game, was undefeated. This could provide a tiebreaker in favor of Louisville.

It looked promising as Louisville added the initial score in the 2nd quarter via the 23-yard Davis pass to White. Davis picked off a late Macon pass to keep halftime 6-0. Macon opened the 3rd quarter with a responding Carroll Walker 7-yard touchdown but the PAT failed. Davis picked off another throw but the ensuing drive ended with Macon's Eddie Permenter blocking a punt for a safety to make it 8-6.

The Tigers then added to the scoreboard with an 11-play drive and Jerry Summerford 2-yarder *"for the clincher"*. Macon picked off a late pass and got to the Cat 3 as the clock ran out.

GAME 6:   LOUISVILLE (3-2) vs MERIDIAN (1-1-1)
                 LOUISVILLE 10 MERIDIAN 14
                 October 13, 1961

An off-week helped in many ways for Louisville. What seemed to be a great year was being held by late mistakes and small margins of victory for their opponents. Now, they seemed to be completely out of contention for another Choctaw title. Meridian, again, seemed beatable with only three lettermen back.

Unlike the previous year, it was competitive in Winston County as the Cats tried to get their first victory since 1944. Louisville was first on the board with a 5-yard Davis pass to Aycock. Meridian bounced back in the 2nd quarter on a Don Rigsby 1-yard plunge and the PAT. Aycock picked off a pass just before halftime to keep hopes alive for the Cats.

Davis added a 26-yard FG in the 3rd quarter to make it better. However, with 4:00 remaining, Meridian got all they needed on another 1-yard Rigsby dive to cap a 60-yard march. As seconds ticked away, Jim Batner picked off a Wildcat pass to ice the contest.

GAME 7:   LOUISVILLE (3-3) vs QUITMAN (4-3)
                 LOUISVILLE 28 QUITMAN 0
                 October 20, 1961: HOMECOMING

The blue and gold Panthers under Coach T.E. Cotton looked similar to Ackerman in that they were 4-6 the previous year and returned eight letter winners. This year, they were already meeting the previous win total and looking to extend that margin. It may have been due to some very large linemen to help pave the way. The previous week they took the measure of Philadelphia 34-14.

Aycock got it rolling in the opening frame from 26 yards. Mike Peterson recovered the ensuing kickoff fumble and Davis hit Aycock from 8 yards to make it 14-0 at halftime thanks to the first of four Davis kicks. Hill recovered a 3rd quarter fumble and Davis found Aycock from 26 yards for another tally. In the finale, Davis hit White for a 19-yard touchdown and Davis made it 4-4 on the night.

GAME 8:   LOUISVILLE (4-3) @ KOSCIUSKO (3-4)
           LOUISVILLE 46 KOSCIUSKO 7
           October 27, 1961

Coach Crawford's Whippets had 10 lettermen back from an 11-0 squad but had already lost to Eupora, Macon, Newton and Philadelphia. This one proved to be a bad sign for the home team after squeaking by the Cats 14-13 the year prior.

Just 5:00 into the game, Yarbrough broke in from 17 yards. An ensuing fumble to Bobby Allman resulted in an 18-yard Davis toss to Aycock. Davis and Aycock again connected for the next tally and, with three Davis kicks, it was already 21-0. Davis added a 10-yarder and kick to put halftime 28-0. That frame ended on his interception.

Kosy added their lone tally via a Richard Jordan pass to Hilliard Jordan to open the 3rd quarter and Avon Frost PAT. Bert Thompson recovered a Whippet fumble but a drive to the Kosciusko 8 ended in a fumble. However, Kosy fumbled it right back to Hull at the Whippet 28. In the 4th quarter, Louisville fumbled again but Boswell then picked off a pass. Three plays later, Garrigues pitched to Doug Cunningham from 8 yards to make it 40-7. Garrigues then picked off a pass and Harry Barnes turned it into a 4-yard tally.

The (Kosciusko) Star Herald gave credit for the touchdowns to White.

GAME 9:   LOUISVILLE (5-3) @ CANTON (6-1)
           LOUISVILLE 33 CANTON 6
           November 3, 1961

The Clarion Ledger thought the game could be a "real test ... that could well be decided by expert kicking toe...". Despite a 1-9 record the previous year, Coach Billy Cooper had 12 letter winners back and were much improved.

The Cats wasted no time on their first drive ending with a 10-yard Davis toss to White for the score. Later, Davis dove in from a yard for the next tally. In the 3rd quarter, Aycock escaped from 71 yards and Davis added his second PAT to make it 20-0. Before the quarter was complete, Humphries blocked a punt and raced 25 yards to paydirt and Davis made it 27-0.

Yarbrough put up the last points on a 9-yard keeper. The lone Canton score went unreported.

GAME 10:   LOUISVILLE (6-3) vs PHILADELPHIA (5-4-1)
           LOUISVILLE 34 PHILADELPHIA 7
           November 10, 1961

Coach Bobby Posey had eight lettermen back but was concerned about the weight of his players. The red and black were 5-4-2 the previous year but did have solid returners to make the season promising. A win in this game meant nothing to conference titles, but would show improvement over 1960. This game was a regular meeting of opponents as far back as 1914; give or take a few years.

Aycock got it going on the opening kick by taking it 85 yards to paydirt. Although the Tornado got less that a yard away in response, the defense held. Before halftime, Ken Broussard recovered a Cat fumble and raced to the end zone to tie it 7-7. There was still enough time for White to run in from 15 yards and intermission sat 13-7.

Davis opened the 3rd quarter with a 2-yarder to increase the advantage. Allman then picked off a Philly pass. Davis eventually found the end zone and converted to make it 27-7. Hull later picked off a pass and Yarbrough took a handoff 41 yards across the stripe. Davis kick proved the last points and subs came onto the field to take their positions. Philly led in first downs (11-10).

All-Choctaw designates included Don Woodward, Jimmy Davis, George Aycock and Freddie White. Honorable Mentions went to James Humphries, Wayne Hull, Bertrum Thompson, and Bernard Fulton. Internal awards went to Jimmy Calvin Davis, George Aycock, Don Woodward, Larry Cunningham and Bernard Fulton.

1962 (10-1)

Fred Morris and assistant Bud Turner now had a new assistant in former player Paul Wood to prepare for bright prospects in 1962. Those that showed for practices were much bigger than in past seasons and Morris was "well pleased with the physical condition of the greater majority of the boys". While there were critical losses, seven letter winners were back to lead the program.

New uniforms awaited the Wildcats with white jerseys, maroon numerals and stripes with "Wildcats" across the back for home games. For away contests, they reversed colors with "Louisville". Voters again picked the Wildcats first in Choctaw Conference play ahead of Macon and Quitman. Mississippi Prep Football had the Cats 11th in the state and Choctaw Conference voters picked them tops.

The new stadium with Tiflawn hybrid sod, new lights and an improved press box would not be open this season, but would for the next.

GAME 1:   LOUISVILLE (0-0) vs EUPORA (0-0)
                 LOUISVILLE 32 EUPORA 7
                 September 7, 1962

Even though Louisville was at least 16-2-1 since 1924, there were no guarantees. Coach James Nichols had only 27 players from a 4-5-1 team a few weeks before kickoff with many young and inexperienced. "Some of (the starters) have never played a game in their life. But you can never tell how the young ones will develop so we are hoping for the best". The Winston County Journal picked it 20-0.

Harry Barnes opened things early for the Wildcats with a 54-yard jaunt and Bobby Allman made it 7-0. The Eagles tied it on the next drive with a two-play score from inside a yard and added the PAT. Fumbles hampered more scoring through halftime. A kickoff fumble stopped a threat at the Eagle 23 and Eupora eventually fumbled to Allman. Robert Garrigues went in from 33 yards to put it 13-0.

Garrigues then picked off a pass and Barnes found paydirt plays later from four yards. Allman's kick made it 20-7. Early in the finale, Garrigues and Barnes hooked up from near midfield for the next. Doug Cunningham then raced 81 yards for another to put It 32-7 with just 4:00 remaining.

GAME 2:   LOUISVILLE (1-0) @ STARKVILLE (1-0)
                 LOUISVILLE 46 STARKVILLE 12
                 September 14, 1962

The win the previous year helped a 3-6-2 record against the powerful Yellow Jackets in the past decade. This one propelled the Cats to what they thought they were capable of doing in 1962.

It took just 2:00 to drive 80 yards with Cunningham getting the last 16 and Allman converting. Late in the quarter, Barnes took a fumble 52 yards to paydirt. Another fumble to Larry Caperton allowed Cunningham a 4-yarder to put it 19-0 early. Cunningham added one more before intermission to make it 25-0.

With 5:30 left in the 3rd quarter, Eddie Foster punched in from 10 yards and Allman converted. Starkville got their first score on a 31-yard William Buckner pass to Jack Kean. The Cats then fumbled near midfield where the Jackets drove for the 8-yard Buckner pass to William Dempsey TD. A long Barnes kick return to the 15-yard line set up a one-play score from Foster and Allman conversion. Foster added the last score late on a 3-yarder and Allman iced it.

Louisville tied Starkville in first downs (11-11), led passing (285-189) and lost the air (41-0). Starkville fumbled six times versus the Cats' two.

GAME 3:   LOUISVILLE (2-0) vs DEKALB (1-0-1)
                           LOUISVILLE 40 DEKALB 6
                           September 21, 1962

Don Goodwin's Panthers were 5-3-1 in the 1961 campaign. This marked the first meeting between the teams since wins in 1951 and 1953. Another game apparently occurred in the mid-1930s though not found.

An opening frame fumble eventually led to Louisville getting back in the groove with a Cunningham 7-yard tally. Allman made it 7-0. An exchange of punts led to another tally with a long Cunningham touchdown. Cunningham then picked off a pass to no avail. However, Foster turned in the next score on a 7-yarder and then converted. In the second half, Cunningham again crossed from nearly 40 yards and again Allman was true. A deep drive to DeKalb territory ended in a fumble at the 15-yard line.

Cunningham then picked off a pass at the 1-yard line to lead to Foster's 13-yard score. Moe Yarbrough intercepted another toss. Bobby Fulcher made it count from 35 yards and with Allman kicks it was 40-0 with a bit over a minute left. As the clock expired, Quarles dashed roughly nearly 90 yards for the DeKalb TD and the PAT provided the finale.

GAME 4:   LOUISVILLE (3-0) @ ACKERMAN (2-0-1)
                           LOUISVILLE 41 ACKERMAN 0
                           September 28, 1962

Although a win over former Choctaw Conference and long-time rival would not help standings, the Cats needed this one. Ackerman was now in the Mid-State Conference. Both Cunningham (first with 42 points) and Foster (tied for second with 30 points) led conference scoring. Barnes was also noted for his 24 points.

The Cats blocked an early Indian punt but got only to the 1-yard line. On the next drive, Cunningham rushed in from 30 yards and Allman made it 7-0. A bit later, Barnes found paydirt from 24 yards to make it 13-0. Rick Peterson then blocked an Ackerman punt and took it to the end zone to the halftime lead 20-0.

Cunningham kept it going in the 3rd quarter with a 60-yarder, Louisville recovered a fumble that led to Foster's 6-yard effort, Foster added a tally late on a 93-yard escape but it came back on a penalty, and Cunningham finally dashed 88 yards for the last. Allman was true on all PATs.

GAME 5:   LOUISVILLE (4-0) vs MACON (4-1)
                           LOUISVILLE 20 MACON 0
                           October 5, 1962

A.J. Kilpatrick and his Tigers were off a stellar season and picked just one slot below Louisville for Choctaw honors. As a side note, they were now called "Noxubee County" by many local papers. In many ways, this was the most important tilt of the season as Macon, Choctaw winners with a perfect 11-0 record in 1961, were also undefeated in the conference. This game went a long way in the event of a tie-breaker.

Called "a hard-nosed blood and guts affair", the Cats scored early on a sustained drive ending with a 2-foot Garrigues plunge and Allman kick. That score held through halftime. Barnes added a 3rd quarter tally from 24 yards and Allman converted. With just 7:00 remaining, Barnes added the last from three yards. Both Cunningham and Lee Castle ended any threats with interceptions late.

Said the visitor paper, "The general impression was that the Tigers played well, but were up against a superior team last Friday night".

GAME 6:   LOUISVILLE (5-0) at MERIDIAN (2-1)
                           LOUISVILLE 7 MERIDIAN 19
                           October 12, 1962

Since 1948, the Louisville Wildcats were a measly 0-5 against the powerful Big Eight version of Wildcats. Many were hopeful that this team could break the losing streak. Their only blemish came in their first game in a one-point loss to Laurel.

A solid opening drive got to the Meridian 19 before Louisville lost the ball on a fumble. Just before the end of the quarter, Meridian's Wayne Bailey recovered their own fumble and raced to paydirt. Just as he prepared to cross, the ball slipped from his hands and out of the back of the end zone. Officials ruled it a touchdown and Bailey's PAT made it

7-0. They added their next just three minutes before halftime on a Kent Busbee dash but Allman blocked their PAT.

Louisville began a comeback in the 3rd quarter on a 1-yard Foster plunge and Allman kick. Meridian responded to start the 4th quarter on a 1-yard Busbee plunge but Allman again blocked the PAT. The home team led in yardage 285-212 with Cunningham responsible to 158 of the Cats' yardage.

GAME 7:   LOUISVILLE (5-1) vs NEWTON (1-3-1)
                  LOUISVILLE 52 NEWTON 6
                  October 19, 1962

It was a down year for Coach Bill Lindsley's Tigers. Not much was expected pre-season as voters had them sixth in conference predictions.

The Wildcats put up three scores in the opening frame alone with Barnes (51), Cunningham (55) and Foster (37) runs. Dave Fair (1) and Cunningham (6-yard reception) joined the books in the 2nd quarter. Newton added their lone tally in the 3rd quarter while Barnes responded with a 65-yarder. In the last frame, Foster (31) and James Smith (36-yard pick-six) ended scoring.

GAME 8:   LOUISVILLE (6-1) @ QUITMAN (2-3-1)
                  LOUISVILLE 25 QUITMAN 0
                  October 26, 1962

Things were not much better for Quitman as they struggled thus far this season. Still, Morris was not taking things for granted. *"We are due for a letdown"*.

That looked like prophecy as Louisville gained only six points in the first half. That came on a 2nd quarter Foster run of three yards. Late in the 3rd quarter, Foster added another; this time from 41 yards. In the final frame, the Cats fumbled to Quitman but the defense held. Barnes (11) and Cunningham (7) each recorded scores afterwards and Allman converted on a lone PAT for the night.

GAME 9:   LOUISVILLE (7-1) vs KOCIUSKO (5-2)
                  LOUISVILLE 47 KOSCIUSKO 19
                  November 2, 1962

An early Cat fumble ended with a Barnes interception to stop the threat. He later added a 32-yard jaunt for a touchdown. A Kosy fumble on the kickoff allowed Foster a 1-yard dive and Allman made it 13-0. The Whippets came back with a 65-yard march ending on Richard Jordan's 38-yard strike with Emmett Sylvester. Hubert Wright ran in for the extra point.

Cunningham got things going in the 2nd quarter on a 5-yard running score, an interception, and a whopping 62-yarder. With Allman's toe, halftime sat 33-7. Potts opened the 3rd quarter for Kosciusko with a 1-yard plunge. Late in the frame, a Cat fumble ended a promising drive. Foster responded in the 4th quarter with his 13-yarder and Allman made it 40-13.

Back came Kosy with a 5-yard pass from Jordan to Jim Henry. However, with less than a minute to go, Foster dashed 45 yards for the last TD. Allman's kick was good.

GAME 10:   LOUISVILLE (8-1) vs PHILADELPHIA (8-2)
                  LOUISVILLE 58 PHILADELPHIA 9
                  November 16, 1962

This was for all the marbles relative to holding the Choctaw crown. Philly started slowly with a pair of losses but since made considerable improvement. The two played one another annually since at least 1948 and perhaps as far back as 1941.

Late in the opening frame, Philly hit the board on a FG, but the Cats came storming back. Cunningham returned a punt 54 yards to paydirt, Foster burst through from three yards, Fair picked off a Jim Haddock pass, and Foster turned it into a 5-yard tally. With three Allman kicks, halftime sat 21-3. Foster added another 3-yarder in the 3rd quarter while the visitors got their first touchdown on a 1-yard Haddock sneak.

The Cats recovered the onside kick and Cunningham made it count from 60 yards to make it 33-9. Substitutes took the field for Louisville but scoring continued. Peterson got across from outside 30 yards and did it again from about the same distance. Fair picked off another pass, Bobby Fulcher got in the books from 19 yards and Allman connected. Finally, a James Smith pickoff led to Fair's 24-yard pass to Fulcher.

This marked the most points scored since potentially 1940 when Louisville beat Ethel 60-0. More importantly, Louisville now claimed their seventh Choctaw title. Cunningham (108) and Foster (102) were points leaders in the circuit.

GAME 11:   LOUISVILLE (9-1) vs MENDENHALL (9-1)
            LOUISVILLE 20 MENDENHALL 9
            November 30, 1962: MISSISSIPPI BOWL; Jackson, MS

Both Louisville and the Little Dixie Conference Tigers accepted invitations to play in the Mississippi Bowl in Jackson. Coach A.J. "Red" Mangum's squad had an identical record to Louisville. "We'll be up against a real tough team". Said Morris, "I know how that Mendenhall club operates. They'll be real tough". His familiarity came as a graduate of the same Mendenhall school.

Mendy struck on their opening drive on a 12-yard Frank Lang run and H.N. Shows' PAT made it 7-0. An ensuing Tiger interception did no damage. Cunningham responded for the Cats early in the 2nd quarter on his 13-yarder and Allman tied the game. Then, Foster "blasted up the middle" for a 38-yard touchdown to make it 13-7 at halftime.

In the 3rd quarter, a Fulcher interception of Shows led to Barnes' 6-yard dash and Allman recorded the last Louisville points. The final tally came on a bad punt snap resulting in a safety for the Tigers by Bob Sullivan. Mendy won first downs (11-9) and passing (99-0) while the Cats held the ground (242-140). Bernard Fulton was chosen Outstanding Lineman in the contest.

Louisville held a number of All-Choctaw honors at the end of the season. First Team players included Larry Cunningham, Larry Caperton, Jerry Taylor, Bobby Allman, Bernard Fulton, Doug Cunningham, Harry Barnes and Eddie Foster. Honorable Mentions went to Gene Fair, Billy Hull, and Jerry Fulcher. Fred Morris was Coach of the Year.

Douglas Cunningham also earned All-State and won the internal MVP and Best Back. Bernard Fulton was Best Lineman.

1963 (4-6)

Fred Morris was back for his fifth season along with stalwart assistant Bud Turner and new addition Bobby Smith. Although the Wildcats had 12 returning letter winners, the schedule was set firmly against them with teams like Hattiesburg and Meridian on the list. Additionally, Treadwell High out of Memphis would make their inaugural visit to Louisville.

Said Turner to The Louisville Business Men's Club, "We have, perhaps, the heaviest schedule this year that the Wildcats have ever faced. We are playing two Big Eight teams. We have Treadwell (Memphis) on our schedule and I understand that this school as 4,600 students in the top three grades. In other words, they have as many in their senior class as we do in our whole high school. Another non-conference game is that with Starkville of the Little Ten. Starkville has an excellent backfield this year and should be a top contender in its conference".

There was good news, however. The Cats debuted their new R.E. Hinze Stadium and were picked by voters to again take the Choctaw Conference title.

GAME 1:   LOUISVILLE (0-0) @ EUPORA (0-0)
            LOUISVILLE 48 EUPORA 6
            September 6, 1963

Annual opponent Eupora was a dismal eighth in the conference pre-season picks. It did not help that Louisville was 16-2-1 all-time against the Eagles. Eupora went just 2-7-1 the previous year but did have two new experienced coaches to get it going.

Louisville recovered an opening onside kick and Eddie Foster made it count later from three yards. Bobby Allman converted on his first of six extra points. James Smith then took the pigskin 63 yards on the ensuing drive. In the 2nd quarter, Robert Garrigues snuck over from two yards next and then took a Buddy Bowen punt 55 yards to paydirt. Jim Boswell picked off an Eagle pass but the halftime clock expired before the Cats could cross.

Another Boswell interception and this time took it 40 yards to the end zone. Late in the 3rd quarter, Foster found the end one from 22 yards while Billy Charles Justice then returned a Eupora fumble from the Eagle 20 across the stripe. After a 4th quarter Bobby Harrison fumble recovery, subs took the field. Bowel found Jim Sones for their lone tally afterwards. The Cats finally put it away on a 60-yard escape.

The (Eupora) Webster Progress was highly critical of the visitors and what they called *"pouring it on an outmanned team"*.

GAME 2:   LOUISVILLE (1-0) vs STARKVILLE (UNREPORTED)
                                    LOUISVILLE 33 STARKVILLE 0
                                    September 13, 1963

Over 6,000 fans joined festivities to open the new R.E. Hinze Stadium. And, their Wildcats gave them something to cheer for!

It took only as long a Garrigues could pull in a Starkville punt and race 75 yards to paydirt. He added a QB sneak before the frame ended and two Allman kicks made it 14-0. Foster added the next midway through the 2nd quarter and Allman made halftime 21-0. Late in the 3rd quarter, Foster plunged across from three yards. Fair then hit Garrigues for the last touchdown.

Foster ran for 148 yards while his team led in first downs (16-3 or 15-4) and rushing (335-27). The win propelled the Wildcats to fifth in the UPI poll, just two spaces ahead of upcoming opponent Hattiesburg.

GAME 3:   LOUISVILLE (2-0) @ HATTIESBURG (1-0)
                                    LOUISVILLE 0 HATTIESBURG 33
                                    September 20, 1963

History was not kind to Louisville as they sustained losses in both 1924 and 1934 (53-20) against the Forrest County team. As a Big Eight squad, they were much bigger in size and school attendance. That gave them a much better chance to selecting more quality athletes. Nevertheless, Coach Reese Snell was not taking the Cats for granted.

"We feel like Louisville is as strong as anyone we play. They are a perennially tough ball club. They have been the Choctaw Conference champion for the past two years". That was inaccurate. *"They lost only to Meridian last year and Meridian has had its hands full with them for the past several years. We must impress our team that this club is not to be taken lightly. We're in a good position to be beat now".*

The Tigers got all they needed in the 2nd quarter when Mickey Edwards found John Huff from 33 yards. Ed Morgan gained the next on a 1-yard plunge to make it 13-0 at intermission. Edwards added another later from 11 yards while Don Wall added the next from 21 yards. The final tally on a 4-yard Edwards (or Danny Geoghagen) pitch to David Simms.

Hattiesburg obviously dominated first down (19-4), rushing (249-116) and passing (80-29).

GAME 4:   LOUISVILLE (2-1) vs TREADWELL HIGH/MEMPHIS, TN (UNREPORTED)
                                    LOUISVILLE 41 TREADWELL 7
                                    September 27, 1963

First-time opponent Treadwell, under Coach Leo Turpin, also lost their previous contest; this to City League leader Messick 26-19.

Midway through the opening quarter, Garrigues' 3-yard keeper counted after his earlier interception. Allman's kick was good. Garrigues then recovered a fumble near midfield but for naught. Steve Rowland found paydirt next from 17 yards for the Eagles and added the PAT to tie it 7-7. It was all Cats thereafter. Fulcher took the kick 88 yards, Garrigues ran in from 84 yards, and Robin McGraw recovered a fumble and took it 26 yards. Allman was true on all three PATs to make it 28-7 at halftime.

A 3rd quarter Garrigues pickoff led to Foster's 1-yarder. In the last quarter, Louisville drove 91 yards with Smith adding the last yard. Allman's kick made it final.

GAME 5:   LOUISVILLE (3-1) @ MACON (4-0)
                                    LOUISVILLE 7 MACON 13
                                    October 4, 1963

Macon was picked second in the Choctaw just six votes behind Louisville as they had numerous key players returning. Now, they had a chance to take sole possession of first place in the conference with a win.

Late in the opening frame, Carroll Walker drove in from a yard for the initial tally. Garrigues responded with a 61-yard scoring dash and Allman put the Cats up 7-6. In the 3rd quarter, Walker dove in on fourth down from a yard for the last touchdown. The last gasp for Louisville came late when Fulcher recovered a Tiger fumble, but the home team held.

GAME 6: LOUISVILLE (3-2) vs MERIDIAN (3-0)
LOUISVILLE 0 MERIDIAN 27
October 11, 1963

It was obviously not a good time to take on a Meridian squad that defeated the Cats six times in a row since 1948. It went about as expected with the other Wildcats scored in each of the last three quarters.

Bruce Newell ran in from a yard, Bob Brunson did it from three yards and Bob Bailey added the next from four yards. The last came on David Goodman's 11-yarder. Richard Armstrong notched three extra points. Garrigues recorded an interception while Meridian had a pair of touchdowns called back on penalties.

GAME 7: LOUISVILLE (3-3) @ NEWTON (2-3-1)
LOUISVILLE 18 NEWTON 27
October 18, 1963

There was still time to turn it around in Louisville but they would have to beat long-time rival Newton in order to get going. The Tigers opened when Ray Nichols picked off a Fair pass and John Melton turned it into an 8-yard touchdown. Fair responded with a 20-yarder to Fulcher.

Another Newton score, this a Bobby Payne 2-yarder and Mike Wood PAT, was followed by Fulcher's 7-yarder. However, a late Tiger scoring drive ending with a 2-yard Gibby Russell dive put halftime in their favor 20-12. Foster opened the 3rd quarter with a 6-yard effort but Russell capped scoring late in the frame on a 7-yard option tally. The final quarter was marred by turnovers on both sides, though Steve White had a Cat interception.

GAME 8: LOUISVILLE (3-4) vs QUITMAN (4-3)
LOUISVILLE 7 QUITMAN 13
October 25, 1963: HOMECOMING

Quitman was a game better thus far than Louisville but playing the Cats in their Homecoming. It ended much like the earlier game with Macon.

Louisville got on the board first for their only points early in the opening quarter on a Smith dash and Allman kick. They later drove to the Quitman 5 but could not cross. Then, Fulcher picked off a pass to kill a threat but the Cats fumbled back to the Panthers. Jim Price eventually turned that into a touchdown from two yards to make halftime 7-6.

Things seemed positive until only 4:00 remained. That's when Quitman mustered a nine-play drive ending on a Price 2-yarder with :41 left. Price then hit Riddell for the extra point.

GAME 9: LOUISVILLE (3-5) @ KOSCIUSKO (4-2-1)
LOUISVILLE 27 KOSCIUSKO 21
November 1, 1963

Kosy enjoyed an open date the previous week to rest numerous injured players. Said Coach Larry Thomas of Louisville after scouting the Cats against Quitman, "They looked big and tough but I think we will be ready for them".

It looked dim as the Whippets scored first midway through the opening quarter on Robert Wright's 2-yarder and White kick. Early in the 2nd quarter, Foster "blasted up the middle" from 42 yards to cut it to 7-6. With 1:00 remaining before halftime, Garrigues hit Rocco Palmieri from nine yards and Allman made it 13-7. There was still time for Richard Jordan to hit Joe Collins from 24 yards and Henry put Kosy back in front 14-13.

Garrigues opened the 3rd quarter with a 6-yard run and Allman added the kick. Back came Kosy with a score courtesy of another Jordan toss to Collins and Henry was again true. A deep Whippet fumble could have been disastrous, but they held. Foster then dashed 43 yards to the end zone and Allman provided the last point of the contest.

Niles McNeel recorded a late fumble and Fulcher notched an interception later.

GAME 10:   LOUISVILLE (4-5) vs PHILADELPHIA (7-2)
                  LOUISVILLE 20 PHILADELPHIA 26
                  November 15, 1963

There was still time to avoid a losing season, but it would take upsetting a tough Tornado squad.

Halftime sat 13-0 in favor of Philly on Jim Haddock touchdown runs of 2 and 6 yards. Midway through the 3rd quarter, Larry Thomas crossed from 12 yards to make it 19-0. Garrigues responded with a 2-yarder and Allman converted. Just before the end of the frame, Joel Triplett hit Palmieri for an 8-yard score while Garrigues added another tally later from 35 yards. Allman's conversion put the Cats up 20-19. It took just four plays afterwards for the visitors to regain the lead when Harry McLemore drove in from the 5-yard line to end the season.

All-Choctaw honors went to First Team members Robert Garrigues and Eddie Foster. Honorable Mentions included Richard Ward, Ricky Peterson and Bobby Fulcher. Macon's perfect record gave them the 1963 Choctaw title.

The football banquet was held in April with five members picking up trophies. They included Billy Joe Long (David Wilson Most Improved), Jimmy Boswell (Paul Mitchell Memorial Best Blocker), Robert Garrigues (Orville Lee Castle Memorial Best Back and D.L Fair Memorial MVP), Robin McGraw (Jesse Ward Memorial Best Lineman) and James Eddie Lee (Fred Morris Scholastic Award).

1964 (3-7)

It came to many as unwelcome news when Fred Morris took the whistle in Natchez around mid-February. In his place was Jack "Pop" Warner. Warner opened the season in August with a speech to The Businessmen's Club at Lake Tiak-O'Khata. *"We have 45 boys out for practices without a single one of them from last year's first team. James Smith, the only first stringer we had this season will apparently be out because of the renewal of an old injury".*

"While our team is unusually small this year, it will be a scrappy, hustling team. Our boys have excellent spirit and they have a great deal of pride in the great football tradition that has been built up here in Louisville".

Though he had eleven letter winners back, it was not enough to keep voters from placing the Wildcats third pre-season in the Choctaw Conference. Long-time rival Philly garnered the vast majority of first place votes ahead of Macon; now Noxubee County.

GAME 1:   LOUISVILLE (0-0) vs EUPORA (0-0)
                  LOUISVILLE 21 EUPORA 7
                  September 4, 1964

Coach Doug Sullivan and his Eagles had 13 lettermen and 12 seniors back from a 3-6 campaign and were looking to beat the Cats for the first time since 1957. Before the game came around, Randy Eaves broke his arm and would be out. *"We'll play one at a time. We'll have eleven men on the field just like the opponents".*

Said Sullivan about the game, *"We're going down there to win and I think we have a good chance. Our team is in fine shape and have shown a lot of spirit. Louisville is bigger than we are, but they lost a lot of seniors and we'll carry more experience into the game".*

Rocco Palmieri finished the opening drive with his 40-yard scamper and James Veazey converted his first of three extra points. On the opening play of the 2nd quarter, James Collum *"barreled in for six points"* from the 6-yard line and Buddy Bowen tied the contest. Veazey recovered a later punt fumble but Eupora's Billy Bailey picked off a Joel Triplett pass at the 5-yard line. With just :22 left before halftime, Triplett snuck in for the 1-yard tally.

It took just nine plays on the opening kick thereafter before Palmieri crossed the stripe from three yards. That ended scoring for the rest of the half and game.

GAME 2:   LOUISVILLE (1-0) @ STARKVILLE (1-0)
                         LOUISVILLE 0 STARKVILLE 26
                         September 11, 1964

        Out-of-conference Starkville was next in Oktibbeha County. They opened their
season with a 13-7 victory over Philadelphia and now sat tenth in the Top 10 in voting. A
win could increase Wildcat confidence, but a loss would not take away from Choctaw
standings.
        The initial Cat drive ended on a fumble at the Yellow Jacket 20. Andy Rhodes
finished their response with a 44-yard dash to make it 6-0. They added to it in the 2nd
quarter on a sustained drive with a Mike Nix 3-yard pass to Bob Baker and, with a Baker
conversion, it was 13-0. A deep Jacket drive ended with the halftime whistle.
        Rhodes opened the 3rd quarter with his 10-yard effort midway through the frame
to make it 19-0. The next Cat drive stalled on Wayne Watson's interception but it went for
naught. Now in the final frame, Nix crossed from eight yards on a keeper. Baker's PAT
finalized scoring on the evening. Louisville fumbles and penalties halted any other efforts.
        The Jackets led in first downs (18-6) and rushing (53-46). The Wildcats held
passing (56-22) on a 9-18 effort.

GAME 3:   LOUISVILLE (1-1) vs HATTIESBURG (1-0)
                         LOUISVILLE 7 HATTIESBURG 14
                         September 18, 1964

        In at least four efforts since 1924, the Wildcats had yet to beat the larger Tigers
from Forrest County. Even still, Coach Reese Snell said of this one, "They will be after us. If
our kids don't get ready, they could go up there and get beat". This one proved much more
interesting than the 33-0 shellacking delivered to Louisville the previous year.
        Both teams traded deep drives early in the game only for the defenses to hold.
Then, a trade of fumbles hampered further efforts. The second recovered by Hattiesburg
led to a 37-yard Tommy Boutwell strike to Ike Farris (or David Sims). The Rick Leard
conversion put it 7-0 midway through the 2nd quarter. It could have been tied at halftime,
but a Palmieri 35-yard touchdown came back on a penalty.
        Louisville did get it back to open the 3rd quarter on a 65-yard march ending on
Prentiss "Bud" Gordon's 35-yard dash. Veazey put the game 7-7. The Tigers quickly
responded on a 69-yard first-play Ed Morgan draw play and the PAT ended all scoring. Cat
fumbles and interceptions killed opportunities to draw closer.
        Hattiesburg led on the ground (199-139) while the Cats held the air (111-50).
Fumble recoveries were even while Hattiesburg had the lost interception.

GAME 4:   LOUISVILLE (1-2) @ MENDENHALL (3-0)
                         LOUISVILLE 0 MENDENHALL 26
                         September 25, 1964

        The tough Little Dixie Conference opponent introduced their new stadium for the
contest to the late Fred Morgan. They well remembered the 1962 Mississippi Bowl defeat
to Louisville 20-9 and were looking to return the favor.
        A first-play Wildcat fumble to Sid Ponder turned two plays later into a Wesley
Bowen 1-yard touchdown and Jaris Patrick PAT. Dennis Caughman picked off a Triplett
throw as the frame ended to kill a response. A late drive before halftime ended on downs.
Mendy then marched 72-yards to open the 3rd quarter with Bowen crossing from a yard.
Ken Revere added the next in the final frame from 31 yards and Patrick made it 20-0.
        The finale came after a Jackie Mullins interception led to a Caughman 2-yarder
with 3:00 remaining in the contest. Caughman rushed for 118 yards and Mendy led in first
downs (17-9), rushing (286-112) and passing (27-22). The Cats lost a pair of interceptions
and a fumble.

GAME 5:   LOUISVILLE (1-3) vs MACON (1-3)
                         LOUISVILLE 13 MACON 3
                         October 2, 1964

        Despite the loss, Louisville was not out of conference contention as they played
three non-Choctaw foes. Meanwhile Coach A.J. Kilpatrick's red and gray Tigers were coming

off a wonderful 10-1 season. However, with six lost All-Choctaw honorees via graduation and only six letter winners back in Noxubee County, their record matched the Cats.

Another opening Cat fumble allowed Macon to get to the 8-yard line before the defense held. The Reinhard Klimkeit FG was unsuccessful. Another fumble moved Macon to the 2-yard line before a Palmieri hit caused a return fumble. Then Steve Davis picked off a Triplett pass and took it to the Cat 7. Klimkeit was true on next attempt from the Cat 18.

Just before halftime, Palmieri burst in from six yards to make halftime 6-3. Palmieri then picked off a pass before Macon's Mitchener picked off another Cat throw. In the 3rd quarter, another Cat fumble kept the frame scoreless. With just seconds left in the final stanza, Triplett dove in from two yards and Veazey added the PAT.

GAME 6:   LOUISVILLE (2-3) @ MERIDIAN (3-0)
                 LOUISVILLE 0 MERIDIAN 27
                 October 9, 1964

Another non-conference foe and another strong competitor. Scheduling for the Wildcats was definitely not in their favor yet again. It had been since at least 1944 that Louisville came out victorious in the battle. In this one, the other band of Wildcats held a three-touchdown lead before halftime rolled around.

The recap is short for obvious reasons. Wayne Lee (10 yards), Bob Brunson (2 yards), and Elwyn James (1 yard) made up the rushing tallies for the 20-0 intermission lead. It did not help that Palmieri and Gordon were sidelined with injuries. The other Cats added a late Steve Holder tally from four yards to ice things. Larry Clark (2) and Bobby Knight (1) added conversions. Louisville lost in total yards (261-101) and first downs (14-7).

GAME 7:   LOUISVILLE (2-4) vs NEWTON (3-3)
                 LOUISVILLE 0 NEWTON 21
                 October 16, 1964

It was now an uphill battle for Louisville to keep up with Choctaw leaders as they welcomed Coach J. L. Nelson's blue and white Tigers. They went a respectable 7-3-1 in 1963 and faced Louisville annually since at least 1948 (if not 1947). Newton was on a 3-1 stretch in the last four games against Louisville.

The Winston County Journal called Newton "underdogs" as they visited Winston County. They responded by marching 63 yards in their first march with Gibby Russell adding the last four. Cliff Booth made it 7-0. Russell then picked off a 2nd quarter throw and finally hit Buddy Weems from 26 yards. Another Booth PAT made it 14-0. While Newton missed a FG attempt, Louisville was not much better with a run play out of bounds for halftime.

Russell added the final touchdown in the 3rd quarter on his 4-yard escape and Booth notched the last point. The Cats marched to the Newton 10 but their defense held. Newton fumbled a late drive to Palmieri.

GAME 8:   LOUISVILLE (2-5) @ QUITMAN (6-1)
                 LOUISVILLE 7 QUITMAN 10
                 October 23, 1964

The Panthers, under Coach William Boone, lost their potential bid for Choctaw honors the previous week to Philly 21-0. They did open with eight lettermen back after 14 graduated, but since the Tornado game (like Louisville) had significant injuries piling.

The low-scoring affair came down to a late 2nd quarter Panther touchdown and PAT to make halftime 7-0. Louisville recovered an opening fumble and Palmieri turned it into an 8-yard touchdown later. The Eaves PAT made it 7-7. Just before intermission, Quitman's Robert Taylor hit a FG from the 20-yard line to make it 10-7. He happened to be on crutches on Wednesday of practices and kicked the first FG in Quitman football since 1926 when John Huggins did the same. Due to injuries in Louisville, the hampered Cats managed only to keep the score equal in the loss.

GAME 9:   LOUISVILLE (2-6) vs KOSCIUSKO (3-3-1)
                 LOUISVILLE 21 KOSCIUSKO 20
                 October 30, 1964: HOMECOMING

Even though Coach Larry Thomas had nine lettermen out of 19, his team finished 4-4-2 the previous season and he was hoping to improve. Thus far, it was not looking like it would. In front of returning alums, it proved a nail-biter until the closing seconds. Louisville was 9-4-2 since 1951 and at least 14-4-2 since 1942 against the neighboring Whippets.

It was Kosy on the initial score in the 2nd quarter when Kuykendall found Frank Simmons from 15 yards and Owens converted. The Cats soon went on a 40-yard march with Fulton getting the last yards and Veazey converting to tie.

Palmieri broke the tie in the 4rd quarter with a 42-yard dash to the end zone and the PAT made it 14-7. Scoring came in waves in the last frame. Billy Joe Long picked off a pass resulting in no points while Kosy took advantage and scored on Self's 6-yarder to Frank Simmons. The Owens PAT evened the game 14-14.

Kosy threatened but Palmieri picked off a Whippet pass. However, Jay Owens did the same and took it back 20 yards for the pick-six. The Owens kick hit the cross bar and fell unsuccessful. Now down with :19 left, Triplett *"lofted a long pass downfield where Billy Charles Justice pulled it in"* at the 38-yard line. An ensuing Cat pass fumble to Justice fell into the hands of Lonnie Fulton who pulled it in for the touchdown. Veazey was true with the kick and the game was essentially over with :09 left to play.

GAME 10: LOUISVILLE (3-6) @ PHILADELPHIA (8-1)
LOUISVILLE 7 PHILADELPHIA 33
November 13, 1964

This appeared to be a bad ending for the 1964 Wildcats. Coach Bobby Posey and his red and black already clinched a tie for the conference crown and a win gave them their first title since 1955. With 15 returning letter winners, they were in position to better an 8-2 record from the previous season.

Just 3:00 into the game, Alex Dees ran in from three yards and kicked the PAT. They nearly did it again as the frame ended but fumbled the opportunity. The Tornado added more later on a 19-yard Larry Thomas run and Dees' conversion. Then, Jim Burkes found Bobby Dees from 29 yards and halftime sat 20-0.

A third quarter Triplett interception paid no dividends. Alex Dees added another tally thereafter on his 3-yard effort to make it 26-0. Despite a Bill Rasberry interception, the Tornado moved in for their final tally of the evening. Louisville could must only a late Niles McNeel 1-yard blast and Veazey conversion.

First Team All-Choctaw Cats included Steve White, Billy Joe Long and Rocco Palmieri.

1965 (4-5)

Second-year Coach Jack Warner, back for his second term, was upbeat about his Wildcats' chances. Voters in the Choctaw Conference picked them as the team to beat followed by Macon and Ackerman. Warner had 17 lettermen back, according to The Clarion-Ledger, along with other newcomers to keep hopes high. A later report by The Winston County Journal noted only eight letter winners back and called the team *"light, inexperienced and lacking in depth"*.

In an August talk with The Louisville Businessmen's Club, Warner called his squad *"a hustling bunch and full of scrap"*. It sounded eerily similar to his 1964 talk to the same crowd at Lake Tiak-O'Khata.

GAME 1: LOUISVILLE (0-0) @ EUPORA (0-0)
LOUISVILLE 19 EUPORA 6
September 3, 1965

Despite even the worst years for Louisville, Doug Sullivan's Eagles were just 2-15-1 against them in the last 18 meetings. This year he returned eleven lettermen from a fine 7-1-3 campaign. Said Warner, *"Barring injuries, I am expecting a good game tomorrow night and a real fine season overall"*.

Louisville opened with a 70-yard drive kept alive by a fake fourth down punt. They finished it with Joel Triplett's 32-yard strike to Rocco Palmieri. Triplett returned a punt over 60 yards to the Eagle 30 from where Palmieri dashed in for the next score. Jim Collum found paydirt for the Eagles in the 3rd quarter from the three for their lone tally while the Cats put it away in the finale on Triplett's 30-yard dash and his PAT.

GAME 2:   LOUISVILLE (1-0) vs STARKVILLE (0-1)
                                     LOUISVILLE 0 STARKVILLE 13
                                     September 11, 1965

Louisville at out-of-conference Starkville played annually since at least 1940 and the Jackets held the better end all-time. This meeting had to be moved to Saturday due to rain and bad playing conditions at R.E. Hinze Stadium.

It appeared a sure Starkville opening touchdown but Jack White picked off a pass to kill the threat. The visitors did the same but also to no avail. However, George Corhern picked off a next Cat pass and ran it in from the 39-yard line. The PAT made it 7-0. Wendell Williamson later recovered a Yellow Jacket fumble but Louisville could get only to the 20.

Williamson got his second fumble recovery in the 3rd quarter but, again, it went nowhere offensively. Starkville took advantage with Mickey Montgomery's 9-yard touchdown run before the frame ended. The last quarter was a defensive battle. Starkville led first downs (11-4), rushing (161-120) and passing (31-3).

GAME 3:   LOUISVILLE (1-1) @ GRENADA (0-2)
                                     LOUISVILLE 14 GRENADA 6
                                     September 17, 1965

Amazingly, Louisville was 3-0 against a usually strong Grenada team with wins in 1941, 1942 and 1946. Now it was time to see if this team could keep the streak alive.

Louisville opened with a pair of fumbles. The last was at the Cat 4. However, a jarring hit caused a fumble to stop things. Although Grenada went on to intercept a Triplett pass, they fumbled it right back to the Cats. Palmieri turned it into a 17-yard touchdown run and his PAT. Triplett then picked off a Grenada pass leading later to his 8-yard tally. Palmieri again nailed the conversion.

Grenada added their score before halftime on a 3-yard run; probably by either Robert England or Ted Johnson. Joe Edwards blocked the extra point. Neither team scored in the second half but Jerry Hill did record an interception.

GAME 4:   LOUISVILLE (2-1) vs MENDENHALL (2-0)
                                     LOUISVILLE 7 MENDENHALL 13
                                     September 24, 1965

This contest promised "to be the toughest test for the Tigers to date", according to The Simpson County News. Coach Carroll Greer enjoyed an open week to prepare for their road game against the Cats. Louisville first met Mendy in the bowl game and came out victorious. The next game in 1964 did not go well for the Wildcats.

An unfortunate opening kick fumble by Louisville allowed Mendy an eventual 8-yard scoring pass from Bob Powell to Ronnie Teter. Powell's PAT gave them a quick 7-0 lead. They increased the advantage to 13-0 before halftime on Wesley Bowen's 1-yarder. Palmieri tightened the game in the 3rd quarter on his 44-yard escape and PAT.

The Tigers tried to respond but fumbled to Williamson. With just minutes remaining, Louisville had a first down at the Tiger 4. However, they could not cross the stripe and the Tigers simply ran out the clock for the win.

First downs were even (12-12) while Louisville led the ground (118-114) and Mendy the air (135-26)

GAME 5:   LOUISVILLE (2-2) @ MACON (3-0)
                                     LOUISVILLE 7 MACON 13
                                     October 1, 1965

Coach A.J. Kilpatrick's Noxubee County squad was not to be overlooked despite coming off a 3-6-1 season. The undefeated red and gray did have 13 letter winners back in Macon and were hosting this affair.

The Cats made a statement on their early drive ending on Triplett's 2-yard dive and Palmieri's PAT. The fired-up defense then stood up with Jerry Justice causing a fumble. Macon got one back the same way and Barney King "powered in for the TD from four yards out" to make halftime 7-6.

Macon got all they needed in the 3rd quarter when Andy Mullins drove his team toward paydirt and Paul Spurgeon got the last four yards on the ground. Barney King had the PAT. A late Macon pick ended any come-from-behind hopes.

GAME 6:   LOUISVILLE (2-3) @ NEWTON (4-2)
                              LOUISVILLE 0 NEWTON 26
                              October 15, 1965

After losing their first pair of games, Newton and Coach Bill Lindsley went on a four-game winning streak. Now the royal blue and white, only 5-5-1 the previous year, were still in contention for the loop title behind undefeated Macon. To make it worse, Louisville won only a pair of games in the annual tilt since 1958. The Cats had a week off to prepare for the important meeting to bring them back to .500.

The opening Tiger drive ended with a 4-yard Bob Gaines dive and Cliff Booth kick to give them a 7-0 lead. They then marched to the 11-yard line from where Bob Douglas found Henley Chapman. Jack White blocked the PAT to keep halftime 13-0. Chapman opened the 3rd quarter with a 63-yard dash for the score. Newton then recovered a dropped pass and Gaines added the final two yards. The Booth PAT finished things.

GAME 7:   LOUISVILLE (2-4) vs QUITMAN (5-1-1)
                              LOUISVILLE 13 QUITMAN 0
                              October 22, 1965: HOMECOMING

The slumping Cats desperately needed a win for pride as they were out of contention for the title. However, the next opponent was going to be a big hurdle for Homecoming affairs. Coach William Boone's blue and gold lost 20 lettermen from their 8-2 team but had a reported 18 back and thus far lost only a lone game.

The first Louisville drive ended 70 yards later with Palmieri's 30-yarder. White blocked a later Quitman FG effort to keep it 6-0 at intermission. Palmieri added the last touchdown in the 3rd quarter on a 41-yard escape and then added the PAT. He attempted a 4th quarter FG but it was blocked.

GAME 8:   LOUISVILLE (3-4) @ KOSCIUSKO (3-4)
                              LOUISVILLE 21 KOSCIUSKO 13
                              October 29, 1965

Despite it a road affair, hopes were high as Louisville was 7-1 in their last eight games against the Whippets. It was not a great season thus far for Kosy as Coach Larry Thomas and his nine lettermen attempted to better their 5-4-1 record from 1964.

On their second drive, the Cats covered 40 yards with Triplett providing the last 30 yards on the ground. The Palmieri kick put it 7-0. The Whippets answered in the 2nd quarter on Kirky Kuykendall's 35-yarder to put it 7-6 at halftime. A huge 3rd quarter hit forced a fumble recovered by the Cats' Rob Bonney. Triplett turned it later into a 5-yard touchdown and Palmieri added the extra point.

An ensuing kickoff fumble put Louisville at the Whippet 25. Triplett headed toward the end zone from 20 yards and Palmieri finished Wildcat scoring. Kosy had one more in them in the finale on Kuykendall's 20-yarder to James Monroe (or Bubba Wiles) and Monroe's PAT.

GAME 9:   LOUISVILLE (4-4) vs PHILADELPHIA (7-2)
                              LOUISVILLE 0 PHILADELPHIA 13
                              November 12, 1965

A win against powerful Philly meant that the Cats avoided their first three-game losing season in decades. Coach Bobby Posey was 10-1 the previous year and had eight lettermen back to keep their program thriving.

It was called "a sparse crowd" for the season finale. A Philly drive to the Cat 1 ended on fourth down when John Galberry dove in for the initial score and 6-0 lead. In the 2nd quarter, and after a deep Cat fumble, Galberry added the last from the 3-yard line and Tim Allen notched the PAT.

Philly led in first downs (15-5), rushing (187-26) and passing (55-51).

Mike Boyles and Rocco Palmieri ended with First Team All-Choctaw honors while Wendell Williamson garnered an Honorable Mention. Palmieri was also named to the Mississippi Sportswriters' All-State squad.

At the banquet in March, internal honors went to Ronnie Eaves (Most Improved), Randall Livingston (Best Blocker), Wendell Williamson (Best Lineman), Joel Triplett (Best Back), and Mike Boyles (Scholastic). Eaves and Williamson were voted team captains.

1966 (8-1-1)

The two-year stint of Jack Warner ended with the hiring of Charles Peets as new head man in Louisville. His squad was *"light and inexperienced"* with only seven letter winners back in Winston County. Gone were Rocco Palmieri and Joel Triplett, both sparkplugs for the Cats.

Choctaw Conference voters picked 1965 champ Philadelphia as pre-season favorites for the title despite tough graduations. Louisville was a predictive second.

GAME 1:   LOUISVILLE (0-0) @ WEST POINT (0-0)
            LOUISVILLE 13 WEST POINT 0
            September 2, 1966

Although not an unfamiliar non-conference opponent, it had been six years since these two met on the gridiron. On the second Cat drive, Jerry Hill found George Fair *"waiting all alone in the end zone"* for the initial tally. In the final frame, Ellis Stewart found a loose ball and Hill eventually hit Jack White for the touchdown. Randy Eaves added the PAT with 3:00 remaining on the clock.

The Cats had first downs (8-5) and total yards (180-87).

GAME 2:   LOUISVILLE (1-0) vs STARKVILLE (0-1)
            LOUISVILLE 13 STARKVILLE 27
            September 9, 1966

The annual rivalry game was here again with the second out-of-conference opponent. The last three years had understandably not been favorable for Louisville but perhaps this was the year to turn it around at R.E. Hinze Stadium.

Louisville marched 80 yards for their initial tally, finishing with a 6-yard run by D.D. Shields to make it 6-0. Later Randy Eaves' pressure on a Jacket punter gave the Cats the ball at the Starkville 13. Hill eventually crossed on short runs and Eaves converted. A late Wildcat fumble to the Yellow Jackets did no damage. They also got as far as the Cat 12 before the defense held for halftime.

Unfortunately, the second half belonged to the visitors. Their first came quickly on an 86-yard burst by Clint Burton to make it 13-6. They then capped a 70-yard drive with Wayne Watson's 29-yarder up the middle. The Frankie Tomlinson PAT tied things. It got worse as Louisville responded with a drive to the Jacket 16 before Burton grabbed an errant pass and took it the distance. It came back a bit on a penalty but Garner eventually found Winston from 23 yards for the 20-13 advantage.

After holding the Cats, Joe Ott found paydirt from a yard and Tomlinson added the last point of the night. The Jackets held yardage 224-179.

GAME 3:   LOUISVILLE (1-1) vs GRENADA (2-0)
            LOUISVILLE 12 GRENADA 6
            September 16, 1966

An early Cat fumble led quickly to a 5-yard James Morris run. Louisville tied in a QB sneak to make halftime 6-6. Late in the 3rd quarter, the Wildcats added their last on a 20-yard escape. Grenada fumbled five times to Louisville. Said their local paper, *"Grenada outplayed Louisville in almost every statistic, but statistics don't count on the scoreboard"*.

GAME 4:   LOUISVILLE (2-1) vs EUPORA (1-2)
            LOUISVILLE 27 EUPORA 0
            September 23, 1966

The Cats held at least 20 wins against just a pair of losses and one tie historically. This season, Doug Sullivan was taking eight lettermen from a 3-7 team into battle. This marked the start of Choctaw Conference play for Louisville.

Despite an early Cat fumble recovery, their first score did not come until the 2nd quarter. That was courtesy of Phil Hart's 6-yarder. A later Eddie Pickett pickoff set up Hill's 1-yard dive and Eaves' PAT. Eupora recovered a fumble but the defense held at the Cat 12. In the responding drive, Homer Fancher drove in from three yards and Eaves made it 20-0.

In the last frame, Fancher crossed again from the 7-yard line. First downs (18-6), rushing (297-132) and passing (60-42) favored the Wildcats.

GAME 5:   LOUISVILLE (3-1) vs MACON (3-0)
                            LOUISVILLE 20 MACON 0
                            September 30, 1966

Unfortunately, much like the Grenada contest, the local game summary is not legible. Fancher's 20-yarder to Pickett and the first of two Eaves kicks made halftime 7-0. In the second half, the Cats tallied again while late in the 3rd quarter they did the same from six yards.

GAME 6:   LOUISVILLE (4-1) @ ACKERMAN (4-0)
                            LOUISVILLE 7 ACKERMAN 7
                            October 7, 1966

The Indians were once a mainstay on the Wildcat calendar. However, after posting a 1-14 record against Louisville in 15 straight games, they moved off the schedule. Now they were back with a reported 17 letter winners from a 10-1 season.

The Winston County Journal called it "one of the hardest hitting high school football games that you would ever want to see". Louisville gained their only tally on their first drive via Hart's 1-yard plunge and Eaves PAT. Ackerman came right back when Black found Mike Wood in the end zone and Wendall Lucas evened things 7-7. Stout defense held the remainder of the game scoreless. The game ended on a Jim Edwards pick for Ackerman.

First downs (14-5) and rushing (212-53) favored Louisville while Ackerman held the air (62-23). As it turned out, a win over the Indians would have given the Cats yet another Choctaw crown.

GAME 7:   LOUISVILLE (4-1-1) vs NEWTON (4-1-1)
                            LOUISVILLE 13 NEWTON 7
                            October 14, 1966

The week would get no easier against James Nelson's Tigers who took the Cats five times in the last six years. This season, they were improved from a 7-3 campaign.

The Wildcats fumbled their first drive away, moved deep into Tiger territory on their next only to be denied, and fumbled their third march. However, they managed to get across on the next when Shields added the last three yards. Newton came back vigorously before halftime. They drove 50 yards with Buddy Weems adding the last couple and the Danny Lindsley kick making it 7-6 at intermission.

While a 3rd quarter lost fumble killed a drive, the Cats came back with under 6:00 remaining. Marching 70 yards, Hill ended it with his 1-yard plunge and Eaves made the kick. They nearly added to it late with a drive to the 1-yard line but were stopped. The defense put it away afterwards.

Louisville led in first downs (18-7) and rushing (211-26). Newton held the air but only by two yards (60-58). The Cats lost three fumbles on the night.

GAME 8:   LOUISVILLE (5-1-1) @ QUITMAN (4-1-1)
                            LOUISVILLE 6 QUITMAN 0
                            October 21, 1966

Coach William Boone, 8-2 the previous year, defeated the strong Philadelphia team the previous week 14-13. They had only six lettermen back but were still in the running for the crown. The game was decisive for both.

A Cat drive to the 5-yard line ended on a fourth down gamble and halftime remained scoreless. Louisville got what they needed in the 3rd quarter on Hill's 30-yard toss to George Fair "all alone in the end zone". The teams traded numerous fumbles in the last frame to hamper efforts and the Cat defense stood tall late to keep Quitman away from the stripe. First downs (10-5), rushing (133-35) and passing (34-30) went to the visitors.

GAME 9:   LOUISVILLE (6-1-1) vs KOSCIUSKO (4-3)
                                     LOUISVILLE 14 KOSCIUSKO 0
                                     October 28, 1966: HOMECOMING

Louisville still hoped for an Ackerman loss but knew they had to continue winning to get their next title. Now, Roy Terry and his 13 lettermen came to Winston County as Homecoming opponents. The Whippets had their hands full against the Cats going 1-8 in the last nine contests.

The Cats scored in the opening frame when Hill hit Fancher from the 12-yard line and "Hotshot" *"literally drove over two of the opponents and into the end zone for the six-pointer"*. Eaves made it an early 7-0 affair. A later Joe Edwards hit and fumble recovery went for naught to end the half.

In the 3rd quarter, Hill "snuck" across the line for 52 yards to paydirt and Eaves converted for the finale. While Kosy picked off a pass in the last frame, Pickett did the same. A late Cat drive to the 4-yard line ended with a Davidson interception.

GAME 10:   LOUISVILLE (7-1-1) @ PHILADELPHIA (4-5)
                                     LOUISVILLE 28 PHILADELPHIA 14
                                     November 14, 1966

The contest against Bob Posey's Tornado, 8-2 the previous year with three consecutive wins over Louisville, came at a good time as they sat with a losing season. Ackerman had yet to lose, so Louisville needed this one and a prayer. Due to heavy rain, the game moved to Monday.

Hart was first across the line from a yard while Hill followed later with a 3-yarder and it was 13-0 at the end of the frame. Hart did it again in the 2nd quarter from five yards. The Tornado answered with second left before halftime on Hale's run and the PAT. In the 3rd quarter, Jerry Hill sacked the Philly QB for a safety. In the finale, Hill hit Randy Eaves for a touchdown and Eaves converted.

Ackerman's fine run, and despite the tie with Louisville, gave them the Choctaw title. Wildcats named to the All-Choctaw team including First Team members Randy Eaves, Joe Edwards and Ellis Stewart. Jerry Hill, Phil Hart and James Hunt were Honorable Mentions.

1967 (9-1-1)

Very little was written about the pre-season efforts of the Wildcats under second-year mentor Charles Peets. Matthew "Bud" Turner was also back as one assistant coach. Despite key losses of 15 lettermen, those returning gave Choctaw Conference voters confidence they would end up as champions. Kosciusko and Quitman followed.

GAME 1:   LOUISVILLE (0-0) vs WEST POINT (0-0)
                                     LOUISVILLE 13 WEST POINT 7
                                     September 8, 1967

The contest against the Green Wave was played *"on a rain-soaked field"*. Conditions such as this could make it low scoring with plenty of turnovers and that happened this night. In all, the Cats had five fumble recoveries and three interceptions.

A solid early drive by West Point ended only in a missed FG effort. Before halftime, a fumble around the Wave 10 allowed Billy Hathorn a 6-yard dash to paydirt and 6-0 lead. Bobby Joe Burton's interception kept halftime the same. An exchange of 3rd quarter fumbles put the Cats deep in their territory and they had to give it back.

West Point fumbled yet again, this time to Dale Stewart, and Homer Fancher hit Jack White three plays later from eight yards for the touchdown. Fancher's conversion made it 13-0. Randy Romedy picked off a 4th quarter pass but Louisville fumbled it back. Finally, West Point avoided the shutout on Gary Echols' 80-yard escape to the goal and they added the PAT. A last gasp by the Wave ended on a Harold Stevens interception.

GAME 2:   LOUISVILLE (1-0) vs STARKVILLE (1-0)
                                      LOUISVILLE 7 STARKVILLE 6
                                     September 15, 1967

The lone loss of 1966 came against the Yellow Jackets; long-time rivals of the Cats. This year proved payback for the four straight losing efforts against the Oktibbeha County squad.

After numerous exchanges of punts, Starkville found the end zone on a Buddy Staggers cross over right tackle to make it 6-0. That held until the clock was nearly expired due to solid defensive play on both sides. However, the Cats had one last chance. They marched 54 yards with Fancher hitting Jack White from six yards with just :37 on the clock. Fancher's crucial PAT was *"perfect"*. The Cats held first downs (12-7) and rushing (117-75).

GAME 3:   LOUISVILLE (2-0) @ GRENADA (1-0)
                                         LOUISVILLE 23 GRENADA 7
                                         September 22, 1967

Next on the schedule was the Delta Valley team that had yet to win against Louisville in five tries. The first score came surprisingly from a Louisville fumble recovery deep in their territory picked up by Hathorn and taken 92 yards to paydirt. Fancher's kick was true but he sustained a leg injury on the play.

The Wildcats opened the 2nd quarter with Keith Giffin's 82-yard explosive run and White added the 14-0 PAT. White picked off a Grenada pass before halftime, but the Cats fumbled it back later. Grenada turned that into a 7-yard Parker touchdown and the PAT put intermission 14-7.

In the final frame, White and Paul Miller sacked the QB for a safety. Later, Hathorn *"lobbed a beautiful 8-yard pass to White for the touchdown"*. White also converted to end scoring. The win also came with a loss as Fancher's injury required a cast and probably eliminated him from further play in 1967.

GAME 4:   LOUISVILLE (3-0) @ EUPORA (1-1-1)
                                         LOUISVILLE 13 EUPORA 0
                                         September 29, 1967

Peets was complimentary of his Wildcats when noting that juniors and sophomores were making good progress. *"I have never had a team that wants to win any harder than this one. This is the best group of boys that I have ever been associated with. They are high-type boys that would be an asset to any community. There are no beatniks or punks among them. They have high moral principles and I am most proud of them"*.

This historical record against the Eagles, this year under Coach Doug Sullivan, was nothing but gaudy in favor of the Cats. Thus far, they showed promise with a victory over Kosciusko, a tie with Macon and their lone loss to powerhouse Little Ten Houston.

The first Eupora possession ended with a Larry Davis punt blocked and then recovered by Andy Woods and taken 30 yards to the end zone. White's toe put it a quick 7-0. That score held until halftime despite a pair of deep threats by Louisville. Hathorn opened the 3rd quarter with his 35-yard run to paydirt to put it 13-0. Defenses held firm afterwards. Joe Edwards picked off a 3rd quarter pass to get into the books.

GAME 5:   LOUISVILLE (4-0) @ MACON (3-1)
                                         LOUISVILLE 23 MACON 0
                                       October 6, 1967

The Noxubee County squad tied Louisville 5-5 since 1956 in games played. Joe Bradshaw's red and gray both lost and returned nine letter winners from their 5-4 team. This year looked more promising thus far.

A late opening frame White interception led later to his FG from the 8-yard line to make it 3-0 in the 2nd quarter. Late in the quarter, Gary Fulton recovered a fumble and Hathorn turned into a 23-yard TD toss to Danny Harris. The White PAT made halftime 10-0. Hathorn found White from 25 yards for the next and White provided the kick. Then, Burton *"swept around end and sped to pay dirt with a 78-yard run"* to finish things. White had one 30-yard FG attempt fail.

GAME 6:   LOUISVILLE (5-0) vs ACKERMAN (1-3)
                                         LOUISVILLE 20 ACKERMAN 0
                                         October 13, 1967

The 7-7 tie with Ackerman the previous season cost the Wildcats yet another Choctaw title. Now they looked to avenge that costly mistake. It may be easier than thought since Coach Dennis Wilson returned only four lettermen from their 9-0-1 team.

An early Keith Giffin fumble recovery went nowhere nor did an Edwards FG attempt for Ackerman. In the 2nd quarter, White picked off a pass and took it in for the touchdown. Later, Fred Nabers found Paul Bryant from 25 yards and White increased the advantage to 13-0. Joe Edwards picked off a pass to keep halftime the same.

In the final frame, Hathorn snuck in from a yard and White added the final point. Ackerman nearly got a late score when Stevens lofted a fourth down pass to Bennie Cherry *"but the receiver failed to hang on to the ball"*.

GAME 7:   LOUISVILLE (6-0) @ NEWTON (1-4-1)
                 LOUISVILLE 34 NEWTON 6
                 October 20, 1967

It had not been a great year for Coach J.L. Nelson's blue and white. They had only four letter winners back from a 6-3-1 campaign and struggled to get back to that mark.

It took little time before Bowman drove in from 10 yards and White converted. Bowman did it again later and White increased it to 14-0. Hathorn recorded the next touchdown in the 2nd quarter and White put it 21-0 at halftime. Randy Romedy found a loose Newton ball at their 10-yard line and Bowman took it in thereafter to make it 28-0.

Louisville followed it with Dale Stewart's 30-yard pick six for the 34-0 final. Newton avoided the shutout as the game neared closing.

GAME 8:   LOUISVILLE (7-0) vs QUITMAN (7-0)
                 LOUISVILLE 0 QUITMAN 0
                 October 27, 1967: HOMECOMING

This meeting was called *"The Big One"* as both were undefeated and the winner took control of their Choctaw destiny. Louisville came close the previous year, but the tie with Ackerman cost them the eventual crown.

The Wildcats originally accepted a bid to host the inaugural Pine Bowl to be held on the home field on November 17. This was according to The Louisville Businessmen's Club on November 2. However, things were to change and the contest did not occur.

The only Cat threat in the opening half came on a drive to the Quitman 15 before a John Gilbert interception killed the threat. The Panthers moved in the second half to the Cat 7 but missed Danny Culpepper's FG effort. Louisville attempted to take the game before another pick ended the drive. None could muster any serious efforts thereafter.

GAME 9:   LOUISVILLE (7-0-1) @ KOSCIUSKO (5-2)
                 LOUISVILLE 27 KOSCIUSKO 13
                 November 3, 1967

Louisville faced Ray Terry's Whippets in a stadium with few spectators, as it was *"cold and damp"*. The Cats jumped out to a 7-0 lead early on a Hathorn sneak and White PAT. Even though White took a later punt 62 yards to paydirt, it came back on a penalty. Early in the 2nd quarter, Bob Jordan found Jerry Pettit in the end zone and the PAT tied things. Before halftime, Hathorn hit Nabers from 32 yards while Jordan found Winfred Shelton to make it 13-13. Now in the 4th quarter, Burton broke through for a 21-yard tally and ran in the PAT. As the game ended, he did it again from 28 yards and White converted.

GAME 10:   LOUISVILLE (8-0-1) vs PHILADELPHIA (3-4-2)
                 LOUISVILLE 41 PHILADELPHIA 0
                 November 10, 1967

Old time rival Philadelphia now came to Winston County and it was essential for the Wildcats to come out with a win to keep Choctaw hopes alive. Quitman was also on a mission with their 27-0 win over Carthage.

The Winston County Journal noted that a Wildcat win made them their first undefeated team since 1944 (11-0). In actuality, that was also an honor of the 1950 squad who also had a tie on their resume (Starkville 6-6). Fancher was back and seniors were preparing to play their last game in Louisville.

An early Bob Livingston punt block set up Fancher's TD toss to Danny Harris for the 6-0 lead. On their next drive, Burton found paydirt and White converted. The Wildcats sat 26-0 at halftime thanks to two more Burton scores. Giffin (23 and 11) added a pair of 3rd quarter tallies and White did damage with the extra points.

GAME 11:   LOUISVILLE (9-0-1) vs QUITMAN (9-0-1)
                  LOUISVILLE 0 QUITMAN 7
                  November 17, 1967

The rematch was held in Philadelphia to determine the 1967 Choctaw Conference winner. This took precedence over the Pine Bowl originally scheduled for the same day. The Wildcats lost the 1966 title due to a tie and were trying desperately to avoid the same fate the ensuing season.

The game came down to the second of two fumbles before halftime. On the last recovery by Larry Riley, Quitman's Larry Mathis went "around the right end" for the touchdown and Ken Woodward added the PAT. White attempted a FG in the 3rd quarter that was not successful. Other deep Wildcat drives in the second half ended the same way.

Said Coach Boone, "It was truly a team effort. We didn't try to change any game plans from the October 27 scoreless tie but simply tried to improve on the execution of play. Louisville has a fine, well-coached team and I feel real happy that we are able to beat them". The Cats outgained their opponents 145-123 on the ground and 8-6 in first downs.

Another one-loss and one-tie squad ended the year without the conference title. Jack White, Joe Edwards, and Bob Livingston all with All-Choctaw honors. Bobby Joe Burton was Honorable Mention. White was named Best Lineman. The Businessmen's Club treated the team to a trip to the Sugar Bowl in New Orleans for their fine season.

1968 (7-3)

Roughly 52 prospects arrived in mid-August in hopes of making the 1968 Wildcat team under returning coach Charles Peets. "We were well-pleased with the spirit and hustle that the boys have showing during early practice sessions this season". Those included football camp at the FFA Camp at Grenada Lake.

While Choctaw Conference voters picked Kosciusko as favorites, the Wildcats and their 16 lettermen were just behind in second place.

GAME 1:   LOUISVILLE (0-0) @ WEST POINT (0-0)
                  LOUISVILLE 28 WEST POINT 13
                  September 6, 1968

It appeared a defensive battle until late in the opening frame when Keith Giffin dove in from two yards and Fancher converted to make it 7-0. He then took a handoff 56 yards to paydirt and the PAT was good. With :02 left before halftime, West Point hit the board on a pass from Gary Echols to Jimmy Hudson but Jeff Jackson blocked the kick.

"Hotshot" Fancher added a 1-yard plunge in the 3rd quarter and his PAT made 21-6. Danny Harris capped Cat scoring in the finale with a 46-yard punt return and the PAT notched the last point. Late in the game, long pass plays resulted in an 8-yard Echols run for the Green Wave touchdown and the Bobby Shelton PAT was true.

Jerry Fuller recorded an early interception in the contest.

GAME 2:   LOUISVILLE (1-0) @ STARKVILLE (1-0)
                  LOUISVILLE 0 STARKVILLE 26
                  September 13, 1968

Five minutes before halftime, Starkville's Bob Buchanan found a loose Wildcat football at the Cat 13 and Paul Millsaps hit David Josey four plays later to make it 6-0. Another fumble allowed a Millsaps touchdown toss to Jim Brown and, this time, the Laughlin extra point. Early in the last frame, Josey added a 27-yard pick-six and PAT to increase the lead. Later, another interception led to their final tally; that a 19-yard Millsaps throw to Ronnie Waldrop.

While the Cats held first downs (8-7) and rushing (94-86), the Jackets controlled the passing game 121-33.

GAME 3:   LOUISVILLE (1-1) vs GRENADA (0-2)
LOUISVILLE 21 GRENADA 6
September 20, 1968

The Bulldogs lost the last three consecutive meetings with the Cats and now featured a new coach in Parkes Johnson. This year had thus far not fared much better.

An early Grenada pickoff killed one threat as did a missed Cat FG, but the Cats found paydirt in the 2nd quarter on a 3-yard Giffin run and Fancher kick. That was set up by a Bob Livingston fumble recovery. Later, a Grenada pickoff by Bubba Vance led to their only touchdown by Mike Parker but the bobbled extra point kept halftime 7-6.

Louisville fumbled to open the 3rd quarter but it did not do damage. Bob Bowman then added a 1-yarder and Fancher the PAT. Tommy Majure 's 60-yard punt return for a TD came back for clipping. Fancher ended scoring with a strike to Benny Hill. The Cats picked off a late pass to end the game. One score went unreported.

GAME 4:   LOUISVILLE (2-1) vs EUPORA (1-2)
LOUISVILLE 20 EUPORA 6
September 27, 1968

Eupora was still searching for a way to overcome a long Wildcat win streak. Doug Sullivan's Eagles had 11 letter winners back from a 6-4-1 squad and were hopeful in this one on the road. This marked the opener for Louisville in Choctaw meetings.

A horrible Eagle punt early allowed Giffin a 6-yard run just six plays. A Cat fumble in the 2nd quarter allowed Eupora a 10-play drive and 3-yard Don Woods touchdown. Giffin blocked the PAT to keep it tied 6-6. Fancher found Fred Nabers from seven yards and then provided the PAT to make it 13-6. Harold Stevens' ensuing interception did no damage.

With 2:04 left in the game, Majure found Stevens on a 26-yard halfback pass and Fancher dotted the board with the final point.

GAME 5:   LOUISVILLE (3-1) vs MACON (2-1-1)
LOUISVILLE 0 MACON 3
October 4, 1968

The Noxubee County team under Coach Joe Bradshaw went just 2-7-1 in 1967 but they did have the services of 11 lettermen back in red and gray. Since 1960, the meetings were tied 4-4 and Louisville needed to keep winning for title hopes.

Louisville threatened early with a drive to the Noxubee County 6. Fancher ended the scoreless half with an interception. The remaining two frames looked similar with strong defensive play. The Cats again drove deep into Macon territory but the Fancher FG failed. On the very last play of the game, and after a 40-yard drive, Moses Vernon knocked home a 23-yard FG with just :04 left for the heartbreaking Wildcat defeat.

GAME 6:   LOUISVILLE (3-2) @ ACKERMAN (3-1)
LOUISVILLE 25 ACKERMAN 6
October 11, 1968

Coach Parker Dykes' blue and gold went just 1-9 in their last season. However, with ten letter winners back, they had a lone defeat and sat second in the Choctaw Conference standings.

An early Harris interception led six plays later to Larry Addkison's 2-yard dive and Fancher kick. Danny Woodward then recovered a deep Indian fumble and Homer Fancher hit Danny Harris from 15 yards for the next. To make it better, Harris took an Ackerman punt 60 yards to paydirt. Before halftime, Nabers hit Hill from the 10-yard line for the last Cat points.

Ackerman avoided the shutout in the second half on a 15-yard pass completion. Fancher picked off a late Indian throw to seal the game.

GAME 7:   LOUISVILLE (4-2) vs NEWTON (3-3)
LOUISVILLE 41 NEWTON 12
October 18, 1968: HOMECOMING

The blue and white for Coach J.L. Nelson lost just five lettermen from a 2-7-1 Tiger squad. While better thus far this year, it was not by much.

Louisville started with a strong drive to the Tiger 35 before fumbling away. Newton returned the favor to Goodin at the 34-yard line. Eight plays later, Giffin got in from three yards. In the 2nd quarter, they drove 69 yards in six plays with a touchdown and Benny Cherry PAT. Penalties helped drive their next score on a 25-yard Fancher toss to Mike Fuller and Cherry kick.

Newton fumbled the kickoff and Louisville found the end zone on Fancher's 7-yarder to Hill. Cherry's kick made it 27-0. The Cats opened the 3rd quarter with a 67-yard march but lost the opportunity. Danny Smith quickly picked off a Louisville throw and took it 93 yards for the tally but Fuller blocked the kick. Fancher and Harris hooked up just before the end of the frame from nine yards and Cherry converted.

In the finale, Davis Kelly picked off a pass and Addkison rushed in later from the 2-yard line. Fancher converted for Louisville. Newton crossed the stripe late in eight plays but Kelly blocked the PAT. Goodin ended the game with a fumble recovery.

GAME 8:   LOUISVILLE (5-2) @ QUITMAN (2-2-2)
                 LOUISVILLE 26 QUITMAN 19
                 October 25, 1968

Since 1961, Louisville was 4-3-1 against William Boone's blue and gold. They were attempting to defend their wonderful 10-0-1 season but lost 17 lettermen and had only six back.

Quitman was first on the scoreboard on Butch King's 6-yard run and Danny Culpepper PAT. Louisville came back on a 10-yard Fancher pass to Majure and then a 21-yard Fancher strike to Larry Livingston to make it 13-7. In the second half, Fancher hit Harris from 34 yards for another touchdown to make it 26-7.

Late in the game, Culpepper picked off a Fancher throw and took it 36 yards to the end zone. Eddie Green added another from seven yards to tighten things. With only :30 remaining, Quitman knocked a ball loose and recovered. Now on fourth down with time only for one more play, Culpepper *"hit the line and the Panthers cheered as they thought they crossed the line"*. However, they were four inches short and Louisville escaped.

GAME 9:   LOUISVILLE (6-2) vs KOSCIUSKO (4-3)
                 LOUISVILLE 0 KOSCIUSCKO 19
                 November 1, 1968

The Cats needed lots of help for hopes of a title. They sat third in the Choctaw but Macon was ahead and held a win over them. Ray Terry's Whippets were just 6-5 the previous year but did enjoy 12 letter winners back in Kosciusko. A loss ended hopes as both Kosy and Louisville held equal 4-1 conference records.

The first of three Cat fumbles to Kosy went for naught but the Whippets soon marched to paydirt on a 28-yard drive in six plays. Wayne Jones crossed from six yards. The next fumble again went nowhere but the next allowed a 10-play drive in 39 yards for a Marion Dees run and 12-0 lead at halftime. The first of a pair of pickoffs occurred before that whistle.

The visitors then went 11 plays for 60 yards for another Jones touchdown; this time from the 3-yard line. Title hopes were now officially over.

GAME 10:   LOUISVILLE (6-3) @ PHILADELPHIA (2-7)
                 LOUISVILLE 27 PHILADELPHIA 0
                 November 8, 1968

It was a miserable year for Philadelphia as Coach Thomas Gaines' Tornado were worse than their 3-5-2 mark in 1967. That was due in part to injuries and having just five lettermen back of 17.

Louisville scored in the opening frame on a 22-yard Giffin run and Fancher PAT. The wet field did not slow the Cats as Nabers found Stevens from three yards and Fancher converted. Just before halftime, the Wildcats blocked a Tornado punt and scored on a 21-yard Fancher strike to Harris. Late in the 3rd quarter, Fancher hit Harris on a 65-yard bomb and then converted. The finale featured only a Stevens interception. The Tornado score went unreported.

First Team All-Choctaw honors went to Bob Livingston. Honorable Mentions included Paul Miller, Robert Goodin and Homer Fancher. Internal awards included Stewart Canty (Scholastic), Benny Hill (Most Improved), Livingston (MVP and 1968 Wildcat Award), Fancher (Best Back), Goodin (Best Blocker) and Larry Livingston (Best Lineman).

1969 (9-1)

After three years, Charles Peets resigned and took the AD and football coaching dues at Cooper High in Vicksburg. Long-time assistant Matthew "Bud" Turner took his place as mentor. Bob Oakley and Paul Wood provided roles as assistant coaches.

Choctaw Conference voters picked the Wildcats second in predictive finish behind favorite Quitman. The Cats did, however, have 17 lettermen back in Winston County and hopes were much higher than perhaps those of others.

Turner addressed the Rotary Club before the first game to discuss 1969 prospects. *"There is more depth in the backfield than last year but less in the line. The workouts have been satisfactory and the team spirit is good. You will have to attend the opening game to learn who plays in the QB position"*.

GAME 1: LOUISVILLE (0-0) vs WEST POINT (0-0)
LOUISVILLE 38 WEST POINT 6
September 5, 1969

In The Little Ten Conference, the Green Wave were picked second behind next opponent Starkville. Consolidation at the school provided them more talent from which to choose. Said Turner, *"West Point is a little bigger (than us). We expect a bit of trouble. Both teams have a similar rating in their conferences. We will undoubtedly have a very strong team. We are just average sized, but we have 17 experienced lettermen returning"*.

Scoring was fast and furious. Larry Addkison added the first on his 35-yard gallop and Tommy Majure added the PAT. West Point gained their lone tally afterwards on a 2-yard Gary Echols plunge. In the 2nd quarter, Keith Giffin crossed (Majure PAT) and Benny Cherry added a FG. Majure got across from twice after halftime on a 60-yard punt return and 65-yard pick-six. Cherry was good on both extra points.

Stanley Cunningham notched the last on his 70-yard dash after the Cats picked off an errant Wave pass. Cherry converted.

GAME 2: LOUISVILLE (1-0) vs STARKVILLE (1-0)
LOUISVILLE 21 STARKVILLE 32
September 12, 1969

This week, Turner spoke with the Businessmen's Club at Lake Tiak O'Khata to discuss the upcoming home game against Starkville. The Yellow Jackets featured 14 returning letter winners from a team that beat the Cats 26-0 the previous season.

The Jackets were first after a Cat fumble and Bill Buckley did the honors from 15 yards to make it 6-0. Louisville came back with a response and PAT to make it 7-6. David Josey took advantage of an 88-yard Buckley return early in the 2nd quarter to take the lead. Buckley picked off a Wildcat pass but the drive stalled on a fumble. Starkville did regather and score again on a Dykes 6-yarder to make halftime 18-7.

Louisville hit the board in the 3rd quarter to put it 18-15 but, eight plays later, Starkville drove 71 yards with Buckley gathering a pass from Paul Millsaps. Dykes had the last Jacket score from 42 yards with David Josey adding two points. Louisville had the last with about a minute to go from Addkison on his 45-yard escape.

The limited recaps from The Winston County Journal noted Danny Harris and Giffin scoring the other touchdowns. Cherry had one PAT while Robert Warner hit Danny Harris for a two-pointer. Both Harris and Addkison rushed for 69 yards while Giffin (42) and Warner (34) followed. Louisville led on the ground 200-176 and air 85-79.

GAME 3: LOUISVILLE (1-1) @ GRENADA (1-1)
LOUISVILLE 17 GRENADA 0
September 19, 1969

Coach Parkes Johnson returned 14 letter winners from his 2-7-1 Delta Valley Conference team this season. The Grenada squad had yet to defeat Louisville in at least the last seven meetings.

Yet another limited recap of the action notes that scoring came from Giffin, Harris and Cherry via his FG and extra points. Scoring was complete by halftime.

GAME 4:   LOUISVILLE (2-1) @ EUPORA (2-1)
                     LOUISVILLE 20 EUPORA 6
                     September 26, 1969

Choctaw play opened in Webster County against long-time opponent Eupora. The Cats were 19-2-1 in consecutive tilts going back to 1947.

Louisville blocked an early Eupora FG attempt by Don Woods. The Eagles jumped out first in the 2nd quarter on David Doolittle's reception from Larry Edwards. Back came Harris with a one-play score to tie it 6-6 at halftime. That tally came via a fumble recovery. Harris added one more from a yard for the Cats and Giffin crossed with :42 remaining. Giffin (or Warner) hit Bobby Bowman for the two-pointer. Louisville led in first downs (12-9), rushing (153-148) and passing (37-12).

GAME 5:   LOUISVILLE (3-1) @ MACON (2-1)
                     LOUISVILLE 26 MACON 16
                     October 3, 1969

It took only minutes before Warner hit Majure from midfield and Harris followed it a 35-yard reception from Warner. Cherry's two kicks made it 14-0. Before halftime, the Noxubee County crew scored on Mike Butler's 45-yarder to Gaylon Koon and added a two-pointer via Butler's pass to Lance Mitchener. However, Giffin answered with a 4-yard rushing tally to make halftime 20-8.

Each team added a last touchdown in the final frame. Davis Kelly did the honors from five yards for the Wildcats while a Butler toss to Brady Whitmore accounted for Macon's. Their two-pointer between the two was successful.

GAME 6:   LOUISVILLE (4-1) vs ACKERMAN (3-2)
                     LOUISVILLE 34 ACKERMAN 6
                     October 10, 1969

The Indians were on the Cat schedule almost every year since the first. Moreover, since the last 1930s, there was very little for them to brag about as they held just two victories and a tie.

Warner passes of 53 and 15 yards to Harris counted for scores. Harris also picked off an Indian pass and raced 95 yards. Warner found Majure for a 50-yard strike and score while Joel Cockrell dashed 40 yards to paydirt for the last. The lone Ackerman score came on Charles Edwards' 80-yarder to Dusty Dendy.

GAME 7:   LOUISVILLE (5-1) @ NEWTON (1-5)
                     LOUISVILLE 47 NEWTON 12
                     October 17, 1969

Harris scored twice in the game on a 57-yard Warner pass and later with a 1-yard plunge. Majure recorded a pair of 25-yard Warner passes for touchdowns. Kelly crossed from two yards, Thad Wright pulled in a 30-yarder from Majure, Cunningham grabbed a 15-yarder from Majure, Giffin added a two-pointer, and Cherry knocked home three PATs.

Louisville reportedly had 473 total yards from scrimmage on the night.

GAME 8:   LOUISVILLE (6-1) vs QUITMAN (3-4)
                     LOUISVILLE 39 QUITMAN 12
                     October 24, 1969: HOMECOMING

The Panthers came to Louisville for Homecoming after losing the previous week to Philadelphia 20-6. The Clarke County Tribune called them *"young"* this year.

Neither newspaper gives specifics about play in the game. Warner hit Majure from 11 yards; Giffin found paydirt from 46 and 2 yards, Addkison did the same from 11 yards, while Harris notched a pair of scores from 15 and 13 yards. Cherry added three PATs for the Cats. Both Quitman scores came from Danny Culpepper.

GAME 9:   LOUISVILLE (7-1) @ KOSCIUSKO (6-1)
                  LOUISVILLE 28 KOSCIUSKO 12
                  October 31, 1969

A win for Kosy was essential to stay in the Choctaw race. However, their six turnovers on fumbles and interceptions killed any hopes that would happen.

An opening fumble could have resulted later on a 43-yard Cat FG, but it was unsuccessful. Louisville then went 67 yards in two plays for the Giffin touchdown and two-pointer. In the 2nd quarter, they picked off a Toby Tyler pass but could not get further than the 25-yard line. Wayne Jones found the end zone from 16 yards for the Whippets but the failed conversion kept it 8-6.

Louisville came back with a 13-yard Giffin tally to make it 14-6. Then, they picked off another pass to kill a threat. However, Kosy later fumbled it back and, one play later, Giffin scored and halftime sat 20-6. In the finale, Jones cut the lead on a 22-yarder to put it 20-12. The last Cat TD came after yet another interception and ensuing Giffin dash and Addkison two-point conversion. The game ended on another Cat pickoff.

Giffin scored all but two points in the game on runs of 70, 15, 20 and 70 yards while adding a two-point conversion. Addkison had the other. Louisville led in total yards a whopping 480-229.

GAME 10:   LOUISVILLE (8-1) vs PHILADELPHIA (7-2)
                  LOUISVILLE 27 PHILADELPHIA 6
                  November 7, 1969

A win on this night gave the Wildcats their first Choctaw Conference title since 1962. If successful, it marked their seventh since 1948.

On the first Cat possession, Giffin took a Tornado punt and raced 61 yards to the end zone. Majure's PAT made it 7-0. Bill Greenleaf swept around the right from 13 yards to cut the lead to 7-6. In the 2nd quarter, Warner hit Bowman from 11 yards and Giffin later dashed 15 yards to make it 19-6 at halftime.

Addkison broke free from 30 yards in the 3rd quarter and Warner hit Bowman for the two-point conversion. Louisville racked up over 300 rushing yards.

All-Choctaw First Team members included Keith Giffin, Robert Warner, and Paul Miller. Honorable Mentions included Bobby Bowman, Mike Younger, Jeff Jackson, Danny Harris and Larry Addkison. Coach Turner was runner up for Coach of the Year.

Internal awards went to Bowman, Miller, Giffin, Bryce Stokes, and Warner.

1970–1979

1970 (6-2-1)

After just one year at Louisville as head coach and numerous years as assistant in football, Matthew Turner moved to nearby Winston Academy as Athletic Director and Head Football Coach. In his place was Paul Wood, long-time assistant mostly with the upcoming players. He had the services of 15 lettermen back in Winston County.

"We feel that we are physically ready to play and now are trying to prepare to be ready mentally. We know that West Pont is going to field a good ball club. I know that our team will represent our school to the very best of their ability". Choctaw Conference voters picked the Wildcats to win the title this year with Quitman and Kosciusko next in line.

GAME 1:   LOUISVILLE (0-0) @ WEST POINT (0-0)
                       LOUISVILLE 28 WEST POINT 0
                       September 4, 1970

Louisville enjoyed six-straight victories over West Point and both clubs were looking to start the season with wins. This was despite it being a non-conference affair.

Larry Addkison opened scoring in the 2nd quarter with a 35-yard dash while Tommy Majure found Thad Wright from 20 yards to make it 12-0. In the 3rd quarter, Majure hit Ronnie Roberts from short yardage. The two-pointer made it 20-0. Majure wrapped up things on their final drive on a 10-yarder to Stanley Eaves for the third passing touchdown.

"I was pleased with the results but feel that we have a great deal of improvement to make, especially if we expect to defeat Starkville". Percy Eichelberger recovered three fumbles on the evening. Majure was 12-20 in the air. First downs (14-10) went to the Cats.

GAME 2:   LOUISVILLE (1-0) @ STARKVILLE (1-0)
                       LOUISVILLE 7 STARKVILLE 33
                       September 11, 1970

Long-time rival Starkville opened their season with a convincing 27-0 win over Kosciusko. The Yellow Jackets were 10-0 the previous year with three straight Little Ten Conference titles. The Cats were just 1-6 against the nearby team since 1963.

Harold Kemp opened the 2nd quarter with a 4-yarder and John Davis converted. Addkison then garnered the lone Cat tally on a 1-yarder and Majure added the point to tie. Kemp then found paydirt from a yard and Davis made halftime 14-7. In the 4th quarter, the Jackets rolled. Henry Vaughn crossed from inside five yards, Dan Glover picked off a pass and Parker hit Mertick Hogan from 37 yards, while Bill Montgomery hit David Jones from 30 yards and Ricky Lemmons for the last. Addkison led rushers with 59 yards.

GAME 3:   LOUISVILLE (1-1) vs GRENDA (2-0)
                       LOUISVILLE 27 GRENADA 6
                       September 18, 1970

The first half appeared to show a Grenada win for the first time, but the second half took away those hopes. Louisville held a 7-6 halftime advantage thanks to Grenada's Jan Collins run with Cat score coming on a 60-yard Roberts punt return and Addkison PAT. Addkison added a 1-yarder in the 3rd quarter while Majure found James Frazier from midfield for the next. Finally, Larry Gamblin picked off a Grenada pass and raced 15 yards. Majure converted on all but one PAT attempt.

GAME 4:   LOUISVILLE (2-1) vs EUPORA (2-0-1)
                       LOUISVILLE 13 EUPORA 7
                       September 25, 1970

Coach Ruben Walker's Eagles returned 12 letter winners from a 9-2 squad. Thus far, it was paying dividends as they outscored opponents 68-19.

The Cats jumped out before most could get a seat when Hervie Hammock dashed 52 yards to the end zone on the first play and Majure converted. Eupora tied it in the 2nd quarter on an 11-yard Eddie Sellars run and Willie Brown PAT. However, Louisville responded with Majure's 35-yard connection with Roberts to end scoring before halftime.

GAME 5:   LOUISVILLE (3-1) @ WINONA (2-1-1)
                               LOUISVILLE 28 WINONA 12
                               October 9, 1970

Things were not all bad for Coach Wally Bumpas thus far in Winona despite the loss of 18 lettermen from a 5-4-1 team. This marked the first contest since the back-to-back games of 1948-1949; both Wildcat victories.

In the opening frame, Majure and Wright connected and the PAT made it 7-0. Willie Love added the next on a 6-yarder and 14-0 lead. Winona got on the board before halftime via a Mike Hardin run. Majure and Wright hooked up again in the second half and the two-pointer put it 22-6.

In the final frame, Majure hit Stanley Eaves on a short pass and the PAT finished Cat scoring. Hardin hit Ricky Raffael for their last. Roberts had an interception in the game.

GAME 6:   LOUISVILLE (4-1) vs NEWTON (2-4)
                               LOUISVILLE 21 NEWTON 6
                               October 16, 1970

The Tigers, under mentor James Nelson, lost only four lettermen from 1969 and were expected to be improved this season. This series had a very long history and would not be taken lightly by either side regardless of records on the season.

Majure opened the contest with a 15-yard toss to Jerome Rash and then added the PAT. Newton answered with a short John Thompson plunge but the missed PAT kept halftime 7-6. In the 3rd quarter, Addkison *"bulled his way over the goal line from the 5-yard line"* and Majure converted. In the final quarter, Joel Cockrell caused a Tiger fumble at the Louisville 1. Later, Majure scampered nearly 80 yards for the last TD and Addkison kicked the PAT.

GAME 7:   LOUISVILLE (5-1) @ QUITMAN (7-0)
                               LOUISVILLE 7 QUITMAN 9
                               October 23, 1970

Coach Benson Holland may have lost 16 lettermen from his 4-6 team, but had ten back. Additionally, they were undefeated, playing at home and coming off a 22-0 shutout over Philadelphia. This one meant the difference in a Choctaw title as the Cat loss to Starkville had no bearing since it was non-conference.

Quitman opened scoring in the first quarter when Willie Moore recorded a safety to give them the 2-0 lead that made the eventual difference. Both hit paydirt in the 2nd quarter. Eddie Cotton found Pete Albritton for the score and added the kick to make it 9-0. Louisville responded with a 10-yard Rash passing reception from Willie Love and Majure conversion. It was all over afterwards. The Cats had a chance after a Majure pick got as far as the one-foot line but the Winston County team could not push across the stripe. Later, Roberts got to the Quitman 1 but, again, to no avail.

GAME 8:   LOUISVILLE (5-2) vs KOSCIUSKO (3-4)
                               LOUISVILLE 20 KOSCIUSKO 20
                               October 30, 1970

Coach Buddy Gardner brought his Whippets to Hinze Stadium for what would be the last home game for 28 Wildcat seniors. Louisville dropped tilts in both 1960 and 1968 but prevailed in every other game going back to 1957. A loss or tie here mathematically eliminated Louisville from the Choctaw crown.

Things looked great for Louisville until just 5:00 remained. Just before halftime, Harvey Hammock pulled in a Majure pass for a 60-yard score and Majure conversion. In the 3rd quarter, Majure hit Roberts for a 25-yarder and Majure again added the PAT. A bit later, Addkison got in from 10 yards to make it 20-0. Now late in the game, Howard Lewis and Robin Swilley connected for a 60-yard tally. They also added the crucial two-pointer.

An intercepted pass soon followed for a touchdown, as did another after a Kosy fumble recovery. The game ended in a 20-20 tie due to turnovers and the two-pointer.

GAME 9:   LOUISVILLE (5-2-1) @ PHILADELPHIA (3-5)
                               LOUISVILLE 27 PHILADELPHIA 7
                               November 6, 1970

Coach Ray Terry's Tornado were much worse than the previous season's 7-3 mark. The question was whether the Cats would end the season with pride since all hopes were now lost and this marked their last game of 1970.

While Philly was first on the board with a 1-yard Guy Nowell touchdown and Don Culpepper conversion, Addkison answered in the 2nd quarter on a 7-yarder and Majure kick. Love followed on his 4-yard dive to make it 13-7. Addkison picked off a Tornado pass in the 3rd quarter and Joel Cockrell later turned it into a 2-yard crossing. The last tally came after Hammock's 55-yard pick-six. Majure found Roberts for the two-point conversion.

The Wildcats ended third in the conference despite losing their critical game by just a safety. First Team All-Choctaw awards went to Mike Younger, Victor Young and Larry Addkison. Honorable Mentions included Thad Wright, Hervie Hammock and Ronnie Roberts.

1971 (11-0)

After a lone season, yet another Wildcat mentor was in Louisville. This time it was A.J. Kilpatrick. In August, he spoke with the Louisville Rotary Club saying, "*Play 100%, play fair and play to win. While more than 70 boys have come out for football, the team will have a number of sophomores in key positions*".

Despite only nine letter winners back while losing 27, and finishing third in the Choctaw Conference the previous season, voters picked the Cats first again.

GAME 1:   LOUISVILLE (0-0) vs WEST POINT (0-0)
           LOUISVILLE 13 WEST POINT 7
           September 3, 1971

This was to be no ordinary win for the Cats as West Point was preseason first in the Little Ten. They featured nine starters among the 18 lettermen back on the team. In this edition, "*neither the Wildcats nor the Green Wave showed mid-season form in fundamentals, but exhibited championship form in desire and determination*".

Sophomore Ray Hisaw got it going in the 2nd quarter on his 89-yard dash to paydirt and Bubba Brown made halftime 7-0. Willie Love "*skirted off right tackle*" in the 3rd quarter to put the Cats up 13-0. Buddy Vance put West Point on the board in the frame and Miller connected to make it 13-7. With 3:00 remaining, West Point drove to the goal but Carl Hathorn's pickoff killed the threat. Hisaw led rushers with 123 yards while Love rushed for 57 more.

GAME 2:   LOUISVILLE (1-0) vs STARKVILLE (1-0)
           LOUISVILLE 19 STARKVILLE 6
           September 10, 1971

Starkville was a tough next opponent with Louisville bragging of only a lone victory (1967) since 1963. The Yellow Jackets opened their campaign with a 35-15 win over Choctaw Conference Kosciusko. Additionally, they held a 21-game winning streak. "*The game was a hard-fought battle before a tremendous crowd, as many people had selected this game as one of the top ones in the state*".

An early Cat punt fumble did no damage thanks to great defense. Hisaw responded with a 66-yard dash to the 15-yard line to set up a Love plunge to make it 6-0. Now in the second half, Starkville fumbled the kickoff to Bubba Brown. Tim Ellis then hit Brown for the touchdown and Earl Carter made it 13-0.

Brown put the game "*on ice with his third pass interception*" and dashed 54 yards to paydirt. Thad Sanders scored late from inside the 1-yard line to avoid the shutout for Starkville. Hisaw rushed for 117 yards of the 266 total to lead the team. Brown had three interceptions, a fumble recovery and the two touchdowns.

GAME 3:   LOUISVILLE (2-0) @ NOXUBEE COUNTY (0-1)
           LOUISVILLE 60 NOXUBEE COUNTY 0
           September 17, 1971

The team Wildcat fans grew up as knowing Macon was now officially Noxubee County. They did not field a team in 1970 and were rebuilding "*but weak*". It was no surprise that Coach Johnson's red and blue Tigers were to be no obstacle in this affair on their home field.

"*Noxubee never threatened in the ball game and could manage to cross the midfield stripe only one time*". Solid rushing allowed Hisaw a 22-yard rushing tally and Carter's first PAT. A blocked punt set up a 2-yard Hisaw run and Carter again converted. With just :05 left in the initial frame, Carl Hathorn dashed 22 yards for the next. A bad punt snap recovered by Mike Goodin allowed a later Tim Ellis 26-0 touchdown run.

With reserves in play, William Earby dove in from three yards to cap a 48-yard march while Leon Pace returned a fumble 33 yards to make it 33-0 in the 3rd quarter. With 1:00 left before the end of the quarter, Earby raced 19 yards for the score and Steve Gladney followed with a 12-yarder to Brown. Gene Roberson added the 11-yard dagger and Carter the PAT.

Love had 89 yards rushing while Hisaw recorded 68 yards. Louisville was 4-9 for 49 yards passing.

GAME 4:　　　　　　　LOUISVILLE (3-0) @ EUPORA (0-3)
　　　　　　　　　　　LOUISVILLE 52 EUPORA 6
　　　　　　　　　　　September 24, 1971

The impressive win for the undefeated Cats pushed them to ninth in Mississippi High School polls. Now they faced Coach Ruben Walker's Eagles featuring only three lettermen back from a 5-3-1 squad.

An early Eupora drive put them at the Cat 10 before Boo Hendrix picked off his first of three passes. Then, the Cats fumbled a punt where the Eagles' Lamar Davis fell in it for their lone tally. Louisville then went 58 yards with Hathorn pulling in a 37-yard Ellis pass and Carter converted. Hendrix picked off his second pass to allow Ellis a 12-yarder to Carter and halftime stood 13-6.

Cockrell added a 3rd quarter touchdown and Carter converted. Love rushing set up an Earby rushing score and Carter put it 27-6 in the frame. In the finale, Ellis hit Hathorn from 25 yards; Bobby Gene Robinson reversed 36 yards to paydirt, and Hendrix had his last pickoff to set up a Donnie Wilson 5-yard plunge. Due to injury with less than 2:00 remaining, the game was called and the PAT was not attempted. Ellis threw for 140 yards. Love rushed for 104 yards.

Unbeknownst to everyone, the long rivalry against Eupora was over. They played 25 consecutive seasons and more stretching back to the early 1920s.

GAME 5:　　　　　　　LOUISVILLE (4-0) @ GRENADA (1-3)
　　　　　　　　　　　LOUISVILLE 14 GRENADA 0
　　　　　　　　　　　October 1, 1971

While Coach Charlie Newell's red and blue Bulldogs were 8-3 the previous season, they had only six letter winners back while losing 21 others. Granted that their record was not stellar, they played tough competition in Greenwood, Winona, Oxford and Tallahatchie.

After recovering an early Bulldog fumble, Hisaw dove in from three yards and Carter converted. The last score came in the 3rd quarter on a 63-yard Ellis connection with Jack McDaniels and Carter PAT. The Cats held Grenada to just 72 offensive yards in total.

GAME 6:　　　　　　　LOUISVILLE (5-0) vs WINONA (3-1-1)
　　　　　　　　　　　LOUISVILLE 40 WINONA 0
　　　　　　　　　　　October 8, 1971

Coach Wally Bumpas was improving his red and gray Tigers from a 4-5-1 mark with the assistance of 14 lettermen back in Winona. History said that there was no way for Winona to win based on the long history of these meetings.

Hathorn opened the game with a 32-yard pick-six. Other early scores came from a 34-yard Ellis toss to Hathorn, 22-yarder to Jack McDaniels, Hisaw run from 15 yards and Love 22-yarder. Other scoring from Cat players was ambiguous in the blowout victory. The Wildcats led in first downs (17-9) while rushing for 254 yards and passing for 208. The Cat defense held Winona to just 173 total yards.

GAME 7:	LOUISVILLE (6-0) @ NEWTON (3-3)
	LOUISVILLE 35 NEWTON 6
	October 15, 1971

Despite the Tigers sitting 3-3, they were undefeated in Choctaw circles and this meant more than just comparative records. Newton had 13 letter winners back from a 2-8 team and could be the spoiler as Quitman did in 1970. Since 1943, Louisville kept a 21-7 hold on games played.

Early in the opener, the Cats marched 63 yards in 10 plays capped by a 2-yard Hisaw dive and Carter PAT. Ellis then hit Carter from 32 yards and Carter made it 14-0 still in the first quarter. Carter (or Hisaw) ran in from 10 yards in the next and provided the 21-0 PAT. Newton got their lone score before halftime on Joe Evans' 2-yard dive.

Late in the 3rd quarter, Leon Pace recovered a fumble and raced 54 yards to set up Love's 6-yarder and Carter kick. In the finale, two Cat FGs of 51 and 58 yards were wide but Hisaw crossed with less than 3:00 left to finalize scoring.

GAME 8:	LOUISVILLE (7-0) vs QUITMAN (7-0)
	LOUISVILLE 19 QUITMAN 16
	October 22, 1971

The previous win against Newton amazingly kept the Wildcats ninth in polling despite only two other teams above them with losses. Greenville (6-0) had 108 voting points for first place while the Cats had only 20 points (7-0). Furthermore, thus far, Louisville stood with a 208-25 record in scoring against opponents.

This contest would prove it all as The Winston County Journal said, "*many football experts consider this version of the Panthers to have the finest football team in the state among the non-Big Eight teams*". All home fans remembered the devastating 9-7 loss from the previous year that kept their Wildcats out of Choctaw contention.

In the first half, Quitman snagged the lead on a 12-yard Eddie Cotton toss to Pete Albritton and their PAT. An ensuing Cat fumble in the end zone led to a Panther safety and 9-0 lead. Late in the half, Love got in from two yards to put it 9-6 at halftime. Later, Donnie Wilson "*jarred the ball loose from Cotton and raced 55 yards*" to make it 12-9. Hathorn then recovered a fumble and Ellis hit Brown for a 20-yard tally. Carter's PAT made it 19-9.

Quitman found paydirt in the 3rd quarter on a Cotton pass to Staten. Cotton's kick was good but was not to be enough. Quitman led in first downs (10-8), rushing (147-101) and passing (136-116) but lost five fumbles and a pair of interceptions in the last half. The win moved Louisville only up a spot to eighth and still far behind five teams with losses.

GAME 9:	LOUISVILLE (8-0) @ KOSCIUSKO (6-2)
	LOUISVILLE 34 KOSCIUSKO 0
	October 29, 1971

Coach Fred Kirkland had only five lettermen back from their 3-4-2 team and prospects for an upset looked dismal in spite of their 6-2 overall record.

Late in the opening quarter, Hisaw dashed 79 yards to paydirt and Carter make it 7-0. Thanks to a pair of Cat turnovers, that score held through halftime. Hisaw opened it up in the 3rd quarter on his 85-yard kickoff return and Carter provided the kick. He scored again later from 22 yards and Carter put it 21-0. An intercepted pass by Brown allowed Hisaw yet another from eight yards while a later Ralph Worth interception allowed Love a short toss from Ellis.

GAME 10:	LOUISVILLE (9-0) vs PHILADELPHIA (1-8)
	LOUISVILLE 54 PHILADELPHIA 6
	November 5, 1971

Unbelievably, Louisville remained ninth in polling despite all but one team above them with a loss. Four other teams had a pair of defeats. Despite that, Coach Ray Terry had 14 lettermen back to improve his odds to beat the Wildcats at R.E. Hinze Stadium. It was a stretch as they had only a lone win on the campaign.

The opening kick was taken by Love 76 yards to the 3-yard line from here he "*blasted*" in for the score and 6-0 early lead. Hisaw's 2-yarder followed with a Carter PAT. Percy Eichelberger picked off a Mike Turner pass and he returned it 38 yards to allow Ellis a TD. Carter made it 20-0. Cockrell then picked off a pass and raced 52 yards to paydirt. He picked off his next in the 2nd quarter but an eventual Cat pass at the 5-yard line was intercepted. A Wildcat FG failed but Brown picked off a pass to allow Hisaw's 2-yarder to make halftime 33-0.

Philly opened the 3rd quarter with a fumble recovery and Mike Turner throw for the lone touchdown. Hathorn then picked off a pass and Gladney found Robbie Roberson from eight yards. Carter put it 40-6. Gladney ran in later from a yard and hit Roberson from midfield for the last. Ellis was 5-11 for 44 yards while Gladney was 2-4 for 67 yards. Hisaw rushed for 152 yards.

GAME 11:   LOUISVILLE (10-0) vs ACKERMAN (10-0)
                  LOUISVILLE 29 ACKERMAN 0
                  November 12, 1971; Philadelphia, MS

It came as a shock that Louisville now faced Ackerman for the Choctaw title. Ackerman lost earlier to West Kemper, but it was determined that their opponent played six ineligible players and could not compete. Art Nester's blue and gold, with eight letter winners back in camp, were much improved from their 7-2-1 record of 1970.

Louisville started with a bang as they took their opening drive to paydirt, finishing on a 48-yard Ellis connection with Earl Carter. The Carter PAT made it 7-0. Later, Hisaw broke away from 63 yards to the 3-yard line from where Love burst through and Carter converted. Now 14-0 in the 3rd quarter, Carter notched a 36-yard FG. Hisaw opened the finale with a touchdown to cap a 69-yard march and Carter added the PAT.

The last score of the season came on Gladney's scrambling 14-yarder to Brown. Hisaw rushed for 167 yards to pace runners. Brown led in tackles and recorded a pair of interceptions. The Wildcats now held their ninth Choctaw Conference championship.

The last undefeated Wildcat squad came in 1950. During that season, they outscored opponents 251-58. This year's edition outscored opponents 369-47. All-Choctaw honors went to Roy Fulton, Bubba Hendrix, Donnie Wilson, Percy Eichelberger, Willie Colter, Ray Hisaw and Willie Love. Honorable Mentions included Joel Cockrell and Bubba Brown.

1972 (8-2)

Second-year headman A.J. Kilpatrick's Wildcats were a unanimous first in pre-season predictions for the Choctaw Conference title. Kosciusko came in second while Winona finished in third place. Despite losing 16 lettermen, his 15 lettermen after an undefeated season meant an easy decision for most coaches.

The coach said of his team before the first contest, "We are much smaller than the championship team of a year ago, but possibly a little quicker. Our schedule is much tougher than it was a year ago so we must have a maximum performance from our young men in order to carry on the winning tradition of Louisville".

GAME 1:   LOUISVILLE (0-0) @ WEST POINT (0-0)
                  LOUISVILLE 28 WEST POINT 6
                  September 8, 1972

The Cats were 9-1 against West Point since 1936. For this year, Coach Travis Langford's Green Wave team finished fourth in The Little Ten conference pre-season votes.

Ray Hisaw got things going for 1972 on their second march with his 3-yarder and Earl Carter nailed the PAT. They then went 60 yards in seven plays with Daryl Coleman finding "daylight off of right tackle from seven yards" and Carter made it 14-0. The Cats made it 21-0 when Tim Ellis found Carter from 12 yards.

In the final frame, with substitutions in play, runs by Boo Hendrix led to a 4-yard Bubba Rogers run and Troy Lee Hardin PAT. The home team avoided the shutout on a 10-yard Carl Griffin reception although the kick was unsuccessful.

GAME 2:   LOUISVILLE (1-0) @ STARKVILLE (0-1)
                  LOUISVILLE 39 STARKVILLE 12
                  September 16, 1972

Despite the Yellow Jackets competing in the Big Ten, this one counted as a Choctaw Conference game for standings. The previous year victory was the first the Cats could proclaim after losing seven of eight recent meetings.

The Winston County Journal called it "an awesome offensive attack and a fierce defense". Ellis engineered a 69-yard drive capped by his 1-yard sneak and Carter PAT. Before halftime, Rogers went in from 14 yards and later notched a 19-yarder. Carter notched another TD pass while recording nine tackles. Hisaw's 75-yard return in the second half set up the score. Roy Miller found paydirt in the 3rd quarter from four yards and Coleman did the same from 52 yards.

Yellow Jacket touchdowns came via a 44-yard Larry Mullins pass to Robert Fabris and Tommy Kettler's 57-yard fumble return; both late in the contest. Compliments on individual performances were numerous. The lone bad result from the contest came because of Joe Letteri's broken arm to put him out for the season.

GAME 3:   LOUISVILLE (2-0) vs NOXUBEE COUNTY (1-1)
                     LOUISVILLE 67 NOXUBEE COUNTY 6
                     September 22, 1972

Although Coach Vernon Vann's team went just 2-7 the previous season, he did like that 26 letter winners were back in Macon. What ended was perhaps the most Wildcat points scored against an opponent since 1940.

Scoring started early with a 15-yard Hisaw run, another from 53 yards, and Robbie Roberson got in to make it 21-0 thanks to three Carter kicks. Roberson grabbed a Steve Gladney throw for the next and Gladney added a 1-yarder later. Hardin added a 7-yard effort and Carter put it 42-0. Before halftime, Hendrix got across from three yards and Hardin converted.

Steve Younger hooked up with Ronnie Hampton in the 3rd quarter from 70 yards while Booker Hathorn tallied twice in the finale. First was a 23-yard toss from Steve Younger while the last was a 2-yard plunge. Noxubee scored on the last play of the game to avoid the shutout. The Wildcats outscored their opponent 355-23 in yardage.

GAME 4:   LOUISVILLE (3-0) @ TUPELO (3-0)
                     LOUISVILLE 0 TUPELO 3
                     September 29, 1972

The last tilt between Tupelo and Louisville came in 1938. It ended a loss for the Cats 33-7. Now, 35 years later, the Cats went on the road to settle the score.

The defensive battle at Robbins Field, under rainy conditions, went into the late final frame where the Cats fumbled to James Barnes at the Golden Wave 3. Though Tupelo fumbled back to Gladney, Louisville again turned the ball over; this time to Roger Davis. The Cats marched late as deep as the Wave 3 before faltering.

With under 2:00 remaining, the Wave began the game-winning march. Now with just :04 left on the clock, Davis booted the 23-yard FG to give them the late heart-breaking win to break a Louisville winning streak of 14 games.

GAME 5:   LOUISVILLE (3-1) vs GRENADA (4-0)
                     LOUISVILLE 14 GRENADA 0
                     October 6, 1972

While the loss to Tupelo was deflating, it meant nothing as it related to the goal of another Choctaw title. Now the Cats welcomed Charlie Newell's Grenada squad. The previous year they were just 3-6 and returned only six letter winners. Nevertheless, the opponent sat undefeated thus far and presented a challenge to Louisville.

Rogers broke the ice in the 2nd quarter with his 6-yard burst and Carter knocked home his first of two PATs. In the last stanza, Louisville put it away with a 13-yard Ellis strike to Carter. The Cat defense held Grenada rusher Greg Harris to just 34 yards while recording two interceptions. Louisville led in rushing (225-51), passing (75-4) and first downs (11-4).

GAME 6:   LOUISVILLE (4-1) vs LEE HIGH (3-2)
                     LOUISVILLE 37 LEE HIGH 7
                     October 13, 1972

Yet another team ranked in the Top 15 made their way to R.E. Hinze Stadium. This time it was the opponent first on the board late in the opening stanza courtesy of a 1-yard Jim Wamble dive and a Derrick Freeman PAT. Eight plays later, the Cats marched 72 yards in eight plays ending on a Rogers run to make halftime 7-6.

The second half was a completely different affair as Louisville amassed 31 points while holding Columbus to just 50 yards of offense. Carter hit a 35-yard FG, Hisaw ran in from four yards and Ellis found Roberson from 60 yards. Two Carter kicks made it 23-7. Roy Miller ran in later from 17 yards while Jimmy Owens took a punt 60 yards to paydirt. Carter's last two kicks proved the final points.

Louisville led in rushing (184-110) and passing (163-15).

GAME 7:   LOUISVILLE (5-1) vs NEWTON (1-5)
                               LOUISVILLE 66 NEWTON 6
                               October 20, 1972

It was not a great season thus far as Coach Gerald Hegan returned just seven lettermen of 21 total from a 5-5 season. The Newton Record said when over, *"No love was lost between the Newton Tigers and Louisville Wildcats as the Winston County mentor A.J. Kilpatrick 'poured on the coal' ..."*

Things started rolling midway through the opening frame when Hisaw dashed 52 yards to paydirt. He followed that with a 9-yarder and two Carter kicks made it 14-0. He then added a 48-yard sprint to make it 20-0. Midway through the 2nd quarter, a Newton fumble deep in Tiger territory allowed Rogers a touchdown dash one play later and Carter made it 27-0. Before halftime, Gladney hit John Goodin for one score while running 30 yards for another. One Carter kick put it 40-0.

Willie Goss opened the 3rd quarter with a 30-yard pick-six and Carter converted. Second later, Hisaw dashed 36 yards to the end one to put it 54-0. In the last frame, Younger hit Jimmy Owens for a 75-yard score. Finally, Lou Eichelberger notched a 30-yard pick-six for the dagger. Newton's late touchdown came when Leon Jackson picked off a Cat aerial and returned it 85 yards to set up a short Hamp Beatty sneak.

GAME 8:   LOUISVILLE (6-1) @ NESHOBA CENTRAL (4-2-1)
                               LOUISVILLE 28 NESHOBA 13
                               October 27, 1972

There were a whopping 12 lettermen of 26 back in red and blue under Coach Bobby Posey. They were 6-3-1 the previous year and expecting to do better. To date, they could reach that goal if they closed out the season with victories. This marked the first meeting between the two teams as the Rockets were formerly in the Sam Dale Conference.

Louisville struck early on a 15-yard Ellis dash. Hisaw soon added the next from two yards and the Cat two-pointer made it 14-0. Owens took a 2nd quarter punt 59 yards to paydirt and Carter made it 21-0. Neshoba then went 70 yards in 15 plays ending on a 4-yard Melvin Yarbrough run and Andy Brantley PAT.

Falling rain in the second half kept the score down considerably. In the last quarter, Ellis hit Roberson for a 50-yard tally and Carter added the kick. Owens could have had another, but his 90-yard kick return came back for clipping. Rufus Latimer (or Brantley) added the last touchdown for NCHS, but the two-point play failed. LHS led first downs (12-10) and passing (82-0) while NCHS held the ground (197-175).

GAME 9:   LOUISVILLE (7-1) vs KOSCIUSKO (8-0)
                               LOUISVILLE 0 KOSCIUSKO 7
                               November 5, 1972

First-year Coach Art Nester was on track to copy the first year of Kilpatrick as his Whippets were undefeated thus far. The winner of this one held their Choctaw future firmly in their grasp and a standing room only crowd was anticipated in Louisville. Said Kilpatrick of Kosy, *"The team will come ready to scrap".*

An estimated 7,500 fans were on hand for the epic battle. An early fumble recovery by Lee Kyles led soon to a Randy Holloway FG attempt from six yards. The Cat defense blocked the attempt to avoid the bullet. Unable to move from deep, the Wildcats had to punt to the Whippets. It was on this drive early in the 2nd quarter that produced a 5-yard touchdown by Evans and Holloway PAT.

Turnovers on both sides killed promising drives. One fumble recovery by Louisville at the Kosy 4 ended in long sacks and losses. Evans sealed the affair with the third Whippet interception of the evening. Kosciusko out-rushed the Wildcats 235-75 while Louisville won the air 124-15. Said Kilpatrick, "*Kosy is the best team in the state*". Added Nester, "*We are the number one team in the state and there are no better, more dedicated athletes in the state*".

GAME 10:   LOUISVILLE (7-2) @ PHILADELPHIA (4-4)
                          LOUISVILLE 54 PHILADELPHIA 0
                          November 10, 1972

Although Coach Ray Terry had 12 letter winners back, they were still a 1-9 team in 1971 and one the paper said, "*lacks experience*". In all, they had 28 players and just four seniors. This season was better despite those obstacles.

The limited recap of the blowout affair noted that Ellis had three touchdown passes. One went to Carter while Goodin snagged a pair. Gladney ran for one tally and hit Ronnie Hampton for another. Hendrix added a 45-yard pick six for good measure. Carter had four extra points and Gladney a pair.

All-Choctaw First Team members included Tim Ellis, Ray Hisaw, Bubba Brown and Earl Carter. Willie Goss was named Honorable Mention. A.J. Kilpatrick was named Southeastern Coach of the Year by the National High School Athletic Association.

1973 (7-2)

Third-year mentor A.J. Kilpatrick posted a respectable 19-2 record in his first couple of years and now hoped to improve that record. He had 13 letter winners back although he lost 17 senior players. The team was "*experienced and confident*" and depended "*on speed and quickness since only four players will weigh in at over 200 pounds*".

GAME 1:   LOUISVILLE (0-0) vs WEST POINT (0-0)
                          LOUISVILLE 34 WEST POINT 6
                          September 7, 1973

Two Wildcat players expected to play despite injuries. Ray Hisaw had a broken finger while Norris Jernigan had a "*gimpy knee*". The Winston County Journal noted, "*since both teams are virtually an unknown quantity, the game will hold a special interest for fans of both teams. It is sure to provide plenty of fireworks*".

On the first Wildcat drive, Tim Ellis found Jimmy Owens from 27 yards and Troy Hardin converted his first of four extra points. A short Ray Hisaw run and Roy Miller's 9-yard effort made it 21-0. Ellis provided a 3rd quarter tally from 12 yards and Steve Younger led the team down the field in the last frame with the finale a 9-yarder to Donnie Glenn.

With 1:26 left, Phyfer hit Marion Bratton from 28 yards to their lone tally. Louisville led in first downs (13-4) and yardage (324-97).

GAME 2:   LOUISVILLE (1-0) vs STARKVILLE (0-1)
                          LOUISVILLE 7 STARKVILLE 0
                          September 14, 1973

Out-of-conference Starkville, like West Point and Grenada, were designated Choctaw Conference games for 1973. Louisville enjoyed a two-game winning streak over the Yellow Jackets but they were a large team this season and featured 55 players. Said Kilpatrick, "*We are expecting a tougher football team than they had last year. They should be bigger and better*".

A promising first drive fizzled, as did other big plays due to penalties and turnovers. With just :15 left before intermission, Ellis and Jimmy Owens hooked up for a short touchdown and the PAT gave them all they eventually needed. The remainder of the second half was a true defensive show on both sides. Louisville led in yardage 288-119 and Hisaw paced rushers with 101 yards.

GAME 3:   LOUISVILLE (2-0) @ NOXUBEE COUNTY (1-0)
                                    LOUISVILLE 29 NOXUBEE COUNTY 12
                                    September 21, 1973

Charles Temkovits and his Tiger squad opened the previous week with a 24-0 win over Heidelberg. Scouting apparently thought this team *"much improved"* over 1972.

In the 1st quarter, Ellis and Owens hooked up for a 37-yard score and 6-0 lead. Back came Noxubee to tie things on Wade Gordon's plunge. In the next frame, Ellis and Owens again connected from nine yards and Hardin made it 13-6 at halftime. Roy Miller added the next from 22 yards on the ground while Daryl Coleman ran in later from five yards to widen the lead.

Hardin, *"in addition to this PATs"*, rammed home a 36-yard FG to give them their 29 points. The other Noxubee touchdown came from James Patterson. The Clarion-Ledger called it *"a highlight of the game"*. Louisville led in first downs (15-9) and yardage (292-110). Hardin averaged 50 yards on his kickoffs. The downside were the 13 Wildcat penalties which amassed 165 yards.

GAME 4:   LOUISVILLE (3-0) vs TUPELO (2-1)
                                    LOUISVILLE 26 TUPELO 0
                                    September 28, 1973

Everyone in Winston County remembered the Roger Davis 23-yard FG with just :04 left on the clock the previous season. This year, Coach Dennis Waites had just seven letter winners back from that 8-2-1 team. Pre-season voting put the Golden Wave fourth in their Big Eight conference.

"They're as good as they were last year or possibly better. We're looking for a real tough ball game", said Kilpatrick. The Clarksdale Press Register picked the Wildcats 13-7 saying, *"With a big question mark beside this game, we'll go with the home field advantage"*.

Hisaw capped the opening 69-yard march with his short run around left end to make it a 6-0 lead. An ensuing Travis Harrington fumble recovery at the Golden Wave 14 led immediately to a fumble back to Bob Rice. However, just before halftime, Ellis found Ray McBrayer from seven yards and Hardin put halftime 13-0.

Scotty Lambert fumbled an opening kickoff to Mike Goodin at the 20-yard line. Daryl Coleman finished a few plays later from seven yards. Roy Miller then got in the books with his 38-yard pick-six and Hardin provided *"the finishing touch"*. Glenn and Randy Hudspeth each recorded other interceptions.

Louisville had 14 first downs and 221 yards of offense. 73 yards came via the air while the 148 came on the ground. Tupelo recorded seven first downs.

GAME 5:   LOUISVILLE (4-0) @ GRENADA (1-2)
                                    LOUISVILLE 16 GRENADA 0
                                    October 5, 1973

The 4-0 start put the Wildcats ninth in the Mississippi High School Poll. Two other teams above them sustained losses, as did the one immediately behind. Now they traveled to Grenada to face Charlie Newell's red and blue Chargers. They went 9-2 the previous year and returned 12 of 25 lettermen.

The Greenwood Commonwealth said that the squad had *"lots of problems this year"* despite their past record. While they did have letter winners back, many others lost were key contributors at critical positions. Said Kilpatrick, *"They're definitely better than their record indicates"*.

It took very little time before Ellis found Owens from 21 yards for the initial score. In the 2nd quarter, Hisaw dove in from a yard and Hardin made it 13-0. As halftime neared, Hardin nailed a 46-yard FG. That ended scoring for the affair. Hardin also recorded an interception while the defense held Grenada at the 1-yard line to kill a drive.

GAME 6:   LOUISVILLE (5-0) @ LEE HIGH (2-2-1)
                                    LOUISVILLE 34 LEE HIGH 10
                                    October 12, 1973

Coach Dwain Acker had a 55-man squad with 16 seniors and 21 lettermen. *"They're bigger and better than last year and we're expecting a tough time"*. The Clarksdale said, "*Louisville has displayed the mark of a winner in more ways than one this season and the Columbus squad has shown only spurts of being tough. Hanging in there, Louisville 21-13*".

The Cats opened with a time-consuming 80-yard drive ending on a 14-yard Coleman run. Midway through the 2nd quarter, Hisaw dodged in from the 6-yard line and Hardin made it 13-0. On the last play of the half, Mark Campbell knocked home a 30-yard FG to make it 13-3. Coleman added a pair of running touchdowns in the second half from 17 and two yards. Roy Miller also added a 38-yard pick-six in the half. The General's lone touchdown late in the game on David Dickerson's throw to Roosevelt Harris while Mark Campbell added the PAT and a FG.

Louisville rushed for 321 of 389 yards while holding Lee to 107 on the ground and 38 in the air. The win pushed Louisville to ninth in high school polling.

GAME 7:   LOUISVILLE (6-0) vs NESHOBA CENTRAL (4-2-1)
                                 LOUISVILLE 48 NESHOBA CENTRAL 13
                                 October 26, 1973

Louisville enjoyed an off-week to prepare for Bobby Posey's Rockets. One report said he had "*a team with more depth and experience in the line than previously and the backs are fast*". This marked the last home game for 14 seniors before the Cats took on their two toughest opponents of the season. The Wildcats now sat seventh in the UPI poll.

Kilpatrick was complimentary of his opponent. "*They've played well all year with losses to undefeated Forest and Kosciusko*". This marked only their second meeting, Louisville having taken the victory the previous season.

Ellis opened the contest with a 54-yard scoring dash and Hardin converted his first of six extra points. A long Goodin punt return then allowed Ellis a 21-yarder to McBrayer. While NCHS on a 9-yard Charles Carter run to make 14-7, the Cats answered on a 1-yard Ellis dive. Owens added a 47-yard scoring reverse while Hisaw did the same from four yards to make halftime 34-13. The Rocket's last tally came on a 1-yard John Stevens plunge.

In the 3rd quarter, Ellis returned a fumble 54 yards to paydirt while Coleman crossed from four yards for the last. Louisville led the ground 301-178 and air 74-62.

GAME 8:   LOUISVILLE (7-0) @ QUITMAN (5-1-1)
                                 LOUISVILLE 10 QUITMAN 12
                                 November 2, 1973

The Wildcats sat sixth behind a pair of teams with losses, but that did not matter on this evening. Coach Benson Holland's Sam Dale Conference squad had 74 players on the roster featuring 26 seniors and 33 lettermen. Their lone loss came to Southeast Lauderdale and the tie was against South Jones.

The Cats hit the board first on Hardin's 28-yard FG but Quitman responded in the 2nd quarter with a Mike Leslie 28-yard pick-six. In the 3rd quarter, William Bennett plunged in from five yards. Louisville made it a game late on Coleman's 7-yard effort but an earlier FG attempt by the Cats failed.

GAME 9:   LOUISVILLE (7-1) @ KOSCIUSKO (8-1)
                                 LOUISVILLE 14 KOSCIUSKO 21
                                 November 9, 1973

The Whippets under Coach Art Nester not only beat the Cats 7-0 in Louisville the previous year, but they also went undefeated (10-0) and took the Choctaw Conference crown. This year, with 10 lettermen back, they were picked to do it again. Like that season, it all came down to this one last game.

Louisville, despite the loss, was still 5-0 in the Choctaw Conference. It would not be an easy scrap as Norris Jernigan suffered a season-ending broken arm against Quitman. Other Wildcats also nursed bad injuries. Said Kilpatrick, "*We feel Kosciusko is as good as last year or better. They have a well-balanced offense and an excellent defense*". Added Nester, "*They have a good, well-balanced, all-around good team. Louisville is well-coached and (I) have nothing but praise for them*".

Kosy hit the board first at Landrum Field when Jeff Moore "*crunched over from five yards*" and Randy Holloway converted. Ellis and Owens answered with an 8-yard touchdown connection and Hardin tied it 7-7. Moore opened the 3rd quarter with a 2-yarder while Ellis ran in from five yards in the final stanza.

The dagger came when Moore added a six-yard crossing for the heartbreaking close to the season. Hisaw had 131 rushing yards.

The First-Team All-Choctaw list was cluttered with Wildcats. They included Ray McBrayer, Norris Jernigan, Mike Goodin, Tim Ellis, Ray Hisaw, Jimmy Owens, Willie Morgan, and Roy Miller. Some also made Honorable Mention on the defense. Others on that list were Ricky Eaves and Cliff Jernigan.

Internal awards went to Miller (Best Defensive Player), Hisaw (Best Back), Daryl Coleman (Best Blocker), McBrayer (Most Improved), Goodin (Wildcat Award), Booker Eichelberger (Most Improved), Eaves (Best Lineman), Ellis (MVP and Scholarship Award) and Steve Gladney (Special Plaque).

1974 (8-1-1)

Fourth-year Coach A.J. Kilpatrick enjoyed 17 returning letter winners as his team broke away from a long relationship with the Choctaw Conference. The Wildcats now competed in the North Mississippi Athletic Conference after winning the previous circuit title nine times.

As with every year, there were key losses, but also great returners from which to work. *"We will prepare for a basic game (against West Point) and hope our youngsters execute and adjust well enough to get through the first game".*

GAME 1:   LOUISVILLE (0-0) @ WEST POINT (0-0)
                 LOUISVILLE 20 WEST POINT 6
                 September 6, 1974

The Green Wave of West Point defeated Louisville only once (1956) out of 13 all-time meetings. Said Kilpatrick, *"West Point will usually field a hard-hitting team and I'm sure this year will be no exception".*

A solid drive of passes and runs allowed Troy Hardin a 1-yard touchdown run in the 2nd quarter to give the Cats a 6-0 lead. Just 2:00 before halftime, West Point responded with a 39-yard touchdown Baird pass to James Otis Doss. The last scoring came in the 3rd quarter on Jimmy Owens runs of eight and three yards, along with a two-point conversion.

Bobby Moore (74) and Travis Herrington (72) led rushers. Steve Younger passed for 98 yards. On defense, Stanley Goss (2) and Hardin (1) recorded interceptions. *"We know more about who can play and where than we did before the game. We made a great many mistakes that we can't afford to make with the people on our schedule".* Louisville rushed for 200 yards and threw for 70 more.

GAME 2:   LOUISVILLE (1-0) @ STARKVILLE (0-1)
                 LOUISVILLE 0 STARKVILLE 6
                 September 13, 1974

Jim Craig's Yellow Jackets had only nine lettermen back and were considered small but quick. Penalties and turnovers made the difference in this contest.

The first half was a defensive struggle. Harold Hughes gained credit for the Cats with a forced fumble, a fumble recovery and a blocked punt. Another fumble came late in the final frame to put Starkville in great position. That is when Jon Fabris hit Tommy Mosley from ten yards for the only score of the game. The last miscue, with the clock expiring, ended hopes.

GAME 3:   LOUISVILLE (1-1) vs NOXUBEE COUNTY (1-1)
                 LOUISVILLE 12 NOXUBEE COUNTY 6
                 September 20, 1974

The Macon team under Coach Charles Temkovits were riding a five-game losing streak to Louisville since 1969. The Wildcats needed this one to bounce back from the previous week heartbreaker.

A bad snap turnover midway through the opening quarter allowed the visitors a quick touchdown run from inside 12 yards to make it 6-0. Back came Louisville with a 65-

yard march and Jimmy Owens 3-yard blast to tie it. It looked as if the Cats would score in the final stanza from three yards but a fumbled killed the opportunity. However, Owens' *"twisting, darting 35-yard sprint"* late gave them the win.

Owens rushed for 119 yards while Harrington added 81 more. Now it was time for conference play. *"We have three films on Grenada and they are a typical Grenada team: play good defense and have some big backs who come right at you. They beat Columbus two weeks ago and we know it will take a good effort on our boys' part to win our first conference game".*

GAME 4:   LOUISVILLE (2-1) vs GRENADA (2-1)
                 LOUISVILLE 6 GRENADA 6
                 September 27, 1974

Coach Charles Newell's Chargers had 12 lettermen back and had wins over Lee High and Winona. Their lose loss was to Greenwood by a 22-0 score. Historically speaking, Louisville sported an 8-0 mark against Grenada since 1941.

Much like another game, a bad snap gave Grenada the ball at the Cat 10 in the 2nd quarter. They ended with a touchdown catch that was semi-deflected but held a 6-0 lead. Steve Younger evened it before halftime on a 15-yarder to Goss. The failed PAT kept the Cats from taking what would have been the game-winning point.

Both Grenada and Louisville missed FGs in the second half. The Cat defense held Grenada to just 65 rushing yards and 34 passing yards. Louisville put up 119 rushing yards. Henry Perry paced runners with 59 yards.

GAME 5:   LOUISVILLE (2-1-1) @ TUPELO (1-1-1)
                 LOUISVILLE 27 TUPELO 24
                 October 4, 1974

This was to be no easy contest as the lone Golden Wave loss was to the second-ranked (Alabama) Grissom High squad 20-10. Coach Dennis Waite had 15 returning lettermen back and an all-time margin of victory over the Winston County squad.

Halftime did not look encouraging for the visitors as they found themselves down 24-6. Tupelo's opening drive went eight plays with a 1-yard Kenneth Jackson touchdown midway through the opening quarter and Tom Baughman conversion. Owens took the ensuing kick 90 yards to paydirt to cut it to 7-6. A Cat punt fumble at the 20-yard line led five plays later to Lea Paslay's 13-yarder to Jeffrey Boyd. Later, they moved 88 yards for a Celester Davis third tally from a yard and 21-6 lead. Baughman capped a 24-yard drive with his 23-yard FG to end the half.

The second half was a different story. First was a 71-yard march and Harrington 4-yard blast. Hardin put it 24-13. A next Cat drive led by Younger made it 24-19 as the 3rd quarter ended. In the finale, Louisville marched 88 yards with Owens adding the last four yards and Younger finding Goss for the two-pointer. Lou Eichelberger ended Wave hopes with a late pass interception.

Tupelo led first downs 13-10 while Louisville held the ground 120-116 and passing 126-115.

GAME 6:   LOUISVILLE (3-1-1) vs LEE HIGH (1-3)
                 LOUISVILLE 21 LEE HIGH 0
                 October 11, 1974

Perineal opponent (Columbus) Lee High was young this season with only six letter winners back. Their losses were by small margins except for a 27-0 defeat to a Tuscaloosa, AL team.

An early Lee interception led eventually to a missed FG effort for what would be their only threat of the night. Midway through the 2nd quarter, Owens *"dazzled"* the crowd with a 75-yard punt return and Hardin gave them all they needed. With just :43 left before halftime, Younger hit Willie Morgan from 15 yards and Hardin provided the extra point.

The Wildcats inserted the dagger late on a 1-yard Younger plunge and the Hardin kick. Despite three missed FGs, the Cats dominated yardage (336-27). Henry Perry led rushers with 90 yards.

GAME 7: LOUISVILLE (4-1-1) @ CALDWELL (4-1-1)
LOUISVILLE 21 CALDWELL 12
October 18, 1974

A second-straight Columbus, MS team was now on the schedule for the first time. This was the inaugural meeting between the clubs and The Winston County Journal said this one would probably give the winner the conference title.

Coach Robert Youngblood's squad jumped out early with a 50-yard Bubba Hill keeper. Louisville marched 95 yards to the Caldwell 3 before running out of gas. The Cats came alive in the 2nd quarter on Younger's 18-yarder to Goss, his one-foot dive for a touchdown, and then his two-pointer to Owens to make it 14-6.

Then, Kenneth Whitehead picked off a Bobcat throw for a 35-yard pick-six. The second Hardin PAT made it 21-6. Sammy Miller's interception ended any hopes of a halftime tie. Caldwell made it closer late in the game on a "disputed" passing touchdown. James Nash picked off a Cat pass to set up Hill's pass to David Boyd. Just one year into the new conference and the Cats held yet another title.

Younger threw for 98 yards while Owens rushed for 86 more. Goss had all 98 receiving yards. "We were most happy for our players that they could win the championship in the conference's first year of existence. We must give credit to all 50 players on the squad for the hard work they have done in coming back from what appeared to be a dismal season in the first few weeks".

GAME 8: LOUISVILLE (5-1-1) @ NESHOBA CENTRAL (3-3-1)
LOUISVILLE 26 NESHOBA CENTRAL 0
October 25, 1974

Coach Bobby Posey's Choctaw Conference team lost 19 letter winners to graduation. This year was break even thus far and they hoped to get better against their former conference opponent.

Wildcat scoring came from Harrington's 1-yarder in the opening frame, Younger's 21-yard pass to Owens in the next, a 1-yard Owens dive, and a 16-yard 4th quarter Younger throw to Owens. "It was a total team effort for us. Our defense played well the entire game. Our backs ran well, especially Harrington and Bobby Moore". Harrington paced rushers with 145 yards. The defense held NCHS to just 93 yards.

Added Posey, "There was just too much Louisville for us. They were the biggest team we've met and maybe the best".

GAME 9: LOUISVILLE (6-1-1) vs QUITMAN (1-6-1)
LOUISVILLE 26 QUITMAN 0
November 1, 1974

This long-time opponent, still in the Choctaw Conference, gave Louisville trouble in the years. In the past few meetings, the final score came down to roughly three points. Fans may have expected the same for 1974 despite the Quitman record.

Travis Harrington's 71-yard burst on the initial drive, along with the Hardin PAT, gave a bit of comfort to the fans. Younger soon followed with an 11-yard keeper and Hardin made it 14-0. Whitehead's 2nd quarter interception led soon to a short Harrington dive to make it 20-0. The final score, with reserves in play, came on a 73-yard Goss "zig-zag" punt return.

Harrington again rushed for over 100 yards while Moore had 96 yards. The defense held Quitman to just 6 first downs and 88 offensive yards.

GAME 10: LOUISVILLE (7-1-1) vs KOSCIUSKO (7-2)
LOUISVILLE 7 KOSCIUSKO 6
November 8, 1974

Coach Art Nester had a machine working in Kosciusko with continuous Choctaw Conference titles. This year his Whippets were projected first in the circuit despite only eight lettermen back. One paper called it "one of the hardest hitting games ever to be played at Louisville".

Owens opened with an 85-yard punt return only to come back for stepping out of bounds at midfield. The first of three fumbles killed the threat on the next play. Kosy took advantage with a later 6-yard Gerry Taylor toss to Larry Harmon to make it 6-0. A second half Perry dash from 26 yards tied it and Hardin gave them the margin of victory needed.

Owens and Miller added interceptions for the defense that held the Whippets to 88 passing yards and -2 rushing. Harrington had 120 total yards while Perry rushed for 62. The score may have been worse aside from the three lost Cat fumbles.

All-Conference honorees included Stanley Goss, Jimmy Owens, Norris Jernigan, Willie Morgan, Cliff Jernigan and Kenny Whitehead. Honorable Mentions went to Travis Harrington, Steve Younger, David Russ, Bobby Moore, and Harold Hughes. Coach Kilpatrick earned the Northeast Mississippi Athletic Conference Coach of the Year.

Internal award included Norris Jernigan (Best Lineman and MVP), Kenneth Whitehead (Most Improved), Gene Stringer (Scholastic), Cliff Jernigan (Best Defensive), Randy Hudspeth (Wildcat Award), Steve Younger (Best Back and Co-Team Captain), Willie Morgan (Best Blocker), and Jimmy Owens (Co-Team Captain Award and Most Versatile Player)

1975 (8-1)

After four years as head coach in Louisville, A.J. Kilpatrick took the position of Athletic Directors and Head Coach at Northwest Junior College in Senatobia. *"There was nothing wrong with the Louisville situation. I just felt that the position and challenge of Junior College football was better"*.

Longtime Kosciusko rival coach Art Nester took his spot as head Wildcat. He posted an amazing 43-7-1 record in recent years including more than one Choctaw Conference title. Still in the Northeast Mississippi Athletic Conference, the Cats found themselves pre-season second to Tupelo by a lone vote. Caldwell, Lee High and Grenada followed behind.

GAME 1:   LOUISVILLE (0-0) vs WEST POINT (0-0)
                    LOUISVILLE 12 WEST POINT 0
                    September 5, 1975

The Wildcats again opened the campaign against the Green Wave of West Point. They expected to be better with 19 starters back. Five of the offensive letter winners were in their spots with seven others on defense. However, Louisville held an impressive 11-0 mark in the last 11 games. *"We'll be ready on Friday nights"*, Nester told the Louisville Rotary Club on game week.

The opening Green Wave drive moved 68 yards before Stanley Goss picked off a Timbo Baird pass to kill the threat. A second quarter Cat fumble deep in West Point territory killed an opportunity and kept halftime scoreless. In the next half, Goss picked off his second Baird aerial and Louisville eventually turned it into a 13-yard Travis Harrington scoring dash and 6-0 lead.

Early in the 4th quarter, a third Goss pickoff set up a 2-yard Tony Triplett plunge for the finale. Louisville had a chance for one more before the end but fumbled one yard short of the stripe.

GAME 2:   LOUISVILLE (1-0) vs STARKVILLE (1-0)
                    LOUISVILLE 14 STARKVILLE 13
                    September 12, 1975

Coach G.T. Thames' Yellow Jackets were the team that spoiled a potential perfect season in 1974 with a tight 6-0 victory. Now the Cats were hoping to do the same to that squad that finished 9-1 and featured 20 returning letter winners from their conference title team. *"The Wildcats will be out for revenge and this promises to be a thriller"*.

Starkville dotted the board first on a 4-yard Breck Tyler reception and Randy Wofford PAT. Foster Glass immediately answered with an 85-yard kick return and Bobby Moore tied it 7-7. A later Clifford Eichelberger interception went for naught due to a later Cat fumble. Starkville eventually found paydirt on a 3-yard Carl Trainer run. The two traded interceptions later with James Harris getting one for Starkville while Goss did the same. The half ended 13-7.

Leon Hoskins found a loose 4th quarter fumble but it did no damage. Later, Tony Triplett did the damage via his *"beautiful spiral"* to Sammie Miller. Moore's crucial PAT was successful. As the clock expired, Goss ended a final threat with his fifth interception of the young season.

GAME 3:   LOUISVILLE (2-0) @ GRENADA (1-1-1)
                        LOUISVILLE 19 GRENADA 12
                        September 26, 1975

Charlie Newell's Chargers, avoiding their tenth consecutive loss to Louisville with a tie the previous year, now had 16 lettermen back of 26 from a 3-6-1 team. It was now time for Louisville to play their first road game of the year.

Grenada scored first on a QB sneak while Moore did the same from 13 yards to end the opening quarter 6-6. Glass' touchdown in the 2nd quarter made halftime 12-6. Now in the final frame, Moore crossed from four yards and Triplett converted. Grenada added a late tally but it was too little and too late. Kenny Yarbrough recorded a Cat fumble recovery.

GAME 4:   LOUISVILLE (3-0) vs TUPELO (3-1)
                        LOUISVILLE 0 TUPELO 6
                        October 3, 1975

The game of the year was at hand in Winston County against Coach Dennis Waite's Golden Wave. They were 6-2-1 the previous year and had nine lettermen back from a total of 25. Their lone loss thus far was to a tough non-conference opponent.

A disputed early call gave Tupelo a second chance at the end zone and they did just that on a 3-yard Tommy Payne dive. Kenny Whitfield blocked the extra point. The dispute came when Louisville was called offside when it appeared a false start on the Wave. It was a "see-saw" game afterwards with neither building much momentum.

GAME 5:   LOUISVILLE (3-1) @ LEE HIGH (2-2-1)
                        LOUISVILLE 6 LEE HIGH 0
                        October 10, 1975

Although Coach Dennis Coleman's Generals were a paltry 0-9 in 1974, they did have 30 lettermen back in Columbus. Voters thought them to be much better this season.

The low-scoring affair at the Magnolia Bowl came down only to Moore's 2-yard plunge. His PAT effort was long but off-mark. Louisville led the ground 159-111 and passing 11-0. Eichelberger picked off a pair of General passes while Robert Walker recorded one for the Columbus team. Glass led Cat rushers with 65 markers and Hoskins recovered a fumble.

GAME 6:   LOUISVILLE (4-1) vs CALDWELL (2-3)
                        LOUISVILLE 18 CALDWELL 7
                        October 17, 1975

Things were not necessarily promising for Coach Waverly King's Bobcats. The Columbus team had 16 letter winners back from a 6-3-1 team but lost 28 others including all-conference players. The Winston County Journal said, "When the fur stopped flying, everyone knew who was the top cat".

Harrington capped the opening 68-yard drive with his 11-yarder to make it 6-0. Caldwell responded before the frame ended on Eugene Bush's 3-yarder and Tim Carter made it 7-6. Triplett put the Cats ahead for good in the 2nd quarter on a 17-yard run. Terry Walker recovered a fumble later to set up an 11-yard Henry Perry dash for the final tally.

Triplett ran for 103 yards while Perry rushed for 104, Sammie Miller picked off a pass, and several others contributed with sacks and touchdown-saving tackles.

GAME 7:   LOUISVILLE (5-1) vs NESHOBA CENTRAL (3-3)
                        LOUISVILLE 28 NESHOBA CENTRAL 10
                        October 24, 1975

Coach Bobby Posey's Rockets were in the Choctaw Conference and coming off a 3-5-1 season. "The Cats are expecting a real tough battle because the Rockets are one of those teams that have had a personal grudge against the Cats for a number of years".

The Cats' first touchdown came on a 4-yard Perry burst and Moore PAT. Glass followed with a 1-yarder and Moore put it 14-0. In the 3rd quarter, Moore "romped into TD land" from four yards and Good returned a punt 60 yards for the next. Mike Land hit Sammie Miller for the two-point conversion.

In the finale, NCHS hit the board on Damon Dunn's 16-yarder to Bobby Byers and Dunn notched the two-pointer. A bad punt snap later gave them a safety. Two other earlier Rocket drives inside the 15-yard line failed on turnovers. Goss picked off his 10th pass while Harold Hughes and Tim Welch picked off others. Terry Walker found a fumble. Harrington paced rushers with 83 yards.

GAME 8:   LOUISVILLE (6-1) vs GREENWOOD (6-1)
                                  LOUISVILLE 7 GREENWOOD 0
                                  October 31, 1975

Coach Hollis Rutter's Greenwood was to be no pushover as the Bulldogs were selected Number One team in Mississippi in 1974 after an 11-1 record and Delta Valley zone Big Eight title. Now, they sat second in the state after losing to Callaway.

The only score came early on a 70-yard drive ending with Moore's 1-yard dive and his PAT. The key play came on a 43-yard Glass pass to Goss. Louisville led in first downs (11-8), rushing (110-73) and passing (108-56). Said Rutter, "*Their defense was strong and that was the strong point of the game*".

GAME 9:   LOUISVILLE (7-1) @ KOSCIUSKO (8-0)
                                  LOUISVILLE 26 KOSCIUSKO 6
                                  November 7, 1975

The win moved Louisville to 7-1 and put them ninth in polling. Greenwood was still two places ahead of them, as were others with worse records. None of that mattered as they faced rival Kosciusko. With Nester now on the Wildcat sideline, Coach Ricky Black took his place had the head Whippet at Landrum Field.

Triplett notched the initial tally on his 74-yard dash to daylight to give Louisville the early 6-0 lead. On the next Kosy drive, Troy Eichelberger fell on a loose Whippet ball to set up Triplett's 26-yarder to Goss for the 12-0 advantage. Kosciusko got their lone touchdown afterwards on Johnny Lee Morris' 36-yarder. An ensuing Cat fumble could have been bad, but their efforts stopped as halftime sounded.

Triplett opened 3rd quarter scoring with his 13-yard effort. Wendell Crockett then recovered a bobbled kickoff and Triplett later turned it into a 36-yard strike to Sammie Miller to finish scoring. Goss wrapped it up with his 13th interception of the season while Cliff Eichelberger recorded his fourth. Troy Eichelberger also added a theft.

Louisville led in first downs (10-8 or 12-11) and put up 366 yards of offense (or 348-271). Harrington rushed for 138 yards and Triplett for 81 more.

The last win moved the Wildcats only up to seventh in the state's best high school football teams. The defense led the NEMAC with just 25 points allowed and 54 in all. The secondary had 23 interceptions.

All Conference nods went to David Russ, Stanley Goss, Terry Walker, Bobby Moore, Clinton Mills, and Harold Hughes. Goss, Russ, Walker and Mills were also on the All-American Prep Team. Internal awards went to Goss (MVP), Moore (Best Offensive Back), Ken Carter (Special Teams), Doug Stokes (Scholastic), Walker (Best Defensive Lineman), Mark Gully (Captain), Sammie Miller (Best Defensive Back), Russ (Permanent Team Captain) and Hughes (Wildcat Award).

1976 (5-3-1)

Prospects looked bright for second-year coach Art Nester as his Wildcats were called "*any coach's dream. The linemen are big and strong and the backs are agile and speedy*". They were, however, now in a division of The Little Ten after a couple of seasons in the Northeast Mississippi Athletic Conference. Therefore, competition would be tougher. Despite this, he was "*still high on the team*" with 15 lettermen back with many starters returning.

The Little Ten actually had 16 teams in two divisions of competition. Louisville was portioned in the southern division. Experts called them perhaps the second-best conference behind The Big Eight. The Wildcats gained a second spot in voting behind Starkville pre-season on that side.

GAME 1:   LOUISVILLE (0-0) @ CALDWELL (0-0)
                           LOUISVILLE 12 CALDWELL 12
                           September 3, 1976

        Since 1966, the opener was always against West Point. Now, the Wildcats
traveled to Columbus for the lid-lifter. It could be worse as Coach Waverly King was in a
"rebuilding year" as they *"lost almost everybody to graduation and then had his top two
quarterbacks move from Columbus this year"*. One report said, *"It could be a long season at
Caldwell"*. Voters picked them last pre-season in the conference.
        The local paper may have been overconfident when they said, *"The Wildcats will
win"*. That came partially from Nester who said, *"We will win Friday night. I feel like we're
ready, the coaching staff has confidence in our young men and our attitude is great. So, I
say once again we will win. Columbus has a good football team; make no mistake about it.
But I know we are better. Our young men are ready"*.
        Bobby Moore opened scoring in the 2nd quarter with a 1-yard plunge to cap a 70-
yard march. Caldwell answered on a 26-yard Gil Earhart pass to Ricky Hill to keep halftime
6-6. Both scored in the 3rd quarter, first after a Cat fumble deep in their territory. Terry
Anderson dove in from a yard but their two-point conversion failed. Foster Glass evened it
with a 95-yard kickoff return but the PAT failed.
        *"There was a rainstorm during the game but it rained on both sides. We just
made too many mistakes to win the football game. The fact is, we failed in our senior
leadership. I take the blame for the tie because it is my responsibility to ensure that the
team has good senior leadership. It was the worst game in my 13 years of coaching. We
were bad on confidence. We thought we could go out there and beat them easily. They
stuck it to us"*.

GAME 2:   LOUISVILLE (0-0-1) vs OXFORD (0-1)
                           LOUISVILLE 32 OXFORD 6
                           September 10, 1976

        The Wildcats now opened against Coach Bobby Sanders, the previous Coach of
the Year in The Little Ten. This year, however, he had only a lone offensive starter back and
only three more on defense. Their opener against Batesville resulted in a 26-0 shutout.
        *"Oxford has a fine QB who throws the ball real well. It's been mighty wet (for
practices) but it's raining all week in Oxford. I think we're going to be ready for Oxford. We
haven't had any injuries and we're in better shape"*.
        Glass gained his first of many early on a 15-yard reception from Triplett to cap an
80-yard drive and make it 6-0. Midway through the next quarter, he ran in from 30 yards.
Minutes later, Moore added another from four yards. Two more Cat scores came back
before halftime due to penalties; one by Ivy Hughes and another Glass run. Nevertheless, it
was 18-0 at intermission.
        Leon Hoskins' pickoff in the 3rd quarter set up another Glass tally and Hughes
pulled in a Triplett two-pointer to make it 26-0. Oxford then drove 80 yards with Randy
Coleman finding Larry Mosley from 21 yards for their lone score. The finale came in the last
quarter when Lou Greer escaped from 46 yards. It could have been worse as Bernard
Jordan took a last-second pickoff 100 yards to paydirt only to have a penalty overturn it.
        Louisville led in yardage (430-111). Rushing was all in favor of them (326 to -15).
Moore recovered a fumble in the affair. Glass rushed for 134 yards and pulled in 56 more in
the air.

GAME 3:   LOUISVILLE (1-0-1) @ STARKVILLE (3-1)
                           LOUISVILLE 7 STARKVILLE 15
                           September 24, 1976

        The two met each year since at least 1940 and the trip was close and familiar for
the Wildcats. Coach G.T. Thames' Yellow Jackets were picked tops in The Little Ten for
1976. *"We could have a super year if all our kids respond. But it is going to be up to them in
the long run. We have some very good athletes; we just have to wait and see if they are
going to use their abilities"*.
        Said Nester, *"Starkville has a fine football team. They're small in size but very
quick. They've got a running back they call 'White Rabbit' and he's considered one of the
best runners in the state. It's going to be a real battle. Our boys are going to be high as a

kite and I know they're going to be the same way. We're going to have to rely on our size to beat them because they're quicker than we are".

It looked positive early as the Cats held a 7-0 halftime lead thanks to a 1st quarter 5-yard Triplett pass to Ivy Hughes. That capped an 81-yard drive. Moore added the PAT. Louisville nearly made it into FG range before the intermission whistle. It fell apart in the 3rd quarter when a fumble at the Cat 5 quickly turned into a David Reed scoop and score and Ronnie Dewberry two-pointer.

In the final stanza, Jeff McDaniel recorded a 20-yard pick-six and Sidney Smith converted the extra point. Louisville led in first downs (10-9), rushing (170-134) and passing (34-17). "We still have a good chance to win the conference. Starkville is in first place right now but if we can beat Tupelo and Grenada and one of them beats Starkville, then we'll win the conference. The most important breaks went to Starkville. We whipped them in every phase of the game except the score".

GAME 4:   LOUISVILLE (1-1-1) vs KOSCIUSKO (3-1)
                   LOUISVILLE 18 KOSCIUSKO 3
                   October 1, 1976

Injuries were starting to take their toll, but there was still enough talent to welcome rival Kosy to Hinze Stadium. Said Nester, "It should be a fine football game. A close, exciting game, and the kind the fans like. I know since I coached there (that) their athletes will be higher. They're going to be high". Added Ricky Black, "We still look for a strong team from Louisville and they will be trying to fight back from a disappointing start".

The only tally of the first half came on a late 1st quarter 25-yard Tim Miller FG for the Whippets. Turnovers stopped both teams from doing much else. One Cat fumble was recovered by Martin Williams while Leon Hoskins returned the favor later. Travis Prisock found another in the 2nd quarter while Miller picked off a Cat throw.

Scoring came alive in the second half. Louisville opened with a 70-yard drive capped by a 41-yard Foster Glass dash. Late in the frame, Henry Perry ran in from 10 yards to make it 12-3. Midway through the finale, Kosy recovered a Cat fumble but fumbled to Riley Murray at the 1-yard line. Perry capped it later on a dramatic 82-yard scamper. Glass and Vic Romedy picked off late passes as Kosciusko attempted a comeback.

Kosciusko led in first downs (12-8) and passing (190-5) while the Cats held the ground (266-100).

GAME 5:   LOUISVILLE (2-1-1) vs LEE HIGH (2-3)
                   LOUISVILLE 38 LEE HIGH 21
                   October 8, 1976

Coach Dennis Coleman proved his Generals to be "another team that could surprise folks" by upsetting Tupelo 10-6 the previous week. Voters had them sixth in the conference pre-season.

Despite freezing temps and light drizzle, Louisville jumped out immediately with Triplett's 35-yard scoring run. Six minutes later, Riley Murray recovered a fumble at the General 26 and Triplett turned it into a 15-yard tally to make it 12-0. Lee responded with a 1-yard Sammie Lowe keeper and John Edwards PAT.

Now in the 3rd quarter, Lee scored on a 60-yard Lowe pass to Elton Cockrell to make it 13-12. The Cats came back with a 30-yard Glass scoring run to re-take the lead 18-13. They increased with another Murray fumble recovery and Glass 6-yarder. Perry plunged in for the two-pointer. Glass added to it with a 35-yarder. Leon Hoskins then picked off a throw for his 45-yard pick-six.

Lee added a final score late against reserves on a 14-yard Mike Cross pass to Frazier. Ray Willis' reception added two points. Glass rushed for 147 yards as Louisville out-rushed Lee 255-158. Lee led in first downs (9-7) and passing (94-9).

GAME 6:   LOUISVILLE (3-1-1) @ TUPELO (4-1-1)
                   LOUISVILLE 7 TUPELO 23
                   October 15, 1976

The Golden Wave were replacing nine offensive starters but that did not mean that Coach Dennis Waite had no lack of talent. This game was crucial as the winner kept conference title hopes alive. "We must win this one. We know someone has to lose but we just hope it's them".

Both scoring and title hopes were over by halftime. Tupelo opened quickly on a 64-yard drive capped by Tommy Payne's 14-yarder and Wesley Baughman PAT. Back came the Cats on a 68-yard march and 2-yard Bobby Moore dive. With both PATs successful, it was tied 7-7. A late 1st quarter turnover to Pat Sneed set up a Payne 1-yarder. In the 2nd quarter, Lee Pasley kept from 10 yards while a late Cat fumble to J.D Townsend set up their 28-yard Baughman FG.

Louisville did not quit but a deep turnover in the 3rd quarter killed what could have been the start of a comeback. Tupelo led in first downs (19-7), rushing (255-169) and passing (74-16). While Glass had 170 yards rushing, Payne recorded 221 yards.

GAME 7:   LOUISVILLE (3-2-1) @ NESHOBA CENTRAL (3-4)
                   LOUISVILLE 25 NESHOBA CENTRAL 6
                   October 22, 1976

There was still an outside chance to end 6-2-1 for a fine season, but Nester thought that, in order to do that, he would have "to go back to the basics". Choctaw Conference Neshoba Central was no pushover. "As far as football rivalries go, Neshoba Central hates us more than just about any other team they play". The Cats had not lost in the four straight games between the two clubs.

Glass got his night going midway through the 1st quarter with an 87-yard escape and Moore converted. They added another in the 2nd quarter via Moore's 4-yarder. NCHS tallied their lone touchdown before halftime on Damon Dunn's 21-yard pass to Ronnie Henry. The Cats added touchdowns in each of the final two frames. Glass had the first from 23 yards and the next from 45 yards.

"We started to show some strong leadership out there. That's something we missed against Tupelo". First downs were tied 8-8. NCHS held the air (85-46) while Louisville held the ground (238-150). Glass was credited with 215 rushing yards.

GAME 8:   LOUISVILLE (4-2-1) vs WEST POINT (7-1)
                   LOUISVILLE 7 WEST POINT 21
                   October 29, 1976

The last 12 meetings all went to Louisville as they traditionally opened the season against one-another. This one was different as the green and white were Little Ten leaders and holding a 7-1 record. Coach Travis Langford returned nine offensive starters and five on defense. Although pre-season fifth, they were showing much more power.

Said Nester, "They started about 80 percent of their players as sophomores three years ago. They paid for it in their last two seasons but now it's paying off".

The cold rain eventually took its toll on the Cats but not before opening with a 60-yard drive capped by Moore's 1-yard plunge and PAT. In the 2nd quarter, West Point recovered a fumble and drove 43 yards with a 1-yard touchdown and Greg Cooke PAT. The 7-7 tie held through halftime thanks to a late David Mullins fumble recovery.

Fumbles again took their toll as an early one led to Timbo Baird's 1-yard dive and Cooke kick. A later one on a kickoff set up Jay Golson's 8-yard run and the final Cooke kick. Romedy picked off a last quarter pass but the Cats eventually fumbled it back. "They whipped us soundly", said Nester. West Point led in first downs (12-10), rushing (219-142) and yardage (219-142).

GAME 9:   LOUISVILLE (4-3-1) @ GRENADA (6-2-1)
                   LOUISVILLE 15 GRENADA 10
                   November 5, 1976

Louisville needed this game to avoid the first non-winning season since 1965. It would have to come without Triplett, injured in the last contest. Coach Charlie Newell's Chargers returned eight defensive and nine offensive starters but were fourth pre-season. They now held a better record than the Wildcats.

Grenada was first on the board via an early 14-yard Chuck Newell FG. The Cats, with Tim Butts behind center, engineered a last-second answer with his 18-yard strike to Glass. Moore's conversion made halftime 7-3. They added more in the 3rd quarter on a 39-yard Butts keeper and Moore ran in for the two points. Grenada came back late in the frame on Barry Harper's 25-yarder to Marvin Stewart and Newell's kick but scoring was over. Sammie Coleman's second interception of the night ended any more threats.

"I am real proud of the team. We never gave up and I think we played one of our smartest games of the year. They kept changing defenses on us and we were able to change our offense without any trouble. Our defense played superior and our secondary got after them from the beginning. It was a great way to end the year".

Grenada led in first downs (15-9) while Louisville led rushing (183-85) and yardage (238-197). Glass eclipsed 1,000 yards for the season.

Foster Glass earned All-Conference First Team while Bobby Moore, Leon Hoskins, Jerry Stokes and Charlie Massey garnered Second Team nods.

1977 (7-3)

Art Nester was *"well pleased with the way the team is shaping up"* in mid-August. *"All of the players are in high spirits and ready to take on Columbus"*. He had 13 returning letter winners back in Winston County of the 55-man squad. If there was deflating news, it came as 18 lettermen were gone and the defense was made up *"mostly (of) juniors and sophomores"*.

A few weeks later, he updated, *"The boys have worked real hard. They are inexperienced but have a lot of confidence. I am well-pleased with their showing and the progress we have made but right now, as is to be expected, we are tired"*. Louisville remained in the South Division of the Little 10 Conference.

GAME 1:   LOUISVILLE (0-0) vs CALDWELL (0-0)
                       LOUISVILLE 34 CALDWELL 14
                       September 2, 1977

After two consecutive wins against the Columbus unit, the Wildcats were mildly *"upset"* in 1976 after a 12-12 tie game. *"Caldwell has 18 returning lettermen. I'm relying on the speed and quickness of both the line and backs, although the Caldwell team is bigger than LHS, we have the advantage over them with speed"*.

There was no better way to kick off a season than with a pair of opening frame touchdowns. Bernard Jordan opened with a 31-yard scoring dash while Willie Hannah did the same from seven yards. Tony Triplett notched both PATs. Triplett started the next frame with a 60-yard strike to Jerry Tiller and his PAT made it 21-0. Both scored before halftime. Caldwell's Terry Anderson dove in from a yard and Dale Upton added the kick. However, Triplett did the same and halftime sat 28-7.

Now in the 4th quarter, Triplett ran in from 12 yards for the last Cat score while Weston found Jerry Earhart from 60 yards for their finale. Their local paper claimed it a late 60-yard Gil Earhart pass to Dewayne Weston. Upton was true on the kick. Louisville led on the ground (260-75) but lost the air (68-60). They also suffered an interception. *"We hit them real quick. We are real proud of our boys for the job they did. They gave a 150% effort and I am just real tickled about the victory"*.

GAME 2:   LOUISVILLE (1-0) @ OXFORD (0-1)
                       LOUISVILLE 20 OXFORD 0
                       September 9, 1977

Heavy rains during practice week pushed the team indoors until they could put on pads Wednesday. Louisville dominated the inaugural matchup the previous year but may be tested this week. *"Oxford (has) a real big and lanky club. We will be using our same type of offense. We are an option ball club and use a balanced attack"*.

All of the scoring came in the initial quarter of play. Triplett recorded the first pair of touchdowns on runs of two and 19 yards. Charles Welch hit Tim Butts for the two-pointer after the second. Jordan finalized with a 10-yard dash. There were other opportunities in the final three quarters but turnovers and penalties killed drives.

"We hit them quick and then really got after them. We are tickled to death over the victory. It was hotter up there than down here the week before. Oxford is an improved ball club and they are still young. I am well-pleased with our offense both in running and blocking. However, we are going to have to eliminate some mistakes".

GAME 3:   LOUISVILLE (2-0) @ KOSCIUSKO (2-0)
      LOUISVILLE 7 KOSCIUSKO 14
      September 16, 1977

  Although Kosy was non-conference, they were definitely no stranger to Cat schedules. The two played consecutively since at least 1951 and others beforehand. *"There will be a lot of rivalry in (this one). We are going to have to be ready to get after them"*. One prognosticator in Kosciusko picked the Whippets 18-15 due to the home field.
  The heartbreaking game at Landrum Field opened with an 87-yard drive culminating on Andrew Carter's 15-yard scamper and Lacey Brooks' PAT. A late frame fumble to the Cats set up Jordan's 1-yarder and the tying PAT. Late in the game, a Jerry Stewart pick fumbled to Tommy Williams put them at the 10-yard line. With :11 left, Michael Harmon hit Robert Williams from there and the Brooks PAT iced it.
  Kosy led in rushing (131-88) while Louisville held the air (64-56). *"I am proud of our team as if they had won it. Kosciusko has a good, experienced team and I wish them the best. We played good ball and really hated to lose, but now we have to put that behind us and get ready for conference play"*.

GAME 4:   LOUISVILLE (2-1) vs STARKVILLE (1-2)
      LOUISVILLE 26 STARKVILLE 8
      September 23, 1977

  It seemed a good year to play the Yellow Jackets as they were young but with 13 letter winners back in Oktibbeha County. *"The Yellow Jackets are a young team, but we are not underestimating anyone with a long and tough season ahead. They have a real good football team. They will be a well-disciplined and well-coached team"*.
  On the third play of the contest, Triplett hooked up with Tiller from 60 yards and Triplett made it 7-0. Jordan added a pair of other scores before halftime on runs of 50 and three yards. One more Triplett kick made it 20-0. Lou Greer put an end to Cat scoring with his 4-yard effort and Triplett kick, while the Jackets got theirs with just :04 remaining on a Joe Carter run.
  Hannah led rushers with 170 yards. *"I felt like we may have a let down a little but after viewing the film I saw that there was not that much of a letdown. I was just tickled to death with our running and blocking and when you give up only eight points, you have to be proud of the defensive unit"*.

GAME 5:   LOUISVILLE (3-1) vs WARREN CENTRAL (2-1)
      LOUISVILLE 14 WARREN CENTRAL 0
      September 30, 1977

  The Wildcats now welcomed the Vikings from Vicksburg, a first-time opponent and Little Dixie Conference power. Nester was still confident. *"I feel we will be ready for anything we have to face. They are a good football team. We have a few aches and bruises, but will be ready for them. It should be a real battle"*.
  Unlike other games, it wasn't until the 2nd quarter that the Wildcats began to amass their lead. Triplett runs set up both touchdowns. The first came from Hannah's 5-yard blast while Greer added a 1-yarder later. Welch and Butts hooked up for a two-point conversion. The remainder of the game turned into a defensive battle.
  "I can't say enough good things about our men and their attitude. We had to come right at those fellows and we had fine running and blocking. They were a well-coached ball club. They really wanted us".
  The Cats led first downs (11-2) and rushing (231-76). Warren Central had two passes intercepted and lost one of their three fumbles.

GAME 6:   LOUISVILLE (4-1) @ LEE HIGH (3-2)
      LOUISVILLE 7 LEE HIGH 0
      October 7, 1977

  Louisville could brag of a long winning history against the Generals of Columbus, but this season they were in contention for the Little 10 title. *"Our biggest worry will be just how to have a full team effort and not to let down or relax as any period of the game"*, said Riley Murray. Added Nester, *"This is a do or die football game for them and we are going to* have to be ready. We have got to have this one". Despite the earlier loss to Kosciusko, the Wildcats were now ninth in the UPI.

A Mullins interception in the game allowed the Cats a 40-yard drive and 5-yard Hannah run. Triplett's toe proved the last point of the game. There was another scoring drive for Louisville but penalties proved the end of the opportunity. The defense came through and kept the seven points enough to take home the win. Louisville led the ground (163-56) but lost passing (76-39).

The win pushed the Wildcats into first place in the Little 10 South. Contender Tupelo ended a loser to Caldwell on the night. "It feels good instead of great. If the race was over and we were still number one, it would be great".

GAME 7:   LOUISVILLE (5-1) vs TUPELO (3-3)
                 LOUISVILLE 7 TUPELO 28
                 October 14, 1977

If Louisville wanted another outright title on their resume, it could well be with a win at Hinze Stadium this Friday night. Regardless of their previous series losses, and that of Tupelo the week prior to Caldwell, all that mattered was this one. "We know all the marbles are going to be out there and this could decide the conference championship. We've got to come out on top in this one".

Fumbles set up the first two opening quarter Tupelo touchdowns. Andre Thomas rushed in from a yard while Malcolm Smith added the next. Two Wesley Baughman kicks were good. While Hannah cut it to 14-7 in the 2nd quarter via his 1-yarder and Triplett kick, Tupelo pulled out a 63-yard Smith pass to Thomas. The Baughman kick was true and halftime sat 21-7. Tupelo added their finale in the final frame on Smith's 9-yarder to Joe Woods.

Total yardage ended in a close 213-208 in favor of the Wave. "Everybody is going to have a bad day once in a while and ours was Friday night. The boys hate it and I hate it but that's the way it goes. They were trying their best. You can't blame it on any one thing but just one of those nights".

GAME 8:   LOUISVILLE (5-2) @ WEST POINT (5-2)
                 LOUISVILLE 35 WEST POINT 2
                 October 28, 1977

A week of rest helped to clear the outline for the remainder of the season and to heal bumps and bruises from a rough schedule thus far. "We are not worried about the loss to Tupelo; just worried about ourselves. We have an exceptionally good group of boys and they are going to bounce back from that loss".

Louisville did bounce back with a pair of touchdowns in each of the first two quarters. Triplett's 30-yard connection with David Mullins allowed him a 1-yarder and the first of two PATs. He then hit Tiller from 30 yards for the next. While West Point recorded a David Caskey safety in the 2nd quarter, back came Hannah on a 15-yard run and Wells and Greer added two more points. Later, Triplett ran in from 25 yards and Butts notched the last in the 3rd quarter from a yard.

"We had a real good ball game. I am real proud of them. We had a lot of folks that did a good job. We played every man we had. We began substituting the JV players midway in the 3rd quarter and West Point was still unable to score on them. I think they did an outstanding job. It was one of our best offensive shows".

GAME 9:   LOUISVILLE (6-2) vs SOUTH PANOLA (8-0)
                 LOUISVILLE 0 SOUTH PANOLA 8
                 November 4, 1977

First-time opponent South Panola wasn't easy. They were defending their Chickasaw Conference title and undefeated. "After getting back into the swing, we will be drilling on timing while allowing a few players to recover from minor aches and bruises. We will be ready for anything or anybody that comes to Wildcat territory".

The Tigers were a bigger school but Nester knew the odds. "This will probably be the most physical game we have played. Them cats come at you. It's going to be headgear and shoulder pads slapping". The deflating loss came late in the game after a fumble put South Panola at the Cat 30. Tillman Valentine made it count from seven yards and Willie Corner added the two-point play.

The good news was that Starkville downed Tupelo and gave the Cats sole possession of first place in the South. *"The players don't have a thing to be ashamed of. We maybe didn't get as high for a non-conference game. We missed several scoring opportunities and didn't look as good offensively. We played good defense and broke only once".*

GAME 10:   LOUISVILLE (6-3) vs GRENADA (4-5)
             LOUISVILLE 35 GRENADA 6
             November 11, 1977

A win clinched South title hopes and everyone knew it. *"We have got to get ready for Friday night. I am greedy and don't want to share the title with anyone. We have to get ourselves ready to win this conference. (Grenada) is a good football team. Overall, they are bigger than we are. They are just a big old physical football team".*

In the end, it was a Wildcat runaway at R.E. Hinze. Early in the game, a reverse pass from Welch to Tiller from 60 yards notched the first touchdown. Triplett added his first of three kicks. In the next frame, Triplett rushed in from five yards as did Hannah. They added another in the 3rd quarter on Greer's 20-yard effort. Grenada avoided the shutout in the finale on a 1-yard Henry Williams dive. Green notched the last touchdown of 1977 from 52 yards while Welch found Mullins for two more points.

"They deserved this thing. They have fought hard all season. I'm proud of every one of our men. This group of young men set their goal at the first of the season to win this thing and they reached their goal. I can't single out any one player. They all did a fine job. I was well pleased with our offense and defense. We executed real well and I think this was our best game of the season".

Bowl or overall conference aspirations went nowhere and Louisville had to settle for the South crown. First Team Little 10 honors went to Tony Triplett, Tim Butts, Tim Hemphill, Clyde Jefferson, Riley Murray, David Mullins and Lavagus Smith. Second Team members included Jerry Tiller, Charles Welch and Willie Hannah. Art Nester received the Coach of the Year award.

Internally, awards went to Bernard Hayes, Butts, Vic Romedy, John Dempsey, James Eichelberger, Triplett, Hannah, Mullins, Jefferson and Murray.

1978 (5-5)

The defending South Little 10 Conference champion Wildcats entered the fourth and final year under Coach Art Nester. They featured only 11 returning letter winners but were a vote higher than Starkville pre-season to repeat. *"With our offensive personnel working hard, we feel pretty secure in that area. We are concerned mainly with our defense to see if we can platoon to avoid our men from having to go both ways"*

"Our ball club is very enthusiastic and I feel we are as strong as any other team. However, we are the next to smallest school in our division and everybody on our schedule will be tough".

GAME 1:   LOUISVILLE (0-0) @ CALDWELL (0-0)
            LOUISVILLE 0 CALDWELL 6
            September 1, 1978

Hopes were high as the Cats had only a tie keeping them from all four matchup victories. However, Caldwell proved to be an improving team in 1977 under first-year mentor Butch Jones and could be an imposing road opener for Louisville. *"It will be tough. We are young and inexperienced but I am well pleased with our desire, hustle and attitude. All that's left is to play".*

The lone notation of the final showed a 55-yard 3rd quarter scoring pass from Scott Smith to Darrell Woods for Caldwell that proved all needed. Louisville led on the ground (111-76) and passing (60-55). The problem came with the loss of three of six Wildcat fumbles all by Tommy Sherrod.

"That bunch was tough on defense and we were inexperienced on offense. We looked real good on defense and didn't break down but that one time. I am proud of our players and the way they got after them. I don't believe this bunch will let this get them down and will come back". Michael Lewis was noted Winston County's Player of the Week.

GAME 2:   LOUISVILLE (0-1) vs OXFORD (1-0)
                 LOUISVILLE 34 OXFORD 8
                 September 8, 1978

The first home contest of 1978 came against a George Blair team reported with "*more experience and more hustle than ever*". Added Nester, "*They are huge, especially the linemen. They are much bigger than we are. They have never beaten us and they want us real bad. We are going to be ready. I have all the confidence in our boys and it is going to be a good football game*".

Tony Baker "*shocked Oxford*" with an early 75-yard dash to paydirt. Glenn Phillips then found the stripe from four yards and added the PAT. Defensive pressure forced a bad punt snap resulting in a safety and 15-0 advantage after only a quarter. The next quarter saw Bernard Jordan escape from 80 yards while Baker did the same later from five yards. Then, Baker hit Jackie Ingram from 10 yards and Phillips put halftime a runaway 34-0.

Reserves found their places in the 3rd quarter and Oxford hit paydirt in the finale after a 60-yard march. That came on a 4-yard Chris Case run. Louisville led on the ground (260-180) and the air (50-37). "*I am real proud of this bunch. We hit them quick and they got shell-shocked. Our experienced players showed great leadership. We are going to have to continue to work. We are not going to change anything but we have to keep improving*".

GAME 3:   LOUISVILLE (1-1) vs KOSCIUSCKO (2-0)
                 LOUISVILLE 19 KOSCIUSIO 0
                 September 15, 1978

Neither Louisville nor Nester were strangers to Kosy football. The pressure may have been even higher this week as Kosciusko, a non-conference foe, was riding a long winning streak. One Kosciusko reporter picked the Whippets 10-7. "*This is easily the toughest pick of the year for the Whippets. Louisville is a strong contender in any game and are better than their 1-1 record. The Whippets will have to work extra hard against an extra-large team to win*".

Baker broke a scoreless half with his 80-yard breakaway to make it 6-0. Tommy Yarbrough's interception set up a later 25-yard Jordan scoring run. In the final frame, James Hannah picked off a ball and Baker broke in from five yards. The Glenn Phillips kick was true. Kosy drove as far as the Cat 18 once but were turned back.

Louisville held rushing (288-104) with Jordan (135) and Baker (133) leading the way. The Cats picked off three passes on the night. "*It was a great team effort, offensive and defensive wise. I just can't praise them enough. For the last two weeks they have shown more leadership than any team I have ever seen*".

GAME 4:   LOUISVILLE (2-1) @ STARKVILLE (1-2)
                 LOUISVILLE 6 STARKVILLE 22
                 September 22, 1978

Only one vote separated the two from pre-season favorites to win the South Little 10 title. Needless to say, his one was crucial for the Wildcats. Said Nester, "*I hope we come out of it alive*". Over the last five years, it seemed the home team came out the best. Moreover, this one was on the Yellow Jacket confines.

Starkville jumped out with a pair of 1st quarter touchdowns to put the Wildcats on their heels for the remainder of the game. Joe Carter had the first from ten yards, a fumble to the Jackets soon set up Bubba Permenter's 23-yarder to Fred Henderson. Carter added both extra points. Their second came after recovery of a Cat fumble. They added their last in the 3rd quarter via Vance Mason's 3-yarder before Baker could cross the stripe from 25 yards. A late safety provided the last Starkville points.

Starkville led in rushing (227-164) and passing (65-26). "*We didn't have the football much. We did have it but about 30 snaps for the whole game and it is hard to score when you don't have the football. We were flat and they were high. They just whipped us. Our young men tried to get themselves ready but it didn't work*".

GAME 5:   LOUISVILLE (2-2) @ WARREN CENTRAL (4-0)
                 LOUISVILLE 7 WARREN CENTRAL 10
                 September 29, 1978

Another road game awaited but this one against Coach Lum Wright's unbeaten Viking team in Vicksburg. *"They always have a good football team and always will. This isn't a small school, with an enrollment of about 1,300 in their top three grades compared to our 700. We are going down there to win. We have real good practices and are physically and mentally prepared. I feel real good over the situation".*

This one apparently came down to penalty yardage as the Wildcats suffered 113 yards on 14 flags to kill numerous opportunities. Warren Central suffered only a pair of flags for 15 yards. A Cat fumble to Willie Taylor in the 2nd quarter led to their first touchdown on John Jackson's 9-yard toss to Art Mordecai. A later Marty Causey interception soon led to Mordecai's 36-yard FG. Jordan, with 137 ground yards on the night, led a 70-yard drive ending with Bakers' 1-yarder for Louisville's only score.

Louisville dominated rushing (216-45) but lost passing (72-16). *"I believe this is the worst we have ever whipped a team and lost the game. I don't believe we have ever been better prepared for a game. We walked all over them and then stopped them cold".*

GAME 6:   LOUISVILLE (2-3) vs LEE HIGH (0-5)
                LOUISVILLE 32 LEE HIGH 12
                October 6, 1978

Said Nester of the upcoming tilt, *"This Columbus Lee ball club has had a lot of costly mistakes so far this season and haven't been able to capitalize on the errors of their opponents. They seem to be coming around, getting a bit more experiences and making less mistakes every game. My men are going to be ready for this game because we realize … they're going to be coming at us full blast".*

Baker opened scoring in the 1st quarter with his 85-yard punt return and Phillips notched his first of a pair of PATs. Lee High responded in the frame with a 1-yard Willie Armistad dive to make it 7-6. The Wildcats piled on a couple of other touchdowns before halftime on Jordan runs of two and five yards to make it 19-6.

They added more in the 3rd quarter on a 10-yard Jordan dash and Phillips' 4-yarder. Columbus answered with their last with :20 remaining on Brett Brewer's 10-yard strike to Danny James. Louisville held the ground (290-83) while Lee claimed the air (34-22). *"Of the 12 penalties (on Louisville), 10 were for off sides. We were simply lining up off sides. This is pitiful. This is the kind of mistake we have got to eliminate if we are going to win football games".*

Jordan rushed for 145 markers and won Player of the Week in Winston County.

GAME 7:   LOUISVILLE (3-3) @ TUPELO (3-3)
                LOUISVILLE 27 TUPELO 23
                October 13, 1978

It was homecoming in Tupelo and Louisville was to be the sacrificial guest of honor. *"We have a lot of nagging injuries that seem to get worse every week. It is nothing serious and mostly just bumps and bruises. We have had good practices this week and should be ready to play. We have got to get mentally ready to eliminate mistakes. They won't give us the ball game. We have got to win it".*

The visitors jumped out early with a 70-yard drive capped by a 10-yard Baker run and Joe Baker PAT. They then marched 50 yards with Jordan doing the honors from five yards and Glenn Phillips making it 14-0. In the 2nd quarter, Tupelo garnered a safety via Tim Webb's QB sack. They then went 45 yards to paydirt to make it 14-9 just before halftime when Baker hit Ingram from 25 yards and Phillips put intermission 21-9.

It was far from over as Tupelo opened the 3rd quarter with a 70-yard scoring march and Thomas 3-yarder though Jordan responded with a 35-yard effort to make it 27-16. Tupelo's final frame touchdown on their 40-yard drive with Jordan running drew it closer but not enough to claim the victory. Baker (153) and Jordan (145) paced Wildcat rushing efforts.

"It was one of our greatest efforts but we only got to enjoy it through Sunday because now we have got to get ready for West Point".

GAME 8:   LOUISVILLE (4-3) vs WEST POINT (5-3)
                LOUISVILLE 14 WEST POINT 7
                October 20, 1978

There was more left to be done for Louisville and it started at home against the Green Wave. *"Our boys are not taking them lightly. They are a good, quick football team, which has lost some close ones but have been in every game. They are larger than we are and their offensive line is much bigger than ours"*. A win here promised the Wildcats no worse than a break-even season.

The only score of the first half came in the opening frame via a Baker run of either three or seven yards along with a Ken Eiland PAT. West Point evened things in the 3rd quarter after a bad punt snap gave them great field position. Avery Young dove in from a yard and Paul Caskey tied it with the extra point. Now in the final frame, Jordan reeled off a 40-yard scoring jaunt and Eiland converted for the finale. Jordan rushed for 153 yards.

"It went right down to the wire. They have a fine football team and they are tough. They have what is probably the finest defensive team we faced all season. We moved the football on them but broke down a couple of times. I am tickled to death with our effort. We are getting a good overall team effort".

GAME 9:	LOUISVILLE (5-3) vs WEST JONES (6-2)
	LOUISVILLE 14 WEST JONES 21
	October 27, 1978

A new opponent awaited in the form of the West Jones Mustangs out of Laurel. They had a strong football tradition and this marked the last home game of the season. *"They have beaten a lot of good folks. On film, they look real good and are big overall. They are not a fancy football team. They come right at you and punish you. West Jones is well-coached and fundamentally sound"*.

It appeared to be a Cat win early with a 75-yard Baker kickoff return for the touchdown, his 55-yard pass to Ezra Dixon and a pair of Phillips kicks. Before halftime, Adolph Duckworth *"streaked 80 yards"* for the response and Eric Johnson's PAT made halftime 14-7. West Jones tied it in the 3rd quarter on Mike Moore's 1-yarder and another Johnson PAT. In the final frame, the Mustangs galloped 99 yards with Duckworth adding the last four and Johnson the PAT.

"They really controlled the ball on us in the second half. We snapped the ball only five times in the fourth period while they were able to snap 16 times. You just can't score when you don't have the football. Duckworth rushed for about 240 yards and that was more than our whole team. They just kept the ball away from us". The Cats ran for 126 yards and threw for 55 more.

GAME 10:	LOUISVILLE (5-4) @ GRENADA (6-4)
	LOUISVILLE 14 GRENADA 21
	November 3, 1978

It was time to bring down the curtain on the 1978 campaign and the Chargers would be no easy foe in Grenada. They threw the football quite a bit and Nester knew that it would probably come down to the defensive secondary and line pressure.

The opening quarter ended tied 7-7. Louisville hit first on an 18-yard dash and Phillips converted. Back punched the Chargers with a 2-yard Russell Clark plunge and Bobby Little kick. In the 2nd quarter, Steve Perkins put Grenada ahead from 45 yards but the blocked PAT kept intermission 13-7. Both finalized scoring in the 3rd quarter. Grenada was first on a 12-yard Clark run and Little's kick. The last points of the year for the Cats came on Jordan's 1-yard effort and Phillips PAT.

"I am proud of them and what they have accomplished this year and give them credit for getting out there and fighting. They accomplished a lot". Baker earned the Player of the Week for Winston County for his efforts.

All Conference nods went to Tony Baker, Donnie Graham and Bernard Jordan. The Winston County Kiwanis Club also honored Baker as their outstanding Louisville High School football player.

1979 (5-4-1)

Much respected and successful coach Art Nester was no longer mentor and the spot went to former assistant Jack McAlpin. His South Little 10 Conference Wildcats did not earn the coveted top spot for conference honors but there were changes in Winston County. The first-place vote went to their opening opponent.

"Our game plan for (the first game) and the season is really not a tricky one but one that will open up our overall picture. On offense, we will run mostly quickies and counters up the middle and go to the outside. Because of our quickness, these plays should work successfully. The team's attitude as a whole is the best it's been in years and they've given me the feeling that they're tired of practice and ready to take the field..."

GAME 1:   LOUISVILLE (0-0) vs CALDWELL (0-0)
                 LOUISVILLE 0 CALDWELL 0
                 September 7, 1979

The Bobcats pulled the 6-0 opening day win over Louisville the previous season and now they returned not only eight All-Conference players, but also 10 of 11 defensive starters. *"We realize that we're up against some very tough competition but my men are showing me that they are ready to play football"*.

The scoreless game came down to strong defensive play and plenty of hard licks and tackles. There were fumbles, but all due to strong contact. The only negative for the Cats was the apparent injury to Tony Baker during the contest.

"I was real pleased with the defense. The coaches did an excellent job of getting them ready. At one time, we had three people in the secondary who were playing for the first time. I was not real disappointed with our offense. We needed to break one for six but it just did not happen. We are bruised up pretty bad. We wanted to win but I guess it's better than getting beat". Eddie Goss was Winston County Player of the Week.

GAME 2:   LOUISVILLE (0-0-1) @ OXFORD (1-0)
                 LOUISVILLE 32 OXFORD 14
                 September 14, 1979

The paper noted that the Wildcats would journey to Oxford to be *"looking eye-to-eye with a herd of big, experienced and fired-up Chargers who are going all out to win"*. The Cats still had the *"bumps and bruises"* but McAlpin focused on other variables.

"The weather may be a factor. We hope it doesn't rain because we think we can stop their passing game. If the field is bad and they are forced to run, it could be bad for us because they are so much bigger".

A scoreless 1st quarter led to a huge offensive output for the Cats before halftime. Tommy Yarbrough got in from 25 yards, Tony Baker hit Jackie Ingram for 60 yards and James Hannah for seven yards to increase the advantage. Then, Ingram recovered a fumble and took it 48 yards to paydirt. The last Cat tally came in the 3rd quarter on a Tracy Owens punt return. The two Oxford touchdowns came late when the game was settled. The first was a Glen Henderson 5-yarder while Teddy Tidwell ran in from 38 yards later. Sidney Henderson added the two points.

"We didn't execute real well. We exploded for scores but our defense looked real good. Our coaches spotted a couple of weaknesses and called the plays to score. We got after them pretty good".

GAME 3:   LOUISVILLE (1-0-1) @ KOSCIUSKO (2-0)
                 LOUISVILLE 0 KOSCIUSKO 6
                 September 21, 1979

This non-conference matchup still meant something to both as this was the second longest consecutive rivalry for the Wildcats. *"We have been working hard on execution this week but almost lost a day when we had to practice outside. The young men will be ready to play tonight and give it their best effort"*.

The (Kosciusko) Star-Herald picked the Whippets, saying *"It's one stern test after another and Louisville represents perhaps the sternest of the season thus far. The Whippets will have to buckle down to pull out a 15-12 win and avenge last year's loss"*.

The lone score came in the opening quarter when Mike McBeath knocked the ball from Tony Baker inside the 20-yard line. It bounced to the 12-yard line from where he picked it up and found paydirt. Another Cat drive ended on a Johnny Williams interception. The Wildcat defense held Kosy to just 188 total yards but put up only 82 themselves.

GAME 4:   LOUISVILLE (1-1-1) vs STARKVILLE (1-2)
                                    LOUISVILLE 19 STARKVILLE 12
                                    September 28, 1979

Perineal rival Starkville was next on the schedule. They featured 65 players on the roster but only eight letter winners from 1978. It seemed that the two teams played best versus one another when at home. This one was at Hinze Stadium.

Like the game against Kosciusko, Starkville opened with a fumble returned 25 yards by Anthony Ward for the opening touchdown. Back came Louisville with Baker's 1-yard dive and Ken Eiland PAT. In the final frame, the Cats pushed out with a Baker 4-yarder while Tracy Owens found the end zone from 85 yards later. The last Yellow Jacket tally came late on a 65-yard Kent Daniel strike to Kirk Perry.

"We played a good game defensively... A big difference was our offense. We were blowing them off the line and controlling the football. This was probably our best performance of this year. They had a lot of talent at skill positions and I think they will get better. Our secondary was also alert. The completed one pass but we intercepted two".

When asked about conference title hopes, McAlpin added, "It is still close and everybody has a shot (at the title). We can't afford to lose another conference game if we are to stay in the race".

GAME 5:   LOUISVILLE (2-1-1) vs WARREN CENTRAL (4-0)
                                    LOUISVILLE 20 WARREN CENTRAL 47
                                    October 5, 1979

An even matchup over two years, McAlpin described the Vikings as "big, bad and tough". The Vicksburg squad was ranked in the top five in a pair of polls and coming off a 35-0 shellacking of Pearl. "It is going to be a real challenge for us to stay on the field with them. I hope we can make a good ball game of it and win. We have some sickness that has hampered practices but hopefully we will be at full strength".

The Vikings, apparently not yielding a point thus far, gave up one early as Charles Triplett broke across from five yards to make the 1st quarter 6-0. It took only until the 2nd quarter before Warren Central began the scoring barrage. Carl Blue ran in from four yards but fumbled to Marty Causey. Clyde Shelley blocked a punt and Ray Mathis found it for the score. A Mathis fumble recovery soon led to Blue's 3-yarder to make it 20-6.

Just before halftime, Scott Allen hit Art Mordecai from five yards and another Mordecai kick made it 27-6. Blue "barreled in from the three" in the 3rd quarter, Harold Pickett recovered a kickoff fumble and Blue got in from six yards. Louisville could muster only a final frame 10-yard Yarbrough run, a 20-yard Baker scoring escape and two-pointer from Yarbrough. The finale came on Blue's last-play 50-yard connection with Mordecai.

"We opened up a little bit in the second half and that seemed to help but that 27 points in the second quarter ... we just couldn't overcome it. We have got to shake off this defeat and now concentrate on our game Friday. We have bounced back before and I know our young men will be ready to play and win this week".

GAME 6:   LOUISVILLE (2-2-1) @ LEE HIGH (5-0)
                                    LOUISVILLE 15 LEE HIGH 0
                                    October 12, 1979

The Generals held top spot in the South Little Ten with a 2-0 mark but Louisville held a strong record of beating them in the last seven outings. The negatives were that it was on the road and Lee High's Homecoming. "We are in pretty good shape. We got beat up pretty good against Warren Central but will be ready to play tonight".

Both Wildcats touchdowns came in the last frame. Triplett ended an 80-yard march from 14 yards while Baker hit Ingram to make it 8-0. Then, Ingram recorded an 18-yard pick six and Eiland converted. Fumbles and a pair of interceptions kept Louisville from making it more of a runaway. The Cats picked off a pair of Lee High tosses.

"Our guys did a real fine job Friday and they beat a good football team. They were ahead of us in the statistics in the first half but we came back to put points on the board. We got excellent play out of people who had not played a lot. We tried to use more people and they came through. We played a lot more young people". Baker won the Winston County Player of the Week for his 150 rushing yards.

GAME 7:   LOUISVILLE (3-2-1) vs TUPELO (2-4)
                        LOUISVILLE 19 TUPELO 8
                        October 19, 1979

        It was not to be an easy game despite their record as Louisville broke a three-game losing streak just the year prior. Like Louisville, they had a new mentor. McAlpin referred to the Wave as *big, strong, and have one of the best coaches in the conference. We have got to have this win before we start thinking about next week. It is going to be a fine football game. We have got to forget last week's win and go out there and perform"*.
        Baker opened scoring in the 1st quarter with his 10-yarder that held through halftime. In the 3rd quarter, he finished a 70-yard Cat march with his 1-yard dive. Owens then picked off a pass and Yarbrough turned it into a 1-yard plunge. Tupelo got on the board late in the game on a Preston Martin's tally and his two-pointer.
        The win left Louisville and Caldwell still tied for the top spot. *"We are real happy with the win. It is very seldom you get to beat Tupelo as we beat them. We should have been ahead by three touchdowns at the half instead of just the one. Every game is a big one for us now and we can't have a let up"*.

GAME 8:   LOUISVILLE (4-2-1) @ WEST POINT (6-2)
                        LOUISVILLE 8 WEST POINT 15
                        October 26, 1979

        West Point was just 1-14 against Louisville in the last 15 tilts, but this was no ordinary Wave team. *"They are a senior-laden ball club with big linemen and real fast backs. They have a big squad and very few boys play both ways"*.
        While West Point opened with Romel Perry's 42-yard reception from Avery Young and Charlie Ledbetter's PAT, Baker topped it with his 8-yard scoring run and two-point conversion. Now in the final frame and with under 3:00 remaining, Young got in from a yard and Wallace Jones added two more points to the board.
        "It was a heck of a ball game but we came out on the short end, our kids being beat up. We had three or four players playing hurt. They stuck in there as best they could. Not having fullback Tracy Glass really hurt but his replacement did a good job. We missed a couple of scoring opportunities and penalties hurt us, but we will be back".

GAME 9:   LOUISVILLE (4-3-1) @ WEST JONES (7-2)
                        LOUISVILLE 8 WEST JONES 28
                        November 2, 1979

        Although a non-conference road game, the defeat from the prior year was still to be avenged. It would not be easy with experienced players led by a host of seniors. *"They beat us last year at home and we're going there to beat them at their home"*.
        Things started well with a 70-yard drive highlighted by a 60-yard Baker run and his eventual 1-yard touchdown followed by the two-point pass to Ingram. However, West Jones took over from there. Adolph Ducksworth was first from five yards along with his conversion while Kip Simpson added a 70-yard pick six. In the second half, Chip Geiger dove in from three yards and Ducksworth added the two-pointer. Finally, Chris Poore took advantage of a Chip Geiger pickoff with his 1-yard plunge.
        "We just didn't look like Louisville at all in the 3rd quarter. They just ran straight at us getting four and five yards at a clip and we couldn't stop them. They had a real good football team but our mistakes killed us. Pass interceptions stopped several drives and penalties also hurt us".

GAME 10:   LOUISVILLE (4-4-1) vs GRENADA (2-6-1)
                        LOUISVILLE 7 GRENADA 6
                        November 9, 1979

        Despite the loss, things were still undecided in the conference standings. It would take Lee High defeating Caldwell to put things into a fray with Louisville the prohibitive favorite. *"We have got to beat Grenada to have a winning season or a possible shot at the conference title. They are a good and big team and we will have to play better than we did against West Jones"*.
        Playing conditions were not optimal but the Wildcats ended the decade on a winning note. Bake and Ingram hooked up in the opening frame from 14 yards and Eiland

toed the PAT. Now in the final frame, Grenada came up with a fumbled punt and took it 30 yards for a touchdown. There was less than :30 on the clock and they opted for the two-point play and the win. It failed.

"We played real (well) under the adverse conditions. We had only one turnover and I thought that was real good. However, we made some mistakes and almost beat ourselves. Any time you play in the rain, it is to the big team's advantage. But, our men responded to the challenge so well the game shouldn't have been close. We had several opportunities to score but just couldn't do it".

Jimmy Metts won Winston County Player of the Week for his efforts. Tony Baker was voted numerous honors for his play over the years.

1980–1989

1980 (4-5)

Jack McAlpin's second year featured a Wildcat team called *"little but quick"*. He added, *"We are a pretty young team and have a lot of juniors starting. We will have 12 returning lettermen and a lot of players going both ways. We should be able to run the ball pretty good but are having to work real hard on our passing game"*.

He called the defense *"pretty fair (but) we have had to move two defensive backs into the secondary and they are doing a good job. We are looking forward to the season and believe we will be playing the type of football that the fans can enjoy"*. In pre-season voting, Louisville came in fourth behind Lee High, Tupelo and West Point.

GAME 1:   LOUISVILLE (0-0) @ CALDWELL (0-0)
                                LOUISVILLE 15 CALDWEL 19
                                September 5, 1980

Caldwell became a formidable opponent over the last couple of years and bragged of defending their Little 10 championship. Now the Cats traveled to Columbus to take on their lid-lifting opponents. *"The kind of practicing has us in great physical condition. The rest of the practices will be spent on improving timing and polishing up the rough spots. The players have worked real hard and they have been showing a real good attitude"*.

The Bobcats jumped out with a 6-0 lead after a 53-yard passing connection between Kirk Reid and Jimmy Gunter. Thomas Eiland later found a loose football and *"scampered 20 yards for the touchdown"*. The PAT put Louisville ahead 7-6. However, Caldwell responded immediately on Reid's 26-yard run to put it 12-7. In the 2nd quarter, they added their last on a Woods run while the Cats could muster only a final period tally. Dwight Graham took a toss and hit Joey Hardy from midfield. The PAT was successful.

"We made a lot of first game mistakes. We made some critical mistakes on defense and didn't move the ball consistently on offense. While made some good gains, we also got some costly penalties. I was real disappointed in our conditioning. I was pleased with the play of our backup people. Our athletes played their hearts out. They really wanted to win".

This marked only the second opening-day loss since 1957. The previous one came to this Caldwell team (6-0) in 1978.

GAME 2:   LOUISVILLE (0-1) vs OXFORD (0-1)
                                LOUISVILLE 7 OXFORD 0
                                September 12, 1980

The Chargers were not a problem in the four meetings since 1976. Now, the Wildcats had to rebound from a disappointing opener. The only score in the contest came when James Moffett recovered an Oxford fumble to allow Charlie Hughes a 2-yard touchdown and Keith Jordan the extra point.

"Our defense played an outstanding game. However, we failed to convert on plays where we needed short yardage to keep the football. We are small up front and our people just can't move them out. Our offensive is looking better. We were able to move the ball real well between the 20s but just couldn't seem to make the third down plays. We were stopped on their 2-yard line in the first half".

Louisville lost three of six fumbles. The offense had 216 of 226 yards on the ground in comparison. Louisville led in first downs (11-4) and rushing (179-41).

GAME 3:   LOUISVILLE (1-1) vs KOSCIUSKO (2-0)
                                LOUISVILLE 20 KOSCIUSKO 7
                                September 19, 1980

The small 6-0 defeat of 1979 still resonated with many players who were involved in the game. The Winston County Journal noted that that those players *"have blood in their eyes already"* as they prepared for the rematch. Even with new coach Charlie Bounds, the Whippets were on a 20-game winning streak. The (Kosciusko) Star-Herald picked the Whippets 13-12.

"The Whippets scraped past Eupora Friday and should be earthbound by now. But it will take more than an earthbound game to produce a winner this week as they visit

Louisville. In this week's toughest pick, I want to call a tie. But, I'll ignore the home field advantage which may make a difference".

An early Cat fumble and tough defense set up a Kosy punt. Rick Triplett rushed in and blocked the effort and recovered for the opening tally. Jordan's conversion made it 7-0 to hold through intermission. Kosciusko fumbled the opening kick afterwards and Jordan *"scooped it up and ripped 22 yards untouched into the end zone"*. Jordan's kick was true. The Whippets answered with a 45-yard march and 20-yard Darrell Jackson pass to Terrance Hull. Jackson's PAT cut it to 14-7.

Back came Louisville when Mac Arthur McCully dashed 75 yards *"though the heart of the Whippets' coverage for the touchdown"*. While Louisville led on the ground (195-117), Kosciusko led in passing (62-0). *"It was an inspired game and we played real good on defense. Our offense played good enough to win. We moved the ball more consistently and controlled it in the fourth quarter. Our defense was really a team effort".*

Players of the Week for Winston County went to Mac Arthur McCully, Keith Jordan and Ricky Triplett.

GAME 4:   LOUISVILLE (2-1) @ STARKVILLE (0-3)
                        LOUISVILLE 8 STARKVILLE 21
                        September 26, 1980

The Yellow Jackets opened 1980 with losses to both Kosciusko and Caldwell, but they still had *"a big team with a lot of talent"*. As it was held in Oktibbeha County, history favored the yellow and black.

Larry Henley had the first Jacket score via interception and Scott Chesser added the PAT. In the 3rd quarter, they moved 80 yards with Bruce Wilson running in and Chesser making it 14-0. The final Jacket tally came on Bob Permenter's 24-yarder and Chesser kick. The lone tally for Louisville came late when Dan Sullivan picked up a Charlie Hughes fumble for the TD. McCully ran in for the two points. Starkville barely held total yards 250-235.

"We played a lot of young folks. We were worried about their passing but they completed only one and we intercepted two. They ran the ball a whole lot better than we thought they could. They just beat us up front. We were held on the Starkville 4 on one occasion and had a screen pass go astray on the 20 another time".

GAME 5:   LOUISVILLE (2-2) @ NESHOBA CENTRAL (1-3)
                        LOUISVILLE 27 NESHOBA CENTRAL 6
                        October 3, 1980

There was a three-year break in the matchup after Louisville dominated all five previous contests. Said McAlpin of this year's NCHS team, *"They are big and slow in the line. Their backs have good size and speed. I hope we can get outside with our runs and do some throwing to our other backs"*.

McCully opened scoring for the Cats with a 2-yarder and Jordan converted. Neshoba came back with Shawn Henry's 3-yard effort but it was all they would muster. Mike Ellis found the stripe in the 2nd quarter and Jordan made it 14-6 at halftime. In the 3rd quarter, Michael Duff ran in from 14 yards and Jordan kicked his last. Hughes had the last from a yard.

Louisville tallied 350 offensive yards and nine first downs while keeping their opponents to only 106 yards and five first downs. McCully paced rushers with 120 yards. The Neshoba Democrat claimed it a 275-179 yardage advantage.

GAME 6:   LOUISVILLE (3-2) vs LEE HIGH (5-0)
                        LOUISVILLE 7 LEE HIGH 24
                        October 10, 1980

This was not to be the usual game against a team the Cats defeated eight consecutive seasons. The Generals were now picked first in the South and undefeated.

An early forced fumble allowed Mike Ellis a 7-yard strike to Dwight Williams and Jordan connected to make it 7-0. Things changed thereafter. Just :03 before halftime, Lee added a 30-yard Danny James FG to make intermission 7-3. Another fumble to Lee in the second half went back 13 yards by Joe Reed Brumley for the tally. Two more pickoffs led to scores by the Columbus team. One came on a 26-yard Kent Willis strike to Terry Welch while James added their last from four yards.

Louisville led in first downs (6-3) and offense (136-102). *"We should have won the ball game. We got good effort from (some) on offense and the whole defensive team really got after them"*.

GAME 7:   LOUISVILLE (3-3) @ TUPELO (4-2)
                          LOUISVILLE 14 TUPELO 34
                          October 17, 1980

The Winston County Journal called the Wave *"a very big school so they always have an extra amount of talent"*. Said McAlpin, *"The game is going to be a tough battle between two teams so the Wildcats will need all of the moral support their fans can give"*.

While the Cats opened with the lead via a blocked punt and 15-yard McCully run (Jordan PAT), Tupelo responded after recovering a fumble at the Cat 20 and scoring later on a Robbie Rial 5-yarder. Halftime ended tied 7-7. The Wave added three more to make it 28-7 before the Wildcats could get their last. Michael Trice (25 yards) had the first while Mike Ellis Wackerfuss had a 24-yard fumble return. The Cat score came from a 4-yard Triplett run and Jordan kick.

The Wave iced it late with their final touchdown on a 46-yard Rial run. *"We are going to get some rest and heal up some bruises. We lost McCully in the first quarter with a dislocated finger but we will be ready (for the next game). We have also got to try and get some more offense out of our wishbone"*.

GAME 8:   LOUISVILLE (3-4) vs WEST POINT (5-3)
                          LOUISVILLE 17 WEST POINT 8
                          October 31, 1980

The last game of 1980 at Hinze Stadium was now here. The Cats were 15-3 against West Point since 1936 and needed this one to keep hopes of a winning season alive.

Things opened well as a punt snap went over the West Point player's head for a Cat safety. They added to it on the next march on a 5-yard Hughes run and McCully two-pointer. McCully's next from five yards along with a Jordan PAT gave them all they needed and a 17-0 advantage. Late in the game, West Point avoided the shutout when they connected on a 32-yard scoring pass to Donnell O'Dneal and his two-pointer.

"We probably played our best game of the season. Charlie Triplett Hughes has 125 yards with Willie Sangster and Keith Jordan turning in an outstanding job on defense. A lot of people played with nagging injuries and I was real proud of them".

GAME 9:   LOUISVILLE (4-4) @ GRENADA (5-3-1)
                          LOUISVILLE 7 GRENADA 21
                          November 7, 1980

The Chargers, picked second pre-season, shocked Lee High with a 14-14 tie game. *"They are probably the most talented team in the conference and have some big and fast backs"*. Louisville needed this one to avoid their first losing season since 1965.

A Cat fumble at the 25-yard line led to the first Grenada score when Ricky Jones scored on a 3-yarder. A Pat Chism dash in the next frame and both Michael Harlow extra points made it 14-0. Hughes found Dwight Graham from 10 yards and Jordan cut it to 14-7. They threatened to tie in the 3rd quarter but got only to the 15-yard line. The home team iced it later with another touchdown by Dwight Graham to end the season.

"They had more talent than anyone we have played. They were big and fast and whipped up physically. We tried hard and would have liked to have played better".

Internal awards went to Marcus Ray (Christian Athlete), Charlie Triplett Hughes (Best Offensive Back), Dwight Graham (Best Defensive Back), William Triplett (Best Offensive Lineman), Thomas Eiland (Best Defensive Lineman), Mark Henderson (Scholastic), John Woodward (Special Teams), Mike Pickett (Husting Non-Letterman), Anthony Brown (Most Improved), Keith Jordan (MVP), Mike Ellis (Wildcat Award), and Mark Henderson and Ricky Triplett (Permanent Team Captains).

1981 (8-3)

Third-year coach Jack McAlpin had a squad of senior-laden starters and practicing hard in hopes of being a much more improved team than from the previous outing of 4-5. Very little else was reported on the team prior to the season in reports found.

GAME 1:   LOUISVILLE (0-0) vs CALDWELL (0-0)
                                  LOUISVILLE 16 CALDWELL 0
                                  September 4, 1981

Since 1974, the battle became one of back and forth as the Wildcats held a slight 3-2-2 advantage. They extended the historical aspect on this night.

Keith Jordan was a one-man wrecking crew this Friday evening, first with a 27-yard FG to make it 3-0. He then recorded a 30-yard pick-six and added to the PAT to make it 10-0. Cal Mayo added to the lead with the last tally in the 3rd quarter on his 1-yard effort. Said McAlpin, "*We were real glad to win and pleased with the defensive effort. We were in good condition... I was not pleased with our offense. We had little blocking. Receivers did not complete their pass patterns and we threw some bad passes. We should have broken the game open in the first half*".

McAlpin reported total offensive yardage as 230 yards but with an interception and a missed FG attempt. Reserves took the field in the final frame. Jordan earned the Player of the Week nod for his accomplishments.

GAME 2:   LOUISVILLE (1-0) vs NOXUBEE COUNTY (1-0)
                                  LOUISVILLE 29 NOXUBEE COUNTY 6
                                  September 11, 1981

After three consecutive games ending in 1974 with all Cat victories, the two teams now met once again at Hinze Stadium.

The opening frame held only one score and that came from Douglas Triplett on a 1-yard effort while Dwight Graham added another later on a 25-yard May toss, a Jordan safety, and Frankie Frazier's 1-yarder. Jordan's PAT made halftime 23-0. Noxubee County found paydirt in the 3rd quarter on Richard Simpson's 1-yard plunge while May and Graham hooked up from 52 yards for the finale at the beginning of the last frame.

"*We got lax in the 3rd quarter. We messed around and let them score. We moved the ball better. We threw less but were effective as (3-7 for 96 yards). We did get too many penalties (four for 15 yards). We played real good defense and the left side of our offensive line looked a lot better. We lost some of our intensity and vigor when we went ahead 23-0. We just haven't played four intense quarters yet*".

NCHS was 4-19 with four interceptions and put up only 18 yards in the first half.

GAME 3:   LOUISVILLE (2-0) @ KOSCIUSKO (2-0)
                                  LOUISVILLE 35 KOSCIUSKO 13
                                  September 18, 1981

Only Starkville held the record for most consecutive games against the Cats. Though Kosy was a Mid-Mississippi Athletic Conference team, this one became a strong rivalry over the decades and meant more than just conference bragging rights. They bragged of an impressive opener over South Panola while just edging Eupora the following week.

The Whippets shocked the Cats on the third play of the game when Terrence Hull grabbed an interception and took it to the Cat 11. Jamie Riley took it in three plays later and Darrell Jackson made it an early 7-0. Back came Louisville early in the 2nd quarter when the Cats went 50 yards with Duff crossing from short and Jordan tying the contest.

Later, a punt taken to the 10-yard line ended when Triplett found the end zone from three yards and Jordan converted. A recovered fumble set up the 4-yard Triplett tally and halftime stood 21-7 for Louisville. In the 3rd quarter, Triplett dashed in from 40 yards to increase the advance and Jordan put it 28-7.

A bad punt effort then set up Stanley Mitchell's 4-yarder and Jordan added the last Cat point. Late in the game, Jamie Riley escaped Wildcat defenders for a 77-yard run to the 3-yard line. Raymond Cotton got in from there to end their night.

"We played real well defensively. Our defensive team just had an excellent ball game. Also, our offense ran the ball real well. We blew some blocking assignments early but finally got on track. They were an extremely big ball club but they made too many mistakes and we took advantage of them". While Louisville suffered an interception, they rushed for 193 yards and held Kosy to 120. Seventy of those came on one play. Triplett, with 117 rushing yards, was Player of the Week.

GAME 4:   LOUISVILLE (3-0) vs STARKVILLE (3-0)
                                LOUISVILLE 7 STARKVILLE 14
                                September 25, 1981

The longest rivalry team, back in conference play, awaited at home for the Cats. Both were undefeated and this one was obviously crucial to conference rights, but would not be easy. Speaking of the 7th-ranked Yellow Jackets, McAlpin said, *"They have a bigger line by about 30 pounds a man, an excellent quarterback who can throw the ball real well and have good speed"*.

Scoring was completed by the time halftime arrived and, unfortunately, not in favor of the home standing Wildcats. An early blocked punt set up a Bruce Wilson 2-yard tally and Artie Cosby PAT. The Cats recovered a 2nd quarter Jacket fumble at the 35-yard line and Frazier did the honors from six yards (Jordan kick). Late in the half, the eventual end came on a 65-yard Wilson dash and Cosby kick.

"We made mistakes in our kicking game. We threw too many interceptions and we let them run inside. We played a pretty decent game against a good football team. It was a big game for us, but we have several big games left. We've got to keep getting after folks. There was some real hitting"

GAME 5:   LOUISVILLE (3-1) vs NESHOBA CENTRAL (0-4)
                                LOUISVILLE 26 NESHOBA CENTRAL 8
                                October 2, 1981 HOMECOMING

Despite the winless record, the opponent kept games close in each tilt. This one was at home and with old alums in packed stands for Homecoming. *"The Wildcats did their part"*, said <u>The Winston County Journal</u>.

Frazier notched the lone tally of the 1st quarter with a 23-yard run and Jordan made it 7-0. They added pair of other scores before intermission on Triplett's 3-yarder (Jordan PAT) and Mayo's 31-yard strike to Anthony Brown to make it 20-0. Mayo and Graham hooked up from 22 yards in the 3rd quarter while the visitors avoided the shutout in the last minute on an 11-yard John Fulton run and the two-pointer.

"We played everybody we had dressed out. Our passing game looked better and we dropped some we should have held on to".

GAME 6:   LOUISVILLE (4-1) @ LEE HIGH (3-1)
                                LOUISVILLE 13 LEE HIGH 22
                                October 9, 1981

Lee High, opponents since the early years of Wildcat football, opened the contest with Frankie Turner's 6-yard run. Terry Welch followed in the next frame from 40 yards and Tyrone Gray did the same from two yards. Kent Willis added two extra points to make it 20-0. Louisville found paydirt before halftime when Joey Hardy took the kickoff 80 yards to the end zone and Jordan added the PAT.

While Frazier tightened things in the final stanza with a 6-yard run, Lee High got some back with a safety as the game expired when *"the Cats snapped the ball out of the end zone on a punt"*.

"We just weren't ready to play football. We were half asleep and by the time we woke up, we were behind 20-0. Penalties really hurt us. They stopped several scoring opportunities. We looked at the game film and just couldn't find the penalties the officials called. They turned two turnovers into touchdowns but we held them to only 33 yards total offensive in the second half". The real loss came as Triplett injured his knee and was feared lost for the season.

GAME 7:   LOUISVILLE (4-2) vs TUPELO (4-2)
                                LOUISVILLE 7 TUPELO 24
                                October 16, 1981

The faltering Wildcats found themselves behind once again. In this one, it was 21-0 at halftime. Two Wave scores came via the long pass and a fumble taken 84 yards to paydirt. The first was a 44-yard Ricky Dilworth pass to Quent Jones and the next a Robbie Rial a yard. Anthony Berry converted on both.

Just before the half, Robert Hadley picked up a loose Cat ball and raced 84 yards to paydirt. Berry made it 21-0. Mitchell put up Louisville's only tally on a 1-yarder and Jordan added the kick. Berry's 29-yard FG in the finale proved the final points.

"They just kept it away from us. We had only 13 snaps in the second half. They did a good job of ball control and we had pitiful field position. We have got to make better adjustments. We are having trouble with the quickies inside. You can't give Tupelo two touchdowns and beat them".

GAME 8:   LOUISVILLE (4-3) @ PHILADELPHIA (4-3)
                 LOUISVILLE 15 PHILADELPHIA 13
                 October 23, 1981

This game was bigger than just because the tilt went back to the earliest days of Wildcat football. In addition, that was despite the lack of playing since 1972. One of the nation's leading runners, Marcus Dupree, was considered the best in the country and held the spotlight. *"Dupree weighs 222 and can run the hundred in 9.6 seconds".*

An early Wildcat interception set up a 15-yard Frazier run to make it 6-0. Philly came back with Dupree's 31-yard score and Mike Green added the PAT to take the lead. Just a couple of seconds before halftime, Jordan knocked home a 35-yard FG to put them ahead 9-7 at intermission. In the 4th quarter, Mayo ran in from 30 yards to make it 15-7. A fumble recovery by Philadelphia at midfield allowed Dupree a 50-yard touchdown pass to Terry Hoskins to make it 15-13. Their late game-winning drive ended on a fumble recovered by James Moffett.

"We had a good ball game. Dupree is the best high school player I have ever seen. We had heard if he was hit real hard he would quit, but we hit that feller plenty hard and he didn't quit. It was good to play Philadelphia and restore a good rivalry. I was real pleased with our effort". Dupree ran for 150 yards on 29 carries while Frazier (97 rushing yards) won the Player of the Week honor in Louisville.

GAME 9:   LOUISVILLE (5-3) @ WEST POINT (4-4)
                 LOUISVILLE 14 WEST POINT 7
                 October 30, 1981

While the conference title was out of reach, the goal was to win the last two games for a respectable 7-3 season. Said McAlpin of West Point, *"They have a good football team and are very quick".*

The home team put up the only touchdown of the first half on their opening drive when Craig Keys pulled in a 24-yard Bryan Tait pass. Dennis Ewing added the point-after. Louisville matched it in the 3rd quarter on Frazier's 1-yarder but the two-point effort failed. Finally, in the last frame, Mayo hit Graham from 15 yards and Frazier converted the two-point effort. A Hal Estes pickoff late got the Cats only as far as the 3-yard line.

"It was like a Dr. Jekyll and Mr. Hyde game. We didn't do anything in the first half (but) really whipped them in the final two quarters. It was like two different ball games. They played the first half and we played the second".

GAME 10:   LOUISVILLE (6-3) vs GRENADA (5-3)
                 LOUISVILLE 7 GRENADA 3
                 November 6, 1981

Despite a great run since 1965, the Chargers took two of the last three against Louisville. This season featured 21 lettermen from a 6-2-1 squad under Coach Jack Holliday. *"We've got great speed this year".* Despite the outcome, Louisville sat assured of no worse than a winning season.

A first half FG effort by the Wildcats was unsuccessful while Grenada scored as the half ended via their 25-yard Michael Harlow FG effort. Now in the finale, Louisville took five plays to set up Frazier's 10-yard score and Jordan PAT. A later drive by Grenada got to the Cat 10 before Mitchell picked off a Charger throw to secure the win.

"Our kids played a hard four quarters. They deserved the victory and the invitation to the bowl. We will be ready for Coldwater Saturday". He was referring to the

announcement that Louisville accepted an invitation to the Mississippi Jaycee Bowl held in Batesville on Friday. Willie Sangster was Player of the Week with 10 solo tackles and 5 assists.

GAME 11:   LOUISVILLE (7-3) vs COLDWATER (6-4)
             LOUISVILLE 36 COLDWATER 13
             November 13, 1981: Jaycee Bowl; Batesville, MS

        In the history of Wildcat football, the team never met Coldwater nor played in a Jaycee Bowl. This one was unique in that Coldwater was very close to Batesville and the Cats had numerous players nursing injuries. The Chickasaw Conference team won their last two contests and' *featured a line larger than Louisville"*.
        "The kids are really excited about getting the bowl invitation. It will be another chance for them to show people what kind of a team we really have. Our people have to get ready to play. If we are mentally ready, we can play a good game. But, if not, they are going to blow us off the field".
        The Cougars opened the tilt with a 95-yard Gerald Futtrell punt return for a touchdown and Bert Odom made it 7-0. Later, Sangster found a loose football at the 17-yard line and Frazier turned it into a 5-yard score. Jordan added his first PAT to tie it. Howard Edmond did the same at their 19 and, six plays later, Bardra Lyons found the end zone from a yard.
        Another Sangster fumble recovery set up an 8-yard Lyons scoring toss to Graham and Jordan put it 21-0. In the 3rd quarter Mitchell scored from ten yards and added the two pointer. The final frame opened with a Lyons and Howard Duff connection from midfield. Coldwater's last came with just minutes remaining on a 45-yard Futtrell dash.
        Lyons received the game MVP while Frazier won Best Offensive Player and Sangster was Best Defensive Player. *"It was a fun game and a fitting game for our seniors to end their high school career. I just regret I had several players who were injured and unable to play"*.

        All Conference honors went to James Moffitt and Willie Sangster. Second team members included Keith Jordan, James Brooks and Frankie Frazier. All District picks include first teamers Jordan, Stanley Mitchell, Hal Estes (Honorable Mention), Frazier, Hilton Miller (Honorable Mention), Moffett, Jerry Hughes, Dwight Graham, Sangster, and Brooks. Kiwanis Club Sportsman of the Year for the Cats was Jordan.

1982 (4-5-1)

        Jack McAlpin, back for his fourth year as head coach, had high expectations despite obvious factors. They lost 19 seniors with only a pair of starters back, faced six teams on the road and were picked fifth out of six District Four teams.
        "A lot of times we have to depend on our tradition to make up for what we lack in size or numbers. We have as good a group this year as I can remember and we hope to have a good season. We have the smallest number of players we have had in years but we have some really good players and have been able to work closer with them to get ready".

GAME 1:   LOUISVILLE (0-0) @ CALDWELL (0-0)
            LOUISVILLE 6 CALDWELL 6
            September 3. 1982

        Caldwell was picked either first or second in conference play prior to the season. Therefore, this would not be an easy lid-lifter.
        The Cats moved inside the Caldwell 20 on their opening pair of marches but lost the opportunities on an interception and fumble. Michael Taylor got it going in the 2nd quarter on his 2-yard dive but the crucial PAT failed. In the 3rd quarter, Glenn Johnson cut into the lead with his 27-yard FG. That was set up by Wildcat penalties. In the final frame, more penalties kept Caldwell going and they finished with a 28-yard Johnson FG to tie.
        Bardra Lyons led Cat rushers with 92 yards and went 5-10-1 in the air. Taylor had 50 yards on the ground. Louisville led stats in rushing (175-150), passing (44-0) and first downs (10-3). *"We played well enough to win, but our mental mistakes cost us. The first three times we touched the ball we gave it away. Our boys could have given up at that point but they didn't"*.

GAME 2:   LOUISVILLE (0-0-1) @ NOXUBEE COUNTY (0-0)
                 LOUISVILLE 0 NOXUBEE COUNTY 6
                 September 10, 1982

Louisville had to be optimistic with four straight wins since 1971. This one came down to a sole tally in the opening frame. That one came via a 5-yard Eddie Harris dash. In the final frame, the Wildcats moved to the Noxubee 5 but fumbled the ball away.

"We just got beat. We played well enough to beat a lot of people in Mississippi but it wasn't well enough to beat Noxubee. They have a good team with plenty of talent and were well-coached and well-prepared. One of our players said it was like hitting trees when he hit one of the Noxubee players".

GAME 3:   LOUISVILLE (0-1-1) vs KOSCIUSKO (2-0)
                 LOUISVILLE 17 KOSCIUSKO 0
                 September 17, 1982

Unlike the first pair of games, the Cats took control with scores in all but the opening quarter. Taylor opened scoring in the second quarter on a 3-yarder and Lyons' kick was true. The Cats opened the second half with Taylor's diving 7-yard reception from Lyons and again Lyons added the extra point. The final dagger came in the last frame when Lyons hit a 25-yard FG.

"We missed the FG because of a mental mistake. We only had the ball placed five yards deep and they were able to block it. I thought we played the last 26 minutes of the game well. But we still had too many mental errors. Our sophomores played a tremendous game. Our defensive backs had their best game but the rest of our defense needs a little work".

Louisville led in yardage (351-161) with Taylor leading the ground with 197 yards. Sangster led the Cats with 10 tackles. Taylor was Player of the Week.

GAME 4:   LOUISVILLE (1-1-1) @ STARKVILLE (3-0)
                 LOUISVILLE 20 STARKVILLE 14
                 September 24, 1982

It was to be no easier as the Wildcats went to Starkville to face a number 5 team. Traditionally, it was a home win and road loss until 1981. Now, it remained to be seen if that would be broken against the longest consistently running Louisville competitor.

The Yellow Jackets opened the game with a 49-yard drive in two plays after a nearly-blocked punt. Ken Cooper did the honors from 37 yards and Scott Chesser's kick made it 7-0. Back came Louisville with a 76-yard drive and Lyons 1-yarder to cut it to 7-6. Starkville responded with a Ken Rogers 5-yarder and Chesser kick and now it was 14-6. In the 2nd quarter, the Cats went 80 yards and Willie Clark found paydirt from nine yards with just :36 on the clock to put halftime 14-12.

The second half looked dismal at first with a pair of close fourth down stops, penalties and an interception. However, Jerry Hughes found a loose football to lead to a 1-yard Lyons plunge and Taylor's two-pointer to end scoring. Taylor had 174 rushing yards of 260 total. Lyons was Player of the Week.

"We had a tremendous effort by all of our players. This is what we practice for. It takes a lot of work to get ready to play and win like we did this week. It makes this kind of win that much better. I thought the team deserved to win. We just hung on and kept fighting back until we won".

GAME 5:   LOUISVILLE (2-1-1) @ NESHOBA CENTRAL (1-3)
                 LOUISVILLE 13 NESHOBA CENTRAL 12
                 October 1, 1982

After a pair of disappointing openers, the Cats were back on track and looking to keep it going at Neshoba Central. However, it would not come until the last 2:00.

The Rockets opened with a deep drive to the Cat 8 before faltering. Neshoba opened with a 2nd quarter 2-yard John Fulton run to make it 6-0. Taylor found Hughes from 35 yards to even things 6-6. With only seconds left, Greg McNair spotted Scott Miller from 40 yards to make intermission 13-6. Now late in the game, a Rocket fumble set the Cats up at the 40-yard line. Lyons hit Tony Fulton for 26 yards and Lyons eventually dove in from a yard. Jimmy Miller's PAT was the game-winner.

GAME 6:   LOUISVILLE (3-1-1) vs LEE HIGH (2-3)
               LOUISVILLE 14 LEE HIGH 7
               October 8, 1982

In a season thus far determined by close games, this long-time rival was to be no exception at Hinze Stadium. Although, it seemed that the Wildcats would run away early.

On the first play of the game, Jeremiah Sangster *"burst through the middle"* for a 56-yard score. The first of two Miller kicks made it 7-0. Despite a long Gerald Hayes run to deep into General territory, the FG failed. However, Lyons found a loose football and, four plays later, he dove in from a foot to make halftime 14-0.

Near the end of the 3rd quarter, a Cat fumble set up the only Lee score. That came on a Jeff Whisenant 7-yarder added with a Willie Neal PAT. *"I thought we played a very good game. Jeremiah and Gerald did a good job of taking up the running slack with Michael Taylor out. Taylor may be able to play this week".*

GAME 7:   LOUISVILLE (4-1-1) @ TUPELO (4-2)
               LOUISVILLE 16 TUPELO 22
               October 15, 1982

The Tupelo squad claimed victories in four of the last six matches and now this one went to their home field. It was to be yet again another close game.

Tupelo jumped out early with a 15-0 lead that could have made the Wildcats give up. Scoring came on Terry Hadley's 10-yard and 27-yard receptions from Mitch Eubank and a 22-yard Danny Grubbs FG. However, Lyons picked off a 3rd quarter pass to set up a 55-yard Jeremiah Sangster scoring dash. They then went 95 yards with a touchdown and both two-point conversions put Louisville ahead 16-15. Questionable calls on the last Wave drive left them at the Cat 15. With less than 3:00 remaining they crossed the stripe on a Eubank pass to Curley Dixon with 1:26 remaining and Louisville dropped the game.

"It's tough on our kids to give so much and then lose a close one like that. We had some very biased officiating and it probably cost us the game. Our boys gave it their all and then had the game taken away from them on some bad calls. That hurts a lot. I'm proud of their effort..." Tupelo led first downs (14-10) and passing (146-62). The Cats held the ground (189-128).

GAME 8:   LOUISVILLE (4-2-1) vs PHILADELPHIA (4-3)
               LOUISVILLE 0 PHILADELPHIA 3
               October 22, 1982: HOMECOMING

The teams resumed a long history that stopped in 1972 with a victory over a Marcus Dupree team the previous season. Now, the welcomed the Tornados to Hinze. The Union Appeal picked Philly 14-13 saying, *"Tornados have won five straight (and) captured the District IV-A North Subdistrict crown... Philly by one".*

Only a short recap of events by The Winston County Journal gives us the outcome. *"The Louisville Wildcats couldn't hang on to the ball long enough to put any points on the board Friday night and a lone field goal by Philadelphia Rodney Kight in 1st quarter) was enough for the upset".* Said McAlpin, *"We just weren't ready to play and they were. We made too many mistakes to win and just couldn't get our game together".*

GAME 9:   LOUISVILLE (4-3-1) vs WEST POINT (8-0)
               LOUISVILLE 0 WEST POINT 23
               October 29, 1982

The two consecutive losses by nine points was demoralizing to everyone. The Wildcats won four of the last five against West Point but now nothing was for granted. In the end, it seemed that showed on the scoreboard.

Robert Smith had the first on 23 yards and Quentin Adams' PAT made it 7-0. In the middle of the 3rd quarter, the Green Wave began adding to their advantage. Smith added another TD from 12 yards while Adams had the last from a yard. Offensively, it may have been the Cats' worst game in years as the Green Wave held them to just three first downs and led in total yardage over 300 to 27. Keith Young added the safety.

"We played a super team and they beat us. I thought we were still in the game up until they scored their second touchdown at the end of the third quarter. We just needed

to get a break and get the momentum going our way. West Point is the best team we've played and deserves their ranking in the state".

GAME 10:   LOUISVILLE (4-4-1) @ GRENADA (2-7)
            LOUISVILLE 6 GRENADA 13
            November 5, 1982

A winning season was in the balance on the road against a team with a worse record that the Wildcats. While Louisville was first on the board on a Lyons pass to Jimmie Horton, a 2nd quarter fumble allowed the Chargers a 68-yard return and PAT to make it 7-6. In the finale, Grenada pulled a 70-yard pick-six for the dagger.

"We won all the battles but lost the war. We only punted one time all night. The rest of the time we fumbled, had passes intercepted or were stopped on downs. We played well enough to win. We just couldn't get the points on the board. We're beginning to set goals and work out programs for next year. I'm proud of our kids' effort this year and know that we will be much improved next year".

At the athletic banquet, honors went to Michael Taylor (Best Offensive Back), Billy Kemp (Special Team), William Watt (Christian Athlete), Jimmy Bowen (Most Improved), Gerald Hayes (Most Improved), John Murray (Permanent Team Captain), Bardra Lyons (MVP and Kiwanis Award), Willie Marshall (Best Offensive Lineman); Willie Sangster (Best Defensive Lineman) and Bobby Shields (Permanent Team Captain).

1983 (4-5)

Jack McAlpin, in his fourth and final year as head coach for the Wildcats, had 20 letter winners back and voted tops in District 4 AA for the coming year. *"We feel that we will have a solid, competitive team. We have seven offensive starters returning and we have some promising younger players who are pushing for a starting spot".*

The Cats had only nine games for 1983, but not for lack of trying. *"We asked everybody within a 100-mile radius to play us but could not get a 10th game".*

GAME 1:   LOUISVILLE (0-0) vs CALDWELL (0-0)
            LOUISVILLE 30 CALDWELL 18
            September 2, 1983

This matchup turned strange since their initial meeting in 1974, as there were three tie games. The last came just the previous year. *"We are going into the game with a virtual blindfold. Even though we saw them in a spring scrimmage with New Hope, we still don't really know what to expect because they changed coaches during the summer. We know they are very fast... We expect them to be tough".*

Chris Eiland began the scoring with an opening 23-yard dash but the Columbus team answered with a Tommy Williams score to make it 6-6 early in the 2nd quarter. Michael Taylor upped the advantage on touchdown runs of seven and 21 yards while Jeremiah Sangster *"gave the home team a comfortable halftime lead"* with a 61-yarder. Caldwell added one just before intermission to cut the lead a bit.

Sangster added the last Cat points in the 3rd quarter on a 79-yard escape while Caldwell managed one more on a 16-yard Don Carodine pass to Mac Turner before the game was over. Sangster, Player of the Week, rushed for 204 yards Taylor pitched in another 114. Travon Neal recorded a pair of pickoffs while Gerald Hayes and Larry Triplett recovered fumbles. The Cats led in yardage by nearly 100 yards.

"I was generally pleased with our performance. Naturally, we found several areas that we will concentrate our work on this week to improve, but we played well considering this was our first game".

GAME 2:   LOUISVILLE (1-0) vs NOXUBEE COUNTY (1-0)
            LOUISVILLE 33 NOXUBEE COUNTY 14
            September 9, 1983

The win against Caldwell shot the Wildcats to eighth in the Mississippi Prep Poll. Future opponent West Point held third place. Now it was time for a Noxubee team that defeated the Cats last year after four straight Louisville wins. *"We have lots of work to do* and will have our hands full Friday. They will be fired up and ready to play, but we should have a little extra incentive this year after losing over there last season".

Eiland again opened scoring with a 4-yarder and added a 1-yarder before the initial frame ended to make it 12-0. In the 2nd quarter, he found Tony Fulton from 29 yards while Taylor dashed 78 yards for another. He also added the two-point play to put halftime in the hands of Louisville 26-0. Taylor opened the 3rd with a 55-yard scoring run.

NCHS finally hit the board afterwards on Elder Dancy's 10-yard toss to Brown and their ensuing two-pointer. In the finale, Robey took a fumble 27 yards to paydirt for their last. "We played really good football. We are still struggling with our kicking game but we had real good line blocking and our secondary played well". Once again, the Wildcats dominated in total yardage.

GAME 3:   LOUISVILLE (2-0) @ KOSCIUSKO (1-1)
                 LOUISVILLE 33 KOSCIUSKO 21
                 September 16, 1983

Another win put the Cats up to sixth in the AP Prep Poll. Now attention turned to longtime rival and non-conference foe Kosciusko. "We are playing good football right now. We need to keep up our momentum this week because we have three important district games remaining. This is our grudge game. Since we are in different classifications and no longer play in a conference, the game has lost some of the meaning standings-wise, but it has lost none of the meaning to the players".

Midway through the opening stanza, Taylor broke through from 28 yards and Jimmy Miller converted. He then added a 7-yarder and Miller was again true. Before the end of the quarter, Sangster plunged in from the 1-yard line to make it 20-0. Kosy answered in the 2nd quarter on a 5-yard Jerry Whitcomb run and James Dotson kick while Taylor got in from 23 yards to make halftime 26-7.

In the 3rd quarter, Neal took a punt 55 yards to paydirt. In the finale, the Whippets put up a pair of scores. Dotson ended a 46-yard march from three yards and Whitcomb did the same later to end a 53-yard drive. Dotson was true on both PATs. Taylor rushed for 165 yards and Michael Miller led the defense with nine solo and four assisted tackles. Miller had a fumble recovery and Neal an interception.

"It was a very physical, bruising game. We have several players banged up a little, but we think we hit them just as hard as they did us. Our defensive front is doing a good job against the run, so people are throwing more and more against us. We had a real good effort from everyone".

GAME 4:   LOUISVILLE (3-0) vs STARKVILLE (1-1-1)
                 LOUISVILLE 13 STARKVILLE 30
                 September 23, 1983

The undefeated Wildcats seemed to be catching the Yellow Jackets at the right time. They were just 1-1-1 and playing at Hinze Stadium. The rivalry was still on after consecutive games since 1940. "We have three consecutive district games ahead of us so we are coming to the real heart of our schedule. The next three are all crucial games for us. (Starkville has) played a tough schedule early and we know they will be tough. We must be ready to play".

The Cats led 13-8 late in the first half thanks to Sangster scoring runs of five and 39 yards. However, a 2-yard Marcus Bush run and Richard Daniel two-pointer turned the momentum. From there, the Jackets seemed to get rolling and dominated the remainder of the contest. Ken Rogers found paydirt from 70 yards, a 6-yard Bush run and 2-yard Rogers plunge ended scoring.

The Yellow Jackets dominated yardage 384-117. Miller led with 10 solo tackles while Harvey Mitchell added a fumble recovery. "Our chances for a district championship are still alive. Last year's champion had a loss on its record and we still have Lee High and Neshoba ahead of us. We have just got to return to some basic, hard-hitting play to stay in it. We just didn't play well on defense. They were able to keep the football and move it up and down the field and our offense was never able to take command of the game".

GAME 5:   LOUISVILLE (3-1) vs NESHOBA CENTRAL (3-0-1)
                 LOUISVILLE 25 NESHOBA CENTRAL 28
                 September 30, 1983: HOMECOMING

With a home tilt and events surrounding the Homecoming week, <u>The Union Appeal</u> picked the Cats 20-14. *"A toss-up with the advantage going to Louisville at home as the Rockets' District 4 AA hopes are dealt a severe blow"*. Said McAlpin, *"We just didn't play our best game last week. We have had a good week's work and our players seem to be responding well. We expect a good effort this week"*.

The Wildcats appeared to have things firmly in hand with a 17-0 lead. Miller opened scoring with a 34-yard 1st quarter FG while Taylor followed with a 25-yard touchdown run and a Sangster dash from 13 yards. The Rockets cut it to 17-14 on two 2nd quarter tallies. One came from Mecedric Calloway from 43 yards on the ground while a blocked punt recovered by James Bell in the end zone garnered the next. Sangster recorded the last of the first half on a two-yard plunge and conversion scamper.

In the final frame, NCHS put up two more to snatch the win. Greg McNair crossed from six yards for the first tally and two-pointer and later from 37 yards. *"It was a very exciting game. Our players were fired up and played as hard as they could. We deserved to win as much as they did and it could have gone either way. I'm always proud of my players when they give their best effort. We are not down after this loss. We have some very big games ahead of us and we plan to get right to work getting ready for them"*.

Taylor paced rushers with 194 yards. Gary Porter had six solo tackles and five assists while Sangster recovered a fumble and picked off a Rocket throw.

GAME 6:   LOUISVILLE (3-2) @ LEE HIGH (4-1)
                                   LOUISVILLE 16 LEE HIGH 7
                                   October 7, 1983

Despite back-to-back losses, Louisville did shine on the ground as Taylor and Sangster accounted for 1,010 total yards. Taylor was just ahead with 519 of those. However, this game came down to how well the defense could stop the General run game.

The Cats jumped out to a 6-0 lead on a wonderful 79-yard Sangster escape but Lee responded with a 5-yard Carl Brown dive and Larry Tate PAT to take a 7-6 lead just before halftime. With seconds remaining, Miller nailed a 24-yard FG to put them ahead 9-7. Now in the last frame, Eiland dove in from a yard and Miller added the icing to the victory.

"We had a very good effort, particularly in the second half. There were several points in the game at which we could easily have given up and got beaten but we hung in there for 48 minutes. We have a good team but we play a tough schedule. These next three games are as tough as we play. Our goal now is to finish 7-2".

Sangster also added eight solo tackles and a pair of assists along with an interception. Billy Kemp also had a pickoff and Gary Triplett blocked a punt recovered by Darren Kincaid. Jimmy Bowen also received credit for a fumble recovery. Sangster's 139 rushing yards earned him Player of the Week.

GAME 7:   LOUISVILLE (4-2) vs TUPELO (6-0)
                                   LOUISVILLE 16 TUPELO 45
                                   October 14, 1983

McAlpin was not kidding about the schedule getting tougher. The Wave were putting up points in bunches with the exception of one contest. *"Coach Ricky Black has really built a tremendous program up there. We are expecting this to be our toughest game of the season"*. Title hopes were gone, but there was still a lot of pride left in Louisville.

Wildcat mistakes led to a quick 17-0 hole. A lost fumble, recovery of an onside kick and interception were simply too much to overcome after a quarter. Before halftime, they added two more touchdowns to make halftime 31-0. After they increased things to 38-0, Eiland and Jimmy Horton hooked up from ten yards and Sangster ran in the conversion. In the finale. Eiland and Henry Coleman connected for a 46-yard score and Eiland found Triplett for the two-pointer.

Golden Wave scores came from two Mitch Eubank passes to Fred Hadley, a Curley Dixon run and two-pointer, two Mack Shell runs and Andy Whitwell run, 35-yard FG and four extra points.

Neal had an interception while Miller led with four solo tackles and four assists on defense. *"We knew we would have to make them earn everything they got if we were to compete with them. We did just the opposite. Tupelo has a very fine football team, we can't, however, be concerned with how good someone else is. We must get aggressive and play our game to be competitive"*.

GAME 8:   LOUISVILLE (4-3) @ WEST JONES (6-1)
      LOUISVILLE 0 WEST JONES 20
      October 21, 1983

The District 6 favorites would not be much easier with a one-loss season thus far. *"We must block, tackle and be aggressive to have a chance. We haven't been doing what we are assigned to do both offensively and defensively. Execution is the key. We must make teams earn what they get and stop giving them so many opportunities to score easily".*

West Jones put up a pair of touchdowns in the 2nd quarter on a Greg Amerson 2-yard run and John Clarke's 1-yarder. John Easterling converted on both. Their last came in the 3rd quarter when Easterling took a fumble seven yards to the end zone. Louisville lost in yardage 299-104. Sangster had 10 solo and 3 assists in tackles. Tim Brown recorded a fumble recovery.

"We played pretty good football but we missed several opportunities to make a big play that would have broken things open for us. We dropped some key passes and had a couple overthrown that would have been big gainers. We just need to settle down, block better and capitalize on our opportunities".

GAME 9:   LOUISVILLE (4-4) @ WEST POINT (6-2)
      LOUISVILLE 10 WEST POINT 34
      October 28, 1983

The season wrapped on the road against the defending AA champions. *"We need to win so the season will end on a sweet note. West Point has a very good team and their two losses were to two undefeated teams (Tupelo and Starkville). If we play good football, we can stay with them".*

Louisville took an early 7-0 lead on a 43-yard Taylor dash. However, halftime sat in favor of West Point 21-10. The home team notched touchdowns in each of the next two frames to pad the final score. Shawn Sykes found the end zone on runs for 9, 21, 16 and 11 yards while Robert Smith added another. West Point led in yardage 289-214 with Taylor rushing for 176 for the Cats. He also led tacklers with five solo stops.

"We played as well as we could. The turnovers hurt us but we hung in there pretty well. They have a very good team and a pair of fine senior running backs. We lost to as good a team as we've played this year".

End-of-season honors were not found for 1983.

1984 (10-1-1)

After five season, Jack McAlpin was now elsewhere and new mentor Mike Justice held the Wildcat whistle. He came from a head coaching stint at Calhoun City where his team were undefeated and district champions the previous season. While he had only six starters back, the team did feature 25 returning letter winners. As such, voters put them first in District IV-AAAA.

GAME 1:   LOUISVILLE (0-0) @ CALDWELL (0-0)
      LOUISVILLE 21 CALDWELL 9
      September 7, 1984

With high expectations, Justice took his Cat squad to Columbus to meet long-time opponent Caldwell. *"We expect Caldwell to be a much-improved team from last year".* David Nelson's team was just 1-8-1 that year. *"I really can't predict what we will do. We know what to do, so we need to play a game to determine how well we can execute. I feel we are well-prepared and our players know how important this game is".*

Caldwell took advantage of a first-drive roughing the punter call to get on the board 6-0. That score came on Tommy Williams' 14-yarder. Back came Jeremiah Sangster with a 68-yard dash to tie it. They took the lead 14-6 after on a 40-yard Chris Eiland keeper and Michael Taylor conversion. Before halftime, a Caldwell 35-yard Roosevelt Poindexter FG put it a tight 14-9. Now in the final frame, Eiland crossed from 12 yards and Jimmy Miller knocked home the PAT.

"I was particularly pleased with the desire and intensity that our players displayed. We didn't execute all that well at times, but we will get better. For the first game with a new offense, I feel we performed well". The Cats rushed for 237 and gained 12 first downs. Sangster (105 yards and Player of the Week) and Taylor (72) paced rushers. Henry Coleman and Warren Miller picked off passes and Vincent Carter recovered a fumble.

GAME 2:   LOUISVILLE (1-0) @ NOXUBEE COUNTY (0-1)
                LOUISVILLE 27 NOXUBEE COUNTY 7
                September 14, 1984

A second district road game was at hand against Coach M.C. Miller's team in Macon. They were just 3-5-1 the previous year but had eight starters and 14 lettermen back. Voters picked them second behind Louisville in District play.
"We need this one badly. We only play three district games and the winner goes to the North State playoffs. We complete our district schedule during the first month of the season so we don't have much room for error".
In the 2nd quarter, Eiland found Willie Thames from 40 yards and Miller converted. A later Cat fumble set up an eventual Wade Taylor 50-yard pass to John Mills. Their PAT tied it at halftime. In the 3rd quarter, Taylor dashed 40 yards to paydirt while Eiland and Henry Coleman hooked up from 20 yards for another. The finale came in the last stanza on a 46-yard Sangster run and Taylor two-pointer.
"We had a very solid performance defensively. We will be very excited about playing at home this week after two dates on the road". The defense held Noxubee to just 78 total yards with -20 of that on the ground. Louisville rushed for 235 of their 318 yards. Taylor paced rushers with 125 yards, Sangster had 85 more, Carter had three sacks, Warren Miller a pair, and Anthony Thames had an interception.

GAME 3:   LOUISVILLE (2-0) vs KOSCIUSKO (2-0)
                LOUISVILLE 14 KOSCIUSKO 7
                September 21, 1984

The 2-0 district start moved Louisville to tenth in the AP Prep Poll. Now, they faced long-time foe Kosciusko, but at least it was at Hinze Stadium. "The rivalry between Louisville and Kosciusko goes back many years and they have a very solid team this year". Said Kosy Coach Abercrombie, "They will be the biggest and most physical team we will see all year. They are solid and are a very sound football team. We will have to be at our very best to even stay close to them".
It didn't take long before Eiland scored from 12 yards and Miller converted his first of three. Sangster then dashed in from 36 yards to make it 14-0. A Cat fumble in the frame led to Jerry Whitcomb's 11-yarder and Robbie McCaffrey's PAT. Louisville added one more in the 2nd quarter on a 5-yard Sangster run. Their last came from Taylor in the 3rd quarter from the 5-yard line
"Kosciusko had given up only three points in the first two games and we were extremely pleased to be able to score 27 on them while stopping them with a good defensive effort. We completely controlled the tempo of the game".
The defense held Kosy to -12 rushing yards (The Star-Herald says 44 yards) while they did get 125 (or 74) in the air. Sangster and Michael Miller picked off passes while Timmy Brown recovered a fumble. On the ground, Louisville rushed for 361 yards with Sangster (176) and Taylor (149) leading the way.

GAME 4:   LOUISVILLE (3-0) @ STARKVILLE (3-0)
                LOUISVILLE 0 STARKVILLE 0
                September 28, 1984

Another victory pushed the Cats to seventh in the Top 20. However, this week brought another road trip to face the top-ranked team in the state. "Starkville is ranked number one in every poll in the state. I have been coaching for nine years and they have the best team I've ever seen. We look at the game as a challenge. We don't know that we can play with them, but we are happy for the opportunity to see if we can. We intend to give them our very best effort".
The best chance for the upset came late in the final seconds of the game. With the ball at the 1-yard line, Justice elected for the FG. Durwood Minor and Keith Thompson, however, blocked Miller's 17-yard effort. There was a chance for overtime, but Justice

declined as the ball would be placed at the 10-yard line and Starkville fared much better odds with their pair of running backs.

"That was the most determined team effort to win that I have ever had in all my years of coaching. We played hard for the entire 48 minutes and didn't make any major mistakes that could have given them the edge. We just got out there and played one fine football game against a very capable opponent. It was really a fan's game and I think everyone got his money's worth". The defense was Player of the Week.

GAME 5:   LOUISVILLE (3-0-1) @ NESHOBA CENTRAL (3-1)
                 LOUISVILLE 12 NESHOBA CENTRAL 6
                 October 5, 1984

A win here at Neshoba Central gave the Wildcats the district title. It would not be easy as Coach Chuck Friend was 9-1-1 the previous year with eight starters back. The Union Appeal picked the Cats 20-6. Said Justice, *"We hope to carry the same intensity, desire and enthusiasm into the game that we showed last week. We have some tough games ahead".*

As expected, the slugfest remained scoreless at halftime. However, Sangster opened the 3rd quarter with an 84-yard kick return to make it 6-0. Taylor followed later with a 3-yarder and now the Cats were up 12-0. Neshoba avoided the shutout in the final frame when Greg Fulton (or Michael Killen) plunged in from a yard after a 65-yard fumble recovery and return by John Moore.

"We had to beat a good team to get the title. I hope this accomplishment by our team gives some credibility to the things we tried to establish when we came in here. They weren't able to drive for a score at all". Sangster led the defense with 11 solo tackles.

GAME 6:   LOUISVILLE (4-0-1) vs LEE HIGH (4-1)
                 LOUISVILLE 31 LEE HIGH 6
                 October 12, 1984: HOMECOMING

Despite sitting fifth in polls, the Cats now had to face yet another strong squad in Lee High out of Columbus. However, both Taylor (581) and Sangster (506) proved a solid rushing combination for any opponent. Eiland also complimented them with 175 yards. *"We will be extremely happy to be playing at home for a change. We have had four very tough games on the road and we are anxious to play before our home crowd. (Lee has) a very solid team. They play a tough schedule and have beaten good teams. We will have to play consistent football and avoid mistakes to play with them".*

The Cats jumped out with a pair of 1st quarter touchdowns on Taylor's 19-yarder and Sangster's 67-yard dash. Miller converted on both. Lee responded with a 3-yard Carl Brown dive while Miller hit a 40-yard FG to make halftime 17-6. In the last stanza, Sangster dashed in from 49 yards while Roderick Baker did the same from 16 yards. Miller was again true on both tallies.

"We had a great effort from everyone. It was our best offensive game of the season and our players were mentally ready to play. They gave a great effort. Our players were extremely happy for the large crowd we had". Sangster (146) and Taylor (126) led rushers. Louisville put up 448 yards with 385 coming on the ground. Sangster again recorded 11 solo tackles while Taylor was second with nine. Coleman and Taylor had picks.

GAME 7:   LOUISVILLE (5-0-1) @ TUPELO (6-0)
                 LOUISVILLE 12 TUPELO 3
                 October 19, 1984

If not tough enough already, now the Cats went to Tupelo to face the second-ranked Wave. Coach Ricky Black went 10-1 the previous year in AAAAA and had 14 lettermen and four starters back. Thus far, they were undefeated and on a 16-game winning streak.

"We consider the game a real challenge for us. We are excited about playing them and we feel that playing a top-caliber team will help up later as we go into the state playoffs. We have played consistent defense this year. We play well together as a team and we haven't given up more than one touchdown in a game all season".

Midway through the opening frame, Eiland *"legged it for a 54-yard TD on an option keeper to finish an 82-yard, four-play march".* In the next frame, they moved 83 yards with Taylor capping it from six yards. Tupelo's only response came in the 3rd quarter on Andy Whitwell's 26-yard FG. It could have been worse as the Cats lost fumbles four times but the defense held. Coleman's interception of Whitwell ended last opportunities for a comeback. Said Coach Black, *"You've just got to praise Louisville. Their defense rose to the occasion..."*

The Cats held Tupelo to 59 rushing yards and 97 passing yards. Taylor (97) and Sangster (84) led Louisville ground efforts. *"It was really a big win for us. We had a super effort from our defense and a solid offensive showing to earn the win. We denied Tupelo every time. We're a defensive-oriented team. That's what we do best. Tupelo has a fine team and they are a well-coached team. It took a tremendous effort from our players to go on their field and whip them on their homecoming".*

GAME 8:   LOUISVILLE (6-0-1) vs WEST JONES (6-1)
                          LOUISVILLE 9 WEST JONES 6
                          October 26, 1984

The upset win pushed the Wildcats to the second spot in prep polls, but that did not matter, as another six-win team was next. The Mustangs, eighth in the state, won the last three against the Cats while also posting successful seasons under Coach Mike Taylor. They were 9-2 the previous season and 8-2 the year prior.

"Our schedule has been exhausting. We have played some very big games and it seems they have all been on the road. (West Jones) led Starkville 20-10 at the half and we have all the respect in the world for them. We know we will have to play one of our better games to beat them..."

Scoring was done by halftime. Miller nailed a 41-yard FG in the opening frame for the difference. In the 2nd quarter, Sangster took off for a 67-yard touchdown while West Jones tallied later on a 17-yard John Clark run. The Cats put up 427 yards on offense. Sangster rushed for 170 yards and Taylor (Player of the Week) another 120. Eiland passed for 53 yards. The visitors managed only 71 rushing and 2 passing yards. Coleman had his sixth interception while Sangster and Gary Porter recovered fumbles.

"West Jones was the most physical team we've played this year. They ran the football well and had the best kicking game we've seen all year. West Jones was a very well organized, well-coached team. They are a leading contender to win South State".

GAME 9:   LOUISVILLE (7-0-1) vs WEST POINT (6-2)
                          LOUISVILLE 14 WEST POINT 13
                          November 2, 1984

Since the two first met in 1936, the Cats were 17-5 against West Point. However, the last two games went to the green and white. Although a playoff position was secured, it meant another challenge against a one-loss team. This marked another tough one as teams were a combined 30-5 in records since coming into the second game of the season.

West Point scored in the opening frame on a 17-yard Lorenzo Fears pass to Jesse Anderson and the Thomas Hosey conversion made it 7-0. The Cats tied it at halftime on a 25-yard toss from Eiland to Thames and Miller PAT. The visitors made it 13-7 in the 3rd quarter via the air but Warren Miller blocked the crucial PAT. Now in the 4th quarter, an Anthony Thames blocked punt set up Sangster's 4-yarder and Miller gave them the margin of victory. The last WPHS score came on an 11-yard Fears toss to Anderson.

Sangster's 105 yards gave him 1,034 on the season. Taylor was close behind (65 yards) with 989. Louisville led rushing 305-41 but lost the air 95-25. *"We did not play one of our better games. However, even though we were not emotionally high, we played sound enough fundamentally to win and that's a credit to our players. It is difficult to be high week after week but our players were able to overcome that and win anyway. West Point had a good, solid team".*

GAME 10:   LOUISVILLE (8-0-1) @ ABERDEEN (2-7)
                          LOUISVILLE 34 ABERDEEN 12
                          November 9, 1984

The regular season was closing on the road, but not the remainder of play. This time they faced Aberdeen, a team that was a regular opponent until their last meeting back in 1971. The 4-A team under Dwight McComb went 3-6 the past year with 18 lettermen back. Eight were starters.

"*Aberdeen is having a tough year. Still, we won't take anything for granted. One of our primary goals right now is to finish the season undefeated and we have put in too much work to go up there and let someone slip up on us. We will be ready to play.*"

It was a quick 21-0 lead in the opening frame on Eiland's 62-yard run, Steven Robinson's blocked punt and recovery for a touchdown, and Eiland's 60-yard connection with Coleman. All kicks by Miller were true. Eiland later ran in from four yards and Michael Taylor crossed from two yards. Victor Hodges (3) and Michael Cockrell to Graham Thompson to Victor Hodges 47-yard flea-flicker accounted for Aberdeen points. The Cats rushed for 350 yards and Eiland threw for 88 more. Taylor (90) and Sangster (73) were now both over the 1,000-yard mark.

"*We are proud to finish undefeated. We played a tough schedule that featured seven top-20 teams and we won six and tied the other. This is a tribute to our players and the pride they have to be able to accomplish this. After we got ahead so quickly, we went to the bench. We tried several combinations and I'm sure that will help us later in our program*". Eiland and Coleman were voted Players of the Week.

GAME 11:   LOUISVILLE (9-0-1) @ CLEVELAND (7-4)
                  LOUISVILLE 27 CLEVELAND 6
                  November 23, 1984

Louisville had a couple of weeks to heal and prepare for the first round of the playoffs. "*The playoffs are like a new season. The first season is over and what we have accomplished to this point is meaningless. When you lose, you are out and we have set our goals to go all the way*". The two met in 1952 and 1953; both Louisville victories.

Scoring came in bunches early and often. Sangster scored on runs of 10 and 31 yards in the first half while Taylor crossed from 2 yards in the opening frame and six yards in the 3rd quarter. Terrance Watt had the last touchdown on a 5-yard pass. Eiland and Coleman found paydirt on a 43-yard connection while Miller added a PAT. The lone Cleveland score came from Jim Earl Thomas' 1-yarder.

Louisville led 407-93 in yardage. Sangster (140) and Taylor (135) paced the Cats to 351 of those yards. Sangster had 10 solo tackles while Warren Miller had an interception and blocked pass. Justice had praise for a number of players while adding, "*We had a fine defensive effort. We are pleased to begin the playoffs with a big win. However, we will have our hands full this week against West Point*".

GAME 12:   LOUISVILLE (10-0-1) @ WEST POINT (8-3)
                  LOUISVILLE 0 WEST POINT 27
                  November 30, 1984

The second meeting in 28 days was now on the road. The Wildcats came out ahead in their first matching but it mattered little today. "*We were very fortunate to beat them before. They were ahead 13-7 in the 4th quarter... Besides, the playoffs are like a completely new season. The fact that we beat them earlier will have no effect on the outcome of this game. They have a very solid team and we must play an emotional game to win. The bottom line is that we must beat them to get to the state championship game*".

A defensive battle led to a scoreless first half, but the game turned completed to West Point thereafter. That's when Lorenzo Fears hit Timothy Green from 27 yards and Thomas Hosey converted. In the last frame, Reggie Williams took a fumble 87 yards to paydirt and Hosey again was true. Fears and Green again hooked up from 19 yards and the game dagger came on Jessie Anderson's 40-yard fumble return to paydirt. Hosey nailed the last point.

"*West Point played a good football game. They deserved the win. Our players really wanted to win but we just couldn't get things untracked and weren't able to do some of the things we wanted to do in the game*".

While internal honors are not found, it is no surprise that Sangster and Taylor were well recognized elsewhere. Sangster was an All-State First Team member while Taylor earned a Second Team nod. Vincent Carter was also a Second Team defensive member.

1985 (11-2)

Mike Justice began his second season as head man with 25 lettermen among 60 players. *"We are trying to establish a solid football program at Louisville. We had a good team last year and the coaching staff and I feel that we will have a good team again this year. Our defensive experience should be a strong plus for us in the first part of the schedule. We have put in a lot of hard work and have had some real good contact work".*

District voters picked the Wildcats first in IV-AAAA.

GAME 1:   LOUISVILLE (0-0) vs CALDWELL (0-0)
                                   LOUISVILLE 12 CALDWELL 0
                                   September 6, 1985

The Columbus district opponent served as the lid-lifter for the Cats since 1976. This season, they had nine defensive and seven offensive starters coming back that lost only 21-9 the previous year to Louisville.

"We feel like the opener is very crucial since it is a district game. We play all four of our district games in the first six weeks of the season and it puts added pressure on our players knowing that this first game means so much. We expect Caldwell to be a much-improved team. We are expecting a very hard-hitting game again this year".

The first Cat score came in the 2nd quarter when Johnny Triplett dove in from a yard to finish a 35-yard march. In the 3rd quarter, Rod Baker finished scoring with his 3-yarder to cap a 75-yard drive. Triplett ran for 139 yards and the defense caused eight fumbles. Louisville led in yardage 202-58.

"We completely dominated them defensively. They had six first downs but three came on penalties. They crossed the 50 only one time and we set that up with a fumble. We were extremely pleased with the (defensive) aggressive style of play... It was a good opening win. It was an important district game and we weren't doing any experimenting."

GAME 2:   LOUISVILLE (1-0) vs NOXUBEE COUNTY (0-1)
                                   LOUISVILLE 48 NOXUBEE COUNTY 7
                                   September 13, 1985

The Wildcats lost only once of seven games since their first in 1972. Still, this was a district game and crucial to repeat as title winners. *"They were very explosive defensively (following an opening 20-6 loss to Heidelberg). They lost five fumbles and had a touchdown called back. We expect a good game from them".*

The first quarter ended 18-7 after Noxubee's only tally on Nathaniel Taylor's 30-yard pass to Perry Tate. Dametrious Wells added the PAT. The Cats tallied on a 10-yard Lashun Wilson run, Triplett's 47-yard dash, and Henry Coleman's 44-yard kick return. Louisville added three more touchdowns before halftime on Triplett runs of six and three yards, a two-pointer from Baker to Anthony Thames, and Baker's 17-yard toss to Thames. Steven Roberson added the PAT.

Roberson added a 32-yard FG in the 3rd quarter while Frank Austin finalized things in the frame with a 2-yard plunge. Louisville rushed for 220 yards alone while the defense held Noxubee to 110 on the ground and 50 more in the air. *"We had a real good game. We had an exceptional effort from our offensive line and our secondary played well, too. Noxubee mixed it up on us a bit with what they did offensively... Our players are in a real good frame of mind right now. We have some big games coming up and we need to have the right attitude to keep things rolling".*

GAME 3:   LOUISVILLE (2-0) @ KOSCIUSKO (1-1)
                                   LOUISVILLE 35 KOSCIUSKO 6
                                   September 20, 1985

Despite a non-conference foe, the Whippets were still accustomed to playing the Wildcats. The win over NCHS put the Cats eighth in the AP Top 10. Said Justice of Kosy, *"We feel they will be a real challenge for us. They have a very solid defense and their offense is improving quickly. We expect them to be fired up and really battle us".*

Triplett had the lone score of the opening quarter on his 25-yard dash. Triplett then ran in from six yards, six yards and another 4-yarder. Roberson added a PAT in the opening frame and a 32-yard FG to make halftime 28-0. In the 3rd quarter, Corey Fuller took an option play 31 yards to paydirt. Midway through the finale, Levon Humphries got in the books on his 4-yard effort. Roberson's kick was true.

Triplett rushed for 160 yards of the Cats' 242 yards. In the air, they added another 165. Anthony Thames had 105 reception yards. On defense, Terrence Watts had eight solo tackles while Vincent Carter added seven more. Buck Thames and Sam Triplett had interceptions and the defense held Kosy to 49 passing and 89 rushing yards.

"We had a fine first half performance but we were sluggish in the second half. I feel that we weren't as intense after we got the big lead so quickly". Added Kosy coach David Abercrombie, *"We played with aggression against a much tougher team than we are and because of that aggression, we got out of position a couple of times and gave up the big play".*

GAME 4:   LOUISVILLE (3-0) vs STARKVILLE (3-0)
             LOUISVILLE 14 STARKVILLE 27
             September 27, 1985

Now sixth in the polls, the Cats welcomed the top-ranked Yellow Jackets to Hinze Stadium. They featured perhaps the top rusher in the state in David Fair. *"Starkville has the best high school team I've ever seen on film. They have size, speed, depth and some extremely talented athletes. Still, we are looking forward to playing them".* Since 1980, the Cats were just 1-3-1 against their local rivals. The tie was the previous season.

The game was closer than the scoreboard showed at the final whistle. While Starkville opened the game with a 4-yard Fair run and Milton Smith kick, Willie Thames pulled in a 12-yard Baker toss and Roberson made it 7-8 at halftime. The Jackets put up another tally in the 3rd quarter on Mike Purnell's 28-yard escape and Smith kick, but Baker hit Coleman from eight yards and Roberson evened it early in the final frame.

The Jackets then went up 20-14 on a 40-yard Fair dash. Baker then drove the Cats to the Jacket 8 in attempt to tie or go ahead. However, Smith picked off a contested pass in the end zone and Fair ran in from 96 yards quickly thereafter to insert the dagger. Smith also added the PAT. The defense was named Players of the Week.

Fair rushed for 208 of Starkville's total 398 yards. Triplett had 87 yards on the ground. *"We played a real good game and had an opportunity to win. We were disappointed that we didn't, but not with the way we played. We felt that if we could hold them to two or three touchdowns, we'd have a chance to win. And we did".* Added Coach Willis Wright, *"This is an intense rivalry. Louisville really played us tonight but David came through when we needed him".*

GAME 5:   LOUISVILLE (3-1) vs NESHOBA CENTRAL (3-1)
             LOUISVILLE 13 NESHOBA CENTRAL 12
             October 4, 1985

The Wildcats lost only once in the last ten games since 1972. *"It's an important game especially because of the district record. We are directing all of our attention in Neshoba and we expect a real good game again this week".* The Union Appeal picked Louisville a 21-7. *"The Rockets do not have the firepower to stifle the Wildcats".*

The game was much closer than they predicted. After a Fred Word fumble recovery, Benny Tingle crossed late in the opening frame from 26 yards to put the Rockets ahead. The PAT was blocked twice by Vincent Carter to keep it 6-0. Louisville could have scored just before halftime on a drive to the NCHS 8 but Triplett's run was stopped. Coleman opened the 3rd quarter with a forced fumble, recovery and 25-yard scamper to paydirt. Roberson put the Cats ahead 7-6.

As the frame ended, Anthony Thames pulled in a 24-yard Baker pass to make it 13-6 Louisville. Midway through the final quarter, the Rockets found the end zone on a 1-yard Tingle run and elected for the two-points for the lead. However, the defense stood tall and kept them out. Late in the game, Neshoba went successfully to the air but, with :14 left, the defense forced a fumble to end the threat.

"I was very surprised they went for two with so much time remaining. We came out fired up to start the second half after being flat for the entire first half. We dealt with it all week after our loss to Starkville. The players felt like they played Starkville well enough to win and a loss like that one stays with the youngsters. Coach Friend's team is a fine football team and they played well".

GAME 6:   LOUISVILLE (4-1) @ LEE HIGH (0-5)
                                  LOUISVILLE 27 LEE HIGH 6
                                  October 11, 1985

A Columbus team that rallied over the previous few years to power now sat winless on the season. It did not hurt the Wildcats as the victory gave them their second title in two years.

Anthony Thames opened scoring in the 1st quarter with a 51-yard punt return and Roberson converted. Lee got in on Ron Carr's 27-yard escape to make it 7-6. Triplett then went in from three yards and Roberson put it 14-6. Before halftime, Coleman pulled in a 21-yard Baker toss and halftime was 20-6. The Cat defense notched the last points in the finale on a safety.

GAME 7:   LOUISVILLE (5-1) @ ABERDEEN (3-2)
                                  LOUISVILLE 40 ABERDEEN 14
                                  October 18, 1985

Louisville dropped only one tilt since 1937 against Aberdeen despite the two not meeting on a regular basis. Now, with the IV-AAA title and playoff position in their hands, they traveled to meet them once again.

Down 7-0, the Wildcats went on to take a 27-7 lead at halftime. Triplett ran in from four and nine yards, Gary Porter recorded an 18-yard pick-six, and Baker topped an 80-yard march for another. Bobby Strong had one Aberdeen tally from four yards while Sean Koehn got in from 18 yards. Other Cat scores came from Triplett on eight and seven yarders.

"We were sluggish early but Aberdeen wasn't. But then our men got fired up and played the best second quarter I've ever had a team play. We knew that Aberdeen would be up for the game with us. They had defeated Number 15 New Hope the week before and were looking to knock off another ranked team in as many weeks".

GAME 8:   LOUISVILLE (6-1) vs TUPELO (7-0)
                                  LOUISVILLE 40 TUPELO 17
                                  October 25, 1985: HOMECOMING

Forget their losing record to seventh-ranked Louisville against Tupelo since 1920, this year's Wave team sat fourth in polls under Coach Ricky Black and proved perhaps one of their toughest opponents of the season. However, The Clarion-Ledger said the team this week *"looked like a hospital ward"* as they had five starters out due to injuries.

Baker and Anthony Thames opened with a 40-yard connection to end a 76-yard march. Back came Tupelo with a 65-yard drive and Ben Floyd 3-yard effort to even the score. Baker and Thames then hooked up for an 89-yard touchdown to make it 13-7. Tupelo added a touchdown before halftime on Mark Lockhart's 17-yard FG to make it 13-10. Afterwards it was all Wildcats. Triplett added touchdowns on nine and 26 yards to go along with a two-pointer from Baker. Thames also had a 23-yard fumble recovery touchdown. Tupelo's last came from a 6-yard Keith Brown reception from Godwin.

Thames led with 196 reception yards and had an interception. Bryant Carter also added one off Chauncey Godwin as Tupelo threw three of them in the 3rd quarter alone. In all, they had four turnovers. Triplett rushed for 15 yards on the evening of Louisville's 363 total yards. *"It was the Anthony Thames Show tonight. He is a hell of a player. He had a once-in-a-lifetime game. Tupelo covered him one-on-one on short yardage and on first downs. You can't cover him one-on-one".*

Added Ricky Black, *"Louisville played outstanding. I'm glad a whipping like this only counts for one loss".* Thames was the obvious choice for Player of the Week.

GAME 9:   LOUISVILLE (7-1) vs CALLAWAY (5-2)
                                  LOUISVILLE 8 CALLAWAY 11
                                  November 1, 1985

Despite their 5-2 record, Coach Charlie Allman's Jackson-area school would be no easy opponent. This marked their first-ever meeting on the gridiron.

Louisville was first on the scoreboard in the 2nd quarter with an 8-yard toss from Baker to Willie Thames to end a 71-yard drive and Baker's two-pointer to Anthony Thames. Back punched Callaway with all 11 points. First was Percy Butler's 70-yarder to Delen

Robinson and Joe Roberson's two-point run. Then Terrell Johnson nailed a 28-yard FG with only :02 left before halftime. All scoring ended thereafter thanks to two late Ricky Henderson interceptions of Cat throws.

"We played well but so did they. Except for just a couple of plays tonight, we beat them. It was important for us to get on the board first and we did that. But they came right back two plays later and took our momentum away. We never regained it. Callaway came up here to get a win and that's just what they left here with. They lost two in a row, almost unheard for Callaway and they were determined not to lose another to us. One big play and FG was the difference".

Added Allman, "I thought their inability to run the ball determined the outcome of the game. Louisville's defense is the best I've seen outside of Meridian". Baker had 117 passing yards of the total 171 yards. Triplett rushed for 59 yards. Louisville led in first downs 10-9.

GAME 10:   LOUISVILLE (7-2) @ WEST POINT (6-2)
                LOUISVILLE 22 WEST POINT 13
                November 8, 1985

It was definitely time for revenge against long-time opponent and eighth-ranked West Point after the Wave ended their season sitting 10-0-1. Once again, it was on the road to Clay County.

A defensive battle held the first quarter scoreless before Baker opened the 2nd quarter with a 1-yard plunge and Roberson made it 7-0. West Point answered with a 77-yard Greg Keller kickoff return and his PAT. Before halftime, the Cats re-took the lead when Baker found Anthony Thames from 80 yards to put it 13-7. The Wildcats had the only score of the 3rd quarter when Baker and Thames again hit from 47 yards and Roberson connected to make the score 20-7.

The Green Wave responded with a 26-yard Jesse Randall throw to Pierre Baker but the failed PAT kept it 20-13. Before it was over, Vincent Carter tackled Randall in the end zone for a safety and the final points. Louisville led 14-8 in first downs, passed for 261 yards and rushed for 91 yards more. Now it was time to try once again for that championship that eluded them in 1984.

GAME 11:   LOUISVILLE (8-2) @ OLIVE BRANCH (9-1)
                LOUISVILLE 20 OLIVE BRANCH 7
                November 22, 1985

First-time opponent Olive Branch was no different otherwise from others the Wildcats faced over the years. They were solid, sitting with a great record and the game was on the road. "Olive Branch beat South Panola, the 5A champs, 21-0. The only loss came at the hands of Grenada on a score in the last seconds of the game. By all rights, they should be undefeated. They're bigger than anyone we played this season and they have two excellent running backs".

The bigger Conquistadors thrilled home fans with an opening tally via Thomas Brown's 7-yarder and Todd Rawson's PAT. Unbeknownst to everyone, it was all they would muster. In the 2nd quarter, Triplett ran in from a yard and later a Baker 11-yard pass to Coleman. Baker's two-pointer to Anthony Thames put it 14-7 at halftime. The last points came in the 3rd quarter on Baker's 45-yard connection with Willie Thames.

"We're a passing team but we became a passing team throughout the course of the season". Baker earned Player of the Week honors for his 11-41 performance.

GAME 12:   LOUISVILLE (9-2) vs WEST POINT (7-3)
                LOUISVILLE 21 WEST POINT 0
                November 29, 1985: Scott Field; Mississippi State University

There probably was not a single Wildcat fan that forgot 1984 when the Cats bested West Point in the regular season only to lose in the rematch when it counted. It was time for Louisville to take that crucial next step and overcome the past.

This one belonged solely to the visitors to advance to another state championship. Before the opening frame was half over, the Cats had a pair of touchdowns on the board. Triplett was first on a 6-yarder to cap a 95-yard march. Then Baker found Anthony Thames from 33 yards and then hit him for the two-pointer to make it 14-0. In the

2nd quarter, Louisville got the last of the game on a 23-yard Baker toss to Thames and Roberson PAT.

West point moved to the Cat 14 in the 3rd quarter but could go no further. In the last stanza, a march to the Cat 35 ended when Triplett picked off a screen pass to allow Louisville to run the clock for the win. *"I'm proud of our team. They played a good game. It took a good game to beat a good team like West Point"*. Triplett won Player of the Week for his 118 yards of rushing to put him over 1,300 on the season.

GAME 13:   LOUISVILLE (10-2) vs PEARL (11-1)
                         LOUISVILLE 23 PEARL 7
                         December 7, 1985: Hinds Junior College; Raymond, MS

The Pirates played 385 games since their first on September 16, 1949; a game they lost to Culkin Academy 25-6. They experienced as many low points as they had high points in their accomplishments, but never sat on the precipice of claiming a state championship. The two teams never faced, and now they did with everything on the line. The Hattiesburg American predicted the following: *"Pearl has been playing super football the last month and will continue to do so at Louisville's expense. Pearl 18 Louisville 13"*

"The main thing about Pearl is they aren't weak in any phase of the game" while Pearl coach Doug Merchant added, *"With a state championship on the line, anything can happen. You never know what kids have on their minds. Our kids surely know Louisville is an outstanding club or they wouldn't be here"*.

The slugfest sat scoreless at halftime. Though Dexter Knight had a pickoff early, a Freddie Northcutt fumble gave it back. Additionally, Mike Berry missed on a 38-yard FG. Louisville hit the board first in the 3rd quarter after a Bryant Carter pickoff of Bailey at the Pirate 30 taken back to the 14-yard line. Baker took advantage of the gift with a 3-yarder and Roberson booted his first of three conversions. Pearl responded in the quarter with a 68-yard march capped by a 1-yard Bailey dive and Berry extra point. Jarvis Jenkins' run of 40 yards set up the opportunity. The game now went into the finale tied 7-7.

Their journey officially ended when Louisville drove 80 yards with Triplett diving in from two yards. They managed two more scores in the end. The first was a 23-yard Baker pass to Anthony Thames while the last was a Porter tackle for safety on Bailey in the end zone. The former came by a Vincent Carter hit on Jenkins forcing a fumble recovered by Porter. Aside from rushing (100-24 for Louisville), the stats were fairly close. First downs (12-11) and rushing (138-110) went to the eventual champions.

Merchant said, *"They really did stop us outside. Most teams won't run enough inside to win and we didn't. The turnovers hurt us. Really, though I think the real difference is that they were more juiced than we were. That is the coaches' job, so I guess it is my fault. They wanted it more"*.

Mississippi Sports Writers Association All-State selections went to Rod Baker (First Team) and Anthony Thames (Second Team). Other voters in The Clarion-Ledger/Jackson Daily News had Vincent Carter and Henry Coleman on their defensive lists. All County awards went to Carter, Gary Porter, Bryant Carter, Willie Thames, Coleman, Baker, Thames, and Johnny Triplett. Honorable Mentions went to Greg Fulton, Walter Davis and Jeffery Smith.

1986 (9-3)

Confidence was high for third-year head coach Mike Justice as his Wildcats sat first in 4-AAAA ahead of Neshoba Central and second in The Clarion-Ledger/Jackson Daily News Super 10 pre-season polls. They featured 36 letter winners back from a state championship squad with four All-State players (Johnny Triplett, Sean Oakley, Anthony Thames and Rod Baker).

"We lost some good athletes. But the thing is, we lost one here and one there. We didn't lose all our players at any one position. I believe in making sure we have players from each of the three classes at every position and believe in playing as many players as I can. We are confident that we will have a good team but we are not over-confident. We are determined to play hard and play well".

GAME 1:   LOUISVILLE (0-0) @ CALDWELL (0-0)
                             LOUISVILLE 7 CALDWELL 0
                             September 5, 1986

The Cats were 4-0-1 against the Columbus team since 1981 and looking to get their season underway on the road. Fumbles were costly in the end and kept this a much closer contest than any expected. The only tally came in the 2nd quarter when Baker hit Thames from 23 yards for the touchdown and Lavon Humphrey added the PAT.

"We had five scoring opportunities but we lost four fumbles. Still, Rod threw the ball well and our players executed the game plan perfectly". Justice also praised the play of the offensive and defensive lines. Triplett paced rushers with 106 yards while Baker and Thames connected on 102 more. The defense held Caldwell to 125 total yards (90 on the ground). Humphrey and Triplett had interceptions and Terrence Watt led tacklers with five solo and eight assists.

GAME 2:   LOUISVILLE (1-0) @ NOXUBEE COUNTY (0-1)
                             LOUISVILLE 27 NOXUBEE COUNTY 8
                             September 12, 1986

Though picked last in 4-AAAA, Noxubee County played a tough game against a good Heidelberg team before coming out on the losing side. Louisville was 7-1 against them since 1971. "We expect them to have a very good team. Noxubee will be ready for us".

Louisville held a 14-0 lead at halftime with touchdowns in each of the first two quarters. Baker and Thames hooked up from four yards to cap a 46-yard march while Baker hit Anthony Clark from 27 yards for the next. Both Humphrey kicks were true. Triplett's 2-yarder made it 20-0 before the home team got on the board with an 8-yard Patrick King run and Howard's conversion pass to Demetrious Jones. Triplett ended scoring in the frame with a 1-yard dive and the Humphrey kick sealed it.

Louisville rushed for 265 and held NCHS to just 151 total yards. Triplett carried for 135 yards while Lashun Wilson added 101 more. Thames recorded an interception. "We had a good effort overall. We are still suffering some turnovers and we are going to work real hard to eliminate those this week".

GAME 3:   LOUISVILLE (2-0) vs KOSCIUSKO (0-2)
                             LOUISVILLE 33 KOSCIUSKO 6
                             September 19, 1986

Louisville won 10 of the last 12 games in a rivalry that went at least back to the 1920s. Now, the Cats met them once again but this time at Hinze Stadium. "We are excited about playing at home. The intense rivalry between Louisville and Kosciusko over the years should create some extra enthusiasm on our part..."

The Cats jumped out early with a pair of touchdowns, first on a 1-yard Baker dive capping a 73-yard march and then via his 62-yard strike to Antonio Smith. Triplett added a 3-yard effort and Humphrey converted on the first tally to make halftime 19-0. In the 3rd quarter, Triplett went over from 32 yards and Thames caught a 73-yarder from Baker to widen the lead. Baker found Anthony Clark for the two points.

Kosciusko could manage only a final stanza score via a 40-yard Mark Woodard and Derwin Johnson connection. "We had a good effort. Kosciusko used different offensive and defensive alignments than we expected, but our players adjusted quickly".

Baker threw for 246 yards with Thames pulling in 131 of those. Watt led tacklers with eight solo and seven assists. Louisville led in yardage 322-244. Baker earned Player of the Week for his efforts.

GAME 4:   LOUISVILLE (3-0) @ STARKVILLE (2-1)
                             LOUISVILLE 9 STARKVILLE 27
                             September 26, 1986

A stunning 21-7 loss by top-ranked Moss Point moved the Wildcats into the driver seat at Number One. However, Justice was not taking the Yellow Jackets lightly. "Starkville seems to have gotten on track after the opening loss. They have a new coach and they beat a good West Jones team. We are expecting a real tough battle up there".

The order differs on the source, but Starkville held a 7-3 lead after the first two scores. While the Cats had a 34-yard Humphrey FG, the Jackets put up an 8-yard Carlos

Kemp run and Rob Frese PAT. With just :09 remaining, Kenny Fair hit John Williams from 55 yards and Frese sent the teams to the lockers 14-3.

Frese increased it in the 3rd quarter with his 37-yard FG. Early in the final quarter, Louisville finally responded with a long march and 4-yard Baker strike to Thames. The home team added two more scores later on a 32-yard Frese kick, 62-yard Kemp dash and Frese PAT.

Louisville led in first downs 18-11 and passing (186-103) while Starkville held the ground (205-94). The Winston County Journal credited Baker with 211 yards passing and 61 yards for Triplett. The Cats fumbled five times on the night. "We seemed to self-destruct. Of course, the big plays they made hurt us. We were just stunned at the half and never adjusted. We are ready to put this behind us and get on with the business of winning a state championship. We got beat by a good team. We've got no problem with that".

GAME 5:   LOUISVILLE (3-1) @ NESHOBA CENTRAL (3-1)
                       LOUISVILLE 19 NESHOBA CENTRAL 21
                       October 3, 1986

This was to be a battle of the district unbeaten. However, NCHS was upset by Quitman the previous week and now everything was up in the air. "Their (Neshoba) loss put them in a must-win situation so we expect them to be very fired up for the game. This game will mean a lot to both sides so we are going to work extra hard this week to get ourselves back on top". The Union Appeal picked the Cats 15-13.

The home team scored on a 46-yard Greg Fulton pass to Derrick Hoskins and Chad Young conversion to take a 7-0 lead but Louisville responded with a 1-yard Triplett dive. The PAT failed. Another NCHS score via Fulton's 6-yarder and Young PAT was followed in the 3rd quarter by Baker's 26-yard pass to Smith. Again, the conversion failed. Another Rocket touchdown in the finale by way of Jimmy Marlowe's 3-yarder put them ahead again but the Cats cut it to a two-point deficit with a 1-yard Baker run and the two-pointer. Defense tightened and scoring was over.

Of the 225 Cat yards, 165 came on Baker throws. "We just got behind and couldn't seem to catch up. Every time we scored, we were still one-point behind. Neshoba has a very good team and they played extremely hard against us. We can still win our district and make the playoffs by beating Quitman by three or more points".

GAME 6:   LOUISVILLE (3-2) vs LEE HIGH (2-3)
                       LOUISVILLE 23 LEE HIGH 7
                       October 10, 1986: HOMECOMING

Most of homecoming week practices allowed some of the more injured to heal and prepare for the Columbus visitors. The Generals held only two victories over Louisville since play resumed in 1972.

A quick safety on Lee was followed by Baker's 15-yarder to Clark to make it 9-0. Baker later crossed from a yard and hit Clark from 30 yards. Three Humphrey conversions added to their total. Lee had a lone touchdown in the contest from Ronnie Richardson's 25-yarder to Willie Williams and Richardson PAT. Baker threw for 121 yards while Triplett rushed for 126 more. Clark was Player of the Week.

GAME 7:   LOUISVILLE (4-2) vs QUITMAN (4-1)
                       LOUISVILLE 13 QUITMAN 0
                       October 17, 1986

Different sources put the margin at either two, three or four points needed as a margin of victory. Regardless, the Cats had to impress against the team picked third in 4-AAAA. "It all comes down to this game for us. If they win, they go to the playoffs. We are playing better. Last week our offense looked better and our kicking game was good. Our defense is playing better, too".

Another opening safety, this on the Quitman punter, quickly put the Cats up 2-0. That small lead held until the 3rd quarter when Triplett found paydirt from eight yards and Humphrey hit Thames for the two-pointer. Finally, in the last frame, Humphrey nailed a 36-yard FG. "The FG was a very important play. We had to win by four points to stay alive in the district and that left us in the position that Quitman would have to score twice to cut our lead..."

Watts led tacklers with eight solo while Thames (2) and Cedric Wooten (1) added interceptions. The Cats held Quitman to 72 passing and 67 rushing yards while putting up 302 themselves. Baker threw for 125 yards and Triplett rushed for 135 yards. *"We were in a must-win situation and our players came through. We played the best we've played so far and I think we're back on track now"*.

Now it was up to the Quitman and Noxubee County game to determine the district champs. A Quitman win gave it to Louisville while a loss gave it to Neshoba Central.

GAME 8:   LOUISVILLE (5-2) @ TUPELO (6-1)
                      LOUISVILLE 28 TUPELO 7
                      October 24, 1986

Despite the non-conference match, it would not be an easy one in Lee County. Tupelo was 8-6 over Louisville since 1972 and suffered their only loss to powerful West Point. Nevertheless, they were fourth in the Super 10 poll. *"We have a very formidable opponent in Tupelo this week. The series has grown into quite a rivalry and it will be their homecoming"*.

The Cats held a 12-0 halftime lead with touchdowns in each of the first two quarters. Baker was first from 19 yards while Triplett added a 6-yarder. They doubled that lead in the 3rd quarter on a 10-yard Baker run, a 2-yard Triplett run, and a two-point pass from Baker to Thames. The last Wildcat tally came via a safety while Tupelo managed only a 5-yard Chauncey Godwin pass to Dennis Presley. Lockhart added their PAT.

Louisville had 196 rushing yards with Baker counting for 100 of those. Triplett had another 83 yards. Baker also threw for 109 yards on a 5-15 night. Thames, Watt and Triplett picked off Wave passes and Todd Fulcher, Shawn White and Ced Baker recovered fumbles. Baker was voted one of The Clarion-Ledger Players of the Week.

"We played as well as we have all year against them. We start eight or sometimes nine sophomores and juniors on defense and they're really beginning to assert themselves. We're playing well right now in all phases of the game."

GAME 9:   LOUISVILLE (6-2) vs WEST POINT (7-2)
                      LOUISVILLE 9 WEST POINT 32
                      November 7, 1986

The win pushed the Cats back into a high spot in Clarion-Ledger/JDN polling. They now found themselves seventh in the state and used their off-week to heal. *"These kids deserve a little time off. We had to give up some blood. We got away from being tough. We're back in the saddle. We didn't panic."*

Now they took on, perhaps, their most powerful opponent of the season. Their only losses were to a Tuscaloosa, AL team and Amory High. *"They have a solid team. We're playing good football right now and we expect a real battle"*.

According to The Clarion-Ledger, the Cats held a 3-0 lead going into the 2nd quarter thanks to a 32-yard Humphrey FG. However, West Point reeled off 13 unanswered points before halftime on a 32-yard Randle run, Taylor PAT, and a 12-yard Grady McCluskey run. They added more in the 3rd quarter on McCluskey's 95-yard hookup with Fred Ward and his 15-yard dash. Their final came on Williams' 15-yarder and Taylor kick. The Cats managed only a 12-yard Baker pass to Triplett.

The good news was that things worked as hoped to give Louisville the district title. *"Our goal at the beginning of the year was to defend our state championship..."*

GAME 10:   LOUISVILLE (6-3) vs WEST POINT (8-2)
                      LOUISVILLE 15 WEST POINT 13
                      November 14, 1986

Said Justice on game week, *"The playoffs are like a new season. We have been inconsistent this year but we have only 11 seniors... We attribute our inconsistency to youth and inexperience but we have still played extremely well at times. West Point has a very good team. We played very poorly against them (the previous week) and we are glad that we have the opportunity to redeem ourselves"*.

It was a completely different story when it mattered. Louisville opened the game with a 1-yard Baker run to cap a 40-yard march and Humphrey added the PAT. In the 2nd quarter, West Point evened it on a 3-yard Williams run and Taylor's kick. That score held throughout the remainder of regulation. Louisville had a chance to take the win late but fumbled it away at the 7-yard line.

Louisville was first to act and scored on a 10-yard Baker pass to Thames. They faked the PAT and Humphrey hit Thames for the two-pointer. Ward pulled in a 10-yard Grady McCluskey toss but their effort to even it failed. The Cats rushed for 207 yards and passed for 102 more. Triplett broke the 1,000-yard mark with his 145 yards but it was Thames voted Player of the Week.

"We didn't play well against them before but we completely turned that around Friday. We ran the ball well and kept their offense in check throughout the game".

GAME 11:   LOUISVILLE (7-3) @ OLIVE BRANCH (10-1)
                     LOUISVILLE 24 OLIVE BRANCH 8
                     November 21, 1986

These two met in this same situation in 1985 with the Cats taking the 20-7 victory. Now, they traveled to take them on again in a repeat match. It would not be easy as the 'Dores had a lone loss. *"They will be a very big, physical team. This is a big challenge for our players and we feel that we can rise to the occasion and play up to our capabilities".*

The Cats led 10-0 at half thanks to a 19-yard Baker run and Humphrey PAT in the 1st quarter. In the next, Humphrey hit a 28-yard FG. Olive Branch had a chance to cut into the lead but missed a FG. Ced Baker opened the 3rd with an interception but Rod Baker threw an interception on the next play. However, Stacy Jimmerson immediately recovered a fumble to set up a Humphrey 23-yard FG attempt. Unfortunately, it was unsuccessful

Not done, the Cats then drove 63 yards with Baker and Clark hooking up from 24 yards. Humphrey made it 17-0. In the final stanza, a Humphrey interception led to a 33-yard march with Baker running from the 2-yard line and Humphrey converting. Donnie Sappington put the Conquistadores on the board late with an 11-yard strike to Kenny Woods and the same two adding the two points.

Louisville rushed for 221 yards with Triplett getting 156 of those. For that, he was voted Player of the Week. *"They were the biggest team we played and we knew that we would have to neutralize their outstanding linemen to be successful, and we did that. Both our offensive linemen and defensive front deserves a lot of credit".*

GAME 12:   LOUISVILLE (8-3) vs SOUTH PIKE (10-1)
                     LOUISVILLE 12 SOUTH PIKE 7
                     November 28, 1986: Robinson Hale Stadium; Clinton, MS

This marked the first meeting between the clubs and it was for all they had worked to achieve this season. *"They are extremely quick and have as good a defense as I've seen in the 4-A league. They've had a great year and should be commended for a 10-1 record after playing such a tough schedule".* Added South Pike Coach Gregory Wall, *"We are the underdog. But we like that. We've been it all year long".* The Hattiesburg American picked Louisville 28-20, noting that it *"could be the game of the year".*

South Pike took advantage of a *"kicking miscue"* in the opening frame in rain when Sidney Felder blocked a Cat punt. Chris James took the loose ball 20 yards to paydirt and Chris Taylor put the contest 7-0. Midway through the 3rd quarter, Louisville drove 56 yards and punched in on a 1-yard Baker sneak to make it 7-6. In the finale, Baker found Smith *"all alone down the left sideline behind the South Pike secondary".* He raced the last 35 yards of 59 yards to the end zone for the game winner.

Louisville had 200 yards of offense. Triplett rushed for 108 yards to finish at 1,335. The defense held South Pike to just 10 passing and 94 rushing yards. Baker threw for 140 yards. Thames earned the Player of the Week. *"It's very, very hard to hold us scoreless. We have a tremendous amount of ability in our skill positions. We're going to break one sooner or later. You know, it would have been easy for them to hang it up, complain, think of excuses and just give up. But they didn't and that's a credit to them".*

All-County honors went to Rod Baker, Sean Oakley, Anthony Thames and Johnny Triplett. All-State awards included First Team members Thames and Oakley while Second Team included Baker and Lee Brown. Thames was also the Player of the Year by the Mississippi Sportswriters Association.

1987 (9-4)

Confidence was high in Louisville as Mike Justice's Wildcats, two-time defending 4A State Champions, returned 36 letter winners and 15 starters. Voters felt the same and voted them first in 4A, second in The Super 10, and fourth in the AP Top 10.

"We have a good-looking football team. We are extremely big and we have some really talented people. We have the caliber of team to win it all again. We have a lot to live up to. Being two-time defending state champs and having the tradition that these young men have puts a little added pressure on our players but we like it like that. We accept the challenge".

This marked the first year since 1972 with no Lee High on the schedule.

GAME 1:   LOUISVILLE (0-0) vs CALDWELL (0-0)
                   LOUISVILLE 27 CALDWELL 6
                   September 4, 1987

These two teams opened the season against one another since 1976. In the end, the Cats were dominant over their Columbus rivals. Lavon Humphrey opened the game with a 10-yard strike to Antonio Smith and a later 12-yarder. Two Michael Frazier PATs ended the 1st quarter 14-0.

Each scored in the 2nd quarter. Caldwell found paydirt on a 4-yard Don DeLoach (or James Moore) run while Lee Earl Jackson got in from the same distance for Louisville. Frazier made intermission 21-6. The Cats added their last in the final frame when Cody Boyd escaped from ten yards for the dagger. Jackson, Player of the Week, rushed for 189 of the 294 Cat ground yards. The defense held Caldwell to 86 rushing and 35 passing yards. Frazier had a pickoff and Todd Fulcher recovered a loose football.

"We had a real good effort. This was probably our best opening night effort ever. We played well on both sides of the football but had especially good effort defensively. We have a good team. This group is big and physical and they have terrific attitudes. We expect them to turn in a very successful year".

GAME 2:   LOUISVILLE (1-0) vs TUPELO (1-0)
                   LOUISVILLE 0 TUPELO 21
                   September 11, 1987

The non-conference power Wave opened with an impressive win over Amory. That caused Justice to say, "Tupelo is evidently better than what many people thought they'd be. We expect a really exciting game". Tupelo held a slight edge in all-time games but the Cats took home victories in the last three meetings.

Tupelo QB Todd Jordan took command of the game with pinpoint scoring passes to three different receivers. They notched a pair of tallies in the 2nd quarter on a 47-yarder to Russell Copeland and an 18-yarder to Jeffery Shoemaker. Their last, along with three Henry Daniels kicks, went 8 yards to Kevin Brooks (or Copeland). Jordan threw for 201 yards while rushers added 52 more. The Cats had 62 rushing and 68 passing yards.

"Tupelo had a good football team and they played extremely well. We seemed to struggle to get the ball all night and Todd Jordan just picked us apart. We'll be back. We had beaten Tupelo three consecutive times and it's just hard to dominate a team of that caliber. We've just got to get going and I'm confident that we will".

GAME 3:   LOUISVILLE (1-1) @ KOSCIUSKO (1-1)
                   LOUISVILLE 20 KOSCIUSKO 13
                   September 18, 1987

Long-time rival Kosy was still on the schedule despite seven consecutive losses to Louisville and 11 of the last 13 meetings. In the end, it turned in to the closest game in three years with the Cats coming out ahead only by a lone touchdown.

Jackson recorded the lone score of the rainy opening quarter via his 19-yard run to make it 6-0. The Whippets roared back before halftime with a pair of scores. Corey Fuller ran in from nine yards while Marc Woodard did the same from four yards. One Michael McCafferty kick made it 13-6, a score that held until the 4th quarter. The Whippets cut the lead to 13-12 in the finale on a 2-yard Humphrey plunge. With :56 left, Boyd dodged in from five yards and Smith pulled in a two-point conversion from Ced Baker for the come-from-behind victory.

"We are playing under a lot of pressure. We have been self-destructive in our past two games and we just need to turn the corner and get everything to fall into place. Though we didn't play our best football, I am confident that we will be alright". Jackson paced rushers with 92 yards of the 158 total. Humphrey threw for 142 yards. The defense held the Whippets to 94 rushing and 45 passing yards.

GAME 4:   LOUISVILLE (2-1) @ YAZOO CITY (1-2)
                 LOUISVILLE 43 YAZOO CITY 8
                 September 25, 1987

Louisville lost a pair of games against Yazoo City in 1954 and 1955. Now 32 years later, they met again in Yazoo County. *"They will probably play their best game against us since it's their homecoming and they will be fired up after winning last week. We expect a tough battle over there".*

Things got out of hand early as Jackson ran in from eight yards and Humphrey dashed 48 yards for touchdowns. Frazier PATs put it 14-0. They doubled the score before halftime on Jackson's 2-yarder, Humphrey's 20-yard strike to Kevin Greer, and two more kicks. YCHS found paydirt in the 3rd quarter on a 90-yard McGhee dash and his two-pointer but Louisville matched it on a 5-yard Hughes run. They added more in the last frame on a Fulcher safety and Jackson's 6-yard run.

Jackson rushed for 126 and Humphrey threw for 183 of the team's 486 total yards. Yazoo City was not unpleasant with 162 rushing and 110 passing yards. Fulcher also had a fumble recovery while Craig Eiland and Alfonzo Childress recorded interceptions.

"I was pleased with our effort. We were better mentally prepared and showed more intensity that we have all year. Yazoo City is in a rebuilding year and I think they were just over their heads a little against us. We were ready to play and we executed well in all areas of the game. I was especially pleased with the play of our younger players".

GAME 5:   LOUISVILLE (3-1) vs STARKVILLE (4-0)
                 LOUISVILLE 21 STARKVILLE 26
                 October 2, 1987

Everyone knew that this non-conference game would be as tough, or tougher, than the Tupelo tilt. The Yellow Jackets were 5-1-1 against Louisville since 1980 and undefeated coming into the contest. Yet, it was tighter than expected at Hinze Stadium.

Starkville opened with a Ricky Gandy 87-yard fumble return for the score to make it 6-0. Before the quarter ended, Louisville countered with a 61-yard Humphrey and Smith connection and Frazier gave the Cats a 7-6 lead. In the 2nd quarter, Louisville increased the advantage with a 66-yard march and 24-yard Humphrey and Smith TD. Frazier made it 14-6, but with :49 left before halftime, either Myron Miller or Troy Nelson shot in from 18 yards to put it 14-12.

The Jackets opened the 3rd quarter with a 1-yard Miller run and his two-pointer to Steve VanLandingham. Back came the Cats with a 60-yard Humphrey pass to Greer and Frazier made it 21-20. Late in the contest, Starkville marched 91 yards and ended things on Miller's 35-yard pass to Nelson. Antonio Smith was Player of the Week for his 185 yards receiving.

"It was a real heartbreaker. It was very unfortunate for our players who had played so well. We played well enough to win and had a great effort but we lost to a good team. This is probably one of Starkville's better teams in recent years. Our players wanted that one... Still, all our district games are still ahead of us and that is what really counts".

GAME 6:   LOUISVILLE (3-2) @ NOXUBEE COUNTY (0-5)
                 LOUISVILLE 34 NOXUBEE COUNTY 0
                 October 9, 1987

A winless Noxubee County team was just the medicine needed for the Wildcats to get back on the winning track. Furthermore, they won only one time (1982) over the Cats in the last nine meetings.

The Wildcats poured it on in the opening frame with a 28-yard Humphrey pass to Tony Grady, a 25-yard Boyd run and Humphrey's 55-yard hookup with Anthony Clark. Two Frazier kicks made it 20-0. They added one more before halftime on a 5-yard Jackson run and Frazier kick. Body added the last in the 3rd quarter with his 5-yard effort and Frazier kick. Humphrey had 112 passing yards while Boyd led rushers with 72 yards.

"We had a good game. We put them away quickly and then let our reserves play. We're playing well right now and we're getting ready to try to defend our state championship. We have been getting good production from both our ground game and our passing attack".

GAME 7:   LOUISVILLE (4-2) @ QUITMAN (1-4)
                                LOUISVILLE 41 QUITMAN 0
                                October 16, 1987

The previous win moved the Wildcats back into the Top 20 at tenth place. Now the Cats journeyed to Quitman to face a team that always played them hard. *"We expect Quitman to play us hard. They always play well at their place so we are preparing for a real battle. We need to keep our momentum going for the division games so this week's game is very important to us. We're gearing up to make another run at a state title".*

Miscues by the Quitman team led to easy tallies by the visitors. Humphrey ran in from a yard, hit Greer from 33 yards, Grady from 13 yards, and Frazier made it a quick 21-0. They added another in the 2nd quarter on Jackson's 1-yarder and Frazier kick. The last two scores came in the second half via a Humphrey pass to Smith (10) and a Frazier surprise to Smith from 5 yards. One PAT meant the end of scoring.

Humphrey threw for 155 yards while Boyd rushed for 57 more. In all, Louisville led in yardage 287 to 69. Greer and Eric Triplett had interceptions while Frazier and Stacy Jimmerson recovered fumbles. *"We executed as well as we have all year. We scored the first three times we had the ball and played just about as well as we could. These past two games should be a boost for us heading into the crucial part of our schedule".*

GAME 8:   LOUISVILLE (5-2) vs NORTHWEST RANKIN (5-2)
                                LOUISVILLE 18 NORTHWEST RANKIN 20
                                October 23, 1987: HOMECOMING

It was homecoming week in Winston County against a first-time district opponent from the Jackson area. *"We're really looking forward to Homecoming this week. This is a very important district game and we feel that we have some momentum and are ready to defend our state championship".*

Midway through the opening frame, Kevin McGee romped in from six yards and Brett Eads added the PAT. Back came the Cats with a 4-yard Boyd run to cut it to 7-6. Louisville took the lead in the 3rd quarter on Humphrey's 3-yarder to make it 12-7. Back came the Cougars on Charlie Hill's 15-yard option run to put it 13-12. The Cats responded in the finale with a 74-yard drive ending on an 11-yard Humphrey run. However, Northwest punched back with McGee's 19-yard pass to Darnell Folsom.

NWR led in first downs 14-12 while Louisville held the ground 192-96. Jackson rushed for 100 yards and Humphries threw for 62 more. The Cougars threw for 168 yards. Said Northwest Rankin coach Don Hinton, *"No question about it. This is the biggest win we've ever had. This is the highest ranked team we've ever played".*

Said Justice, *"We simply could not stop them defensively. They had a great game plan and converted nine third down situations. I didn't think we played poorly. They just sustained their drives with a well-executed offensive effort. Our playoff hopes are now (on the Northwest Rankin and Neshoba Central game). We can get in by winning our last two provided we beat Neshoba by more than two points".*

GAME 9:   LOUISVILLE (5-3) vs NESHOBA CENTRAL (6-2)
                                LOUISVILLE 17 NESHOBA CENTRAL 14
                                October 30, 1987

While other teams may have been more powerful, this one meant all hopes for the Wildcat football team this season. *"To say that (this) is a big one would be a gross understatement. All our hopes of defending our state title depend on our winning this game. I think we will be ready and we know that Neshoba will be fired up, too. It should be another great game between two good football teams".*

The Union Appeal picked Neshoba 20-14. *"Really taking a stab here, with Neshoba playing on the road, but I like the Rockets by six".*

An early loose Wildcat ball was recovered by the Rockets and led to a 12-yard Tyrone Rush run and Chad Young PAT. Frazier cut into the advantage before the end of the frame with his 29-yard FG; a kick that would be meaningful when the game ended. As the 2nd quarter ended, Derrick Hoskins pulled in a 10-yard pass from Tony Holmes and Young made halftime 14-3.

The Cats responded in the 3rd quarter with a 92-yard drive ending on a 3-yard Humphrey run. Now in the final frame and still behind, Louisville went 56 yards with Humphrey diving in from a yard and then hitting Smith for the two-pointer. Louisville led in first downs (13-9) while Boyd paced rushers with 51 of the Wildcats' 95 yards. Humphrey, Player of the Week, threw for 138 yards with an interception. Neshoba ran for only 47 yards.

"We won the game we had to win by the margin we had to win it. The Jim Hill game is now the biggest game of the year for us".

GAME 10:   LOUISVILLE (6-3) @ JIM HILL (3-6)
                                     LOUISVILLE 33 JIM HILL 0
                                     November 6, 1987

Playoff hopes were on the line against first-time opponent and Jackson-area Jim Hill. Playoff rules changed to the top two teams and this would mean a guarantee of post-season play. *"Our playoff hopes are riding on this game and we are expecting another great effort from our players".*

Louisville established dominance with a 1st quarter 10-yard Jackson run, a 2nd quarter Humphrey 5-yarder and 50-yarder to Greer, and a pair of Frazier kicks. They added seven more points in the 3rd quarter on Humphrey's 7-yard pass to Clark and Frazier kick. In the finale, they wrapped it up with a 3-yard Humphrey run.

Louisville led in yardage 346-107. Humphrey threw for 160 while Boyd carried for 84 yards. *"We played real well and we have begun to play much better in our last two outings. With the playoffs underway, we are hoping that we are getting ready to peak at the right time".*

GAME 11:   LOUISVILLE (7-3) @ CLEVELAND (6-3)
                                     LOUISVILLE 35 CLEVELAND 6
                                   November 13, 1987

This marked the third meeting between the teams with Louisville having never lost. Those victories came in 1952, 1953, and 1984. Nevertheless, this was a new season and it was *"one and done"* if they wanted to retain their rights as champions. *"We know that Cleveland is a great passing team. From here on, there are only good teams remaining and we know that Cleveland will be a real challenge for us".*

Once again, the Cats came to play and jumped out to a 7-0 lead after a quarter thanks for a 1-yard Humphrey run and the first of five Frazier kicks. They notched another 14 points before halftime on a 63-yard Humphrey pass to Greer and a 34-yard Fulcher pick-six. Seven more points came in the 3rd quarter on Humphrey's 44-yarder to Smith while Boyd added their last in the final frame. Cleveland avoided the shutout late on a 27-yard Dwight Cox run.

The Wildcats rushed for 160 (or 147) and passed for 192 (or 177) yards. Boyd led rushers with 103 (or 89). Cleveland passed for 192 yards but suffered interceptions to Greer, Fulcher and Craig Eiland. *"We were ready to play. Our team was well-prepared and we had a very sound effort on both sides of the football".*

GAME 12:   LOUISVILLE (8-3) vs OLIVE BRANCH (11-0)
                                     LOUISVILLE 21 OLIVE BRANCH 7
                                   November 20, 1987

While Louisville was 2-0 against Olive Branch in the past two seasons, this edition of the Conquistadores sat undefeated. Said Justice, *"This is the best team we've seen in a while. Their speed is awesome and they average about 35 points per game".*

Olive Branch had the only score of the first half in the 2nd quarter when Kenny Woods ran in from five yards and Gary Sullivan converted. However, the Cats were determined to take control in the next half. First, they went 90 yards with Humphrey finding the stripe from six yards and Frazier kicking his first of three extra points. Then, they moved 95 yards with Humphry and Smith hooking up from seven yards. In the last frame,

Boyd capped a 54-yard drive from two yards to send the Wildcats to the North State title game.

"We played an inspired second half. They had an exceptionally good team but our players went out and did what it takes to win. I'm very proud of them". Both Jackson (136 rushing) and Boyd (114 rushing) were named Players of the Week.

GAME 13:   LOUISVILLE (9-3) @ WEST POINT (9-2)
                              LOUISVILLE 12 WEST POINT 29
                              November 27, 1987

It seemed as if long-time opponent West Point always provided the obstacle to Wildcat hopes. This year would be no different. Though they did not have the same record as Olive Branch, everyone knew this one was not going to be easy. *"We know we will have a very tough battle up there. They will be fired up and are hungry for a state title, but so are we. It should be a classic matchup between two good teams"*.

Louisville took a 3-0 lead after a quarter on a 26-yard Frazier FG. Then, Dexter Jackson recorded a 29-yard pick-six and Frazier put the Cats up 10-0. They actually made it 12-0 shortly thereafter when Walter Graham sacked Grady McCluskey for a safety. After that, West Point strengthened and kept Louisville out of the end zone.

A fumble led to a 3-yard Danny Sherrod run and Shaun Taylor PAT. Now in the final frame with Louisville ahead 12-7, West Point went on a scoring barrage. Fred Ward pulled in a 16-yard McCluskey pass and Sherrod ran in for the two points. Darick Moore added a 30-yard pick-six and Treddis Anderson escaped from 46 yards. Taylor added both of the extra points.

Four interceptions and two fumbles led to the demise. Louisville led in first downs (9-8) but West Point held the ground (72-66) and the air (67-34). The Winston County Journal gave the Cats credit for 146 offensive yards with 104 rushing.

"We had a real good effort. We had a good year from a real good group of players who worked very hard. We are proud of our 21 seniors who posted a record of 30-9 for three years and we will remember them as a great group of people. We defended our title a long way. We are not going to let this last game ruin our year. We worked hard and reached many of our goals. I'm really proud of our players and we appreciate the great support we had throughout the year".

All-County honors went to Antonio Smith, Lavon Humphrey, Shaun White, Stacy Jimmerson, Steven Yarbrough, Rodney Cistrunk, Todd Fulcher and Anthony Clark. Honorable Mentions included Cody Boyd, Walter Graham, Larando Metts and Dexter Jackson. White, Jimmerson and Smith earned All-Stars. All-State went to Brown and Smith.

Internal awards went to Boyd (Christian Athlete), Jackson (Best Offensive Back), Jackson (Best Defensive Back), Paul Mitchell (Best Offensive Lineman), Lee Brown (Best Defensive Lineman), Jimmerson (Scholastic), Kevin Greer (Most Improved), Water Graham (MVP), Humphrey (Leadership), Ced Baker and Michael Frazier (Offensive Play of the Year), Smith (Defensive Player of the Year), and White (Senior Award).

West Point beat South Jones 35-7 for the 4A title.

1988 (11-2)

Fifth-year mentor Mike Justice started practices in mid-August with 26 letter winners back including 11 starters and 82 candidates for spots in Wildcat uniforms. One, Lee Brown, earned a preseason Super Prep All-American nomination. As such, Justice again expected a great team with aspirations of 4A title honors.

"We have a good football team. We will be a contender for state honors without a doubt, despite a very demanding schedule. Our division is the toughest 4A league in our state. Two of our four teams are in the top five and (the others) are strong as well. We have lots of experience and the most team speed we have ever had. Though we are not as big overall as we have been, we do have some big people in key positions".

GAME 1:   LOUISVILLE (0-0) @ CALDWELL (0-0)
                              LOUISVILLE 34 CALDWELL 0
                              September 2, 1988

Once again, the Wildcats opened with the Columbus team that struggled to come away with a victory. This one would not help their cause. At Saunders Field, the Cats poured it on the Bobcats.

Willie Love opened with a fumble recovery but it went nowhere. Later, they blocked a punt to allow Lee Earl Jackson an 11-yard TD scamper. On the kickoff, Andrew Payton recovered a fumble and one play later Ced Baker found Tony Grady from 33 yards. In the next frame, Baker capped a 46-yard drive with a 22-yard toss to Scott Reed. With a flag on the play, Caldwell then picked off a pass to kill the threat.

A fine defensive effort forced a punt and Terry Hughes took it 65 yards to paydirt to make intermission 18-0. Bernard Ball opened the second half with an interception. Just plays later, the Cats scored again and converted the two-pointer. Myron Moore found another loose ball, but again, to no avail. In the finale, Andre Hayes ran in from two yards and Jeffery Hawthorne added the 34-0 PAT.

Said Coach Randy Martin, "*You cannot make mistakes against a team like Louisville and win*". Added Justice, "*Caldwell has a spunky football team*".

GAME 2:　　　　　　　　LOUISVILLE (1-0) @ TUPELO (1-0)
　　　　　　　　　　　　LOUISVILLE 0 TUPELO 28
　　　　　　　　　　　　September 9, 1988

Much like the previous season, the Wildcats now faced the powerful Tupelo squad in their second game of the season. The previous year, Louisville went down 21-0 after coming off two consecutive 4A titles. This one looked eerily similar.

An opening Cat fumble led to a 1-yard Harold Roby run for the touchdown and the first of four Henry Daniels kicks. A Craig Eiland interception of a Wave pass was for naught. Louisville tried a 2nd quarter FG but was unsuccessful. However, Todd Jordan found Russell Copeland from six yards to cap an 80-yard march for another touchdown to put halftime 14-0.

In the 3rd quarter, Robert Allen dove in from a yard to increase the advantage. They added the dagger in the last frame on an 8-yard Scott McCoy reception. Tupelo led in first downs (16-11), rushing (149-90) and passing (146-105).

GAME 3:　　　　　　　　LOUISVILLE (1-1) vs KOSCIUSKO (2-0)
　　　　　　　　　　　　LOUISVILLE 39 KOSCIUSKO 0
　　　　　　　　　　　　September 16, 1988

After two road contests, long-time rival Kosy was next at Hinze Stadium. It did not take much time before Baker found the end zone from five yards to make it 6-0. They added three more tallies before the quarter ended. Baker hit Grady from 41 yards, Greer from 38 yards and then ran in another from five yards. They also converted a two-pointer on Baker's pass to Scott Reed.

The 26-0 score stayed that way until the 3rd quarter when Jackson dodged in from a yard. Hughes followed in the final quarter with a 12-yard run and Frazier notched the last point. Both Eiland and Keith Dailey recorded interceptions. The Cats put up 464 offensive yards with Jackson rushing for 207 of their 229 yards.

"*We were embarrassed last week. But we've got a real good football team here. We just wanted to come out in our first home game and show that we can play well, and we did*".

GAME 4:　　　　　　　　LOUISVILLE (2-1) vs YAZOO CITY (1-2)
　　　　　　　　　　　　LOUISVILLE 38 YAZOO CITY 0
　　　　　　　　　　　　September 23, 1988

This, the second meeting in two years, was never close. Terry Hughes had the 1st quarter score from 12 yards and Frazier converted his first of four extra points. Two more touchdowns came back for Louisville, but they still added 21 more points before halftime. Baker and Greer hooked up from 14 yards, a recovered fumble led to a 16-yard TD from Jackson, and Baker found Reed from 25 yards.

Up 28-0, they added more scores. First was a 3rd quarter 20-yard Jackson scoring run after a Cat pickoff. They wrapped it up in the last frame after a Bruce Smith interception with Chris Peterson's 32-yard FG.

GAME 5:   LOUISVILLE (3-1) @ STARKVILLE (2-2)
                  LOUISVILLE 24 STARKVILLE 7
                  September 30, 1988

The Yellow Jackets were easily the longest consecutive opponent for Louisville with games going back to at least 1940 and some before. The three-straight wins over the Cats made this one uncertain, but it was Louisville taking control.

A long opening Wildcat drive got only to the Jacket 3 before failing. However, Frazier recorded a sack safety for the two points. Starkville picked off an ensuing Cat throw but could not make it count. Louisville came back with Baker's 54-yard dash to paydirt and Frazier converted. Starkville cut it to 9-7 before the frame ended on a 6-yard John Rice carry and Adam Teater PAT.

Now in the 3rd quarter, Louisville took a fumble and turned it into an eventual tally on Baker's 1-yard dive. Amazingly, Dewey Lee followed that with another safety by recovering a fumble in the end zone. In the final quarter, Baker and Greer hooked up from 30 yards and Frazier iced it with the kick.

GAME 6:   LOUISVILLE (4-1) vs NOXUBEE COUNTY (0-5)
                  LOUISVILLE 42 NOXUBEE COUNTY 12
                  October 7, 1988: HOMECOMING

After five consecutive victories over Noxubee, and with their winless record and now at Hinze Stadium, hopes were high. The Wildcats did not disappoint old alums for the Homecoming affair.

They put up four touchdowns in the opening quarter on a 29-yard Jackson dash, a 1-yard Hughes run and Baker's two-pointer to Greer, and two more Hughes runs of 11 and 4 yards. Frazier converted on the last two.

Noxubee had the only tally of the 2nd quarter when Davis got in from four yards to make halftime 28-6. Louisville padded the lead in the 3rd quarter with a 38-yard Hughes run and a 7-yarder by Baker. Frazier connected for one PAT and Peterson the other. Noxubee ended scoring in the 4th quarter on an 85-yard Riley run.

Jackson led rushers with 16- yards while Hughes added another 104. Baker threw for 184 yards with one interception and Jackson pulled in 93 yards of receiving. The defense held the visitors to a (-13) rushing total and 149 passing with three interceptions.

GAME 7:   LOUISVILLE (5-1) vs QUITMAN (2-4)
                  LOUISVILLE 41 QUITMAN 0
                  November 14, 1988

Louisville was 8-3-1 against Quitman since 1965 but this one was never in doubt. Baker opened the game with a 2-yarder while Jackson ran in from the same yardage after. Both Frazier kicks, and two more later, gave them a 14-0 lead. Derrick Glenn's fumble recovery in the 2nd quarter led five plays later to Jackson's 5-yard score. Before halftime, Frazier picked off a Quitman pass but the Cats eventually fumbled it back. Nevertheless, the defense held and Baker turned it into an 18-yarder. As the half neared the end, Baker hit Greer for a 61-yard touchdown to make it 35-0.

The last Cat score came in the final stanza where Peterson found daylight from three yards. Jerome Ball ended hopes of avoiding a shutout with a sack. Jonathan Johnson and John Carter intercepted Wildcat passes in the first half for Quitman.

GAME 8:   LOUISVILLE (6-1) @ NORTHWEST RANKIN (3-4)
                  LOUISVILLE 22 NORTHWEST RANKIN 12
                  October 21, 1988

The mentor at Northwest Rankin called their upset victory in 1987 their biggest win in program history. Now, it was time to pay them back in the Jackson area. Two more victories assured Louisville of the playoffs.

Baker opened the game with a 2-yarder and Frazier notched the first of a pair of extra points. Northwest Rankin's only response was a Davis FG. In the 2nd quarter, Baker rushed in from 27 yards. Again, only a Davis FG put NWR on the board before halftime. The final Cat tally came in the 3rd quarter when Hughes dashed 40 yards and Jackson added the two points. Northwest finished the game with a 40-yard Andre Newsom escape.

GAME 9:   LOUISVILLE (7-1) @ NESHOBA CENTRAL (8-1)
                          LOUISVILLE 28 NESHOBA CENTRAL 12
                          October 28, 1988

On paper, this was no easy step to assuring a title and playoff berth. The Union Appeal picked Neshoba 20-17 saying, "*Both teams are just about even in total points scored and allowed. They both have beaten common opponents. Sounds identical and evenly matched? They are. The best game of the week in our area*".

A 1st quarter punt fumble gave the home team their eventual touchdown on a Tony Holmes 23-yard dash to make it 6-0. Louisville roared back in the 2nd quarter on a 12-yard Baker run and the first of four Frazier kicks. Baker added the next from six yards while they finished with a 13-yard Baker and Greer connection for the 21-6 halftime lead.

Neshoba fumbled an early 3rd quarter punt and Jackson turned it into a 34-yard rushing TD. The last score came from Neshoba on a 6-yard Holmes toss to Dwayne Pickens. Louisville led in first downs (13-10), rushing (162-139) and passing (134-72). Both teams fumbled twice but the home team lost both compared to Louisville's one.

Said Justice, "*The intensity level was the thing for us. Two down and one to go*".

GAME 10:   LOUISVILLE (8-1) vs JIM HILL (2-7)
                          LOUISVILLE 34 JIM HILL 0
                          November 4, 1988

A two-win Jim Hill team visited Hinze Stadium in attempts to stop the seven-game winning streak by Louisville. It would not be as they hoped as the Cats took the title.

Scoring was steady as the Cats recovered an opening Hill fumble. Jackson turned it into a 2-yard touchdown and Baker's run put it 8-0. In the next frame, Baker found Grady from 22 yards to make halftime 14-0. The two hooked up to start the 3rd quarter from 18 yards while Hughes rushed in from 11 yards for the last score. Another report says that came on a Lavond Wilson reception. The two-pointer to Russ Nowell finished scoring.

GAME 11:   LOUISVILLE (9-1) vs NEW HOPE (5-5)
                          LOUISVILLE 60 NEW HOPE 20
                          November 11, 1988

First-time opponent New Hope opened the playoffs for Louisville but were highly out-classed as the Cats scored the most points since the Newton game of 1972.

It seemed different as New Hope was first on the board with a 1-yard Tommy Cribbs run and Lance Moore kick. However, Louisville was just getting started with Baker going in from two yards and Frazier converting his first of three kicks. Baker then hit Green for a 65-yard tally while New Hope kept hopes alive in the next frame with Moore's 30-yarder to Britt Glenn. Moore also added the PAT. The Wildcats went back to work with two more scores via a 2-yard Baker run and his 53-yarder to Greer. Halftime sat 27-14.

Things got worse for the visitors in the 3rd quarter as Hughes ran 65 yards for a score, Jackson added a 6-yarder and then a 15-yard dash. Baker found Grady for two more points. New Hope added their last on a 2-yard Moore run but Louisville responded with a 43-yard Hawthorne reception from Hughes. Leading the ground for the Cats were Hughes (154) and Jackson (129).

GAME 12:   LOUISVILLE (10-1) vs CLEVELAND (9-1)
                          LOUISVILLE 27 CLEVELAND 6
                          November 18, 1988

Despite meeting twice in the early 1950s, it seemed like the road to the title always ran through the Cleveland team. They never defeated the Cats in all four attempts and this would fare no better.

A long drive gave Louisville the early lead on Jackson's 3-yard effort but Cleveland came back with an answer of a 21-yard Taylor King pass to Mitchell to make it 7-6 in favor of the Cats. In the 2nd quarter, another long march ended on Baker's 8-yard pass to Jackson. Greer then picked off a pass to allow Baker an eventual 5-yarder to put it 21-6.

Now in the final frame, the defense stopped a Cleveland threat and set up a later 1-yard Baker rush for the finale. Frazier converted on three extra points. The entire defense was voted Players of the Week.

GAME 13:   LOUISVILLE (11-1) vs WEST POINT (12-1)
                LOUISVILLE 0 WEST POINT 28
                November 25, 1988

As always, West Point stood in the way of the bragging rights for the title. This year's team was different in that they outscored their two playoff opponents 83-3 in those games. Their last against Olive Branch ended 44-0. No doubt, it would be a tough road. Both lost only to top-ranked Tupelo. Much like previous years, including the previous, West Point proved too much for the one-loss Wildcats.

A Willie Love sack ended a promising West Point drive in the opening stanza, but the visitors got on the board in the 2nd quarter on a 49-yard march ending on a 3-yard Dannie Sherrod run and Shaun Taylor PAT. Three plays later, they finished the half with Brad (or Fred) Ward's 42-yard pick-six and Taylor kick to make it 14-0 despite an Eiland interception.

West Point scored in each of the last two frames. First was a 3-yard Sherrod run after a Robert Young interception, followed by his 2-yarder. Taylor was true on both kicks. West Point led in first downs (15-4), rushing (198-52) and passing (38-2). Louisville had four interceptions and lost a fumble.

Said Justice, "*Nobody in the state has been able to play with either of us in 4A the last several years. I think West Point will win it. I know we just played them and we don't want any more of them. They are a big, fine football team and whipped us on the line*". He was right as West Point went on to beat Laurel 3-0 for the state title.

1989 (8-3)

Coach Mike Justice, back for his sixth season as head coach of the Wildcats, had a lot to be excited about for the coming year. Not only were they ranked first in the district ahead of Neshoba Central, they also had other rankings pre-season. The Super 10 had the Cats 8th, 4A had them 2nd behind Laurel, and the AP Top 20 put them 7th. Not to mention that Louisville featured a Dandy Dozen winner in Alfonso Childress. With 12 returning starters and 35 letter winners, it was easy to understand by confidence was high.

Perhaps also notable was the absence of Kosciusko, a team that played Louisville consecutively since at least 1952 and many years beforehand.

GAME 1:   LOUISVILLE (0-0) vs TUPELO (0-0)
                LOUISVILLE 10 TUPELO 7
                September 1, 1989

Tupelo held a 6-3 advantage in their last nine meetings and now the Wildcats opened with the highly-ranked Wave instead of annual lid-lifting Caldwell. It would quickly tell Winston County fans how their team looked from the start. The Clarion-Ledger picked Louisville 21-14 over Tupelo despite them also having a Dandy Dozen player in Stacy Wilson.

The Cats jumped out to a 7-0 lead in the 1st quarter on a 33-yard Kendrick Coleman reception from Daralyd Hughes. Chris Peterson notched the PAT. Tupelo answered in the frame on Robert Allen's 2-yard run and a Nat Leathers kick. That score held until the final quarter as, with 2:15 on the clock, Peterson nailed a 30-yard FG.

Louisville led in first downs (17-15) while Lawrence Sangster rushed for 117 of their 266 yards. The defense held Tupelo to 211 rushing yards while they put up 88 more in the air. The Cats lost three fumbles but picked off one pass. "*Everyone expected to see two good defensive teams but they were surprised to also see two very good offensive teams. Tupelo has a very good team and they are tough. We played a tough game and I am proud of our team*".

GAME 2:   LOUISVILLE (1-0) @ ITAWAMBA AHS (0-1)
                LOUISVILLE 35 ITAWAMBA AHS 10
                September 8, 1989

The Fulton school was a first-timer on Wildcat schedules. Meanwhile, the win over Tupelo pushed Louisville to first in 4A and fifth in The Super 10 polls. It was no contest as Louisville rushed for 330 yards compared to their 124 yards under Coach Craig Cherry.

Louisville led after a quarter 14-0 and 21-0 at halftime. They added a couple of other scores while Fulton tallied their lone TD in the 3rd quarter and FG in the finale.

Sangster had the first from six yards and added the two-pointer. Hughes was next from 38 yards to make it 14-0. Midway through the 2nd quarter, Sangster dove in from a yard and Peterson notched the PAT.

The last Wildcat scores came in the 3rd quarter on a 5-yard Hughes run and Reed's 63-yard pass from Hughes. Peterson connected on both extra points. A Neil Brown fumble recovery and 52-yard return gave IAHS their initial score later (Trae Wiygul PAT) while another fumble set up Wiygul's 26-yard FG to finish it. Hughes threw for 141 yards with a pick.

GAME 3:   LOUISVILLE (2-0) vs WEST POINT (2-0)
                                    LOUISVILLE 9 WEST POINT 20
                                    September 15, 1989

Another tough contest and one against a third-ranked Super 10 team that held a 6-4 record since 1982. However, it was non-conference and the Cats seemed much better prepared for this encounter. The Clarion-Ledger picked Louisville 16-14 over the 5A team.

Louisville started strong with a 63-yard Hughes strike to Sangster to make it 6-0. In the 2nd quarter, Peterson added a 21-yard FG while West Point closed the halftime gap to 9-6 via Chris Jefferson's 33-yarder to James Walker. The visitor defense held the Cats out of the end zone after while putting up tallies in each of the last two frames. First Jefferson ran in from four yards while Dannie Sherrod added a 3-yard TD and the two-pointer to close it.

Stats vary, but The Clarion-Ledger gave credit of first downs (17-15), rushing (244-135) to West Point and 126-65 passing to Louisville. West Point's Sherrod paced all runners with 116 yards while the Cats lost three fumbles. A cryptic notation from The Hattiesburg American noted that LHS, not the MHSAA, suspended Justice afterwards "because of unsportsmanlike conduct".

GAME 4:   LOUISVILLE (2-1) vs GREENVILLE (0-3)
                                    LOUISVILLE 29 GREENVILLE 0
                                    September 22, 1989

The games in 1924 and 1944 both ended in Louisville victories. Despite the absence of Justice, it was never a game in doubt. Sangster opened with a 19-yard touchdown and Peterson the first a pair of extra points. Then, Peterson added a 24-yard FG while Coleman hauled in a 21-yard Hughes toss to make it 16-0 after a quarter.

Sangster then escaped from 85 yards on a punt return in the 2nd quarter and Scott Reed caught a 30-yarder (or 80-yarder) from Hughes. That ended scoring for the evening. Louisville held first downs (16-9).

GAME 5:   LOUISVILLE (3-1) vs STARKVILLE (1-3)
                                    LOUISVILLE 9 STARKVILLE 10
                                    September 29, 1989

In the Cats' longest-running consecutive rivalry, Hughes found paydirt from eight yards for the lone tally of the opening frame. Both tallied in the second quarter on a 23-yard Joe Macon pass to Eric Jones and Scott Denson kick for the Jackets, while Peterson added a 37-yard FG. Halftime sat a tight 9-7 in favor of Louisville. The game went scoreless until late when Denson nailed a 23-yard FG to win it. Louisville led in yardage 188-173 with Hughes rushing for 122 yards.

GAME 6:   LOUISVILLE (3-2) @ NOXUBEE COUNTY (0-5)
                                    LOUISVILLE 30 NOXUBEE COUNTY 0
                                    October 6, 1989

After posting a 2-2 record after their opening shocker against Tupelo, the Wildcats looked to get back on track. A winless Noxubee County team picked fifth preseason in the district seemed just the thing needed.

As the opening quarter ended, Sangster broke free from 47 yards and Peterson made it 7-0. They increased halftime to 17-0 when Hughes and Coleman hooked up from 20 yard, and Peterson added the PAT and a 31-yard FG. In the final frame, Sangster ran in from two yards and later threw an 8-yard pass to Reed. Peterson ended scoring with the kick.

Hughes passed for 128 yards while Sangster rushed for 70 yard and caught 55 more. Coleman led receivers with 63 yards. The defense held Noxubee County to a measly 26 offensive yards.

"*We are always glad to win a division game on the road. We did not look real good in our execution of things but sometimes the other team just won't cooperate. We are not going to allow ourselves to fall into the old standard line of 'well, we are young this year but next year we will be good'. Our program is built to operate on a high level every year, not just when the athletes are better. This is next year and we are going to play hard and get better every day*".

GAME 7:   LOUISVILLE (4-2) vs LEE HIGH (2-4)
                LOUISVILLE 41 LEE HIGH 3
                October 13, 1989: HOMECOMING

The win brought the Wildcats back to sixth in The Super 10 and first in 4A polls. Now they faced familiar Lee High who was picked third in the district preseason. "*We are looking forward to a big game against Columbus Lee. Lee will be a district game and we will also be celebrating Homecoming...*"

The only 1st quarter score came on a 15-yard Hughes and Reed connection. Lee's lone points came in the 2nd quarter on a Joe Ayema 24-yard FG but Louisville roared back before halftime. Willie Porter ran in from three yards while Hughes and Reed again connected from 15 yards. The two then added the two points to make it 20-3.

They scored 18 more in the 3rd quarter on Sangster runs of 52 and 4 yards while Hughes hit Coleman from 26 yards. With reserves on the field, the last points came on a 32-yard Peterson FG. Sangster's 203 rushing yards led the Cats to a 355-156 lead on the ground. Coleman led receivers with 76 yards. "*Reserves Charles DePriest, Jerome Ball and Eric Triplett combined for 67 yards rushing*".

GAME 8:   LOUISVILLE (5-2) @ CALDWELL (4-2-1)
                LOUISVILLE 26 CALDWELL 6
                October 20, 1989

Normally the Columbus team was the season-opener for Louisville. This season, they were fourth preseason in district picks and trying to make a strong push at Saunders Field to end the season.

Sangster opened the tilt with a 22-yard score and Peterson the PAT. Hughes then got in from two yards and Paterson made it 14-0 to end the half. Louisville notched scores in each of the last two quarters. Sangster had the first from 11 yards while Hughes wrapped it up with a 1-yarder. With just :26 left, Lee added a score for their last points.

Sangster's 226 yards were the big part of their 361 rushing total yards. Overall, the Cats led in yardage 294-191. "*We felt our team played with great intensity and strong determination. Our players know how to play a big game and this one put us in the playoffs*".

GAME 9:   LOUISVILLE (6-2) vs NESHOBA CENTRAL (3-5)
                LOUISVILLE 25 NESHOBA CENTRAL 8
                October 27, 1989

The victory over Caldwell moved Louisville to third in The Super 10. The Union Appeal picked Louisville 17-14. "*Both teams have earned playoff berths but the winner of this game will get the home field advantage to start the playoffs*". Said Justice, "*This game will determine first and second place in our division. We are supposed to have great weather and we really need support from our fans*".

The Cats opened the 2nd quarter on a 3-yard Hughes run and Peterson PAT, but Neshoba answered on a 51-yard Jerry Welch run and his two-point conversion to take the 8-6 advantage. However, as the half ended, Sangster "*unleashed a 51-yard bomb to hit Scott Reed in full stride*" to make it 13-8.

The last scores came in the 4th quarter. Derrick Glenn's interception led to Sangster's 34-yard scoring dash while Keith Dailey added a 29-yard pick-six. The Cats led in first downs 18-3 while the defense created the pair of interceptions. Louisville held Neshoba to just 97 total offensive yards while compiling 366 yards (200 via the air).

GAME 10:   LOUISVILLE (7-2) @ JEFFERSON COUNTY (UNREPORTED)
                              LOUISVILLE 28 JEFFERSON COUNTY 14
                              November 3, 1989

A report from the November 8 Winston County Journal noted that Louisville went to Jefferson County during their off-week and won 28-14. Scores reportedly came from Hughes on a 9-yarder and the first of three Peterson PATs, a Dewey Lee 4-yard effort and a Sangster 14-yarder to make it 21-6 at halftime. Sangster ran in from 89 yards for their last while Jefferson County added a QB sneak at the end. Louisville led in yardage 450-37.

GAME 11:   LOUISVILLE (8-2) vs CLEVELAND (6-4)
                              LOUISVILLE 24 CLEVELAND 14
                              November 10, 1989

It seemed the road to a title ran through a Cleveland squad despite their meeting five times overall. Now they visited Hinze Stadium to see if history would change. It looked good for them after a frame as a 55-yard Alvin Vence run and John Easley PAT gave them the 7-0 lead. However, Louisville came back to make halftime 14-7. A punt snap recovered by Keefer Triplett set up a 6-yard Sangster tally and a later 3-yarder. Both Peterson kicks were true.

Now in the 4th quarter, Peterson nailed a 36-yard FG to answer a 58-yard Payne run and Easley PAT. Sangster wrapped it up with a 33-yarder and Peterson kick to finish the contest and move the Wildcats to the next step.

GAME 12:   LOUISVILLE (9-2) @ OXFORD (10-2)
                              LOUISVILLE 13 OXFORD 15
                              November 17, 1989

In order to go further, the Wildcats now had to travel to Lafayette County to face a team they defeated in all five of their previous contests between 1976 and 1980. It would not be easy as Oxford was 10-2 on the season and playing at home.

They opened with a long kick return to set up a seven-play march and 22-yard Rontae Bass run. To make it worse, they blocked a Cat punt and Mike Stark took it 64 yards to paydirt to make it 12-0. Before the 1st quarter ended, Louisville drove 70 yards with Sangster adding the last three yards and adding the extra point. Neither scored in the next quarter to keep halftime 12-7.

Louisville took the lead in the 3rd quarter on a 62-yard sequence with Sangster getting across the stripe from five yards. It looked as if the 13-12 lead would hold as there was only 1:46 remaining. However, Joey Verlangieri hit a 35-yard FG to seal the playoff win. That kick *"hit the upright and fell through"*. The Cats had a desperation attempt to win with a FG but Stark blocked it to ice the game and season.

"We felt like we accomplished a great deal this season. We are trying to convince our players that we had a very good year. After winning state championships in 1985 and 1986, our players are only satisfied with a state championship. Our 9-3 record, along with our sixth straight district championship highlights a good year. Although we do not want to lose sight of our ultimate goal, a state championship".

Lawrence Sangster earned Offensive Player of the Year in district play while Justice got Coach of the Year. Other honorees included Roger Caperton, Keith Smith, Daryald Hughes, and Scott Reed. On the defense, they included Myron Moore, Keith Dailey, David Coleman, Derrick Glenn and Dewey Lee. Honorable Mentions went to Chris Peterson, Kendrick Coleman, Bernard Ball, Yancy Burn and Bruce Smith.

Internal awards went to Moore (MVP), Hughes (Best Offensive Back), Reed (Big Play), Caperton (Best Offensive Lineman), Coleman (Best Defensive Lineman), Dailey (Best Defensive Player) and Sangster (Best Offensive Player). Keefer Triplett (Christian Athlete), Derrick Glenn (Leadership), Keith Smith (Coaches Award), Russ Nowell (3D Award), Donnie Laine (Best Blocker) and Coleman (Most Improved) also took home awards. Permanent Captains were Moore and Reed.

1990–1999

1990 (7-4)

The departure of six-year head coach Mike Justice to Madison Ridgeland opened the door for Bobby Hall. He reportedly had 17 seniors, 18 juniors and 25 sophomores to make up his Wildcat squad. Voters had them second to Neshoba Central in 2-4A but first in overall 4A and sixth in the AP Prep Poll.

"Basically, we're new. I didn't get to practice with the boys through spring. We're at the stage we would normally have our team the third week of spring practice. These kids have good attitudes and they've worked real well. I'm pleased with that aspect. I'm excited about the program we have... We are looking forward to a successful year..."

GAME 1:   LOUISVILLE (0-0) @ TUPELO (0-0)
                          LOUISVILLE 7 TUPELO 17
                          October 31, 1990

After a pair of consecutive defeats, the Cats came back to beat the Wave in 1989. Said Hall about the opponent, *"Tupelo has an outstanding football team and will be a good team"*.

He was accurate as Tupelo had a 10-0 halftime lead courtesy of an opening quarter tally via Adam Paxton's 10-yarder to Mike Williams and the Hardin Patterson PAT. Patterson also added a 33-yard FG before halftime. In the 3rd quarter, Chris Jones dashed 54 yards and Patterson converted to make it 17-0. The Wildcats found paydirt only in the last frame on a 4-yard Daryald Hughes pass to Keith Dailey. Slade Fancher notched the PAT.

Tupelo edged Louisville in yardage 218-211 while Hughes threw for 106 yards and Lawrence Sangster paced rushers with just 55 yards.

GAME 2:   LOUISVILLE (0-1) vs ITAWAMBA AHS (0-1)
                          LOUISVILLE 38 ITAWAMBA AHS 0
                          September 7, 1990

The second-time opponents from Fulton marked the Wildcat home opener for 1990. The Cats dominated the Indians in 1989 with a 35-10 win. Louisville took advantage with a blowout win.

The home team was already up 14-0 after a frame via a 2-yard Sangster run, Hughes' 18-yard pass to Dailey and Hughes' two-point conversion. They added 12 more in the next frame on a 4-yard Charles DePriest run and a 4-yarder by Willie Porter. Porter added another from five yards in the 3rd quarter while Ollon Carter did the same from six yards after a fumble recovery.

"We felt like the five changes we made in defensive personnel during practices would help us attack the ball and play more consistently. I was extremely pleased to see the defense play more aggressively and, although they are learning a new system, there were many positive things I saw tonight that lead me to believe this defense can be a great bunch".

Louisville amassed 18 first downs and 352 offensive yards. Hughes passed for 127 yards, Brad Hathorn led receivers with 53 yards and Porter put up 63 more on the ground to lead rushers.

GAME 3:   LOUISVILLE (1-1) @ WEST POINT (1-1)
                          LOUISVILLE 25 WEST POINT 21
                          September 14, 1990

In a contest going back consecutively since 1966 consisting of 27 games, West Point was 3-0 against Louisville in the last three meetings. Their 31-0 loss the previous week to Starkville ended a 23-game winning streak. The Clarion-Ledger picked Louisville 21-14 saying, *"Historically, it is one of the hardest-hitting games played in Mississippi"*.

There were an estimated 5,000 fans in a place called *"the hole"* to watch this one. It seemed an early home team runaway as Mike Edwards took the opening kick 95 yards to paydirt and Jay Criddle converted. Not much longer Chris Jefferson hit Orlando Robertson from six yards and Robertson put it a quick 14-0. The Cats responded with a Sangster run of 58 yards to the 3-yard line from where Porter crossed. West Point came right back with a 2-yard Jefferson run and Criddle kick to end the frame 21-6. It was all Louisville thereafter as Hughes found Dailey from 23 yards and Lemond Wilson added two more points. Tim Herrington then hit a 32-yard FG to make halftime just 21-17. In the 3rd quarter, "Vicious hits were taken by West Point players as the 'killer bee' defense was taking no prisoners". In the finale with just around 4:00 remaining, West Point moved to the 20-yard line. However, Chuck Hunt picked off a pass.

That put the Cats on a drive ending with under two minutes left on the clock when Hughes hit Sangster for a 36-yard touchdown. Sangster also added the two points to seal the come-from-behind win. "We caught a West Point team a week after Starkville hurt their pride and feelings. They had something to prove. This victory was a total team effort".

GAME 4:   LOUISVILLE (2-1) @ GREENVILLE (0-3)
                           LOUISVILLE 12 GREENVILLE 19
                           September 21, 1990

What seemed to be an easy trip to Greenville to face a winless Hornet team that had yet to beat the Cats in three meetings turned out otherwise. However, not without Hall calling it "the worst officiated game I have even been involved with in 13 years of coaching. When you come to the Delta, you have to expect that and play well enough to overcome the adversity. We did not, and it wound up costing us the game at the end".

Flags seemed to call back every big Cat play, yet Louisville ended the half up 12-0 on a 3-yard Sangster run and a 49-yarder by Willie Porter via a lateral from Dailey. The Winston County Journal called them "listless" for the second half. A pair of fumbles led to a tie ball game by the final frame. One came from a 1-yard Tommy Redd plunge and an Anthony Moore run from the same distance. On the last play of the game, Redd hit Keith Mills from 20 yards to take the win.

"Our team seems to play good one week and average the next. We told the players all week that Greenville had a talented and dangerous football team. We came on in the second half and didn't protect the football and let them gain momentum to come back on us and, at the end with the game on the line, we couldn't make the plays offensively nor defensively to get the job done".

GAME 5:   LOUISVILLE (2-2) @ STARKVILLE (4-0)
                           LOUISVILLE 16 STARKVILLE 0
                           September 28, 1990

After such a disappointing road effort the week prior, now the Cats traveled up Highway 25 to face a team that bested them four of the last five contests. The Clarion-Ledger picked top-ranked Starkville 29-14. "While the Jackets were pelting Callaway 28-6 a week ago, Louisville was being upset by Greenville 19-12. And this one is in Starkville".

Louisville took a 6-0 lead to the lockers with a 2nd quarter Sangster run from 26 yards. In the 3rd quarter, he ran in from three yards while Hughes found Dailey for two more points. In the finale, the Cats recorded a safety for what turned to be the last points. Sangster ran for 178 yards on the evening.

"I am very proud of our team, to say the least. We are not intimated by anyone, anywhere or any place. These kids played extremely hard, one play at a time, just like we talked about all week. In the end analysis, we controlled the game at the line of scrimmage and did not turn the football over all night. This kept our defense rested and enabled them to have three takeaways at crucial time. Honestly, the game was not as close as the final score might indicate".

GAME 6:   LOUISVILLE (3-2) vs NOXUBEE COUNTY (0-5)
                           LOUISVILLE 52 NOXUBEE COUNTY 0
                           October 5, 1990: HOMECOMING

Noxubee County, also called Macon Central in some reports, sat last in 2-4A in preseason voting. It was for an apparent reason as they were winless thus far on the year. The Tigers were to be no match for the homecoming affair in Louisville.

The Lawrence Sangster Show begin with two 1st quarter scoring runs of 15 and 8 yards. He added three more before halftime on carries of 5, 18 and 12 yards. A pair of Weems kicks put intermission 32-0. The last Sangster score came in the 3rd quarter from 12 yards while Undra Glenn notched a pair of touchdowns on 12 and 36-yard runs. Slade Fancher was true on both kicks.

"I thought we played well even through Noxubee was obviously not a real strong team. Again, we got a chance to look at a lot of our young kids and give them some valuable game experience".

GAME 7:   LOUISVILLE (4-2) @ LEE HIGH (2-4)
        LOUISVILLE 32 LEE HIGH 7
        October 12, 1990

With only a pair of wins over Louisville since 1972, this season was not shaping up to be one that changed course. As with the prior game, the Cats tallied in each of the four frames. Derrick Loving recorded an early safety and Hughes found Brad Hathorn for a 46-yard scoring strike. A Fancher kick made it 9-0.

Louisville mustered only an Ollon Carter safety before halftime but came on stronger in the 3rd quarter. Sangster broke away from 71 and 42 yards before adding the last Cat tally in the finale from 21 yards. Fancher was true on each PAT. Lee High avoided the shutout late on a 13-yard Anthony Thompson dash and Jason Bigelow PAT.

"I thought this game was a very mediocre performance by our team. We just did not play extremely well, although we had several individual efforts on both sides of the ball". Louisville led in yardage 396-182. Sangster rushed for 171 yards while Hathorn pulled in 57 more. Hughes threw for 112 yards.

GAME 8:   LOUISVILLE (5-2) vs CALDWELL (5-2)
        LOUISVILLE 28 CALDWELL 14
        October 19, 1990

Picked third in 2-4A, the Columbus team had a record equal to that of the Wildcats. Nevertheless, they bested the Cats only twice since 1974.

Louisville jumped out to a 14-0 lead after a quarter, first when Keith Dailey fell on a Sangster fumble for a touchdown. Sangster then dashed in from nine yards while Fancher converted on both scores. Caldwell responded with a 35-yard Donya Green pass to Kenneth Verdell and Edwards PAT. The Bobcats also had the only score of the 2nd quarter courtesy of a 3-yard Edwards run and his game-tying kick.

The last two scores came from the home team. In the 3rd quarter, Sangster took it in from 13 yards while Hughes crossed from 10 yards and hit Dailey for the two points. Louisville dominated yardage 412-113 and Dailey recorded interceptions. The victory secured a playoff berth for the Wildcats. *"We probably played as well on both sides of the ball as we have all year. We got another great effort from our offensive line and our defensive front dominated the game. Except for turning the ball over so many times, I thought our team really played a great ball game".*

A report from 1991 noted this as Sangster's best rushing game with 226 yards.

GAME 9:   LOUISVILLE (6-2) vs NESHOBA CENTRAL (5-3)
        LOUISVILLE 14 NESHOBA CENTRAL 15
        October 26, 1990

A win tonight over division foe Neshoba Central secured the 2-4A title. It ended as one of the stranger heartbreaks in Wildcat history. Neshoba took a 7-0 lead to halftime thanks to a 2nd quarter Cepeda Moore run of 65 yards and a Lundy Brantley PAT. Louisville responded in the 3rd quarter with a 6-yard Sangster run.

Now in the final frame, the Cats widened the lead when Sangster took a punt 65 yards and then added the two-pointer to lead 14-7. As they drove the field late for the dagger, a fumble at the Rocket 25 gave NCHS a chance. What appeared to be a sure stop defensively, ended as a 75-yard Jonathan Day dash to the end zone. Deciding for the win, Day hit Wells in the corner of the end zone and hopes died.

"I've never seen such a phenomenal series of events that took place for us to lose this game".

GAME 10:   LOUISVILLE (6-3) vs JEFFERSON COUNTY (1-8)
        LOUISVILLE 53 JEFFERSON COUNTY 18
        November 2, 1990

Frustrations were taken out on the visiting Jefferson County team. In a short recap of a tremendous amount of scoring, Sangster ran for five touchdowns from 6, 1, 2, 55 and 65 yards. Hughes ran in from three and five yards for others while Glenn finished it with a 61-yarder. Neshoba Central defeated Caldwell to claim the 2-4A title.

GAME 11:   LOUISVILLE (7-3) @ OXFORD (9-1)
                    LOUISVILLE 6 OXFORD 9
                    November 9, 1990

      While Louisville took the first five contests (1976-1980), the Generals defeated the Cats the previous year by two points to continue in post season. This season, they were an admirable 9-1 and hosting for the first round of the playoffs.

      The Winston County Journal noted that Oxford *"overcame rain, wind and their own mistakes to beat the Cats in a game that was played in almost unbearable weather conditions on a field that resembled a pig sty"*. Louisville marched inside the Oxford 10 on three occasions before halftime only *"to lose the football via a fumble"*. Oxford, too, turned the ball over but the Wildcats could not make it count. They even missed a short FG effort.

      Louisville put up the lone points of the 3rd quarter on a 7-yard Sangster run to make it 6-0. In the all-important finale, the game was decided. Pinned deep, Hall decided on a safety instead of turnover. With the ball back in their hands, they marched 55 yards and, with just under 3:00 left, Randy Johnson crossed from two yards and Culotta added the PAT. That meant that three of the four losses came with less than 3:00 left in the games.

      Lawrence Sangster garnered numerous honors during the year outside of the program. He earned First Team All-State, First-Team Mississippi Sportswriters All-State, Second Team Clarion-Ledger All-State, and WCBI TV Player of the Year.

      All Division awards went to Keith Dailey, Sangster, William Cistrunk, Scott Ruth, Roger Caperton, James Edmond, Chuck Hunt and Ollon Carter. Honorable Mentions included Brad Hathorn, Charles DePriest, Daryald Hughes, Andre Hayes, Patrick Landers, Britt Goodin and Lamond Wilson. Edmond also earned Defensive MVP.

1991 (12-2)

      The Wildcats under Bobby Hall were tabbed the *"team to beat"* in 4A as they sat first in that poll and sixth in the overall Prep Poll. He said, *"Personally, I think we are the team to beat in the Class 4A. I don't feel we have any glaring weaknesses. We're two-platooning all the way; something we think gives us an advantage. Because we have so many players who can play, we are able to do this without sacrificing quality"*. He featured a Dandy Dozen player in Lawrence Sangster after 2,125 all-purpose yards and 1,449 rushing yards and nine defensive starters back in uniform.

GAME 1:   LOUISVILLE (0-0) vs TUPELO (0-0)
                    LOUISVILLE 7 TUPELO 27
                    September 6, 1991

      Tupelo, under the tutelage of former Clinton head man James Sloan, sat third in the Super 10 pre-season and went 12-2 in 1990 after losing the 5A championship 34-22 to Vicksburg. The Clarion-Ledger picked Tupelo 20-12. *"Tupelo has speed to burn from a team that was 12-2 and second in 5A"*.

      Said Hall, *"They have always been a great team, a larger school with a new coach. They will be going through a transition period this season. If you like big-time high school football, then Louisville is the place to be Friday night. There will some fierce collisions out there"*.

      It was not a great start to the season as Tupelo recorded the lone points on the opening frame via Zoe Freeman's 3-yarder and Hardin Patterson's PAT. By halftime, they put up 20 more points on a 27-yard Patterson FG, Kirk Presley's 3-yard pass to Daniel Sanders, a 16-yard Freeman run, and a two Patterson PATs. Defenses were stout afterwards as the 3rd quarter remained scoreless.

      Louisville avoided the shutout in the final frame when Brad Peterson found Moine Nicholson from 44 yards and Payton Weems added the conversion. Tupelo held Lawrence Sangster to 110 yards. *"We never really got going. Tupelo whipped us on both sides of the ball. I want to give Tupelo all of the credit. They had a lot to do with the way we looked. We really didn't rise to the occasion"*.

GAME 2:   LOUISVILLE (0-1) @ PEARL (1-0)
                 LOUISVILLE 3 PEARL 10
                 September 13, 1991

Although mentor Doug Merchant notched a 9-4 record in 1990, losses both in graduation (along with some unexpected others) depleted the strength he expected for this campaign. Now he was playing fewer personnel, including underclassmen, and many both ways. *We've got some good people to fill in and, if we can stay injury-free, we can be a good football team hopefully. But a serious injury at the right place could be very crippling to us"*.

He added, *"Some kids are going to have to step forward and play both ways. We've got a group of sophomores and juniors who are good players. By the middle of the season, they will be able to take up some of the load and help us. I feel like we'll be able to compete at 5A. Overall, we have a much tougher schedule than we've had in the past several years. We have a lot of leadership and desire from these guys. I think they'll accept the challenge, myself"*. Voters felt the same and had Pearl tops in their division pre-season.

Said Hall, *"(Pearl is) an outstanding team with one of the top running backs in the state. They will be quality"*. The only previous meeting had been in the 1985 playoffs where they ended Pirate dreams of a State Championship by a 23-7 margin. Pearl sat eighth in The Super 10. The Clarion-Ledger picked Pearl 21-10.

The game was known more for turnovers and penalties than for the win. A scoreless first half saw Keeth Taylor pick off a Cat pass. The Wildcats returned the favor but lost the opportunity due to a penalty. In fact, they had more flags before Pearl fumbled back to Louisville at the 27-yard line. Three plays later, Brant Mitchell fell on a loose ball at the 36-yard line, but Pearl could not make it count. Subsequent yardage gains by Louisville were also met with yellow flags for miscellaneous fouls.

Pearl had a nice 3rd quarter opportunity but lost the chance with a Darrell Hobson fumble at the 6-yard line. Louisville took the ball and marched to Pearl's side of the field from where Peyton Weems hit a 33-yard FG with :33 left. Another Pirate fumble blew a 4th quarter opportunity, but they rebounded when Dominic Brown *"knocked down a Wildcat pitch"* with Darrell Larkin taking the ball 20-yards to the end zone. B.J. Helms' PAT was good with 8:45 remaining.

Then, Chris Poole picked off a Peterson throw. With the aid of more flags, Pearl turned it into a 23-yard Helms FG for the last points. After Sylvester Houston's pickoff of Louisville, Hall was incensed at officiating. For his outburst, penalties totaled 53 yards against Louisville as the game ended.

Pearl won first downs (15-9) and rushing (168-148) but lost the air (46-0). Louisville suffered 20 flags for 220 yards. Said Merchant, *"Certainly both teams hurt themselves with mistakes. I was disappointed in the way we played. I wanted us to really get after them, but we didn't. They dominated our line in the first half then we shot ourselves in the foot in the second half. We sputtered all night long. We played with no emotion in the first half"*.

The game came under scrutiny after Hall let the officials know his thoughts on calls during the game. *"Every single big play we had, without exception, was called back on a penalty. That seems strange. When I went out on the field, I was doing it because I have to take up for my kids"*. For that, he received a reprimand from the MHSAA due to his complaint of 220 penalty yards and declined to make further statements.

GAME 3:   LOUISVILLE (0-2) @ WEST POINT (2-0)
                 LOUISVILLE 10 WEST POINT 7
                 September 20, 1991

Rival West Point was undefeated and hosting the Cats this Friday evening. The disappointing start to the season, along with the Pearl particulars, could impact this team greatly. They put it behind them and started to win.

Louisville had the only touchdown on the opening frame on an 85-yard drive ending on a 10-yard Peterson toss to Undra Glenn and Weems PAT. West Point tied it at halftime on a 3-yard George Elliot run and Jon Murray kick. After a scoreless 3rd quarter, Weems gave the Cats the needed win with a 27-yard FG. A later roughing the kicker call on Louisville led to no points as the defense stood tall.

GAME 4:   LOUISVILLE (1-2) vs NOXUBEE COUNTY (0-3)
                 LOUISVILLE 55 NOXUBEE COUNTY 6
                 September 27, 1991: HOMECOMING

Not only was it Homecoming in Winston County, but also the start of district play. Louisville dominated NCHS the previous season 52-0 and hoped for the same.

Noxubee opened with a 24-yard passing score to make it a quick 6-0 but it was all they could muster the remainder of the evening. Sangster answered with a 70-yard dash to paydirt and added touchdown runs of 35 and 5 yards before halftime. Peterson found Marlon Goss from 35 yards for another and Nicholson from 15 yards for the last. With reserves in play, Ryan Hudson ran in from five yards while Sangster put up a 1-yarder. The last came from Travis Coats.

GAME 5:   LOUISVILLE (2-2) @ LEE HIGH (0-4)
                   LOUISVILLE 56 LEE HIGH 7
                   October 4, 1991

Much like the previous game, the Wildcats faced a winless team and wanted to prove a point to 4A skeptics. Sangster got in from five yards to start the parade, and Glenn took advantage of a Generals kickoff fumble to pull in a 10-yarder from Peterson. Yet another fumble set up Sangster's second score and the game was fairly secure.

Peterson and Goss then hooked up for an 80-yard tally, while another Sangster run put the 1st quarter 35-0. Michael Carr put Lee High on the board in the next with a late 26-yard tally. Hudson ran in for a touchdown later and found Nicholson for the next. Coats got the last tally for the Cats in a blowout road win.

GAME 6:   LOUISVILLE (3-2) vs CALDWELL (1-3)
                   LOUISVILLE 48 CALDWELL 0
                   October 11, 1991

Another week against a team with a less-than-stellar record thus far on the season. And, much like the past two weeks, it seemed easier than in the first two weeks.

Sangster started the scoring with a 20-yard dash while Peterson found Goss from that yardage later for another. Weems connected on his first of six extra points. Peterson ran in from five yards to open the next frame while hitting Nicholson from 20 yards for the last before halftime. Now 28-0, the Wildcats poured it on for the last scoring of the game in the 3rd quarter. Nicholson put up runs of 20 and 38 yards for touchdowns while Sangster notched the last from 15 yards. Scoring was mercifully over.

This was the last season for the Caldwell football team.

GAME 7:   LOUISVILLE (4-2) @ SHANNON (2-4)
                   LOUISVILLE 37 SHANNON 0
                   October 18, 1991

Only a scant recap notes the results of the shutout over first-time opponent Shannon. Nicholson scored from five yards, Sangster took a punt 55 yards and Weems' 30-yard FG and PATs put halftime 17-0. Sangster added two more in the second half (six yards and 39 yards) to finish things. Eddie Shell added a pick-six on the last play of the game for the final tally. Sangster rushed for 135 of the 241 total ground yards.

GAME 8:   LOUISVILLE (5-2) @ NEW HOPE (4-3)
                   LOUISVILLE 23 NEW HOPE 7
                   October 25, 1991

Eddie Hunt stopped an early New Hope drive with his interception and Weems booted a 17-yard FG to make it 3-0. Duan Johnson then gave the Trojans the lead with his 1-yard dive and Kelly Hunt made it 7-3. Sangster then ran 80 yards for the response and against from 21 yards.

Now in the 4th quarter, Sangster found paydirt from three yards to give him 122 rushing yards on 18 carries. Nicholson had 58 yards. Nothing more is found on other game specifics.

GAME 9:   LOUISVILLE (6-2) vs STARKVILLE (7-1)
                   LOUISVILLE 20 STARKVILLE 10
                   November 1, 1991

This would be no easy night for the Wildcats as the Jackets sat second in The Super 10. And they opened well on their first drive ending on a 30-yard Lee Miller FG. In the 2nd quarter, Sangster ended a march with his 28-yard escape to make halftime 6-3.

Starkville jumped ahead with the only 3rd quarter points. A fumble recovery ended on Donnell Jordan's 4-yard plunge and a Miller PAT. However, it was all Louisville in the last stanza. Tim Herrington found a loose football and Nicholson crossed a few plays later from six yards. Herrington then picked off a Joe Malon throw at the 5-yard line. Peterson ran in from there and Weems converted on both scores.

A number one-ranked Vicksburg loss 21-14 to rival Warren Central put the Vikings in the top spot. However, Louisville's win put them second in the Super 10.

GAME 10:   LOUISVILLE (7-2) vs ABERDEEN (8-1)
                     LOUISVILLE 14 ABERDEEN 0
                     November 8, 1991

Aberdeen was back on the Louisville calendar after sporadic meetings over the decades. History was good to the Cats as they were at least 7-1 since the 1930s. The home tilt marked the end of the regular season.

In weather described as "near freezing", scoring came down to just two quarters. A Herrington fumble recovery of the opening kick led to Peterson's 1-yarder and Weems kick. In the 3rd quarter, Peters and Goss connected from 47 yards and Weems nailed the last point. Louisville led in first downs (13-6) and yardage (253-99). Sangster rushed for 100 yards for the Cats.

"We played well for nine straight weeks now. I think it's a wide-open race in North Mississippi. There's still a lot of teams left that can play. There's a whole lot of folks ranked ahead of us, so I guess we'll be the underdogs". Hall, now with 100 career wins, earned Clarion-Ledger Coach of the Week.

GAME 11:   LOUISVILLE (8-2) vs JIM HILL (8-2)
                     LOUISVILLE 37 JIM HILL 7
                     November 15, 1991

After victories in 1987 and 1988, the Tigers now met the Cats in the first round of the playoffs. The contest eerily matched those of the previous meetings as Louisville held a solid lead by halftime.

Louisville scored on their initial drive via a 1-yard Sangster plunge and the first of four Weems kicks. In the next, Nicholson pulled in a 6-yarder from Peterson while Goss did the same from 40 yards. Weems opened the 3rd with a 25-yard FG followed by Peterson's 7-yard pass to Reed Herrington. In the last frame, both tallied. Louisville found paydirt on a 13-yard Sangster run while Euell hit Sean Woodson from 11 yards and Frierson converted.

GAME 12:   LOUISVILLE (9-2) @ LAFAYETTE (10-0)
                     LOUISVILLE 21 LAFAYETTE 14
                     November 22, 1991

This could be the biggest game of the season as the Cats not only faced an undefeated team on the road, but also without Sangster. He injured his foot during the practice week and could not get in the game.

Louisville opened the game with a 1-yard Peterson dive and the first of three Weems kicks. In the next frame, Peterson hit Nicholson from 14 yards to make halftime 14-0. They tacked on their last in the 3rd quarter when Peterson escaped from four yards. The Commodores did not quit and tallied a pair of scores in the last frame. The first was on a 2-yard pass from Glenn Downs to James Tyson while they added another on Downs' 37-yarder to Marlin Pearson. Heath Trost added both extra points.

They had time for one more score with a minute remaining, but the defense stood tall. Bo Miller recovered a fumble for Louisville in the game. Robbins rushed for 146 yards on the evening.

GAME 13:   LOUISVILLE (10-2) vs CLEVELAND (11-0-1)
                     LOUISVILLE 24 CLEVELAND 23
                     November 29, 1991

Between 1987 and 1989, the playoff road always went through the Cleveland squad. In each, the Wildcats came out victorious. This one would not be as easy with the team undefeated with only a tie game. The Clarion-Ledger picked Louisville 21-12.

Louisville had to kick and claw with determined effort in order to pull out the win at home. The visitors struck first on a 2-yard Earnest Edwards plunge to make it 6-0. Back came the Cats with a 20-yard Sangster dash and a Weems PAT. The 2nd quarter belonged to Cleveland. Steven Rose found Gary Thigpen from 19 yards and Edwards converted the two-pointer. John Easley then drilled a 41-yard FG to put halftime a disappointing 19-7.

Cleveland started the 3rd quarter with a fumble recovery and Bobby Payne later turned it into a 39-yard scoring run. However, Sangster came back with a 2-yard tally and Weems added the kick. Scoring in the crucial final frame started with Nicholson's 55-yard punt return and Weems made it 23-21.

"With two seconds left on the clock, Peyton Weems trotted onto the field to attempt a game-winning 18-yard FG. Weems' kick was perfect and his jubilant teammates mobbed him in the middle of the field". Louisville led in first downs (14-12) and yardage (252-241). Sangster rushed for 153 yards. Said Hall, "I'm kind of empty right now. That was amazing. I don't want to sound mushy, but I'm really proud of our kids. They never really gave up".

The end was not without controversy as Cleveland filed a formal complaint about fan activity after the kick. For that, the Cat fans received a reprimand from the MHSAA.

GAME 14:   LOUISVILLE (11-2) vs STONE COUNTY (12-1)
                  LOUISVILLE 6 STONE COUNTY 3
                  December 7, 1991: Robinson-Hale Stadium; Clinton, MS

There was a lot of mutual respect between Hall and Coach Larry Easterling. Both were complimentary of the players on the other teams. Due to the tremendous talent on the Tomcat squad, Hall said Louisville would need "a wish and a prayer to defeat Stone County". This marked the first meeting between the two clubs.

In a defensive battle, it was Louisville first on the board courtesy of a 32-yard Weems FG. The Tomcats evened it late in the 3rd quarter when Brent Huff hit a FG from the same distance. Now with just :08 remaining, Hall called on Weems to win a second-straight game for the Cats. His 27-yarder sailed through the uprights and Louisville now had another 4A Championship.

Sangster rushed for 86 yards to give him 1,569 on the season with 20 touchdowns. Porter also recorded a 4th quarter interception. The Tomcats had only 63 offensive yards on the night. Said Hall, "Weems basically won us a state championship. He can kick them when the money is on the table. He has ice water in his veins". The Cats ended fourth in The Super 10.

Lawrence Sangster earned The Clarion-Ledger Player of the Year and Mississippi Sportswriters' Association Offensive Player of the Year. Other First Team members of the MSWA All-State team included Keith Smith and James Edmond.

WLSM All-County awards went to Smith, Damon Fulcher, Britt Goodin, Reed Herrington, Brad Peterson, Moine Nicholson, Sangster, Willie Porter, Ollon Carter, Purvis Holmes, Tim Herrington, Randy Miller and James Edmond.

1992 (11-2)

Third-year Louisville mentor Bobby Hall, coming off a state championship, returned 29 lettermen including six offensive and five defensive starters. The Wildcats also sat third in the Mississippi Prep Top 30 preseason.

"We've got experience on offense and a strong kicking game, but one area of concern in our lack of experience on defense. But I'm confident that these young players, defensively, will get the job done". On the tough schedule ahead, he said, "We wanted to play a tough schedule this year to prepare for the playoffs. By playing 'up' we will be prepared. When the playoffs start, we will have played in adverse conditions and will be ready".

PRESEASON: LOUISVILLE (0-0) @ VICKSBURG (0-0)
                 LOUISVILLE 7 VICKSBURG 23
                 August 28, 1992: Red Carpet Bowl

The Winston County Journal called this *"a preseason game"* on August 26. That was fortunate, as it would have started the season off on a poor foot. Said Hall before the game, *"Vicksburg has been in the South finals for the last two consecutive years in the 5A playoffs. They have a rich football tradition there and are a formidable opponent. They will be a challenge for us"*.

Louisville opened their first two drives with fumbles. The last to Marlon Nixon set up a 3-yard Mark Smith run and Tracy Tullos PAT. On the next march, the Cats moved 81 yards with Undra Glenn romping in from four yards. Peyton Weems tied the game. In the 3rd quarter, the Gators went 58 yards to allow Tullos a 32-yard FG and 10-7 lead.

The Wildcats had a chance later on a drive to the 3-yard line but could get no further. Vicksburg went the other way to paydirt with Damian Slaughter getting the last yard and Tullos the PAT. On the last play, Brad Peterson launched a desperation throw but Joffery Holloway grabbed it and took it 45 yards for the score.

Louisville led in rushing 136-129 with Moine Nicholson gaining 56 of those. Peterson threw for 87 yards but suffered a pair of interceptions. Other reports show the final to be 17-7.

GAME 1:   LOUISVILLE (0-0) @ TUPELO (0-0)
                                    LOUISVILLE 14 TUPELO 10
                                    September 4, 1992

If the warm-up game against Vicksburg was not enough, now the Wildcats traveled to Tupelo to face a Wave team second in The Super 10 and featuring Dandy Dozen QB Kirk Presley. Said Coach James Sloan, *"We'll find out right quick what we are made of. It won't take long"*. The Clarion-Ledger predicted a 21-7 victory.

The home team took a slim 3-0 lead after a quarter on Hardin Patterson's 20-yard FG. Back came Louisville with a 77-yard Nicholson punt return and Weems PAT. Tupelo answered with a 3-yard Chris Thomas dive and Patterson extra point. However, before the halftime whistle sounded, Nicholson dodged in from 16 yards to cap a 77-yard march and Weems converted.

Drama unfolded late in the game as Hall opted for a fourth down play. It failed and put the Wave at the Cat 35. However, the defense held and Daren Middleton sacked Presley on their fourth down attempt to seal it. Tupelo dominated first downs (18-7) and rushing (154-76) while Louisville controlled the air (140-111). The lone turnover was a Tupelo fumble. The Clarion-Ledger voted Hall Coach of the Week.

GAME 2:   LOUISVILLE (1-0) vs PEARL (2-0)
                                    LOUISVILLE 48 PEARL 13
                                    September 11, 1992

The next contest came against a Pearl team ranked one spot (7th) below Louisville in The Super 10 and one that defeated the Cats in 1991. That was the last loss the Wildcats suffered aside from the pre-season game against Vicksburg. Said Coach Larry Merchant, *"Louisville remembers that (1991) game. I know if I'd had 220 yards in penalties, I'd have been upset, too. Louisville is deep talent-wise everywhere. It worries me going into this game. Louisville certainly has some athletes"*. Said Hall about the Pascagoula game, *"I thought I was watching a horror movie. Pearl was totally awesome"*. The Clarion-Ledger picked Pearl 17-14.

The Wildcats had only one score in the first quarter via a Johnny Robbins 4-yard run and Weems PAT courtesy of a Pirate fumble. They stacked scores on quickly in the next. Peterson's 1-yarder was followed by another Pirate fumble to put Eddie Hunt on the receiving end of a 31-yard Peterson toss. Another fumble led to a 44-yard Nicholson run and, with :47 left, Peterson hit Rod Dismuke from 45 yards. The only Pirate bright spot came on the kickoff when Darrell Larkin took the football 99 yards to paydirt. B.J. Helms' conversion cut halftime to 34-7.

A 3rd quarter Chad Harvey pickoff led to their last points when Jason Cox hit Matt Raphelt from the 17-yard line. However, Louisville put up two more tallies in the 4th quarter to ice it. Robbins escaped from 30 yards while Bo Miller picked off a Pearl pass and took it 44 yards to the end zone. Stats favored Louisville in first downs (17-9) and rushing (287-56) but Pearl led in passing (142-104).

Said Merchant, *"We came up here sleep-walking and Louisville was ready to kill us. They just knocked the dog out of us and we laid it on the ground. You just can't keep* doing that. Mentally we were not ready to play. All night long we were one step from making the tackle or one step from making a big play on offense. We had too many turnovers and you can't afford that against a team as talented and well-coached as Louisville. Part of it was them; a lot of it was us".

GAME 3:   LOUISVILLE (2-0) vs WEST POINT (3-0)
                 LOUISVILLE 31 WEST POINT 24
                 September 18, 1992

Wins over Pearl and Tupelo put the Cats fourth in the Top 10 but it may not last long as the next opponent was second-ranked and undefeated West Point. They were not unknown as they played consecutively since 1966 and other games prior. "This will be toughest one yet. You know they're back to the West Point of old. They start 10 seniors on offense". The Clarion-Ledger picked Louisville 17-14 but called it a "toss up".
        The Cats jumped out in the opening frame on a 38-yard Weems FG and a 1-yard Johnny Robbins plunge. Weems converted his first of four extra points. They added one more touchdown before halftime via Peterson's 18-yard strike to Robbins. Nicholson increased the lead in the 3rd quarter from four yards while Kee Banks did the same for West Point from three yards and added the two-pointer.
        Nicholson got the points back in the finale from six yards, but West Point did not quit. They added a 1-yard Carlton Smith run, Jeremy Goins two-point play, Anthony Fair 9-yard reception from Banks and a Darwin Gandy two-point conversion. However, it was too little and too late. Nicholson (143) and Robbins (103) paced rushers while the defense caused an interception and three fumble recoveries.
        First downs were tied (14-14), Louisville held the ground (271-216) and West Point the air (91-40). "We've had our backs against the wall for a month. I'll challenge anybody to be 3-0 against the schedule we've played. We're physically and emotionally drained after these three games. I'm proud of our kids for coming through in this stretch".

GAME 4:   LOUISVILLE (3-0) @ NOXUBEE COUNTY (0-2)
                 LOUISVILLE 49 NOXUBEE COUNTY 6
                 September 25, 1992

The tough stretch and victories moved the Wildcats to tops in The Super 10. "I feel like we've earned it. We have no apologies with the schedule we've played. Our kids have rung the bell. The kids are very proud of being number one but they understand how they got there. We've still got a lot of areas to improve on. It's harder to stay there than it is to get here. Everybody will be really gunning for us".
        The first division game could not have been better for Louisville. Glenn opened with a 24-yard run and Weems the first of seven PATs while NCHS gained their only tally after on a 1-yard Mason run. It was all Cats afterwards. Nicholson ran in from a yard to end the frame while Robbins put up a 3-yarder in the 2nd quarter and Peterson found Freddie Love from four yards for the last.
        In the 3rd quarter, Glenn recorded his second touchdown on a 16-yard effort while Nicholson (8) and Travis Coats (1) finished things in the last frame.

GAME 5:   LOUISVILLE (4-0) vs COLUMBUS (0-5)
                 LOUISVILLE 45 COLUMBUS 7
                 October 2, 1992: HOMECOMING

This marked the initial meeting between Louisville and the Falcons. They previously played a pair of Columbus teams in Caldwell and Lee High but now it was time for their fourth 5A opponent.
        An early Falcon fumble to Bo Miller set up a 3-yard Nicholson tally and Weems' first of six extra points. Nicholson then pulled in a 17-yard Peterson pass while Love grabbed a 3-yarder from him to end the 1st quarter. In the next, Weems nailed a 42-yard FG and Love added a 5-yard touchdown reception. Halftime stood 31-0.
        Darrell Robbins took the 3rd quarter kickoff 97 yards to paydirt while Nicholson broke away from 34 yards to pad the lead. The last score came in that frame when Cornell Miller (or Cyrus Conner) crossed from four yards and Pfeiffer converted. Said Coach David Rush, "They have a lot of weapons and they're extremely hard to prepare for".

GAME 6:   LOUISVILLE (5-0) vs MERIDIAN (2-3)
               LOUISVILLE 38 MERIDIAN 16
               October 9, 1992

Louisville now found themselves in the national spotlight with a 25th ranking in The USAToday Super 25. Still, Hall was concentrating on always-tough Meridian. "*Meridian could very easily be 4-1…. Meridian is arguably the finest 2-3 team in the state*". The Clarion-Ledger picked the Cats 22-10 saying, "*Louisville is at home and should have enough firepower to run its win streak to 18 games*".

The home team jumped out 10-0 after a quarter via a 37-yard Weems FG and a 9-yard Nicholson run. Trey Cooper cut into the Cat lead in the 2nd quarter with his 25-yard FG but Robbins came right back with a 9-yard run. Peterson followed with a 1-yard dive while Meridian closed the half on Reggie Little's 17-yarder to George Hart. Cooper's PAT, along with three from Weems made it 24-10.

Louisville had the only tally of the 3rd quarter on Peterson's 8-yarder to Glenn while their last came in the 4th quarter on a 24-yard Nicholson dash. Both Weems kicks were true. Meridian closed with a 1-yard Adrian Smith plunge. Nicholson rushed for a career-best 174 yards while Shalawn Miller added an interception. First downs were tied (17-17) while yardage favored Louisville 304-281.

GAME 7:   LOUISVILLE (6-0) vs SHANNON (5-1)
               LOUISVILLE 47 SHANNON 0
               October 16, 1992

Now 24th in the national poll, the Cats met the Red Raiders for the second encounter. The first the previous year ended 37-0 for Louisville.

This one was never in doubt with scores in each frame. Nicholson had the only of the opening frame from five yards. In the 2nd quarter, Coats ran in from two yards while Peterson and Hunt connected from 12 yards. Weems converted on two kicks. The 3rd quarter brought one more via an 18-yard Glenn run. The firepower came in the finale on a 6-yard Nicholson run, another from four yards and Bo Lewis' 40-yard fumble return.

Nicholson put up 180 yards on the ground while Bo Miller joined Lewis with a fumble recovery. The Sun Herald gave Nicholson credit for 200 yards. Said Hall, "*I have to commend Shannon. Their kids played hard under adverse conditions*".

GAME 8:   LOUISVILLE (7-0) vs NEW HOPE (1-6)
               LOUISVILLE 41 NEW HOPE 0
               October 23, 1992

The one-win New Hope team was a welcome sight as the Wildcats had run a gauntlet of tough opponents. This one seemed over before it started. Peterson opened with a 57-yard dash to paydirt, Nicholson took a punt 55 yards and later ran in from two yards. With one Weems kick and a two-point Peterson toss to Cornell Miller, it was 21-0 as the opening frame ended.

Before halftime, they added 14 more points on Peterson's 17-yarder to Robbins and his 8-yarder to Love. The last merciful tally came in the 3rd quarter when Peterson and Glenn connected from eight yards. Chris Carter added an interception in the game. Coach Dale Hardin noted, "*They gave a really good effort. I'm proud of them. Louisville is an outstanding football team and I wish them the best of luck*".

GAME 9:   LOUISVILLE (8-0) @ STARKVILLE (6-3)
               LOUISVILLE 6 STARKVILLE 7
               October 30, 1992

While many focused on the winning streak and national ranking, Hall knew that these two met annually since 1940 and then more before. "*I assure you our rivalry with Starkville is much more important to us than the winning streak. Starkville is our biggest rival. It will be exciting high school football*". The Clarion-Ledger picked Louisville 28-14.

Scoring was over by halftime as defenses took control on both sides of the field. Starkville had the opening tally in the 1st quarter when Kevin Randall found Calvin Daily from five yards and Lee Miller knocked through the PAT. Louisville answered in the 2nd quarter after a Jacket fumble on an 11-yard Peterson toss to Eddie Hunt. The crucial extra point amazingly failed.

With just about 47 seconds left, Weems attempted a long 48-yard FG but it was wide left and the streak was over. First downs were even (9-9), Starkville led the ground (140-90) and Louisville the air (91-13). Both lost a fumble. Said Starkville Coach Tommy Lucas, *"Louisville has a hell of a team. I'm pinching myself to make sure I'm not dreaming"*. Added Hall, *"Starkville just outplayed us. I really tip my hat to them. They did a great job and deserved to win"*.

GAME 10:   LOUISVILLE (8-1) @ ABERDEEN (7-2)
                         LOUISVILLE 14 ABERDEEN 0
                         November 6, 1992

The surprising one-point loss dropped Louisville to third in The Super 10 but still first in 4A. Tupelo, a previous victim, now assumed the top spot. The Clarion-Ledger said the Cats *"must show more fire than it had at Starkville or could have a two-game losing streak"* but still picked them 24-12.

This one ended only with Weems field goals in three of the four frames. First was a 31-yarder and two more in the 2nd quarter from 27 and 30 yards made halftime just 9-0. A bad punt snap that sailed out of the end zone gave the Cats a 3rd quarter safety while Weems finished things in the last stanza on a 33-yarder. The win gave Louisville home field advantage to start the playoffs.

Louisville led in first downs (18-7), rushing (182-118) and passing (105-10). Nicholson, despite an ankle injury, rushed for 106 yards. *"We would have been in serious trouble if we had not won tonight. Our egos were crushed after we lost last week. We had a totally different approach in practice. We strapped on the pads and got after it"*.

GAME 11:   LOUISVILLE (9-1) vs CLEVELAND EAST SIDE (6-4)
                         LOUISVILLE 28 CLEVELAND EAST SIDE 20
                         November 13, 1992

Louisville faced a Cleveland team five times since 1972. Now they faced Cleveland East Side. They proved *"a worthy opponent"*.

The Cats put up 14 points in the opening frame. After a fumble recovery, Nicholson dashed 17 yards to paydirt and Weems added his first of four kicks. Then, Peterson hit Glenn from 10 yards. Cleveland bounced back by controlling the 2nd quarter with touchdowns from Ken Kizart (3) and Tony Murray (or Ricky Randall) via a fumble recovery. Ronald Gee knocked through both kicks to tie halftime 14-14.

Louisville took a slim lead at the end of the 3rd quarter. Robbins dove in from a yard while Kizart hit Twan West from 16 yards. Their missed PAT made it 21-20. In the finale, Paul Sangster hauled in a 33-yard Peterson pass to insert the dagger. Rodney Wraggs recovered a last-minute fumble. Nicholson (156) and Robbins (101) paced Wildcat rushers.

"I think East Side really deserved to win, to be honest with you. We'll take it, but they played their hearts out".

GAME 12:   LOUISVILLE (10-1) @ MADISON CENTRAL (10-1)
                         LOUISVILLE 17 MADISON CENTRAL 13
                         November 20, 1992

It had to come eventually and that time was here. Former successful Louisville coach Mike Justice now squared off with his past team in the second round of the playoffs. He said, *"There's no emotion about it. I don't work there anymore. I'm not the least bit concerned about Louisville. I'm concerned about Madison Central. Bobby Hall has done a great job and he's to be commended for it. I'm trying to win a state championship and Louisville is the next game. It's just another game on the road to the championship"*. The Clarion-Ledger predicted a 24-14 Louisville victory.

Louisville opened on a *"muddy, rain-soaked field"* with a 63-yard Nicholson touchdown, a Weems PAT and then Weems' 37-yard FG. Madison Central responded with a minute left before halftime on D.D. Cowan's 55-yard touchdown and Jeremy Gunalda PAT. Now in the final frame, the Cats were up just 10-7. Late in the quarter, a bad snap to Lee Wylie allowed the Jags the ball at the 16-yard line. Cowan eventually crossed from a yard but the PAT failed.

Just about as last as you can get, Louisville drove 69 yards with Nicholson adding the last 15 yards. Weems nailed the PAT. Louisville led in first downs (12-9), rushing (250-181) and passing (32-15). Nicholson rushed for 147 yards while Bo Lewis had an interception and Morris Scott a fumble recovery. *"We're two games away and one game closer"*. Said Justice, *"We played hard and took it to the wire. We just didn't win"*.

GAME 13:   LOUISVILLE (11-1) @ NESHOBA CENTRAL (10-3)
                                 LOUISVILLE 14 NESHOBA CENTRAL 21
                                 November 27, 1992

The *"one step closer"* now included long-time opponent Neshoba Central. They came a long way since the first encounter in 1972 where the Cats started a 13-3 overall run against them. A win put the Wildcats into another shot at the state championship.

It appeared to be an easy Wildcat win as Louisville scored in the opening frame on a 6-yard Peterson run and in the 2nd quarter on his 13-yarder to Love. Weems added both kicks to make intermission 14-0. However, the Rockets were better in the second half. They put up 14 points in the 3rd quarter on a 62-yard Johnny Nash escape and a 65-yarder by Demarco Fox. Lundy Brantley's PATs evened things.

In the finale, they took the North title when Nash dashed in from five yards and Brantley converted. Louisville tried in vain to come back but Johnny Vaughn ended hopes with an interception. Louisville led in first downs (11-10) and passing (69-67) while Neshoba held the ground (233-178). Each suffered an interception while the Cats lost two fumbles.

"We did not execute in the second half. My hat is off to Neshoba. They played a good ball game and I wish them well next week".

Despite a successful year with a disappointing end, numerous Wildcats earned spots on the All-District Team. Among those were Kendrick Hughes, Randy Miller, Morris Scott, Bo Lewis, Peyton Weems, Lee Wylie, Moine Nicholson, Kendrick Hickman, Derrick Coleman, Brad Peterson, Eddie Hunt, Eddie Shell and Johnny Robbins.

Honorable Mentions included Eric Sullivan, Freddie Love, Marcus Holmes, Maurice Slaughter and Derrick Brown.

1993 (14-1)

After posting a 30-8 record in his three years at Louisville, Bobby Hall returned to Amory to take the same position there. In his place stepped former Aberdeen mentor Lynn Moore. *"Louisville has a great tradition. The kids know how to win. It's a great challenge to carry on that kind of reputation, the kind of challenge I was looking for..."*

Preseason voters put the Wildcats first in 4A and 10th in the AP Top 10. Additionally, Moine Nicholson earned a Dandy Dozen honor for his 2,236 all-purpose yards, 1,372 rushing yards, and 19 touchdowns in 1992.

GAME 1:   LOUISVILLE (0-0) vs YAZOO CITY (0-0)
                                 LOUISVILLE 19 YAZOO CITY 6
                                 August 27, 1993

Every so often, Yazoo City would suddenly re-appear on Louisville football calendars. While the Cats won the last pair in 1987 and 1988, this one could be different. The Clarion-Ledger said, *"This might be Yazoo City's best team in years. Can the Indians, however, slow Louisville's running game?"*

Bryan Childress got the Indian train going in the opening frame on his 5-yard touchdown run. Down 6-0, Nicholson dashed 51 yards to the Cat 5 and then in from there on the next play. Peyton Weems added the PAT. A muffed punt caused by Bo Miller and Shalawn Miller resulted in a safety to make it 9-6.

Travis Coats notched the second score in the 3rd quarter from five yards and Weems converted. In the finale, Weems nailed a 45-yard FG to end things. Coats led rushers with 91 yards while the defense held YCHS to just 65 offensive yards.

GAME 2:   LOUISVILLE (1-0) vs TUPELO (0-0)
                                 LOUISVILLE 7 TUPELO 6
                                 September 3, 1993

The win in 1992 gave Louisville an overall 5-4 record against Tupelo since 1984. Now the Cats were facing the defending 5A champions whose last loss came that year to Louisville. The Clarion-Ledger picked the Golden Wave 17-16.

The Cats garnered their only points on the first drive. Darnell Robbins hit Nicholson on passes to set up a 23-yard Coby Miller dash and Weems PAT. With about a minute remaining, Jarious Jackson dodged in from nine yards but the Blaine Gray extra point attempt was blocked. Miller recovered their onside kick effort to seal the win.

Tupelo led in first downs (12-9) and rushing (192-109) while Louisville dominated the air (147-13). Nicholson had 143 all-purpose yards (119 on receptions), Miller and Chris Carter had interceptions, and Morris Scott had a pair of sacks. "Beating Tupelo is a big win for us. I thought we made some great plays on defense. We're going to live and die with the big play. That's how we are".

GAME 3:   LOUISVILLE (2-0) @ GREENVILLE WESTON (0-2)
                 LOUISVILLE 38 GREENVILLE WESTON 8
                 September 10, 1993

While the Wildcats faced a Greenville team in previous years, this was the first against Weston. It would not be close as Louisville jumped out to a 14-0 lead at Charles S. Kerg Field after a quarter. Nicholson found paydirt from 10 yards and returned a punt 70 yards for another. Weems was true on both conversions and three more later.

In the 2nd quarter, Robbins hit Nicholson from 24 yards while Carter added a 42-yard pick-six. Halftime sat 28-0. Weems made it 31-0 on a 40-yard FG while Charles Henton later dashed across from eight yards. The only Weston tally came in the finale on a 10-yard Nathan Kennedy run and Larry Kennedy two-point conversion.

Louisville led in first downs (14-7) and yardage (239-167) with 102 coming from Robbins throws. Morris Scott and Judd Boswell found fumbles for the Wildcats,

GAME 4:   LOUISVILLE (3-0) vs WEST POINT (0-2)
                 LOUISVILLE 20 WEST POINT 0
                 September 17, 1993

The two squads faced one-another over the past 80 years and consecutively since 1966. In that period, the Cats were 21-9 but West Point was traditionally not an easy team to beat. This season afford them some bad breaks to start winless after two games.

An opening West Point fumble to Scott set up Coby Miller's 37-yard run and Weems PAT. Eric Rush gathered up another fumble and rambled 45 yards to the end zone. Weems made it 14-0; a score that sat until the 3rd quarter when Nicholson cross from ten yards. Cornell Miller added an interception, Maurice Slaughter led in tackles with 10 solo, and Coby Miller led rushers with 90 yards.

GAME 5:   LOUISVILLE (4-0) @ STARKVILLE (2-2)
                 LOUISVILLE 20 STARKVILLE 7
                 September 24, 1993

The Yellow Jackets served as the longest consecutive rival for Louisville going back to 1940 with other contests prior. They were a break-even 2-2 this season and hoping for the big upset at home.

Solid defense on both sides kept each out of the end zone in the first half. The only score of the half came on a 2nd quarter 47-yard Weems FG. Starkville took the lead in the 3rd quarter when Mike Duck scored on a 9-yard dash and the Kenny McDonald PAT made it 7-3. Louisville turned up the heat in the finale, first with a 63-yard Coby Miller dash and Weems PAT. A fumble recovery then led to a 29-yard Weems FG. Carter then picked off a pass that set up Coby's 1-yard plunge and Weems kick.

Miller (114) and Nicholson (107) led rushers. The total offensive output by Louisville came to 317 yards compared to 183 for Starkville. Scott recovered a fumble in the game. "It was a great team effort. Our boys came out in the fourth quarter and did what they had to do to win the ball game".

GAME 6:   LOUISVILLE (5-0) vs HOUSTON (3-1)
                 LOUISVILLE 28 HOUSTON 7
                 October 1, 1993: HOMECOMING

Few remembered their only other meeting in 1945 where Louisville came out on top 47-13. The Hilltoppers served as Homecoming victims on a night where the Cats scored on their first three drives.

Nicholson was first from 20 yards on the ground and then 71 yards on a Robbins strike. He then crossed from 21 yards, and with Weems kicks, it was 21-0. They added more in the 2nd quarter on a 24-yard Robbins pass to Gideon Kelly. Weems made halftime 28-0. Houston scored in the 3rd quarter on a Tony Johnson 3-yarder. Their PAT was good.

Bo Miller and Slaughter recorded fumble recoveries, Nicolson put up 224 yards with 91 on the ground, and Robbins threw for 133 yards. The defense held Houston to only 33 passing yards.

GAME 7:   LOUISVILLE (6-0) @ CHOCTAW COUNTY, AL (4-1)
                                 LOUISVILLE 21 CHOCTAW COUNTY 6
                                 October 8, 1993

The first-time opponent across the state line in Butler, AL was an unknown quantity for Louisville. Despite the 5A team proving *"a worthy adversary"*, the Cats scored in each of the first three frames.

Nicholson had the first late in the opening quarter on a 28-yard run, Coby Miller had the next on a 73-yard escape, and Nicholson wrapped it up with a 62-yarder. Late in the contest, Reginald Ruffin scooped up a Cat fumble and took it 64 yards to the end zone. Scott stopped their two-point effort. Louisville rushed for 291 of their 351 yards with Nicholson leading with 129 yards. Carter added his fifth interception.

GAME 8:   LOUISVILLE (7-0) @ NEW HOPE (0-6)
                                 LOUISVILLE 49 NEW HOPE 0
                                 October 15, 1993

The New Hope team, a relative newcomer to the Wildcat football schedule, had yet to win against Louisville in three tries since 1988. This one would not fare well.

Nicholson started the barrage midway through the opening frame with a 1-yard run. Shortly thereafter, Kenyon Smith grabbed a fumble and took it to the end zone. With a pair of Weems kicks it was already 14-0. One more tally came before the quarter ended via a 2-yard Nicholson run and it was quickly 21-0. Robbins and Anthony Glenn hooked up for the only tally of the 2nd quarter from five yards and halftime sat 28-0.

With reserves in play, Nicholson broke through from 26 yards while Steve Henley got the next from four yards. Gideon Kelly had the last merciful tally in the finale from a yard to end things. Weems was true on all PATs for the night. Henley led rushers with 117 yards while Nicholson was close with 108. Robbins threw for 54 yards and the Cats led first downs (16-6). Carter picked off his sixth pass while the defense held New Hope to 73 yards.

GAME 9:   LOUISVILLE (8-0) vs NOXUBEE COUNTY (1-6)
                                 LOUISVILLE 34 NOXUBEE COUNTY 0
                                 October 22, 1993

In 15 encounters, only once (1982) had Noxubee come out victorious in the meetings. This year, they seemed at a low point and the undefeated Cats took advantage.

The Cats made it look easy as they opened with a 1-yard Coats run after a bad NCHS punt. Kenyon Smith blocked a later punt and Carter took it six yards to paydirt. The Weems kick, his first of four, made it 13-0. Robbins had the next the 2nd quarter from 25 yards while Henley got across after from 25 yards. In the 3rd quarter, Nicholson broke through from 41 yards to finish Cat scoring.

Louisville put up only 202 yards but all came on the ground. Nicholson led rushers with 68 yards. The Wildcats lost first downs 12-6 but the defense held Noxubee to just 154 total yards. Carter recorded a pair of interceptions while Smith had another.

GAME 10:   LOUISVILLE (9-0) @ NESHOBA CENTRAL (7-1)
                                 LOUISVILLE 0 NESHOBA COUNTY 10
                                 October 29, 1993

The real test of the season was now at hand as Number 3 (Super 10) and Number 5 (AP) Louisville faced two Dandy Dozen players at their home confines. Those included both running back Jamie Day and quarterback Domarco Fox. However, the contest against Number 8 was miniscule this this week as Gideon Kelly, second leading receiver for Louisville, sat in a coma after a car accident. Coach Moore noted, *"Kelly is breathing on his own. It could be a long, drawn-out deal. The kids have responded well. They understand the seriousness of it".*

The Union Appeal picked Neshoba 15-14 knowing that Neshoba had to win to get in postseason and were hosting. The Clarion-Ledger did the same 20-17 noting, *"The Rockets will prove up to the test".*

All scoring in the defensive contest was completed by halftime. Neshoba's first drive ended in Brandt Winstead's 29-yard FG to make it 3-0. In the 2nd quarter, Fox scrambled and hit Brian Madison from 59 yards for their only touchdown. Winstead nailed the PAT and it was over. *"Penalties and an interception killed Wildcat drives"* afterwards. Though Carter recovered a later fumble that led to a drive to the NCHS 15, it went nowhere as time expired.

"We can't blame it on the weather. Neshoba Central has a great team. We could never get untracked. They hit the big one right there before halftime and that was the difference". Neshoba led first downs (9-8), rushing (158-115) and passing (72-54). Robbins led the ground with 42 yards. Kelly succumbed to his injuries in September of 1996.

GAME 11:   LOUISVILLE (9-1) vs ABERDEEN (1-8)
                   LOUISVILLE 28 ABERDEEN 7
                   November 4, 1993

The seventh place Super 10 ranking meant little as the Wildcats recovered from their first loss in attempt to march to another title. Now Aberdeen was next as the Cats finalized the regular season. It did not hurt as they had only one win on the campaign.

Though both squads seemed to move the football in the opening frame, nothing ended on the scoreboard. Midway through the 2nd quarter, Robbins hit Ray Ivy for a touchdown and Weems put it 7-0. In the 3rd quarter, Randall Rowe found open ground for his 21-yard scoring run and Scott Rowe tied it. A pair of Aberdeen fumbles later led to scores.

Nicholson was first from 17 yards and, late in the game, Coats had the last from 21 yards. Weems was true on both. The defense allowed only 116 yards on five first downs. Morris Scott and Carter had fumble recoveries. Nicholson rushed for 104 yards to pace the total 292 offensive yards for Louisville.

GAME 12:   LOUISVILLE (10-1) @ OLIVE BRANCH (9-1)
                   LOUISVILLE 38 OLIVE BRANCH 7
                   November 12, 1993

In the three contests against the Conquistadors from 1985-1987, the Wildcats came out victorious in all. None of the three were blowout wins. Now, the season started again on the road to another state title. The Clarion-Ledger picked Louisville 24-10.

Despite a 49-yard opening possession with Nicholson dashing 49 yards, the Cats had to settle for a 45-yard Weems FG. Scott blocked an ensuing punt and Robbins made it count from eight yards. Before it the frame ended, Nicholson ran in from 10 yards and Weems put the Wildcats up 17-0. Their only tally of the 2nd quarter came on another Scott blocked punt and Darren Middleton recovered it in the end zone. Weems made it 24-6.

In the 3rd quarter, Anthony Mitchell picked up a loose fumble and rambled 35 yards to paydirt. In the finale, Robbins took off from 39 yards again Weems again converted. The Dores' only tally came via a Chris Milam 14-yard run and Larry Mullins PAT. Nicholson ran for 121 yards in the total 202 offensive output. All of it was on the ground. Olive Branch had a total of 189 yards. Cornell Miller had an interception.

GAME 13:   LOUISVILLE (11-1) vs GRENADA (9-3)
                   LOUISVILLE 37 GRENADA 0
                   November 19, 1993

Number six Super 10 Louisville welcome a Grenada team coached by Neil Hitchcock with an overall Cat record of a 14-3-1 going back to 1965. Nevertheless, each game counted as much as the last of the season. The Clarion-Ledger picked Louisville 30-14.

This second round game could not be better for the Wildcats. Coats got scoring underway with a 15-yard touchdown. Weems soon added a 22-yard FG to make it 9-0. In the 2nd quarter, Robbins kept it from five yards while Nicholson added a 6-yarder, with Weems kicks, to make halftime 23-0.

A second half Charger fumble turned into a 1-yard Nicholson scoring dive while the Cats inserted the dagger in the finale when Henley crossed from two yards. Weems was true on all kicks. The last touchdown came via a Marcus Slaughter fumble recovery. Nicholson rushed for 102 yards to put him at 1,025 on the season while Robbins added 76 more on the ground. Louisville rushed for 281 of 355 total yards. Fumble recoveries went to Scott, Slaughter, and David Crowder.

GAME 14:   LOUISVILLE (12-1) vs NESHOBA CENTRAL (11-1)
                            LOUISVILLE 27 NESHOBA CENTRAL 0
                            November 26, 1993

Just four weeks previous, the Rockets beat the Wildcats to spoil a run at a perfect season. Now the two met again for the North 4A championship and a spot in the state finals. The Hattiesburg American picked Louisville 20-16 in the rematch while The Clarion-Ledger favored Neshoba Central 14-13.

Louisville recorded the only tally of the half on their first drive. Moving 66 yards, Robbins capped it with a 13-yard strike to Martez Triplett and Weems converted. Both teams missed FGs in the half. Neshoba seemed poised to score in the 3rd quarter but the Cats recovered a Demarco Fox fumble at the 34-yard line. Then, Darren Middleton blocked a Rocket punt to put them at the 8-yard line. Coats got across from four yards two plays later and it was 14-0.

Both Nicholson (28) and Henley (44) found the end zone as the clock wound down. Neshoba led in first downs (12-10) while Louisville controlled the ground (251-149) and air (26-16). Fumble recoveries went to Rodney Wraggs, Judd Boswell, Bo Miller and David Crowder. Robbins led rushers with 101 yards.

GAME 15:   LOUISVILLE (13-1) vs MAGEE (13-0)
                            LOUISVILLE 25 MAGEE 6
                            December 4, 1993: Memorial Stadium; Jackson, MS

Unbelievably, this was the inaugural matchup for these two teams on the football field. Said Coach Perry Wheat, *"They're the best team, by far, we will have played. We have a lot of respect for them. We know what we're up against"*. The Winston County Journal picked Louisville 20-13 as did The Clarion-Ledger 19-16.

Magee ran into a first-half buzz saw on this Saturday morning. Louisville took their opening drive to paydirt on Robbins' 30-yard keeper. The Trojans moved as far as the Louisville 13 before faltering. In the 2nd quarter, they went 73 yards in six plays with Coats bursting in from a yard out. Later, they moved 72 yards in only three plays with Coby Miller escaping from 57 yards for the touchdown to make halftime 18-0. In the 3rd quarter, Chad Grayson hit Charles Johnson from 46 yards away to cut into the lead. However, Louisville had another left in them when Nicholson darted 62 yards on a QB keeper. Weems's extra point was true.

Magee led in first downs (14-11) and passing (179-72) but were dominated on the ground 267-105. Nicholson rushed for 105 yards, Bo Miller recovered two fumbles and Middleton another. *"We knew Louisville would move the ball on us. We gave up three long runs and a long pass. You just can't do that against Louisville. They physically took the ball game. We had hoped to throw the ball a good bit, but our pass protection broke down. Defensively, we just didn't get the job done early"*.

Said Moore, *"We've been working towards this for a long time. We got our chance and we got the job done. This is a great bunch of football players"*.

Moine Nicholson garnered a slew of honors. Those included Clarion-Ledger All-State, Mississippi Gatorade Player of the Year, and Mississippi Sports Writers Association All-State, among others. Morris Scott also grabbed a Clarion-Ledger All-State and MSWA All-State nod.

1994 (12-2)

The defending 4A champions entered the 1994 campaign with 22 lost letter winners from that squad. Voters still had the Wildcats second in 2-4A and overall 4A behind Starkville. They also sat fifth in The Clarion-Ledger Super 10 with three Top 100 Seniors on the squad: Darrell Robbins, Coby Miller and Anthony Mitchell.

"We're not going to be bad. The players have really responded and worked hard and it will be very tough because we play in a tough division. We are going to play hard and do the right things and winning will take care of itself".

GAME 1:   LOUISVILLE (0-0) vs YAZOO CITY (0-0)
                      LOUISVILLE 30 YAZOO CITY 7
                      August 26, 1994

New coach Bennie Tillman spoke about this contest during game week. *"The squad will be opening with one of the toughest teams in the state... but I feel that we are more than prepared for the challenge and will fare well. We can play against any team in the state and we will get a chance to see what we are made of in the contest".* The Clarion-Ledger fairly accurately picked Louisville 27-6.

The Indians surprised home fans with the first touchdown via a 19-yard Ladon Moore run and Michael Carter PAT. However, it was all Louisville thereafter. Coby Miller dashed 71 yards to cut the end of the first 7-6. Before halftime, they added a safety, a 16-yard Darrell Robbins pass to Charles Henton, Miller's two-point conversion, a late 39-yard Marcus Thames reception. Jason Burchfield converted to make it 23-7.

The last tally came in the 3rd quarter on a 33-yard Henton dash and Burchfield PAT. Reserves then took the field. Louisville led in first downs (15-9), rushing (323-165) and passing (91-0). Miller rushed for 176 yards in just three quarters. The bad side was the five fumbles in the opening half. Said Moore, *"We weren't losing the game. But we were letting them stay in it.*

GAME 2:   LOUISVILLE (1-0) @ TUPELO (0-1)
                      LOUISVILLE 19 TUPELO 3
                      September 2, 1994

This meeting was traditionally a very tough one for both sides. It was now time to see what the Cats looked like against strong competition. Much like the opening contest, the opponent scored first before Louisville got it going and took over.

The Golden Wave held a 3-0 lead after a frame thanks to a 20-yard Michael Key FG. The Cats put up 13 points before halftime for the lead they would not relinquish. Miller's early departure due to a separated shoulder opened the door for Peter Thames. He rushed across for scores of 13 and eight yards and Makoto Narahama added an extra point. A scoreless 3rd quarter led to the final tally from Tony Thompson on his 17-yard dash.

The Cat defense held Tupelo to just 107 offensive yards and Dandy Dozen QB Jarious Jackson to minus 16 rushing yards. *"It was a great win. Any time you can go to Tupelo and get a win, it's a great win".* Added Coach James Sloan, *"That's the worst whipping I've ever been involved with. We got whipped in every phase of the game".*

GAME 3:   LOUISVILLE (2-0) vs GREENVILLE WESTON (0-2)
                      LOUISVILLE 27 GREENVILLE WESTON 6
                      September 9, 1994

Their inaugural meeting the prior year was a 38-8 bloodbath. This season proved a bit closer. Louisville got going on a first-play fumble recovery by Jonathan Burt but it was to no avail. However, they still managed points some plays later when Tyler Peterson hit Henton from 23 yards and Kevin Aycock converted. Burchfield then recovered a loose football and Peterson used it to run 13 yards to paydirt.

The Wildcats added seven more points before halftime when Peterson hit Ray Ivy from 24 yards and Aycock added the kick. Their last points came in the 3rd quarter on Miller's 8-yard effort and Aycock kick. The Golden Eagles avoided the shutout in the finale on a 1-yard Ghuneen Redmond plunge.

GAME 4:   LOUISVILLE (3-0) @ WEST POINT (0-2)
                      LOUISVILLE 13 WEST POINT 10
                      September 16, 1994

The green and white seem to be having a down year but any meeting would be tough in a rivalry. This one proved to be just that.

An early Robbins interception at midfield led to 1-yard Torrence Young QB sneak, Jason Moore PAT and 7-0 West Point advantage. Only a fumble later in the frame stopped them from increasing the lead. In the 4th quarter, Robbins drove across from a yard and the successful PAT tied the affair. The defense recovered a late West Point fumble to seal regulation.

West Point opened overtime with a 23-yard Moore FG. Now the Cats managed to snatch the win when Robbins again plunged through from a yard. *"You're looking at a win and we were six inches away from the goal line. We just felt like we had as good a chance to score from six inches away as we did to kick a field goal. It was two or three yards away; we probably would have kicked..."*

GAME 5:   LOUISVILLE (4-0) vs STARKVILLE (4-0)
                             LOUISVILLE 6 STARKVILLE 45
                             September 23, 1994

Prior to the season, Moore noted, *"Starkville is going to be very good"*. Even he may not have realized how strong they were to be in competition. True, Louisville was third in The Super 10, but the Jackets were second. The Clarion-Ledger picked Starkville 22-17.

The Yellow Jackets dominated the ball game from start to finish. An opening frame 5-yard Kevin Randall run and the first of seven Jake Arians kicks made it 7-0. They added more in the next frame on a 1-yard Randall run, a 34-yarder by Chris Rice and a 37-yard Arians FG. Two more tallies came in the 3rd quarter and Antwan Edwards' 48-yard escape and a 20-yard Randall toss to Rice.

Both scored in the finale. Marque Campbell found the stripe from two yards while Peter Thames found it from 26 yards for Louisville. Said Moore, *"We just got whipped tonight by a heck of a football team. Starkville was just a better team than us tonight"*. Starkville dominated first downs (18-9), rushing (327-60) and passing (98-47).

GAME 6:   LOUISVILLE (4-1) @ HOUSTON (1-3)
                             LOUISVILLE 28 HOUSTON 13
                             September 30, 1994

A win over Houston the previous year came at Hinze Stadium. Now the Wildcats journeyed to Houston with homes of rebounding from a sound defeat.

An early fumble to Houston set up their fourth down 1-yard dive by Tony Johnson and the Sanderson PAT to make it 7-0. As halftime neared, Peterson took the reins and hit Marcus Thames from 24 yards to close it to 7-6. The defenses held in the 3rd quarter but the finale was much different. An early fumble to Louisville ended on an 18-yard Thompson run and Robbins two-pointer.

Thompson then added an 11-yarder and Aycock the PAT. Houston tried to claw back into it with a 70-yard Johnson kickoff return. However, with just around 3:00 remaining, Cortez Miller blocked a Hilltopper punt and Judd Boswell recovered. Robbins ran 26 yards to the 1-yard line from where he dove in after. Aycock knocked home the kick.

GAME 7:   LOUISVILLE (5-1) vs CHOCTAW COUNTY, AL (3-0)
                             LOUISVILLE 26 CHOCTAW COUNTY 21
                             October 7, 1994: HOMECOMING

It was Homecoming in Winston County and the opponent was the Butler, AL squad meeting Louisville for just the second time. It was closer than fans wanted.

Robbins got it going early on his 18-yard dash and Aycock kick. Then Peterson hit Darzine Thames from 57 yards and Aycock made it 14-0. The Tigers answered with the only points of the 2nd quarter on a 2-yard Fitch dive. Louisville matched the six points in the 3rd quarter with a 45-yard Thompson run. Now 20-6 in the 4th quarter, Hasson Ruffin found the end zone for Choctaw County from 48 yards and Jamal Blakely hit Joe Parker for the two-points.

While Thompson answered with a 16-yard scoring run, Ruffin again broke away from near midfield for a 52-yard touchdown. Parker's kick made it 26-21. As the clock neared expiration, the visitors sat at the Cat 2. However, the defense held and the win was secured. Thompson led rushers with 154 yards while Robbins had 104 more. *"I think this is what we definitely needed. Our defense made the big stop when we had to"*.

GAME 8:   LOUISVILLE (6-1) vs NEW HOPE (1-6)
                             LOUISVILLE 41 NEW HOPE 0
                             October 14, 1994

It seemed that New Hope had no hope against Louisville as the Cats outscored them 173-27 in their only four meetings. This made it no better for the Trojans.

Strangely, the Wildcats had only one tally in the first half. That came on an early 17-yard Robbins run after Kenyon Smith recovered a bad Trojan snap. New Hope managed a drive to the Cat 5 but to no avail. In the 3rd quarter, Peterson ran in from 62 yards, Robbins from 60 yards, Zack Grady had a 25-yard pick-six, and Coby Miller ran in twice for the last from seven yards and one yard.

Miller (106) and Robbins (101) led rushers while Marcus Thames has 125 receiving yards. "I think we got started slow but we came on and scored a lot of points in the second half. We just hope to not get started so late in the game".

GAME 9:   LOUISVILLE (7-1) @ NOXUBEE COUNTY (0-7-1)
                 LOUISVILLE 40 NOXUBEE COUNTY 6
                 October 21, 1994

This was not much of a test against a team trending in the wrong direction. The field described as "a quagmire" may have held the final down even more.

While Noxubee started well with a 90-yard Pippen kick return, Louisville went on a scoring barrage soon after. Robbins crossed from three yards, Thompson from 26 then added a two-pointer to make it 14-6. In the 2nd quarter, Henton had a 40-yard pick-six and Cortez Miller a 25-yard fumble return. Aycock was true on the first touchdown. In the 3rd quarter, Darzine Thames pulled in a 28-yard pass while Robbins scored from a yard later. All was done by the end of the 3rd quarter.

"We will be ready by Friday (for Neshoba Central). There is no pressure on the players to win the game. Pressure is something you put on yourselves and we are not going to do that".

GAME 10:   LOUISVILLE (8-1) vs NESHOBA CENTRAL (6-2)
                  LOUISVILLE 34 NESHOBA CENTRAL 7
                  October 28, 1994

The game was essentially a playoff contest as the winner made the post season with Starkville while the loser's season ended. The Union Appeal chose Neshoba Central 14-7 and said they had "the better defensive ball club and that's where this game will be decided. Neshoba in a mild upset". The Clarion-Ledger disagreed and picked the Cats 22-14.

The Wildcats posted 21 unanswered points in the 1st quarter. Scores came on a Ray Ivy 68-yarder to Marcus Thames and Aycock PAT, a 5-yard Robbins run, and 1-yard Peterson dive. He then hit Robbins for the two points. The last tally came after an Anthony Mitchell blocked punt. Robert Yarbrough scored for the Rockets in the 2nd quarter from three yards and Jason Spears converted.

Back came Louisville with Thompson's 27-yard run and Aycock kick. The last points came in the 3rd quarter when Peterson found Thames from 27 yards. Louisville led in first downs (13-11) and passing (204-0). NCHS held the ground (198-148). "It got us back to where we need to be. It got us in the playoffs. We are exactly where we were a year ago".

GAME 11:   LOUISVILLE (9-1) @ ABERDEEN (2-7)
                  LOUISVILLE 32 ABERDEEN 2
                  November 4, 1994

The regular season finale against the Bulldogs was never in doubt as the Cats scored all of their points in the first three quarters. Peterson opened with a 71-yarder to Marcus Thames while Coby Miller dashed 77 yards for the next. Now 12-0, they added one more before halftime when Robbins crossed from four yards and Narahama added the PAT.

Thames opened the 3rd quarter with an interception and later grabbed a 27-yarder from Peterson. Miller wrapped it up for Louisville from 13 yards and Aycock converted. Aberdeen got on the board late on a safety. Thames had a pair of pickoffs.

GAME 12:   LOUISVILLE (10-1) @ MENDENHALL (8-3)
                  LOUISVILLE 28 MENDENHALL 7
                  November 11, 1994

In their only three battles, the Wildcats won in 1962 while losing in both 1964 and 1965. The Simpson County team was traditionally tough but this one proved to be a stellar second half showing for the visitors.

Mendy had the only touchdown of the first half when Larry Shower got across the stripe from two yards and Brian Barlow converted. The second half proved different as the Cats posted 14 points in each frame. Peterson and Thames connected from 13 yards, Henton had the next from 44 yards, and Aycock was true on both. In the finale, Robbins crossed from five and four yards and Aycock nailed both extra points. Both of the last Robbins scores came on Louisville fumble recoveries.

GAME 13:   LOUISVILLE (11-1) vs OXFORD (11-1)
                LOUISVILLE 47 OXFORD 16
                November 18, 1994

While losing contests to the Cats from 1976-1980, Oxford got revenge in both 1989 and 1990 with victories to end title aspirations. Said Moore, "*Oxford will be a challenge for our young men, being so well-balanced*".

Louisville started the scoring with a 7-yard Peterson run while Oxford managed only a 23-yard Wesley Flake FG. The Cats poured in 21 more points in the 2nd quarter on Peterson's 15-yarder to Thames, a safety, Robbins' 7-yarder, and Peterson's 22-yard throw to Henton. Aycock added the PAT.

Now 27-3, Peterson found Thames from 55 yards and Ivy from 21 yards. Oxford's only answer was a 3-yard Walt Hill run and Flake PAT. In the finale, Peter Thames crossed from three yards and Kevin Aycock converted. Oxford closed with a 38-yard blocked punt return by Blair Webb. Louisville amassed 350 total yards on offense. Peterson, now with 955 passing yards, earned a Clarion-Ledger Player of the Week nod.

The game was not without controversy. One Cat player was found to have a knife in his sock in the 2nd quarter. In the end, he was determined to have been cutting his stockings on the sidelines and just shoved it in his sock as he ran on the field. The MHSAA said, "*We feel this is something that was very isolated and there was no malice intended*".

GAME 14:   LOUISVILLE (12-1) @ STARKVILLE (13-0)
                LOUISVILLE 0 STARKVILLE 28
                November 25, 1994

Everyone remembered the severe beating the Wildcats endured in the fourth game of the season to Starkville. The Jackets were now first in the polls, 24th by The USAToday, and riding an 18-game winning streak. As such, The Clarion-Ledger picked them at home 24-20.

The game was much like the first, but a bit closer. Antwan Edwards had the only score of the opening quarter from five yards while Chris Rice added runs from ten and 34 yards before halftime. Jake Arians was true on all conversions and the one after. That score came in the 3rd quarter when Kevin Randall hit Edwards from 41 yards.

Again, the Jackets dominated stats in first downs (17-9), rushing (274-102) and passing (82-13). "*They've dominated us two games. They've got a great football team. They have no weaknesses. There's nothing they don't do well. They've got a great opportunity to win it (and) I hope they do well*".

Anthony Mitchell garnered a Clarion-Ledger All State honor, an Orlando Sentinel Dixie Dozen place and a spot on the Gatorade Super 35 list.

1995 (11-3)

After great success as head man in Louisville, Lynn Moore moved on to another job. Now taking the whistle was long time assistant Tony Stanford. "*Here at Louisville, there's always pressure. The kids expect to win and the town expects to win. We've got such a great tradition that the kids give an outstanding effort. We will have a chance to win most Friday nights when we step on the field*".

He added, "*We've got a lot of people back on defense and we feel like our linebackers are our strong point. We've got only two starters back on offense...*" Voters had the Cats first preseason 2-4A, second in 4A and seventh in The Clarion-Ledger Super 10.

GAME 1:   LOUISVILLE (0-0) vs TUPELO (0-0)
               LOUISVILLE 14 TUPELO 16
               September 1, 1995

The Wildcats carried three consecutive wins over Tupelo but their season openers against the Golden Wave ended in losses. *"This town expects these kids to go out there and have a winning team and the kids know it. And these kids have grown up used to winning. They will go out there on Friday nights and try to win the best they can"*. The Clarion-Ledger picked Louisville 22-14.

Names of scorers from The Clarion-Ledger and The Winston County Journal differ completely. The Clarion-Ledger said that Tupelo started strong with a 4-yard Jackson touchdown run, a Stevens kick, and his later 20-yard FG. The Winston County Journal put it as a 22-yard Kevin Scott FG and Michael Osborne's 1-yarder after a fumble recovery early in the 2nd quarter. Louisville came back with Tyler Peterson's 19-yarder to Karlton Hampton and Jason Burchfield PAT. Before halftime, the Cats took the lead when Steve Henley went untouched to paydirt from 11 yards. Burchfield made it 14-10.

After a scoreless 3rd quarter, Tupelo scored with just 3:56 on the clock when Charles Penson hit Sammy Brooks for a touchdown. The Golden Wave ended any comeback hopes with a pair of interceptions. Peterson had 186 passing yards with Jeremy Eiland hauling in the most with 64 yards.

GAME 2:   LOUISVILLE (0-1) @ GREENVILLE WESTON (1-1)
               LOUISVILLE 31 GREENVILLE WESTON 0
               September 8, 1995

The lone report of the contest came from the opponent newspaper wherein they called the final 34-0. The Cats opened with a Cornelius Goss fumble return and Rajevski PAT. A bad snap gave Louisville a safety and 9-0 lead.

Martin Hathorn added a 38-yarder and Rajevski made it 16-0. Patrick Hudson's 14-yarder put halftime 22-0. Another bad snap by Weston added yet another safety. Late in the contest, Paul Harrison crossed from three yards and Rajeski nailed the last point. Peterson was 1-22 for 138 yards. Hathorn led receivers with 63 yards.

GAME 3:   LOUISVILLE (1-1) vs STARKVILLE (3-0)
               LOUISVILLE 19 STARKVILLE 55
               September 15, 1995

The 5A Yellow Jackets, ranked second in The Super 10, were not missing much of a stride as they held a 23-game win streak and completely dominated the Wildcats in 1994. Thus far, Meridian, Noxubee County and West Point fell to them. *"I'll be honest with you. Starkville may be better than last year. They've got so much more speed than we do"*. The Clarion-Ledger picked the Jackets 28-14.

The game turned out far worse than even the 1995 meeting as the Jackets ran wild. It was quickly 21-0 on a 44-yard Carl Fair dash, Surhaven Fair's 26-yarder, and a 36-yarder from Carl. Ken McDonald added the first two extra points while Jake Arians added the next. Louisville swung back with a 7-yarder to Petey Thames. However, Starkville came right back with a Carl Fair 58-yarder and Arians kick to end the 1st quarter 28-6.

The 2nd quarter was not much better. After an interception by Alex Peterson, Carl dashed 82 yards to paydirt. That was followed by Tanny Flowers' 16-yarder and 69-yarder with PATs by McDonald and Arians. Peterson could only get in from two yards before halftime.

Both scored lone touchdowns in the last two frames. Starkville was first on a 3-yard Flowers run and Arians kick while Henley got in from a yard with Martin Rajevksi adding the last extra point. The last was benefit of a fumble recovery. Starkville led in in rushing (565-114), Louisville in passing (202-0), and first downs were even (19-19). Henley led Cat rushers with 97 yards and Eiland in the air with 70 yards. Carl Fair put up 232 yards on just six carries.

"It didn't surprise me at all. We did all we could do. We knew all week it was going to be rough. Let somebody else try to stop them. I ain't got to do it no more. I've had my dang whipping. You never know what can happen in 5A, but they are good enough to win it all".

GAME 4:   LOUISVILLE (1-2) @ NEW HOPE (2-1)
                 LOUISVILLE 21 NEW HOPE 7
                 September 22, 1995

The hopeless home team welcomed Louisville with a game closer than many in the past. However, the Cats did bounce back from a humiliating defeat.

Louisville opened with a 70-yard march ending on a 5-yard Henley run and Rajevski kick. Late in the half, Martin Hathorn ran in from seven yards to make it 14-0 at halftime. Henley crossed again from a yard after for the Cat's last. Michael Bailey recorded the lone New Hope TD on a 65-yard pitch and Blake Koeingherbger converted.

Henley had 156 rushing yards and 189 all-purpose yards while Peterson threw for 88 yards. LHS led first downs 16-7, rushing (284-79) and passing (88-85).

GAME 5:   LOUISVILLE (2-2) vs ABERDEEN (1-4)
                 LOUISVILLE 21 ABERDEEN 6
                 September 29, 1995

Aberdeen's only win in 12 meetings since 1937 came in 1956 (38-14). This one ended almost exactly like the last Wildcat game of 1995.

An opening drive ended in a failed FG effort but Martin Hathorn's blocked punt set up a an eventual 3-yard Peterson scoring run and Rajevski added his first of three PATs. Three minutes later, Peterson and Hathorn connected from 32 yards. Derek Hopkins runs in the 3rd quarter set up a 1-yard Henley dive and scoring for Louisville was complete. The Bulldogs got their only tally on the next possession via a 68-yard Frederick Fields run.

Louisville led in offensive yards 277-125. The defense allowed only 83 of those. One play gave them 67 yards of the total. Petey Thames led rushers with 62 yards while Peterson had 98 in the air. Hathorn also pulled down 57 receiving yards.

GAME 6:   LOUISVILLE (3-2) @ WEST POINT (1-5)
                 LOUISVILLE 35 WEST POINT 7
                 October 6, 1995

The recap from the game is surprisingly short despite a strong Louisville showing against their longtime opponent. Zack Grady recorded a pair of touchdowns in the opening half via a blocked punt return and a 20-yard fumble return. Henley ran in twice from a yard while Peterson found Hathorn from 13 yards in the 2nd quarter. The lone West Point tally came in the 2nd quarter on a 1-yard Robertson dive and Chris Jenkins PAT.

GAME 7:   LOUISVILLE (4-2) @ HOUSTON (0-7)
                 LOUISVILLE 42 HOUSTON 3
                 October 13, 1995

Both prior meetings saw the Wildcats walk away with wins. This contest proved the greatest margin of victory in any of those. Late in the opening stanza and after a fumble recovery, Peterson hit Desmond Baker from six yards and Rajevski put it 7-0. Peterson upped it to 14-0 later with an 80-yard scamper.

Another recovered fumble midway through the 2nd quarter led to Peterson finding Petey Thames from 28 yards and Rajevski kicks put it 21-0. Before the game was over, Henley crossed from 10 yards, Peterson threw for another touchdown, and Grady found a fumble in the end zone for the finale. Extra points were true.

Houston avoided the shutout late on a 36-yard Paul Sanderson FG. The Cats led in first downs (5-4) while rushing for 105 and throwing for 181. Henley led rushers with just 51 yards. Houston lost three fumbles and the Wildcats a pair.

GAME 8:   LOUISVILLE (5-2) vs NOXUBEE COUNTY (1-6-1)
                 LOUISVILLE 38 NOXUBEE COUNTY 8
                 October 20, 1995

Going back to 1972, the Wildcats took 15 of 16 meetings. This one proved no different as Thames crossed from 18 and 10 yards. With Rajevski kicks, it was quickly 14-0. In the 2nd quarter, Grady recorded a 24-yard pick-six and Henley got across the stripe from six yards. Rajevski kicks put it 28-0 at intermission.

Rajevski added a 24-yard FG in the 3rd quarter and Peterson finished the evening in the last on a 46-yard connection with Henley. Again, Rajevski was true. Noxubee County found paydirt only late with a 79-yard Connor kickoff return to avoid the shutout against reserves. Harden's two-pointer proved the last points.

GAME 9:   LOUISVILLE (6-2) @ NESHOBA CENTRAL (6-2)
LOUISVILLE 14 NESHOBA CENTRAL 13
October 27, 1995

The Wildcats were 15-5 since the teams began play, but the Rockets were proving stronger opponents each game. As usual, The Union Appeal picked them 14-13. *"Win and they probably have a playoff berth. Lose and they stay home. That's what is on the line for Neshoba Central..."*

Their prediction was accurate but for the wrong team and Louisville secured the playoff berth. Henley tallied both Wildcat touchdowns and Rajevski both extra points. For Neshoba, Billy Singleton had two (12 and eight yards) for the Rockets, but Brant Winstead converted on only one, and that made the difference.

Peterson threw for 76 yards while Thames led rushers with 74 yards. The defense held NCHS to no passing yards in a 283-191 offensive yard comparison. *"Our guys played well. The defense did a great job. Offensively we made some mistakes and I feel that if we had not made those mistakes, Neshoba would have never scored on us. The turning point of the game was when our offensive line controlled their defensive front".*

GAME 10:   LOUISVILLE (7-2) vs KOSCIUSKO (7-3)
LOUISVILLE 7 KOSCIUSKO 14
November 3, 1995

Kosy was one of the longest-serving matchups in Wildcat history. In fact, they played from 1951 to 1988 without interruption with many games before. Now, they were back after a six-year delay and a power awaiting to continue their success. *"It's going to be a tough ball game. Kosciusko has a good throwing game and they have two real good running backs who can run the ball hard. Offensively we are going to have to maintain and control their defensive front because they have some big players".*

It was Kosciusko taking the 2-4A title on this evening despite a scoreless opening frame in cold temperatures. Cornelius Thames had an interception but soon R'dele Olive *"returned the favor"*. Neither were to any avail. Peterson had the first tally on a 35-yard keeper and Rajevski kick put them up 7-0. Sam Potts evened it before halftime on an 8-yarder to Bill Roundtree and Jackson Jordan kick.

Kosciusko found the last points on a Demetric Armstead 10-yard toss to Lakendrick Williams and Jordan put them ahead with 2:26 left in the 3rd quarter. Kosy had the ball last deep in Cat territory and simply ran the clock for the division win. Kosciusko led on the ground 290-120. Letron Overstreet had an interception and Peterson threw for 99 yards. *"They just beat our butts, any way you look at it. They were better than us tonight. The cold weather didn't have anything to do with it. They just whipped (us). It was nothing we did to ourselves. They just ran over us".*

GAME 11:   LOUISVILLE (7-3) @ YAZOO CITY (6-5)
LOUISVILLE 42 YAZOO CITY 7
November 10, 1995

While the first contest came in 1940, four more were played since 1988. In all five the Wildcats exited victorious. This one was over early.

Midway through the 1st quarter, Peterson took off from 33 yards and Rajevski added his first of many extra points. Before the quarter ended, Henley broke free from 18 yards. Midway through the 2nd quarter, Louisville made it 21-0 on a 1-yard Petey Thames plunge. YCHS notched their lone score after recovering a fumble when Kerry Hodges dove in from a yard and added the PAT.

The Cats put up only one touchdown in the 3rd quarter via a Henley 18-yarder. In the finale, Peterson nailed the coffin with runs from six and three yards. Louisville led in first downs (11-6) and rushing (285-40) while Yazoo held the air (44-0). *"This is a must-win situation for us to continue looking for our State Championship. Our kids will have the ability to rebound after the tough loss to Kosciusko".*

GAME 12:   LOUISVILLE (8-3) vs MAGEE (9-3)
                  LOUISVILLE 17 MAGEE 13
                  November 17, 1995

There were still some from the 1993 squad that remembered their first meeting. In that game, the Wildcats beat the undefeated Trojans for the state championship. For a long while, it looked as if Magee would get their revenge.

Midway through the 1st quarter, Henley got through numerous defenders for a 33-yard Cat touchdown and Rajevski converted for the 7-0 lead. Three minutes later, Fred Patrick bested the effort with a 69-yard dash and Marcus Myers tied the contest. Louisville's return drive stopped inside the 20-yard line and Rajevski nailed a 35-yard FG. However, Magee punched back with a 70-yard march capped by James Mangum's 1-yard plunge. That kept halftime 13-10 in favor of Magee.

The best chance for a score in the 3rd quarter came from Magee but they could move only to the 16-yard line. Early in the final quarter, Peterson found Mark Clement for 39 yards to put the ball at the 10. From there, Henley ran in from 7 yards and Rajevski provided the PAT. After recovering a fumble with 2:35 remaining, Magee was unable to move and ran out of downs to end their season.

First downs (7-6) and rushing (182-171) went to Magee. Henley led Cat rushers with 114 yards. Boswell (12) and Kenyon Smith (11) led tacklers. Peterson threw for 58 more yards, per The Winston County Journal. Magee claimed a Trojan advantage 63-39.

GAME 13:   LOUISVILLE (9-3) vs PEARL (9-4)
                  LOUISVILLE 24 PEARL 0
                  November 24, 1995

In 1985, Louisville ended Pearl championship hopes 23-7. Since then, the two met in 1991 and 1992 with the teams splitting wins. Said Coach Bruce Merchant, "We're just elated to be playing right now. They're going to try to line up and run over us".

The home team hit first at the end of the opening frame when Peterson escaped from the 44-yard lane. Rajevski's PAT was his first of three. Pearl came right back with a 77-yard drive to the Cat 3 before Rodrecus Rand fumbled at the one-foot line. After the Pirate defense held, the Wildcats went to the bag of tricks on fourth down at the 12-yard line. Instead of punting, they ran the ball for a first down. The drive moved to the Pirate 14 but ended when Sean Keyes picked off a pass as the half ended.

Louisville opened the 3rd quarter with a 64-yard drive capped midway through the frame on a 1-yard Henley run. Now in the finale, the home team scored on a 23-yard Rajevski FG. An ensuing Rand pass was intercepted, but it produced no points. However, Rand's ensuing fumble on the next drive led to a 1-yard Henley scoring run.

Said Merchant, "They physically won the game at the line of scrimmage. That's where ball games are won and lost. The second half, they came out and rammed the ball down our throats. That was the difference in the game. In the playoffs, we didn't have any turnovers until tonight. I don't know if our fumble at their 1-yard line would have had a lot of bearing on the outcome of the game, but I would like to think it did".

Added Stanford, "This was a defense-controlled game. Our defense just shut them down all night". Louisville held the advantage in first downs (17-10), rushing (319-90) and passing (34-29). Peterson rushed for 134 yards to pace the ground game.

GAME 14:   LOUISVILLE (10-3) vs McCOMB (9-4)
                  LOUISVILLE 14 McCOMB 7
                  December 1, 1995: Veteran Memorial Stadium; Jackson, MS

The previous meeting between the teams came in a 1938 Wildcat defeat. Prior to this one, Stanford said, "I think McComb is the best team to come out of the south division in ten years. They are a physical team on offense. Defensively they are really quick. Our defensive front and offensive line will have to control the line of scrimmage". The Clarion-Ledger (19-14) and The Hattiesburg American (24-7) chose Louisville.

"Unranked and seemingly forgotten when the postseason began, Louisville won perhaps its most unlikely state championship yet". Louisville recorded the only score of the first three quarters in the first frame when Peterson hit Jeremy Eiland from 23 yards and Rajevski added the PAT. It seemed McComb tied it with a 2-yard run but it came back for clipping. Their FG opportunity failed thanks to a Grady block.

At the end of the 3rd quarter, Smith picked off a Derrick Pittman pass to end a threat. That led to Henley's 1-yarder and Rajevski kick. With 1:54, McComb dotted the board on Brian Crimeal's 10-yarder and Hart PAT. After recovering the onside kick, it was Letron Overstreet's interception sealing the 4A title.

Said Stanford, Clarion-Ledger Coach of the Week said, "We've ruled 4A since it started. It hurt our kids when everybody dropped us after we lost a couple of games. Our kids took it on themselves to prove we're as good as anybody in 4A. We came together as a team and are just proud of ourselves".

Added McComb mentor Lee Bramlett, "We couldn't overcome the mistakes. We're a ball-control offense and when we don't make the mistakes, we give ourselves a better chance of winning. Either team could have won. We played hard but we got a TD called back. Louisville's just got a fine team".

Louisville led in rushing (156-111) but lost passing (107-49) and first downs (13-9). Henley paced Cat rushers with 83 yards.

The Clarion-Ledger All-State Second Team Defense included Judd Boswell and Kenyon Smith. 2-4A honors went to Tyler Peterson (MVP), Boswell and Smith (Most Valuable Defensive Backs), Kendrick Ball, Brad Bradford, Kelvin Goss, Steve Henley, Cortez Miller, Cornelius Thames and Jason Wallace. Honorable Mentions included Gary Ashford, Kelvin Cistrunk, Chris Crosby, Josh Davenport, Zack Grady, Adam Lowrey and Petey Thames.

Internal awards included Peterson, Kendrick Ball, Davenport, Cistrunk, Ashford, Boswell, Smith, Petey Thames, Monty Thames, Kelvin Goss, Bradford, Jason Wallace and Chris Crosby.

1996 (8-6)

Tony Stanford came back for his second year with a state title under his belt in his inaugural season. With 10 returning starters, voters put the Wildcats first in 2-4A and ninth in The Clarion-Ledger Super 10 preseason.

Relative to Louisville having never missed the playoffs, he said, "Our players don't want that streak to end. If it did, the community would run me out of town and might shoot half of them. I think a lot of our success has to do with the community. They instill it in their kids. The kids grow up believing they are supposed to win. You have to attribute it to the parents".

On the coming campaign, he added, "I think we've got the players to have a great ball club but the biggest thing is our defense has to come around. Year in and year out, a lot of the top 4A teams come from this area".

GAME 1:   LOUISVILLE (0-0) @ AMORY (0-0)
                   LOUISVILLE 14 AMORY 34
                   August 29, 1996

While the two schools traded coaches over the decades, they had yet to meet on the gridiron. The 3A Panthers, with former Wildcat mentor Bobby Hall in charge, were 15-0 the previous year and state champion. The Clarion-Ledger picked Louisville 21-14.

An early Cat fumble to Erby Hampton led to a 1-yard Chris Jones dive. Another fumble to Wade Polk resulted in a 4-yard Steve Griffin escape and Jones added the two-pointer for a 14-0 lead after a frame. Louisville had the only points of the 2nd quarter when Elliot Carter found the end zone from two yards. The second half was not going to go well for the visitors.

Michael Goss started things with an interception to allow a Carter cross from 14 yards. He also found paydirt for the game-tying two-pointer but Amory took control afterwards. They notched touchdowns on a Griffin 11-yard run and 1-yarder. With David Mooneyham kicks, it was 28-14. In the finale, Griffin dashed 85 yards for the only score of the quarter.

Louisville actually led in first downs (16-9) and passing (35-0) while the Panthers held the ground (253-222). Amory's Hampton recovered two fumbles and had a Tyler Peterson interception. "We had missed opportunities in the first half and they took it to us in the second half. They were better than us tonight".

GAME 2:   LOUISVILLE (0-1) @ TUPELO (1-0)
                               LOUISVILLE 21 TUPELO 39
                               September 6, 1996

It would not be easier as the Wildcats journeyed to Tupelo to face the Golden Wave. After a scoreless 1st quarter, Tupelo exploded with 32 points. Luke McAlpin (1), a Jason Miller two pointer from Jack Hill, Kevin Williams (18), Lanauda Bolden 55-yard reception from McAlpin, Detricks Beckley 41-yarder from McAlpin, and three Scott Weatherly PATs and a 26-yard FG made up their scoring.

The lone tally from Louisville was Mark Clemons' 1-yarder and Michael Smith's PAT. In the 3rd quarter, Goss pulled in a 24-yard Peterson toss and Smith converted. Now 32-14, Goss scored from 14 yards and Smith added the extra point.

Tupelo put it away in the last with a touchdown and PAT despite a blocked punt by the Cats. Tupelo led in rushing (288-186) while the Cats held the air (222-157). Peterson threw for the 222 yards with just one interception. *"We had four fumbles and an interception. We also had 11 penalties, which cost us 100 yards. When you have that many turnovers and that many penalties, you just cannot win a game"*.

For the Wave, Williams had a touchdown and 274 rushing yards (according to The Clarion-Ledger).

GAME 3:   LOUISVILLE (0-2) vs GREENVILLE WESTON (0-2)
                               LOUISVILLE 35 GREENVILLE WESTON 12
                               September 13, 1996

The last 0-2 start came just in 1991 when the Wildcats eventually took home the 4A state championship. It was a good time to get a win against a winless Weston squad that was 0-3 against Louisville. It also marked the first home game of 1996.

Louisville wasted no time with 14 points in the opening frame. First, Terrance Yarbrough pulled in a 19-yard Peterson toss while Carter later ran in from 12 yards. Smith added both kicks. In the 2nd quarter, Thames crossed from nine yards to make it 20-0. While Weston added either a 65-yard Scott run to paydirt or a 65-yard Jermaine Johnson pass to Jimmy Davenport, Louisville responded with a 22-yard Peterson pass to Goss and Peterson's two-point run. Halftime stood 28-6.

Now in the finale, both found scores. Weston's Quintarius McCray took a fumble 63 (or 40) yards but the extra point failed. Thames found the end zone from three yards and Smith converted. Louisville passed for 102, rushed for 179 and had 15 first downs. Thames led with 117 yards on the ground while Kelvin Cistrunk led tacklers with 12.

"Overall, we played better. We still had a lot of mistakes. With the upcoming Starkville game, we are going to have to play a mistake-free ball game. It's a very big game for our team".

GAME 4:   LOUISVILLE (1-2) @ STARKVILLE (2-1)
                               LOUISVILLE 0 STARKVILLE 17
                               September 20, 1996

Said Stanford on game week, *"Offensively, Starkville is better than last year. Defensively, they are not quite as good. They're blessed with good athletes. Right now, they are hard to handle. Probably if we bring out the National Guard, then we would have a chance. The biggest thing that hurt us is turnovers. We've got to play an error-free game. Defensively, we haven't stopped anybody yet. We're going to play hard, though, and anything can happen"*. The Clarion-Ledger picked Starkville 31-14.

Halftime sat only 3-0 in favor of the Yellow Jackets thanks to an 1st quarter Neil Couvillion 28-yard FG. The Cats moved to the Jacket 2 in the next frame but a missed FG kept the lead the same. Starkville scored touchdowns in each of the last two frames on a 42-yard Freddie Milons run and 3-yarder by Dewayne Carter. Couvillion was true on both kicks. The home team led first downs (16-12) and rushing (314-148). Passing went to the Cats 74-66.

"Even with the loss, we played a much better game than we have in the last few. We still want to work on penalties (only 2 for 15 yards). They really hurt us at crucial times. The next game is the one that counts. Starkville controlled the second half of the game. Our offense had only 12-15 plays total. Our defense got a little tired". Thames led rushers with 68 yards while Martin Hathorn paced tacklers with 13 total.

GAME 5:   LOUISVILLE (1-3) vs NEW HOPE (3-1)
                                  LOUISVILLE 20 NEW HOPE 21
                                  September 27, 1996

This was no regular "No Hope" opponent at Hinze Stadium as the Trojans were 3-1 thus far to open district play for Louisville. Said Stanford, "*In a way, we are starting 0-0 this week*". The final must have come as a disappointment to all Wildcat players and supporters.

The Cats struck first in the 2nd quarter thanks Chad Steele's blocked Blake Koenigsberger FG effort taken 85 yards to paydirt. Smith's PAT made it 7-0. In the 3rd quarter, Demetrius Shirley dashed in for 80 yards to close the gap 7-6. Peterson then hit Terrence Yarbrough from 16 yards to make it 14-6. With :47 left, Scott Kappler hit Lawrence Porter from 13 yards and then hit Lance White for the tying two points.

In overtime, Shirley scored from seven yards and Koenigsberger converted. The Cats answered on a 15-yard Peterson pass to Thames, but the PAT failed. Shirley had 125 yards in the contest. Letron Overstreet rushed for 89 yards, Peterson passed for 112 yards, and Jerrell Thompson led with eight tackles on defense.

"*In 1986, we lost our first district game. Then we came back and won every game afterward and ended up winning the state championship. All we have to do now is win the rest of them. We dominated most of the game*".

GAME 6:   LOUISVILLE (1-4) vs ABERDEEN (2-3)
                                  LOUISVILLE 30 ABERDEEN 0
                                  October 4, 1996

In 1956, the Wildcats began 1-7 to start the season. This year, the Wildcats could shape up the same if things did not change. Of Aberdeen, Stanford said, "*They have a real good ball team. We are going to be trying to get down offensively. From here on out, we gotta win the rest of them*".

Peterson opened with a 1-yard dive and Smith converted. The half ended 10-0 thanks to Smith's 33-yard FG. Petey Thames increased it in the 3rd quarter from 60 yards, as did Overstreet from 10 yards. Zack Grady recorded a 40-yard pick-six and the Smith conversion finished scoring.

"*Defensively we couldn't ask for a better game. This was the best game our defense ever played. It was a good game and because we were ahead, we put our subs in during the 4th quarter; mainly sophomores and juniors but we saw a lot of potential there. We're going to be up all night with what's coming up*".

GAME 7:   LOUISVILLE (2-4) vs WEST POINT (2-4)
                                  LOUISVILLE 28 WEST POINT 26
                                  October 11, 1996

It seemed strange that West Point lost the last six meetings against Louisville. They were traditionally tougher but Louisville always seemed ready. This one was close.

The Cats scored on the first offensive play when Peterson ran 73 yards to paydirt and Smith converted his first of four extra points. Back came West Point with a 1st quarter touchdown on Kelvin Strong's 50-yard dash while adding a 2nd quarter tally on a 3-yard Derry Hammond plunge and both Nick Dimino PATs. Now 14-7, Louisville tied it before halftime when Peterson ran in from 15 yards.

Peterson opened the 3rd quarter with a 35-yarder to Mark Clemons but West Point came back with a Strong 15-yard scoring dash. The crucial extra point was blocked. Overstreet found the end zone from 12 yards to increase the lead. West Point got across in the last frame via Jeremy Bell 6-yarder but their two-point effort to tie failed.

GAME 8:   LOUISVILLE (3-4) vs HOUSTON (1-5-1)
                                  LOUISVILLE 60 HOUSTON 20
                                  October 18, 1996: HOMECOMING

The only win by the Hilltoppers this year came by two points over Aberdeen. Due to no submission of game activity by the writer for The Winston County Journal nor The Clarion-Ledger, there was no substantial recap of the activity in the blowout.

The local paper from Houston noted their touchdowns came from Chico Chandler (2) and Jamye McIntosh. Marcus Hoskins had a two-pointer.

GAME 9:   LOUISVILLE (4-4) @ NOXUBEE COUNTY (5-3)
                 LOUISVILLE 22 NOXUBEE COUNTY 14
                 October 25, 1996

A district win was crucial to keep playoff hopes alive after losing their first to New Hope. Moreover, things looked good on paper, as the Wildcats were 17-1 against the Tigers since 1972.

Noxubee controlled the ball ten minutes of the opening stanza, scored and converted the two-pointer to make it 8-0. Peterson, however, finished the frame with a toss to Mark Clemons for the touchdown and Marques Braggs recovered a loose ball for the two-points to tie. Overstreet opened the 3rd quarter with his 30-yarder and Smith put it 15-8. Peterson and Overstreet hooked up from 14 yards after for the next.

Noxubee managed a lone tally before the end of the contest to tighten the final but it was too late. Peterson threw for 92 yards while Clifton Smith led tacklers with 15.

GAME 10:   LOUISVILLE (5-4) vs NESHOBA CENTRAL (5-3)
                 LOUISVILLE 54 NESHOBA CENTRAL 35
                 November 1, 1996

This battle was in favor of Louisville 16-5 since 1972 but none of that mattered now. Neshoba Central was 3-3 in their last six meetings and some for big outcomes. The Union Appeal picked the Cats 21-20 saying, "The Rockets may be able to steal a win here if they can control the football and make a couple of big plays in the kicking game". A Wildcat win secured a playoff spot despite less than a less than stellar record thus far.

Overstreet began the scoring early with a 41-yarder and Smith converted. Neshoba came right back with Karl Washington's 2-yard plunge and Jason Spears PAT. Louisville went on a scoring barrage before halftime. Petey Thames got in from 35 yards and Smith put it 14-7. Overstreet them rushed in from 25 yards and Smith converted. Midway through the frame, Peterson dashed 71 yards to paydirt to make it 27-7.

Marcus Holmes then crossed from eight yards before Washington took the kickoff 96 yards for a touchdown. Spears was true to put it 33-14. Holmes "struck again" from a yard to make halftime 39-14. Neshoba had the only score of the 3rd quarter on a Kea Homes 40-yarder and Spears kick. Scoring continued into the last quarter. Peterson was first on a 44-yard run and added the two-pointer. Washington answered from 17 yards as did Spears.

Petey Thames had the last Cat score from 62 yards and Josh McNeill notched the PAT. As the clock expired, J.B. Morrow tallied for the visitors and the PAT was the end. The Cats were led with 244 rushing yards by Thames, 34 passing and 131 rushing yards by Peterson, while the defense had four fumble recoveries and two interceptions.

GAME 11:   LOUISVILLE (6-4) @ KOSCIUSKO (9-1)
                 LOUISVILLE 21 KOSCIUSKO 24 (OT)
                 November 8, 1996

While Louisville was guaranteed post-season, there was a rivalry here for the regular season finale. After a six-year hiatus, Kosy took the last meeting 14-7. Said Stanford, "We've got a chance. The biggest thing is we have to play a lot better on defense. We've got to quit breaking down mentally and giving up the big play".

Said Head Coach Rodney Jones, "No doubt about it, this is a big one Friday night. They have one of the best programs around and year-in and year-out they are tough. This was a big rivalry for Kosciusko way back and it's turned into one again".

Kosy notched the only tally of the opening stanza on Armon Quarles' 14-yarder and Sam Potts' PAT. Louisville answered in the next on a Petey Thames 17-yard dash and the PAT tied it. The Whippets, however, recorded one more before halftime on a 3-yard Potts dive and his kick.

The home team increased it to 21-7 in the 3rd quarter. Chris Kern grabbed a loose football to no avail but soon Whitt Lewis found the end zone off a 5-yard Potts pass and Potts converted. The Cats tied it once again in the final frame on Thames runs of 14 and four yards. Smith's kicks sent it to overtime. While the Cats faltered on the first possession, Kosy did not. Potts nailed the FG to snatch the division title win.

GAME 12:   LOUISVILLE (6-5) @ OLIVE BRANCH (10-0)
                LOUISVILLE 42 OLIVE BRANCH 14
                November 15, 1996

Louisville faced the Conquistadors from 1985 to 1987 and won all three contests. Now, however, Olive Branch was undefeated for the second time under Coach Leslie Pool. Said he, "We've played Louisville in the playoffs four times and they won all four ball games. We expect to be competitive. If we don't turn the ball over and don't give up the big play on defense, I think we can be in the game".

The Cats opened up well with a 71-yard march and 5-yard Thames TD run that, with the first of six Smith PATs, made it 7-0. The Dores opened poorly when Grady tipped a pass to Anthony Paten who took it 39 yards for a pick-six. The 14-0 score held through halftime. Louisville kept going in the 3rd quarter with a 15-yard Overstreet run and 1-yard Peterson run while Steve Harwood's 37-yard reception from Bobby Anderson marked their first score.

The finale looked similar to the 3rd quarter. Although Willie Anderson ran in from eight yards and added two points, the Cats scored on Thames runs of seven and 14 yards for the surprise blowout final.

GAME 13:   LOUISVILLE (7-5) vs CLEVELAND EAST SIDE (11-0)
                LOUISVILLE 34 CLEVELAND EAST SIDE 16
                November 22, 1996

The only meeting between the clubs came in 1992 when Louisville took a 28-20 playoff win over East Side. Like Olive Branch, Cleveland was undefeated. It was to be a huge challenge for the Wildcats.

Louisville had the lone score of the opening frame with Overstreet's 4-yarder to make it 6-0. In the 2nd quarter, he took off again from 17 yards and Peterson dodged in for two points. Marcus Holmes added the next from 16 yards and Smith made intermission 21-0. The first play of the 3rd quarter was a Peterson pass to Thames that resulted in a 46-yard touchdown and Smith kick.

East Side dotted the board with a 6-yard Smith run and his two-pointer to end the stanza. The last quarter was roughly similar as Peterson hit Demon Baker for a 73-yard tally. The visitors had the last on an 11-yard Smith run and two more points. Louisville had 356 total yards with Peterson throwing for 159 of those.

GAME 14:   LOUISVILLE (8-5) vs KOSCIUSKO (12-1)
                LOUISVILLE 14 KOSCIUSKO 19
                November 29, 1996

The only team standing in the way of a trip to the state championship was the rival Whippets that took the overtime win over Louisville just three weeks prior. Said Coach Jones, "It's simple for us. We've got to play a near-perfect game to win".

The Cats had a pair of scoring opportunities in the first half. A Peterson touchdown run came back on a penalty and a Smith FG effort was just short of the mark. That kept intermission scoreless. In the 3rd quarter, Armon Quarles crossed from five yards and Sam Potts made it 7-0. While the Cats crossed and converted to tie it, Robert Huffman came back with a 22-yard TD run. Louisville blocked the PAT to keep it 13-7.

An ensuing Cat fumble allowed Quarles a 22-yard dash to put it 19-7. The last Wildcat touchdown came with just :04 on the clock, but the onside kick went to Kosciusko. Said Jones, "Louisville came to Kosciusko to win the football game but our kids just went out and gave them all they had".

All Division honors went to Tyler Peterson, Kelvin Cistrunk, Eric Whitehead, Adam Lowrey, Jeffery Wraggs, Demon Baker, Petey Thames, Zack Grady, Letron Overstreet and Cedric Vaughn. Honorable Mentions included Mark Clemons, Michael Goss, Emmit Ellis and Mike Smith.

Internal awardees included Peterson, Anthony Jimmerson, Whitehead, Cistrunk, Lowrey, Thames, Overstreet, Vaughn, and Grady.

1997 (9-4)

For third-year Coach Tony Stanford, youth held the *"key to winning"* for 1997. He did have 16 seniors of 39 returning letter winners, but there would be many younger players on the field for the Wildcats. Voters had them only second in 2-4A with no other rankings from the media.

The road would, as usual, be a tough start. *"We use the first six games as a kind of pre-season in an attempt to get better so we can win the games we have to win to get into the playoffs. Everyone in the state knows that the road to the 4A championship goes through Louisville, Mississippi. LHS is gunning for its 14th straight year in the playoff and sixth state championship"*.

GAME 1:   LOUISVILLE (0-0) @ MADISON CENTRAL (0-0)
                                      LOUISVILLE 21 MADISON CENTRAL 13
                                      August 29, 1997

Louisville hit the road to Madison for the lid-lifter to face former mentor Mike Justice and his number four Super 10 Jaguars. Their only previous meeting came in the 1992 playoffs where the Cats took home the win. In this one, The Clarion-Ledger picked the home team 24-10.

It took just four plays before the Cats struck on a *"dazzling"* 62-yard Michael Goss dash and Brett Smith PAT. MC was up for the fight and scored on Anthony Ephrom's 2-yarder and Dale PAT. A Cat fumble led to Ephrom's 8-yard pass to Johnny Pate to make it 13-7. Louisville controlled the 2nd quarter on a 9-yard Marcus Holmes run, a fumble recovery, and Justin Reed's 24-yard pass to Demon Baker. Smith added both extra points to make halftime 21-13.

Scoring was over by intermission as both defenses held firm. Louisville led on the ground (161-118) and the air (73-62). The Cats forced four fumbles and recovered three. Clifton Smith found a pair of them. The defense also had five sacks. Terrance Yarbrough led tacklers with five solo and four assists while Cornelius Goss added an interception. *"The offense set the tone in the first half and then the defense took complete control of the game"*. Stanford was voted one of The Clarion-Ledger Coaches of the Week.

GAME 2:   LOUISVILLE (1-0) vs TUPELO (1-0)
                                      LOUISVILLE 12 TUPELO 15
                                      September 5, 1997

While Tupelo was just 14-11 all-time against Louisville, everyone knew that a game at fourth-ranked Tupelo would be just as tough as the opener. *"I'm going to be honest with you. We felt we had a chance to be pretty good, but we are so young. We may still be a year away and we may look like the devil Friday night, but we are excited. One thing about a young team: you either play real good or real bad.*

Tupelo is a lot bigger than us and it look like they are stronger than us. They are a lot quicker on defense than us (and) those suckers are big". The Clarion-Ledger picked the Golden Wave 21-17.

The opening quarter was a defensive battle with numerous Wave fumbles and a missed Cat FG keeping it scoreless. Mark Clemons kept from eight yards to give them a 6-0 lead but Tupelo came back with a 1-yard Luke McAlpin dive and John Michael Marlin PAT. Just 7-6 to start the 3rd quarter, Louisville rallied in the 3rd quarter for the only score on a 63-yard Goss escape to put it 12-7.

In the finale, Tupelo provide what would be the final points on another 1-yard McAlpin plunge and his two-pointer to Brent Heavener. A late comeback attempt failed via a Maury Long interception to run the clock. Tupelo led in first downs (15-7), rushing (174-153) and passing (144-56). Latron Overstreet led rushers with 73 yards. *"We're a year away but we still got after them. It's no disgrace getting beat 15-12 by Tupelo. They playing in the toughest league in the state"*.

GAME 3:   LOUISVILLE (1-1) @ YAZOO CITY (1-1)
                                      LOUISVILLE 36 YAZOO CITY 22
                                      September 12, 1997

The Cats won six games against Indians aside from the consecutive losses of 1954 and 1955. This seemed an easy one despite being on the road for yet another week.

Yazoo City's opening march was stymied by an Eddie Smith sack while the Wildcats missed an ensuing FG opportunity. Back came the home team with an 80-yard drive capped by Corey Freeman's 8-yard run and the Wilson PAT. Tacorey Patie evened it on a 67-yarder and Smith made it 7-7. In the 2nd quarter, Louisville blocked the punt but fumbled it back soon afterwards. Freeman found Wilson from 28 yards later and Wilson put them back in the lead.

The visitors responded when Clemons and Goss connected from 30 yards and Justin Reed hit Clemons for the two-point fake PAT. Halftime stood just 15-14. On the first possession of the 3rd quarter, Louisville drove 50 yards with Homes adding the last four and Smith converting. In the finale, Louisville went 11 plays with Clemons crossing from six yards and Smith splitting the uprights.

After forcing an Indian fumble, Reed hit Clemons from 11 yards and Smith again was true. A late Cat fumble allowed Felton a 34-yard reception from Freeman and Freeman's two-point run to finish the evening. Holmes led rushers with 148 of the 250 yards. Clemons threw for 108 yards while Goss pulled in 97 yards.

GAME 4:   LOUISVILLE (2-1) vs STARKVILLE (3-0)
                 LOUISVILLE 6 STARKVILLE 28
                 September 19, 1997

Another top-ranked team was now at hand but in Louisville. Long-time foe Starkville, ranked second in The Super 10 and in 5A, was on a march for their third state championship in four years under Coach Chuck Friend.

An early drive to the Jacket 4 fizzled but the opponents drove the other way with Dorsey Randal's 94-yard dash to paydirt to make it 6-0. They opened the 2nd quarter with a 45-yard march and 20-yard Freddie Milons run. Milons and Randle connected for the two points. Louisville drove to the Jacket 5 before fumbling the ball away. Late in the frame, Milons' runs put the ball at the 3-yard line from where Randle drove across. Neil Couvillion's kick put halftime 21-0.

Now in the 4th quarter, Clemons hit Goss from 10 yards for six points. Starkville put up one more to end it afterwards on Henry Vaughn's 1-yarder and Couvillion kick.

GAME 5:   LOUISVILLE (2-2) @ AMORY (3-1)
                 LOUISVILLE 17 AMORY 20 (OT)
                 September 26, 1997

It would get no easier as the Wildcats now traveled to 3A Amory to face a formidable team under former Coach Bobby Hall that beat Louisville in their only meeting the previous season 34-14. If the goal was to face the hardest teams early, it was working.

A Smith sack stopped the first Panther drive while Louisville got deep but had to settle for Smith's 32-yard FG and 3-0 lead. Both put up scores in the 2nd quarter. Louisville was first on a 5-yard Holmes run while Amory added a 28-yard David Mooneyham FG as time expired. Halftime sat in favor of the Cats 9-3.

Amory opened the second half with an 83-yard drive capped by Will Hall's 36-yarder and Mooneyham kick. The Cats responded with Clemons' 90-yard touchdown connection with Goss and a Holmes two-pointer to put it 17-10. A late Wildcat fumble allowed Amory a long 66-yard drive in eight plays with Deshaun Fields adding the last 13 yards and Mooneyham the PAT to tie. An ensuing Panther interception sent it to overtime.

Mooneyham put up a 27-yard FG on their first possession. The Cats could only manage a tying 32-yard FG but the low snap allowed a block and heartbreaking defeat.

GAME 6:   LOUISVILLE (2-3) @ WEST POINT (1-4)
                 LOUISVILLE 38 WEST POINT 3
                 October 3, 1997

The season was about to turn dramatically in favor of Louisville after tough tests early in the campaign. First was a West Point squad that lost their last seven to the Cats.

It was never close as an early Elliot Carter sack gave Louisville great field position. One play later, a Cat fumble gave it back. Still, the defense gave the Cats better position, Goss drove in from 17 yards, and Smith put up his first PAT. Another short field allowed

Smith a 42-yard FG. Before the frame ended, Overstreet picked off a pass and Holmes turned it into a 4-yard TD. Smith again was true.

Clemons had the next from three yards and Smith put it 24-0. With :33 left, Nick Dimino added the only West Point tally on a 22-yard FG. In the 3rd quarter, Louisville ended scoring. Reed found Bruce Sims from seven yards and Smith made it 31-3 while Cornelius Goss picked off a pass and took it 35 yards to paydirt. Smith kicked the final point. Holmes led rushers with 76 of the 116 ground yards and pulled in 40 more in the air.

GAME 7:   LOUISVILLE (3-3) @ CANTON (1-5)
                                 LOUISVILLE 55 CANTON 0
                                 October 10, 1997

Canton was a mainstay on the Wildcat schedule from 1944 through 1961. Now, they faced each other again on the gridiron. During that earlier span, the Wildcats dominated.

Late in the opening quarter, the Cats put up their first on a 13-yard Clemons run and the first of a number of Smith kicks. In the next, Goss took the punt 52 yards to set up an 8-yard Holmes score. The second half started with 35 points in just the 3rd quarter. Scores came from Patie's 9-yard run, a 12-yarder from Clemons to Baker, Clemons to Goss from 10 yards, a fumble to allow Holmes a 3-yard dash and a 40-yard Goss escape.

With reserves in play, Mario Smith added the last on a 1-yarder. Holmes led rushers with 59 of 155 yards, Clemons threw for 117 and Goss dominated with 185 yards in punt returns. The defense had given up only 37 rushing and two yards passing.

GAME 8:   LOUISVILLE (4-3) vs NOXUBEE COUNTY (7-0)
                                 LOUISVILLE 31 NOXUBEE COUNTY 16
                                 October 17, 1997: HOMECOMING

An undefeated Noxubee team, in hindsight, was not an optimal opponent to schedule for homecoming at Hinze Stadium as NCHS allowed only 32 points on the season.

The only score of the opening quarter came on Mike Smith's 27-yard FG but they added two more touchdowns before intermission. Clemons was first from 14 yards, Chris Eaves recovered a late fumble and Holmes turned it into a 4-yarder. Brett Smith added both kicks to make it 17-0. Noxubee County had the lone points of the 3rd quarter after a Cat fumble. Six plays later, Hardin drove in from a yard and then ran in for the two points.

In the last quarter, another Louisville fumble led to a 36-yard Johnson run and Hardin's toss to Johnson for the conversion. The Cats, however, took over with Clemons' 17-yard toss to Goss, a 1-yard Holmes dive and a pair of Smith conversions. Holmes again led on the ground with 106 yards of the 225 yards. Clemons threw for 32 more while the defense held NCHS to 137 yards.

GAME 9:   LOUISVILLE (5-3) vs WINGFIELD (6-1)
                                 LOUISVILLE 33 WINGFIELD 12
                                 October 24, 1997

Louisville faced a number of other Jackson-area teams in their history. However, none had come against Wingfield High School. Their record was impressive but the visitors knew they had a big obstacle to climb to continue.

Said Coach Dan Fails, *"We've never done enough consistently for people to know about us. I'm hoping Louisville is thinking were a bunch of city boys who can't play football. Playing at home and their winning tradition are two major things in Louisville's favor. Remember, they've won five state championships and nobody else is even close"*. The Clarion-Ledger picked the Wildcats 22-17.

It did not start as a runaway win as Wingfield held a 6-0 advantage after the first frame. Johnny Lindsey took the first possession 76 yards to paydirt for the upset alert. Louisville managed only to tie before halftime on a 58-yard drive and Holmes 18-yarder. In the next frame, Clemons hit Goss from five yards and Clemons dashed across for the two points.

Louisville took control in the finale with a 38-yard Clemons run and a 38-yard Clemons toss to Goss but Wingfield's Minor took a Cat fumble 33 yards to paydirt. Goss added a 7-yard run to wrap up the game. Louisville led in first downs (16-10), rushing (249-201) and passing (59-36). Holmes had 135 yards rushing.

GAME 10:   LOUISVILLE (6-3) @ KOSCIUSKO (6-3)
                         LOUISVILLE 27 KOSCIUSKO 12
                         October 31, 1997

After a six-year hiatus, the Whippets came back to win three games in the last two seasons over the Wildcats. However, this was a new year and Louisville was up for the test. A win guaranteed the Cats yet another playoff spot.

The game was essentially won in the first half. The opening drive covered 79 yards with Clemons running in for the last two yards and Smith connecting. A fumble in the next quarter was immediately returned to Terrance Yarbrough. Clemons ran in from 19 yards four plays later. Clemons and Goss finished it with a 13-yard connection and Smith added both PATs.

Kosy had the lone score of the 3rd quarter on Reggie Mayfield's 53-yard dash to make it 21-6. They added their last in the 4th quarter on Brent Tyler's 7-yarder to Demetric Armstead while another fumble recovery led to Clemons' 14-yard escape. Clemons ran for 172 yards while Holmes added 135 more. Clemons also threw for 57 yards.

GAME 11:   LOUISVILLE (7-3) vs NESHOBA CENTRAL (3-6)
                         LOUISVILLE 40 NESHOBA CENTRAL 14
                         November 7, 1997

The Rockets claimed only five wins over Louisville going back to 1972. The Union Appeal chose Louisville 21-8 while noting that there was still a chance for Neshoba Central to make the playoffs.

Lacey McBeath scooped up an early Cat fumble and took it 43 yards to paydirt. The Timothy Fieber PAT gave them a 7-0 lead. Louisville punched back with a 15-yard Holmes run set up by Patie's 54-yard dash and the Smith extra point tied the affair. The next quarter belonged solely to the Wildcats.

Holmes was first on his 41-yard run while Clemons found Goss from 67 yards for the next. The last came with just seconds to play via Clemons' 47-yarder to Overstreet. One Smith kick put halftime 26-7. Horace Daniels opened the 3rd quarter with a 49-yard fumble return to allow Clemons a 9-yard touchdown and Smith the PAT.

In the finale, both hit the board. Patie found paydirt from nine yards and Smith converted. With reserves in play, Derrick Pickens found daylight from 22 yards and the conversion was true. Holmes rushed for 147 yards while Clemons threw for 164 yards. Goss led receivers with 111 markers. The defense held the Rockets to just 163 total yards.

GAME 12:   LOUISVILLE (8-3) vs OXFORD (9-2)
                         LOUISVILLE 29 OXFORD 24
                         November 14, 1997

Though Louisville was 6-2 all-time against the Chargers, losses in both 1989 and 1990 ended those Wildcat seasons.

This one appeared to be an Oxford runaway at halftime. Another opening Cat fumble was plucked by Ken Mathis and taken 32 yards to paydirt. Ben Boatright was true on his first of three extra points. Derrick Johnson followed that with a 70-yard escape and the quarter ended 14-0. They added ten more points in the 2nd quarter on a 20-yard Richard Cross pass to Lee. A pair of ensuing interceptions led to a 35-yard Boatright FG.

A seemingly different Wildcat team took the field afterwards. The second of two Charger fumbles led to a 6-yard Holmes run. He recorded the next from 17 yards and added the two-pointer. Clemons soon followed from six yards and Chris Eaves dashed in for two more points. The big score came in the last stanza when Clemons hit Baker from 11 yards and Smith converted. A Cornelius Goss interception late in the game sealed the surprising win. Holmes rushed for 104 yards of the 237 total.

GAME 13:   LOUISVILLE (9-3) @ ABERDEEN (8-4)
                         LOUISVILLE 28 ABERDEEN 16
                         November 21, 1997

The Wildcats traditionally dominated the Aberdeen eleven. Going back to 1937, they held a 13-1 record with the only loss coming in 1956 (38-14). It was one of the worst seasons in Louisville history as that team finished just 1-10.

As in other games this season, it was the opponent hitting the board to start. An errant Clemons pass was picked off and soon led to a 10-yard Irons run and two-pointer by Billy Blanchard. Louisville stormed back in the 2nd quarter. Holmes ran in from fifteen and five yards, converted the two points, and Clemons hit Goss (or Reed) from eight yards after an Aberdeen fumble. Intermission sat 20-8.

Louisville fell on an onside kick to start the 3rd quarter. They moved 56 yards with Clemons adding the last yards and two-pointer. The last points came in the frame when Blanchard dodged in from 14 yards and then hit T. Blanchard for the conversion. Overstreet pulled in a 4th quarter interception but scoring was complete. Holmes rushed for 154 yards of the 227.

GAME 14:   LOUISVILLE (10-3) @ CLARKSDALE (11-1)
                         LOUISVILLE 12 CLARKSDALE 40
                         November 28, 1997

The only previous known meeting came in a 13-12 squeaker in 1939. The North State playoff game was not to be easy on the road and The Clarion-Ledger picked the home team 24-17. Said Coach John Murphree, "We're excited about but we know it's going to take a heck of an effort to get by these folks. Louisville has set the standard in 4A since the playoffs have been in. They have a tremendous program".

The Wildcats seemed up to the fight as they held a 6-0 lead after a frame. That score came on a 49-yard Clemons strike to Goss. Despite a recovered fumble, the Cats could not make it count. Clarksdale, on the other hand, put up 27 points before halftime. Tarnakay Counselor was first from four yards, Mikale Ahi nailed his first of four PATs, Orrden Williams stripped the ball and raced 55 yards to paydirt for the next, then recovered the fumbled kickoff and Counselor crossed from six yards, and Mario Haggan picked up a final fumble and raced 33 yards for the touchdown.

The rainy second half slowed Clarksdale to just a lone 3rd quarter score on a 3-yard Counselor run. Both tallied in the last quarter. Louisville recovered a fumble in the end zone for a score while Michael Gammell hit Kacy Williams from 58 yards for the last of the night. First downs were even (11-11) while Clarksdale led in yardage (266-135).

District 2-4A honors were plenty for Louisville. Michael Goss (Most Valuable Offensive Player), Chris Eaves (Most Valuable Defensive Player), Marcus Holmes (Best Offensive Back), Letron Overstreet, Demon Baker, Roderick Thomas, Mark Clemons, Elliot Carter, Ricky Edwards, Mon Houston, Eddie Smith, Cornelius Goss and Terrance Yarbrough all received recognition.

Honorable Mentions included Mike Smith, Rico Wraggs, Anthony Paten, Ken Jernigan and Terrance Johnson. Goss also received All-State Honorable Mention.

Internally, awards went to Justin Reed, Carter, Yarbrough, Clemons, Baker, Smith, Holmes, Cornelius Goss, Thomas, Emmitt Ellis, Wraggs, Eaves, Michael Goss, Houston, Johnson, Baker and Marquis Bragg.

1998 (9-4)

Voters had the Wildcats under fourth-year mentor Tony Stanford as high as eighth in The Clarion-Ledger Super 10, second in overall 4A and eighth in the AP Poll. Of the 25 seniors, many who had "started since they were sophomores", only Michael Goss earned the prestigious Dandy Dozen list. The road was not easy as three of their first four opponents were as highly ranked.

Starkville was fourth (Super 10) and fifth in the AP, Tupelo was sixth (Super 10) and sixth in the AP, and lid-lifting Madison Central was 10th (Super 10) and ninth in the AP. Said Stanford, "At LHS, we have only one goal: to win the state championship. We have a winning tradition. Kids and parents respect that. They have grown up watching these teams and they want to be part of that".

GAME 1:   LOUISVILLE (0-0) vs MADISON CENTRAL (0-0)
                         LOUISVILLE 20 MADISON CENTRAL 2
                         August 28, 1998

The previous year, the Wildcats surprised everyone by beating former coach Mike Justice and his Jaguars 21-13 in Madison. Now the Jags traveled to Hinze Stadium for revenge. Fans were eager to see if longshot Louisville could do it again.

An early Madison Central fumble to Ricky Edwards earned a five-play drive ending with Marcus Holmes' 3-yarder and Brett Smith PAT. Another fumble recovery gave them a chance but it went back the same way. Another loose Cat ball ended their last opening quarter threat. A last-second play before halftime ended just a yard short.

Scoring was done after the 3rd quarter. Louisville was first on a Justin Reed 8-yard toss to Goss and Smith PAT. Late in the frame, the Cats forced and recovered another fumble to no avail. However, a bad punt snap gave the Jags a safety to make it 14-2. Before it was over, and after stopping a deep visitor drive, Goss dashed 54 yards for the finale. Goss led rushers with 135 yards while Holmes gained 104 more.

GAME 2:   LOUISVILLE (1-0) @ TUPELO (1-0)
                  LOUISVILLE 0 TUPELO 10
                  September 4, 1998

The tough road planned by Stanford now took the Wildcats to Tupelo to compete against a squad that bested them three straight seasons. The Clarion-Ledger expected the Golden Wave to come out victorious 17-14.

It appeared Tupelo was marching to their first touchdown but for the interception from Adrian Eiland. Louisville marched to the Wave 28 before losing yardage on sacks. As the clock expired in the 1st quarter, John Michael Marlin nailed a 37-yard FG to make it 3-0. Now in the 4th quarter, Kelly Shumpert dashed 12 yards to paydirt and Marlin provided the last point.

Both defenses were the key to the contest as Louisville forced seven Tupelo fumbles. Holmes led rushers with 101 yards.

GAME 3:   LOUISVILLE (1-1) vs YAZOO CITY (0-2)
                  LOUISVILLE 57 YAZOO CITY 7
                  September 11, 1998

Not since 1955 had the Indians defeated the Cats. Since that time, Louisville won five straight. After consecutive games against 5A opponents, it was time to flex Cat muscles in front of home fans.

It was over after a frame despite an opening John Wilson 70-yard touchdown escape and his PAT. From there, it went south for the Indians. Scoring came in waves thereafter. Goss ran in from 65 yards, the Cats blocked a punt for a safety, Goss took the ensuing kick 67 yards to the end zone, Horace Daniels ripped a ball away and took it 17 yards, and Smith converted on all kicks.

Eiland recovered a 2nd quarter fumble for a 29-yard TD and Bryant Thomas drove in from four yards. Another Indian fumble led to Reed's 4-yarder to Goss, Louisville blocked a punt, Eiland ran in from 12 yards and Drew Massey converted. Edwards soon recovered another fumble and Holmes crossed from five yards to make it 55-7 at halftime.

Reserves, already in play, held Yazoo City scoreless in the second half. The last score came in the finale on a bad punt snap out of the end zone for a safety. Louisville rushed for 254 yards while the defense held Yazoo City to just 16 rushing yards after the first touchdown, forced four fumbles, blocked two punts and picked off a pass.

Said Coach Lewis Tillman, "Our guys just got their heads down. We made mistakes and they took advantage of it. Louisville was able to show us what will happen in you don't do your job. I think we've probably learned more from this game than anything else we have done so far".

GAME 4:   LOUISVILLE (2-1) @ STARKVILLE (3-0)
                  LOUISVILLE 7 STARKVILLE 21
                  September 18, 1998

Coach Chuck Friend downplayed the success of his 5A Yellow Jackets before the game. "Our offense has made so many mistakes. We hardly have a starter back on offense. Everybody is kind of in a different position this year with almost no experience at all. If it had not been for our B team, we would really be in a mess. Without question, this is the best Louisville team we've faced since I've been at Starkville".

Despite his comments, The Clarion-Ledger still picked them 21-19. Perhaps it was because they knew that Goss would not suit for this game. Perhaps it was because Starkville, playing in their Homecoming game, won six of the last seven since 1992.

The first half was all defense with neither passing the others' 23-yard line and total yardage in favor of Starkville 61-59. In the 3rd quarter, Holmes broke the scoreless tie with a 4-yarder and Smith the kick. Back came the Jackets with a 20-yard Fred Fair toss to Fred Edmonds and the first of three Joey Sherrard kicks. Starkville's Robert Outlaw soon recovered a Cat fumble and Fair found Eric Tucker from 25 yards to make it 14-7.

A late fumble to Louisville led to a decision. With 1:43 left and fourth down at their 10-yard line, the Cats went for it unsuccessfully. Fair turned it into an 8-yard tally for the last touchdown. Starkville led in yardage 272-131. The Cats rushed for only 80 yards. *"Any time you don't have your game breaker (Goss out with a cut knee) in there, it will affect you. I thought our defense played about as well as they could, but they just wore us down in the second half".*

GAME 5:   LOUISVILLE (2-2) vs AMORY (4-0)
                    LOUISVILLE 32 AMORY 34
                    September 25, 1998

Although a 3A squad, Amory was a force under former Cat mentor Bobby Hall. For game week, they were already sixth in The Super 10 and first in 3A. This one was a fight all the way to the heartbreaking end.

An opening Amory deep drive resulted in just a 23-yard David Mooneyham FG and 3-0 lead. Louisville responded with a long march and Marquess Ledbetter reception from either Thomas or Reed to make it 6-3. Amory came right back with a 90-yard Steve Griffin kick return and the PAT made it 10-6.

Louisville responded to open the 2nd quarter with an 80-yard drive ending with a 4-yarder from Reed to Goss. Amory punched back with a 72-yard march ending in Will Hall's 15-yarder to Rory Thornton and a Mooneyham kick to make it 17-12. Again, the Cats scratched a response when Reed and Goss hooked up from 17 yards and Smith cut it to 19-17 at halftime.

Holmes opened the 3rd quarter with a 2-yard dive. A Cat fumble gave Hall time to hit Mooneyham from 31 yards and the game sat 25-23. Disaster hit in the final frame when Antonio Scott picked off a Thomas pass and raced 80 yards to the end zone. Fields' two-point conversion put it 31-25. With 1:34 left, Holmes found paydirt from two yards and Smith converted.

Amory quickly drove deep with :03 left on the game clock from where Mooneyham hit a 24-yard FG to steal the win. Holmes raced for 194 yards on 30 carries. Louisville led in yardage 391-233.

GAME 6:   LOUISVILLE (2-3) vs WEST POINT (0-5)
                    LOUISVILLE 41 WEST POINT 3
                    October 2, 1998

This was this last non-division contest of the season but Louisville wanted to continue an eight-game winning streak against a team they played consecutively since 1966.

It took just three plays on their first possession for Corey Sanders to find paydirt on a 28-yard dash and the first of four Smith kicks. Great field position after led to a 5-yard Holmes run and 14-0 lead. Goss then pulled in a 49-yard Reed pass for a touchdown to put it 21-0. Finally, Holmes dove in from three yards and halftime was 28-0.

In the second half, a Cat fumble led to a 31-yard Nick Dimino FG but Louisville was not done. Despite a West Point interception and fumble recovery, Louisville added more via a Holmes rush and Drew Massey kick. Holmes added the last score of the game in the finale on a 14-yarder. Holmes rushed for 124 yards while Reed threw for 113 yards. Goss pulled in 109 passing yards. Yardage went to Louisville 327-105.

GAME 7:   LOUISVILLE (3-3) vs CANTON (1-5)
                    LOUISVILLE 56 CANTON 3
                    October 9, 1998: HOMECOMING

In 1956, Canton was able to take advantage of a weak Cat squad to take home the win. Since then, Louisville won all six meetings. The Tigers put the "Can't" in Canton for this affair.

As the final score suggested, it got out of hand early. Holmes started things with an 8-yarder and Smith converted. Goss had the next from nine yards while Canton tallied their only points on a 26-yard Tomber Fleming FG. Goss responded with a 99-yard kick return to end the 1st quarter 19-3. They added 16 more points before halftime after Elliot Carter recovered a fumble and Holmes used it to run in from 18 yards and add two points.

A bad Canton punt attempt gave Louisville great position and Reed capitalized from two yards. Holmes again converted for two more. Another Tiger fumble led to Thomas' 15-yard dash and his two-pointer. In the 3rd quarter, the Cats put up the final points. Holmes crossed from six yards and Massey converted while Holmes dashed in from a yard. Reserves held the Tigers scoreless in the last frame.

Holmes rushed for 144 of the 231 yards while the defense held Canton to 138 yards on the ground and 76 passing. Said Coach Patrick Henderson of Louisville, "That's the type of team we want to be".

GAME 8:   LOUISVILLE (4-3) @ NOXUBEE COUNTY (5-2)
               LOUISVILLE 20 NOXUBEE COUNTY 8
               October 16, 1998

Noxubee County, coached for former Wildcat assistant M.C. Miller, just suffered a 24-0 shutout to Kosciusko. However, this game was significant as it was a 4-4A tilt. Goss had a reported 1,601 all-purpose yards in just six games.

The game in Macon was a bit tighter than perhaps expected. An early fumble halted the initial drive. However, a fumbled NCHS punt snap put Louisville on the Tiger 3. Holmes ran in from there and Smith provided the kick. Holmes opened the 2nd quarter with a 14-yarder and Smith made it 14-0. Another Cat fumble stalled any more scoring.

The Tigers had the only tally of the 3rd quarter on a first-drive Johnson dash of 55 yards. He also added the two-pointer. Two more fumbles ended any Cat hopes of getting the points back. In the finale, Louisville drove 86 yards with Holmes adding the last 13 yards. Jermaine Miller ended things with an interception. Holmes rushed for 211 yards and Reed threw for 40 more. The defense held Noxubee to 144 total yards.

GAME 9:   LOUISVILLE (5-3) @ WINGFIELD (1-6)
               LOUISVILLE 51 WINGFIELD 6
               October 23, 1998

This contest in Jackson ended much like the one against Canton a few weeks before. It took little time for Holmes to break away from 31 yards and Smith to convert his first of five extra points. The Falcons cut into the lead thereafter when Johnson dashed 50 yards to paydirt.

Louisville poured it on from there starting with Reed's 31-yard toss to Goss. The Cats recovered a fumble and Sanders eventually crossed from five yards. There was still more to come as Reed and Goss connected from 59 yards and Holmes scored from three yards. Halftime sat 35-6.

The Cats added more in the second half on an 8-yard Holmes run, Massey PAT, Holmes run from 13 yards and Smith finally nailed a 33-yard FG to ice it. Louisville dominated yardage 444-150. Holmes led rushers with 117 yards.

GAME 10:   LOUISVILLE (6-3) vs KOSCIUSKO (8-1)
               LOUISVILLE 20 KOSCIUSKO 7
               October 30, 1998

Kosciusko, despite losing to the Wildcats the previous year, still made it to the 4A title contest. This year they looked to seek revenge and capture the title. The winner of this meeting claimed the 4-4A title while the loser secured second place.

A late 1st quarter Lakendrick Huffman interception set up Robert Huffman's 12-yard score and Matt Mims' PAT. Down 7-0, Louisville responded quickly with an 80-yard drive ending on a 4-yard Holmes run and Smith kick. Goss later pulled in a 25-yarder from Reed and Smith was again true. In the finale, Elvis Idom recovered a Whippet fumble leading to a 9-yard Thomas score.

Holmes rushed for 107 yards while Reed threw for 43 and rushed for 53 yards.

GAME 11:   LOUISVILLE (7-3) @ NESHOBA CENTRAL (4-5)
                    LOUISVILLE 45 KOSCIUSKO 7
                    November 6, 1998

For a couple of years, Neshoba Central became a thorn in the Wildcat side. However, four consecutive victories eased that pain somewhat. For the sixth straight time, the Cat defense held opponents under eight total points as the offense scored often.

Holmes started with a 4-yarder, Louisville recovered a fumble, Reed hit Goss from 15 yards, another fumble went to the Cats, and Holmes dashed in from eight yards for the third touchdown to make it 18-0. Miller then picked off a Rocket pass but the Cats had to eventually punt. Idom found another fumble and Holmes turned it into an 18-yard score. Smith's PAT made it 25-0. Before halftime, Goss crossed from six yards and Smith ended the first half 32-0 with his kick.

Thomas, playing with many reserves, opened the second half with a 55-yard dash and Massey put it 39-0. An interception gave Neshoba a FG opportunity but it failed. In the finale, Ken Love blocked a Rocket punt, recovered and raced for the touchdown. Neshoba avoided the shutout after on a 68-yard run and extra point.

Thomas led rushers with 80 yards of the 224 total. Reed threw for 47 yards.

GAME 12:   LOUISVILLE (8-3) vs NEW HOPE (7-4)
                    LOUISVILLE 33 NEW HOPE 0
                    November 13, 1998

Louisville held a 5-1 record against New Hope with their only loss coming in the last meeting in 1996 (21-20). Regardless, a chance for another state championship with losses only to the top teams in Mississippi had to include one here on playoff night.

It was elementary for a bit despite rainy conditions. An opening Trojan fumble led to a 17-yard run by Goss and the first of three Smith kicks. Goss added more from 38 yards to end the opening frame 14-0. A poor Trojan punt gave Louisville great position. Holmes nearly crossed from 18 yards but fumbled to Hilliard Hudson for the score. That meant a 21-0 halftime Cat advantage.

Louisville put up tallies in each of the last two frames. Holmes was first from three yards and a late one from the same distance. He led rushers with 158 yards, Goss pulled in 47 yards receiving and Reed threw for 60 yards. In all, Louisville rushed for 315 yards on the evening.

GAME 13:   LOUISVILLE (9-3) @ CLARKSDALE (10-1)
                    LOUISVILLE 27 CLARKSDALE 19
                    November 20, 1998

Every Wildcat supporter remembered the season-ending blowout to Clarksdale in 1997 (40-12). *"They (the team) wanted me to put them on our schedule this year. Ever since we pulled out of Clarksdale last year, that's all our kids have talked about"*. Now they had their wish against Coach Jesse Murphree's state championship team. *"Clarksdale has a great ball club. They are probably the best team we've played all year. They are just loaded with talent"*. The Clarion-Ledger picked Clarksdale by a close 21-20 final.

It took only minutes for Tarkaka Counselor to dash 29 yards to paydirt and Byron Johnson to annex the PAT. In the 2nd quarter, Holmes crossed from a yard and Smith converted to tie the game. However, the other Wildcats had two more touchdowns in them before halftime. The first was a 63-yarder from Michael Gammel to Brian Barnes and the Jackson PAT. After an unsuccessful 31-yard Smith FG effort, Counselor found paydirt from a yard and Jackson put intermission 21-7.

Louisville then dented the lead with an 80-yard march and Holmes ended it from five yards. Before the quarter could end, Gammel and Barnes hooked up from 68 yards and the score sat 27-13. Anthony Paten found a loose football in the finale but it was to no avail. However, the Cats managed an 85-yard drive ending with Reed's 3-yard pass to Goss. That would be the last points of 1998. A Mandrell McGregory pass interception with 1:00 left iced it.

Holmes rushed for 141 yards of the total 219. Louisville led in first downs (14-11) and rushing (219-170). Passing went to Clarksdale 203-74.

All Division 4-4A honors went to Marcus Holmes (Offensive MVP), Mon Houston (Defensive MVP), Chris Eaves (Most Valuable Linebacker), Justin Reed (Most Valuable

Punter), Terrance Johnson, Ken Jernigan, Reginald Cistrunk, Michael Goss, Anthony Paten, Emmit Ellis, Rick Edwards and Elliot Carter.

Honorable Mentions included Allen Stroud, Jermaine Miller, Adrian Eiland, Horace Daniels, Robert Finch, Corey Crosby, Bruce Sims and Ken Love. Goss earned a Clarion-Ledger All-State nod.

1999 (11-2)

Tony Stanford entered the season with high optimism for his fifth year at the helm. Voters had the Wildcats first preseason in 2-4A and third overall in 4A by The Clarion-Ledger. Nevertheless, he started four sophomores on the offensive line and others in the backfield. Nothing more was reported about activities before the kickoff of the season.

GAME 1:   LOUISVILLE (0-0) vs FOREST (0-0)
                LOUISVILLE 3 FOREST 0
                August 27, 1999

Jack French entered his 13th season in Forest with a Bearcat team that came just shy of a state championship the season before. He had 17 starters back from that 11-2 squad, picked first in 7-3A, overall 3A and 20th in the AP. *"On paper, these guys look real good and it looks like we'll be alright. But I don't know anybody who wants a paper championship. A lot of teams with talent don't make the state finals. A lot of teams with talent don't make the playoffs. We're still pretty young, but we have enough speed to keep us in some contests"*.

The Scott County Times said, *"The contest looms as the toughest regular season test that Forest has faced in the last 20 years"*. Forest met Louisville back in 1930 and 1934, both ending in Bearcat victories. The Clarion-Ledger thought Louisville best 17-14.

Said French, *"When you play somebody like Louisville, it means great football. We couldn't find anyone else and Louisville's not too bad of a drive. It's a great opportunity for us. It speaks well of our program that Louisville would consider playing us. It's a challenge and an opportunity for us. I think we're legitimate and that we're capable of winning this game. We go into this with the expectation that we can win this game"*.

The first Bearcat drive moved as far as the Cat 22 but got no further. Both exchanged fumbles early in the 2nd quarter but Forest gave up another late to Horace Daniels. However, Matt Smith picked off a Wildcat pass to kill the threat. Louisville attempted a late FG but the *"snap slipped through the holder's hands"* and fumbled it away. Fortunately, Forest gave it right back the same way. Now late in the game, another Bearcat fumble to Elijah Pippen put Louisville at the Forest 23 with 1:43 remaining. Ken Triplett attempted another from 39 yards with 1:29 left and it was *"more than long enough"*.

Louisville led in first downs (6-3) and passing (28-0). Forest was best on the ground (102-89). Forest fumbled seven times (losing four) while the Cats dropped it twice and had the interception. French was *"proud of how our players came up here, accepted the challenge and played without any sign of intimidation. But we obviously hurt ourselves out there with the turnovers and we've got to go back and work on that. We can brag on our defense. We just have to eliminate a few fumbles"*. Added Stanford, *"It was a great game. I think our defense was the difference but both teams gave a good effort and it was a hard-hitting contest on both sides"*.

GAME 2:   LOUISVILLE (1-0) vs TUPELO (1-0)
                LOUISVILLE 6 TUPELO 24
                September 3, 1999

It was commonplace in recent years to schedule strong opponents for the beginning stretch of play as it prepared the Cats for what was to come. 5A Tupelo was no exception with four consecutive victories over Louisville. The Clarion-Ledger picked the Number Six Golden Wave 14-13.

A solid opening drive spurred by Glenn's 49-yard dash ended in a 42-yard Triplett FG. On the next drive, they moved deep but had to settle for Triplett's 40-yard FG to make it 6-0. Tupelo took advantage of a bad punt snap in the 2nd quarter to allow Stan Hill a 16-yard toss to Kevin Caldwell. John Michael Marlin added his first three extra points. Late in the frame, and after two missed Wave FG attempts, Hill tossed a 4-yarder to Caldwell and halftime stood 14-6.

Tupelo added a 3rd quarter touchdown via a 45-yard Hill strike to Antonio Dilworth. The game ended in the last frame on Marlin's 25-yard FG. Louisville rushed for 184 yards and threw for 39 more. The defense held Tupelo to 66 ground yards but allowed 228 more in the passing game. Worse, Jermaine Miller fractured his leg in the game.

GAME 3:   LOUISVILLE (1-1) @ YAZOO CITY (0-2)
                     LOUISVILLE 26 YAZOO CITY 6
                     September 10, 1999

A much-needed break was at hand as the Cats traveled to Yazoo County to face a team they defeated seven straight times. Though winless, the Indians put up a battle in the opening frame to keep it scoreless.

Louisville exploded for 14 points before halftime on a 78-yard Glenn dash, a Vent Jackson pickoff, Glenn 5-yarder, and finally a Chris Eaves two-point conversion. Both tallied in the 3rd quarter, Yazoo City marched 85 yards and finished with a 23-yard Jimmy Simmons run. Louisville answered with a 5-yard Rory Sanders plunge. In the finale, the Cats put up the last on a 95-yard drive ending on Thomas' 14-yarder.

Glenn led rushers with 123 of the 354 yards. The defense held the Indians to just 75 rushing yards and 34 passing yards with one interception. Said Yazoo City Coach Bennie Tillman, "Louisville is a strong, physical team and we knew we were going to have a battle on our hands".

GAME 4:   LOUISVILLE (2-1) vs STARKVILLE (3-0)
                     LOUISVILLE 16 STARKVILLE 8
                     September 17, 1999

Another tough opponent awaited. Starkville was the longest-running opponent in Wildcat history with a streak going back to at least 1940 and some prior. With Dandy Dozen linebacker Jason Clark and a ranking of third in the state, The Clarion-Ledger predicted a Yellow Jacket win 21-10.

The Cats took the 1st quarter lead when Eiland finished a 66-yard drive from eight yards. Eaves added the two points. Eaves then caused and recovered Jacket fumble at the Cat 7. Starkville's Jason Clark later intercepted a Louisville throw to kill a threat and turned it into an eventual 52-yard drive and 1-yard Thurman Ward run. David Yeates tied things with his two-point play. Before halftime, the Cats went 74 yards with Thomas finding E.W. Thames from 16 yards. The Thomas two-pointer proved the games last points.

Triplett attempted an unsuccessful 33-yard FG in the 3rd quarter, Corey Crosby recovered a fumble at the Cat 2, and Jarrod Vaughn ended the last threat with his interception on the Cat 5. Starkville led in first downs (13-12) and rushing (186-90) while Louisville held the air 153-61. Stanford was a Clarion-Ledger Coach of the Week.

GAME 5:   LOUISVILLE (3-1) vs KOSCIUSKO (1-3)
                     LOUISVILLE 47 KOSCIUSKO 13
                     September 24, 1999

Familiar foe Kosciusko was next for the Wildcats. It was not projected to be an easy contest as Coach Rodney Jones, 11-3 the previous season, was picked second in 2-4A pre-season. However, at kickoff the Whippets had only a lone victory on the campaign. Meanwhile, Louisville climbed to 9 in The Super 10 and 11th in the AP Poll.

Glenn opened scoring early with a 78-yard breakaway and Drew Massey hit his first of five extra points. Despite a later fumble, the defense held. Thomas turned the opportunity into a 68-yard scoring dash. In the 2nd quarter, Cornelius Hathorn drove in from five yards to make it 19-0. Eiland then found paydirt from two yards to make intermission a 26-0 Cat lead.

Hathorn opened the second half with a 65-yard escape for points, Vaughn recovered a Kosy fumble, and then rambled the necessary 17 yards to put it 40-0. Reserves took the field and the Whippets finally found the end zone on a 30-yard Lakendrick Huffman pass to George Castine. Daniel Kirkendall added the PAT. Crosby answered with an 80-yard kickoff return for the last Cat points. The Whippets took their final possession 88 yards and finished with a 1-yard Cory McElwain run.

Louisville dominated yardage 472-123. Thomas led rushers with 141 markers while Glenn had 133 more. Said Jones, "Louisville has a real strong defensive team".

GAME 6:   LOUISVILLE (4-1) @ NESHOBA CENTRAL (2-2)
                     LOUISVILLE 21 NESHOBA CENTRAL 17
                     October 1, 1999

        Preseason third 2-4A Neshoba Central posed a bigger threat this week on the road. Louisville was 19-5 all-time with five straight victories, but this was not easy.
        The back-and-forth contest sat tied after each of the first two frames. Louisville was called *"emotionally flat after several big games"*. Louisville blocked a punt and later lined up for an apparent FG. However, Thomas rolled out and hit Bruce Sims from 15 yards and Massey converted his first of three. A later fumble to Marlos Cole by the Cats to led to an 8-yard Anthony Steele touchdown toss to Bran Lillis and Timothy Fieber PAT. Neshoba opened the 2nd quarter with a 9-yard Marco Cole run and Fieber kick to take the lead, but the Cats came back Glenn raced 66 yards to paydirt with a minute remaining to tie.
        In the 3rd quarter, Thomas hit Thames from eight yards for the only points of the frame. A Rocket interception in that quarter ended another Cat threat. In the finale, Neshoba's Feiber hit a 35-yard FG for their last tally. Crosby picked off a late Rocket pass to allow Louisville to simply run the clock for the win.
        Louisville rushed for 226 yards with Glenn having 146 of those. Thomas threw for 76 more yards. The defense held the opponents to 90 rushing and 9 passing yards.

GAME 7:   LOUISVILLE (5-1) vs WEST POINT (1-5)
                     LOUISVILLE 36 WEST POINT 6
                     October 8, 1999: HOMECOMING

        This one seemed a "breather" as West Point was not only a one-win team, but also picked last in 2-4A preseason.
        The rainy Homecoming game was essentially over after a quarter. The Cats put up points in the opening frame on an 8-yard Glenn run, another from 65 yards and a Thomas two-pointer, and finally on a 58-yard Thomas keeper and the second Massey kick. A pair of 2nd quarter fumbles and a Jackson interception kept the 2nd quarter scoreless.
        Now in the final frame, James Shelton recovered and returned a fumble 64 yards to paydirt for six points. The Cats came back with a pair of scores on Glenn's 61-yarder, a Crosby 20-yard fumble return and two Massey extra points. In all, Louisville fumbled four times. Louisville rushed for 381 yards (Glenn had 176 and Eiland 115) and passed for 61 yards.

GAME 8:   LOUISVILLE (6-1) @ NEW HOPE (2-4)
                     LOUISVILLE 33 NEW HOPE 7
                     October 15, 1999

        New Hope, formerly called by many "No Hope" until their shocking 21-20 win in 1996, was next-to-last preseason in 2-4A. Now they had just a pair of wins but played the Wildcats in the home confines.
        Bryant took care of all of the opening possession yards with his 68-yard dash to paydirt. Glenn then ran in from nine yards and Eiland got the two points to make it 14-0. Martez Hopkins recovered a late fumble but the drive moved only to the NH 3. Glenn added the lone 2nd quarter points on his 4-yard plunge and Massey put halftime 21-0.
        Sanders claimed the first touchdown on the 3rd quarter on a 10-yard run, but New Hope got their only points thereafter on a 33-yard Demarco Hunter run and Carpenter kick. The last tally came in the 4th quarter and after a Crosby fumble recovery. Hathorn turned it into a 33-yarder. Glenn led rushers with 102 of 341 yards. Thomas threw for 36 yards. The defense held the Trojans to 100 ground yards and 41 passing yards.

GAME 9:   LOUISVILLE (7-1) vs ABERDEEN (1-6)
                     LOUISVILLE 48 ABERDEEN 0
                     October 22, 1999

        After a 4-7 season, Coach Steve Herring knew he had an uphill fight for 1999. Voters put them fifth in 2-4A and they had now just a lone win. These two first met in the 1930s but claimed one win (1956) of 15 known contests.
        Scoring came in waves against a seemingly hapless Aberdeen squad. Glenn put up a 3-yarder for the 6-0 opening quarter lead. In the next, Thomas ran in from 14 yards and Glenn from 24 yards. Massey was true on two scores to make halftime 20-0. The 3rd

quarter got out of hand. Eaves took a fumble 10 yards, Massey converted, Triplett on his a 48-yard FG, Sanders ran in from six yards and Massey added his last.

Thomas and Sims also connected from 52 yards while Clifton Harris added the last points courtesy of a 26-yard Thomas toss. The story of the game was the defense. They allowed only 28 rushing yards and 51 passing yards. Meanwhile, Louisville put up 363 total yards. Of those, 285 came on the ground.

Said Coach Steve Herring, "*Louisville is definitely a team on a different level than we are and Friday's score is indicative of what happens when you up against a team of Louisville's caliber*".

GAME 10:   LOUISVILLE (8-1) @ NOXUBEE COUNTY (3-7)
                        LOUISVILLE 22 NOXUBEE COUNTY 14
                        October 29, 1999

A loss did not matter except for pride as Louisville already held another district title. Kosciusko was two games behind. Noxubee County defeated Louisville only once (1982) since play began in 1972. The other 20 games went to the Wildcats. It seemed on paper to be an easy affair, but things were quite different.

The trip to Macon ended with a scoreless opening stanza. Thomas opened the next with a 10-yarder to Eiland and Massey put it 7-0. Quickly, Thomas added an 80-yarder and Massey put it 14-0 midway through to end it for halftime. Now in the final quarter, and after a failed Triplett 36-yard FG failed, the score was the same. Knowing they could not run, Noxubee drove 80 yards and ended it with a 12-yard touchdown pass and two-pointer to make it 14-8.

The Tigers then blocked a Cat punt and took it 25 yards to the end zone. That put it 14-14. Thomas saved the Wildcats later with a 7-yard touchdown and Eaves added the last two points. Noxubee moved to the Cat 9 late before Ken Love picked off a pass and took it to the Tiger 23. They allowed the clock to expire and come out victorious.

Thomas rushed for 157 yards and threw for two touchdowns. Glenn added 68 more yards on the ground. The defense allowed only 24 rushing yards but gave up 237 more in the air.

GAME 11:   LOUISVILLE (9-1) vs LAFAYETTE COUNTY (8-3)
                        LOUISVILLE 21 LAFAYETTE COUNTY 0
                        November 12, 1999

After an open date, the Cats now welcomed Lafayette County to Hinze Stadium for the first round of playoffs. In 1991, the Wildcats defeated a team called just Lafayette, so the assumption is that it is the same team eight years apart.

It ended as a relatively low scoring affair with Cat scores in the first two frames and the last. Eaves led the "*heavy set*" into the end zone from a yard to make it 6-0. Lafayette County moved as far as the Cat 2 before the defense held. In the 2nd quarter, Louisville marched 71 yards with Thames pulling in an 18-yarder from Thomas. Thomas added the two points and halftime sat just 14-0.

With time running out and after a timeout from Lafayette with :10 remaining, Eiland hit Thames from 26 yards, along with a Massey conversion, for the final tally. Louisville rushed for 104 yards and 91 passing. The defense held Lafayette Count to just 75 yards on the ground and 15 in the air.

GAME 12:   LOUISVILLE (10-1) vs PEARL (9-3)
                        LOUISVILLE 49 PEARL 26
                        November 19, 1999

The Pirates faced Louisville four times. They were 1-4 all-time with Louisville ending Pirate playoff runs in 1985 and 1995. Head Coach Marcus Broyles was intimately familiar with Louisville as he had been an assistant there for a couple of seasons. Unfortunately, his return to Louisville marked the decade finale for Pearl football.

The Cats hit on just the second play of the game when Glenn escaped for a 66-yard tally and Massey converted. The 7-0 score held until the 2nd quarter when Pearl tied it on Derrick Alexander's 2-yard run and Aaron Katzenmeyer PAT. However, Louisville increased the pressure with three scores before halftime. A 2-yard Eaves run, and more Massey PATs accompanied a 10-yard Ledbetter reception from Thomas, and a Thomas' 3-yard plunge. Their second TD in the frame came by a Pirate fumble.

Another Pirate fumble in the 3rd quarter led to a 38-yard Thomas dash. Louisville then added another from Sanders from 19 yards. Now down 42-7, Pearl finally began their response. Alexander's 80-yard run and Earl Clowers' 22-yard toss to Lawrence Jackson in the 4th quarter made it 42-20. With the ball back quickly after a bad punt snap, Alexander ran for 65 yards to the 3-yard line from where Clowers scored with 5:08 remaining. However, Louisville ended the drama when Thomas broke away for a 93-yard touchdown and Massey converted. The last Pirate drive got to the Wildcat 13 but ended in a Jackson interception to finish the Pirate season.

The Pirates put up 362 yards while Louisville had 429. Thomas rushed for 168 while Glenn had 102 yards. Thomas also threw for 92 more. Said Broyles, *"Louisville had a great team. On top of that, we didn't come out ready to play. Overall, we had a good season. We started out 0-3 and a lot of people wrote us off. We kept battling back and won nine games in a row"*. Thomas earned a Clarion-Ledger Top Performer honor.

GAME 13:   LOUISVILLE (11-1) @ CLARKSDALE (10-2)
                           LOUISVILLE 0 CLARKSDALE 34
                           November 26, 1999

The last two chases for the state title ran through a tough Clarksdale squad. The Clarkdale Press-Register thought their Wildcats better 34-14. Now it was up to the Cats to break the streak to make it to another 4A title game. They could not as the Clarksdale team took out an offensive and defensive stronghold on the Louisville squad to end the 20th century and 85 years of Wildcat football.

The Coahoma County team put up 14 points in the initial frame on a 62-yard Curtis Kemp strike to Tamera Allen and the first of four Lamarcus Milton extra points. John Hawkins then pulled in a 12-yarder from Kemp. They added another touchdown before halftime after a Brandon Downing interception when Adari Hanley crossed from two yards. They continued in the 3rd quarter with a 41-yard William Reynolds fumble return while finishing the last frame on a Kemp 32-yarder to Allen.

While Louisville led in first downs (16-10) and rushing (160-124), Clarksdale held the air 168-75. Louisville lost one fumble and had an interception. Said their coach John Murphree, *"I was really surprised in the score. That's a great Louisville defense that we scored those points against"*. Added Stanford, *"I didn't think they were as good as they have been in the past. They have a great ball club and good skilled people..."*

2000—2009

2000 (11-2)

Sixth-year Coach Tony Stanford had reason for optimism as his Wildcats garnered a number of preseason honors. Voters put them first in 2-4A, first in 4A overall, sixth in the AP Top 20, and seventh in The Clarion-Ledger Super 10. Some of that may have had a great deal to do with the 25 returning seniors.

"Our strength has to be our seniors. Most of them have started for three years. We will be fast on defense this year. I would say this is the fastest defense we've had since 1993. The backfield has a lot of speed, our offensive line is big and our receiving corps returns so we should be able to throw the ball better. We have a tough schedule. We're going to be a road team this year. Four out of our first five are going to be on the road. We have one goal at Louisville. That is to win the State (title). But we will have to get by Clarksdale because they are the team to beat in the north half".

Stanford told The Clarion-Ledger, "We feel like we have a chance to have a good ball club but you never know. Anything can happen. We had a real good spring".

GAME 1:   LOUISVILLE (0-0) @ FOREST (0-0)
                     LOUISVILLE 41 FOREST 6
                     August 25, 2000

The defending 3A state champions under Coach Jack French started highly regarded for the coming season. The Mississippi Prep Poll had them 18th while 7-3A preseason votes had them either first or second. On the other hand, the team lost 15 seniors including four offensive and six defensive starters. Said French, "We're not overly concerned about the pre-season rankings either way. I'm not sure how these decisions are made, but we tell our folks that we won the championship on the field last year and that until somebody takes it from us on the field, it's still ours".

French knew what he faced in Louisville. "They will be a tough opponent. They may well be the best team overall in the state right now. They only lost six starters from last season. We've got a chance to really accomplish something but this is a real challenging way to get our season underway". The Clarion-Ledger thought Louisville was only a point better (14-13).

What may be most memorable was off the field and before kickoff. The Supreme Court apparently ruled against organized prayer from athletic events. Instead, the crowd "initiated a heads-bowed, hands-linked recitation of The Lord's Prayer immediately prior to the playing of The National Anthem".

Louisville opened quickly with Bryant Thomas' 6-yard dash. The Bearcats tied it in the next frame with Mario Thomas' 27-yard strike to Jerry Bowie. Thomas answered with a 30-yard dash and Horace Glenn added two more points. They increased the advantage 20-6 before halftime on Thomas' 22-yard pass to Kentay Eiland. An opening 3rd quarter Forest fumble allowed Rory Sanders a 1-yard dive with Thomas and E.W. Thames adding the conversion. Still in the 3rd quarter, Thomas connected with Gabe Snow from 18 yards and Drew Massey toed the PAT. Finally, in the final stanza and after an Adrian Eiland pickoff, Anthony Stanford found Thames from three yards for a touchdown.

Louisville led in first downs (13-8), rushing (283-132) and passing (165-61). Thomas had 243 total yards (97 on the ground) and earned a Clarion-Ledger Top Performer.

GAME 2:   LOUISVILLE (1-0) @ TUPELO (0-1)
                     LOUISVILLE 28 TUPELO 0
                     September 1, 2000

The next road tilt for the Cats was one that proved unsuccessful in the past five seasons. The Wildcats had confidence after soundly defeating the defending 3A champions and looked to break this trend, as well.

Kentay Eiland opened scoring with a 17-yard scamper and Massey added the PAT. Thomas then found Gabe Snow as the opening frame expired and Massey added the kick. A Tupelo fumble in the 2nd quarter ended a threat to keep halftime 14-0. Nick Frazier picked up another 3rd quarter fumble in the air and returned it the necessary 25 yards. Thomas added the last from 66 yards and Massey converted his second of the half.

Louisville rushed for 299 yards with Thomas having 141 of those. He also threw for another 61 yards. The defense held Tupelo to just 179 yards on the night. The victory moved the Wildcats to fifth in the Top 20 and fourth in The Super 10.

GAME 3:   LOUISVILLE (2-0) vs YAZOO CITY (0-2)
                       LOUISVILLE 58 YAZOO CITY 0
                       September 8, 2000

        Yazoo City had not been a threat to Louisville since the mid-1950s and this one
proved to be out of control early. The Cats blocked a first-possession punt attempt to put
them at the 11. Eiland took it in from there and added his first of four extra points.
        Eiland also recorded the next in the quarter from 13 yards to make it 14-0.
Before halftime, they moved 85 yards with Eiland adding his third touchdown from three
yards. Thomas and Marcus Hibbler hooked up for the last from 21 yards to put intermission
27-0 in favor of Louisville. The rout continued in the 3rd quarter with scores from Glenn (14
yards), Glenn from a yard, and Cornelius Hathorn from two yards. A pair of those
touchdowns came on fumble recoveries.
        Up 46-0, the Cats added more in the finale on a 50-yard Thames punt return and
a 6-yard Glenn dash. Hathorn led rushers with 87 yards of the 366 total. Thomas threw for
94 yards to make it 460 total on the night. Ken Triplett caused a fumble and recovered
another. The defense held YCHS to just 70 total yards.

GAME 4:   LOUISVILLE (3-0) @ STARKVILLE (2-1)
                       LOUISVILLE 23 STARKVILLE 30
                       September 15, 2000

        The Yellow Jackets opened their 2000 campaign with a loss to Meridian but were
still ranked 11th in polling. The Louisville victory the previous year broke a six-game streak
of defeats, but it would not be easy to repeat the feat.
        Starkville welcomed the Cats to their new stadium with the visitors opening with
a 77-yard drive and Eiland 8-yarder. Then a fumble to the Jackets put the home team at the
45-yard line. That led to a 45-yard Deangelo Dantzler touchdown run and Jason Read PAT
to make it 7-6. In the 2nd quarter, an interception led later to a Dantzler 1-yarder and Read
PAT to make it 14-6, but Louisville responded before halftime on a 43-yard Thomas escape
to make halftime 14-12.
        Ken Triplett attempted a 3rd quarter FG from 39 yards but Starkville was able to
block it to put them at the 32-yard line. A later fumble to Louisville ruined another
opportunity. Another FG from 33 yards was true and put the Cats ahead 15-14. A later
fumble by Louisville ended with an Adrian Eiland pickoff at the 11-yard line.
        Now in the final frame, the defense held Starkville to a Read FG and 17-15 deficit.
Starkville later picked off a pass to set up a 1-yard Dantzler touchdown run to put it 23-15.
Late in the game, Jereme Milons took a punt 38 yards to the end zone. Down 30-15,
Louisville got their last on a 69-yard Thomas pass to Eiland.
        Louisville led 212 in passing from Thomas and 113 more on the ground. The Cats
had 372 yards in total offense. Deangelo Dantzler had three of the Jacket touchdowns.

GAME 5:   LOUISVILLE (3-1) @ KOSCIUSKO (2-2)
                       LOUISVILLE 35 KOSCIUSKO 7
                       September 22, 2000

        In a series that stretched back to at least 1929, the Cats were dominant with a
12-3 advantage in their last 15 meetings. Coach David Woodfin's Whippets were just 5-6
the previous year, but projected just behind Louisville in preseason 2-4A polling.
        The division opener proved all Wildcats despite the loss of Thomas from an injury
against Starkville. An opening drive Cat fumble came back to them via Jermaine Miller's
interception. Reserve QB Anthony Stanford then hit Eiland from 13 yards and Massey
converted his first of many. Marquess Ledbetter then picked off a Whippet pass and, on the
first play of the 2nd quarter, Stanford snuck in for a 14-0 lead.
        Nick Frazier then recovered a Kosy fumble, but they soon intercepted the Cats.
Before halftime, Rory Sanders crossed from a yard and Massey made it 21-0, a score that
stayed the same despite a Corey Crosby pick late. The home team opened the 3rd quarter
with their only tally on a 9-yard Marcus Estes run and Jeremy Lepard PAT to put it 21-7.
Two long Glenn runs set up a 3-yard Stanford touchdown. Stanford finished scoring with a
30-yarder to Snow and Massey remained true on the night.

Glenn rushed for 176 yards of the 259 total. Stanford threw for 111 yards. The defense held Kosy to 227 yards with 109 coming via the air. Said Woodfin, *"Louisville has a good football team"*.

GAME 6:   LOUISVILLE (4-1) vs NESHOBA CENTRAL (2-2)
                          LOUISVILLE 35 NESHOBA CENTRAL 9
                          September 29, 2000

With six consecutive wins since 1994, the Cats now welcomed Coach Pat Davis' Rockets to R.E. Hinze Stadium. They ended the previous year 5-5 but started this one ranked preseason fourth in 2-4A. Thus far, they were break-even but it would get no better.

An opening bad punt snap by Neshoba put the Cats at the 25-yard line. Eiland ended with a 3-yarder and Massey added his first of five extra points. Louisville then went 82 yards with Thomas and Hibbler hitting to make it 14-0. Crosby picked off a pass on their next attempt to end a threat. Just before halftime, the Cats moved 97 yards with Thomas and Eiland connecting from three yards.

Late in the 3rd quarter, Adrian Eiland partially blocked a Rocket punt to put it at the 20-yard line. Thomas found Hibbler from 41 yards for the only score of the frame. Hibbler finalized Wildcat scoring in the finale from 51 yards on a punt return. A bad Louisville punt snap gave NCHS a safety and they finished on a 75-yard Jacob Townsend fumble recovery and return. Timothy Feiber added the extra point.

Louisville had 127 ground yards and 202 Thomas passing yards. Stanford added 25 of those. Hibbler led receivers with 159 yards. The defense held Neshoba to 137 yards. Hibbler earned a <u>Clarion-Ledger</u> Player of the Week nod for his efforts.

GAME 7:   LOUISVILLE (5-1) @ WEST POINT (1-5)
                          LOUISVILLE 35 WEST POINT 9
                          October 6, 2000

Coach Dennis Allen had a 2-9 club from 1999 and projected fifth in 2-4A. That was holding as they had just a lone victory on the season. Unbelievably, the Wildcats matched the exact score from the previous week in the runaway road win.

An opening 66-yard Cat drive ended deep with a fumble. However, they moved 43 yards to paydirt on their next with Glenn adding the last 11 yards and Massey his first of four kicks. In the 2nd quarter, Louisville suffered a safety to make it 7-2. A solid drive put the Cats at the Wave 5 from where Eiland dashed in to make it 14-2. Thomas added to the lead with a 35-yarder to Hibbler late to make it 21-2. A West Point fumble allowed Glenn a 9-yard scoring run.

West Point opened the 3rd quarter with a 55-yard T.C. Harris punt return and PAT, but Louisville answered in the stanza when Thomas *"eluded the West Point defenders and ran 67 yards for a touchdown"*. Scoring was done with many reserves already in play. Thomas rushed for 137 yards and threw for 70 more. While Louisville had 315 yards, the defense held WP to just 206 yards.

GAME 8:   LOUISVILLE (6-1) vs NEW HOPE (2-5)
                          LOUISVILLE 55 NEW HOPE 0
                          October 13, 2000

New Hope proved in 1996 that this was no off-week. They did finish just 4-6 in the last campaign and voters put Rick Cahalane's squad next to last in 2-4A to start this season. As many anticipated, it was a blowout from start to finish.

Louisville opened with a 14-yarder to Thames and Massey hit his first of three kicks. The next march was from 38 yards and all on a Thomas strike to Hibbler. In the next frame, Eiland ran in from two yards, Cornelius Hathorn crossed from 15 yards, a bad punt snap resulted in safety, and Eiland got across from 14 yards. Halftime now sat at a comfortable 36-0 lead.

The Cats added more in the 3rd quarter on Hathorn's 5-yard run and Anthony Stanford's 15-yard dash. Ben Clark added two kicks to make it 49-0. Reserves took the field, but Hibbler took a last frame punt 75 yards to paydirt to end scoring. While the offense had 422 total yards, the defense held New Hope to just 24 yards.

Both Thomas (125) and Eiland (102) passed the 100-yard mark, Thomas threw for 50 more, Ken Dawkins led tacklers with 11 solo to creep up on Marquess Ledbetter's 77 solo on the season. He also caused a pair of fumbles and recovered one.

GAME 9:   LOUISVILLE (7-1) @ ABERDEEN (1-6)
                           LOUISVILLE 42 ABERDEEN 0
                           October 20, 2000

        Another shutout game awaited Louisville against a one-win team under Coach
Lee Doty that went just 2-8 the previous year and was selected last in 2-4A preseason.
        It got ugly quickly as Louisville jumped out on their first possession with an 80-
yard march ending on Glenn's 48-yard dash. Glenn then ran in from three yards to make it
12-0. Eiland had the next from 15 yards and Thomas' two-pointer put it 20-0. In the 2nd
quarter, they added scores from a Thomas 8-yard run and Sanders two-point conversion
along with Thomas' 16-yarder to Snow. The last came courtesy of an Adrian Eiland pick.
Massey added his first of a pair of kicks.
        The last score came in the 3rd quarter after another Eiland interception when
Stanford hit Snow from 27 yards. Scoring was done thanks to the fine efforts of the younger
reserves. Glenn rushed for 140 yards of the 329 total. Thomas threw for 58 more and
Stanford for 28 yards. The defense held Aberdeen to 89 yards.
        Said Doty, "*Coach Stanford was good to us tonight but he beat us in every way
there is to be beat in the game of football*".

GAME 10:   LOUISVILLE (8-1) vs NOXUBEE COUNTY (5-4)
                           LOUISVILLE 35 NOXUBEE COUNTY 0
                           October 27, 2000

        A third consecutive shutout was next as the Wildcats met former assistant M.C.
Miller. His Noxubee County squad was just 3-8 the previous season and third in 2-4A by
voters preseason. A win gave Louisville the division crown.
        Scoring did not start until the 2nd quarter when Eiland crossed from 11 yards and
Massey converted for his first of five. Before halftime, the Cats moved 48 yards with
Thomas and Eiland connecting from 13 yards to make intermission 14-0. Glenn finished the
opening 3rd quarter drive with a 2-yarder while Glenn ran in from 17 yards. Hathorn "*put
the finishing touches on the Wildcat victory*" from 40 yards.
        Glenn ran for 193 yards of the total 334 Cat yards and was a Clarion-Ledger
Player of the Week. The defense held Noxubee County to just 96 total yards.

GAME 11:   LOUISVILLE (9-1) @ OCEAN SPRINGS (1-9)
                           LOUISVILLE 62 OCEAN SPRINGS 3
                           November 3, 2000

        The Greyhounds proved not only a first-time opponent, but perhaps the longest
road game in Louisville history. When the game was scheduled, it was not assumed that
Ocean Springs would hold just a lone win on the 2000 season. In 1972, the Wildcats
defeated Noxubee County 67-6. This was the best since that time.
        The recap would be tedious except for scoring particulars, with even The (Biloxi)
Sun Herald calling Louisville "*worthy of their reputation*". Eiland started with a 2-yarder,
Jermaine Miller picked off a pass with Thomas finishing from 15 yards. Glenn added the
next from three yards. Crosby then picked off another pass to set up a 3-yard Eiland dash
and Massey added his fourth conversion to make it 28-0.
        Adrian Eiland joined with an interception to set up a 38-yard Thomas run and
Clark PAT. Thomas and Eiland added the following with a 12-yarder and Clark put it 42-0.
While Ocean Springs added a Jeremiah Noack 35-yard FG to avoid the shutout, Stanford and
Hibbler connected from 38 yards. Eiland then went 47 yards and Stanford and Jonathan
Kemp added the last from 29 yards. Clark was again true with the PATs.
        Louisville rushed for 356 yards with Thomas leading with 130. Eiland almost
broke the 100-yard mark with 91 yards. Thomas also threw for 78 yards while the defense
held Ocean Springs to just 81 yards.

GAME 12:   LOUISVILLE (10-1) vs WINGFIELD (8-3)
                           LOUISVILLE 35 WINGFIELD 6
                           November 10, 2000

        The two teams began play in 1997 with Louisville holding two wins in both
meetings. In both games, the Cats were always at least 21 points better than Wingfield.

While the opening frame proved a 6-0 Wildcat lead via a 27-yard Hathorn run, they immediately garnered much more before halftime. Thomas hit Snow from 27 yards, Glenn added two more points, Thomas *"broke free on a beautiful 50-yard run"* and Massey made it 21-0. Crosby picked off a Wingfield pass with Thomas finding Thames from 24 yards, Ledbetter recovered a fumble and Thomas ran in later from five yards. Massey kicks were true and it was now 35-0.

Despite an early second half Adrian Eiland interception, the only score after halftime came from Wingfield midway through the finale. Louisville rushed for 271 yards with Glenn going for 109. In all, the Cats had 338 yards on offense while the defense held Wingfield to just 124 yards. Thomas won a <u>Clarion-Ledger</u> Player of Week honor.

GAME 13:   LOUISVILLE (11-1) @ CLARKSDALE (10-1)
                     LOUISVILLE 28 CLARKSDALE 36
                     November 17, 2000

Said Stanford before the season began regarding their last three playoff meetings, *"We just can't seem to get by them. They have a little more speed than we are used to seeing"*. Despite the Wildcats having a better record, the other Wildcats seemed always have a way of beating the Winston County squad.

By game week, Stanford said, *"Our feeling is if we don't beat Clarksdale this year, we're not going to beat them. This is the best team we've had in my six years as head coach. We're excited about it. We've got a good ball team this year. If we can't beat Clarksdale, we can't win the state"*.

Said Clarksdale head man Jesse Murphree, *"They are the best Louisville team that we've had to face. I can't see any weaknesses"*. <u>The Clarion-Ledger</u> picked Louisville the winner 21-14.

A wet field led quickly to a bad Louisville punt snap and good field position for Clarksdale. Chris Liddell turned it into a 2-yarder and 6-0 lead. Louisville tied it immediately with Thomas' 8-yard toss to David Schwanebeck. Before the end of the frame, Thomas escaped for a 54-yard touchdown and then hit Thames for two more points.

Clarksdale took control in the 2nd quarter with 14 points courtesy of a 2-yard Liddell plunge, Casey Clark's 4-yarder to Marvin Young, and a two-pointer between the two. Halftime stood 20-14. Louisville had the initial score of the 3rd quarter on a 12-yarder from Thomas to Eiland and Massey PAT. However, Clarksdale answered via Truman McBride's 50-yard pick-six and Clark two-pointer to Darren Williams

Hibbler started the last stanza with an interception and Glenn turned it into a 5-yard score and Massey tied it 28-28. With 7:40 remaining, Clarksdale ended a 69-yard drive with Clark's 29-yard strike to Young and the two combined for the conversion. Clarksdale's Williams picked off another pass but fumbled it back to the Cats. The last gasp ended in yet another home team interception, this by LaMarcus Hicks.

First downs (12-11) and passing (223-89) went to Clarksdale while Louisville held the ground 169-67. Thomas led Louisville with 125 yards.

All Division 2-4A honors went to Brant Thomas (Offensive MVP), Marquess Ledbetter (Co-Defensive MVP), Eddie Harsh (Best Offensive Lineman), Adrian Eiland (Best Defensive Back) and Tony Stanford and staff (Co-Coach and Staff of the Year). Others selected included Horace Glenn, Tyler Rogers, Kentay Eiland, Rhyne Thompson, Davis Carter, Ken Dawkins, Ken Triplett, Jarrod Vaughn, Jermaine Miller, Corey Crosby, Drew Massey and Marcus Hibbler.

The Mississippi Association of Coaches All-State 4A team included Triplett, Ledbetter and Miller.

2001 (8-5)

After a wonderful 11-2 campaign, Tony Stanford and his Wildcats focused on returning to the playoffs. Voters put them tops in the 2-4A division in their pre-season rankings to set the stage. <u>The Winston County Journal</u> thought they had *"quite a chore in replacing last year's big graduating class (26 seniors)"*.

GAME 1:   LOUISVILLE (0-0) @ STARKVILLE (0-0)
                     LOUISVILLE 2 STARKVILLE 21
                     August 31, 2001

It was a tall task to take on a Starkville squad on the road that bested the Wildcats in the last seven of eight contests. This one proved to be no different.

On the Yellow Jackets' third possession, DeAngelo Dantzler hit Lynn Terry to put them at the Cat 1. Xavier Collier snuck in and Zach Bost PAT. An ensuing interception by Julius Randle produced the next Jacket score on a 4-yard Collier crossing. Louisville marched as far as the Starkville 6 but could not cross. A later 3rd quarter snap over Jacket punter Brooks Crabtree's head gave the Cats their only two points of the night. In the finale, Dantzler hit Tee Milons from 17 yards and the PAT closed scoring.

Louisville had only 72 yards on the ground as Horace Glenn paced with 25 yards. Anthony Stanford's lone completion for 37 yards gave the Cats only 109 total yards to go along with two interceptions. Meanwhile, Starkville rushed for 70 and passed for 219 more. Leron Yarbrough had three interceptions for Louisville.

GAME 2:   LOUISVILLE (0-1) vs TUPELO (1-0)
                                     LOUISVILLE 7 TUPELO 12
                                     September 7, 2001

The Golden Wave came to Louisville after a 28-0 whipping of Shannon in their season opener. It also marked the second consecutive week against a 5A school, and a second defeat.

Tupelo's Will Cline hit Kevin Caldwell from 68 yards on their opening possession to make it a quick 6-0. The Cats took the ball to the Wave 1 but could move no further. Leron Yarbrough, picked off a Wave pass but, again, with no results. Before halftime, Kentay Eiland pulled in a 5-yard Stanford toss and Ben Clark put Louisville ahead 7-6.

As the 3rd quarter ended, Tupelo recovered a Louisville fumble near midfield. Two plays later, Davious Gillespie dashed across from five yards for the eventual final points. Louisville outgained Tupelo in yardage (250-182). Eiland paced rushers with 97 of the total 203 yards.

GAME 3:   LOUISVILLE (0-2) vs MERIDIAN (0-2)
                                     LOUISVILLE 13 MERIDIAN 21
                                   September 14, 2001

Another week and another 5A team. If anything, the Wildcats were facing perhaps their toughest competition of the year early. After seven straight losses from 1959-1966, the Cats finally came back with a win in 1992. That marked only their third win in the long history of meetings (1920, 1921 and 1947).

Meridian scored their first in the 2nd quarter on a 4-yarder by Fred Patton and a Leslie Rush PAT. Yarbrough answered immediately with a 97-yard kickoff return and Clark tied the contest. However, Meridian punched back before halftime when Ken Mitts found Torry Bates from 22 yards and Rush converted.

After a scoreless 3rd quarter, Louisville closed the gap with a 15-yard Stanford strike to David Schwanebeck, but the PAT failed. Meridian closed it with Patton's second tally, this from three yards. Rush dotted the board for the final point. Meridian led in rushing 234-119. Derrell Ashford had an interception.

GAME 4:   LOUISVILLE (0-3) @ ABERDEEN (1-2)
                                     LOUISVILLE 12 ABERDEEN 6
                                   September 21, 2001

Louisville opened division play against Lee Doty's Aberdeen team picked sixth in the division after a 2-8 campaign. On their second possession, Stanford escaped from 44 yards to make it 6-0. Aberdeen tied it in the 2nd quarter after a Cat penalty when Fred Hinton hit Jonathan Williams from five yards.

Louisville wrapped it up in the final stanza after strong defensive plays from Lentrell Eiland (interception) and fumble recoveries. Horace Glenn iced things on his 2-yard dash but the two-point attempt failed. The defense stood tall on the next two Bulldog efforts to run the clock for the win.

Glenn rushed for 68 of the 179 yards while the defense held Aberdeen to just 67 rushing yards. They did, however, pass for 124.

GAME 5:   LOUISVILLE (1-3) vs NESHOBA CENTRAL (1-3)
                           LOUISVILLE 32 NESHOBA CENTRAL 0
                           September 28, 2001

          Coach Jim Ray's Rockets were 5-4 the previous season and projected fourth in 2-4A for the coming year.
          Glenn got things going with just over 4:00 remaining in the half when he galloped 76 yards to paydirt. Stanford and Kentay Eiland connected on the next possession from 23 yards. Unbelievably, Louisville added one more between Stanford and Eiland from 27 yards. They added another in the 3rd quarter after a Derrell Ashford pick when Stanford hit Yarbrough from 20 yards and Clark converted.
          The last came in the fourth quarter after a fumble recovery. Stanford and Eiland shared the love from eight yards and Clark notched the final point. The Cats had 329 total yards with Glenn rushing for 178 and Eiland for 90. Stanford threw for 108 yards. The defense held NCHS to just 115 yards.

GAME 6:   LOUISVILLE (2-3) @ NOXUBEE COUNTY (4-1)
                           LOUISVILLE 19 NOXUBEE COUNTY 21
                           October 5, 2001

          Noxubee County was not to be the same team faced previously. Coach M.C. Miller received a second-place position pre-season despite the 5-6 season of 2000. The Cats won 22 of the 23 games played, dropping only the 1982 tilt. Said Stanford, "I think they're the team to beat. They've got a lot of talent and they'll be at home".
          The Cats carried a 13-0 lead to the lockers on a 1-yard Stanford dive and Clark PAT. Kerry Miller followed that from 37 yards for the next. The weather changed quickly into a downpour and coaches knew it could change things. Said Miller, "Once we got two touchdowns down and the rain got so bad, I was worried". Added Stanford, "I felt pretty good when all that rain came. But we lost field position after that and it really hurt us".
          Now in a 4th quarter of "driving wind and rain", Omarr Conner found Joey Sanders from 15 yards and Javar Dooley hit the PAT. On their next possession, they started with a 69-yard Conner pass to Sanders and Conner ran it in from four yards later. The Dooley PAT put it 14-13. They made it 21-13 with under 2:00 remaining on a Vincent Dancy 48-yard pick-six and the kick. Louisville managed a 30-yard Stanford scoring pass to Derrell Ashford with :22 left but the two-pointer failed after a sack.
          Conner had 373 all-purpose yards, throwing for 205. He also rushed for 130 and had a 38-yard kick return. First downs were even (13-13). Glenn led rushers with 58 yards while Stanford threw for 115. Ashford pulled in 59 yards of those.

GAME 7:   LOUISVILLE (2-4) vs NEW HOPE (3-3)
                           LOUISVILLE 33 NEW HOPE 7
                           October 12, 2001

          New Hope was not expected to be much better than their 2-9 season of last year. Coach Dale Hardin's team was chosen last in 2-4A but were at least .500 thus far. This Cat win secured their playoff invitation.
          The home team took their first possession 78 yards and ended it on Carey Miller's 5-yarder. New Hope shocked fans when Donte Jones took the kickoff to paydirt from 95 yards and Ballard converted for the lead. Louisville took control afterwards but scored only once more before halftime when Glenn crossed from two yards and then added the two-pointer. Late in the 3rd quarter, Glenn scored from 15 yards to make it 20-7.
          In the finale, Miller dodged in from three yards and Gabe Snow added the PAT. With just over a minute remaining, Miller got in from two yards to end it. Glenn rushed for 241 yards of the total 426 offensive yards. The defense held the Trojans to just 51 yards. Glenn earned a Clarion-Ledger Player of the Week nod.

GAME 8:   LOUISVILLE (3-4) @ WEST POINT (4-3)
                           LOUISVILLE 7 WEST POINT 0
                           October 19, 2001

          Normally tough West Point under Coach Dennis Allen went just 3-8 the previous year. This season they were fifth in polling. The game proved tougher than expected.

The lone score came in the opening frame when Miller dashed 60 yards through the line of scrimmage to score and Snow converted. Other drives got deep but ended on turnovers and time. West Point had a chance to tie or win with :32 left, but Martez Hopkins picked off a Wave pass to secure the win.

The Cats rushed for 256 with Miller gaining 136 of those. West Point rushed for 163 and passed for 72 more. Ashford caused one fumble in the game.

GAME 9:   LOUISVILLE (4-4) @ NORTHEAST LAUDERDALE (1-7)
                 LOUISVILLE 34 NORTHEAST LAUDERDALE 0
                 October 26, 2001

Just two minutes into the inaugural game between the clubs, Miller ran from eight yards and Snow converted. The Trojans responded with a drive that fizzled at the Cat 17. In the 2nd quarter, Eiland got across from 12 yards to make it 13-0. Lauderdale moved only to the Cat 10 before bowing.

In the 3rd quarter, Eiland escaped from 57 yards and Miller added two more points. Brian Dotson later crossed from three yards. Ken Bragg wrapped it up with a 2-yarder and Clark the PAT. Louisville rushed for 374 yards in the blowout while the defense held the Trojans to just 104 total offensive yards.

GAME 10:   LOUISVILLE (5-4) vs KOSCIUSKO (6-3)
                 LOUISVILLE 19 KOSCIUSKO 7
                 November 2, 2001

Kosy was already better than their 5-5 campaign of 2000. Coach David Woodfin's squad was projected third in the division this season but had to play in Winston County. A win guaranteed the Cats no worse than second place in the playoffs and a first round home field advantage.

On their first possession, Louisville drove to paydirt ending on Eiland's 15 yarder and Snow PAT. They added another before the next frame on Stanford's 17-yard burst to make it 13-0 at halftime. The defense held Kosy and forced a fumble during that period. In the 3rd quarter, the Whippets moved to the Cat 27 but stalled.

Early in the finale, they moved 89 yards and scored on a 1-yard Adrian Riley run and Jeremy Lepard kick. Stanford ended it with an 18-yard scoring pass to Chris Perry. Eiland rushed for 100 yards. Kosciusko rushed for 127 of their 188 total yards. Louisville led first downs 13-12. Said Woodfin, "*We had the opportunities to score but could not make the plays. We played hard. We would stop them twice and then miss a tackle*".

GAME 11:   LOUISVILLE (6-4) vs OXFORD (5-5)
                 LOUISVILLE 38 OXFORD 14
                 November 9, 2001

The Chargers finished third in 1-4A and came to R.E. Hinze Stadium for the first round of the playoffs. Louisville was 7-2 all-time against Oxford since 1972.

The Wildcats put up the majority of their points before halftime while holding Oxford scoreless. On the third play of the game, Glenn dashed in from 11 yards. Stanford then hit Snow from 27 yards to end the quarter. The next was just as bad as Miller broke free from 30 yards, Lentrell Eiland picked off a Charger pass, the Cats recovered a fumble, and Brandon Dotson ran in from 13 yards. Clark added the kick. Finally, Stanford ran 39 yards to the 2-yard line from where Miller dove in.

Oxford's Jason Keller took the opening kickoff 88 yards to paydirt for six points. However, Louisville came right back with an 80-yard march and 7-yard Stanford run. Oxford's last came in the frame on a 1-yard Turner Barnes run and his two-pointer. The Cats rushed for 366 and passed for 104. The defense held Oxford to just 89 total yards. Miller led rushers with 130 while Glenn had 94 yards.

GAME 12:   LOUISVILLE (7-4) @ SHANNON (10-1)
                 LOUISVILLE 44 SHANNON 38
                 November 16, 2001

The Red Raiders had won 35 of their last 38 games, losing only to Tupelo this season in their opener. Their Dandy Dozen quarterback, Ken Topps, was "*considered the best in the state at his position by many*". This marked their initial year in 4A.

The home team opened with a bang when Green took the opening kick 81 yards to paydirt and Jones converted. The Cats came right back with a 2-yard Miller run but the two-pointer failed. In the 2nd quarter, Topps hit Bogan from 22 yards and Jones added another of his eventual five extra points.

Louisville moved as far as three yards from the end zone before penalties caused the drive to fail. Shannon then went 92 yards in four plays with Topps and Brown hooking up from 27 yards. While Glenn came back with a 15-yarder and Miller the two points, the Raiders moved 80 yards and ended it on a Topps 15-yarder to Brown.

Shannon seemed to continue the momentum in the 3rd quarter but only after the Cats cut it to 28-20 on a 23-yard Stanford pass to Snow. The home team moved ahead on a 58-yard screen pass from Topps to Ivy and followed it with a 28-yard Jones FG. It seemed lost in the finale down 38-20, but Louisville started to punch back. Stanford found Perry from 13 yards and Stanford added two more.

A fake punt by the Cats gave them a chance for Stanford to hit Ashford for a later 71-yard touchdown to put it 38-34. A bad punt snap gave the visitors two more points. Taking the ensuing possession, Eiland dashed in from 3-yard score and Stanford the two-pointer. Louisville led in yardage (482-385) and rushed for 312 of those.

GAME 13:   LOUISVILLE (8-4) @ HERNANDO (11-1)
            LOUISVILLE 28 HERNANDO 36
            November 23, 2001

Another first-time opponent welcomed the Wildcats in the form of formidable Hernando. An early fumble to Louisville quickly led to Glenn's 8-yarder to make it 6-0.

Kevin Dockery responded for Hernando on the next possession with an 18-yard dash combined with the first of four Niklas Baumberger kicks. An ensuing turnover led to a 65-yard Dockery bomb to Larry Henderson. Back came Louisville on Eiland's 57-yard punt return to make it 14-12. Then, a Yarbrough interception set up Glenn's 4-yarder and Stanford two-point conversion to put them ahead 20-14.

As the half ended, Dockery ran in from a yard and then *"disaster struck"* with only seconds remaining when Stephen St. John took a Cat fumble 45 yards to paydirt. Their two-point conversion from Kyle Cleveland to Rob Ramage put it 29-20. A 3rd quarter Hernando fumble to Louisville led to Glenn's 1-yard cross and Stanford's two-pointer.

Questionable penalties stalled a final frame march that got as far as the Hernando 10. Dockery ended things with a 44-yard escape and the PAT proved their last. The Cats rushed for 158 with Eiland gaining 105 of those. Louisville led in yardage 288-274.

All-Region 2-4A honors went to Davis Carter (Co-MVP Offensive Line), Martez Hopkins (MVP Defensive Line), Horace Glenn (MVP Running Back), Courtney Smith (Sportsmanship Heart of a Champion), Gabe Snow, Kentay Eiland, Ryan Thompson, Tilmorris Jackson, Mantrel Ashford, Durrell Ashford, Ken Shields, Laron Yarbrough, and Anthony Stanford.

2002 (8-5)

Though Coach Tony Stanford's Wildcats were picked second in polling, he was not overconfident. *"Thirty five of our sixty players on the varsity have never been a varsity field before. Many of them played junior high and junior varsity ball but we've got some that have never played before. We're going to be very young this year"*.

Despite only three offensive starters and seven on defense, Stanford was a bit more optimistic as August ended. *"I think we're coming together real well right now. Defensively we should be strong. The five starters that we have on the offensive line are just going to have to mold together quickly. The first three or four games, they may not look all that great, but by the middle of the season, they should be coming together nicely"*.

GAME 1:   LOUISVILLE (0-0) vs STARKVILLE (0-0)
            LOUISVILLE 6 STARKVILLE 28
            August 30, 2002

Hopes must have been small for fans at R.E. Hinze against the much-bigger Yellow Jackets under Coach Ronnie Cuevas that carried an 8-1 record against Louisville in their last nine contests. In addition, they won the 5A title the previous year but did have the loss of 18 starters and 34 total letter winners.

To everyone's surprise, the first half was scoreless. One Jacket FG was blocked by Lentrell Eiland. That changed in the 3rd quarter as Starkville went 77 yards in 12 plays ending with a 22-yard Roger Armstead run and Zach Bost PAT. Back came Louisville with an 84-yard drive and Derrell Ashford 33-yarder. Before the frame ended, the Jackets drove 53 yards and capped it with a 25-yard Rodney Hampton reception from Barry Doss and the Bost PAT.

In the last frame, Starkville put up two scores. First, a fumble led to Nate Hughes' 30-yarder and Ben Rush later via a 35-yard catch from Will Sneed. Ashford had 136 of 219 yards of rushing. Starkville rushed for 245 yards and threw for 152 more.

GAME 2:   LOUISVILLE (0-1) @ TUPELO (1-0)
                LOUISVILLE 19 TUPELO 21
                September 6, 2002

The Golden Wave opened the game with a 92-yard Davious Gillespie kickoff return and Tommy Pharr PAT. In the 2nd quarter, the Cats tied it on a 24-yard Ashford dash and the PAT. Back came Tupelo on a 1-yarder by Gillespie and Pharr kick.

The Cats had the only score of the 3rd quarter when Cornelius Colter dove in from a yard to make it 14-13. The Wave responded in the finale on a 4-yard Gillespie run and Pharr kick. Louisville tried to send it to overtime on a 47-yard Ashford run but the two-point effort failed to seal the loss.

Ashford ran for 166 yards in the losing effort while Anthony Stanford added another 64 yards.

GAME 3:   LOUISVILLE (0-2) @ MERIDIAN (0-2)
                LOUISVILLE 33 MERIDIAN 17
                September 13, 2002

Despite a tremendous record against the Cats, turnovers spelled the defeat of the home team on this night. In the 2nd quarter, Stanford found Mantrell Ashford from 19 yards and Stanford added the PAT.

Meridian answered with a Andrew Gambrell 29-yard FG midway through the frame to put halftime 7-3. Ryan Kimbrough found a loose Cat ball in the 3rd quarter and took it 42 yards to paydirt to put it 10-7 after a Gambrell conversion. Back punched Louisville with Ashford's 55-yard escape and it was now 14-10.

While Meridian got their last to open the finale via a 65-yard Ken Mitts pass to Courtney Lynch and Gambrell kick, the Winston County squad was just getting started. A fumble recovery led to Stanford's 1-yard dive. Another at their 18-yard line set up a 5-yard Colter run while he did it again from nine yards before the contest ended.

Louisville had 320 offensive yards with 266 coming on the ground. Dotson led with 103 while Stanford went 3-4 for 54 yards.

GAME 4:   LOUISVILLE (1-2) vs ABERDEEN (2-1)
                LOUISVILLE 30 ABERDEEN 0
                September 20, 2002

Now the Wildcats welcomed a team ranked fourth in polls but now ninth in the state to start the season to see if they could not only break even on the year but win their first division game.

Chris Perry took the opening kick 93 yards to the end zone and Stanford quickly made the rainy night score 7-0. Brandon Dotson added a 13-yarder and Stanford the kick in the same frame. By halftime, Dotson found paydirt from a yard and it was 20-0. Derrell Ashford crossed from 44 yards in the 3rd quarter and Stanford converted. He later added a last-frame 37-yard FG to close it.

GAME 5:   LOUISVILLE (2-2) @ NESHOBA CENTRAL (0-4)
                LOUISVILLE 17 NESHOBA CENTRAL 3
                September 27, 2002

Dotson started the win with a 3-yarder and Stanford made it 7-0. Kyle Vowell's 18-yard FG in the 2nd quarter cut it to 7-3. Now in the final stanza, Stanford nailed a 23-yard

FG and Dotson dashed in later from 10 yards. Stanford added the PAT. The Cats led in yardage 137-95.

GAME 6:   LOUISVILLE (3-2) vs NOXUBEE COUNTY (4-1)
                               LOUISVILLE 22 NOXUBEE COUNTY 36
                               October 4, 2002

Since Noxubee County under Coach M.C. Miller was voted first in the division, it was no surprise that The Clarion-Ledger picked them 22-20. It took only as long as the kickoff for Joey Sanders to take it 84 yards to the end zone to make it a quick 6-0 game.

Dotson responded on the next drive for the Cats from 25 yards and Stanford gave them the 7-6 lead. Four plays later, Louisville got to the Tiger 22 only to fumble it away. They then drove to the Tiger 2 only to fail. Turnovers on both sides stalled drives for the frame. An Omarr Conner 56-yarder to Sanders set up a 1-yarder by Conner and his two-pointer to Sanders.

In the 3rd quarter, an early Cat fumble allowed Conner to find Brandon Tate from 13 yards and it was now 20-7. Conner found Sanders again in the frame from 13 yards and Roberto Jordan made it 28-7. Louisville came back with an 85-yard march ending with Dotson's reception from three yards and the PAT cut it 28-14. Back came NCHS with a 69-yarder to Sanders and Jordan two-pointer.

Louisville responded with a 71-yard drive and Corey Goss 3-yarder and his two-pointer with 5:55 left. Chris Perry then picked off a Conner pass late but the Cats could go nowhere. Louisville rushed for 300 yards with Dotson (101) and Derrell Ashford (91) leading the way. Noxubee had 269 total yards.

GAME 7:   LOUISVILLE (3-3) @ NEW HOPE (1-5)
                               LOUISVILLE 57 NEW HOPE 0
                               October 11, 2002

The Trojans were picked last to start the season and had just a single victory on the year. It got no better for this one.

An early sack on New Hope QB Chas Brown led to the 2-0 lead. Ashford then dashed in from 15 yards to end the 1st quarter 8-0. The Cats added 21 more before halftime on a 6-yard Goss run, Stanford's 41-yarder to Hunt, and another 30-yarder to Eiland. Stanford also added all three kicks.

Goss added a 71-yard dash in the 3rd and Ashford notched one from 38 yards. In the finale, Goss crossed from 11 yards and Perry from 44. Stanford was true on all kicks. While the defense held New Hope to just 92 total yards, the Cats put up 533 yards. Goss ran for 133 while Derrell Ashford added 111 more. Louisville had 379 on the ground.

GAME 8:   LOUISVILLE (4-3) vs WEST POINT (6-1)
                               LOUISVILLE 7 WEST POINT 17
                               October 18, 2002: HOMECOMING

It was not to be a wonderful Homecoming as West Point opened with a 1-yard Vernon Morton run and Scott Hughes PAT. Hughes then added a 23-yard FG before Stanford hit Rod Ingram from 78 yards and Stanford converted. The last tally came in the 4th quarter with 1:08 left on Cedric Wells' 2-yard burst and Hughes extra point.

GAME 9:   LOUISVILLE (4-4) vs NORTHEAST LAUDERDALE (3-5)
                               LOUISVILLE 38 NORTHEAST LAUDERDALE 7
                               October 25, 2002

The recap from the local paper notes only the win and that seniors were honored for the contest. The Clarion-Ledger gives a bit more in their box score. Hunt put the Cats up in the opening frame on a 9-yard run while Stanford hit Perry from four yards and Allen from six yards in the next frame. With his extra points, it was 21-0 at halftime.

While Northeast dotted the board in the 3rd quarter on a 47-yard Betts run and Rodrigues kick, Louisville came back with Ashford runs of 33 and 11 yards. In the finale, Stanford booted a 32-yard FG. With that and his 5-5 on kicks, he earned a Player of Week nod from The Clarion-Ledger.

GAME 10:   LOUISVILLE (5-4) @ KOSCIUSKO (2-7)
                          LOUISVILLE 38 KOSCIUSKO 7
                          November 1, 2002

Kosciusko, ranked sixth in polls preseason, expected a tough home game against the Wildcats. Said Coach David Woodfin, *"Louisville is a good football team. They are not as strong as in the past, but they are still good"*.

An early Whippet fumble allowed Stanford a later 1-yard scoring dive and PAT. Then, a punt over Eli Dew's head gave the Cats a safety for 9-0 advantage. Dotson then found the end zone from 45 yards and Stanford put it 16-0. Before halftime, Derrell Ashford crossed from 64 yards and Stanford added two more points.

In the 3rd quarter, Dotson went in from 54 yards and Stanford put it 31-0. Kosy avoided the shutout after when Antron Dotson recovered a fumble to set up a 33-yard Adrian Riley dash and Allen Howell PAT. Goss later found paydirt from 25 yards and Stanford's PAT ended it.

Said Stanford, *"We played well for the win. I felt like we had the game under control"*. Woodfin added, *"We had to play young kids before they were ready to play. We tried to simplify things offensive and defensively"*. Louisville led in yardage 304-192. Dotson, a Player of the Week, rushed for 160 yards while Derrell Ashford added another 100. Mantrell Ashford led tacklers with 15.

GAME 11:   LOUISVILLE (6-4) @ PEARL (6-4)
                          LOUISVILLE 22 PEARL 0
                          November 8, 2002

Pearl was jinxed against Louisville, going 1-4 all-time against them since 1985. And, it was Louisville that ended Pearl playoff hopes in both 1995 and 1999. However, the Wildcats had to travel to Rankin County and Pearl was prepared to play as tough as they could for the home fans in wet conditions.

After a scoreless opening quarter, Chris Shoto recovered a Cat fumble. They drove to the Cat 23 but Justin Roberts' 44-yard FG on a muddy field was unsuccessful. Louisville came back with an 80-yard drive capped by a 35-yard Stanford run and his extra point. It may have been worse after a Pirate fumble at the 21-yard line, but the Pirate defense held and kept halftime a slim 7-0 deficit. Pearl opened the 3rd quarter with a drive to the Wildcat 19, but again a Roberts FG attempt failed.

Just before the quarter's end, Louisville blocked a Pearl punt out of the end zone for a safety. They took the ensuing kick and threatened again, but Leon Seals' interception thwarted the effort. Louisville put the game away in the final quarter of play. An interception led to a 1-yard Stanford run and, with just 1:51 remaining, Dotson escaped from 25 yards for another tally. Stanford's kick ended the Pirate season.

Derrell Ashford rushed for 214 yards and earned a Player of the Week honor.

GAME 12:   LOUISVILLE (7-4) @ NOXUBEE COUNTY (10-1)
                          LOUISVILLE 21 NOXUBEE COUNTY 20
                          November 15, 2002

The playoff rematch would not be an easy one. Omarr Conner and NCHS not only had the earlier win over the Cats, but Conner now had 51 touchdowns on the year. His passing equaled 3,141 coming into the game. Said Coach M.C. Miller, *"I know Louisville is going to be up and ready. When we left, they said 'We'll see you in the playoffs'. I hope we can get up because there is no tomorrow"*. The Clarion-Ledger picked his squad 28-24.

A muddy field slowed progress somewhat but the Cats eventually crossed the stripe when Stanford snuck in from a yard and converted. Noxubee answered with a 23-yard Conner pass to Joey Sanders to put it 7-6. The Cats took a 14-6 lead to intermission when Rod Ingram pulled in a 55-yarder from Stanford and the QB converted.

Conner answered for the Tigers in the 3rd quarter on his 6-yard run but Louisville came back in the finale with Derrell Ashford's 18-yarder and Stanford kick. The last tally came on a 1-yard Conner run and his two-pointer to Brandon Tate.

The Cats led first downs (20-15) and rushing (271-53) while Noxubee held the air (233-55). *"I've said all year that the only way you're going to beat Noxubee County is to control the football and keep Omarr off the field. We tried to do it the first time but we had turnovers that killed us. It was just old-fashioned football out there tonight"*. Dotson, with 136 rushing yards, earned a Player of the Week nod.

GAME 13:   LOUISVILLE (8-4) @ WEST POINT (8-4)
                  LOUISVILLE 0 WEST POINT 6
                  November 22, 2002

The Wildcats now traveled to face another opponent that bested them (17-7) just over a month previous. The history was long between these two. In some years, the first to win also lost the post-season battle, while other times it was reversed. Either way, there was nobody on either sideline taking this one for granted.

In the end, it came down to just one touchdown in the final frame. That came when David Webber found paydirt from three yards after a long and arduous defensive struggle between both teams. The Cats had a chance to steal the win with 18 seconds left but Taz Carter picked off an errant Stanford throw in the end zone. West Point held yardage 204-62

All-Region 2-4A honors went to Derrell Ashford (MVP Offensive Back), Anthony Stanford, Brandon Dotson, Greg Hathorn, Jordan Kemp, Brandon Doss, Chris Perry, Lentrell Eiland, Mantrell Ashford, Isaac Triplett, Courtney Coleman, Joseph LeBlanc and Alvin Coleman (Heart of a Champion).

2003 (9-4)

After eight years at the helm of Louisville football, beloved Tony Stanford announced his retirement. Late in the season, he noted that "*it was one of the toughest decisions he ever had to make*". The move was, according to him, to help his family and see his son play at the next level. Assistant Coach John Mullins was immediately named acting head coach while the school evaluated options for replacement.

Eventually the school named Joe Gant as mentor. Gant had five state titles at 1A Weir and 224 games to his credit. "*I think I'm hitched up onto a good bus. The most attractive thing is that's it's 17 miles from my house in Weir. Louisville just reminds me of where I've been. They're the same kind of kids. You don't have to beg them. They want to win. You don't have to pressure on them. The community puts pressure on them*".

As kickoff neared, Gant said "*I think we're a little behind, especially on offense because of the coaching change. But that's definitely not because of a lack of effort on the part of the kids. These kids have been putting in the effort and this coaching change has thrown them behind*".

GAME 1:   LOUISVILLE (0-0) @ STARKVILLE (0-0)
                  LOUISVILLE 12 STARKVILLE 7
                  August 29, 2003

Coach Ronnie Cuevas, in his second year, was coming off of a 9-3 campaign and now eighth in The Super 10 and fifth in 5A. The Clarion-Ledger thought the new adjustment too much for the Wildcats and picked Starkville 24-12.

The visitors opened with a 1-yard Barry Doss dive to make it 6-0. Starkville came back in the 2nd quarter to put halftime 7-6 when Isaac Smith ran in from five yards and Matt Grable converted. The Cats pulled it out in the finale on a 4-yard LaKendrick Coleman dash. Starkville had a chance to win late but penalties and an incomplete pass dashed hopes.

The Cats rushed for 134 yards and passed for 32. Doss paced rushers with 62 yards while Coleman was close with 58 yards. The Jackets had 164 total offensive yards with 109 of those coming on the ground.

GAME 2:   LOUISVILLE (1-0) @ NOXUBEE COUNTY (0-1)
                  LOUISVILLE 6 NOXUBEE COUNTY 16
                  September 5, 2003

The win over Starkville moved Louisville to eighth in the Associated Press Top 20. This one now matched the Cats against a team they faced twice the previous year and bested in their last match.

This time was not as successful. Jordan opened the 1st quarter for the home team with a 1-yarder to make it 6-0. Both tallied in the 2nd quarter. A safety by Campbell put them ahead 8-0 while Coburn picked up a loose Noxubee ball and raced 95 yards to paydirt. The extra point attempt failed.

In the 3rd quarter, Tate widened the gap on a 37-yard dash and added a two-pointer from Bryant to Tate to finalize things.

GAME 3:   LOUISVILLE (1-1) vs WEST POINT (2-0)
                           LOUISVILLE 7 WEST POINT 10
                           September 12, 2003 (OT)

Coach Dennis Allen's West Point club was a 4A team in 2002 and ranked second with an overall 12-3 finishing season. Now they moved to 5A and sat seventh in The Super 10 and fifth in Class 5A voting by kickoff. The Clarion-Ledger said, "West Point has more offensive punch" and picked them 21-14.

It was a tough battle as the only score came in the 2nd quarter courtesy of a Doss 38-yarder and Josh Black kick. In the 3rd quarter, Chris Matthews found the goal on an 18-yarder and Scott Hughes tied it. Now in overtime, Hughes knocked home a 17-yard FG but Louisville could not respond and gave West Point their third consecutive win over the Cats.

GAME 4:   LOUISVILLE (1-2) vs NESHOBA CENTRAL (1-2)
                           LOUISVILLE 30 NESHOBA CENTRAL 3
                           September 19, 2003

The last Rocket win over Louisville came back in 1993 when the two teams split the pair of meetings. Now they met with equal records but in Winston County.

Though the opening frame was scoreless, the Cats tallied in the 2nd quarter on an 11-yard Doss run and Josh Black PAT. Neshoba Central's only response came in the form of a Kyle Vowell 22-yard FG to make halftime 7-3. Louisville took control in the second half, first with a 3rd quarter 16-yard LaKendrick Coleman dash and Black PAT.

In the final frame, the Cats scored on a 21-yard Black FG, a 6-yarder from Doss to Chris Terry and finally Coleman's 89-yard escape. Coleman's 188 rushing yards made him a Clarion-Ledger Player of the Week.

GAME 5:   LOUISVILLE (2-2) @ KOSCIUSKO (3-1)
                           LOUISVILLE 26 KOSCIUSKO 20
                           September 26, 2003

The Whippets were 3-15 against Louisville in their last 18 encounters. While close, this one extended the advantage.

Kosy jumped on the Wildcats early and held a 14-0 lead after the initial quarter. Chris Herron broke free from 33 yards and did it again later from a yard. With two Evan Thrasher extra points, the Cats felt the pressure. They responded in the 2nd quarter with a 14-yard Coleman dash and a 16-yard Doss strike to Rod Ingram. Two Black extra points knotted the game 14-14 at intermission.

Channing Kern put the Whippets back up via his 54-yarder to make it 20-14. Louisville took over in the finale on an 80-yard Doss bomb to Ingram to tie and then a 21-yard dash by Doss to finish scoring. The win kept the Wildcats tied for first in 4-4A with Pearl; a team they would face later. It also kept them 19th in The Top 20.

GAME 6:   LOUISVILLE (3-2) vs BAILEY (0-5)
                           LOUISVILLE 40 BAILEY 0
                           October 3, 2003: HOMECOMING

Only the box score from The Clarion-Ledger is found recapping the inaugural matchup. The Cats had a 13-0 lead after a frame via a 10-yard Dotson run and 6-yarder by Coleman. Black added the PAT after the second score.

In the 2nd quarter, Perry dove in from a yard, Doss from five yards and added a 6-yard pass to Dotson. Black was true on each. The final tally came in the 4th quarter when Tavaris Welch ran in from 10 yards.

GAME 7:   LOUISVILLE (4-2) vs TUSCALOOSA NORTHRIDGE (0-6)
                           LOUISVILLE 42 TUSCALOOSA NORTHRIDGE 7
                           October 10, 2003

Another first-time opponent found their way to R.E. Hinze to face the Wildcats. While the name may sound imposing, their record thus far was far from the same.

Coleman opened with a 53-yard run, Doss crossed from two yards and then found Ingram from 16 yards. Black's kicks made it a quick 21-0 contest. They added another in the 2nd quarter on a 53-yard Perry run and Dotson two-pointer before the visitors could find paydirt on a 14-yard pass and PAT.

Louisville put up scores in each of the next two frames. First was a 5-yard Dotson run while the last was a 17-yard Doss pass to Antoine Triplett. Black dotted the board for the final point.

GAME 8:　　　　　LOUISVILLE (5-2) @ PEARL (5-2)
　　　　　　　　　LOUISVILLE 0 PEARL 33
　　　　　　　　　October 17, 2003

The Cats knocked the Pirates out of the playoffs in 1985, 1995, 1999 and 2002. The Clarion-Ledger picked Louisville 23-13. "Pearl is fighting to stay in the race for one of four playoff spots and a win over Louisville would put the Pirates in a three-way tie for first place. It won't happen".

Though an opening Pirate fumble gave the Wildcats a FG opportunity, Isaac Bryant's tackle of the kicker after a bad snap erased the opportunity. Pearl then drove 77 yards and capped it with a 6-yard Ty Weems run. They moved 70 yards in the 2nd quarter and scored on a 7-yard Fred Scott run. Though Pearl scored once more before intermission, it came back and the Pirates then later fumbled the ball away. The 3rd quarter opened with a Wildcat fumble to Terrell Hobson but it produced no points. However, later in the quarter, Weems hit Rico Brown from 30 yards to make it 18-0.

In the 4th quarter, a bad punt snap gave Bryant a safety. Jaron Bell took the ensuing free kick 65 yards to the end zone and Weems made it 27-0. Pearl added one last TD when a Hobson hit popped the ball into Phil Wheeler's hands and he raced 48 yards to paydirt. First downs (10-5), rushing (159-139) and passing (68-7) went to Pearl.

Said Coach Larry Weems, "This one was huge. We've got one more division game against Canton in two weeks. If we win that, we win the division. If we had lost, we would have been the number 3 seed at best. In football, sometimes it works and sometimes it doesn't. Our kids played hard. We did some things and got off to a real good start and carried that momentum throughout the game". Added Gant, "When you whip somebody like they whipped us, there ain't no key. They whipped us every way we could be whipped".

GAME 9:　　　　　LOUISVILLE (5-3) vs CANTON (3-5)
　　　　　　　　　LOUISVILLE 55 CANTON 7
　　　　　　　　　October 24, 2003

Drama unfolded in Louisville during the week following the Pearl tilt. According to sources, Gant was fired by superintendent Harry Kemp over the removal of pics of Rod Baker and Moine Nicholson from the fieldhouse. Says Gant, "The letter I've been given says I'm being fired for verbal abuse and profanity in dealing with football players and for insubordination by repeatedly refusing to follow specific directions from the superintendent". The school had no comment at the time.

Interim Coach John Mullins and the Wildcats still had no trouble preparing and demolishing their next opponent. Scoring came in bunches with the Cats putting up 21 points in the opening frame on a 14-yard Coleman run, another from a yard, a 6-yarder by Dotson, and three Black extra points. They added another touchdown in the next quarter on Doss' 31-yard keeper and Black kick.

Coleman opened the 3rd quarter with a 41-yard escape and 7-yard Stanley Frazier carry. Black again converted. Frazier did it again in the finale from 18 yards while Daniel Eichelberger found the end zone from 48 yards. Black converted on the last. Canton finally scored on a Gary Johnson 51-yard dash and Roderick Hardy kick.

GAME 10:　　　　LOUISVILLE (6-3) @ RIDGELAND (4-5)
　　　　　　　　　LOUISVILLE 16 RIDGELAND 7
　　　　　　　　　October 31, 2003

First-time foe Ridgeland had to have a win and other factors come into play in order to progress to the playoffs. Coach Kenny Burton said, "We haven't made any changes as far as how we are approaching this game. We're here to win games and we are trying to even our record. Louisville is Louisville. They have a good team and good athletes. We feel if we show up and play like we can play, we have a chance".

It ended a tough-fought contest in Ridgeland. Doss had the lone tally of the 1st quarter on his 20-yard dash. Both scored in the 2nd quarter, first on a 12-yard Dotson carry and Frazier two-pointer. Ridgeland found paydirt on a 78-yard Blake Hitchcock strike to Derek Holmes and a Roberts PAT. The last score came when Louisville recorded a safety.

GAME 11:   LOUISVILLE (7-3) @ AMORY (8-2)
                  LOUISVILLE 20 AMORY 7
                  November 7, 2003

The first-round draw was not optimal for Louisville as Amory bested them in their only three meetings (1996-1998). However, this one belonged (finally) to the Wildcats.

Coleman got Louisville going in the opener with his 34-yard dash. Doss added a 26-yarder and Black converted both while the defense held Amory scoreless. In the 3rd quarter, Matthew Randle found Sergio Wallace from nine yards and a Randy Earnest kick made it 14-7, but the Cats soon answered with a 56-yard Doss bomb to Coleman. It proved the end of scoring.

GAME 12:   LOUISVILLE (8-3) vs CLARKSDALE (9-2)
                  LOUISVILLE 20 CLARKSDALE 9
                  November 14, 2003

The other "Wildcats", ranked sixth in The Super 10, proved to be a thorn in the Louisville side via their elimination of the Cats from playoffs four times since 1997. Said Coach Jim Hughes, "It's going to be a war". The Clarion-Ledger picked Clarksdale 20-16.

Doss ran in from 45 yards to start the game and Black converted. Shortly thereafter, Sebastion Morton hit Champ McGregory for 57 yards and the Ahmad Salameh PAT evened things. Black nailed a 22-yard FG in the 3rd quarter while Dotson put up a 7-yarder in the last frame. Black made it 17-7 and then added a 24-yard FG. The last points came on a Clarksdale safety.

Ironically, Clarksdale led in first downs (10-9), rushing (181-126) and passing (167-0). This was according to The Clarksdale Press-Register.

GAME 13:   LOUISVILLE (9-3) vs OXFORD (8-4)
                  LOUISVILLE 13 OXFORD 14
                  November 21, 2003

Louisville was an all-time 7-2 against Oxford with losses coming only in 1989 and 1990. The Chargers defeated Kosciusko 28-6 in the second round to advance.

Oxford had a chance to be first on the scoreboard when Anton Anderson "stripped the ball" to give them a shot that failed. Nevertheless, they tallied in the 2nd quarter on Chris Cutcliffe's 64-yarder to Anthony Mitchell. Kevan Wright made it 7-0. The Cats then went 80 yards with Coleman finding paydirt from a yard and Black adding the PAT to even things at intermission.

On their first march, Oxford's Ken Smith dodged in from six yards and Wright put up the 14-7 kick. That came on "a questionable pass interference call against the Wildcats". Louisville then used Coleman to run 58 yards to the 1-yard line and Cornelius Colter dove in from there, but the crucial PAT failed. Louisville drove as far as the Oxford 5 in the last frame before penalties and a fumble killed the opportunity.

Coleman rushed for 94 yards while Dotson added 88 more. The Wildcats led in yardage (280-207) but the season was over. "We made too many mistakes. We missed an extra point and had a fumble deep in their territory when a FG would have won the game. You can't make those types of mistakes and expect to win, especially against good teams. There isn't any doubt that these kids could have quit any time during this year. But they fought through it, pulled together as a team and did what they had to do to reach the playoffs. I'm very proud of these kids".

2004 (2-7)

New head man John Mullins had a new era for the Wildcats who were ranked 15th preseason in the Top 20. "We have had real good practices. We look to play good defense and have a strong running game. We have several good running backs and our offensive and defensive lines are both very solid. The kicking game will require some work. We still have to find a kicker due to injuries".

GAME 1:   LOUISVILLE (0-0) vs STARKVILLE (0-0)
                 LOUISVILLE 7 STARKVILLE 14
                 August 27, 2004

The win the previous year hopefully ended a string of Starkville victories over Louisville that went back to the early-to-mid 1990s with only another win sandwiched in between. This contest at home didn't help against the sixth-ranked Yellow Jackets.

It took Starkville only their first drive to find the end zone when Alonzo Bush hit Monterio James from 57 yards and Wade Spurlock connected. A failed 31-yard FG by LaKendrick Coleman kept it 7-0. In the 2nd quarter, the Cats missed a 21-yard FG but did block a 25-yarder by Starkville. Though Louisville immediately fumbled back, Caleb Reed picked off a Jacket pass leading to a 2-yard Cornelius Colter dive and Coleman PAT.

In the final frame, and after a Charles Wraggs fumble recovery, the Cats turned it back over via interception. With just over a minute left, Glover Young crossed from three yards and Spurlock added the last point. Kevin Cane ended Cat hopes with a pick.

GAME 2:   LOUISVILLE (0-1) vs NOXUBEE COUNTY (0-1)
                 LOUISVILLE 8 NOXUBEE COUNTY 26
                 September 3, 2004

After going years dominating Noxubee County, the Tigers came back to win three of four consecutive matches. They jumped on the Cats early in this one, starting with a second-drive 5-yarder by Bobby May and Shields PAT.

They added another in the 2nd quarter on a 56-yarder from James Patterson to Darryl Walton to make halftime 13-0. Patterson added an 11-yard run in the 3rd quarter and Shields the kick. Yet another Cat fumble, one of many, led to May crossing from five yards to end the frame 26-0.

Louisville dotted the board in the finale after a Kenneth Whitfield fumble recovery led to Colter's 5-yard run and Coleman's two-point conversion.

GAME 3:   LOUISVILLE (0-2) @ WEST POINT (2-0)
                 LOUISVILLE 0 WEST POINT 22
                 September 10, 2004

Undefeated West Point moved up to fifth in The Super 10 after beating Canton 39-0. Now they welcomed Louisville to West Point after three-straight wins over them.

Things were going from bad to worse as the green ended the evening with a shutout. WP got going in the 2nd quarter on a 16-yard pass from Cliff Bailey to Travis Walker and soon followed that with a safety to put halftime 8-0. They added their next in the 3rd quarter via a 6-yard Chris Matthews run and their last on a 33-yard Bailey pass to D.D. Young. Tyler Weston added both extra points.

GAME 4:   LOUISVILLE (0-3) @ NESHOBA CENTRAL (0-3)
                 LOUISVILLE 18 NESHOBA CENTRAL 7
                 September 17, 2004

With ten straight wins over the Rockets, hopes were high for the first win of the year. Reed got it going with an early fumble recovery and Coleman turned it into a 75-yard touchdown run. Ahmad Greer recovered a later fumble but Louisville gave it back the same way. Strong defenses kept halftime just 6-0.

Reed started the 3rd quarter with a 35-yard fumble return for the lone points of the frame. That was also courtesy of a Michael Sims fumble recovery. Both tallied in the last quarter. Neshoba got theirs on a 2-yard Kevin Marshall dive and Derek Crenshaw conversion. The Cats put it away after picks by Reed and Daniel Eichelberger when Eichelberger hit Corey Miller from 32 yards. Reed, a Clarion-Ledger Player of the Week, sealed it with another pickoff.

GAME 5:   LOUISVILLE (1-3) vs KOSCIUSKO (3-1)
               LOUISVILLE 20 KOSCIUSKO 30
               September 24, 2004

Kosciusko was perhaps one of the longest serving rivalries stretching back to 1929 with some years without a matchup. The question was whether the Cats could bounce back from a 1-3 season thus far to climb the ladder.

It looked promising early as Louisville held a 12-7 lead after a quarter. Despite an early Whippet fumble recovered by the Wildcats, they could not advance. On their next possession, Kosy took the lead on a 30-yard Chris Herron pass to Terry Levy and Taylor Putt PAT. The Cats then responded with a 65-yard drive ending with a 1-yarder by Colter. Now 7-6, Colter recovered another Kosciusko fumble and took it 35 yards to paydirt to make it a Louisville advantage.

It was short-lived as the Whippets put up a pair before halftime. While a Carey Miller pick did no damage, Herron took a punt 45 yards to paydirt to put them ahead 13-12. Herron bettered the previous punt return with an 80-yarder and Putt converted. Markevius Hoskins recovered yet another Kosy fumble to set up a 4-yard Deon Hickman run. Miller found Coleman for the two-points to tie it 20-20.

Kosciusko answered before the quarter ended on a 68-yard Earlson Costine run and Putt connected. The lone tally of the finale came on a 27-yard Putt FG. The Cats tried to come back and got as far as the 5-yard line but an interception to Malcolm Tolliver ended any hopes.

GAME 6:   LOUISVILLE (1-4) @ BAILEY (2-3)
               LOUISVILLE 31 BAILEY 0
               October 1, 2004

A game at Bailey meant a chance for the Wildcats to get some sort of rhythm to get a winning streak underway. It was about as expected as Louisville held a 19-0 lead at intermission.

Hickman opened with an 8-yarder and Colter PAT while the Cats tallied twice in the 2nd quarter. Frazier ran in from 14 yards while Jermaine Glass grabbed a Bailey fumble and raced 87 yards to paydirt. The last scoring came on a pair of 3rd quarter Cat tallies. First was a Daniel Eichelberger 12-yard reception from Miller and a 35-yard Glass pick-six.

GAME 7:   LOUISVILLE (2-4) vs PEARL (5-2)
               LOUISVILLE 14 PEARL 27
               October 15, 2004: HOMECOMING

Fifth-year Coach Larry Weems took his Pirates to a 9-3 record based in large part on the play of his defense. That unit allowed only 98 points on the season. *"We had a tremendous defense. If we didn't make too many mistakes, not a lot of teams could drive on us and score"*. This year brought not only losses due to graduation, but a drop in interested players. Weems would be without seven starters on both sides of the ball and forced to play many Pirates in dual capacity.

"We've got some pretty good holes to fill on both sides of the ball. We've got guys who can do it, but it takes time and repetition. We've got good players; kids who will make plays for us. We just don't have enough. Depth is our biggest concern. Against the better teams on our schedule, we will have to play many of our guys both ways on offense and defense. That usually gets to you in the second half. Fatigue sets in and the tackles you were making don't get made because you're worn down and not as quick.

We laid out for our guys if you want to win, you've got to push. We're working hard on conditioning but you can only go so far so fast, especially the big ole boys. In the fourth quarter we're going to get tired, but that's what it's going to call for. Those guys will make or break us. Our guys know what the challenge is in front of them. We asked them to learn a lot on both sides of the ball and they are trying for us. With us, it's a numbers game. We'll take what we've got, line up and play. Then the next week, we'll take what we've got, line up and play". Voters slotted Pearl second in 4-4A preseason.

A win against the Wildcats assured Pearl of post-season play for another year. A loss would not necessarily exclude them, but the road would be more difficult. *"It's a big game, crucial for both of us. We're looking forward to it. It's an opportunity for us to go on the road and show that we can beat a good team. If they want in, they have to win.*

Louisville's in the same spot we are. They have athletes who can run the football and get after it". The Clarion-Ledger picked Pearl 14-13.

It was a great start as Clint Coleman picked off an errant throw and took it 35 yards to paydirt. Lakendrick Coleman booted the PAT. Pearl rebounded in splendid fashion by tacking 27 points to the board. The first pair were via the ground from Phil Wheeler (25) and Reggie Chancellor (1). After Trey Coleman recovered a Carey Miller fumble, Wheeler added his next from three yards. He tallied his third of the game afterwards on an 18-yard scamper. Mark Buchanan (or Matthew Logue) was true on the first three kicks.

Though the defense held Louisville at the Pirate 6 in the 3rd quarter, a fumble back to Louisville's Kris Welch allowed them a 9-yard Miller pass to Jeremy Gill and Coleman PAT. It was, however, the last. While Pearl put up 156 passing and 286 rushing yards, the defense held Louisville to a combined 21 markers. *"It's a big win for us as far as our playoff situation goes. We didn't finish them off like I wanted us to, but I'm proud to get the win. Our defense played a solid game. I'm glad, too, because our offense gave them some chances. I'm proud of our kids. I hope we finish out the season like we should"*.

GAME 8:   LOUISVILLE (2-5) @ CANTON (5-3)
               LOUISVILLE 21 CANTON 27
               October 22, 2004

This one turned out to be a battle between third and fourth place 4-4A squads. It came down to the final frame to determine the winner.

Canton opened with two touchdowns in the opening frame. Desmond Ratliff raced in from 21 yards for the first with Ramon Small adding the PAT. Then Ratliff hit Domique Puckett from 39 yards to make it 13-0. In the 2nd quarter, Coleman ran in from six yards and added the PAT. While Ratliff responded with a 10-yard pass to Jamarcus Jackson and added his two-point pass to Richard Worthy, the Cats scored twice to tie it at halftime.

Frazier dashed in from 38 yards, Coleman did the same from nine yards, and both Coleman kicks put it 21-21. However, in the finale, Ratliff found open space from 38 yards to provide the winning points.

Said Mullins, *"We got in the red zone twice in the 3rd quarter and didn't stick in after rip and roaring all down the field all night. That's plagued us all year. We can get into the red zone and just can't put it in the end zone when we need to"*. Lakendrick Coleman rushed for 282 yards but Frazier's 200 yards earned him a Player of the Week nod.

GAME 9:   LOUISVILLE (2-6) vs RIDGELAND (3-6)
               LOUISVILLE 14 RIDGELAND 34
               October 29, 2004

A dismal end of the season awaited the Wildcats against Ridgeland. The Cats went to the playoffs 21 consecutive years but this year would prove the end of the streak.

The Titans found paydirt in the opening frame when Taylor Watkins hit Derrell Moore for the 30-yard touchdown and Brandon Walls converted. An Eichelberger interception stalled a potential Ridgeland threat. In the 2nd quarter, Moore dashed in from 17 yards and Walls made it 14-0. Louisville found the board with a 60-yard pick-six by Wraggs.

Louisville had three turnovers in the second half and all three produced Titan scores. Watkins had a 1-yarder, Walls nailed a 34-yard FG, Moore a 9-yard run and two Walls conversions. Coleman provided the last Cat score of the season when he dove in from a yard and added the two-point conversion while Walls added a 35-yard FG.

2005 (2-8)

After the worst year since 1956, the Cats had to be more optimistic about 2005. Some of that had to do with the change in head coach as Brad Peterson now took the reins. Peterson was a former Wildcat and enjoyed successful stints at other schools in Mississippi. *"I'm trying to do what is best for the kids, the program and our Wildcats"*.

GAME 1:   LOUISVILLE (0-0) @ STARKVILLE (0-0)
               LOUISVILLE 7 STARKVILLE 42
               August 26, 2005

It was no easy opener for Peterson as his Wildcats journeyed to Starkville. Louisville lost nine of the past eleven matches going back to 1994.

The Yellow Jackets wasted no time in distancing themselves from the Cats. In the opening frame, Patrick Shed scored from four yards and Wade Spurlock added his first of many PATs. Fiero Watts soon added the next from two yards to make it 14-0. The 2nd quarter was scoreless thanks in part to a Starkville interception.

The 3rd quarter was even tougher for Louisville as the home team scored three times. Those came on a Decorey Goss 31-yard fumble return, another fumble to set up Lavinea Brooks' 5-yarder, and a 6-yarder by Shed. Charles Wraggs did recover a Jacket fumble in the frame. The Jackets got their last TD in the final frame on a 40-yard Brad Henderson pass to Michael Lindsey. The Cats avoided the shutout on Clint Coleman's 90-yard kickoff return and Deon Hickman conversion.

GAME 2:　　　　　　　LOUISVILLE (0-1) vs TUPELO (1-0)
　　　　　　　　　　　LOUISVILLE 12 TUPELO 17
　　　　　　　　　　　September 9, 2005

Though at home, things got no easier as traditionally powerful Tupelo came to Winston County. They notched a 1st quarter touchdown on a 2-yard Ken Davis plunge and Adam Ruff kick. Tupelo added a pair in the next frame via a 21-yarder from Eric Jones to Jeffrey Cameron and a Cameron interception ending with a 40-yard Ruff FG.

Down 17-0, the Wildcats tallied in each of the next two frames while holding the Wave scoreless. An early fumble did no damage and Hickman eventually found paydirt from 17 yards. In the finale, Justin Moore recovered a Tupelo fumble while Terrion Young blocked a Wave punt. Carey Miller hit Fred Glass from five yards to the last score.

GAME 3:　　　　　　　LOUISVILLE (0-2) @ LAFAYETTE COUNTY (2-0)
　　　　　　　　　　　LOUISVILLE 7 LAFAYETTE COUNTY 31
　　　　　　　　　　　September 16, 2005

Lafayette County opened the game with touchdowns in each of the two first quarters. Ricky Wadlington was first from six yards before returning a fumble 26 yards for his second. Taylor Maddux was true on both kicks to make halftime 14-0.

They added a 24-yard Maddox FG in the 3rd quarter while Josh Fondren ran in from six yards in the final stanza. He did it again later from 12 yards and Maddux added both conversions. The lone Cat score came late on a 68-yard Dennis Thames breakaway and Brandon Fulton extra point.

GAME 4:　　　　　　　LOUISVILLE (0-3) vs NEW HOPE (1-2)
　　　　　　　　　　　LOUISVILLE 31 NEW HOPE 12
　　　　　　　　　　　September 23, 2005: HOMECOMING

Louisville notched their initial win of 2005 with alums back for Homecoming. The opening quarter resulted only in a 24-yard Stanley Frazier dash. The Cats added 13 points before halftime on Frazier runs of 22 and 89 yards. Kris Welch added one extra point.

Another six points came in the 3rd quarter on a 95-yard Eichelberger reception from Miller while their last tally came on Frazier's 27-yard effort. New Hope managed their only points in the final quarter. The first was on a fake punt taken 51 yards to the end zone and 4-yard Brent Hallmark run.

Frazier's 265 rushing yards earned him a Clarion-Ledger Player of the Week mention. Ernie Triplett and Clint Coleman recorded interceptions in the game and Triplett also added a fumble recovery.

GAME 5:　　　　　　　LOUISVILLE (1-3) vs WEST POINT (3-1)
　　　　　　　　　　　LOUISVILLE 12 WEST POINT 35
　　　　　　　　　　　September 30, 2005

West Point, winners in the last four meetings, came to Winston County ranked seventh in The Top 10 after a convincing 41-0 smothering of New Albany.

The Wildcats took a 6-0 lead after a frame on Miller's 90-yard connection with Eichelberger. However, West Point put up 14 before halftime, first on Travis Walker's 10-yarder to Eldrick Hogan and Phillip Dimino kick. Chris Matthews added the next from 19 yards and Dimino made halftime 14-6.

Matthews added a 3rd quarter score on his 19-yard scamper and Dimino converted. Now in the 4th quarter, Walker and Hogan hooked up from 25 yards with Dimino kicking. A Mark Hoskins fumble recovery soon led to Miller's 12-yarder to Eichelberger. West Point closed things on Jamar Shelton's onside kick recovery and return from 52 yards and Dimino PAT.

GAME 6:   LOUISVILLE (1-4) @ NOXUBEE COUNTY (2-2)
                    LOUISVILLE 0 NOXUBEE COUNTY 29
                    October 7, 2005

NCHS had their 29 points via scores in each quarter. First was a 1-yarder by Patterson and next a 13-yard run by Shields and Patterson two-point run. In the 3rd quarter, Harmon found the end zone from seven yards. Finally, a safety, a 5-yard Patterson run, and a Shields PAT closed scoring.

GAME 7:   LOUISVILLE (1-5) vs KOSCIUSKO (4-2)
                    LOUISVILLE 14 KOSCIUSKO 28
                    October 14, 2005

This one was described as "*a heartbreaker*" by The Winston County Journal. Kosy held a slight 7-0 lead after a half courtesy of Terry Levy's 13-yard run and Taylor Putt extra point. They added two more in the 3rd quarter on a 48-yarder by Levy and 34-yarder from Jemariey Atterberry. Putt was true on both kicks.

Louisville garnered only a single score in the frame on Frazier's 10-yard effort. Now 21-6, both found paydirt. Kosy crossed on a 40-yard Jonathan Worrell pick-six and Putt kick while the Cats did likewise on a 10-yarder by Frazier and Dennis Thames' two-pointer.

GAME 8:   LOUISVILLE (1-6) @ WEST LAUDERDALE (6-0)
                    LOUISVILLE 0 WEST LAUDERDALE 39
                    October 21, 2005

A first-time opponent, West Lauderdale sat undefeated and welcomed a deflated Louisville team to their field. They showed their power with 17 points in the opening quarter. Josh Hanible got in from 11 yards and then from 17 yards. Dimitri Uhl added both kicks and Michael Pogue notched a 34-yard FG.

They added eight more before halftime on a 12-yard Jon Hunter dash and Dameon Baylor two-point conversion. West Lauderdale added scores in each of the following quarters. Baylor ran in from four yards and Darren Farmer ended things with his 1-yard dive. Uhl converted after each.

GAME 9:   LOUISVILLE (1-7) vs NESHOBA CENTRAL (1-7)
                    LOUISVILLE 34 NESHOBA CENTRAL 30
                    October 28, 2005

Neshoba Central sat last in 4-4A, just behind a 2-6 New Hope team. A Wildcat win here actually kept playoff hopes alive.

It was not as easy as hoped as the 1st quarter ended 14-14. Frazier got it going with an early 25-yard touchdown run. Neshoba responded with Ken Robinson's 85-yard kickoff return and Derek Crenshaw PAT. Miller came back with a 35-yard pass to Triplett and Miller found Glass for the two-pointer. Tyler McNeal punched back with a 20-yard strike to Emmanuel Moore and Crenshaw tied it with the kick.

The 2nd quarter was just as tight. Thames took a reverse 15 yards to paydirt but the PAT was blocked. Frazier then crossed from 18 yards and added the two-pointer. The Rockets struck with another kickoff return by Robinson from the same distance as the first. Crenshaw closed the gap with the kick and later added a 25-yard FG. Louisville had the only score of the 3rd quarter. An Emmanuel Thomas fumble recovery allowed Frazier to dash in from seven yards. In the finale, NCHS added their last on Robinson's 10-yarder.

GAME 10:   LOUISVILLE (2-7) @ NORTHEAST LAUDERDALE (7-2)
                    LOUISVILLE 21 NORTHEAST LAUDERDALE 41
                    November 4, 2005

The game was close until the final frame. While Northeast struck first on a 1-yard Scott plunge and White kick, the Cats answered with a 10-yarder by Frazier and Fulton boot. The home team recorded the only score of the 2nd quarter when Cortney Scott broke through from two yards and Jason White converted.

Each tallied in the 3rd quarter. The Cats crossed on a 73-yard escape by Thames and Futon kick while Lauderdale got theirs on a 2-yard Elijah Lee run. Things got out of hand in the 4th quarter. While Frazier crossed from 13 yards and Fulton made it 21-20, the home team put up three more touchdowns to finish it. Those came on a 19-yard Maurice Langston dash, his two-pointer, another from 34 yards and White kick, and lastly Lee's 2-yard run. It was a merciful end to a second season in which Louisville won only a pair of games.

All-Region 4-4A honors went to Stanley Frazier (Co-Best Offensive Back), Dennis Thames (Co-Best Linebacker), Charles Wraggs (Co-Best Defensive Lineman), Clayton Moore, Steven Hunt, Emmanuel Thomas, Deon Hickman, Jamaal Coburn and Clint Coleman.

2006 (8-4)

Brad Peterson was back for his second year and his Wildcats were slotted fourth in Region 4-4A. Certainly, the year had to be better than his first. *"We feel like physically and mentally we are in a much better position than we were last year. We are stronger. The kids still know the tradition and still know the history. They understand the importance of what needs to be done".*

GAME 1: LOUISVILLE (0-0) vs STARKVILLE (0-0)
LOUISVILLE 0 STARKVILLE 3
August 25, 2006

The previous year's meeting in Starkville was a disaster for the Wildcats. Now they hosted the Yellow Jackets and hoped to even the score.

Both defenses had solid performances throughout the night. While the Cats had their chances, penalties and turnovers killed drives. The lone tally came in the final frame on a 40-yard Lindsey FG. Clayton Moore was 10-18-1 for 104 yards in the air. *"We really had a good physical football game. Missed opportunities were the theme of the night. We got down into the red zone twice and turned it over. We moved the sticks but there were a lot of penalties (113 yards)".*

GAME 2: LOUISVILLE (0-1) @ TUPELO (0-1)
LOUISVILLE 31 TUPELO 27
September 1, 2006

The Golden Wave opened the 2006 campaign with a 17-10 loss to Clinton. Now they welcomed a Wildcat team they bested seven of the last eight times. Said Peterson, *"Starkville just comes right at you and Tupelo is more of a 50/50 pass and run type of team".*

Moore opened the game with a 25-yard FG. Tupelo answered with a 1-yard Ken Davis run and his two-pointer made it 8-3. Louisville came back in the next frame with a 6-yard Stanley Frazier dash set up by a 48-yard double-pass from D.Q. Farmer to Dennis Thames. Back came Tupelo with a 55-yard Davis run to daylight. The Cats struck quickly with a 5-yarder by Frazier and his two-pointer to make it 17-14.

Tupelo was next in the 3rd quarter on Chris Garrett's 1-yard dive and Backstrom PAT. The Wildcats' Moore then crossed from two yards and added the PAT. In the final frame, Rod Zinn pulled in a pass and took it 80 yards for the pick-six. The Cats' Michael Hudson blocked their extra point attempt. With just under 6:00 remaining, Louisville drove to the Tupelo 5. With about a minute left, Frazier crossed from three yards and Moore converted.

Frazier led rushers with 63 yards while Moore went 10-19 for 173s. Howard led receivers with 99 yards. The Wildcats had 341 total offensive yards. *"We had a really big win. Any time you beat a team like Tupelo, you have to feel good about it. We are not to the point where we need to be, but we are getting closer to being back to where Louisville football is supposed to be".*

GAME 3:   LOUISVILLE (1-1) vs LAFAYETTE COUNTY (2-0)
                 LOUISVILLE 21 LAFAYETTE COUNTY 23
                 September 8, 2006

          Peterson was wary of Lafayette County and knew they would be just as tough as
the first two opponents. *"Lafayette may be better on the defensive line than (Starkville or
Tupelo). And offensively they are solid. They will run it right at you"*.
          An early Cat fumble led to a 30-yard Webb FG. Back came the Cats with a 99-
yard drive and 27-yard Moore pass to Kentareas Howard. Moore then hit Thames from 11
yards and added both extra points to make it 14-3. Lafayette County came back with a pair
of scores to make halftime 16-14. Wadlington was first from three yards while Ivy dashed
52 yards to paydirt and Webb converted. They put up another touchdown in the 3rd quarter
on a 3-yard Wadlington run and Webb PAT.
          The Wildcats had the lone tally of the finale on Moore's 12-yarder to Clint
Coleman and the Moore PAT. That was set up by a 50-yard Thames run. Louisville had 334
yards of offense with 189 coming in the air. Another report gave Moore 291 of passing
yards. Thames paced rushers with 90 yards and Coleman receivers with 69 yards. Moore
was again a Clarion-Ledger Player of the Week.

GAME 4:   LOUISVILLE (1-2) @ NEW HOPE (1-2)
                 LOUISVILLE 48 NEW HOPE 8
                 September 15, 2006

          The lone New Hope win came in an overtime battle with Caledonia. Thus far,
they were giving up an average of 35 points per game. Said Peterson, *"This is what we have
been playing for. But honestly, this may sound strange, but our number one concern is not
New Hope. It's the Louisville Wildcats. Our kids know we are a pretty good football team"*.
          The Wildcats scored early and often, starting with Frazier's 2-yarder and Moore's
kick. New Hope drove deep but Clint Coleman blocked their FG effort. Frazier then ran in
from 20 yards and Moore converted. Moore threw touchdowns of 58 and 66 yards and
added the kicks to make halftime 28-0.
          New Hope gained their only tally to start the 3rd quarter on a 10-yard Jonques
Wells run and two-point conversion. Moore came back with a 10-yarder to Frazier, found
Thames from 14 yards, and D.Q. Farmer ended it with a 1-yard run. In all Moore was 15-29
for 291 yards, Frazier led rushers with 75 yards and Thames receptions of 122 yards.
          *"There were some things we needed to see going into the game. Knowing we
were the favorite; I was curious to see if we could put the game away. We did that"*.

GAME 5:   LOUISVILLE (2-2) @ WEST POINT (4-0)
                 LOUISVILLE 20 WEST POINT 14
                 September 22, 2006

          West Point was not only third in 4A rankings, but also fourth in The Top 10 polls.
Said Peterson, *"Our kids will be fired up to play West Point. They are the defending state
champions. We know what we are facing. They have one of the state's best players and
they love to get him the ball"*.
          West Point hit the board for the only 1st quarter score on a 1-yard Shelton run
and Dimino extra point. Louisville came back to tie it in the 2nd quarter on a 6-yard Moore
toss to Howard. Moore's extra point ended the half. West Point did have a chance for the
lead but missed a FG effort.
          The home team put up another tally in the 3rd quarter via a 26-yard Ward dash
and Dimino kick. Down 14-7 in the last stanza, the Cats did what they had to do. Moore hit
Thames from 10 yards and Moore added the PAT. Then, Frazier darted in from six yards
with :25 remaining and scoring was finalized.
          Moore was 13-30 passing, Frazier led the ground with 57 yards and Coleman
pulled in five receptions. Deon Hickman and Thames each has 10.5 tackles defensively.
Peterson was Clarion-Ledger Coach of the Week. *"West Point's defense, for the most part,
dominated the game. But when we had to, we moved the ball. We didn't fumble the
football a single time. That was it"*.
          This game marked the end of a streak stretching back to 1966.

GAME 6:   LOUISVILLE (3-2) vs NOXUBEE COUNTY (4-1)
                 LOUISVILLE 36 NOXUBEE COUNTY 16
                 September 29, 2006

        The Clarion-Ledger picked Louisville 24-21 over M.C. Miller's Noxubee County
squad. Said Peterson, "There is no difference between them, Starkville, West Point and us.
It should be a good football game".
        The visitors started with a quick 5-yard Harmon touchdown run and a two-
pointer by Patterson. The Cats came back with a 1-yard Frazier run and Moore kick. Moore
then nailed a 27-yard FG and Thames grabbed a 37-yard Moore pass to put it 16-8. Before
halftime, Medford Hardin took a fumble 46 yards to paydirt and Moore put it 23-8. NCHS
added a 3rd quarter safety but Frazier answered with a 4-yard scamper and Moore added
the PAT. While Neshoba had a 4th quarter touchdown and conversion, Ernie Triplett added
a 57-yard pick-six to ice it.
        Moore was 6-19 for 117 yards while Frazier ran for 175 more. Thames led
tacklers with 11. Coburn and Hardin also had fumble recoveries. "We go into every game
with a good plan. After the first drive when they marched down the field on us, we went to
plan two. Once we got it going defensively, we put them in a lot of long yardage situations.
We probably didn't throw it five times in the second half. We didn't want to beat ourselves
at that point".

GAME 7:   LOUISVILLE (4-2) @ KOSCIUSKO (4-2)
                 LOUISVILLE 9 KOSCIUSKO 35
                 October 6, 2006

        The Whippets and Wildcats faced one another all but eight times since 1929.
This time, the opponent was projected much tougher than their 4-2 record. "Kosciusko is so
close to being undefeated. They are a really good football team. We have got a heck of a
division. The fifth team in our division could beat a lot of playoff teams. We need to focus
on this game to move to 3-0 in the region. If you win that, then you can start playing for the
region championship".
        While Moore opened with a 24-yard FG, Kosy answered with a Kendrick Presley
24-yard pass to Dandrick Weatherby for the touchdown. Taylor Putt added his first of five
extra points. In the 2nd quarter, Presley dove in from a yard and found Weatherby from 13
yards to make halftime 21-3. The Whippets notched another in the 3rd quarter on a 5-
yarder by Kembe Harris.
        The finale was no better as Moore ran in from 12 yards but Kosy notched a 2-
yarder by Martin Peteet. Frazier rushed for 98 yards, Moore was 9-24 for 116 yards,
Coleman had 25 receiving yards, and Foster paced tacklers with 15.5. "We played our worst
game of the year and played a really, really good team. You have to be ready to go to war
every Friday night and we weren't. Our kids were not focused going into the game and
(they) knew we played a terrible football game. That all falls back on me. That's my fault.
I've got to do a better job".

GAME 8:   LOUISVILLE (4-3) vs WEST LAUDERDALE (7-0)
                 LOUISVILLE 31 WEST LAUDERDALE 28
                 October 13, 2006: HOMECOMING

        It did not get easier as Louisville now faced an undefeated Knight team at Hinze.
This one came down to the wire.
        West Lauderdale struck first in the 2nd quarter on a 13-yard Austin Davis toss to
Darren Farmer to make it 6-0. Thames returned a kickoff 67 yards to set up Frazier's 2-
yarder and Moore's PAT. The 7-6 score remained through halftime. The visitors then tallied
on Donathan Fortner's 6-yarder and his two-pointer. Louisville answered on Moore's shovel
pass to Frazier taken 62 yards and Moore making the kick to tie it 14-14.
        Moore and Thames then hooked up from 14 yards and Moore converted. Late in
the frame, WLHS tied it on Fortner's 1-yarder and Davis PAT. Now midway through the final
stanza, Farmer pulled in a 7-yard Davis pass and Davis converted. With 2:50 left, Louisville
re-tied the game on Thames' 8-yarder and Moore kick. With about a minute left, the
Knights elected to go for fourth down but the Cat defense held.
        A long Moore run and a personal foul penalty put Louisville at the Knight 12.
Moore then "split the uprights" from 30 yards for the upset win. Said Peterson, "This was
not a unique situation for us. We have played four down-to-the-wire ballgames. We know

what it takes to win those kind of games". Moore was 14-24 for 261 yards while Frazier rushed for 149 yards and led receivers with 76 more.

GAME 9:   LOUISVILLE (5-3) @ NESHOBA CENTRAL (3-5)
       LOUISVILLE 42 NESHOBA CENTRAL 0
       October 20, 2006

   The Wildcats jumped all over homestanding Neshoba Central early with two tallies in the opening frame.
   Thames started with a 6-yard run and Moore added a 20-yarder with two extra points. That held through halftime to keep it 14-0. In the 3rd quarter, they added three more on a 3-yard Frazier run, Moore's 36-yard strike to Coleman, and a Kris Welch 8-yard dash. The three Moore kicks made it 35-0. Their last came in the finale on a 2-yarder by Arnold Henderson combined with a Matthew Graham PAT.
   "We really dominated the game early. We did a good job of keeping the ball on offense and controlling the clock. We probably could have scored more in the final half but we didn't take advantage of our opportunities". Frazier led rushers with 168 yards while Moore was 12-22 for 179 yards. In all, he accounted for 278 yards and earned a <u>Clarion-Ledger</u> Player of the Week mention. Coleman led with 132 yards in receptions and Thames on tackles with 9.5. Deon Hickman had nine others.

GAME 10:   LOUISVILLE (6-3) vs NORTHEAST LAUDERDALE (7-2)
       LOUISVILLE 35 NORTHEAST LAUDERDALE 14
       October 27, 2006

   Northeast Lauderdale could win and finish second in the division, but a loss put them out of the playoffs. *"Their whole season is on the line (and) they will come in ready to play. We better be ready. It's going to be a tough game. This is a tough division. There are five teams that could beat each other on any given night".*
   The Cats jumped out to a 6-0 lead after a quarter on Rion Young's 34-yard fumble return. Northeast took the lead on Maricius Anderson's 25-yarder and White PAT. Louisville came right back on a 65-yard drive ending on a 9-yarder by Thames and Frazier two-pointer. They then went 54 yards with Moore adding the last yard with seconds remaining to make it 21-7 at halftime
   Northeast Lauderdale struck first in the 3rd quarter on a 5-yarder by Scott and White kick. Louisville bettered the effort with Moore's 5-yard dash after a bad Trojan punt, a 41-yard Foster pick-six and two Moore extra points. Frazier rushed for 141 yards and Moore was 9-13 for 60 yards.

GAME 11:   LOUISVILLE (7-3) vs TISHOMINGO COUNTY (8-2)
       LOUISVILLE 32 TISHOMINGO COUNTY 7
       November 3, 2006

   The Wildcats hosted the first round of the playoffs against a first-time opponent. Said Peterson about the opponent, *"Tishomingo is a good football team. They only lost to West Point by 10 points at West Point. They are as sound of a football team as we have played all season. They don't make mistakes and they play hard".*
   The Cats opened with scores on a 6-yard Moore pass to Thames and a 7-yarder from Triplett to Henderson. Tishomingo retaliated with a Tyler Walker fumble in the air returned 25 yards for the tally. Steven Atkins added the PAT to make it 12-7. But Louisville had one more left before halftime when Moore hit Thames from 27 yards and added the extra point.
   Louisville added a touchdown in each of the last two quarters. Moore and Thames hooked up from 54 yards while Frazier added the last from two yards. Moore's kicks were true. Moore, a <u>Clarion-Ledger</u> Player of the Week, was 10-18 for 220 while Thames pulled in 170 of those. Frazier rushed for 117 yards and the offense was perfectly balanced with 227 each way. Thames also led tacklers with six while Hickman was close behind with five.
   "It was like they had been there before and they went out and took care of business against a good Tishomingo County football team".

LOUISVILLE (8-3) @ CLARKSDALE (10-1)
        LOUISVILLE 20 CLARKSDALE 35
        November 10, 2006

The only Clarksdale loss came in their opener 19-13 against South Panola, a team finishing a fifth-straight undefeated status. Now the other Wildcats were second in 4A and third in The Super 10. *"They are extremely fast on defense"*. As for the trip to Coahoma County, he added, *"(The home field) doesn't have much value. If you are prepared, you can play good football either place. Once the game gets started, you sort of even forget where you are"*.

Many Louisville fans remembered the four consecutive meetings between 1997 and 2000 in which the other team prevailed. Only in 2003 did Cat fans celebrate a victory. In this one, Brandon Williams opened the game with a 12-yarder and Abdul Salameh added the extra point. In the 2nd quarter, Charles Mitchell blasted in from three yards and Salameh converted. Tim Jackson then found the end zone from a yard and Salameh made it 21-0. Louisville came back with a 5-yard Frazier dash to put halftime 21-6.

Clarksdale had the only score of the 3rd quarter when Mitchell dashed in from 25 yards. The Cats cut it to 28-12 when Moore hit Fred Glass from 12 yards. But Clarksdale added their last on a 2-yarder by Jackson. The final points of 2006 came later when Moore hit Coleman for a touchdown and the two-pointer.

"We lost to a really good football team. They were the most physical team we have played all year and that says a lot considering the type of teams we played this season. It wasn't like we made terrible plays. We were in the game but they had control of the game. We had a good season".

All-Region 4-4A honors went to Stanley Frazier (Co-Best Offensive Back), Dennis Thames (Co-Best Linebacker), Charles Wraggs (Co-Best Defensive Lineman), Clayton Moore, Steven Hunt, Emmanuel Thomas, Deon Hickman, Jamaal Coburn and Clint Coleman.

Internal awards included Jarred Fleming and Romeo Miller (Hustle Award), Kentareas Howard (Ironman Award), Emanuel Goss (John Matthews 3D Award), Derrick Underwood (Most Improved), Emmanuel Thomas and Hedrick Foster (Head Hunter Award), Clint Coleman (Hands Award), Kyle Donald and Steven Hunt (Best Offensive Linemen), Jamaal Coburn (Best Defensive Lineman), Ernie Triplett (Best Defensive Back), Deon Hickman (Best Linebacker), Dennis Thames (Play Maker Award), Drew Smith and Medford Hardin (Special Teams MVP), Charles Wraggs (Defensive MVP), Clayton Moore (Offensive MVP), Stanley Frazier (Overall MVP), and Kris Welch, Stanley Frazier, Deon Hickman and Jamaal Coburn as Team Captains.

2007 (12-3)

After a much better season, Brad Peterson was hopeful for one even better. They were also now a 3A team but with a smaller roster. *"The players are excited and ready to play. We are improving with each practice. We will be ready for our tough schedule. Expectations are really high especially based on last year's playoff results. The players have really accepted the challenge and have worked hard to get to this point"*.

In the preseason rankings, the Wildcats were second behind Franklin County.

GAME 1:   LOUISVILLE (0-0) @ STARKVILLE (0-0)
        LOUISVILLE 13 STARKVILLE 14
        August 31, 2007

The annual matchup now featured a 3A Louisville against a 5A Starkville club. Before the season, Peterson said, *"The Starkville matchup is always a measuring stick of the direction we are going. We plan to work on minimizing mistakes and playing tough each play. Our players will get on the field and fight to win and go at it full speed"*.

Now at game week, he added, *"Two of our four guys who play along the defensive line are injured. We really don't know what their status will be Friday night"*.

Starkville scored both of their touchdowns in the 1st quarter. Brad Henderson found Patrick Shed for a 96-yard tally while Talmalcom Kemp added a 65-yard pick-six. William Arick was true after each score. The first came after a Cat fumble at the Starkville 4. Louisville closed the gap in the 2nd quarter when Arnold Henderson pulled in a 35-yard Clayton Moore pass and Moore converted to make halftime 14-7. The final touchdown came very late in the game when Henderson rushed in from 11 yards. The PAT failed to tie the contest and gave Starkville the win.

Said Peterson, "*We as coaches felt like we dominated the game. We could have played a weaker team and beat them by 30 points but that's not going to do us any good*". Louisville recorded 418 total offensive yards in the loss.

GAME 2:   LOUISVILLE (0-1) vs WAYNE COUNTY (1-0)
                    LOUISVILLE 21 WAYNE COUNTY 39
                    September 7, 2007

First-time foe Wayne County was not only third in the Top 10, but also reigning 4A State Champions. Said Peterson, "*We're just going to have to work hard and get ready for the game*".

Wayne County opened scoring in the opening frame on Tracy Lampley's 5-yarder and the first of four Storm Seawright extra points. They increased the lead to 14-0 in the 2nd quarter on Shaurice Cunningham's 15-yard reception from Calvin McDougle. The Cats clawed back on a 1-yard Moore dive. The last score of the half came on a 20-yard Seawright field goal to make it 17-6.

Lampley scored again from six yards to start the 3rd quarter but Louisville blocked the PAT. Back came LHS with a 1-yard Henderson plunge and Moore conversion, but the War Eagles had more points before the frame ended via a safety and Lampley 4-yard effort. The visitors garnered their last in the finale on McDougle's 15-yard escape after Henderson found paydirt from seven yards. Dennis Thames pulled in a Moore pass for two points.

Moore was 13-22 for 173 yards while D.Q. Mays went 4-6 for 52 more. Thames had 48 receiving yards while Henderson led rushers with 35 yards. Said Peterson, "*We knew it was going to be tough*".

GAME 3:   LOUISVILLE (0-2) vs KOSCIUSKO (2-0)
                    LOUISVILLE 16 KOSCIUSKO 7
                    September 14, 2007

It was time once again for the rival Whippets at Hinze Stadium. Of the schedule, Peterson noted, "*It doesn't ease up. If you look at The Clarion-Ledger, they have Wayne County at Number 2, Starkville at Number 8 and Kosciusko at Number 9. We have to take the approach that this is a rival game and they are going to be ready to play us*".

Moore started the scoring with a 31-yard FG. That was soon followed by a 58-yard Moore strike to Thames and Moore made it 10-0. Kosy closed the gap in the 2nd quarter on a 3-Martin Peteet run and Duncan PAT but it was all they would get. The last tally came in the 3rd quarter when Moore found paydirt from 11 yards.

Moore went 11-23 for 242 yards while Thames had 155 receiving yards. "*We came out with the same game plan we had last year but this year we just executed. The balls we caught for touchdowns were dropped last year*".

GAME 4:   LOUISVILLE (1-2) @ NETTLETON (3-0)
                    LOUISVILLE 42 NETTLETON 14
                    September 21, 2007

Coach Scott Cantrell's Nettleton team was third in 2-3A and undefeated thus far. The previous season they were 14-1, 3A State Champion runner-up and looking to continue their success. Still, The Clarion-Ledger picked Louisville 30-20.

Henderson opened the victory with a 1-yarder to make it 6-0. Back came Nettleton with a 7-yard Jami Boland toss to Jeremy Jones. Thomas Peredo's kick gave them a 7-6 lead. Louisville retook the lead in the 2nd quarter via Moore's 2-yard plunge and his two-pointer to Emmanuel Thomas. It was soon tied 14-14 when Boland crossed from a yard and Peredo converted. However, the Cats tallied twice before halftime on an 11-yard Thames run, a Moore 5-yarder, and his two extra points.

The last points came in the 3rd quarter courtesy of Moore's 40-yard breakaway, another from 16 yards by Thames, and a pair of Moore kicks. Thames (107) and Moore (155) had the majority of the 355 total rushing yards. Moore was 7-9 for 79 passing yards. "*The first 20 minutes was pretty tight. Even at halftime we didn't feel comfortable by any means. Then we scored to go up by 21 and we breathed a little sigh of relief*".

LOUISVILLE (2-2) @ HOUSTON (1-3)
LOUISVILLE 55 HOUSTON 13
September 28, 2007

Coach Buz Boyer was coming off a 6-5 season but dropped their first three games of 2007 before finding a division win. Said Peterson, *"We know it's a division game so it's an important game. They are 1-0 in the division. That's what matters"*.

An early Cat fumble at the Hilltopper 1 soon came back when Thames recorded a 9-yard pick-six. Moore added his first of seven extra points. Houston's Malcolm Stanfield then took a pickoff 15 yards to the end zone. The Torres extra point was good. Back came Louisville with a 67-yard Moore pass to Carlos Hunt to make it 14-7. Houston did not go away. Malcolm Hogan took the ensuing kick 86 yards to put the game 14-13.

Moore followed that with a 27-yarder to Markeese Triplett and 16-yarder to Thames to end the frame 28-13. The Cats added three more before halftime. The first was a 32-yard Moore pass to Thames followed by a 2-yard Delande Johnson run and a 1-yarder by Henderson. The half was out of control 49-13. The last Cat score came in the final frame when Jarrad Ball dashed 91 yards to daylight with just 2:00 remaining.

Moore was 8-11 for 210 yards, Hunt pulled in 80 yards of receptions and Ball rushed for 106 more. In all, Louisville rushed for 292 of the 502 total yards. Dra Hughes led tacklers with 10 and had a fumble recovery and sack.

"We knew we were dominant and we just needed to settle down. They couldn't move the ball. They had run six plays and hadn't done anything. We are going to focus on not slacking off and improving this week. We don't want to overlook anybody".

GAME 6:   LOUISVILLE (3-2) vs SOUTH PONTOTOC (1-3)
LOUISVILLE 43 SOUTH PONTOTOC 0
October 5, 2007: HOMECOMING

Coach Jack Clark's South Pontotoc squad finished the previous campaign 5-6. This game was not expected to provide much excitement as the school welcomed back alums for Homecoming.

While the opening quarter was scoreless, the Wildcats unleashed a scoring barrage in the next. Moore crossed from a yard and May added two more points. Moore then hit Hunt from 23 yards and added his first of many extra points. Moore then found Henderson from 12 yards and Hunt from 24 yards. Halftime sat 36-0. Their last came in the 3rd quarter when Chris Wraggs hit Evan Dailey from five yards.

Moore was 21-29 for 321 yards while Carlos Hunt added 161 receiving yards. Ball paced rushers with 73 yards. *"We struggled early but it was just a matter of time. Obviously South Pontotoc is in kind of a rebuilding phase. We wanted to jump out of them and put them away"*.

GAME 7:   LOUISVILLE (4-2) @ NOXUBEE COUNTY (4-2)
LOUISVILLE 26 NOXUBEE COUNTY 40
October 12, 2007

Said Peterson before the game, *"This game is going to have a playoff type atmosphere. They have a great defense. They fly around after the football. They have a good football team. It is a lot easier to become number 1 than to stay number`1"*.

Eight total turnovers stalled any chance of a Wildcat victory. NCHS opened with a 3-yarder by Jontae Skinner but Moore soon found Carlos Hunt from 20 yards to tie it 6-6. The Tigers answered with two scores before the quarter ended. Patreon Hopkins recorded a 15-yard pick-six while Andre Wright followed with a 67-yard pick six. Patrick Patterson added a 32-yard FG.

Louisville fought back in the 2nd quarter on Moore's 57-yard connection with Thames but the Tigers notched a 32-yard Patterson FG. Louisville again closed the gap with Moore's 22-yarder to Thames and a two-point reception from Henderson. Now 22-20, another interception soon led to Vincent Sanders finding Temarkus Conner from 44 yards. Terrance Hardin then picked off a Tiger pass to set up Henderson's 2-yard dive and halftime stood 28-26

Noxubee County added touchdowns in each of the last two quarters. First was a 73-yard pass from Sanders to Patterson while Demarkus Harmon dashed in from three yards for the final points. Moore was 10-19 for 195 yards, Thames rushed for 104 and caught 115 more. In total, Louisville had 474 total offensive markers. *"I've never coached a team with that many turnovers. In fact, I've never coached in a game where either team made that many turnovers".*

GAME 8:   LOUISVILLE (4-3) @ ABERDEEN (5-2)
                             LOUISVILLE 41 ABERDEEN 7
                             October 19, 2007

Though the Wildcats still needed another division win to be assured of the playoffs, their next opponent under Coach Chris Duncan was a woeful 0-10 the previous year. They were better now with a 5-2 card. Frustrations from the Noxubee County game spilled over into this one as the Cats rolled easily.

The Cats jumped out to a 20-0 halftime lead, first on a 2-yard Henderson run. In the 2nd quarter, he added runs of 41 yards and a 1-yard plunge to go along with a two-pointer. Aberdeen answered on the first drive of the 3rd quarter on a 12-yard Marcus Hinton toss to Erik Buchanan and a Griffin PAT.

Louisville then added a safety by Jimmy Owens and followed with a 24-yard Moore strike to D.Q. Mays. In the finale, Moore dove in from a yard while Delande Johnson crossed from the same yardage. Moore was 16-26 for 250 yards while Henderson rushed for 89 yards. *"I thought our defense played extremely well. Offensively, I'm not going to say we played great, but we had so many snaps that we were able to score a lot of points".*

GAME 9:   LOUISVILLE (5-3) vs AMORY (3-5)
                             LOUISVILLE 35 AMORY 0
                             October 26, 2007

Amory, under the tutelage of Coach Pat Byrd, was going backwards from their previous 7-5 season. *"Friday night is important for us because if we win, it will clinch a home game in the playoffs. But win or lose, Winona will be for the region championship".*

After just one frame, Louisville held a 21-0 advantage. Scores came on an 80-yard march ended with a 19-yard Moore run and his first of four extra points. Dennis Thames then picked off an Amory pass for a 38-yard pick-six. Recovering a fumble, the Cats found the end zone again on Henderson's 3-yarder.

The last two touchdowns came in each of the final two stanzas. A 99-yard drive became possible on Hendrick Foster's goal-line stop. Moore and Carlos Hunt ended it with a 31-yard pass. Finally, Henderson got in from two yards and Zach McGarr added the PAT. Moore was 13-17 for 168, added 115 on the ground, and Hunt had 74 receiving yards. *"The defense played extremely well".*

GAME 10:   LOUISVILLE (6-3) vs WINONA (8-1)
                             LOUISVILLE 34 WINONA 7
                             November 2, 2007

Ken Challenger dramatically improved his Winona squad, taking them from a 5-5 season to one now with a lone loss. Undefeated in conference play, they just shut out South Panola 28-0. *"There is no question that they are the best team we will have played in the division. We are going to have to do a great job of staying down and locking* up". The Clarion-Ledger picked Louisville 40-23.

Henderson had the lone tally of the opening frame on his 3-yard blast and Moore added his first of a pair of kicks. In the next frame, Moore found Mays from 24 yards to make it 14-0 at the half. Winona cut the score on their opening drive of the 3rd quarter to end a 70-yard drive with Harry People's 11-yarder to Jamondrick Hobbs. The Kent PAT put the game 14-7.

Back came Louisville with an 80-yard march and 4-yard Moore run and extra point. The Cats dominated from there with two 4th quarter scores. Thames had the first from two yards while Frank McNeal added a 3-yarder after. McGarr added last PAT. The Cats rushed for 238 and threw for 112 more. Moore led rushers with 118 yards. *"I thought (yet again) our defense really stepped up and took control of the game. I thought we had opportunities to put the game away in the first half. Then I thought we came out a little flat in the second half".*

GAME 11:   LOUISVILLE (7-3) vs KOSSUTH (5-5)
                             LOUISVILLE 47 KOSSUTH 12
                             November 9, 2007

The first-round draw found the Cats welcoming the Kossuth Aggies, first-time opponents, to Hinze Stadium. Said Peterson, *"This is what we have been playing for. We got a number one seed in the playoffs and that's what we wanted"*.

It proved to be all Louisville as Moore and Thames hooked up from 31 yards for the first score. They added three more before halftime to make it 28-0. Moore hit Thames from 10 yards, Moore dove in from a yard and then hit Thomas from 17 yards. Moore was true on kicks.

The Wildcats opened the 3rd quarter on Moore's 38-yard TD to Henderson. Kossuth got on the board on a 15-yard run and followed it with an interception leading to a 14-yard scoring toss. Louisville added two more before the end of the frame on a 20-yard Moore pass to Hunt and Markese Triplett's recovery of a McNeal punt block taken 23 yards to paydirt. McGarr was true on the last tally.

Moore was 24-35 for 416 yards, Henderson led receivers with 98 yards and Jerrick Ball rushed for 34 yards. Medford Hardin also had two interceptions. The win pushed Louisville to second in overall 3A voting. Moore earned a Clarion-Ledger Player of the Week mention.

GAME 12: LOUISVILLE (8-3) vs CHARLESTON (7-4)
LOUISVILLE 42 CHARLESTON 9
November 16, 2007

Charleston finished 13-2 the previous year, losing the championship to Hazlehurst 14-0. *"They are good. They are as athletic as anybody we have played all year. They are big and they can run. We do know that Charleston will be one of the best teams we have played"*.

This matchup started badly for the homestanding Cats. Charleston opened with a 28-yard Marcus Bernard FG. Louisville answered with a 16-yard Moore pass to Hunt. However, the visitors re-took the lead 9-6 on Quontarian Murry's 2-yarder. The Cats came back with a fury starting in the 2nd quarter. Ernie Triplett's pick led to a flea-flicker Clayton Moore pass from 38 yards to Henderson. They then went 70 yards with Moore finding Hunt from 20 yards and Moore adding the PAT. Finally, a Jimmy Owens fumble recovery allowed Moore to hit Mays from 17 yards.

They notched two more touchdowns in the 3rd quarter. Moore and Henderson hooked up from 14 yards while an Owens blocked put gave Thames a 14-yard tally. McGarr was true after both. Moore was 16-21 for 219 yards and rushed for 62 more. The Cats had 362 total offensive markers. Moore, again, was a Clarion-Ledger Player of the Week.

GAME 13: LOUISVILLE (9-3) @ RIPLEY (12-0)
LOUISVILLE 28 RIPLEY 22
November 23, 2007

Getting past this game would be a tough task. Amory, winners in three or four meetings all-time were now undefeated. Said Peterson, *"It's going to be a real challenge for us. We have played at home for four straight weeks so this is going to be a little different. But we'll be fine. We know how to play and win on the road"*.

Less than 2:00 into the contest, the Tigers struck on a 43-yard Rashun Adams pick-six and Will Wallis kick. Another pick led to a Jaquise Cook 23-yarder. Down 13-0, the Cats then drove 70 yards with Thames' 1-yarder and Moore kick. The 2nd quarter was also close. Another Cat turnover quickly led to Michael Poole's 14-yard effort. Louisville put halftime 19-14 when Thames darted in with :40 left and Moore added the PAT.

Louisville took the lead in the 3rd quarter on Hunt's 6-yard reception from Moore and Thames two-pointer. Now in the finale, Wallis nailed a 37-yard FG to tie it 22-22. Ripley could have scored from five yards if Clay Geter hadn't sacked the QB. Thames garnered the last when he dashed 22 yards to give the Cats a 6-point lead. Ripley attempted a fake punt late but Owens stopped the effort and the clock ran out.

Thames had 156 rushing and 64 receiving yards. Moore was 12-19 for 167 yards. Medford Hardin and Malcolm Kincaid paced tacklers with 10 each and Owens also had a fumble recovery. *"Ripley played a real good football game but we just didn't do very well at all, to be honest. If we had played our A game, then the outcome would never have been in doubt. Hats off to Ripley. They took it to us. We didn't have man answers but our kids kept fighting. They never quit"*.

GAME 14:   LOUISVILLE (10-3) vs CORINTH (9-4)
                   LOUISVILLE 48 CORINTH 14
                   November 30, 2007

This North State Championship match gave the Wildcats to play for the State title. Coach Jimmy Mitchell's Corinth team was riding an 8-game winning streak to make matters worse. However, The Clarion-Ledger picked Louisville 28-14.

The Cats had the lone tally of the opening frame when Moore hit Kincaid from a yard and added the first of five extra points. Corinth grabbed an errant Wildcat throw but Antwan Bragg stopped a potential gain with a big hit later. Moore found Thames from 43 yards while Thames broke away from 53 yards. Corinth crossed on a 1-yard Zerrick Payne run and Parker kick, but Louisville added one more before halftime on a 1-yard Moore dive.

In the 3rd quarter, Ernie Triplett grabbed a 57-yard pick-six, Henderson ran away from 20 yards, McGarr notched the kick, and Henderson ran in from 31 yards. Corinth had their last in the finale on a 1-yard Payne run and Parker kick. Moore was 8-13 for 130 yards while Henderson rushed for 97 more.

"I thought we came out and really played well. We came out and established ourselves from the beginning. Those (defensive) guys have really stepped up for us. If you aren't physical and you don't run to the ball, you can't play defense for us".

GAME 15:   LOUISVILLE (11-3) vs FRANKLIN COUNTY (12-2)
                   LOUISVILLE 21 FRANKLIN COUNTY 7
                   December 8, 2007

Before the season began, Peterson said of his opponent, "Franklin County is just hard-nosed and very athletic. They get after you. I'd love to be in Jackson playing them". He now had his wish. FCHS won two straight 3A championships and were hoping to be the first team since Collins to pull off the trifecta. The Clarion-Ledger's Todd Kelly picked Louisville.

The long drought to being close to competing for the crown was now over and the result brough bragging rights back to Winston County. Thames was the star in this with his opening 67-yard pick-six and one of three extra points. He did it again in the 2nd quarter with a 31-yard pick-six and halftime sat 14-0. In the 3rd quarter, Moore hit him from 11 yards and it was now 21-0. The Bulldogs hit the board their only time in the quarter when Jamie Collins crossed from a yard and Carlock converted. The rest of the game went scoreless.

Moore threw for 30 yards on a 5-8 evening, Carlous Hunt led receivers with 20 yards and Henderson paced rushers with 66 yards. Thames earned a statewide Clarion-Ledger Athlete of the Week. Said FCHS Grady McCluskey, "To me, the better team won. Louisville was really good defensively. They're hard to run the ball on".

Added Peterson, "It has been a long 18 weeks but now I am just kind of sitting back and watching our kids celebrate. It's the best thing in the world. They got to experience what so many kids never get to experience – a state championship".

All-State Honors went to Dennis Thames while The MSHC All-State roster included Clayton Moore (Offensive Player of the Year), Brad Peterson (Coach of the Year), and Thames, Jarred Fleming and Steven Hunt (First-Team Offense).

2008 (12-3)

Coach Brad Peterson knew that teams would be focused them as defending 3A Champions. "No question that we are one of the favorites to win since we are coming off a state championship. Going back-to-back is something special. But really, we are approaching this year like we do every season. This year is no different".

The Wildcats still had a formidable team highlighted by a pair of Dandy Dozen players in Clayton Moore and Dennis Thames. The usual tough openers would make it tough to start well, but that was no concern. "It puts your guys to the test, see what they do when they have to fight. Going undefeated has never been a goal of ours. No Louisville team has gone undefeated and won a state championship".

GAME 1:　　　　　　LOUISVILLE (0-0) vs STARKVILLE (0-0)
　　　　　　　　　　LOUISVILLE 32 STARKVILLE 10
　　　　　　　　　　August 29, 2008

　　　　The Cats opened third in 3A preseason ranking and eighth in The Super 10 but that would be tested against powerful Starkville. The Clarion-Ledger, nevertheless, picked Louisville 28-13.

　　　　Louisville took a quick 6-0 lead via Clayton Moore's 17-yarder to Antwan Bragg and then Moore found Markese Triplett from 57 yards. Up 12-0, the Jackets were able to turn a Cat miscue into a Cody Berryhill 24-yard FG. Louisville continued to pour it on in the 2nd quarter. Moore was first on a 14-yard run and later a 7-yarder. This time, the Moore PAT was good.

　　　　A Bragg interception set up a 9-yard Moore strike to Evan Dailey and Moore converted. The last gasp by Starkville came afterward on a 14-yard Jay Johnson run and William Arrick PAT. Moore was 14-24 for 153 yards and rushed for 113 more. Triplett led receivers with 64 yards and Randy Hornesburger paced tacklers with seven. Interceptions came from Bragg, Zan Carter and Triplett.

　　　　"Anytime you can beat a 5A opponent, it's good. And throw in the fact that it's Starkville, and it's even better. We have definitely closed the gap on them. We still have a ways to go. We just made too many mistakes".

GAME 2:　　　　　　LOUISVILLE (1-0) vs WAYNE COUNTY (1-0)
　　　　　　　　　　LOUISVILLE 3 WAYNE COUNTY 28
　　　　　　　　　　September 5, 2008

　　　　Coach Marcus Broyles bragged of three state titles and sat seventh in the Top 10 and first in 4A rankings. Said Peterson, *"I told the kids Wayne County may be the best team in the state, period. It's a big game for us because we know we'll have to fight for four quarters. Louisville has always scheduled the big boys for a reason; to find out where we're at".* The Clarion-Ledger thought the home team better 27-13.

　　　　This time, the shoe was on the other foot against the powerful War Eagles. WCHS opened with a 3-yarder by Tracey Lampley and Storm Seawright knocked home his first of four extra points. Calvin McDougle then escaped from 33 yards to end the opening frame 14-0. While Moore hit a 29-yard FG, the Eagles crossed again before halftime when Lampley ran in from 11 yards. Now 21-3, the added their last when Lampley got away from seven yards.

　　　　"They are one of the best football teams in the state, if not the best. We tried to tell everybody that. They just dominated us. We just have got to do better. Everybody thought we were going to be the team to beat. But we are not there. We are not the team that won a state championship last year. We have to get to that point. We have got to find another gear if we are going to make a run at this thing".

GAME 3:　　　　　　LOUISVILLE (1-1) @ KOSCIUSKO (1-1)
　　　　　　　　　　LOUISVILLE 37 KOSCIUSKO 10
　　　　　　　　　　September 12, 2008

　　　　Rival Kosy was just 3-8 against Louisville in the last 11 years. This one was meaningful to both. One was for bragging rights while the other wanted to get back on track for another state title.

　　　　Fred Parker opened scoring with a 14-yard run and Moore converted. Kosy cut it to 7-3 on a FG. Later the Cats moved to the Kosciusko 1. Then a fumble was returned 99 yards to make it 10-7. They could have widened the gap but fumbled the FG snap to Markese Triplett who took it 70 yards the other way. Moore put it 14-10 at halftime.

　　　　In the 3rd quarter, Moore hit a 28-yard FG to make it 17-10. In the finale, Triplett's blocked punt set up a 6-yarder by Parker. Moore and Triplett then connected from 23 yards while Chris Wraggs dashed 34 yards for the last. Moore was 9-12 for 168 yards, rushed for 120 yards, and Triplett pulled in 128 receiving yards. Malcolm Kincaid had five sacks and Montricus Goss recorded a pickoff.

　　　　"It was a tight football game at the half and that's something we haven't had all year. It was good to see how we would react in a close game".

GAME 4:   LOUISVILLE (2-1) vs NETTLETON (2-1)
                    LOUISVILLE 35 NETTLETON 0
                    September 19, 2008

Peterson was aware of the recent strength of Nettleton and commented about the game, "(Nettleton) will be ready to play". Their only meeting came the year before in a Wildcat victory.

The Cats "ripped off 23 first-quarter points" to jump on Nettleton early. Moore opened with a 10-yarder to Triplett, Frank McNeal and Damon Triplett caused a safety, Fred Parker dashed 33 yards, Chris Wraggs found Jordan Christion for the two-pointer, Zan Carter returned a punt 50 yards and Lamarcus Cistrunk added the PAT. Wraggs, now at QB, found Triplett from 10 yards to make halftime 29-0.

Parker ended Cat scoring in the 3rd quarter on his 3-yard effort set up by an Antwan Bragg punt return. Wraggs led rushers with 85 yards while Triplett added 40 receiving. Blake Cunningham had an interception and Tyler Griffin recovered a fumble. "We have to keep getting better because all of (the upcoming games) will tough ones".

Notable is that both Thames and Moore were out due to injuries.

GAME 5:   LOUISVILLE (3-1) vs HOUSTON (1-3)
                    LOUISVILLE 21 HOUSTON 0
                    September 27, 2008: HOMECOMING

Still without the two key players, Louisville was determined to keep their run for the title alive while keeping their all-time 6-0 record intact versus Houston for Homecoming.

All scoring came in the opening half. The Wildcats put up 14 points in the first frame. Cunningham's first of two interceptions helped Bragg find paydirt from 25 yards. Cistrunk connected on his first of three PATs. Parker then added the next from 20 yards. Wraggs added the last on his 41-yarder to Bragg. Cunningham had seven tackles while Malcolm Kincaid had three sacks, eight tackles and a fumble recovery.

"We still feel like we have a great football team. Our defense is playing well enough that we have a chance. The positive with having two starters out is that other guys are having to step up and play and it is helping us develop some depth".

GAME 6:   LOUISVILLE (4-1) @ SOUTH PONTOTOC (1-4)
                    LOUISVILLE 41 SOUTH PONTOTOC 0
                    October 3, 2008

The next foe was not having a great season thus far. Meanwhile, Louisville was yet again without Moore and Thames.

The Wildcats led 34-0 at the break thanks to 14 points in the opening frame. Parker had a 3-yard run and then pulled in a 21-yarder from Wraggs. Cistrunk was true on both and another later. In the 2nd quarter, Wraggs and Bragg connected from 27 yards, Jeffery Moore ran for 47 yards and Parker found the end zone from 14 yards. Tevarius Hardin added the last two PATs.

In the 3rd quarter, Wraggs dodged in from 15 yards and Hardin converted again. Wraggs was 12-20 for 116 yards. The team rushed for 232 yards and Kincaid recorded eleven tackles. "We are really about to hit the home stretch. We have the Number 3 ranked team in the state and then we play Aberdeen, who folks think may be a little better than that. But we take a little offense to that. You want to be peaking going into the playoffs".

GAME 7:   LOUISVILLE (5-1) vs NOXUBEE COUNTY (5-0)
                    LOUISVILLE 0 NOXUBEE COUNTY 32
                    October 10, 2008

As Peterson feared, Noxubee County would be no pushover. The Tigers held serve in contests since 2001 with a 6-3 record. Before that, Louisville dominated the matchup with all but two wins since 1972.

The two defenses held one-another to a scoreless half. Things changed rapidly starting in the 3rd quarter. A fumble recovery led to a 31-yard Temarcus Conner pass to Patrick Patterson. They added the two-pointer on a pass between the two. Another fumble allowed them to connect from 16 yards and Patreon Hopkins' run made it 16-0. Conner then found Vincent Sanders from 21 yards and Hopkins two-pointer.

It continued with a final frame Conner 10-yarder to Sanders and a Toddrick Tate run. Louisville had only 103 offensive yards with Moore running for 39 yards and passing for 29 more. *"We knew we had to play a perfect game and in the first half we played pretty well. But in the second half, it really snowballed on us. Of course, that happened because they made some plays"*.

GAME 8:   LOUISVILLE (5-2) vs ABERDEEN (7-0)
                               LOUISVILLE 35 ABERDEEN 12
                               October 17, 2008

Knowing that Aberdeen was blown away the previous season, The Clarion-Ledger picked the Wildcats a remarkably accurate 35-16. *"They are a good football team. A lot of people are saying they may be the best team in 3A, so I guess we'll have our hands full. We are ready to go. This is the biggest game of the season for us right now. We are going to work hard all week to get prepared for a big football game"*.

When over, The Clarion-Ledger said, *"Just in case anyone was wondering, Dennis Thames and Clayton Moore are feeling just fine these days"*. The two hooked up from 29 yards for the initial score and Moore connected on his first of five kicks. Thames then dashed 53 yards to paydirt to make it 14-0. Aberdeen came back with a 68-yard Jamerson Love escape to make it 14-6. Late in the half, Moore kept for the 18-yard tally.

Aberdeen drove 65 yards and scored on a 2-yarder by Marcus Hinton to open the 3rd quarter. The Cats answered with a late 44-yard Moore strike to Thames and finished things in the finale on a 5-yarder between the two. Thames had 86 yards on the ground, Moore was 13-21 and Triplett grabbed 58 yards of receptions.

"We want to get better. We are far from peaking. We have work to do to get to where we need to be. We're going to just keep working at it".

GAME 9:   LOUISVILLE (6-2) @ AMORY (4-4)
                               LOUISVILLE 24 AMORY 7
                               October 24, 2008

Louisville opened with a 55-yard drive ending on a 19-yard Moore pass to Markeese Triplett and Moore converted. Kincaid recovered a late 2nd quarter fumble while Jordan Christon *"went up to haul in a 20-yard scoring pass from Moore with time expired"*. Moore made it 14-0.

Moore broke free late in the 3rd quarter from 35 yards before the Panthers tallied in the 4th quarter on a 20-yard TD pass. Moore ended scoring with his 23-yard FG. Moore was 19-28 in the air and rushed for 111 yards. Thames was close behind with 100 rushing yards. Triplett led receivers with 90 yards. Thames, Terrance Hardin and Kincaid each had six tackles and Hardin had two sacks.

"We knew we had to make a statement and we did. We are still the Louisville Wildcats. (Amory) just kept on playing. They never quit and they never gave up". Moore earned a Player of the Week mention for his performance.

GAME 10:   LOUISVILLE (7-2) @ WINONA (6-3)
                               LOUISVILLE 27 WINONA 30
                               October 31, 2008

The Wildcats took one step closer to claiming the 2-3A Championship but now had to go to Winona. *"It's really good that the last game has meaning. We now have to go out and play with focus"*. Despite being a road game, it did not seem like a big hurdle with Louisville holding wins in all six meetings.

Winona scored on all four of their first possessions and held a 23-20 halftime advantage. Louisville struck first on a 30-yard pass to Triplett and Moore made it 7-0. While Winona then added a 35-yard FG, Louisville increased the lead on Moore's 36-yarder to Evan Dailey.

Winona got going before intermission. They recorded a touchdown to make it 13-10 and then scored again to make it 16-13. Thames then crossed and Moore converted but Winona added another touchdown :20 before halftime to put them ahead. Harry Peoples opened the 3rd quarter with yet another Winona tally while LHS could garner only a 22-yarder from Moore to Triplett.

"After the loss, some people told me it may be a good thing. I told them that if we responded well, it will be a good thing. But it was going to depend on how we

responded. We had a pretty good meeting and the players responded well. It can be a real good thing".

GAME 11:   LOUISVILLE (7-3) vs McCLAIN (7-3)
                     LOUISVILLE 21 McCLAIN 14
                     November 7, 2008

The first-time opponent out of Lexington, MS was not to be taken lightly. "It's going to be a tough ball game for us. They have been beaten by three good football teams. They are very athletic. It's definitely going to be a tougher than normal first-round game".

McClain was the aggressor and held a 14-0 halftime lead thanks to a 3-yard Calvin Smith plunge, a 1-yard LeKendol Cox sneak and two extra points. Back came the Cats in the 3rd quarter, first with a 58-yard drive capped by a 15-yard Wraggs pass to Triplett. Josh Hardin's kick was true. Brandon Hendrix then picked off a pass to set up a 6-yard Thames dash. The blocked PAT kept it 14-13. Finally, Wraggs "lofted the ball down the right sidelines" and found Triplett for a 39-yard touchdown. Triplett pulled in the Wraggs pass for the two points.

Wraggs was 11-17 for 175 yards and Thames held the ground with just 30 yards. "The defense really stepped it up. They just pushed us around in the first half and did what they wanted to do. They really took it to us. We knew we had to come out and score in the second half or we were going to be in big trouble".

GAME 12:   LOUISVILLE (8-3) @ SENATOBIA (7-4)
                     LOUISVILLE 20 SENATOBIA 7
                     November 14, 2008

This marked the first meeting between the two schools. "To go to the State Championship game, you have to win on the road and, most of the time, you have to play a game in some wet weather".

Surprisingly, the Warriors were first to the board after a Cat fumble set up a touchdown and PAT. Louisville then went 70 yards ending on a Thames 3-yarder and Jimmy Owens PAT. In the 2nd quarter, Christion grabbed an 18-yard Wraggs pass and it was 14-7. Finally, a solid Markese Triplett punt return set up a 6-yarder by Thames.

Thames ran for 111 yards while Wraggs went 8-16 for 77 yards. "By the end of the first quarter, we were playing in a monsoon. It was a driving wind that had the rain really whipping around".

GAME 13:   LOUISVILLE (9-3) @ CORINTH (12-0)
                     LOUISVILLE 51 CORINTH 28
                     November 21, 2008

The Wildcats jumped out to a 14-0 lead on two Wraggs passes to Thames from 14 and 72 yards. Owens connected on both. In the next frame, Triplett pulled in a 5-yarder from Moore before Corinth hit the board on a Williams 9-yard pass from Frazier and Parker PAT. But Louisville had more to add. Moore hit Thames from 51 yards (Owens PAT) and Triplett from 60 yards. Finally, Moore hit Thames from 24 yards to make halftime 39-7.

Corinth put two tallies on the board in the 3rd quarter via a 1-yard Frazier run, his 22-yard strike to Payne and a pair of Parker kicks. Louisville added one tally on a 6-yard Moore run and Wraggs dodged in from four yards in the finale. Crawford's 9-yarder and Parker kick finished scoring.

Wraggs went 8-11 for 129 yards while Moore was also 8-11 for 195 yards. Thames pulled in 188 receiving yards. Moore was named a Clarion-Ledger Player of the Week. "I thought the offense clicked extremely well. We had a couple of turnovers or we would have scored more. Other than that, I thought we played extremely well".

GAME 14:   LOUISVILLE (10-3) vs ABERDEEN (10-2)
                     LOUISVILLE 41 ABERDEEN 21
                     November 28, 2008

Earlier in the season, the Cats defeated Aberdeen 35-12. This one was up for grabs as the winner moved on to play for the state championship. "There are 20 great football teams playing across the state on Friday night. There are no upsets at this point".

Thames broke away from 70 yards and Owens made it 7-0. Aberdeen responded with a 1-yard Marcus Hinton run and Crayton kick to tie it. In the next frame, Blanchard hauled in a 63-yard Hinton pass and Crayton put them ahead 14-7. Louisville cut it down with a 40-yard Moore toss to Triplett. Before halftime, the two hooked up from 80 yards and a safety from Glendrell Miller put intermission sat 21-14.

An Aberdeen punt miscue led to a 4-yard Thames run and Owens kick to make it 28-14. Aberdeen responded with a 49-yard Hinton pass to Buchanan and Crayton kick. In the finale, the Cats put up a pair of scores on two 1-yard Thames runs and an Owens PAT. *"You always hear how hard it is to go back-to-back and it's been an unbelievable journey to get to this point. This is the toughest year I have ever had to go through. This is a great ground of kids who have fought and battled".*

While Thames won a Clarion-Ledger mention for Player of the Week for his 108 rushing yards and four touchdowns, the biggest news came afterwards. There was apparently a disagreement between Moore and Peterson somewhere around halftime on an audible call that eventually led to the dismissal of the QB. There was a lot written about this incident in numerous newspapers, but the end result was that the Wildcats would play the last contest without their starting quarterback.

GAME 15:   LOUISVILLE (11-3) vs TYLERTOWN (12-0)
                     LOUISVILLE 26 TYLERTOWN 21
                     December 6, 2008

This marked the first trip to the 3A championship for the Chiefs. Said Peterson before, *"Last year it was just smooth sailing. Everything jelled. Everything came together. You always hear it's harder to go back-to-back than it is to win the first time. At times we questioned our kids as to how hungry they were. After the Winona loss, things started coming together, but then we had other distractions. I think we are a good football team. Tylertown has a good football team. We know it's going to be a challenge".*

As the game drew near, he added, *"In our opinion, Tylertown is a better football team than Franklin County was last year. I may be wrong, but I don't think Tylertown is going to throw two interceptions. We have to be in the right place at all times. We're going to have to make good decisions on covering their pass routes and we've got to stop the running back".*

Tylertown took the lead late in the opening frame on an 18-yard Deon Howard dash and Larome Holmes PAT. Louisville answered in the 2nd quarter with a 43-yard Wraggs pass to Triplett. The Chiefs made it 14-6 after on Jameon Lewis' 35-yard pass to Brandon Thompson. Back came the Cats with a double pass and 32-yard Thames connection with Triplett. Still down 14-12, they added one more before halftime on a 14-yard Wraggs toss to Christion. Thames added the two-pointer to make it 20-14.

Late in the 3rd quarter, Lewis gave the Chiefs the lead again via his 17-yarder to Thompson and a Holmes kick. Louisville made it 26-21 in the finale on Wraggs' 11-yarder to Christion. It appeared the Wildcats were putting it away late in the game on a Thames escape, but his fumble was recovered by Tylertown. They drove as far as the Cat 10 but a Kincaid sack on Lewis allowed the clock to expire.

Wraggs was 16-22 for 171 yards, Triplett had 126 receiving yards, and Thames ran for 110 yards. First downs were even at 18 each and total yardage was almost the same. Louisville edged that part 342-327. *"I just can't tell you how proud I am of these guys. They overcame so much to get here. Now we are a team. When it mattered most, we pulled together. It's been a tough, long, hard year. But we pulled through it and did what we set out to do".*

Peterson was 3A Coach of the Year. Dennis Thames earned a First Team Offensive award. Randy Hornesburger was a first Team Defense member. Second Team Offense included Tate Rogers.

2009 (8-5)

After two years in 3A with both ending in state championships, the Wildcats now found themselves back in 4-4A. Voters still thought Brad Peterson's team strong and voted them second in overall 4A. *"You have to have good senior leadership and you have to catch some breaks to (win another title). Our kids expect to win and believe they are going to win and they are going to work their butts off. We always have some great players here".*

GAME 1:   LOUISVILLE (0-0) vs NORTHWEST RANKIN (0-0)
                   LOUISVILLE 41 NORTHWEST RANKIN 21
                   August 21, 2009

The two split games in 1987 and 1988. The Cougars this season were coming off a 10-3 campaign and a second-round playoff loss to eventual champion South Panola. The Clarion-Ledger picked the Cats 27-17.

An opening drive fumble by Louisville led to a Chase Taylor sneak and quick 7-0 Cougar lead. The Cats came back with an 80-yard march and Chris Wraggs 7-yarder. Zach McGarr added the game-tying PAT. NWR then went 82 yards and tallied on a 10-yard Taylor strike to Jonathan Hailey. Now in the 2nd quarter down 14-7, Wraggs hit Blake Cunningham from 17 yards to tie it. Minutes later, Wraggs dove in from two yards and added another passing TD to put halftime 28-14.

Louisville pulled a lateral pass from Tahj Ford to Markese Triplett for a 68-yard touchdown to start to pull away. Dava'is Schaffer add a 1-yarder in the finale while Eddie Abraham did the same from ten yards for NWR with :16 remaining. Wraggs, a Clarion-Ledger Player of the Week mention, was 12-14 for 196 yards and rushed for 94 more. Triplett grabbed 154 receiving yards. In all, Louisville had 413 offensive yards and 16 first downs.

GAME 2:   LOUISVILLE (1-0) @ STARKVILLE (0-1)
                   LOUISVILLE 26 STARKVILLE 21
                   August 28, 2009

The Yellow Jackets opened their season with a 30-0 loss to Number One 4A Noxubee County. Said Peterson, "Starkville is always a big game for Louisville. It doesn't matter what the records are". The two faced one another each year since 1940 and some before that.

Triplett opened the tilt with a great catch that covered 87 yards and McGarr put the Wildcats up 7-0. The Jackets then tied it on Jaquez Johnson's 3-yard dive but Louisville responded with a 22-yard Cunningham dash. Johnson obtained his second touchdown for the home team but Wraggs and Triplett hooked up for a 60-yard TD to make it 20-14. Zan Carter's interception in the end zone killed a Jacket threat.

Early in the 4th quarter, the Cats scored their last on a Ford 13-yard reception from Wraggs before Johnson pulled in a short Justin Rogers toss for their finale. Triplett had 192 receiving yards while Wraggs went 16-26 for 302 more. Triplett earned a Clarion-Ledger Player of the Week nomination.

GAME 3:   LOUISVILLE (2-0) @ QUITMAN (2-0)
                   LOUISVILLE 25 QUITMAN 42
                   September 4, 2009

The 2-0 start put the Wildcats eighth in the Super 10. However, their next opponent would make it tough to continue to climb. "If Quitman is not the best 4A team in the South (part of the state), then they are in the top three or four. They have a legitimate shot to get to Jackson". The Clarion-Ledger still picked Louisville 30-20.

Things appeared to go the Cats' way early as Triplett returned a Quitman fumble 41 yards to paydirt and McGarr made it 7-0. However, Dyar Ealie then took a Cat punt 90 yards to the end zone and DeAnthony Pickens added the two-pointer. Louisville came back with a 1-yard Wraggs plunge to retake the lead, but Ealie hauled in a 58-yard Wesley Warren pass. Adrian Moore's 14-yard pick six late in the 2nd quarter made halftime 21-13.

Four plays into the 3rd quarter, Pickens dashed 50 yards to daylight and Carlos Davis added the 28-13 kick. Louisville did not quit. Wraggs hit Jordan Christion from 36 yards and it sat 28-19. However, Quitman had a 66-yard drive end on a 2-yarder by Pickens. They then added a 9-yard Warren pass to Dyar. The final Cat tally came on Cunningham's 7-yard effort.

The Cats had just 51 rushing yards while Wraggs was 17-29-3 for 164 yards. Christion led receivers with 73 yards. "We didn't play great and Quitman did. I thought they played a heck of a football game. We had an opportunity to make some plays and didn't. It's another week. We have to put that one behind us and get ready for Tupelo".

GAME 4:   LOUISVILLE (2-1) vs TUPELO (0-2)
                   LOUISVILLE 20 TUPELO 17
                   September 11, 2009

     Tupelo was 20-13 against Louisville in their last 33 meetings. While the usually powerful Golden Wave was winless thus far, it would still not be an easy affair.

     An early Wave interception led to Luke Hobson's 29-yard FG and 3-0 lead. Late in the 2nd quarter, Louisville hit the board on Wraggs' 1-yarder and McGarr kick. Just before halftime, McGarr nailed a 27-yard FG to make it 10-3. In the 3rd quarter, Tupelo blocked a Cat punt to allow Chris Donald an eventual 6-yarder and 10-9 deficit. The Wildcats answered with a 29-yard Wraggs toss to Triplett and McGarr kick.

     Tupelo tied it 17-17 on Donald's 4-yard run and two-point conversion. The winning points came on a 29-yard McGarr FG. Tupelo had a chance late but dropped a fourth down pass at the Cat 5 to seal the win. Wraggs was 12-25 for 155 and rushed for 71 more. Christion pulled in 46 receiving yards. *"People had the mindset that we were supposed to blow everybody away. I would love for that to be the case, but we are going to have close games"*.

GAME 5:   LOUISVILLE (3-1) @ COLUMBUS (1-2)
                   LOUISVILLE 34 COLUMBUS 20
                   September 18, 2009

     The lone win thus far for the Falcons came in their 27-26 opener over Aberdeen. *"It's not a game where we are thinking it's an easy win. They are going to line up and try to run over us. They want to pound us and hold the ball"*.

     While Columbus scored first on a 25-yard Cedric Johnson toss to Deontae Jones, Zan Carter answered with an 83-yard kickoff return to tie it. In the 2nd quarter, the Cats tallied three times. Wraggs put up a pair of 1-yard runs and added a 12-yarder to make it 28-7. The Falcons added a pair of touchdowns on runs of three and five yards to cut it to 28-20. Wraggs pulled out the win with a 65-yard bomb to C.J. Bates to ice it.

     Wraggs was 8-12 for 110 passing and rushed for 39 yards. Leading the ground was Schaffer with 84 yards while Bates pulled in 71 passing receptions. *"We break the season into three parts. We have the non-division games which we call the preseason, then the division, and then the playoffs. We are still working on things, trying to get better. We are making some progress, but we still need to get better at taking advantage of our opportunities"*.

GAME 6:   LOUISVILLE (4-1) vs WEST LAUDERDALE (3-2)
                   LOUISVILLE 18 WEST LAUDERDALE 19: OT
                   September 25, 2009

     In their only two meetings (2005-2006), the teams split wins to make this a more competitive contest historically. Now West Lauderdale had only one more loss than the Wildcats. Said Peterson, *"This will be our last chance to get ready for division play. We look at this as our last pre-season game"*.

     Louisville scored first on an 11-yard Wraggs pass to Triplett and added two more points on a Wraggs pass to McGarr. McGarr made it 11-0 at halftime with his 27-yard FG. Nate Hodges cut into the lead with his 26-yard FG after a turnover. Later, he dove in on a keeper and converted the two-pointer to tie things.

     Now in overtime, Wraggs hit Carter from eight yards and McGarr converted. West Lauderdale, however, tallied on a 7-yard Dennis Lewis run and went for the win. Robert Sillimon dove in from a yard and a half for the comeback victory. Wraggs went 15-25 for 155 yards, Christion led receivers with 58 yards and Schaffer rushers with 42 yards. *"We really played well in the first half and had the game under control. We had a couple of turnovers that hurt us"*.

GAME 7:   LOUISVILLE (4-2) @ HOUSTON (1-5)
                   LOUISVILLE 48 HOUSTON 28
                   October 2, 2009

     Coach Buz Boyer's Hilltoppers finished 2008 at 2-8. This campaign was not better thus far. In fact, the previous week provided Houston a 73-7 shellacking at the hands of Aberdeen. *"We have to go up there and take care of business. We just need to play our game and not worry about anything else".*

Though Louisville jumped out with a 19-yard TD pass from Wraggs to Triplett and McGarr PAT, Houston roared back with a pair of touchdowns and PATs. The first was on a 33-yard run and the next a 65-yard halfback pass. Back came the Cats with Triplett's 53-yard dash to tie it. He then ran in from 21 yards while Wraggs hit Montricus Goss from 18 yards. The two-pointer was from Wraggs to Christion. The last came after an Anthony Davis fumble recovery.

Schaffer made it 35-14 with a 6-yard scamper but Houston answered with a 60-yard "hitch play". Just before the half, the Cats scored on a 13-yard Wraggs pass to Bates. In the finale, Wraggs dashed in from five yards while the Hilltoppers scored on another "hitch play", this time from 50 yards.

Triplett, now at running back, had 116 rushing while Wraggs paced them all with 126 yards. Schaffer's 104 yards put three Cats over the century mark. Wraggs was 5-12 for 78. Jamie Sanders and Jonathan Coleman each had seven tackles. *"Any time you get a win in region play, it's a big one. We are excited about it. They were never going to stop us".*

GAME 8:   LOUISVILLE (5-2) vs KOSCIUSKO (2-5)
                                   LOUISVILLE 46 KOSCIUSKO 22
                                   October 9, 2009: HOMECOMING

The Cats were 18-6 in the last 24 meetings in a rivalry that stretched at least back to 1929. Coach Stan McCain's Whippets were just 3-7 the previous year and a defeat of Louisville in Winston County would be big in more ways than one. *"Kosciusko will come in ready to play. This is a huge rivalry for them. It's Homecoming for us and could be a little bit of a distraction".*

Louisville got a huge lead after a frame. Bates opened with a 31-yard dash and McGarr put it a quick 7-0. Triplett took a punt 54 yards and Davis took a fumble to the house from 37 yards. The Cats made it 34-0 on a 15-yard Triplett dash and 21-yard Bates toss to Ford. While John Kern put Kosy on the board from three yards, Schaffer took the kick 74 yards to paydirt. That made halftime 40-7.

Goss earned the last Cat tally in the 3rd quarter from 24 yards while Kosy scored once in each of the two frames. Bates went 5-9 for 59 yards and rushed for 79 of the 275 total yards on the ground. Christon had 18 receiving yards. *"I thought you saw a different Louisville team out there Thursday night. I thought we were playing with the passion that we have to play with to make a run at it. Once division play starts and the playoffs start, you want your kids more focused and playing with more of that passion and desire".*

GAME 9:   LOUISVILLE (6-2) vs CALEDONIA (0-7)
                                   LOUISVILLE 43 CALEDONA 6
                                   October 16, 2009

If Caledonia and Coach Jason Forrester thought the previous 1-9 campaign was bad, this one was worse. The Wildcats made it no better on this Friday night.

It was out of control early as Carter's blocked punt put the Cats at the 6-yard line from where Bates hit Deangelo Willis for the score and McGarr converted. A safety over the Caledonia punter's head was followed by a 3-yard Bates run to make it 15-0. Then, Bates hit Christion from 20 yards after Triplett took a punt 25 yards to paydirt. Bates later hit Jordan Fleming from 23 yards and ended the opening half with Schaffer's 3-yarder. The Confederates found paydirt with just two minutes left.

The defense held Caledonia to just 35 total yards. Marcus Odom led the charge with six tackles. Bates was 8-10 for 126 passing yards.

GAME 10:   LOUISVILLE (7-2) @ NOXUBEE COUNTY (8-1)
                                   LOUISVILLE 0 NOXUBEE COUNTY 28
                                   October 23, 2009

The Noxubee County game matched their third ranking in the state against the seventh place of Louisville. The Tigers just shut out Houston 44-0. In fact, they shut out the last four out of seven opponents on the season under Coach M.C. Miller. Only West Point tallied back on September 18th in a 20-12 victory. However, it was the two defending state champions against one another.

"It's a huge game this week. It is what we have been looking forward to. The biggest thing is you want to win the region. It kind of gives you a leg up in the playoffs. While it is hard to beat a team twice, at the same time if you beat them the first time, it does put some doubt in their minds". The Clarion-Ledger picked NCHS 20-12.

It actually turned out worse as the home team scored in each of the last three quarters. They made it 8-0 at halftime after a Cat fumble was scooped up by Tommy Lane and taken 57 yards to the end zone. William Jarrad Johnson found Victor Sanders for the two-pointer. They added another in the 3rd quarter on a 1-yard Earnest Harmon dive after Johnson and Sanders hooked up from 20 yards.

Now in the finale, Sanders dashed in from 15 yards and added a 28-yard reception from Johnson. Carmichael added a pair of PATs in the game. Bates and Wraggs combined on an 8-24 night for only 95 yards. Triplett had 42 yards receiving and recorded a pair of interceptions. Schaffer led rushers with just 29 yards. *"We have got to get consistent. I was pleased with our effort early. We just didn't make the plays. We have to get where we make those plays".*

GAME 11:   LOUISVILLE (7-3) @ AMORY (2-8)
                LOUISVILLE 19 AMORY 14
                October 30, 2009

The Winston County Journal called this one a *"stunning 19-14 decision"* against Coach Pat Byrd's Amory team that finished 6-5 the previous season and came into the game with just a pair of wins.

Louisville jumped out early with an 11-yard Wraggs toss to Triplett and McGarr put it 7-0. Wraggs then dashed 32 yards to paydirt and McGarr put it 14-0. The home team cut into the lead when Frank Carter took the opening second half kick 70 yards to daylight. A Cat turnover soon led to Forest Williams' 20-yard strike to Josh Andress to make it 14-13. Late in the game, Joreel Freeman found the end zone from five yards and Amory snatched the upset.

Louisville led in yardage 335-96. Wraggs was 9-20 for 116 and rushed for 95 more. Bates led receivers with 38 yards. While Broam Ashford paced the defense with four tackles, a sack, and two fumble recoveries. Rod Clark (8) and James Sanders (6) were leading on tackles. *"We barely got off the bus and we were up 14-0. But we just never could get anything else going. We shot ourselves in the foot a bunch. It was just one of those games where I truly felt like we gave it away".*

GAME 12:   LOUISVILLE (7-4) vs PONTOTOC (8-2)
                LOUISVILLE 28 PONTOTOC 21: 2 OT
                November 6, 2009

On paper, Pontotoc appeared the stronger of the two. Their only previous meeting came in a 1930 6-6 tie game. *"We are definitely the underdogs through the eyes of everybody in the state. If there was a line on the game, we would be the underdog. Of 4A football they are the best Number 3-seed there is. Itawamba had to score with two minutes to go to beat them. It's going to be a challenge, for sure".*

The Cats started with a 76-yard march ending on a 1-yard Wraggs sneak. Pontotoc came back in the next frame with a 91-yard drive with Camden Dallas falling *"on a teammate's fumble in the LHS end zone".* The Michael Bounds PAT made it 7-6. The Warriors made it 14-6 at the half when Dallas found paydirt from three yards with just seconds remaining and the conversion.

Louisville tied it 14-14 in the 3rd quarter on an 11-yard Wraggs pass to Bates and two-point pass to Carter. Now in the first overtime, Randall Crayton dashed in from six yards but Wraggs found Triplett to tie it 21-21. In the second OT, Schaffer grabbed a Wraggs pass for a 10-yarder. Just two plays later, Bates picked off a Warrior pass to move the Cats to the next round.

Wraggs was 16-25 for 160 yards, Schaffer rushed for 108 more and caught 74 yards in the win. *"We knew we were going to have to be able to run the ball in order to be able to win. That's not in my nature, but that's what we were determined to do. (That last interception was) a terrible way to end the game, but what a heck of a job by our guys. They fought their hearts out and played really, really well".*

The Commodores' only loss came early in the season to Itawamba by a small score, but they managed to record every victory thereafter. Though Lafayette won in both 2005 and 2006, it still proved a heartbreaking end to the 2009 campaign.

Three Cat throws were intercepted by the 'Dores on their home-standing evening to prove an eventual defeat. LCHS was first on the board on a 2-yard Dominique Price run and the first of a pair of Jackson kicks. Ontario Phillips' interception set up an Anfernee Gooch 19-yard reception from Jeremy Liggins made it 14-0. The last tally came from the Cats in the finale on a 4-yard Schaffer dash.

Wraggs was 9-18 for 130 yards while Bates went 6-11 for 66. Triplett had 76 receiving markers while Rod Clark paced tacklers with nine. Carter had a pickoff. *"I thought we were the better team and I thought we outplayed them on the field. The three turnovers cost us the game. When you get 366 yards you are supposed to score some more points. We have been in some 14-0 games before, so we had that experience on our side. We weren't down and out. We just had to come back and make some plays. Going back-to-back is hard. Winning three in a row is extremely hard"*.

Markese Triplett earned a First Team All-State Defense honor at year's end.

2010—2019

2010 (8-5)

After five seasons at his alma-mater with a 50-28 record and two 3A championships, Brad Peterson took the head job in Brandon. In his place stood long-time Noxubee County mentor M.C. Miller.

Miller's Wildcats were not ranked in the Top 5 in 4A to start the season, but he had high hopes for his team and planned to rely on a passing attack. *"We want to throw the ball every time we can, but it's all going to come down to the offensive line. That's what we are working hard to find more than anything else"*.

GAME 1:   LOUISVILLE (0-0) @ NORTHWEST RANKIN (0-0)
               LOUISVILLE 14 NORTHWEST RANKIN 22
               August 20, 2010

Coach David Coates' Cougars finished 4-8 the previous year, including a loss to Louisville. Said Miller, *"That first game's going to be a tough one. They are all going to be tough ones for us until we get everything figured out. We are just going to try to get better each week but right now we are looking at the first one"*. The Clarion-Ledger thought NWR better 21-14.

Things appeared to be going in favor of the Cats as they held a 14-0 lead after a quarter. Wyatt Roberts hit Blake Cunningham from 12 yards and Dava'is Schaffer dodged in from two yards to accompany a pair of Tajh Ford kicks. They were driving for another but a fumble gave NWR the chance to get back into the fight.

Bo Thomason got in from a yard later and they evened things on his touchdown pass to Reid Humphries. The last touchdown came from the Cougars when Kurterrius Taylor found paydirt ran in from seven yards. Roberts went 13-28 for 170 yards, Ford led receivers with 76 yards, Schaffer rushed for 49, Kevin Washington led tacklers with 13 and Anthony Davis recorded a fumble recovery.

GAME 2:   LOUISVILLE (0-1) vs STARKVILLE (0-1)
               LOUISVILLE 0 STARKVILLE 34
               August 27, 2010

Starkville opened their year with a close 14-7 loss to Noxubee County. This long-time rivalry game was always a tough one. *"I think it is very important that we bounce back and play well so that we can build some momentum for the rest of the season. It is very important that we pull out a win in one of these tough games to show that we can do it"*.

It was never in doubt as mistakes plagued the Cats. Jaquez Johnson ran away from 23 yards only to fumble into the end zone where Eddie Brown recovered for the score. Fumo was true on the kick and three others after. They made it 21-0 at intermission on Johnson's 27-yard strike to Gabe Myles and a 4-yarder by Jakarta Agnew.

Starkville added a score in each of the last two frames. Johnson had a 1-yard dive in the 3rd while Agnew crossed from nine yards in the finale. Starkville rushed for 388 yards and had 18 first downs. Schaffer led rushers with 59 of the total 102 offensive yards. To make matters worse, Roberts fractured his left wrist and was due out for four weeks.

"We just couldn't make a play at the right time and a lot of times we had the opportunities. Every time we had them on third down, we would have a mishap and give them new life. That keeps the defense on the field when they should be off and the offense should be on".

GAME 3:   LOUISVILLE (0-2) vs QUITMAN (2-0)
               LOUISVILLE 26 QUITMAN 14
               September 3, 2010

It was now time for number 14 Louisville to meet up in Winston County with the 15th-ranked Quitman team. Believe it or not, the two had numerous previous meetings going back to at least 1930. It was time for the Wildcats to get in the win column.

C.J. Bates put Louisville up early on a 69-yard escape. Quitman took the lead on a 1-yard dive and PAT still in the opening frame. Zan Carter put the Cats up 12-7 at halftime when he recovered a loose football and raced 42 yards to daylight. In the 3rd quarter, Ford dashed in from eight yards and three yards for the next scores. Quitman added a late tally to make it respectable.

Bates led rushers with 131 yards with also going 3-6 for 18 in the air. *"It was a good win for us. It was good for our guys to actually finish a game"*.

GAME 4:   LOUISVILLE (1-2) @ TUPELO (2-0)
                        LOUISVILLE 0 TUPELO 17
                        September 10, 2010

Larger Tupelo, a common foe for the Wildcats on the gridiron since 1920, was ranked 14th in 6A. *"It is going to be a very important game for us. They are a good team. It will be a challenge"*. As usual, the Wildcats were getting a fill of higher-ranked opponents to start the season.

Tupelo held a 10-0 lead at the half thanks to a 49-yard Hunter Raines FG and a 19-yard fumble recovery and return by Terrell Pinson. Another fumble in the 3rd quarter led to Ashton Shumpert's 1-yard dive to cap a 40-yard march. Bates was 11-17 for 124 yards and led rushers with 53 more. Ford led receivers with 68 yards and Jonathan Coleman paced tackers with 10.

"The schedule has been kind of tough. As far as competition, it should help us. The team is getting more comfortable. Right now, we just have to keep calling plays to help them be more successful. We are trying to simplify things to ease the transition".

GAME 5:   LOUISVILLE (1-3) vs COLUMBUS (2-1)
                        LOUISVILLE 36 COLUMBUS 28
                        September 17, 2010

Playing a Columbus team was normal for the Wildcats as numerous schools around that city fielded teams as opponents. For this one, it proved a chance to begin getting Wildcat feet firmly on the ground.

The opening quarter ended with a 6-0 Cat lead courtesy of a 5-yarder by Schaffer. In the next, Schaffer dashed in from 20 yards while Cunningham pulled in a 45-yard Ford pass. Ford and Bates connected for a pair of two-pointers. Marcus Odom had a 3rd quarter 38-yard fumble return and Schaffer a 3-yarder as time drew near. Ford and Bates added the two points.

Columbus scored on via a pair of 3rd quarter Cedrick Jackson passes to Deonte Jones from 51 and 66 yards. Damian Baker dashed in from four yards in the finale to tie it but the conversion failed. Schaffer, a <u>Clarion-Ledger</u> Player of the Week mention, led rushers with 114 yards of the 252 total. Ford was 4-6 for 57 yards and Coleman led tacklers with nine sacks. Carter, Cunningham and Jim Goss each had interceptions. *"We knew it was going to be tough. But we are just trying to keep getting better and to be ready to (play) our district games. Those are the ones that count the most"*.

GAME 6:   LOUISVILLE (2-3) @ WEST LAUDERDALE (0-5)
                        LOUISVILLE 21 WEST LAUDERDALE 7
                        September 24, 2010

West Lauderdale stood with victories in two of the three contests played to date against Louisville. This season, however, now they were winless. This one marked the last non-division game for the Cats.

Louisville was up a quick 7-0 on Ford's first-play 85-yarder to Bates to make it 7-0. That score amazingly held through the first half. The Knights opened the 3rd quarter with a 65-yard march ending on a 6-yard Warren Trussell tally and it was 7-7 with the kick. Back came Louisville with an 80-yard drive ending on Ford's 10-yarder and two-pointer. They finished with a 64-yard march and Ford 1-yard sneak for the finale.

Ford ran for 85 of his total 231 yards and was a <u>Clarion-Ledger</u> Player of the Week mention. In the air, he went 6-12 for 149 yards while Bates was 3-3 for 25 yards. Bates also had 87 receiving yards. *"Right now, this is a new season. We are lucky to come out of it 3-3 because it was a tough schedule from the start and we had so few players coming back. I am proud of the young men for picking up and working so hard. We are on the right track now"*.

GAME 7:   LOUISVILLE (3-3) vs HOUSTON (1-5)
                        LOUISVILLE 29 HOUSTON 7
                        October 1, 2010: HOMECOMING

The Cats welcomed Houston to their Homecoming tilt in front of alums. Louisville was 8-0 against the Hilltoppers since their first meeting in 1945. *"We want to go in there and make a statement in this first game starting off region play"*.

It was a fast 8-0 lead when Ford hit Cunningham from 26 yards and Bates for the two-pointer. The Cats put up three more touchdowns in the 2nd quarter on a 3-yard Ford strike to Isaiah Waldrip, a 35-yard Roberts pass to Ford, and Bates' 54-yard punt return. Houston got on the board via a 3rd quarter tally to avoid the shutout.

Ford was 11-17 for 188 yards and caught 73 more yards. Roberts was 9-16 for 148 yards, Bates pulled in 86 markers, and Cass Love ran for 126 yards. Coleman led tacklers with 12 while Carter picked off a pair of passes. Jim Goss and Chaffin Triplett each recovered fumbles.

GAME 8:   LOUISVILLE (4-3) @ KOSCIUSKO (3-4)
                     LOUISVILLE 8 KOSCIUSKO 6
                     October 8, 2010

The Wildcats now hit the road to Attala County to face long-time foe Kosciusko. It was to be a big game for both as well as a hard-fought contest.

Louisville's lone tally came in the 2nd quarter when Ford found Bates from nine yards and then ran in the two-pointer. Kosy opened the 3rd quarter with a 74-yard drive and 21-yard Jeremy Williams dash. The two-point attempt was intercepted. The Whippets drove as far as the Cat 29 late but Chaffin Triplett recovered a loose football to seal the win.

Ford was 8-16 for 96 yards, Cunningham pulled in 56 receiving yards, and Schaffer rushed for 48 yards. *"I just knew we would put up 21 or 28 points on them. Man, in the second half, we weren't even coming close to scoring. We dropped some passes we were supposed to catch. The offensive line also didn't do what it was supposed to do. They played us hard"*.

GAME 9:   LOUISVILLE (5-3) @ CALEDONIA (1-7)
                     LOUISVILLE 31 CALEDONIA 0
                     October 15, 2010

The Confederates met the Wildcats only once. That ended in a 2009 beating by Louisville 49-6. This was a bit closer. In the opening frame, Louisville put up a pair of scores. Those came on Roberts passes of 30 and 11 yards to Bates. In the next, Roberts and Bates hooked up from nine yards while Love dove in from two yards to make halftime 25-0. Finally, a 3rd quarter Bates pass to Ford from six yards ended the scoring.

Roberts went 8-14 for 168 yards. Bates was 3-8 for 79 yards. Ford recorded 138 receiving yards, Montricus Goss led rushers with 70, and Desmond Underwood led tacklers with 13.

GAME 10:   LOUISVILLE (6-3) vs NOXUBEE COUNTY (8-1)
                     LOUISVILLE 12 NOXUBEE COUNTY 19
                     October 22, 2010

It was now time for a game fans on both sidelines had circled early in the season. Coach Tyrone Shorter's Tigers were 12-2 under now-Louisville Coach Miller. Now, they were second in 4A and 10th in The Super 10. Only two teams had yet to score on the Tigers. One was West Point in a 28-13 defeat.

When asked about playing his former team, Miller said, *"We talk about it. Louisville hasn't scored on Noxubee County in the last three years. We are trying to motivate them to change that. (One of our goals) was to be district champs and we are in a position to do that on Friday night"*. That was incorrect as Louisville not only beat Noxubee County in that span, but also scored in losses. The Clarion-Ledger picked NCHS 27-14.

The Tigers opened the game with a 63-yard drive and 1-yard Corey Williams dive to make it 7-0. Bates picked off a pass on their next possession to kill a threat and Ford eventually found paydirt on his 15-yarder to Bates. Halftime stood 7-6.

A short 3rd quarter punt allowed NCHS to score on a 26-yard Deangelo Ballard strike to Terrance Brarron. Daquarrius Mallard then *"stepped in front of a Ford pass and raced 84 yards for the touchdown"*. Now 19-6, the Cats put on a furious attempt to come back. Schaffer took the ensuing kick 82 yards and the game was 19-12. They were in good field position late but another interception killed the opportunity.

Schaffer led rushers with 67 yards and Bates pulled in 60 receiving markers. *"We had our chances. We just made some mistakes and didn't make the plays when we needed to. We just have to get ready to bounce back"*.

GAME 11:   LOUISVILLE (6-4) vs AMORY (3-7)
                              LOUISVILLE 40 AMORY 7
                              October 29, 2010

Once tough Amory, holding an all-time 4-3 record over Louisville since 1996, was now just 3-7. The Cats took out frustrations on them this evening.

Louisville was up 20-0 after a quarter and 28-0 at halftime. Jordan Fleming started with a 1-yarder while Bates (47) and Jim Goss (14) returned interceptions. In the 2nd quarter, Montricus Goss crossed from four yards and Roberts found Dalton Hudspeth for the two points. They made it 34-0 in the finale on a 22-yard Roberts toss to Desmond Goss. Amory garnered their lone tally after on a 13-yard Dylan Nicholson run.

Schaffer led rushers with 118 yards, Roberts was 8-15 for 89 yards, Goss led receivers with 54 yards and Jeremy Sangster led tacklers with nine. *"The main thing we wanted to do was get the seniors a lot of good reps on Senior Night and then turn it over to the young guys so they could get some experience headed into the playoffs"*.

GAME 12:   LOUISVILLE (7-4) vs GREENWOOD ELZY (7-3)
                              LOUISVILLE 32 GREENWOOD ELZY 8
                              November 5, 2010

Said Miller of first-time opponent Elzy, *"They are pretty good. They have a Dandy Dozen player... It is going to be a pretty good challenge for us. It's a good game to start the playoffs with in order to get the guys into the mood of playing big playoff games"*.

The Cats jumped out with an 11-yard Roberts toss to Bates followed by a 4-yard Schaffer run. Ford added a pair to two-pointers and Jim Goss added a safety to make it 18-0 after a frame. It was 26-0 at halftime thanks to Schaffer's 3-yard effort and another Ford two-pointer. Carter pitched in the finale on an 18-yard pick-six in the 3rd quarter. Elzy hit the board in the last frame.

Roberts was 17-26 for 262 yards, Ford hauled in 116 receiving, Schaffer ran for 47, Washington led tacklers with nine, and Carter, Cunningham and Jeremy Sangster each had interceptions. *"We made a lot of key defensive plays in key situations to keep the ball out of their hands. We knew going in that their coverage would benefit our receivers a whole lot. We have three great receivers and they just couldn't cover all of them"*.

GAME 13:   LOUISVILLE (8-4) @ LAFAYETTE COUNTY (12-0)
                              LOUISVILLE 12 LAFAYETTE COUNTY 44
                              November 12, 2010

Despite the larger teams played to open the season in preparation for other games, Lafayette County would prove the measuring stick. Finishing 13-2 the previous year, they entered 2010 ranked first in overall 4A and now sat undefeated. *"I think if we come out with the motivation and the intensity we had this past week, we will be OK. We are going into the playoffs battle-tested. We just need to turn it up another notch"*.

Unfortunately for the Wildcats, the journey ended on this November evening. LCHS jumped out to a 14-0 advantage on a 15-yard Demarkus Dennis run, another from Jamel Dennis from a yard and two Jackson kicks. The Cats didn't quit, adding scores from Schaffer on a 38-yard run and a 30-yard Roberts pass to Bates. Lafayette soon added another Dennis 1-yarder and the Jackson kick made it 21-12 at the break.

Jeremy Liggins assisted LCHS with 10 more points in the 3rd quarter on a 59-yard escape while Jackson knocked home a 24-yard FG. Their last came on a 1-yard Liggins run, a 30-yard D.Q. Reynolds fumble return, and a Jackson PAT. Roberts was 11-21 for 143 yards while Schaffer rushed for 60 more. Bates led receivers with 65 yards and Underwood led tacklers with 15.

"I think Lafayette is going to be tough to beat. They are very balanced and very disciplined. When you have a team that is consistent, disciplined and knows what it is doing and couple that with experience, it's going to be tough to beat them. Overall, looking back, we think we had a great season. We ended it by going to play the defending North State champions who went to Jackson last year and have it on their minds to go back. We have worked through a lot of things and I think gotten better as the season wore on".

2011 (12-2)

Second-year Coach M.C Miller's Wildcats were gaining momentum before running into Lafayette County in the post-season of 2010. *"Nobody expected us to get that far with what we had last year. But with our coaching staff and players improving all season long, we were able to make the second round of the playoffs".*

GAME 1:   LOUISVILLE (0-0) vs NEW HOPE (0-0)
                        LOUISVILLE 12 NEW HOPE 17
                        August 19, 2011

New Hope was always called *"No Hope"* as they won only once (1996) out of 13 previous meetings. This season would prove different for the Cats' lid-lifter. <u>The Winston County Journal</u> said after the final whistle, *"Both teams had opportunities to take over the game with neither capitalizing and dominating. It was the Trojans at the end, though, making just enough plays to by the Wildcats on their home field".*

The Cats struck first when Desmond Underwood recorded a 69-yard pick-six but the failed PAT kept it 6-0. The visitors struck back on a Jameel Johnson 27-yarder and Horace Carr two-pointer to make it 8-6. In the next frame, Louisville grabbed the lead on a Wyatt Roberts 65-yard connection with Desmond Goss. A failed two-point conversion meant their last points.

Meanwhile, the Trojans drove down and scored on a 12-yard Johnson run and Austin Oswalt PAT for what was the game's final touchdown. New Hope added a safety in the end to push the margin ahead of a potential game-tying FG. Roberts was 11 of 27 for 186 yards. Louisville led in total yards 237-158.

GAME 2:   LOUISVILLE (0-1) @ DEMOPOLIS, AL (0-0)
                        LOUISVILLE 24 DEMOPOLIS, AL 17
                        August 27, 2011

The Wildcats journeyed to Hoover, Alabama at Spain Park High School to take on first-time opponent Demopolis. The Alabama squad was as competitive in this one as others had been in pre-division contests.

Great defensive pressure caused an opening Demopolis fumble to Marcus Odom. Steven Hunt made it count from four yards later to make it 6-0. The Wildcats fumbled it back on their next possession and the Alabama squad tallied with a FG late in the frame. The defense caused another fumble at the Tiger 1 and Roberts dove in from there a play later. The two-pointer put Louisville ahead 14-3.

Another forced fumble later fell to Underwood. Goss then gathered in a 44-yard Roberts pass and the two-pointer put the Cats ahead at intermission by a score of 22-3. In the second half, the Cats forced a safety to put it 24-3. Then, Nick Shields picked off a Tiger throw but it went for naught. Midway through the contest, James Wilson crossed from two yards for the Tigers and the PAT made it 24-10. Tucker Jones then scored on a running play and the PAT proved the eventual final point.

Demopolis did get to the Cat 13 but the defense held on fourth downs with *"only a minute left in the game".* Roberts ran out the clock and Louisville escaped.

GAME 3:   LOUISVILLE (1-1) @ NESHOBA CENTRAL (1-1)
                        LOUISVILLE 53 NESHOBA CENTRAL 35
                        September 2, 2011

Neshoba Central, a nearly annual opponent from 1972 to 2007, was back on the schedule. They just defeated West Lauderdale 20-11 and hoped to turn history around as Louisville won 13 consecutive matchups. The contest put up their most points in a game since 2003 when they scored 55 against Canton.

The Cats jumped all over the Rockets with 26 unanswered points in the opening quarter. Roberts hit C.J. Bates from 24 yards, Roberts ran in from seven yards, Odom took an interception 48 yards to the end zone, a safety was added to the board, and Underwood took a fumble 35 yards to daylight. Neshoba Central scored twice in the 2nd quarter to ease the pain at 34-14.

Bates pulled in another Roberts throw from 38 yards and their two-point play increased their advantage. The two hooked up again from 63 yards to continue the pressure. Now, Steven Brown added a 63-yard pick-six while their last came in the 3rd quarter on Roberts' 5-yarder to Goss. The Dalton Hudspeth PAT was true.

Neshoba took advantage of reserves in the finale with three touchdowns to make it respectable.

GAME 4:   LOUISVILLE (2-1) @ KEMPER COUNTY (2-1)
                        LOUISVILLE 42 KEMPER COUNTY 18
                        September 9, 2011

It was now time to travel to another first-time opponent also called Wildcats. The DeKalb team lost their opener to Lumberton but came back to beat Nanih Waiya and Noxapater. This one was not close, either.

Dava'is Schaffer opened with a 1-yarder in the 1st quarter and then added Desmond Goss' 13-yard reception from Roberts and a Goss 3-yarder. With one KCHS tally, halftime sat 22-6. Roberts hit Bates from midfield in the 3rd quarter and the Cats added a pair in the finale. Schaffer ran one in from nine yards and Roberts hooked up with Hudspeth from 18 yards for the last. Roberts was 11-17 for 166 yards while Schaffer rushed for 94.

GAME 5:   LOUISVILLE (3-1) vs COLUMBUS (3-0)
                        LOUISVILLE 22 COLUMBUS 10
                        September 16, 2011

Ex-Louisville mentor Tony Stanford's 6A Falcons came into the contest undefeated with wins over New Hope, Aberdeen and West Point. The tough contest proved to be their first loss in what ended in a 7-4 campaign.

In the end, the Cat defense forced four turnovers to make it easier. Their first came via a safety from Anthony Davis and Chaffin Triplett on Cedric Jackson. After the kickoff, Schaffer dodged in from two yards and the two-pointer put it 10-0. In the 2nd quarter, Ricky Hackler hit a 25-yard FG to close the gap to 10-3 at halftime.

An early Columbus fumble ended in a 16-yard Roberts scoring run and 16-3 lead. The Falcons took advantage of a Jimmy Cockrell 37-yard pick-six and Hackler kick in the finale to add their last points. However, Schaffer escaped from 77 yards afterwards to end scoring. The defense held Columbus to just 129 of offense while Louisville notched 289. Schaffer rushed for 125, Roberts was 13-31 for 121 and Goss pulled in 55 yards receiving.

GAME 6:   LOUISVILLE (4-1) vs ABERDEEN (2-3)
                        LOUISVILLE 14 ABERDEEN 6
                        September 23, 2011: HOMECOMING

Homecoming in Winston County brought not only old alums back to Hinze Stadium, but also the Aberdeen Bulldogs. The opponent won only once (1956) in 22 games since 1937. This one was closer than expected.

On their second possession, the Dogs obtained their lone touchdown via a 1-yard run and failed two-pointer. Though a 2nd quarter Brown interception did not produce points, the Cats tallied on their next via Roberts' 33-yarder to Bates to tie it 6-6.

Anthony Davis forced a 3rd quarter fumble but Louisville gave it back via turnover. This time, Underwood picked off a Dog pass. That led to Roberts and Bates connecting from 28 yards and again for two points. Cass Love rushed for 66 yards, Roberts was 12-24 for 126, and Bates grabbed 81 yards in the air.

GAME 7:   LOUISVILLE (5-1) @ HOUSTON (3-3)
                        LOUISVILLE 26 HOUSTON 23
                        September 30, 2011

Coach Franklin Rogers had already improved the Hilltoppers' 2-9 mark from 2010. This one turned into yet another close matchup.

An early blocked punt by Louisville set up a Love 16-yarder to make it 6-0. Houston attempted to cut the lead, but Emmitt Dendy's 36-yard FG effort failed. In the 2nd quarter, Roberts hit Goss from 42 yards and it was 12-0. The half ended on Houston's safety for two points. The Cats added more in the 3rd quarter when Roberts found Bates from 47 yards. The two-point play put them up 20-2.

Houston kept fighting and found paydirt in the frame when Kantrell Murry crossed from six yards and the PAT put it 20-9. The Cats answered with an 11-yard Roberts toss to Bates for their last points. Meanwhile, Houston rallied with a 7-yard Quon Brown run and Dendy PAT. After holding, Murry escaped from 55 yards and the Dendy PAT ended scoring. The defense held Houston from attempting a FG to tie.

Roberts went 12-25 for 180 yards, Bates had 120 receiving yards and Schaffer led rushers with 21 yards. Hudspeth had three punts downed inside the Houston 10.

GAME 8:   LOUISVILLE (6-1) vs KOSCKUSKO (0-7)
                    LOUISVILLE 33 KOSCIUSKO 0
                    October 7, 2011

Coach Stan McCain's Whippets were not nearly as solid as their previous 7-6 team, sitting winless on the season thus far. Louisville was riding a four-game winning streak over Kosy after losing three straight tilts.

Schaffer led the 1st quarter charge with 4-yard and 32-yard touchdown runs and the Cat two-pointer made it 14-0. They added one more before halftime when Roberts hit Bates from 11 yards. Up 20-0 in the 3rd quarter, Love dashed across from nine yards while Roberts and Bates hooked up from 30 yards. Hudspeth added the final PAT.

Roberts went 9-19 for 173 and Schaffer rushed for 121 yards. The win moved the Cats to fifth in overall 4A rankings. Noxubee County, an upcoming opponent, sat second while Lafayette County was first at 8-0.

GAME 9:   LOUISVILLE (7-1) vs CALEDONIA (3-5)
                    LOUISVILLE 42 CALEDONIA 0
                    October 14, 2011

The Confederates under Coach Richard Kendrick were much better thus far than their 1-10 record of the previous season. Nevertheless, they were no match for Louisville.

According to the Caledonia report, Schaffer ran 68 yards on the first play of the game and followed it with a 1-yard dive after a Cat fumble recovery. Roberts then hit Goss from three yards to make it 21-0. In the 2nd quarter, Willie Carter drove across from a yard and halftime was 28-0. In the finale, and after a missed James Longmire FG effort by Caledonia, Brown returned a fumble 75 yards. Finally, Murray galloped 79 yards for the tally. Hudspeth was perfect on kicks.

Roberts was 4-6 for 42 yards and Goss pulled in 34 yards of receptions.

GAME 10:   LOUISVILLE (8-1) @ NOXUBEE COUNTY (8-1)
                    LOUISVILLE 14 NOXUBEE COUNTY 12
                    October 21, 2011

Coach Tyrone Shorter was complimentary of Louisville before the season started. *"Louisville will be a really strong team. They're solid. They have a great coaching staff"*. The Cat mentor served as NCHS head man from 1979 to 1987 and 1996-2009. This would be no easy meeting. Voted second preseason in 4A after a 13-2 record, they were now fifth in The Super 10. The Clarion-Ledger picked the Tigers 21-13 in the televised event.

Said Miller, *"It will almost be like I'm coaching against myself. Because, I know the players over there. We know they are going to be good. It is a great challenge for me because I knew they were going to be tough for the next few years. I know Coach Shorter is going to do a great job with them"*.

After pregame festivities including fireworks and flyovers, the Cat defense held on a crucial fourth down attempt. Louisville then drove the remainder of the field and scored on a 1-yarder by Schaffer and Hudspeth PAT. Odom caused a 2nd quarter fumble that led immediately to a 31-yard Roberts pass to Bates and Hudspeth PAT. With 2:00 before halftime, DeAngelo Ballard found Lamadrick Macon from five yards but their extra point attempt was blocked to keep halftime 14-6.

Noxubee closed the gap early in the 3rd quarter when Darrell Robinson found paydirt from a yard. Their two-point effort to even the game failed. From there, defenses stiffened. That included a late Tiger effort in the Cat red zone to seal the win. Bates was voted C-Spire Player of the Game for his 84 receiving yards and interception on defense. Roberts was 10-18 for 118 yards.

"It feels good to come back and beat them because I know they are a good ball club and I know they were quick. It was just a matter of us hanging in there".

GAME 11:   LOUISVILLE (9-1) @ LEAKE CENTRAL (4-6)
                    LOUISVILLE 37 LEAKE CENTRAL 0
                    October 28, 2011

Louisville was now second in overall 4A and tenth in The Super 10 poll. It was important to keep winning district games and they now traveled to meet Coach John Sallis' Gators now sitting with a losing campaign. Unfortunately, no write-up of game specifics is found. The only local notation is the final score and a look-forward to the playoffs.

GAME 12:   LOUISVILLE (10-1) vs SENATOBIA (5-5)
                    LOUISVILLE 42 SENATOBIA 14
                    November 4, 2011

The two teams met only in 2008 when Louisville ended their playoff run 20-7. Now it was time to take that first step toward Jackson.

Louisville opened the game with a 5-yard Roberts toss to Bates and Hudspeth PAT. On their second drive ending in the early part of the 2nd quarter, Love dove in from a yard and Hudspeth converted again. Senatobia then dotted the board on a run but missed the PAT to keep it 14-6. The Cats pounced back with Roberts' long TD pass to Goss. As the halftime clocked neared expiration, Roberts found Bates for the TD and the two-pointer put the board at 28-6.

The Warriors opened the 3rd quarter with a touchdown pass and two-pointer. As time expired in the frame, Schaffer dodged in from a yard and Hudspeth made it 35-14. In the finale, Nick Shields found a fumble and raced for the touchdown. Hudspeth's kick was true for the last point.

Roberts was 17-23 for 185 yards; Schaffer ran for 137, and Bates hauled in the same amount in receptions.

GAME 13:   LOUISVILLE (11-1) vs CORINTH (6-5)
                    LOUISVILLE 34 CORINTH 17
                    November 11, 2011

Another set of Warriors was next on the list. They just defeated Yazoo City in the first round 38-6. The Cats first played Corinth in 1939 and came out ahead, much like they did in their only other two meetings in 2007 and 2008.

Louisville showed dominance with 21 points in the opening quarter. Schaffer dashed in from 49 yards, Roberts hit Goss from 56 yards, and the two hooked up again after Louisville recovered a Warrior fumble. One Hudspeth PAT and a two-pointer added to the total. Corinth mustered only a FG in the frame. The only score of the 2nd quarter came from Corinth and their PAT made halftime 21-10.

The Wildcats hit the board again in the 3rd quarter when Roberts hit Schaffer from 24 yards and Hudspeth converted. Schaffer dashed 25 yards for another in the last frame while Corinth managed one more tally. Roberts went 10-17 for 153 yards while Schaffer rushed for 171 yards and passed the 1,000-yard mark.

GAME 14:   LOUISVILLE (12-1) @ LAFAYETTE COUNTY (13-0)
                    LOUISVILLE 6 LAFAYETTE COUNTY 28
                    November 18, 2011

Familiar LCHS was defending 4A champions and featured Dandy Dozen player Jeremy Liggins. Additionally, they were on a 29-game winning streak. The Clarion-Ledger thought LCHS best 35-14.

The only notation of game events noted that halftime stood 21-6. Liggins ran for touchdowns from 10, 7 and 34 yards. The lone Cat tally came on a 35-yard Roberts pass to Goss. Once again, Lafayette County had dashed Wildcat title hopes.

2012 (10-5)

M.C. Miller's Wildcats came into the season picked fourth in 4A preseason rankings. The fourth-year mentor still had reservations. *"We lost a lot of people on defense. The defense is what carried us last season. And this season we are going to be young due to* the fact we lost eight starters on that side of the ball. We will be a little young, but I think as the season goes along, they will get better. Offense should be our strong point this time. They didn't lose as many. (They) should be able to carry the defense for a while until the defense gets ready".

GAME 1:   LOUISVILLE (0-0) @ NEW HOPE (0-0)
                 LOUISVILLE 26 NEW HOPE 43
                 August 17, 2012

After the 2011 opening loss of 17-12 to New Hope, Miller was anxious about meeting them again for the lid-lifter. "New Hope has everybody coming back. This year they are expecting to beat us again. But we are going up there to beat them. Playing the big schools makes you better when you start playing the district".

This one marked the only time in history that New Hope bested Louisville in consecutive years. The home team jumped out with two 1st quarter scores to make it 13-0. The first was a 53-yard Brady Davis strike to Trae Collins and Jerrod Bradley PAT while the next was a 10-yarder from Davis to James Hill. Cass Love answered in the 2nd quarter from a yard and the PAT closed the gap. However, New Hope tallied again to put it 19-7 at halftime courtesy of a 67-yarder from Davis to Lee.

New Hope increased the lead in the 3rd quarter with a 32-yard Austin Oswalt FG while Wyatt Roberts bested the effort with a 10-yard option keeper to make it 22-13. The Trojans quickly responded with an ensuing Juaquin Weatherspoon 86-yard kickoff return to paydirt. Though the Cats blocked the PAT, it was still 28-13. Louisville came back with Roberts' 20-yarder to Lathomas Brown and the PAT put the score 28-20.

In the final frame, Desmond Goss crossed from six yards to put them just behind 28-26. However, a Roberts throw was picked off by M.J. Shirley and returned for a TD. Ryan Lee's two-pointer was also good. The same happened shortly after to end scoring. Both Love and Drew Lee rushed for 27 yards, Roberts was 15-37 for 235 yards, Brown had 76 receiving yards, and Jeremy Sangster led tacklers with 12.

GAME 2:   LOUISVILLE (0-1) vs RIDGEWAY, TN (1-0)
                 LOUISVILLE 42 RIDGEWAY 41
                 August 25, 2012

The Mississippi/Tennessee Showcase featured the Wildcats and the first-time opponent Roadrunners on a Saturday matchup in Noxubee County.

Like the opener, the opponent tallied twice for a 14-0 lead after a frame. They scored another 14 in the 2nd quarter before Roberts hit Dontae Jones from five yards and Hudspeth converted. The two hooked up again after from nine yards and Hudspeth connected. Now halftime sat 28-14.

Each tallied in the 3rd quarter. Goss pulled in a 5-yard Roberts throw for the Cats and Hudspeth made it 35-21. Down two scores going into the finale before Ridgeway scored yet again, the Cats stormed back. Roberts and Goss accounted for all three scores on passes of 78, 19 and 20 yards. With successful extra points, the Cats snatched the win.

Goss ended with 164 receiving yards, Roberts (a Clarion-Ledger Player of the Week) was 19-30 for 275 yards and six touchdowns, Love dashed for 131 yards, and Sangster led tacklers with 18.

GAME 3:   LOUISVILLE (1-1) vs NESHOBA CENTRAL (1-1)
                 LOUISVILLE 21 NESHOBA CENTRAL 3
                 August 31, 2012

It had been since 1993 that the Rockets bested Louisville. On this evening, the Cat streak of victories continued.

A Roberts touchdown called back on a penalty and an interception gave Neshoba an early 3-0 lead on their FG. Starting in the 2nd quarter, Louisville got back on track starting with a 1-yard Love run. Roberts and Goss then hooked up from 61 yards and the Roberts two-point pass to Jones made halftime 14-3. Now in the finale, Roberts hit Jones from nine yards and the PAT proved the last point.

Roberts was 13-21 for 196 yards, Love rushed for 83 yards, Goss pulled in 71 yards of receptions, and Sangster again led tacklers with 11 and a sack. Roberts was a Clarion-Ledger Player of the Week mention for his efforts.

GAME 4:   LOUISVILLE (2-1) vs KEMPER COUNTY (1-2)
               LOUISVILLE 49 KEMPER COUNTY 8
               September 7, 2012

This game against Kemper County, their second all-time, ended as the first did. Despite an opening fumble that went for naught, the Cats found paydirt on Love's 30-yarder and Hudspeth PAT.

After another defensive stand, Roberts scrambled in from 18 yards and Hudspeth again converted. As the quarter ended, Roberts hit Goss from 23 yards and Hudspeth put it 21-0. In the 2nd quarter, Tathomas Brown pulled in a 16-yard pass for the tally and Hudspeth was true on the kick. That 28-0 score held through the half.

Another KCHS fumble in the 3rd quarter recovered by Channing Hughes soon led to a 46-yard Demarcus Brooks dash. After the Hudspeth PAT, it was 35-0. Kemper muffed a Cat punt and Hughes fell on his second loose football. On the same drive but in the final frame, Brooks crossed from three yards and Hudspeth put it 42-0. The last Louisville score came on a 9-yard T.J. Hudson dash while Kemper County added a late touchdown and two-pointer to avoid the shutout.

GAME 5:   LOUISVILLE (3-1) @ COLUMBUS (2-1)
               LOUISVILLE 13 COLUMBUS 21
               September 14, 2012

Louisville visited Columbus with an undefeated 4-0 record all-time against the Falcons. But this meeting would end that streak.

After a scoreless opening stanza, LaWilliam Carter hit paydirt from a yard and Hudspeth converted. Columbus responded immediately with a 6-yard Trace Lee pass to Dalon Moore and a Greg Sykes PAT. Now in the finale, the Falcons tallied twice while the Cats could only cross once. Lathomas Brown dove in from a yard for six points and Kendrick Conner dashed 22 yards to daylight with Lee and Clark hooking up for the two-pointer. The last hurrah came with just seconds remaining on a 40-yard Roberts dash.

Love had 36 rushing yards, Roberts was 16-26 for 226 yards, Jones caught 126 of those, while Sangster led tacklers with 15.

GAME 6:   LOUISVILLE (3-2) @ ABERDEEN (3-2)
               LOUISVILLE 21 ABERDEEN 32
               September 21, 2012

The road tilt against the Bulldogs meant the end of non-division play. One of their three wins came against 2A West Bolivar 45-28. Louisville was 22-1 all-time against their foes in Aberdeen.

It proved another disappointment as the Dogs scored in the opener to make it 6-0 and added another touchdown and two-pointer in the second to widen the advantage. Back came the Cats with a Roberts 25-yarder to LaThomas Brown and Hudspeth connected. They tied it before halftime on a short Roberts toss to Hudspeth and the PAT was true.

An early Louisville fumble led to a 27-yard John Williams strike to Sammie Burroughs but the PAT failed. They added a Williams pass to Justin Lucas and now it was 26-14. On the first play of the 4th quarter, Sangster grabbed a Dog fumble and raced 38 yards to the end zone. Hudspeth's kick put it 26-21. However, the Dogs drove 70 yards ending on a 17-yarder from Williams to Lucas.

Love rushed for 48 yards, Brown had 80 yards receiving, Roberts was 18-35 for 258 yards, and Sangster had 15 tackles and a fumble return.

GAME 7:   LOUISVILLE (3-3) vs HOUSTON (6-0)
               LOUISVILLE 35 HOUSTON 14
               September 28, 2012: HOMECOMING

Coach William Cook's Hilltoppers were making big strides in 2012. The previous year they went a break-even 6-6. Now they were undefeated and looking for their first win over Louisville in ten all-time meetings.

Goss opened the game with his 19-yard dash and Hudspeth made it a quick 7-0. Love added more in the 2nd quarter from 22 yards after Louisville recovered a Houston fumble. Then, Roberts hit Goss from 40 yards and, with two more Hudspeth extra points, halftime sat 21-0 in favor of the Wildcats.

Love added another score in the 3rd quarter from three yards and Hudspeth converted. Houston finally hit the board in the finale on Sharone Wright's 22-yarder to Gavin McQuary. They then returned a punt 48 yards to make it 28-14. However, the Cats recovered another fumble and added a late 11-yard Love scoring run and Hudspeth PAT to put it away.

Love led rushers with 146 yards, Roberts was 12-25 for 209 yards, Goss had 96 receiving yards, and Raquel Graham led tacklers with 15. Both Dylan Nicholson and Nicholas Shields had interceptions, while Sangster, Julius Love, Channing Hughes and Shaquille Shumaker recovered fumbles.

GAME 8:   LOUISVILLE (4-3) @ KOSCIUSKO (2-5)
                                LOUISVILLE 28 KOSCIUSKO 20
                                October 5, 2012

After going 0-11 the previous year, Tyler Peterson now manned the Whippet team. He was familiar with the Kosy-Louisville rivalry after playing for the Cats in the mid-1990s and hoped dearly for a Kosy win this time.

It was the Whippets first into the end zone on a 1-yarder by Jabri Selmon but the blocked PAT kept it 6-0. Louisville stormed back with three touchdowns in the 2nd quarter. First was Roberts' toss to Goss from 31 yards, Anthony Gund blocked a Kosy punt to set up a 1-yard Roberts sneak, Roberts hit Jones from 30 yards, and Hudspeth provided PATs to put the Wildcats ahead at halftime 21-3.

Now in the final frame, Kosciusko added another touchdown but Goss took the ensuing put 76 yards to the Kosy 17. Roberts soon dove in from a yard and Hudspeth converted. The home team added their last with just seconds to go. Love led rushers with 108, Roberts went 5-16 for 94 yards, Jones had 38 yards, Sangster had 12 tackles, and Stefan Brown had an interception.

GAME 9:   LOUISVILLE (5-3) @ CALEDONIA (4-4)
                                LOUISVILLE 33 CALEDONIA 13
                                October 12, 2012

The Confederates under Coach Richard Kendrick were just 4-8 the previous year. Now they had a chance to better that mark with games yet to play. This one would be a big feather in their cap as they had yet to beat Louisville in three previous attempts.

Like other contests, the opponent jumped out with a 40-yard FG by Joshua Kugel and added a 2nd quarter Randy Randall run from 12 yards and a Kugle PAT. Demarcus Brooks took that kickoff 90 yards to paydirt and Hudspeth put it 10-7. Then, Roberts hit Goss from 33 yards to make halftime 13-10.

The two hooked up again to start the 3rd quarter from 50 yards. Caledonia answered with a 46-yard Kugel FG for their last points. Louisville went on a tear after when Roberts found Jones from 15 yards and Rodneal Smith for the two-points. Midway through the last frame, Love crossed from a yard to finalize scoring.

Love rushed for 43 yards, Roberts was 19-29 for 313 yards, Goss had 208 receiving markers, and Sangster led tacklers with 16. Anthony Gund blocked a punt.

GAME 10:   LOUISVILLE (6-3) vs NOXUBEE COUNTY (9-0)
                                LOUISVILLE 28 NOXUBEE COUNTY 41
                                October 18, 2012

Like so many years previously, the season really balanced on this particular game. Coach Tyrone Shorter, 10-3 the previous year, had eight starters back on both sides of the ball. Preseason he said of the Cats, *"They've got a great team coming back and we feel that they took it from us last year so we have it coming for them this year"*. This one effectively decided the 4-4A crown and The Clarion-Ledger gave the nod to NCHS 27-13.

Unfortunately for the home crowd, Noxubee put up 28 unanswered points in the opening half. Darrel Robinson accounted for all four tallies. First was his 4-yard run and two-pointer, next a 40-yard escape, a 15-yarder and finally from three yards. Roberts brought the Cats back in the 3rd with a 7-yarder to Jones and Hudspeth PAT, while Love opened the 4th quarter with his 4-yard score. Down 28-13, Roberts dove in from a yard and Darius Haynes' kick made it 28-20.

The Tigers and Robinson put up a pair of other touchdowns before Louisville could add their last on a 38-yard Roberts pass to Jones and his two-pointer to Goss.

Louisville had 409 offensive yards. Love rushed for 124, Roberts went 24-41 for 274 yards, Goss had 94 yards receiving, and Sangster put up a whopping 20 tackles. Brown had a pickoff, while Graham had a sack and Drew Lee had a blocked punt.

GAME 11:   LOUISVILLE (6-4) vs LEAKE CENTRAL (3-7)
                              LOUISVILLE 44 LEAKE CENTRAL 7
                              October 26, 2012

Leake Central was staying about like the 2011 team that finished 4-8 with a shutout loss to Louisville. Coach John Sallis was hoping that this one brought his team a big win and even that record for the current season.

The Cat defense stood tall early and recorded a safety to make it a quick 2-0. Then Roberts hit Jones from 35 yards and Hudspeth converted. Leake got theirs from 20 yards to make it a close 9-7 Cat lead. That was all they got as the Cats took over the game.

Love ran in from 45 yards, Corey McCullough added the PAT, and it was now 16-7. Sangster soon blocked a LCHS punt at their 15 and Roberts hit Hudspeth from there for the score. With just 3:00 left in the half, Roberts hit Goss from 45 yards and McCullough added the PAT.

It wasn't long into the 3rd quarter before Julius Love ran in and J.J. Waldrip grabbed a scoring toss from Roberts. With two McCullough kicks, it was the final 44-7. Love rushed for 161, Roberts was 7-13 for 109 yards, Goss pulled in 42 yards, and Sangster led with 12 tackles. Julius Love had a fumble recovery.

GAME 12:   LOUISVILLE (7-4) vs CORINTH (8-2)
                              LOUISVILLE 42 CORINTH 19
                              November 2, 2012

Corinth entered the playoff picture with a 20-14 win over Shannon the previous week. The Wildcats bragged of four straight wins all time, including the first in 1939. This one extended that streak of no losses despite their 8-2 year.

On the first Cat possession, Love ran in from eight yards and McCullough converted. He did it again later from 10 yards. A failed 2nd quarter Corinth FG effort gave Louisville the chance to allow Love a later 8-yarder and Roberts a two-point throw to Jones. Corinth answered late before halftime with a score, but with seconds left, Roberts hit Brown for a score and McCullough widened the lead to 28-6.

While Corinth battled bravely with a pair of touchdowns, Louisville matched them. An interception allowed Drew Lee an 8-yard dash. And, in the final frame, Roberts hit Goss for the last. In all, the Cats had 584 yards of offense. Love rushed for 191, Roberts was 21-28 for 305 yards, Goss caught 127 yards, and McCullough went 5-6 on kicks.

GAME 13:   LOUISVILLE (8-4) @ NEW ALBANY (8-4)
                              LOUISVILLE 38 NEW ALBANY 13
                              November 9, 2012

The previous week's 34-0 win over Gentry sent up the Cats' travel to New Albany to face the Bulldogs.

The Dogs actually found the end zone first in the oping frame on a 20-yard Day pass to Howard. Rainey provided the PAT. Louisville responded in the quarter to tie it when Roberts and Jones hooked up from 70 yards and McCullough's kick was true. The Cats poured on the coal in the 2nd quarter with scores via a 1-yarder from Love, a Shields fumble recovery leading to a 21-yard Roberts pass to Jones, their two-pointer, Roberts' 82-yard hookup with Goss and McCullough PAT, and 20-yard connection from Roberts to Jones. The McCullough kick put intermission 35-7.

After a scoreless 3rd quarter, Newsome found the end zone for New Albany from seven yards while McCullough nailed a 28-yard FG. Love ran for 67 yards and Roberts, a Clarion-Ledger Player of the Week, went 9-15 for 242 yards. Jones received 133 yards, Sangster recorded 22 tackles, and Dylan Nicholson and Lakendrick Vaughn had pickoffs.

GAME 14:   LOUISVILLE (9-4) vs HOUSTON (11-2)
                              LOUISVILLE 46 HOUSTON 21
                              November 16, 2012

A previous encounter this season with an undefeated Hilltopper team resulted in a Cat win 35-14. Now the two met again. The only other loss by Houston came to rival Noxubee County 40-13.

This one was similar to the previous meeting relative to differential in scoring. Future NFL star Chris Jones started the game for Houston with a 71-yard pick-six and the PAT put them up 7-0. Roberts came right back with a 73-yard hookup with Goss to make it a one-point game. Late in the 2nd quarter, Brown had a 43-yard pick-six, Christian Wraggs forced a fumble and Jalon Sangster took it back to the 5-yard line. Roberts crossed from four yards and it was now 18-7.

Jeremy Sangster immediately picked off a Houston pass to set up Roberts' TD throw to Goss. The two-pointer from Roberts to Jones was good to make halftime 26-7. Roberts snuck in from a yard in the 3rd quarter while Jalon Sangster added an interception for the 23-yard pick-six. McCullough's kick was true.

Now up 39-7, the Hilltoppers found paydirt twice on scoring passes. In between, Demarcus Brooks hit the end zone and McCullough converted and scoring was done. "Our defense came out and played hard. We've been getting better each game we play and it seems like we're peaking at the right time in the season. We have a young team and, at the beginning of the year, we struggled. But it's finally coming together. We knew by the middle of the season we would be better, and right now they are rising to the occasion".

Roberts went 10-17 for 201, Goss pulled in 158 receiving, Sangster had 11 tackles to match an interception and a fumble recovery, and J.J. Waldrip rushed for 58 yards. Both Goss and Roberts were Clarion-Ledger Players of the Week.

GAME 15:   LOUISVILLE (10-4) @ NOXUBEE COUNTY (15-0)
            LOUISVILLE 21 NOXUBEE COUNTY 41
            November 23, 2012

Louisville was just 4-9 against the Tigers in their last 13 meetings. That was a big turn 18 straight game before that point. As for the previous encounter, Miller said, "We have improved a whole lot since then. I know (they) have too. Those guys are good and the senior group is the last group that I coached so it's good that we are playing for a North State championship. But we are going over there to get it. We want (this) momentum to carry over into the game this Friday".

Unfortunately, the road to Jackson came to an end in Macon. Noxubee County started with a pair of Darrell Robinson touchdowns on 6-yard and 20-yard runs. Late in the opening frame, Roberts hit Goss from 50 yards and McCullough made it 14-7. Robinson then dashed 45 yards to make it 20-7. In the 2nd quarter, Roberts and Jones hooked up from 40 yards and McCullough put the game 20-14. On the kick, Robinson took it 85 yards to paydirt as halftime stood 26-14.

The last Cat touchdown of 2023 came in the 3rd quarter when Roberts and Jones hooked up from 40 yards and McCullough connected. In finale, Robinson crossed twice to end the affair and the season. Love ran for 46, Roberts was 11-33 for 170, Jones grabbed 80 yards of passes, Sangster had 22 tackles, Gund and Vaughn had a fumble recovery, and Nicholson an interception.

In all, Roberts hit on 205 passes for 3,247 yards with 34 touchdowns. Goss has 1,312 receiving yards, Love rushed for 1,261 yards, Sangster had 228 tackles, and Brown had five interceptions.

2013 (16-0)

The Wildcats under Coach M.C. Miller were now back in 4-3A. While The Clarion-Ledger had them 2nd in state 3A, the Mississippi Public Broadcasting Top 25 had Louisville 13th. Said Miller, "There are a lot of expectations. Everybody is looking at us. It's not going to be easy. Everybody will be ready to play us. We have a lot of players coming back; a lot of weapons on offense".

GAME 1:   LOUISVILLE (0-0) @ JIM HILL (0-0)
            LOUISVILLE 47 JIM HILL 0
            August 23, 2013

The only three meeting came between 1986 and 1991, each ending with Wildcat victories. In this one, the offense jumped out to a 40-0 halftime lead before letting reserves take the field for the second half.

In the opening frame, Malik Slaughter's tackle gave them a safety after a deep Cat fumble earlier. Corey McCullough tacked on a 32-yard FG and Demarcus Brooks crossed from a yard with McCullough converting. They put up four touchdowns in the 2nd quarter. Avonte Harris and Drew Lee in each got in from a yard, Wyatt Roberts hit Dalton Hudspeth from 10 yards and Travian Hudson from the same distance later. The last score came via a 15-yarder from Hudson to Dontae Jones.

Roberts was 13-23 for 198 yards while Hudson was 1-1 for 15 yards. Goss pulled in 104 yards. *"I think we played pretty well. They were up and ready to play. They were tired of hitting each other and ready to play somebody else and they showed it. We feel good about our offense and what it can do"*.

GAME 2:   LOUISVILLE (1-0) vs WILKINSON COUNTY (1-0)
                 LOUISVILLE 30 WILKINSON COUNTY 12
                 August 30, 2013

Wilkinson County was a first-time foe for the Cats but Miller was wary. *"Wilkinson County is pretty good. They beat Natchez 34-32 and they have a lot of offensive weapons. It's not going to be hard to get them ready to play. It never is when you are playing a good team. We need to be ready for the challenge"*.

Roberts opened the game with touchdown passes of 35 yards to Jones and 23 yards to Goss. McCullough was true on all four PAT efforts this evening. The team from Woodville came back with *"a long touchdown pass"* to put it 14-6. However, Roberts and Goss connected for a 60-yarder for the only tally of the 2nd quarter.

The visitors added their last in the 3rd quarter to make it 21-12. The last two scores came from Louisville on an 8-yards safety sack by Channing Hughes and a 38-yard escape by Books. Roberts was 18-27 for 258 yards, Brooks rushed for 89 yards, and Goss had 94 in receiving. Jeremy Sangster ran his tackle total to 21 along with 12 sacks.

"We got off to a good start, but they began to come back. I really think they took us a little lightly and didn't think we are as good as we are. After they got behind, they started playing better and made a ball game out of it".

GAME 3:   LOUISVILLE (2-0) @ NOXUBEE COUNTY (1-1)
                 LOUISVILLE 28 NOXUBEE COUNTY 6
                 September 6, 2013

Big-time foe Noxubee County was second in 4A while Louisville sat 1st in 3A. The history between the two had become one that either made or ended title dreams. *"It's a big deal. It's always been a big deal. These are two good programs who both want to win championships and both play hard and want to be the best. It's always a good, hard game with a lot of challenges"*.

The Cats scored in each quarter to take the win. First was a 3-yard Brooks run and the first of four McCullough kicks. NCHS came back with an 89-yard kick return and 1-yard Darrell Brandon dive to make it 7-6. Roberts and Jones hooked up from 25 yards in the 2nd quarter and Roberts found Brooks from 17 yards in the 3rd quarter. In the finale, Sangster added a 40-yard pick-six to seal the win.

Roberts was 12-26 for 143 yards; Jones pulled in 53 yards, Brooks rushed for 82 yards, and Sangster had six tackles.

GAME 4:   LOUISVILLE (3-0) vs PHILADELPHIA (3-0)
                 LOUISVILLE 19 PHILADELPHIA 6
                 September 13, 2013

The win boosted the Cats to 9th in The Super 10. Now back on the schedule was Philadelphia, ranked third in 3A. Most fans would not remember that these two squads met almost every season between 1915 and 1972, and with a few games after in 1981 and 1982. Now Coach Teddy Dyess had his Tornadoes 54-3 in regular season games in six years.

"Philadelphia has a good football team. They are quick and they have a good offense. They score more than 40 points a game. Playing good teams isn't going to do anything but help us. It will get us ready for the playoffs and just make us better".

While Philly was first on the board, back came Louisville with a 57-yard Roberts strike to Goss to tie it 6-6. The Tornados drove to the Cat 10 late in the half but the defense forced a FG that was unsuccessful. A Sangster hit forced a fumble picked up by Nicholas Shields and taken to the end zone for the next touchdown. Up 12-6, Louisville added their last on a 2-yard plunge by Roberts and McCullough PAT.

Roberts was 13-24 for 193, Brooks rushed for 103 yards, Goss caught 114 more and Sangster led tacklers with 15. Shields also had a pick in the game. "*I knew it was going to be a physical game. The main thing was to come out on top and we did that. We knew we had to stop their offense*".

GAME 5:   LOUISVILLE (4-0) vs COLUMBUS (2-2)
                                 LOUISVILLE 21 COLUMBUS 10
                                 September 20, 2013: HOMECOMING

The Wildcats now sat 7th in The Super 10. As for common opponent Columbus, Miller said, "*It's isn't getting any easier. I think Columbus is better than Philadelphia. They are big and strong. We have a lot of bumps and bruises (but) hopefully we can be ready for them Friday night*".

Conditions were not ideal for Homecoming as heavy rain poured on fans and alums. Brooks opened the game with a 95-yard kickoff return for the touchdown to set up scoring. Later in the frame, Roberts found paydirt from six yards and McCullough kicks put it 14-0. Columbus added a 2nd quarter 29-yard FG. In the last frame, Roberts and Goss connected for a 14-yard tally while Columbus crossed with less than a minute on the clock on Moore's 4-yarder to end it.

Roberts was 7-18 for 101, Goss had 61 receiving yards, Brooks rushed for 38 yards and Sangster had 13 tackles and caused two fumbles. Darius Dora and Nick Shields picked off passes with Dora also adding a fumble recovery. "*I think they handled it pretty well. The rain did make a difference. The ball got heavy and it was pretty hard to throw. Both teams were a little more cautious than usual because of the weather. Once we got ahead, we just tried to control the ball*".

GAME 6:   LOUISVILLE (5-0) @ KOSCIUSKO (2-3)
                                 LOUISVILLE 28 KOSCIUSKO 0
                                 September 27, 2013

After winning their first pair of games, the Whippets were now on a three-game losing streak. Miller noted, "*We want to win this game because it helps us get ready for the district. They are not winning right now but they still have a pretty good team. This is a big game for them (and) you know they are going to be ready to play*".

It was a quick 14-0 Cat lead on Roberts' 15-yard pass to Hudspeth and a 62-yard Goss punt return paired with McCullough kicks. Brooks put them up 21-0 at halftime on a 25-yard escape. In the final stanza, Roberts and Hudspeth connected from 10 yards and McCullough was true yet again.

Roberts was 16-34 for 190, Hudspeth had 74 receiving yards, J.J. Waldrip rushed for 81 yards and Sangster had 13 tackles. Dyquan Jordan had three sacks and an interception. Lakdendrick Vaughn also had a pickoff. "*We have been playing real physical and that has made the difference for us. We have been able to control things defensively and given our offense a chance to score*".

GAME 7:   LOUISVILLE (6-0) vs WINONA (1-5)
                                 LOUISVILLE 35 WINONA 0
                                 October 4, 2013

After a 5-7 campaign that featured a 46-21 loss to Louisville, Coach Ken Chandler's Winona squad was now with just a lone victory. Said Miller, "*Everybody is out there trying to beat you. They would love to do it*".

Roberts and Goss helped the Cats to a 21-0 lead after a frame on a 62-yard connection, a 20-yarder and finally a 30-yard Roberts pass to Hudson. The last of the frame came on Roberts' 3-yard toss to Goss. McCullough was true on all kicks on the night. Roberts was 6-9 for 179, Lee rushed for 38, Goss caught 85 yards, and Ty Hathorn (a Clarion-Ledger Player of the Week) led tacklers with 11 and a fumble recovery. Darius Miller and Shields also had fumble recoveries while Dora added an interception.

"We got a chance to play everybody. We needed a game like that. Our games have been so tough that we have had to play the starters for four quarters, so we were hoping to be able to rest some of the seniors and give our younger guys a chance to get some experience".

GAME 8:   LOUISVILLE (7-0) @ SOUTH PONTOTOC (3-4)
                              LOUISVILLE 63 SOUTH PONTOTOC 0
                              October 11, 2013

Coach Roger Chism's team was much-improved over the previous 1-10 season. The only two previous games in 2007 and 2008 ended in Wildcat wins. *"We just have to stay focused and take care of business. We can't fool around".* This proved the most Cat points in game since 1972 against Newton.

It was 37-0 after just one quarter of competition. Roberts hit Goss from 36 yards, Brooks ran in from 14 yards, Vaughn had a 54-yard pick-six, Hathorn took a fumble 47 yards to paydirt, Roberts hit Jones from three yards and Darius Miller had a safety. McCullough, good on all extra points, added a FG while Shields took a punt 47 yards to daylight. Hudson also tallied from 11 yards.

Miller added a second-half 81-yard pick-six and the team added a safety. Roberts was 8-14 for 129, Hudson rushed for 52 yards, Goss caught 88 yards of passes.

GAME 9:   LOUISVILLE (8-0) vs ABERDEEN (4-4)
                              LOUISVILLE 39 ABERDEEN 13
                              October 18, 2013

Aberdeen defeated Louisville the previous year en-route to an 11-3 season. This year, Coach Mark Bray's team was not as strong thus far. Said Miller, *"They have some skill people who can play. They are as quick as we are. They have a good team and are going to play hard. If we can (play hard), that will knock a little of the air out of them and put us in control of the game".*

Louisville scored on their first two plays via a 41-yard Roberts pass to Hudson and a 55-yard Brooks dash to match a pair of McCullough kicks. Aberdeen moved to the Cat 8 but Anderson Gund sacked them for a 10-yard loss. The Cats increased the lead on Roberts' 10-yarder to Goss and Hudson finding LaWilliam Carter for the two-pointer.

In the 3rd quarter, McCullough hit a 27-yard FG to make it 25-0. The Bulldogs moved to the Cat 6 but stuffed the opportunity with tackles, incomplete passes and a sack. Midway through the frame, Gund blocked a punt, picked it up and raced 18-yards to the end zone. Aberdeen finally scored on a Josh Williams 69-yard pass to Jerrick Orr. With :45 in the quarter, Gund picked up a blocked punt and took it three yards for another score.

With :05 remaining, Tramonte Prather dove in from two yards for their last tally. Books rushed for 68 yards, Roberts went 6-18 for 66 yards, and Hudson had 41 receiving yards. In all, Gund returned a pair of blocked kicks for scores and blocked a punt himself. Sangster and Rodneal Smith blocked other punts against a team and that had yet to give up one on the season.

GAME 10:   LOUISVILLE (9-0) @ KEMPER COUNTY (7-2)
                              LOUISVILLE 42 KEMPER COUNTY 6
                              October 25, 2013

After a 1-10 season, Kemper County looked to Chris Jones to lead the team. He dramatically turned them around thus far. *"Almost all of his coaching staff are my former (Noxubee County) players. It's his first year and he's doing a good job down there".* As for prospects of his Wildcat team ending undefeated, he added, *"It's not an easy thing to do. It's really not. Especially here at Louisville where we play tough teams in our non-district games. We look to win championships; going undefeated is just something a little extra".*

The Wildcats scored four unanswered touchdowns in the opening frame. Shields dashed 40 yards off a fake punt, Brooks dashed 43 yards, Roberts hit Goss from 18 yards and Lee escaped from 18 yards. McCullough hit on three PATs and another later. Sangster added a safety in the 2nd quarter while Goss caught another Roberts pass. Brady Anderson finished things with a 7-yard run.

Roberts was 9-16 for 116 yards, Brooks rushed for 82 yards and Jones pulled in 45 yards in receptions.

LOUISVILLE (10-0) vs NETTLETON (6-4)
LOUISVILLE 46 NETTLETON 0
November 1, 2013

The Wildcats played Nettleton only in 2007 and 2008 and both were victories. Though they went 2-9 the previous season, Coach Mike Scott did have them improved this season with six victories.

The Wildcats scored three times in the opening frame. Roberts had the first on runs of two yards and a 45-yard dash by Goss. McCullough connected on all three and two later. At halftime, it was 35-0 with scores from a Roberts' 60-yarder to Goss and a 43-yarder to Jones. In the 3rd quarter, Rodrick Roberts grabbed a 30-yard toss from Roberts and Hudson ran in the two-pointer. McCullough finished things with a FG.

Roberts (a Clarion-Ledger Player of the Week) was 15-22 for 273 yards, Brooks ran for 89, Goss pulled in 112 receiving yards, and Sangster led tacklers with five tackles. "They weren't quite as strong as we thought they were, but we played well. They played us hard. We just had the right things happen for us early in the game".

GAME 12:   LOUISVILLE (11-0) vs RULEVILLE CENTRAL (2-8)
LOUISVILLE 69 RULEVILLE CENTRAL 0
November 8, 2013

Ruleville was a first-time opponent for the now-third Super 10 Cat team, but Miller was not taking them for granted. "I really don't know anything about them. But they are just really very good. We just let the players know that this is the playoffs and everybody has a chance to beat you. You just can't slip up and have a bad game. We need to go out and take care of business early and get control of the game. We have to let them know that we are better than they are. We don't want to let them hang around".

The Cats scored four times in the 1st quarter and led 48-0 at intermission. Goss had a run from 10 yards, Roberts and Goss hooked up from seven and 32 yards and Roberts dashed in from eight yards. McCullough added 20-yard and 24-yard FGs to go along with nine extra points, Hudson ran in from seven yards, and Cam'ron Harrington had a 20-yard pick-six.

In the 3rd quarter, Waldrip crossed from eight yards, Avonte Harris did likewise from five yards in the finale and Keon Coleman ran in from 10 yards. Hudson rushed for 58 yards, Goss and Jones both pulled in 53 yards of receptions and tackles were split at five between Sangster, Jalon Sangster and Malik Slaughter. Roberts was 10-14 for 154 yards. This game was the most points scored by a Wildcat team since 1916 (Macon 79-7).

GAME 13:   LOUISVILLE (12-0) vs WATER VALLEY (11-1)
LOUISVILLE 56 WATER VALLEY 27
November 15, 2013

Water Valley was another first-time opponent, but no pushover as they sat with just one loss on the campaign. "They have a pretty good ball club. I know we will have to play to beat them. If we want to keep this going, we have to win here. They know they are playing a good team and we know we are... We are going to have to step it up and play four quarters. That's something we haven't had to do in quite a while..."

Details are scant, but Brooks put up touchdowns on runs of 50, 7, 3, 10 and 2 yards. Jones had three receiving touchdowns from 61, 10 and 22 yards. McCullough was true on all kicks this evening. In all, Brooks rushed for 118 yards, Roberts (a Clarion-Ledger Player of the Week) was 24-33 for 355 yards with Jones catching 165 yards of those.

GAME 14:   LOUISVILLE (13-0) @ CLEVELAND EAST SIDE (10-3)
LOUISVILLE 40 CLEVELAND EAST SIDE 6
November 22, 2013

While East Side was 0-2 historically against Louisville, this was to be no easy matchup as they sat with just three losses on the campaign. And, the game was in their home confines.

The opening frame ended 14-0 via Roberts' 49-yard pass to Goss and a 2-yard Harris dive. They made it 21-6 at halftime on Roberts' 26-yarder to Jones after Cleveland found the board for their only touchdown. Roberts added runs of one and two yards and hit

T.J. Hudson from 26 yards. McCullough added four extra points on the night. Roberts was 11-24 for 215 yards, Harris rushed for 54 more, and Jones caught 89 yards.

GAME 15:   LOUISVILLE (14-0) @ CHARLESTON (12-1)
                        LOUISVILLE 35 CHARLESTON 0
                        November 29, 2013

The Clarion-Ledger thought these were *"two of the top teams in 3A"* and picked the Cats 35-28. In 2007, Louisville knocked Charleston from the playoffs in their only previous meeting. Said Miller, *"They have a pretty good football team. They are big and they are strong"*.

This proved a win for the defense as they held their one-loss opponent scoreless. Louisville notched 21 points in the 2nd quarter to begin to pull away. The opening frame saw Roberts hit Goss from 17 yards to end a 76-yard march. McCullough was true on all five kicks. Sangster then dove in from a yard to make it 14-0.

Darius Miller caused a fumble and Vaughn took it 38-yards to paydirt. Roberts then found Jones from 15 yards to make halftime 28-0. The last tally came in the 3rd quarter from 35 yards between Roberts and Goss. Roberts (a Clarion-Ledger Player of the Week) was 10-16 for 251 yards and rushed for 82 markers. Goss had 109 receiving yards while Sangster led tacklers with 16. Miller had an interception on defense.

Said Miller, *"They always rise to the occasion. They did that against Charleston. We had to keep our players in the game. We had seen where Charleston had come back from way behind the week before and we had to make sure that didn't happen"*.

GAME 16:   LOUISVILLE (15-0) vs HAZLEHURST (14-1)
                        LOUISVILLE 30 HAZLEHURST 28
                        December 7, 2013: Veterans Memorial Stadium; Jackson, MS

The final game of the season came in Jackson against the defending 3A champions. Said Miller of the challenge, *"We are just going to have to get some of that determination back on our side. We're not done yet"*. The Clarion-Ledger thought Louisville best 35-27 while The (Biloxi) Sun Herald picked them 21-18.

An early Wildcat fumble allowed Dycelious Reese a 15-yard scoring reception from Jarvis Warner. Despite fumbling again, Louisville tied it in the frame with a 3-yard Sangster crossing. Jalon Sangster went on to intercept a Hazlehurst pass to put them at the Hazlehurst 25. One play later, Roberts hit Goss and McCullough converted his second of four extra points.

The opponent was not going away. They drove 80 yards and wrapped it was a 27-yard connection between Warner and Reese. Slaughter added a 2nd quarter safety to put Louisville up 16-14. They took the free kick to paydirt on four plays ending on a 19-yarder between Roberts and Jones. In the 3rd quarter, Hazlehurst cut the game to 23-22 on an 87-yard Reese run and a John Bridges catch for the two-pointer. Roberts added another tally in the frame on a 4-yard effort.

The Indians had a chance with 41.7 left when Warner and Dedrick Reese hooked up from 14 yards. Going for the two-pointer to tie, Slaughter raised his hands and knocked down the effort to seal a state title. Roberts (a Clarion-Ledger Player of the Week) was 12-22 for 159 yards and Goss pulled in 72 yards in the air. Harris led rushers with 110 yards, but Brooks put up 62 yards to push him to 1,016 on the season.

"We took what they were giving us. We talked about it coming into the game that we might be running the ball a lot and whatever they gave us, we were going to take whether it was running or passing".

Louisville now had yet another State Championship and ended sixth in the final Super 10 poll. M.C. Miller was named Coach of the Year while Jeremy Sangster was Defensive Player of the Year. First Team Offense Cats included Desmond Goss, Anderson Gund, Tyler Hickman, Demarcus Brooks and Wyatt Roberts. First Team Defense included Anthony Gund, Nicholas Shields, and Dalton Hudspeth.

Second Team Offense had Dontea Jones and Second Team Defense included Lakendrick Vaughn. Both Jeremy Sangster and Wyatt Roberts played in MS/AL All-State Game while Goss played in Bernard Blackwell All-Star Classic

2014 (9-5)

It was always tough to repeat as state champions, but this would be even tougher with the loss of some key starters. Said Miller, "*I still think we are going to be pretty good. We lost a lot of starters, but we have some good young guys. They just need some experience. I like the talent we have on the field*". One of the key returners was Mississippi State commit Dontae Jones, also named a Clarion-Ledger Dandy Dozen.

GAME 1:   LOUISVILLE (0-0) vs JIM HILL (0-0)
                   LOUISVILLE 41 JIM HILL 18
                   August 22, 2014

The Wildcats emerged victorious in all four previous meetings going back to 1987. Now they welcomed Jim Hill to Winston County to kick off a run for another title.

It wasn't the best start for Louisville as they held a slim 20-18 lead at intermission. It was a Cat lead 14-6 after a frame due to a 2-yard Demarcus Brooks dive and a 49-yard Brody Anderson strike to Chris Blair. Corey McCullough added both extra points. The only tally of the 2nd quarter came on a 12-yarder from Brody Burchfield to Demarcus Frazier.

They added 21 points in the 3rd quarter, the first on a 1-yard Anderson keeper. A fumble recovery at the Jim Hill 10 allowed Anderson to find Jones from there. The last tally came when Rod Jackson added a 55-yard pick-six. McCullough went 5-6 on kicks. Jones led receivers with 98 yards, Brooks rushed for 84, Anderson went 9-16-1 for 172 while Brody Burchfield was 4-7-1 for 40 yards.

"*They just didn't play very well in the first half. They were a little better than I thought, but we are so youthful and inexperienced and made a lot of mistakes. After I got through raising hell at halftime, we came out and played a little better. The defense stopped them and we made some things happen on offense*".

GAME 2:   LOUISVILLE (1-0) @ WILKINSON COUNTY (0-1)
                   LOUISVILLE 40 WILKINSON COUNTY 19
                   August 29, 2014

The win pushed Louisville to first in 3A polling. Now they traveled to play a Wilkinson County squad coming off a lopsided loss at Natchez.

Louisville's only tally of the opening frame came on a 64-yard pass from Anderson to Frazier and McCullough's first of five kicks. However, Wilkinson County ended the frame up 13-7. Though WCHS added another tally in the 2nd quarter, Louisville notched a 14-yard Burchfield to Jones score and a 14-yarder from Burchfield to Blair. Jalon Sangster added a safety sack and McCullough a 40-yard FG to make it 26-19 at intermission.

Charles Moore, an eight-grader "*scooped up a fumble and raced 20 yards to the end zone for a touchdown*". Finally, Burchfield ran in from five yards to end scoring. "*We are still making a lot of penalties and a lot of mistakes. It's not going to be pretty Friday night (against Noxubee County) if we keep doing that. We can't hope to make those kinds of mistakes and get away with it against Noxubee County*".

GAME 3:   LOUISVILLE (2-0) vs NOXUBEE COUNTY (1-1)
                   LOUISVILLE 14 NOXUBEE COUNTY 49
                   September 5, 2014

Miller knew that this meeting could spell trouble for his Wildcats. He even referenced it the previous week. He added about this one, "*They are going to come in here fired up and we are going to have to be ready to play. We are very young, we know that. But we need to start getting better*". The Tigers whipped Columbus after losing to Number One 6A Starkville in their opener. The Clarion-Ledger picked Noxubee 34-24.

Noxubee County was ahead of the hapless Wildcats 21-0 midway through the opening frame. Javarcus Walker took the opening kick 90 yards to paydirt and Zack Kaufman converted. They then blocked a punt and Kavorkian Brewer took it the eight yards for the next to make it 14-0. On their first offensive play, the drove 67 yards with Tamorris Conner finding Walker from 33 yards. Kaufman again converted.

Burchfield then found Frazier from 39 yards for a score, but Shannesy Sherrod scored from four yards and added a two-pointer to make it 29-8. Burchfield then hit Blair from 11 yards to put halftime 29-14. Conner opened the 3rd with a 9-yarder to Tarmarcus Silvers, Kaufman added a 24-yard FG, and Daveon Bell added a 75-yard pick-six.

Burchfield went 7-25 for 81, Anderson 6-12 for 45, Frazier caught 50 yards of passes, and Demester Harrington paced Cat rushers with just 13. The Tigers intercepted four Cat passes and held Louisville to just 21 ground yards while putting up 248 of their own. *"We were in a bad spot early and, really, we didn't play well. We had a bad game against a good team. We are going to have to keep working hard and get better. We have some good athletes. They just need some experience and have to listen to what we are telling them"*.

GAME 4:   LOUISVILLE (2-1) @ PHILADELPHIA (3-0)
                               LOUISVILLE 17 PHILADELPHIA 21
                               September 12, 2014

Unbelievably, the loss did not drop the Cats from the top spot in 3A. *"We have to come out against Philadelphia and show something. We know we had a bad game this week and have to got to work correcting it starting Monday"*. The Tornado were no strangers to the Louisville schedule. In fact, they once played almost consecutively from 1914-1972. They resumed meetings in 1981-82, but had since fallen from the schedule. Overall, it was never an easy affair.

Philly was first to the board on a Kenshon Henderson 2-yarder to end an 84-yard march. Rod Jackson then picked off a Tornado pass and raced 94 yards to daylight. McCullough's PAT put them up 7-6. He added a 22-yard FG and, thanks to a turnover, Burchfield found Jones from 13 yards just before halftime to make it 17-6.

However, the 3rd quarter was not kind as Philly went 75 yards with Donerrius Poe finding paydirt from two yards. Jonathan Edwards hit Kaylon Gray for the two points to make it 17-14. Now in the finale, the home team got the break they needed via a blocked punt recovered by B.J. Boler. Poe dove in from a yard and John Smith converted with the kick. Edwards picked of a Louisville pass with :30 remaining *"as the Wildcats were moving across midfield"*.

Philly had 324 rushing yards. For Louisville, Brooks led with 72 yards of the 90 total rushing yards. Burchfield was 12-25 for 119 and Jones pulled in 42 yards in the air. *"We played hard, but we should have won that game. If we handle that punt, everything could have been different. We better be ready for Columbus. We came back and worked hard after Noxubee and we are just going to have to come back and work hard this week. We have some improvement to make and we need to do it"*.

Philadelphia Coach Teddy Dyess added, *"I've been coach here for eight years and this is our biggest regular season win"*.

GAME 5:   LOUISVILLE (2-2) @ COLUMBUS (0-3)
                               LOUISVILLE 20 COLUMBUS 43
                               September 19, 2014

This seemed to be an easy win not just because of their winless season, but because the Cats won four of the only five meetings with the Falcons. It was not to be.

The Falcons jumped out with a 24-yard Kylin Hill run, a 3-yarder by Jay Jay Swanigan, and a 2-yarder by Keondre Conner to go along with a safety to make it 22-0 after a frame. Swanigan tallied again in the 2nd quarter from four yards and Hill added a 20-yarder in the 3rd quarter to build a 36-0 lead.

In the finale, the Cats came alive with a 1-yard Burchfield dive, a 4-yard run by Devonte Glenn, and a 37-yard Anderson pass to Michael Frazier. McCullough converted on two of those. Columbus added a 4th quarter 32-yard run by Rod Hogan. Burchfield was 10-18 for 119 yards and led rushers with 37 yards while Anderson was 4-6 for 59. Jones caught 71 yards in the loss. Columbus rushed for 304 and passed for 110 in the win.

"We have come to the conclusion that it's just a lack of experience and understanding of how to be ready to come out and play. It just seems like it takes us a while to get going and when you start slow against good teams, you get behind. I'm not sure if we have stopped a team on their first possession all year".

GAME 6:   LOUISVILLE (2-3) vs KOSCIUSKO (4-1)
                               LOUISVILLE 14 KOSCIUSKO 21
                               September 26, 2014

Before the contest, Miller noted that *"Kosciusko has a really good football team. It will be another challenge for us. But that's what we are looking for. We are playing solid ball clubs and a strong schedule that we just aren't ready for yet. But if we were playing a weak schedule and winning, we wouldn't see where we are and what we have to improve upon. With the teams we are playing, you find out where your problems are"*. Kosciusko was primed for a rivalry win after dropping seven in a row to the Wildcats.

The Cats actually held a 7-6 halftime advantage before caving in the second half. Anderson dove in from a yard and McCullough provided those points for the lead. Their last came on an Anderson pass to Devon Lee but they failed in recovering the on-side kick to give them a chance to snatch the comeback. McCullough was true on both kicks.

"I was really hoping we would have two more wins. I think Noxubee County and Columbus really beat us, but we should have won Philadelphia and Kosciusko. But that part of the season is over with. We are going into district play and that's what really matters. We are getting better each game. If we were losing and getting worse, I would be mad about it, but these young guys are beginning to learn".

GAME 7:   LOUISVILLE (2-4) @ WINONA (1-4)
                                LOUISVILLE 39 WINONA 0
                                October 3, 2014

Regardless of the fact that Winona sat with just one victory thus far, nothing was taken for granted. Miller was a bit more optimistic, saying *"It should be a tough game ... but if we play well, we should be able to handle it"*. The Wildcats did just that.

The Wildcats held a 16-0 lead after a frame on a 5-yarder by Brooks, a 39-yard Burchfield strike to Blair, two McCullough extra points and an Isiah Latham safety. It went to 30-0 at halftime with Burchfield finding Demarcus Frazier from 14 yards, and Brooks hitting paydirt from nine yards.

The 3rd quarter found the Cats marching 88 yards and ending it on a 1-yard Burchfield dive while Dylan Gill *"was credited with a safety"*. Brooks rushed for 72 yards, Burchfield was 6-14 for 113, Anderson was 4-4 for 87 yards, Devonte Glenn grabbed 87 passing yards, and McCullough was true on all kicks. Defensively, Lajordin Anderson led with 13 tackles while Julius Love had a pair of sacks and a forced fumble. Kamron Jackson had an interception.

"The offense really moved the ball for us the first time. We really haven't been doing that, so that was good to see. We made some stops on defense, so overall we played pretty well. We just need to continue to get better. I think once we get a little success and start to feel a little bit better about ourselves, we will continue to improve".

GAME 8:   LOUISVILLE (3-4) vs SOUTH PONTOTC (2-5)
                                LOUISVILLE 52 SOUTH PONTOTOC 0
                                October 10, 2014: HOMECOMING

Concerning this one and the upcoming Aberdeen tilt, Miller said, *"those two games right there will probably tell who is going to win the district. We have to go out and play a real solid game and get ready for Aberdeen"*. The two teams met only three times historically, but each ended in a Wildcat victory.

It was a quick 21-0 halftime lead after a frame courtesy of a 34-yard Burchfield pass to Frazier. McCullough converted his first of seven kicks. Then came Brooks' runs of 21 and 76 yards to strengthen the advantage. In the 2nd quarter, Anderson found Blair from 11 yards and McCullough's 47-yard FG put halftime 31-0.

Herrington ran in from 30 yards in the 3rd and Keon Coleman did the same from 55 yards. The final tally came in the 4th quarter on a 15-yard Pervis Frazier dash. Brooks rushed for 156 yards on just six carries.

GAME 9:   LOUISVILLE (4-4) @ ABERDEEN (6-2)
                                LOUISVILLE 37 ABERDEEN 6
                                October 17, 2014

The Bulldogs were not to be taken lightly on the road as they sat fifth in 3A voting. However, the Bulldogs were losers to Louisville in the last 23 of 25 games. To make it more confusing, a win over Louisville and another over Kemper County gave Aberdeen the region title. The Clarion-Ledger picked Aberdeen 26-23 since Josh Williams had already throw for 1,268 yards and 13 touchdowns and the game was in Aberdeen.

"This is what we have been playing for. We hoped we could work things out and get ourselves to this point. Now we just have to take care of our own business. You want to win all of your games, but the district games are the ones that matter most". Louisville proved those who picked totally wrong.

While Aberdeen hit the board with six points to open the contest, the Cats came back with 37 to answer. In the 2nd quarter, they "hung 24 points on the board". Anderson hit Glenn from seven yards, McCullough nailed a 38-yard FG, Brooks dashed seven yards, and Anderson found Glenn from 75 yards. In the final frame, Anderson and Frazier connected from 44 yards while Coleman ran in from four yards.

Brooks rushed for 168, Anderson went 11-13 for 256, and Lee pulled in 131 receiving yards. Jones suffered a separated shoulder and was now lost for the season. Said Miller, "They looked like they really wanted it on Friday night. They looked more like the old Wildcats. They were real aggressive from the start. We had to beat Aberdeen to stay in the district and they went out and did it".

GAME 10:   LOUISVILLE (5-4) vs KEMPER COUNTY (7-2)
                  LOUISVILLE 31 KEMPER COUNTY 24
                  October 24, 2014

A win over Kemper County, a team that had lost three consecutive games to the Wildcats, was imperative. "This game will be for the championship as far as we are concerned. We need to beat Kemper County to win the district outright. With every win, we get more confidence".

Louisville was first on the board in the opening frame on a 23-yard Anderson toss to Blair. Kemper answered with Eric Clark's 8-yard scamper and a Devonte Scott two-pointer. Then, they added a 3-yard Scott dash and Otis Cross two-pointer. McCullough notched a pair of FGs, one from 47 yards, to make halftime 16-13.

Scott added a 3rd quarter touchdown from 13 yards and another two-point conversion. Now 24-13, the Cats made their comeback. McCullough started with his third FG. Now in the finale, Brooks escaped from ten yards and Anderson converted the two points to tie it 24-24. With just :11 remaining, Anderson snuck in from a yard for the win and outright divisional championship.

McCullough hit FGs of 30, 47 and 25 yards, Anderson was 17-28 for 160, Frazier led with five receptions and Brooks rushed for 87 yards. "It was a good comeback and something we needed. Kemper had a good team and they played us hard. We have just got to keep it going. It is the first time we have had a close game like this and come out on top. That's a big effort for us".

GAME 11:   LOUISVILLE (6-4) @ NETTLETON (3-7)
                  LOUISVILLE 35 NETTLETON 6
                  October 31, 2014

Nettleton was yet another opponent without a win over the Wildcats after three attempts. This was not their best year but the game was in their confines. "We really aren't where we should be. We are still really young and we are small. When you start playing some strong teams, that's tough".

It was never in doubt as the Cats jumped out to a quick 35-0 lead. Brooks darted 69 yards for the first touchdown, added a 37-yarder, Coleman notched one from 17 yards and three kicks put it 21-0. Then Anderson and Frazier connected from 65 yards while the last came on an 80-yard march capped by Coleman's 1-yard dive. McCullough was true on all attempted extra points.

Brooks ran for 110 on four carries, Anderson was 3-5 for 83 yards, Burchfield was 2-3 for 53 yards and Frazier had 105 receiving markers. "I wish they had been a little better than that. We needed our work and really weren't able to get it. I wasn't able to play the starters as much as I would have liked to".

GAME 12:   LOUISVILLE (7-4) vs HOLLY SPRINGS (6-5)
                  LOUISVILLE 38 HOLLY SPRINGS 8
                  November 7, 2014

Holly Springs was an unknown quantity for the Wildcats. Said Miller, "Those seniors are going to have to step up and encourage the other guys. They know what the playoffs are all about and what it takes to win. We are just going to have to continue to get better each week".

Louisville started quickly with a 6-yard Brooks run to finish an 85-yard march. Anderson then found him from 30 yards and McCullough booted both for a 14-0 lead. McCullough added a 29-yard FG to widen the advantage. The last trio of touchdowns came on a 68-yard hook-up between Anderson and Brooks and Coleman runs of 17 and 6 yards.

"We didn't start off like we should have started. We picked it up and played better In the second half. I need them to get going from the top of the game and play hard. That's a problem we have had all year. That's eventually going to get us. In fact, it has already caught us a couple of times this year. I know we are young, but we have to get ready to play from the first snap".

GAME 13:	LOUISVILLE (8-4) vs MOOREVILLE (8-3)
	LOUISVILLE 42 MOOREVILLE 28
	November 14, 2014

First-time foe Mooreville won their second-round playoff game 35-0 over Greenville O'Bannon. Though significantly better in season records than the previous opponent, Miller noted of the Troopers, "They have a pretty fair team".

Brooks opened with touchdown runs of four and 81 yards and McCullough put it 14-0. Anderson and Brooks hit from 25 yards while Frazier took a punt 59 yards to the end zone. In the 2nd half, Dylan Gill added a 51-yard pick-six while Coleman dodged in from five yards. Anderson was 11-18 for 130 yards and Brooks rushed for 182. Blair had 39 yards on receptions.

"I thought the offense played well and, as a group, the whole team did a good job. We are getting better".

GAME 14:	LOUISVILLE (9-4) @ CHARLESTON (10-2)
	LOUISVILLE 13 CHARLESTON 35
	November 21, 2014

Charleston may have been winless all-time against Louisville, but this season was different. Their only two losses came to 6A Olive Branch and 4A Noxubee County, both by a 26-16 final. The Clarion-Ledger picked Charleston 24-20 since the home team was averaging 329 running yards per game.

"They are a good running team. They have the same boys running the ball they had last year but we don't have the same boys trying to stop them. But we have gotten better on defense and we have been playing hard and giving it all they have. I can live with that. It should be a good game".

The only notation of game activity came from The Winston County Journal, saying "LHS was actually in the game (by) cutting the Tiger lead to 21-13 before the winners took advantage of turnovers to pull away and take the win". The Clarion-Ledger noted that Javonte Jones ran for 223 yards and three touchdowns. Miller said, "It was close for a while, but we made a few mistakes. They are a more experienced team than we were and it showed. The one thing I like about this team is their attitude. They played hard and kept a good attitude. That will really help us in the future if they can keep that up".

As for the season, he continued, "We have really improved a lot this season. If we had been playing at the start of the year the way we were at the end, we would probably still be playing. They really worked hard and got the things corrected that needed to be corrected. It was really just about getting experience and learning what to do and how to do it. We had three 9th graders, an 8th grader and a bunch of 10th graders out there. Even some of our seniors really didn't have a lot of experience".

2015 (8-5)

Coach M.C. Miller returned for his sixth season in Louisville with a Wildcat team picked fourth in The Clarion-Ledger Top Five pre-season. He suffered through lots of youth and inexperience the prior season but his squad ended with a respectable 9-5 campaign. "Our strong point is that we have some good skill people. We are going to be able to run and throw the ball. We are going to throw the ball but probably not as much as we used to. We want to be able to run the ball, as well. We have some good running backs".

He still scheduled tough teams as openers to prepare the team for district play and post-season. *"That's what we do every year. We are used to it. Everybody on our schedule is looking good. We are just going to have to bow up and play".*

GAME 1:   LOUISVILLE (0-0) vs NEW HOPE (0-0)
                                   LOUISVILLE 20 NEW HOPE 3
                                   August 21, 2015

After a long and successful matchup with New Hope, the opponent came back with back-to-back wins over the Cats. It was now time to see what 2015 held.

Five turnovers by the guests spelled disaster for the Trojans. Louisville led 7-3 after a stanza on two Keon Coleman runs of 13 and 11 yards, a Corey McCullough FG and his extra points. McCullough later added another FG to ice the win.

Daylen Gill led tacklers with 12, Isaiah Latham had two interceptions, and both Gill and Montravious Johnson recovered fumbles. The Cats had 320 offensive yards (171 rushing). Brody Burchfield was 12-20 for 149 and Chris Blair led receivers with 70 yards.

"We played OK at times but we need to continue to improve on offense. We need to get the ball into the end zone. The lightning delay hurt us a little bit. We kind of got out of rhythm. Our defense is small and they were able to move the ball on us some, but we were able to get some stops and make some plays when we had to".

GAME 2:   LOUISVILLE (1-0) vs WEST POINT (0-0)
                                   LOUISVILLE 7 WEST POINT 46
                                   August 28, 2015

After playing consecutively from 1966 to 2006, powerful West Point was back on the schedule. The Clarion-Ledger picked them 27-14. Said Miller, *"We know West Point is going to be a tough challenge because they always are. They are going to be physical and try to control the line of scrimmage. It is going to be an old-school type of game".*

West Point opened with a 39-yard Marcus Murphy bomb to D'Marrio Edwards and Joe Garcia put them ahead 7-0. The Cats tied it 7-7 late in the 1st quarter on a 38-yard Coleman pass to Devon Lee and McCullough PAT. West Point, however, was relentless. Murphy's 3-yarder and their PAT put it 14-7 and it snowballed.

Murphy added a 57-yard escape, Trey Brownlee added a 38-yard pick-six, and Murphy ran in from 20 yards. They finished the game with second-half scores on Andre Lane's 10-yarder and a 1-yard Trevino Harris dive. Burchfield was 8-24 for 104 yards, Demarcus Fair caught 62 yards in the air, and Kendrick Holmes paced rushers with 28. LaJordin Anderson led tacklers with 10.

Said Miller afterwards, *"We have Kemper County next week and we have to work and prepare. We have got to put this one behind us and move on from here. That's all you can do. That's what you have to do. That's a good offensive line they have. They went right down the field on us and we couldn't make any tackles. Any time we got down to third down, we just gave up a big play".*

GAME 3:   LOUISVILLE (1-1) @ KEMPER COUNTY (1-1)
                                   LOUISVILLE 27 KEMPER COUNTY 20
                                   September 4, 2015

The Wildcats had to flush the previous week performance and prepare for Kemper County, a team they four straight times.

The home team hit the board 6-0 midway through the 1st quarter via a 17-yard Eric Clark strike to D.J. Clayton. McCullough cut into the lead with a 39-yard FG but KCHS came back with a 15-yarder by Elijawhan Cole to make it 12-3. The Cats bounced back with a late tally on Burchfield's 30-yard pass to Blair and McCullough kick. Kemper had a chance to widen the lead at halftime but their 24-yard FG effort was unsuccessful.

In the 3rd quarter, McCullough nailed a 39-yard FG to put them ahead and Keon Coleman crossed from two yards. Then, Latham recorded a 31-yard pick-six. Down 27-13, Jameez Sims came in to lead an 80-yard drive ended by Cole's 2-yarder. Their two-pointer to Clayton made it a one-score game. They tried a valiant comeback but Jay White picked off a Sims pass. With one opportunity left in the game, Daylen Gill knocked away a potential TD throw to ice it.

Burchfield was 9-16 for 106, Coleman had 26 receiving yards and led rushers with 36 yards. In total, the Cats had 175 offensive yards and nine first downs. *"They were* blocking us and kicking us out. They were getting four or five yards every play. At halftime, we had to change that. We got the right personnel in there and went to a 40 defense and we faced up over their guys so that they couldn't double us up".

GAME 4:   LOUISVILLE (2-1) vs PHILADELPHIA (2-1)
                       LOUISVILLE 51 PHILADELPHIA 0
                       September 11, 2015

The previous year, Philly picked up their first win over Louisville since 1982. It was time for payback against an old rival. The Clarion-Ledger picked the Wildcats 28-13.

Devante Glenn found the end zone before many could find seats as he took the opening kick 87-yards for "all the points they would need". That propelled the Cats to a 28-0 halftime advantage. Pervis Frazier found Glenn from 20 yards, Demarcus Frazier ran in from 16 yards, and Kenneth Knowles crossed from seven yards to match the extra points. Midway through the 3rd quarter, Frazier hit Lee from 70 yards, Tyrone Stallings blocked a punt for a safety and Lee raced 70 yards for yet another tally.

William Sullivan added the last points on his 1-yard dive and McCullough was true on this and all other kicks. Burchfield was 6-8 for 132, Lee led receivers with 70 yards, Pervis Frazier led rushers with 26 yards, and Stallings paced tackles with nine. He also had three sacks, a forced fumble, two blocked kicks and a safety. Latham had an interception and a fumble recovery.

"We finally came around. We have been starting out slow and we wanted to come out and play hard against them. I didn't think we were going to beat them that bad. I looked at the film and knew we had a better team. I felt like we were going to win, but I didn't know we were going to beat them like that".

GAME 5:   LOUISVILLE (3-1) vs LAFAYETTE COUNTY (3-1)
                       LOUISVILLE 10 LAFAYETTE COUNTY 27
                       September 18, 2015

This one proved a real test as to Wildcat strength. Despite an 8-5 record the previous year, Lafayette County came in third preseason in The Clarion-Ledger Top Five. "It will be another tough game against another tough team. We will have to be ready and we will need to play well to have a chance to beat them". The same newspaper picked Lafayette County 24-14.

Lafayette County was already up 20-0 at halftime on a 2-yard Tyrell Price run and his two scores in the 2nd quarter. Those came on runs of 17 and five yards to go along with a pair of Robbie Langley extra points. The extended the lead to 27-0 after three quarters when Tay Tay Owens found paydirt from 11 yards and Langley converted.

Louisville put up their only points in the 4th quarter on a 49-yard Latham pick-six, a McCullough PAT and his later 34-yard FG. LCHS led in yardage 431-100. Pervis Frazier was 3-9 for 25 yards while rushed for 40 more. Gill paced tacklers with 7.5. "We played better in the second half. The defense played pretty well most of the game but we did have problems stopping their big running back".

GAME 6:   LOUISVILLE (3-2) @ AMANDA ELZY (1-4)
                       LOUISVILLE 44 AMANDA ELZY 2
                       September 25, 2015

Miller was not very impressed by first-time opponent Amanda Elzy. "It's very important that we win and get some momentum heading into the district. I think they are an average team, but we need to play well".

It was already 21-2 after a frame with Latham's 46-yard interception return setting up Coleman's 25-yarder. McCullough was true on his first of six. Gill then had a 36-yard pick-six and a later 24-yard fumble recovery and return. The lone Elzy score came on a sack on Pervis Frazier. Jakevious Whitfield added a safety after and Frazier dashed in from seven yards. Anderson then took a kick 38 yards to daylight and, finally, Ken Holmes dodged in from five yards.

"I thought we played better. I need the offense to play a little better, but it looks like the defense is improving. We have most everybody back now and we are getting better every game. We are getting into region play now (and) this is what matters". Frazier was 6-14 and Coleman rushed for 53 yards.

LOUISVILLE (4-2) vs LEAKE CENTRAL (4-2)
                    LOUISVILLE 22 LEAKE CENTRAL 9
                    October 2, 2015: HOMECOMING

Homecoming in Winston County brought alums and fans as well as a prior-year 6-5 squad yet to defeat the Wildcats in two attempts.

Leake County was first on the board via a safety but the Cats came back with a 26-yarder from Frazier to Lee and his two-pointer to Mike Frazier. Holmes then added a 3-yarder and McCullough added the first of his two extra points to make it 15-2. The Gators made a *"late surge"* starting with a 30-yard scoring pass and PAT. Back came Ken Holmes with :35 left on an 8-yarder to seal the home victory. Frazier was 13-22 for 151 and Coleman rushed for 28 yards.

"From here on out we are playing pretty good football teams and we are just going to have to play better. The offense struggled and that leaves the defense on the field too much. We had homecoming and that might have something to do with it. You have so many distractions and they have their minds on a lot of different things, but homecoming is over. We have to get ready to play".

GAME 8:   LOUISVILLE (5-2) @ CALEDONIA (4-2)
                    LOUISVILLE 38 CALEDONIA 13
                    October 9, 2015

Caledonia was next on the list, albeit on the road. They faced the Cats four other times but none came out to their advantage. The previous year, they were 6-6. Said Miller, *"They like to throw the ball, but they have been running it more as well. They have a good receiver and a good quarterback".*

Caledonia jumped out to a 6-0 lead on Caleb Comer FGs of 33 and 25 yards. Louisville stormed back on a 22-yard Pervis Frazier dash and McCullough PAT. Caledonia also responded with a 43-yard Zion Ford scoring run but Kenneth Knowles soon crossed from 10 yards. Demarcus Frazier added the two points to make it a 15-13 contest. It was all Wildcats thereafter. Pervis found Demarcus from 18 yards and McCullough added a 43-yard FG. In the 3rd quarter, the Fraziers connected from 16 yards while Pervis added a 10-yarder later.

Frazier was 13-17 for 241 yards and rushed for 83 more. Lee caught 134 yards of passes and Dylan Gill led tacklers with 9.5. *"We are playing OK. We just haven't come together as an offense. We have got to keep our defense off the field. Also, we are banged up. We just don't know who will be healthy enough to play. But we have to go and play with what we have, no matter what".*

GAME 9:   LOUISVILLE (6-2) @ NOXUBEE COUNTY (4-4)
                    LOUISVILLE 7 NOXUBEE COUNTY 33
                    October 16, 2015

The "Toothpick Bowl" now awaited against a team that went 14-2 in 2014, won two of the past three 4A titles, and started first in The Clarion-Ledger preseason 4A rankings. Thus far, they faced a difficult schedule and lost some tough battles. *"It will be a big game for both teams. We have just got to get ready to play hard and hope we can pull it out. We just hope we can hang in there with them. They have gotten beat by some good teams. They have a good ball club...."*

In division standings, Louisville and Noxubee County were tied at 2-0, despite the Cats having a better overall record. The Clarion-Ledger picked the Tigers 21-17 and Noxubee's offense *"seems to be on the mend".*

An early Tiger fumble recovered by Zach Vaughn allowed a drive to the Noxubee 1 but the Cats could not cross. Noxubee went the other way to paydirt in 17 plays ending on Ladaveon Smith's 3-yarder and Samuel Lowrey's PAT. A later Wildcat punt block by Art Davis was recovered and returned by Kalmorris Robinson for a 24-yard score and 14-0 lead. Louisville cut into it before halftime on Pervis Frazier's pass to Glenn.

However, Tilmorris Conner found Kymbotric Mason from 29 yards in the 3rd quarter to make it 20-7. They added more later on Conner's 29-yarder to Mason, his 10-yard run, and a later 10-yard pass to Javarcus Walker. Frazier was 7-24 for 120 yards and led rushers with 38. Lee had 103 receiving yards and Gill an interception. *"We have got to pick it up. We have got to get ready to go. The season is not over yet. We have got to pick it up and go from here. No matter what it takes, we have got to do what we have got to do to get better".*

GAME 10: LOUISVILLE (6-3) vs HOUSTON (7-2)
LOUISVILLE 14 HOUSTON 10
October 23, 2015

After a losing 5-7 season, the Hilltopper now sat 7-2. Their first meeting in 1945 ended in a Cat win as did the past 10 others. Now it would be tighter than some previous meetings as both geared up for playoff runs.

It was a meager 2-0 Cat lead in the opening frame after a *"botched Houston punt attempt"*. Houston eventually added a 21-yard FG to make it 3-2. McCullough answered with a 21-yarder of his own to put it 5-3. Late in the 3rd quarter, Houston added a 5-yard touchdown run and kick to mark the first crossing of the evening. Things looked bleak despite a 44-yard McCullough FG with about 7:00 left in the contest.

Now with just under 3:00 remaining, Anderson stepped in front of a Hilltopper pass and took it 35-yards to paydirt. Though the two-pointer was not successful, the Wildcats were. Houston led in first downs 10-5. Frazier was 10-18 for 73 yards and Coleman led rushers with only 25 yards. Demarcus Frazier led receivers with 60 yards while Stallings and Gill each had six tackles. Antrous Glenn had an interception, too.

GAME 11: LOUISVILLE (7-3) @ KOSCIUSKO (7-2)
LOUISVILLE 21 KOSCIUSKO 46
October 30, 2015

Rival Kosciusko went 11-3 the previous season and now had losses only to Forest and Noxubee County. The game meant more than rivalry records. *"The winner gets a home game"*, said Miller as both raced for second place in the division behind Noxubee County. *"That's what we are playing for. If we lose, we have to go on the road. We are struggling, but the other guys are picking things up and getting better and better. We are just finding a way to win. We just have to keep doing what we can do".*

The Cats were down 13-0 before taking a 14-13 lead just before the half. Gill's 1-yarder and Pervis Frazier's 9-yarder marked the Louisville scores. But just before the intermission whistle, the Whippets tallied on a 48-yard Josh Dodd strike to Taquan Winters to make it 19-14.

Dodd added runs of 11 and a yard to increase the advantage to 33-14 after three quarters. Winters later ran in from four yards and Dodd hit Stefan Harmon from 51 yards to end things on their side. The last Wildcat score came on a Charles Moore 75-yard fumble return and the third McCullough PAT.

GAME 12: LOUISVILLE (7-4) @ ITAWAMBA AHS (7-3)
LOUISVILLE 36 ITAWAMBA AHS 9
November 5, 2015

The two met only in post season in 1989 and 1990 and both were Louisville victories. IAHS finished in a three-way tie for second in 1-4A and lost to Kosy only 32-26. Now the Wildcats traveled north to try to regroup and keep moving on. Due to inclement weather, this game and others were moved to Thursday affairs.

Thought IAHS held an early 3-0 lead, Louisville came back with 24 points in the 2nd quarter. Kendrick Holmes crossed from two yards, McCullough converted and added a 42-yard FG, Gill took a fumble back 20 yards, Pervis Frazier ran in from two yards and then hit Coleman from midfield. Cam'Ron Herrington finished it with a 3-yarder. Gill led tacklers with eight.

"That is the best game we have played all year. The offense really played well and the defense did a good job as well. We had to go on the road and win and we did it. I hope our offense can keep improving but our defense needs to improve as well".

GAME 13: LOUISVILLE (8-4) vs GREENWOOD (10-1)
LOUISVILLE 12 GREENWOOD 13
November 13, 2015

These two faced each other on in 1947, 1954 and 1975. The first two were losses but the most recent was a victory. Said Miller, *"The main thing we have to do is stop* their running attack. They have a pretty good team with a good quarterback and good receivers. They are pretty balanced, but it's the run you have to stop. That is what we are going to have to be prepared to do".

A McCullough 47-yard FG held until midway through the 2nd quarter when Damarius Ray hit Jermarcus Weatherall for an 80-yard touchdown. The Marquiss Spencer PAT put them ahead 7-3. McCullough cut it to 7-6 late in the 3rd quarter with one from 29 yards, but Greenwood came back with Transelon Tribblett's 63-yarder to John Derrick Smith. That 13-6 lead held until Frazier hit Tyrique Carter from 20 yards with 1:36 left. The crucial PAT was a bit high and the holder went for the two-pointer. It failed and the run for another title was over.

Louisville rushed for only 49 yards and 205 of total offense. Frazier was 14-30 for 156. Greenwood had 278 offensive yards with 143 coming on the pair of touchdowns plays. Said Miller, *"The game shouldn't have been even close. We will just have to take our loss and go from here, but we should have won the game. We kept them pinned back but just couldn't get anything out of our offense and it just killed us. The defense played great. We felt like if we tied it up, we could beat them in overtime because they had a hard time moving the ball and we have a good kicker. Even though we knew it had rained last week, we expected better"*.

2016 (7-6)

As always, key players graduated for Coach M.C. Miller's next class of Wildcats. *"The line is bigger and stronger this year. That should help us get some tough yardage offensively. We weren't very effective on first down last year. We are hoping we come out this year and get positive yardage and put ourselves in better situations"*.

Regarding the outlook of the season, he added, *"It's going to be another tough schedule for us. Noxubee County is the 4A State Champion and Kosciusko is going to be pretty good. The whole district is going to be tough"*.

GAME 1:   LOUISVILLE (0-0) @ NEW HOPE (0-0)
                                   LOUISVILLE 26 NEW HOPE 27
                                   August 19, 2016

Unlike games from 1988 to 2006, this had become a tougher battle for Louisville. Now they traveled to New Hope for the opener to face a team that came out victorious in the last two of three meetings.

The Wildcats jumped out to a 13-0 lead via a 19-yard pass from Pervis Frazier to Devon Lee and a 2nd quarter Frazier run from three yards. New Hope tied it in the 3rd quarter on Stevens' touchdowns passes of 19 and 54 yards to Tate. The Cats regained the lead in the finale 20-13 on a 10-yard Cam'ron Harrington run but Stevens' strike to Andrew Erby from 20 yards put it back into a stalemate.

Late in the game, Erby pulled in a 75-yarder to put them ahead. Frazier managed a 1-yard dive but the PAT failed. Harrington led rushers with 108 yards, Frazier was 9-18 for 87 yards, and Devon Lee pulled 87 passing markers. *"We just made too many mistakes, especially on defense. We have got to work with them. (New Hope) kind of hurt us passing the ball"*.

GAME 2:   LOUISVILLE (0-1) @ WEST POINT (0-0)
                                   LOUISVILLE 13 WEST POINT 33
                                   August 26, 2016

After losing six of the last seven to the Wave, everyone knew this road tilt would be tough. *"We have been watching them on film but you don't see much in a jamboree. We know they will mix it up, but they really like to run the ball"*.

Pervis opened with a Cat score on his 12-yard run and Elijah Wilkes PAT. West Point tied it thereafter in the 2nd quarter on a 14-yard Chris Calvert run and Jose Garcia kick to keep it 7-7 at intermission. In the 3rd quarter, Clayton Knight found Calvert from 18 yards and Garcia converted. Louisville cut it to 14-13 on a 94-yard Frazier bomb to Ladarius Luckett.

Marcus Murphy then put the Wave back on top with a 48-yard escape before Jeremy Browless picked off a Frazier pass for a 55-yard pick-six. Then, Xavier Fair picked off another Frazier throw to set up a 1-yard Andre Lane dive. Frazier went 10-24 for 157,

Luckett pulled in 111 yards, and Harrington led rushers with 51 yards. *"We knew it was going to be tough, but that's what we wanted. We wanted to be challenged. You can learn quickly what you have to work on and where you stand".*

GAME 3:   LOUISVILLE (0-2) vs KEMPER COUNTY (1-1)
                     LOUISVILLE 27 KEMPER COUNTY 32
                     September 2, 2016

After five straight wins over Kemper, this one may have seemed easier than it was. Miller was wary. *"They are putting together a good program down there. They have a lot of talent and (Coach Chris Jones is) getting a lot out of them. It's going to be another challenge for us".* In the end, it proved perhaps the most heartbreaking loss in Wildcat history.

An early safety put Kemper ahead 2-0. In the second quarter, LHS came back with a 7-yard Frazier pass to Dontae Yarbrough and Wilkes added the PAT. KCHS retaliated with a 15-yard Eric Clark toss to Gus Nave to make halftime 8-7. In the 3rd quarter, LHS added a pair of tallies on a 33-yard Frazier strike to Tyler Kincaid and Harrington's 15-yarder.

Back came the visitors with a Clark 2-yard run and his 80-yard bomb to Clayton to make it 24-21. With :18 remaining, the Cats looked to have shocked fans when a bad punt snap rolled into the end zone and was recovered by Jakevious Whitfield for the shocking touchdown. However, Kemper took the ensuing kick and Nave raced the length of the field and added the two-pointer for good measure.

"We just weren't supposed to win. This is the toughest loss I've had. These are three tough losses to deal with. We have just got to pick it up and move forward. It will turn somewhere down the line because we are playing too good of ball right now. We just have to keep it going".

GAME 4:   LOUISVILLE (0-3) @ PHILADELPHIA (3-0)
                     LOUISVILLE 32 PHILADELPHIA 7
                     September 9, 2016

After starting with three consecutive losses, older Wildcat football alums could have told you that there could be no better way to change than to beat Philadelphia.

Although the Tornado held an early 7-0 advantage at home, the Cats were not to be denied with 32 unanswered points. Frazier, now at wingback, cut the lead to 7-6 with his 1-yard effort. That turned into an 18-7 halftime lead via a 2-yard Kenneth Knowles burst and a 3-yarder by Kendrick Holmes. The first was set up by a blocked punt.

Now in the final frame and after solid defensive play by Louisville, penalties put the Wildcats at the Philly 2. Knowles ran in from there late in the game. An ensuing kick fumble by Philly allowed Anderson a 46-yard romp for the finale. Harrington rushed for 107 of the total 329 offensive yards. Eric Sudduth and Ashanti Cistrunk paced tacklers with seven while LaWilliam Holmes also picked off a pass.

"We really needed that win. We have been getting beat by good people and playing hard, but what we needed was a win. That will help us a lot".

GAME 5:   LOUISVILLE (1-3) @ LAFAYETTE COUNTY (1-2)
                     LOUISVILLE 7 LAFAYETTE COUNTY 42
                     September 16, 2016

Though a *"down year"* for powerful Lafayette County thus far, they still held six consecutive wins over the Wildcats. And, injuries were mounting with four Cat starters sidelined for the game. Said Miller, *"It's going to be a big test for us. They have a good running back and a big offensive line, so it's going to be a challenge".*

The home team was already up 14-0 before Yarbrough broke through from a yard to make halftime 14-7. Lafayette put it away in the 3rd quarter on scoring runs of 51 and 60 yards to match and 11-yard passing touchdown. They added another TD later. Yarbrough was 7-17 for 134, Ladarrius Luckett had 46 receiving yards, and Harrington rushed for 31 yards.

"We have got some boys beat up and hurt and that's what really hurt us. We didn't have any middle linebackers who had played and they just took advantage of that. We know they are going to be out now, so we have to get ready".

GAME 6:   LOUISVILLE (1-4) vs AMANDA ELZY (1-3-1)
                    LOUISVILLE 49 AMANDA ELZY 0
                    September 23, 2016

It was hard to miss the inaugural final tally of 44-2 over Elzy the previous season. Said Miller, *"We have a good team. We just have to keep playing hard. This is our last game before district and it's very important to be able to get a win. We beat them pretty good last year but they are playing much better and will be a challenge for us"*.

It was already 28-0 after a quarter and 42-0 at halftime. Knowles dove in from a yard, Yarbrough from six yards, Whitfield and Desmond Love returned fumbles, Holmes crossed from seven yards and Knowles from 25 yards. The last touchdown came on a 4-yarder by Harrington. Santos Espinos was true on all seven extra points.

Knowles ran for 93 yards, Yarbrough was 5-9 for 96 yards, and Luckett recorded 45 yards receiving.

GAME 7:   LOUISVILLE (2-4) @ LEAKE CENTRAL (4-2)
                    LOUISVILLE 42 LEAKE CENTRAL 11
                    September 30, 2016

Leake Central out of Carthage was 4-7 the previous season and welcomed Louisville with three consecutive losses against the Cats. Said Miller, *"We need to win these next two games. If we can do that, then we will know we are in the playoffs, we won't have as much pressure on us and it will allow us to play better"*.

A scoreless opening stanza soon led to Lee's 11-yarder and Santos PAT. Leake Central hit a 34-yard FG but Louisville and Lee came back with a 65-yard kickoff return. Frazier hit paydirt from two yards and Yarbrough hit Frazier from 32 yards later. Now in the finale, Knowles rushed in from two yards.

The home team blocked a punt for a touchdown to make it 35-11, but Yarbrough *"closed out the scoring"* via his 20-yard dash. Yarbrough was 6-12 for 151, Knowles rushed for 79 yards, Luckett grabbed 60 yards in the air, and Charles Moore led tacklers with 4.5. In all, the Cats had 351 total offensive yards.

GAME 8:   LOUISVILLE (3-4) vs CALEDONIA (3-3)
                    LOUISVILLE 42 CALEDONIA 35
                    October 7, 2016: HOMECOMING

After finishing break-even 5-5 the previous year, Caledonia came to Louisville on track to match or better that campaign. Both desperately needed wins in this tilt.

The Cats went up 14-0 in the 2nd quarter on Harrington runs of six and three yards on his way to 121 rushing on the night. Espinos converted his first two of four. Wilkes added a pair of others. However, in the last three minutes before halftime, Caledonia hit paydirt three times to make intermission a surprising 21-14.

Louisville tied it midway through the 3rd quarter on a 1-yarder from Knowles and took the lead on a Yarbrough dive later from the same distance. Back came the visitors to tie it 28-28. However, Harrington ran in from five yards in the finale and Knowles did the same afterwards. The last Caledonia touchdown came with 1:10 remaining.

Of the total 469 offensive yards, Knowles rushed for 169 and Yarbrough went 7-14 for 63 yards. Cistrunk led tacklers with 6.5.

GAME 9:   LOUISVILLE (4-4) vs NOXUBEE COUNTY (4-4)
                    LOUISVILLE 26 NOXUBEE COUNTY 34
                    October 13, 2016

The "Toothpick Bowl", dubbed for Miller's penchant for having a toothpick in his mouth on the sidelines, appeared about as even as could be expected as both teams sat 4-4 and the game was in Winston County. The previous season, the Tigers were 12-4 including a 33-7 win over the Cats. By mutual agreement, the football game was played on a Thursday.

It was not a spectacular start for the Wildcats as the Tigers went up 14-0 after a frame. Those tallies came on Kaddarrion Outlaw's 21-yarder to Maliek Stallings and the first of four Samuel Lowrey extra points. They, Armoni Clark hit Kyziah Pruitt from six yards. They increased it to 28-0 before halftime on a Kymbotric Mason 31-yard reception from Clark and Clark's 49-yarder to Pruitt. The lone Wildcat tally came on Frazier's 67-yard bomb to Yarbrough to end the half 28-6.

In the 3rd quarter, Louisville had the lone tally when Frazier and Yarbrough hooked up from 19 yards. Now in the finale, Ty'Quintin Ramsey dodged in from four yards before Louisville found paydirt twice. Lee grabbed a 27-yarder from Yarbrough, Yarbrough added the two-pointer, and then he hit Luckett from seven yards.

Louisville had 412 offensive yards to 328 for NCHS. Yarbrough was 11-18 for 234, Harrington rushed for 83 yards, Frazier recorded 137 receiving yards, and Anderson led tackles with 5.5.

GAME 10:   LOUISVILLE (4-5) @ HOUSTON (8-1)
             LOUISVILLE 27 HOUSTON 23
             October 21, 2016

The Hilltoppers were obviously moving in the right direction. They went a respectable 9-5 the year before but now had only an opening night 24-14 loss to Pontotoc. It was obvious that this one for a second-place lock in 4-4A would be tough as the Wildcats tried to continue an all-time 12-0 streak against Houston.

Houston's starting FG made it 3-0, but Louisville answered on a 5-yard Jackson run and Espinos PAT. The Hilltoppers ended the frame, however, with a 20-yard scoring pass and PAT to put it 10-7. Early in the 2nd quarter, Yarbrough dove in from a yard but the extra point was blocked. Houston then took the lead at intermission via their 1-yarder.

In the 3rd quarter, Yarbrough and Luckett connected from 27 yards to put it 19-16. Late in the frame, Houston scooted in from five yards and it was now 23-19. The Cats recovered in the finale via a 4-yard Harrington run and his two-pointer. Knowles led rushers with 123, Yarbrough was 6-17 for 108 yards, Luckett grabbed 82 yards, and Anderson led tacklers with nine.

GAME 11:   LOUISVILLE (5-5) vs KOSCIUSKO (1-8)
             LOUISVILLE 27 KOSCIUSKO 24
             October 28, 2016

A win here at home against a rival team finishing 10-3 the previous season meant an opening home game in the first round of the playoffs. To most, the 1-8 record of Kosy was a reason to smile but the Whippets had victories over the Cats in the last two games. It turned out as a tighter contest than their 1-8 record would have many think. However, the win gave the Cats home field in the opening playoff round and a chance to meet back up with Lafayette County down the road.

The Winston County Journal called the game "back and forth" as Kosy went up 6-0 early "only to have LHS come back" on Yarbrough's 30-yarder and Espinos PAT. The Whippets re-took the lead on a 1-yard dive but the Cats answered before halftime on Yarbrough's 11-yarder to Lee. Yarbrough hit Frazier in the 3rd quarter from 39 yards while the visitors did the same later from midfield. The last punch came from Louisville on Knowles' 9-yarder in the 3rd quarter. Yarbrough was 6-11 for 91, Knowles 89 on the ground, and Lee 67 in receptions.

GAME 12:   LOUISVILLE (6-5) vs RAYMOND (3-7)
             LOUISVILLE 35 RAYMOND 6
             November 4, 2016

The first-ever meeting with Raymond was a welcome opening playoff night at Hinze Stadium as the Rangers were just 3-7 thus far. Of course, other teams with worse records gave Louisville a fight this year, too.

Cat scoring started with Harrington's 10-yarder and Espinos PAT. Then, Jackson crossed from a yard, Knowles ran in from 13 yards, and Espinos added both extra points. Raymond added a 9-yard TD pass just before halftime but there was enough time for the Wildcats to add a 34-yard Yarbrough strike to Frazier. Harrington's two-pointer made intermission 29-6. The last tally came in the 3rd quarter when Harrington found daylight from 10 yards. Yarbrough was 6-14 for 149 yards and Anderson led tacklers.

GAME 13:   LOUISVILLE (7-5) @ LAFAYETTE COUNTY (9-2)
             LOUISVILLE 7 LAFAYETTE COUNTY 24
             November 11, 2016

The rematch was now set. Earlier in the season, Lafayette drummed the Cats 42-7 to extend their winning streak against Louisville to seven. Despite a rough start to the season, this one kept hope alive. While closer than the first, the result ended the same.

Lafayette scored twice in the 2nd quarter to open and then moved it to 17-0 via a 23-yard FG in the 3rd quarter. Late in the game, Yarbrough dodged in from a yard and Espinos tacked on the PAT. Nevertheless, Lafayette County added one more on a short run to finalize Wildcat dreams of another title.

LCHS led 382-266 in yardage and 17-14 in first downs. Yarbrough was 8-20 for 78 yards and rushed for 98 yards. Harrington pulled in 30 receiving yards, and Moore paced tacklers with just five. It was a disappointing start and, now, a finish to the 2016 season.

2017 (12-3)

M.C. Miller hoped his Wildcats could rebound from a season of injuries and close losses. *"It was a tough season. We had a lot of players get hurt and that really hurt us. We were young in some positions and by the end of the year we had a lot of guys playing out of positions. (With returners, it) should make us better this season. I know that we look a lot better at this point than we did this time last year. We just have to stay healthy".*

Those returning players accounted for 24 seniors, seven offensive starters, and eight on defense. One poll had the Wildcats 3rd in 4A.

GAME 1:   LOUISVILLE (0-0) @ HOLMES COUNTY (0-0)
                            LOUISVILLE 24 HOLMES COUNTY 0
                            August 18, 2017

Unbelievable, only the final score is found for the inaugural game against Holmes County and the 2016 lid-lifter for Louisville. Either way, the Wildcats had a 1-0 record as they journeyed north to face a rugged Green Wave squad.

GAME 2:   LOUISVILLE (1-0) vs WEST POINT (1-0)
                            LOUISVILLE 7 WEST POINT 27
                            August 25, 2017

Powerful West Point won seven on the last eight contests against the Cats, but Louisville was still scheduling meetings against the larger school to prepare for the upcoming season.

Louisville was first to the scoreboard on Pervis Frazier's 44-yard pass to Deonte Yarbrough and Elijah Wilkes converted. West Point and Marcus Murphy added a pair Murphy runs of five and 50 yards to put halftime 14-7. They increased the lead in the 3rd quarter on a 10-yard Semaj Harris reception from Jake Chambless. Chris Calvert had the last in the finale on his 7-yard effort.

Daylen Gill led tacklers with 10, Eric Sudduth and Ashanti Cistrunk recovered fumbles, and Knowles rushed for 50 of the 107 ground yards. *"That was a good football team. We won't play anybody that good for a while. I thought their offensive line was good and wore us down. I didn't think (our) defense played that bad. They just needed more rest. We needed the offense to keep the ball longer to get them a rest. But I'll give West Point credit. They have a heck of a football team".*

GAME 3:   LOUISVILLE (1-1) @ KEMPER COUNTY (0-2)
                            LOUISVILLE 42 KEMPER COUNTY 12
                            September 1, 2017

The next opponent won the 3A title the previous season but started this one with a pair of defeats. The Wildcats made it a bit worse for them on the road.

Louisville made it a quick 8-0 via Cistrunk's 35-yard pick-six and the Cat two-pointer. In the 2nd quarter, Yarbrough found Ladarius Luckett from 46 yards to make it 14-0. Their next came on a Yarbrough 5-yarder and his two-pointer to made it 22-0. In the 3rd quarter, Kenneth Knowles plowed across. Kemper finally got on the board but Yarbrough soon found D.Q. Haynes from 25 yards for a tally.

Daylen Gill led tacklers with 12 while Kedarius Dixon and Desmond Love added interceptions. *"It was a good win for our guys. I thought we played a lot better than last week. Kemper has a good team but they are not like what we were playing last week. I* thought the defense played real well and the offense picked it up this week. We are getting better every week on both sides of the ball".

GAME 4:   LOUISVILLE (2-1) vs RIPLEY (1-2)
                           LOUISVILLE 49 RIPLEY 6
                           September 8, 2017

The one other contest between the two came in 2007 where the Cats took home the win. "I have seen them on film and they are looking pretty good. We have to be ready to play. They are a good fundamental football team. We have them at home and have to come out and hit them in the face and not mess around with them. I think if we can do that, we will be OK".

A 2nd quarter stop of a fake punt put the Cats at the Ripley 29. Kevon Jackson crossed later from 20 yards and Wilkes made it 7-0. Jackson then ran in from 15 yards while Yarbrough later hit Luckett from 57 yards. With Wilkes kicks, it was 21-0. Jehmiah Harden picked off a Ripley throw allowing Yarbrough to hit Frazier from 47 yard with :11 left to ice the opening half.

In the next, they added a pair of others on two Knowles runs. Ripley added a touchdown early in the finale, but the Wildcats came back with a 38-yard Drea Shumaker dash. Ken Holmes had 68 of the total 296 rushing yards for Louisville. Yarbrough was 9-13 for 171 yards, Luckett grabbed 88 air yards with Frazier just behind with 83. Tackles were abundant with Cistrunk, Gill and Harden each recording eight.

"I thought we whooped up on them pretty good. We started a little slow but finally got rolling in the second quarter. We knew that they had a pretty good team but didn't have that depth and speed that we have. They had about four or five players going both ways and we just wore them down. I thought we ran the ball a lot better than we have. Good things are starting to happen on offense".

GAME 5:   LOUISVILLE (3-1) vs GRENADA (1-3)
                           LOUISVILLE 22 GRENADA 17
                           September 15, 2017

Next was a Grenada team that first faced Louisville in 1941. Since then, Louisville was 18-3-1 against them. "We have been playing a lot of bigger schools and have to be able to step up and beat those (upcoming) schools. (Grenada) beat Kosciusko last week (52-14) in a tight game and we have to be ready to play. Their coach came from here so it will be a big game for them".

The Chargers put up the first two touchdowns and PATs of the contest, the second coming on a 30-yard pass. Late in the 2nd quarter, Yarbrough hit Frazier for a score and Wilkes cut it to 14-7. Before the halftime whistle, Grenada added a FG to make it 17-7. Yarbrough came back in the 3rd quarter with his touchdown to Shumaker and Haynes added two more points to put it 17-15. Thereafter, he hit Luckett with :33 left in the frame and Wilkes put them ahead to stay 22-17.

Yarbrough went 9-20-1 for 122 yards with Luckett receiving 60 of those. Knowles led rushers with 93 of the 234 total yards. Gill led tacklers with a big 17 solo while others had big numbers, too. Gill also had an interception.

"It was a good win. It was important for our kids to win a game like this. Normally when we get behind like that, we would give up. But the kids hung in there. Then we went into halftime and gave them a good talk and got some things straight. We told them not to panic, that we were going to correct those mistakes and that's what we did".

GAME 6:   LOUISVILLE (4-1) @ GREENWOOD (4-1)
                           LOUISVILLE 34 GREENWOOD 18
                           September 22, 2017

Greenwood was not an unfamiliar team over the history of Wildcat football. Since their first meeting in 1947, the Cats were just 1-3 against them. "They look really good on film. We have to go over there and be ready to play. They like to run right at you". The Greenwood Commonwealth noted that The Clarion-Ledger second-ranked Wildcats and fifth-ranked Bulldogs were both bracing for "a tough test". Said Bulldog Coach Clinton Gatewood, "This will be our toughest game to date. They have athletes all over the field".

While Knowles opened with a 5-yard run and a Wilkes PAT, it was the defense leading the way with three interceptions and a fumble recovery. After recovering that fumble, Yarbrough snuck in from a yard and Wilkes put it a quick 14-0. Louisville had their own mistakes with a pair of picks and a lost fumble. One allowed the Dogs' Jaylen Stanley an 88-yard scoring pass to Kobe Chambers to make halftime 14-6.

Ken Holmes found paydirt from 14 yards late in the 3rd quarter and Wilkes put the Wildcats up 21-6. Greenwood added a 15-yard scoring run from Cardaryl Johnson but Frazier crossed later from four yards late in the finale. Walter Ivory found the end zone later from five yards. The Cats put up 385 offensive yards. Knowles had 111 rushing, Frazier led receivers and Cistrunk tacklers with 12. Gill, Lakevias Daniel and Kedarius Dixon had interceptions.

"I was surprised how well we handled them. I thought the offense played the best they have all season. We didn't even have a penalty on offense. I thought we ran the ball really well. We ran it right at them all night long".

GAME 7:   LOUISVILLE (5-1) vs NEW HOPE (4-2)
                 LOUISVILLE 48 NEW HOPE 7
                 September 29, 2017: HOMECOMING

This home matchup featured New Hope for Homecoming. Miller was not a big fan of the event as it related to football games. "It's our first district game and that's always important. It's also homecoming and you have to deal with those things. (New Hope) moved from 5A to 4A and I'm sure they are thinking they can dominate. We just have to keep our minds on the game".

The Cats opened with two touchdowns and Wilkes extra points. The first came on a 19-yard Yarbrough pass to Frazier. Jonteavis Garnett then intercepted a pass to set up a Knowles 15-yarder and 21-0 lead. The Trojans found the end zone on Ryan Burt's 7-yard keeper and the PAT put intermission 21-7.

Knowles opened the 3rd quarter with a 30-yard dash, a 10-yard Wildcat tally then came midway through the frame before Knowles rushed in from 15 yards early in the finale. Tyrell Thames added the last on his 6-yard effort. The Wildcats led offensive yards 389-267. The air attack provided 149 of those. Yarbrough was 5-8 for 80 yards while Drea Shumaker was 4-5 for 67. Knowles rushers with 80 and Luckett caught 73 more. Sacario Goss had a fumble recovery and Darius Hopkins an interception.

"I know they thought they were going to come down here and be the kings of 4A. I honestly thought they were going to be better than they were. They were big but we were so much quicker that they were. I thought the defense did a good job and they couldn't stop our offense. That was probably our best game of the season".

GAME 8:   LOUISVILLE (6-1) @ NOXUBEE COUNTY (2-4)
                 LOUISVILLE 30 NOXUBEE COUNTY 35
                 October 6, 2017

Noxubee was quickly becoming a replacement for the Kosciusko rivalry among fans. With eight of the last 11 games going their way, it was easy to see why. That is not to mention that Miller was the former Tiger coach for 27 years. "I know their record isn't that good, but they have played some good people. Noxubee will be our toughest test since we played West Point. They are our biggest rivalry game and we have to be prepared for them".

The Cats recovered an early Tiger fumble, their first of five, but settled for a 33-yard Wilkes FG. The Tigers were ready with a scoring touchdown and PAT to end the frame. Then, they took a Cat fumble back 40 yards to paydirt, took advantage of another fumble and drove 60 yards to score on a 1-yard QB sneak. Their two-pointer made it 21-3.

A 4-yarder midway through the 2nd quarter made it 28-3 before Louisville came back with a Frazier scoring run and a 10-yard Yarbrough toss to Alvis Haynes. Intermission sat 28-16. Luckett took a Tiger punt 35 yards for the tally but Noxubee added a pick-six to make it 35-23. Jakevious Whitfield recovered a late fumble for a touchdown to end it.

Louisville led in offense 227-222. The Cats ran for 152 and Jackson led with 66 yards on the ground. Shumaker was 4-11 for 51 yards while Frazier led receivers with 29. Gill had 14 tackles and Cistrunk a pair of interceptions. Whitfield, Cistrunk and Dixon recovered fumbles in the affair.

"They came out here and hit us in the mouth. They had two weeks to prepare for us and I think they were more ready to play. We were a little banged up and they had two weeks to get healthy and work on what we do. We came out slow and they came out on fire and took it to us".

GAME 9:   LOUISVILLE (6-2) @ FOREST (6-2)
                          LOUISVILLE 35 FOREST 0
                          October 13, 2017

Forest had a strong history of great teams. In fact, since 1930 the series against the Bearcats was even 2-2. This season, they lost only to Jackson Prep and Ridgeland. *"Forest looks really good. We have to be ready to play them on the road and have to be ready for them. They play a good schedule".* Louisville was without Frazier for at least another couple of weeks.

Louisville put things in high gear with a 35-0 lead when Shumaker found Frazier from 29 yards. The defense blocked a Bearcat punt and Antrous Glenn took it seven yards to paydirt. Shumaker then hit Luckett from 28 yards and J'Kevious Hibbler's two-pointer made it 21-0. Shumaker then dashed 35 yards and Wilkes provided the PAT. A pickoff allowed Shumaker to hit Knowles from nine yards and the Wilkes PAT finished scoring.

The Wildcats led in yardage 312-164. Shumaker was 14-17 for those yards, Knowles rushed for 46 and Luckett caught 95. Gills and Whitfield led with ten tackles each, Cistrunk and Love had interceptions and Eric Sudduth led with a pair of sacks.

"They played a lot better this week. We knew that Forest was going to be pretty good. We wanted to go and have a good first half. They really couldn't stop us in the first half and the defense played really good,, too. We really shut down their passing game. The defense did a good job. I thought it was our best first half of football this year. The kids were playing hard and it seemed like everything was clicking for us".

GAME 10:   LOUISVILLE (7-2) vs KOSCIUSKO (2-7)
                          LOUISVILLE 41 KOSCIUSKO 7
                          October 20, 2017

The Kosciusko Star Herald noted that *"Louisville comes into the Friday night contest after thrashing a good Forest team".* The 76th meeting, starting in 1929, between the Whippets and Cats would mean a lot for both squads in Winston County this evening.

The first Wildcat march went 55 yards with Shumaker adding the last 10. Wilkes made it a quick 7-0. Cistrunk was next from 60 yards on a direct snap. After a fumble recovery, Yarbrough found Luckett from 60 yards to put the game 19-0. Finding yet another loose ball, Yarbrough and Frazier connected from 31 yards and his two-pointer to Jy'Kevious Hibbler made halftime 27-0.

The home team put up a pair in the 3rd quarter via a 25-yard Shumaker dash and an 18-yarder by Jackson. One came via a blocked punt. The lone Whippet TD came on Clark Dean's 74-yard bomb to Kadarius Banks and Jake Cockroft's PAT. Yarbrough was 4-5 for 123 of the 140 passing yards. Shumaker had the rest on a 2-4 night. Shumaker led rushers with 63 of the 219 yards, Luckett paced receivers with 74, Derius Hopkins led tacklers with 11, and Dixon and Jehmiah Harden had fumble recoveries.

"We jumped on them from the start and shut them down pretty good. We played well on both sides of the ball. We are playing pretty good right now. We did a good job running the football and played really well on defense".

GAME 11:   LOUISVILLE (8-2) @ LEAKE CENTRAL (4-5)
                          LOUISVILLE 34 LEAKE CENTRAL 0
                          October 27, 2017

It was not a stellar season in Carthage, not to mention that Leake Central had yet to defeat Louisville in four attempts. *"I really don't think Leake is in the same class as we are but they have played everybody pretty hard. I know we have to be ready to play and can't be slouching around".*

It is said that bad weather is the equalizer. On this night it was not. Louisville put up three scores in the first half via Yarbrough to Frazier from 15 yards, Knowles from 25 yards, a Dixon pick to set up Yarbrough's 10-yarder to Frazier, and two Wilkes kicks. A Whitfield fumble recovery in the 3rd quarter allowed Knowles a 3-yard run and Wilkes the PAT. A later Leake fumble gave Yarbrough a 5-yard dive and Wilkes the extra point.

Knowles rushed for 84 of the 223 total yards. Louisville passed for only 40 yards. Defensively, the Cats caused six turnovers. Dixon and Harden had interceptions while Whitfield, LaWilliam Holmes, Hopkins and Hibbler recovered fumbles. Hopkins paced tacklers with 10.

"I thought the defense played really well and the offense is doing well. We did what we had to do to win the game. I'm glad it rained because we needed to see that because we have more rain coming Friday night. I thought we ran the ball hard. The line has gotten better as the season has gone on…"

GAME 12:   LOUISVILLE (9-2) vs SHANNON (6-5)
                     LOUISVILLE 41 SHANNON 6
                     November 3, 2017

The Red Raiders, though losing to the Cats in all three previous meetings, was expected to provide stiff competition at Hinze Stadium to open the playoffs. *"Shannon is a pretty good team and we still have to play to beat them. They do more stuff than all the 12 teams we have played combined. We have to do a lot of preparation".*

Shannon fumbled their first snap to Dickie Hunt. In all, they had seven turnovers on the evening. Two plays later, Yarbrough found Haynes from 16 yards and Wilkes converted his first of many extra points. In the same frame, Yarbrough found the end zone from 10 yards. Knowles was next from 19 yards and it was 20-0. Despite two interceptions thrown by Louisville, Cistrunk blocked a punt to set up Yarbrough's 11-yarder to Luckett.

Just before intermission, Shannon found paydirt after an interception led to a short drive. In the second half, Shemar Eiland took a fumble 35 yards while Dixon added a 35-yard pick-six. Yarbrough was 7-16 for 117 for the total 142 passing yards. Jackson led the ground with 82 of the total 206 yards. Frazier had 51 in receptions.

Defensively, Dixon and Gill had seven tackles each. Dixon had two picks and Sudduth, Eiland, Harden, Hunt and Whitfield recovered fumbles. *"We took it to them right off the bat. I thought we played well on offense and defense. Right now, we are playing really well. I just hope we can keep it up. I thought we shut down their passing game and didn't give them much room to run and created some turnovers".*

GAME 13:   LOUISVILLE (10-2) @ SENATOBIA (8-3)
                     LOUISVILLE 42 SENATOBIA 14
                     November 10, 2017

Like a few others before, Senatobia had yet to defeat the Wildcats. However, this game was in Tate County and not a short trip against a Warrior team with just three losses. *"They are going to have a good team. I don't think they have played anybody like we have, though. They do a lot of different stuff on offense. We're just trying to figure out how we are going to attack them. That's the furthest we have traveled this season".*

The Cats took their opening possession 70 yards with Yarbrough finding Frazier from 17 yards and Wilkes made it 7-0. Louisville forced a punt and fumble but also missed a 30-yard FG. However, Knowles soon found the end zone from 21 yards to make it 14-0. Two plays on their next possession, Yarbrough and Frazier hooked up from 54 yards and Wilkes added another PAT.

Senatobia found the board midway through the 2nd quarter on a 41-yard run and PAT, but Jackson later crossed from five yards and halftime sat 28-7. Back came the Warriors in the 3rd quarter on a 39-yard march and the two then traded turnovers. Louisville tallied two more times to put it away. Knowles crossed from two yards while Whitfield recovered a blocked punt for the last.

Louisville rushed for 194 and threw for 217. Yarbrough was 12-18 while Frazier hauled in 148 yards in the air. Knowles rushed for 100 yards and Hopkins led with 9 tackles. Cistrunk had an interception. *"We played hard right off the bat and continued to play hard. I thought the offense and defense did well and I hope we can continue that. It's like we are getting better every game and we are trying to keep it going. Everybody is coming around and playing together as a team".*

GAME 14:   LOUISVILLE (11-2) vs GREENWOOD (10-2)
                     LOUISVILLE 21 GREENWOOD 13
                     November 17, 2017

Coach Clinton Gatewood was accurate after their first meeting when he noted, *"I guarantee you we will see them in the postseason".* Now their time had arrived to see if the first tilt was just a fluke. *"They have been talking about how much better they have gotten since we beat them. But we feel like we have gotten a lot better ourselves. I have warned* our kids to not overlook Greenwood. They are a good football team. We can't backslide or we will be sitting at home next week".

Gatewood was anxious for the rematch. "So many people considered Louisville a favorite to win the North and I knew our team was better than what we showed that night... We still have a very bitter taste in our mouth from that game. We are excited for this one".

It wasn't until the 2nd quarter that Knowles finished a 65-yard march with his 1-yarder and Wilkes provided the 7-0 lead. They then went 46 yards with Yarbrough hitting Tyrique Carter from 25 yads to allow Yarbrough a 4-yard tally and Wilkes the PAT as halftime closed. Greenwood fumbled deep in their territory to start the 3rd quarter and Hopkins recovered. Two plays later, Knowles plunged in from 10 yards and Wilkes put the game 21-0.

The Dogs then went 42 yards and finished on a QB sneak and PAT. A Cat fumble allowed them to score again in the finale to put the contest 21-13. They had chances to come back yet again before Claretravious Triplett ended one threat. Louisville had 195 rushing and 56 passing. Knowles led the ground (101) while Gill led tacklers with 16.

"We knew it was going to be tough to beat them two times in one season. They played us hard. I thought when we got ahead 21-0, we sort of coasted a little bit and let them back in the game. But you never felt like the game was in danger. I thought the defense stepped up and played well and we ran the ball".

GAME 15:   LOUISVILLE (12-2) @ NOXUBEE COUNTY (9-4)
                LOUISVILLE 28 NOXUBEE COUNTY 35
                November 24, 2017

The North State finals now had yet another rematch with a familiar opponent. Noxubee County was on a roll and beat the Wildcats 35-30 earlier this year. "The kids are looking forward to it. We have made it here and now have to get ready to play. We just have to go over there and not make the same kinds of mistakes we made the first time. We need to control the ball and not put ourselves in a bind. If we can control the ball and not throw interceptions and not fumble, I think we will be OK".

The Tigers found the end zone early in the 2nd quarter on Armoni Clark's 47-yarder to Rashad Eades and Samuel Lowery PAT. A trade of turnovers soon led to a 2-yard Kyziah Pruitt dive to make it 14-0. They added to it when Clark hit Jaquaylan Smith for a 54-yard score and 21-0 lead. Louisville answered when Jackson dashed 31 yards and Wilkes converted to make it 21-7 at the half.

Noxubee added their next in the 3rd quarter on a 17-yard fade from Clark to Eades and the Lowery PAT put it 28-7. Louisville tried to storm back with Yarbrough's 21-yarder to Jackson, a Dixon pick to set up a 9-yard Jackson dash and Wilkes' PAT. An apparent TD was called back and JaQuarius Jackson immediately took an interception 92 yards to the Cat 3. L.C. Clemons took it in from there.

The last tally came on a 94-yard connection from Yarbrough to Frazier. Though they got the ball back with under 2:00 remaining, an interception ended hopes of another title. Yarbrough was 7-15-2 for 132 yards. Knowles led with 63 of the 99 rushing yards and Frazier pulled in 107 in the air. Gill led with 14 tackles.

"We made too many mistakes early in the game and couldn't make any tackles. The kids didn't give up and we just couldn't get the offense to do the right things at the right times. The one think about it is they never quit and kept battling back and kept putting themselves back in the game. We knew it was going to come down to the wire and knew our kids would keep playing hard. That was our break and it was taken away from us and killed our momentum".

2018 (15-1)

The Winston County Journal believed at the beginning of August that ninth-year Coach M.C. Miller's Wildcats were "getting ready for possible 4A title run". As opening practices began in late July, Miller noted "We got after them pretty good today. We went three hours and some of them got tired towed the end. So right now, we are trying to get them into shape and get them ready to play. That first day is always the toughest".

Their opening jamboree was against Starkville to give them "a chance to find out where we are right off the bat". They defeated the Yellow Jackets 17-16. "I felt good coming out of there ... about the way we played... And the main thing is we didn't get anybody hurt".

GAME 1:   LOUISVILLE (0-0) @ NAVARRE, FL (0-0)
                                LOUISVILLE 14 NAVARRE 6
                                August 17, 2018

The opener was to be against Holmes County *"but asked to back out of the game. Then Navarre called and Miller said he jumped at the chance to play"*. He added, *"This will be a good trip for us. Most of these kids have never been to Florida so it's a big deal for them. The kids all wanted to go and are motivated"*.

This marked the longest road trip for a Wildcat team in history as they traveled to face a Raider team that went 9-2 the previous year and featured 102 roster players. They were apparently motivated as Drea Shumaker found Alvius Haynes for a 47-yard tally in the 2nd quarter and Elijah Wilkes made it 7-0. The Raiders moved to the Cat 10 but the defense moved them back far enough to force a punt. Navarre found paydirt in the finale from eight yards but missed the PAT.

In the 3rd quarter, the Raiders picked off a pass to put them at the 37-yard line and moved to the Cat 40 before Shemar Eiland's sack ended the threat. Then, Kevon Jackson broke free for a 70-yard touchdown and Wilkes put them ahead 14-6. Though Navarre later moved to the Wildcat 25, Jehmiah Harden picked off a pass to ice it.

Shumaker was 7-12-1 for 96 of the total 106 yards. Haynes pulled in 73 air yards while Jackson rushers for 75 of the 132 total. Kristian Hopkins led tacklers with 13 while Cistrunk had 12. *"That was a big win for our guys. That was a big school and we had to play like the devil to come out of there with a win. The defense made things happen. They played hard and we shut them down pretty good. We didn't even let them get close in the first half"*.

GAME 2:   LOUISVILLE (1-0) @ WEST POINT (1-0)
                                LOUISVILLE 10 WEST POINT 26
                                August 24, 2018

Tough 5A West Point opened with a 55-6 beating over Columbus to start their season. *"They are tough again. They have a good offense. They look like they are just as strong as they were last year. That's a tough place to play and you had better be ready when you go in there. We can't take a break this week. We have to be prepared to play"*.

An opening tackle on punter Wilkes at the 13-yard line set up a Jose Lemus 22-yard FG. Early in the 2nd quarter, Brandon Harris hit T.J. Anderson for a 23-yard TD and it was now 10-0. Wildcat runs put the ball deep enough to add a 31-yard Wilkes FG, Shemar Eiland recovered the squib kick, but a pass was picked off by Kentavious McMillan to end the half. Early in the 3rd quarter, Anderson found paydirt on a 25-yard reception and Kam Marin followed it with a 3-yard tally. In the finale, Dantaryius Cannon ran 57 yards to the end zone. A later safety by the Cats on Camden Sanders then led to a Claretavious Triplett 66-yard punt return as the game ended.

Shumaker was just 3-10-2 for 14 yards while Jackson rushed for 54. Ashanti Cistrunk led tacklers with nine. In all, West Point had three interceptions, five sacks, 11 tackles for loss and extended their winning streak to 30 games. Louisville had 134 yards of total offense compared to the 180 of the Wave. *"Defense really played well. We played a good team in West Point. The offense didn't play well enough. We just didn't come out like we should have. We didn't play up to par like we should have. We just have to work on it and get better. West Point is a good football team"*.

GAME 3:   LOUISVILLE (1-1) vs KEMPER COUNTY (0-2)
                                LOUISVILLE 48 KEMPER COUNTY 0
                                August 31, 2018

Kemper was having a bad season with a pair of lopsided losses and won only one contest (2016) in seven meetings against Louisville. *"They have a new coach over there and I don't know that much about him. I saw film on them. They're doing the same thing everybody else is doing. We're trying to put stuff in so we can be ready to play and pick it up and play a lot better than we did last week"*. It was another blowout from start to finish.

Scoring came in "bunches" as Michael Foster (11) scored while Claretravious Triplett set up and 2-yard Jackson run to make it 13-0. Cistrunk then recorded a 25-yard pick-six, Jackson crossed for five yards and then grabbed a punt and *"flipped it back"* to Triplett for the 33-yard tally.

Now with the clock running, Jace Hudspeth hit David Haynes from 56 yards. Camden Sanders then found Niselbyion Kirk from 56 yards for the final tally. Hudspeth and Sanders both had 56 passing yards. Michael Foster ran for 47 yards.

"Overall, offense and defense played pretty good, but we didn't play like we should have played. Defense especially played well, because we didn't let them score. Kemper didn't have the strength they usually have. I don't know if we are that much more powerful or whatever, but they're a young bunch and ours is a senior bunch".

GAME 4:   LOUISVILLE (2-1) @ RIPLEY (2-1)
                                  LOUISVILLE 55 RIPLEY 7
                                  September 7, 2018

Ripley's only two meetings with Louisville came in a 2007 playoff defeat 28-22 and last year's drubbing 49-6. *"They're a really good ball club and they're really fundamentally sound. We're just trying to get prepared for them. We will practice every day and try to get prepared for Ripley".*

Two minutes into the contest, Shumaker escaped from 56 yards and then hit Niselbyion Kirk later after a Marcus Glenn interception. They made it 21-0 on a 69-yard Michael Foster run late in the frame. Cistrunk then recorded a pick-six for his first of a pair of interceptions on the night. Cistrunk later dashed in from 42 yards to make it 35-0 after a frame.

They opened the 2nd quarter with a Jy'kevious Hibbler forced fumble while Laquarrious Taylor scooped it up and took it to paydirt. Jackson added a 46-yard run and halftime was already 49-0. Jackson had the last on a run midway through the 3rd quarter. The defense forced four interceptions and two fumble recoveries. Rankevious Johnson also had a pick while Taylor and Hopkins had fumble recoveries. Hopkins led with 10 tackles.

"We played some good ball on offense and defense. My defense played well and my offense picked it up and played a little better, too. We just shut them down and they couldn't get anything going".

GAME 5:   LOUISVILLE (3-1) @ GRENADA (1-3)
                                  LOUISVILLE 32 GRENADA 14
                                  September 14, 2018

The Wildcats' victory moved them to tenth in The Clarion-Ledger Super 10 poll. All that mattered now were the Chargers. *"We have to get them ready to play because we are playing a better team. They have a good running game and they can throw the ball pretty good. We have to be ready to play balanced football".*

Shumaker opened with an 8-yard dash up the middle for a 6-0 lead but Grenada punched back with a 70-yard Demarquese Gibson escape and Remington Smith put them ahead 7-6. Less than a minute later, Jackson dashed 51 yards to paydirt and the two-pointer put it 14-7. In the 2nd quarter, Shumaker hit Markie Haynes to set up his 9-yard run. Shumaker and Haynes hooked up in the 3rd quarter from 11 yards to put it 26-7.

In the finale, Grenada cut the lead to 26-14 on Abbott Hankins' 15-yarder to Christian Wortham. However, Shumaker put the game away with his 30-yard keeper. Johnson, Hibbler and Hopkins had sacks, Omauri Macon and Antrous Glenn recovered fumbles and Johnson had a pick. Jackson rushed for 100 yards.

GAME 6:   LOUISVILLE (4-1) vs GREENWOOD (4-1)
                                  LOUISVILLE 21 GREENWOOD 0
                                  September 21, 2018

Louisville upset a confident Coach Clinton Gatewood twice the previous year. Said Miller about this one, *"Greenwood has a pretty good team and they try to run and throw the ball a lot. We're going to have to be able to offset what they do".* Gatewood added, *"It's a test to see where our program is right now. We're trying to see how we stack up to the best. Louisville is one of the best teams in 4A. We are going there to knock them off. Yes, it's in their back yard but I can promise that we won't back down".*

Cistrunk ended the first frame with a fumble recovery and, in the 2nd quarter, the Cats blocked a Bulldog punt at their 20-yard line. Five plays later, Jackson dodged in from five yards and Triplett converted his first of three extra points. As the half approached, Shumaker hit David Haynes from 25 yards to make it 14-0.

The 3rd quarter saw Cistrunk with another fumble recovery and an interception. Shumaker tallied the last points of the game in the final stanza on a 9-yard run. The Cats had 253 total yards in the contest. Shumaker was 6-23-1 for 67 yards and 90 rushing. Haynes pulled in 51 yards while Cistrunk and Hopkins led tacklers with 12 each.

"My defense played great. We've been playing well all the time. Sometimes we put our second string in and we'll mess up and let the other team score and stuff like that, so we've been pushing that point with them. They played their assignments and did everything they were supposed to do. We just cut the run off. They were driving the ball down the field and we stood up and stopped them".

GAME 7:   LOUISVILLE (5-1) @ NEW HOPE (0-6)
                        LOUISVILLE 54 NEW HOPE 0
                        September 28, 2018

District play now started for the Wildcats and their first opponent was a road trip to face New Hope. *"New Hope is going to play us hard no matter what and we just have to be ready to play. Our main thing is to stop the run. If we stop the run, we think we can handle them".*

With many looking ahead to the Noxubee County tilt, this could have been a let-down against the winless Trojans. Shumaker got it going early with an 11-yarder and Triplett the first of many kicks. Jackson ran in late in the frame to make it 14-0. Shumaker and Alvius Haynes connected from 38 yards to set up a Jackson 2-yard plunge. The two hooked up again to set up Shumaker's 27-yarder to David Haynes.

Before halftime, Shumaker and Jackson hit from 47 yards and Jackson added a 55-yard dash to put the break 41-0. With a running clock, Jackson added a 67-yard run and Jace Hudspeth found Jamar Haynes from 60 yards to ice it. Jackson rushed for 170 yards and caught 108 more. Shumaker was 8-19 for 227 yards. Hudspeth was 2-2 for 73 yards. In all, the Cats had 537 offensive markers with 300 coming on the ground.

"They played pretty well. As long as we can keep them going like they're going. We have a lot of injured people out so hopefully we'll have them all back this week. We just have to keep the ones we have focused now".

GAME 8:   LOUISVILLE (6-1) vs NOXUBEE COUNTY (3-4)
                        LOUISVILLE 27 NOXUBEE COUNTY 26
                        October 5, 2018

All eyes were on this rival meeting and history noted that this could be one to derail Wildcat hopes yet again. The Tigers had an 8-2 record over Louisville in the last ten contests. *"If we can play good for the first quarter, we will be OK. We always have a bad first quarter against them. They always get us down in the first quarter and then we have to battle back. We want to try to make them bounce back from behind".*

Just seconds into the 1st quarter, the plan went awry when Kyziah Pruitt's 21-yard TD reception made it 6-0. Elijah Wilkes nailed a FG midway through the frame while Cistrunk garnered his fifth interception of the season. Noxubee's Trillo Brown grabbed a loose Wildcat football and took it to paydirt and it was 12-3 still in the opening frame. Then, Jackson pulled in a Shumaker screen for a 65-yard dash to daylight and Wilkes made it a 12-10 game.

In the 2nd quarter, Kedarius Shell added a pick-six and, with Wilkes' PAT, gave Louisville a 17-12 advantage. Jackson added a 35-yarder early in the 3rd quarter to put it 24-12. The Tigers scratched back with a 4th quarter safety followed by a Savion Price touchdown reception to put it 24-20. Then, JaQuaris Jamison took a blocked Cat punt for a touchdown with 2:25 left and appeared to have completed the comeback upset. However, with just :02 left in the game, Wilkes calmly nailed a 19-yard FG for the game-winner.

Antrous Glenn, Kedarius Glenn and Cistrunk all had interceptions. Charles Moore led tacklers with 11, Shumaker was 10-25 for 177, Jackson rushed for 106 and led receivers with 74 yards. *"Defense set the tone but we did mess up down the line. It really was just a tough game. Our main thing going into the game was not letting them score early because, normally, they used to score early in the game and get a big lead on us and we always have to battle back. And that's what I talked to them about".*

GAME 9:   LOUISVILLE (7-1) vs FOREST (5-3)
                        LOUISVILLE 49 FOREST 3
                        October 11, 2018

After losing to the Bearcats in 1930 and 1934, Louisville rebounded with three wins. The last was a 35-0 whitewash the previous year. This game was moved to a Thursday tilt. Said Miller, *"They have a balanced team. They can throw the ball a little bit and run the ball a little bit. I think we can handle that pretty good. We just need to go into there and play basic, fundamental football and we will be alright"*.

Added the Forest mentor, *"Playing a team like Louisville is a good challenge for us because they will hold us accountable for every mistake we make"*. That is just what the Wildcats did as the second-ranked 4A team in Mississippi.

Shumaker was first across the stripe from eight yards and Wilkes made it 7-0. He then hit David Haynes from 18 yards, Triplett took a punt 60 yards to paydirt and Wilkes gave the Cats a 21-0 lead at intermission. Forest got their only points midway through the 3rd quarter on Alejandro Aguillar's FG but Shumaker immediately hit Alvius Haynes from 60 yards to put it 28-3.

Still in the 3rd quarter, Derius Hopkins took a fumble 25 yards while Menyon Sanders ran in from 45 yards to start the finale. Jace Hudspeth soon added a 6-yard run and Wilkes converted on the extra points. Louisville rushed for 190 and passed for 191. Shumaker was 6-9 for 147, Yarbrough (now back from an injury sustained in the first game) went 3-9-1 for 44. Kristian Hopkins led tackers with 14, Shemar Eland had a pick and Omauri Macon forced a fumble.

Alvius Haynes led receivers with 76 yards while Triplett ran for 51 more. Wilkes went 7-7 on extra points.

GAME 10:   LOUISVILLE (8-1) @ KOSCIUSKO (3-5)
                        LOUISVILLE 46 KOSCIUSKO 23
                        October 19, 2018

With 80 previous meetings, Kosciusko's Whippets were once the Wildcat's number one rival. That cooled down over the past decade and was now seemingly replaced by Noxubee County for a host of reasons.

"I'm expecting it to be a good game because they played Noxubee County in a tough game last week in the first half and I think that was at Noxubee County, too. We have to go there and you know they're going to play better when they're at home. We just have to get ready to play and get up early. Because if we don't, and we play around and hang in there, we might be in trouble".

Wilkes opened with a 42-yard FG and Jackson followed it on his 19-yarder to put the Cats ahead 10-0. Kosy's Cody Pope added a 30-yard FG late in the frame to cut into the lead. Yarbrough dove in from three yards and Wilkes converted. Derius Hopkins then blocked a Whippet punt and Jackson turned it into a 9-yard TD to put halftime 24-3.

Yarbrough opened the 3rd quarter with a 5-yarder to Haynes while Wilkes hit Eiland for the 32-3 two-pointer. Kosy came back with Zavier Miller's 7-yard toss to Ethan Wood and make it 32-9, but Jackson opened the finale with a 25-yard scamper and 39-9 lead. Antonio Harmon for the Whippets added their next on a 70-yard fumble return and Pope converted. Wood then hit Marlon Dotson late in the game, but Shumaker responded with a 58-yard escape and Wilkes PAT to end things.

"We did pretty well. I was out there telling my guys not to go out there slow playing and let Kosciusko jump up on us. As long as we play like we're supposed to, we will be alright. We usually have trouble with people in that first quarter (but) they hung in there and played good".

GAME 11:   LOUISVILLE (9-1) vs LEAKE CENTRAL (0-9)
                        LOUISVILLE 43 LEAKE CENTRAL 0
                        October 26, 2018

Said Miller of the last regular season game against a winless team, *"We're getting ready … to grind it out and do what we have to do to get ready, get healed and ready for the playoffs. That's what we want to do. Hopefully we can keep everybody playing hard this week. We don't want to have any days off. I want to keep them playing hard"*.

Derius Hopkins started the affair by pulling *"the football from a Leake Central carrier"* for a 72-yard touchdown and Wilkes converted his first of many. Yarbrough then found Haynes from 45 yards and then hit Shumaker from 25 yards as the frame ended. The Cats added a safety followed by a 23-yard Yarbrough dash to paydirt.

Starters were replaced by reserves with the score already 29-0. Camden Sanders found Kirk from six yards and Terrance Luckett from five yards for the final. Yarbrough was 3-7 for 84 yards, Sanders 5-8 for 68 yards and led rushers with 52 more, Shumaker had 47 receiving yards, while Hopkins, A.J. Hardin (fumble recovery) and T.J. Graham (interception) led the defense. Laquarrious Taylor had six tackles.

"They came out, offense and defense, and did a good job. They didn't play as hard as they could have but they played good right off the bat".

GAME 12:　　　　LOUISVILLE (10-1) vs BYHALIA (6-5)
　　　　　　　　LOUISVILLE 41 BYHALIA 0
　　　　　　　　November 2, 2018

This marked the first meeting between the two squads. *"Byhalia is coming in as the number four team. We have to get ready to play them like we're supposed to. We have to play them hard. We can't let them get their momentum going. This is the playoffs. All of the weak are at home. Anybody can beat you on a given night".*

Even with Miller absent due to health issues, the Wildcats ran roughshod over the visiting team from Byhalia. In the 2nd quarter, Yarbrough ran in from three yards and Wilkes made it 7-0. Kristian Hopkins recovered a fumble and Yarbrough used it to find Alvius Haynes from 23 yards. Late in the half, Yarbrough broke across from two yards to make intermission 20-0.

In the 2nd half, Menyon Sanders escaped from 45 yards, Yarbrough hit Shumaker from 12 yards, and Shumaker hit Jackson from 20 yards. The Wilkes PAT proved the last point. Yarbrough was 8-15 for 94. Haynes led receivers with 50 and Jackson rushers with 78. In total, the Cats had 143 total offensive yards.

GAME 13:　　　　LOUISVILLE (11-1) vs CLARKSDALE (7-6)
　　　　　　　　LOUISVILLE 59 CLARKSDALE 0
　　　　　　　　November 9, 2018

The Coahoma County squad was no pushover with four wins over Louisville in their last five meetings. Their journey continued the previous week with a win over Itawamba AHS 21-16. Said Miller, *"It's going to be a little bit more of a physical game than we've had in the last two games. They are going to try to run. They're going to try to pass and they're going to mix it up".*

Yarbrough opened with a 2-yarder to end a 98-yard drive while Kedarius Dixon (or Billy Houston) took a fumble back to paydirt later and Wilkes converted both. In the next frame, Yarbrough rushed in from 18 yards, Jackson dashed in from six yards after a Cat fumble recovery, Yarbrough dove in from a yard, Kevon Jackson crossed from 38 yards and Wilkes' kicks put it 42-0. He also added a 42-yard FG to put intermission 45-0.

Yarbrough opened the 3rd with a 15-yard toss to Alvius Haynes and Wilkes converted. Sanders' 10-yarder put the final 59-0. Dixon, Kristian Hopkins and Cistrunk had fumble recoveries. Louisville put up 503 offensive yards with 271 coming on the ground. Jackson rushed for 133, Haynes pulled in 121 in the air, Yarbrough ran for 71 and threw for 232 with 12 completions.

"They're playing good ball right now. Everything is coming together. It just felt like everything went our way on offense and defense. We're not as banged up as we were. We're getting back our physical strength and all of them are playing really well right now. We just have to keep them going".

GAME 14:　　　　LOUISVILLE (12-1) @ PONTOTOC (11-2)
　　　　　　　　LOUISVILLE 56 PONTOTC 7
　　　　　　　　November 16, 2018

The Warriors were coming off a 31-6 win over Senatobia. Said Miller, *"Pontotoc has a good team. They play good fundamental, sound football. We have to go up there, be balanced ad play them like we're supposed to play. We can't go up there and make a whole lot of mistakes and stuff. We just have to settle down and play hard-nosed football".*

Scoring came in bunches in the blowout victory. An early safety was followed by a Charles Moore pick-six. Yarbrough found Alvius Haynes from seven yards, Moore picked off another pass and Yarbrough hit Kirk from 30 yards. Wilkes converted on one score. Jackson then rushed in from four yards and Wilkes put halftime 28-0.

Yarbrough then ran in from two yards before Pontotoc found paydirt to avoid the shutout. Jackson later rushed n from 45 yards, Jontea Garnett recorded a 55-yard pick-six and Wilkes put the board 49-7. Jackson ended things with a 65-yard dash. Louisville had 425 offensive yards with 279 coming via the ground. Jackson led rushers with 171, Yarbrough was 13-17 for 146, and both Kirk and Haynes had 50 receiving yards.

Defensively, there were four turnovers. Claretavious Triplett also had an interception to join Moore and Garnett. Cistrunk had eight solo tackles. *"Our defense has played well all year and our offense has gotten it together and now they're playing good. I had them fired up when they went on the field and they were ready to play the whole game. They did a good job".*

GAME 15:   LOUISVILLE (13-1) vs GREENWOOD (11-2)
                 LOUISVILLE 17 GREENWOOD 14
                 November 23, 2018

Much like the previous season, the Wildcats would have to beat Greenwood twice in order to have a chance at the championship. *"When we played them, they said they were going to meet us again and I said 'OK'. We have to get ready to play them. We beat them 21-0 but they've improved. But, we've improved, too".*

Late in the 1st quarter, Wilkes hit a FG to make it a slim 3-0 game. In the next quarter, Yarbrough broke through from 10 yards and Wilkes put them up 10-0. However, a pair of 3rd quarter turnovers *"proved costly"*. One fumble was taken 35 yards by Quiontavious Lymon to paydirt and an Omar Emmons 75-yard pick-six gave them the 14-10 lead.

Now in the final frame, Jackson rushed in from three yards on fourth down and Wilkes nailed the PAT. The Cats forced a turnover with 2:00 remaining to ice it. Yarbrough rushed for 134 yards and was 4-10-1 for 62 more. Jackson rushed for 31 while Shumaker led receivers with 48. Hibbler, Hopkins and Glenn each had sacks while Marcus Glenn had an interception. Cistrunk led tacklers with nine.

"I told the guys we can't afford to lose a game like this. The defense has played their heart out. Greenwood hadn't come close to scoring. You all have to do better than this. If we stop them here... They have to pick it up and do their job".

GAME 16:   LOUISVILLE (14-1) vs POPLARVILLE (13-1)
                 LOUISVILLE 25 POPLARVILLE 20
                 December 1, 2018: M.M. Roberts Stadium; Hattiesburg, MS

Since Louisville began play in 1913, these two teams had yet to meet. The Hornets, on a 13-game winning streak, were very run-heavy with nearly no passing attack. *"What we have to do is stop the running attack because they have a good offensive line. And when you have a good offensive line, you can run that way and get pretty good at it".*

This one seemed to get out of hand the wrong way early. Tyson Holston put up a pair of rushing touchdowns and the extra points gave them a 14-0 lead. The Cats came back in the 2nd quarter with an 80-yard drive capped by Yarbrough's 9-yarder to Alvius Haynes. Now in the 3rd quarter and Louisville down 14-6, Jackson with his 4-yarder to make it 14-12. Poplarville responded with a 44-yard Holston run to push them back on top 20-12.

The Wildcats responded with a 14-yard dash by Jackson and it was now 20-18. The last tally came after an unsportsmanlike penalty put the Cats at the 28-yard line. Yarbrough hit Kirk from there for yet another State Championship. Said Poplarville coach Jay Beech, *"I thought we laid it all on the line. We believed we could do it. Nobody doubted. To come up short, that's a hard pill to swallow".*

Yarbrough amassed 140 passing and 160 rushing yards and was named MVP of game. Kristian Hopkins (18) and Cistrunk (15) combined for 33 tackles on the day. *"The guys said they wanted to do it for me and they did it. Every time we play for it, we're going to win it. I feel so happy now winning, it makes me feel good".* At the end of the season, Miller announced his pending retirement.

Jy'Kevious Hibbler earned an All-State nod. PowerCats Choice Awards included Donte Yarbrough as Comeback Player of the Year, Ashanti Cistrunk was "Boys Leader of the Year", Alvius Hayes, was "Boy's Breakthrough Athlete of the Year", and Elijah Wilkes earned "Play of the Year" for his last-second FG against Noxubee County.

Other internal awards included Derrion Dora (Best Offensive Lineman), Charles Moore and Antrous Glenn (Best Defensive Lineman), Claretavious Triplett and Jehmiah

Harden (Best Linebacker), Hibbler and Kedarius Shell (Best Defensive Back), Alvius Haynes (Best Wide Receiver), Yarbrough and Shumaker (Best Offensive Player), Cistrunk (Best Defensive Player), Kevon Jackson (Offensive MVP) and Derius Hopkins (Defensive MVP).

2019 (11-3)

After years of competing against Coach Tyrone Shorter and his Noxubee County Tigers, Shorter now stepped in as Wildcat mentor. After 20 years at Noxubee, Shorter was 89-28 and had four 4A titles. *"It's gone really well. I thought coming in would have been a whole lot different. But it wasn't. We came in and the kids started buying into everything that we've asked them to do. It wasn't a hard transition at all. These kids are winners"*.

He added more as the first game approached, *"They're the same kids I'm used to. They are very talented. You find so many more diamonds in the rough here and there's a larger talent pool to pull from here. I like physical kids. They're not the country kids I'm used to, but they're very similar. If they can handle me and my coaching staff, everything else will take care of itself"*.

GAME 1:   LOUISVILLE (0-0) @ NOXUBEE COUNTY (0-0)
               LOUISVILLE 0 NOXUBEE COUNTY 2
               August 23, 2019

It was poetic justice that Shorter's first contest came against Noxubee County. He guided the Tigers to a 7-2 record against Louisville in the last nine meetings, and now he patrolled the other sideline. After meeting consecutively since 1981 and then more prior, this one may have been the most unanticipated ending in the series.

The entire defensive struggle between the clubs came down to a fumbled 3rd quarter snap that gave the Tigers a safety. It was just one of three on the night for the Cats, but most definitely the costliest. They also suffered an interception. On the positive side, the defense allowed just 63 total offensive yards.

"We're still learning this team. We knew that we could play defense and our defense pitched a shutout. We plan on doing that a lot this season. Our offense struggled. We moved the ball up and down the field but we had too many mistakes. We've got to correct the mistakes that we made offensively and move forward".

GAME 2:   LOUISVILLE (0-1) vs WEST POINT (1-0)
               LOUISVILLE 38 WEST POINT 28
               August 30, 2019

The season did not get easier and the Wildcats now faced 5A West Point. The three-time state champions were coming off a 34-6 drumming of 6A Horn Lake and beat Louisville their last four encounters. *"West Point is going to be West Point and I'm very familiar with them. They're not going to beat themselves. We might stop them for three quarters and then they might hit three big runs. They capitalize on your mistakes so we most definitely have to correct (our) mistakes"*.

Louisville jumped on the Wave early as, midway through the opening frame, Rankevious Johnson had a sack-fumble and Drea Shumaker quickly used it for an 8-yard TD. The Wave came back before the end of the quarter to tie it 7-7. Roper Stoots then hit a 30-yard FG in the 2nd quarter. Shumaker later found Niselbyion Kirk from 26 yards but West Point responded to put halftime 17-14.

West Point took the lead in the 3rd quarter to make it 21-17, *"but Louisville showed its resiliency"* when Shumaker and Mosley connected from 35 yards. Ty Cooper later picked off a Green Wave pass to allow Michael Foster a 3-yard TD run. The visitors came back once more in the finale to close it to 31-28. Louisville then went 95 yards with Shumaker and Mosley again hooking up. The defense closed affairs with solid play after.

The Cats had 437 offensive yards. Shumaker was 19-26 for 341 while Mosely had 165 receiving. *"It's what we have been expecting. I told them from the beginning that if they would just trust the process, it works. Last week I just came in and challenged the kids. I told them that they could either quit and tuck their tails or they could learn from their experience and move forward. They came back to practice and worked hard. Noxubee County didn't beat us. We beat ourselves. We showed them that and we came back. I felt good all week about it"*.

GAME 3:   LOUISVILLE (1-1) @ COLUMBUS (0-2)
                              LOUISVILLE 32 COLUMBUS 6
                              September 6, 2019

The win over West Point launched Louisville into eighth in the Mississippi Prep Poll. West Point, despite the loss, sat sixth. *"We can't let this (Columbus) be a trap game. We've just got to continue to get better. Columbus has a new coaching staff and they're trying to get better. We've just got to do what we do and get ready for the next one. We're going to prepare our team and get them ready to roll. We don't take anybody lightly"*.

An early Jamarcus Eland fumble recovery ended only in a 30-yard Stoots FG. Later in the frame, Foster took the ball to the 5-yard line and Shumaker eventually crossed from two yards to make it 10-0. Foster later added a 30-yarder and halftime stood 17-0. Now in the finale, Tyrell Thames garnered a 60-yard pick-six and the two-pointer put it 25-0. Jaden Triplett finished it with a 36-yard dash while the Falcons tallied only in the last ten seconds on a 1-yard Ethan Conner dive.

Louisville had 332 offensive yards. Shumaker was 9-14 for 124, Foster rushed for 141 yards, Mosley grabbed 66 passing yards, Kristian Hopkins led with 16 tackles and Thames a pair of interceptions. *"Coming off a big win like we did, you're playing against an 0-2 team. You're playing teenage kids and they take teams lightly sometimes. We just have to play our style of game and play our football"*.

GAME 4:   LOUISVILLE (2-1) @ STARKVILLE (1-2)
                              LOUISVILLE 7 STARKVILLE 35
                              September 13, 2019

The long-time 6A foe Yellow Jackets were just defeated by West Point 41-35 the prior week. Said Shorter, *"I knew that was going to be a really good game. I told my coaches that it would go down to the wire and whoever made the least amount of mistakes would win. The only thing I was surprised by was West Point had the rushing yards they did"*. Of this one against Coach Chris Jones, he added *""We're excited to play Starkville in a big-time football game. There are certain games that should be played in this area and this is one of them"*. <u>The Clarion-Ledger</u> predicted a Jacket victory.

Starkville and QB Luke Altmyer took a 14-0 lead on a pair of drives over 70 yards. Foster cut into the lead for the only Cat tally via his 31-yard escape. In the 3rd quarter, Keyshawn Lawrence bulled in from a yard despite a plea from the Wildcats that he fumbled before crossing the stripe. The Jackets added a pair of last-quarter touchdowns that made *"the score worse than the game actually was"*.

Shumaker was 11-24 for 106, Mosley had 76 receiving, and Foster recorded 119 rushing. *"I'm pleased with this team. We fought. Starkville is a big 6A school and we were in there for a minute and then they started making some plays. We're fine. This is a good football team that we played and it showed tonight"*.

GAME 5:   LOUISVILLE (2-2) vs SHANNON (1-3)
                              LOUISVILLE 28 SHANNON 8
                              September 20, 2019

Before the season, the Wildcat schedule (perhaps incorrectly) had Morton as the visitor for this weekend. Instead, Shannon was back on the schedule for the fifth time since 1991 having never recorded a win over Louisville. *"We're going to have to regroup and get a good game plan together. It's just good to be back to playing 4A football. These guys just have to stay healthy and hold their heads up"*.

A 28-0 halftime lead led to a running clock in the second half. Foster was first from 10 yards, Foster added the next from 29 yards, Shumaker hit Dantavius Triplett from 18 yards and later Mosley from 48 yards. The Red Raiders had their lone tally late as reserves garnered valuable experience.

Shumaker was 11-19 for 157, Mosley grabbed 101 of those, and Shumaker (68) and Foster (66) paced rushers. The defense allowed just 78 total yards and had nine sacks and an interception. In all, the Cats had 307 offensive yards with 140 on the ground.

"I'm pleased with the way our kids responded after last Friday night. We wanted to be balanced and we were. That's what we took out of it. I like the way they're handling adversity. Sometimes a loss can help your team. We evaluated the film and each position after last week and saw that we just got worn out at the end of the game against Starkville so I liked the way we responded from that".

GAME 6:   LOUISVILLE (3-2) vs YAZOO CITY (0-5)
                   LOUISVILLE 49 YAZOO CITY 0
                   September 27, 2019

The pair first met in 1939 with a Wildcat victory and repeated that feat in 1940. However, the Indians bested Louisville in 1954 and 1955 before losing the next nine. Said Shorter about the winless opponent, *"Looking at Yazoo City, they're big and they have athletes. We just can't allow them to come in here and us play down. They can slip up on you. We want to take care of business and (do it) early. We're trying to train their mind and get ready for the division play. This is the last game before division and we want to come out and play really well. We want to eliminate mistakes"*.

The night started with a recognition of every Wildcat team to win state championships and ended with a resounding non-conference victory. An early Yazoo City turnover soon led to Foster's 6-yarder. They quickly made it 28-0 after just a frame and 42-0 at intermission. Afterwards, the clock ran for the second half.

Shumaker crossed from five yards and a later from 26 yards. Louisville recovered a fumble in the end zone for the next touchdown, Kirk opened the 2nd quarter with a 75-yard dash while Foster got in later. Jace Hudspeth took over at QB in the 3rd quarter and had a 25-yard scoring pass. Camden Sanders also saw playing time at QB. In all, the offense had 326 offensive yards, Shumaker was 7-11 for 134 and 40 rushing yards, and Kirk had 92 receiving.

"I thought we came out and played really well. We wanted to focus on being balanced and have our mindset on there being no tomorrow. We want to treat every game like it's a playoff game. We could meet Yazoo City again in the playoffs, so we wanted to play well".

GAME 7:   LOUISVILLE (4-2) @ NORTHEAST LAUDERDALE (2-4)
                   LOUISVILLE 35 NORTHEAST LAUDERDALE 7
                   October 4, 2019

With a 3-1 all-time record against NEL on the line, one could wonder whether the Wildcats were tested and ready for this road tilt. This one started the division series and a win was all that mattered. *'I like where we are right now. We're healthy going into this division stretch. We've been battle-tested and know what our kids can do. We have to be disciplined on defense because they can hurt us"*.

Surprisingly, Louisville trailed early as Northeast tallied. But the Cats got it going in the 2nd quarter with a 2-yarder by Foster and he followed that with another from three yards. Shumaker later hit Kirk from 25 yards while Omauri Macon found a fumble afterwards. Shumaker turned it into a 13-yard TD and 28-7 lead at halftime. Reserves again got the call for the second half. Jaquez Thames added 3-yarder to wrap up the game.

Of the 312 total offensive yards, Foster rushed for 120 of them. Shumaker was 9-16 for 163. *"For us to come out and play like that in all three phases in the first district game, we were very pleased. Those first six ball games prepared us for division and it was important for us to win that first division ball game, especially on the road"*.

GAME 8:   LOUISVILLE (5-2) vs CHOCTAW CENTRAL (3-3)
                   LOUISVILLE 43 CHOCTAW CENTRAL 14
                   October 10, 2019: HOMECOMING

Now fourth in the latest polling, Louisville welcomed first-time opponent Choctaw Central for Homecoming. The Warriors were break-even thus far but still a division opponent in front of returning alums. Due to impending weather conditions, this tilt was moved to a Thursday affair.

Louisville was already on the board after a few minutes when Shumaker found Jaquayvius Hawthorne from 15 yards and a two-pointer. Foster then found paydirt from a yard while Shumaker had the next on a 20-yard run. A Cat fumble into the end zone gave the Warriors a touchdown, but Shumaker rushed in from six yards and followed it with a 15-yarder late to make halftime 36-7.

The benches emptied again and allowed Choctaw Central one more touchdown. However, Jace Hudspeth found Thames from 25 yards to end it. Of the 272 total yards, 194 were via the air. Shumaker was 11-20-2 for 159 and 61 rushing yards. Foster had 106 rushing and Mosley 92 receiving.

"We're getting better. We played three phases of the game really well. We were balanced. We don't want to be one-dimensional because we want people to prepare for a lot. I want a lot of different things on film for people to prepare for. I like the way we're passing and I think our offensive line is doing a great job".

GAME 9:   LOUISVILLE (6-2) @ WEST LAUDERDALE (5-3)
                          LOUISVILLE 12 WEST LAUDERDALE 0
                          October 18, 2019

Up next was an undefeated 2-0 team in the district. Moreover, it was on the road. *"This game is going to be for the district championship. West Lauderdale has tradition. They've been in the playoffs year in and year out. They've got a good football team so we've got our hands full. They're impressive so we've got to go on the road and it's always hard to win there".*

The first tally for the Wildcats didn't come until the 2nd quarter. Touchdowns came from both Shumaker and Thames. Shumaker was 6-10 for 61, Foster ran for 117 and Eiland recorded an interception.

"I thought going into the game that they were going to have a good football team and they did. I thought we played really well defensively and gave up just 143 yards. Offense played well but we stalled in the red zone a couple of times. It's always good to go on the road in that environment and get a win. They had a good scheme. I've got to give them credit. They gave us problems up front but we moved the ball up and down the field and then just got a couple of goal line stands...".

GAME 10:   LOUISVILLE (7-2) vs LEAKE CENTRAL (4-5)
                          LOUISVILLE 39 LEAKE CENTRAL 0
                          October 25, 2019

A win tonight against Leake Central gave the Cats yet another 4-4A division title. *"Watching them on film, they have a very good QB and some talent and speed. I don't know what they're going to do because they've played two styles of offense and a couple of different QBs. We can't allow them to be spoilers. We've been telling (our kids) all along that we want to be division champs and have the number one seed. We've got to finish these last couple of ball games out".*

Under a consistent rain at Hinze Stadium, the Wildcats did not fade as they took Leake Central to the wet woodshed. Other teams moved their games to Thursday. Foster put up the first two touchdowns against the Gators while Mosley pulled in a 19-yarder from Shumaker for the next. In the 3rd quarter, Shumaker hit Kirk from 45 yards and later a 25-yarder to put it 32-0. Jaden Triplett dashed 20 yards for the finale. The defense allowed just 29 total yards while Shumaker went 14-20 for 169. Thames rushed for 92 yards and Kirk pulled in 72 receiving.

The reason I didn't move the game to Thursday is that I wanted to see how this team could handle weather. Lat year's team handled it really well, but this is a different team. I wanted to see how we handled the elements and we did a great job. We didn't have any turnovers or even a bad snap. You never know what you're going to get in the month of November so I wanted to see them in those elements".

GAME 11:   LOUISVILLE (8-2) @ KOSCIUSKO (3-6)
                          LOUISVILLE 55 KOSCIUSKO 7
                          November 1, 2019

With games going back to at least 1929, this one was never to be taken lightly. At one time, this was the biggest Wildcat rivalry. Now the Wildcats traveled to Kosy to see where they stood against a team with a losing record. Nevertheless, the Whippets were coming off back-to-back conference victories.

"We've got to prepare for both offenses that they're going to give us. They're clicking at the right time and they're going to be fired up on senior night. It's one of those games we'll have to play our A-game. We'll treat this game like it's our first playoff game".

The Whippets drove to the Cat 5 before the defense forced a turnover. Hopkins took the ball 95 yards to paydirt despite it coming back on a penalty. Foster eventually made it count from five yards for the 7-0 lead. Though Kosy put up their only tally after on a 14-yard Ethan Wood pass to Zavier Miller and Will Carter PAT, Louisville came back with a 26-yard Shumaker pass to Kirk and it was 13-7 after a frame.

Shumaker then added a pair of tallies and Jaquez Thames had a running touchdown to lead the Cats to a 42-7 halftime lead. Thames garnered another in the second half from 18 yards while Hopkins *"strip sacked"* to set up a 40-yard Ty Cooper return for the finale. The Cats rushed for 125 yards, Shumaker was 10-14 for 214, Haynes had 117 receiving and Joshua Nunn had an interception. Kristian Hopkins led tacklers with 13.

"We wanted our guys to come in and treat it like a playoff game. We started to gel together in all three phases of the game and that's where we want to be at this point in the year. We wanted to start off fast and we did. Our defense has been playing really well all year... My staff is doing a great job and we've got some guys where we want them to be. We're fast and physical and play smart football".

GAME 12:   LOUISVILLE (9-2) vs YAZOO CITY (2-8)
                            LOUISVILLE 30 YAZOO CITY 12
                            November 8, 2019

Shorter noted in late September that the two teams could meet again in the playoffs. He was correct, and this one was much closer than the first meeting.

The Indians had the first score on their opening possession but Shumaker took in the responding touchdown and the Cat PAT put them ahead 7-6. Hibbler then took a fumble in for the next before Yazoo City returned the favor and halftime sat 13-12. The Wildcats took control in the next half.

Foster's two quick scoring runs gave the Wildcats some breathing room. Shontez Thames then picked off a pass and the defense added a safety. Foster later dashed in from 65 yards to finish it off. Foster ran for 239 to pass the coveted 1,000-yard mark with 1,192. Shumaker was 8-17-1 for 76 yards. That put him at 1,887 passing yards thus far.

"Looking at them on film, I knew that they were a much-improved team. They did a lot of things different than the last time we played them. They came to play and we knew that they had talent. They had a really good game plan. We went in at halftime and the adjustment that we made was with our personnel. They caught us with some different mismatches against our defense. We changed some of our personnel around".

GAME 13:   LOUISVILLE (10-2) vs PONTOTOC (6-5)
                            LOUISVILLE 52 PONTOTOC 0
                            November 8, 2019

After starting 0-4, the Warriors roared back with victories to put them in the position to upset Louisville at Hinze Stadium. Though they tied Louisville in 1930, they lost their only two other matches with the Cats. *"You can throw out the records when you hit the playoffs. They have a good football team. They're well-coached and they are going to play hard. We've just got to come out and hit them early and use our speed. We've got to tackle well against them".*

Shumaker found Mosley early from eight yards and Kirk from 25 yards to make it a quick 12-0. Then, Shumaker and Kirk hooked up from 60 yards and Mosley from 17 yards to make it 24-0. The last touchdown came after an Eiland interception. Mosley opened the 2nd quarter with a 70-yard reception while a fumble recovery by Louisville led to a 12-yard Jehmiah Harden dash. A later Rankevious Jonson pick soon led to a 2-yard Foster dive and 45-0 lead at intermission. Kylan Triplett added the last score from three yards to ice the contest.

Shumaker was 12-18 for 286 yards, Mosely had 179 of those in the air and Kirk rushed for 107 yards. Foster rushed for 182. *"Our guys came out really focused and played a lot better than we did in the first round. That's what it's going to take. We wanted to be balanced. We wanted to establish a passing game from the beginning. We thought we could hurt them that way and we did. We started fast".*

GAME 14:   LOUISVILLE (11-2) @ GREENWOOD (12-0)
                            LOUISVILLE 6 GREENWOOD 14
                            November 15, 2019

The Bulldogs had not been to the state championship game since 1988. They had chances in the recent past, but Louisville was the one to end those dreams. Said Greenwood Coach Clinton Gatewood, *"This is the game we have been waiting on for a full year now. We felt like we were the better team a year ago but we had some key calls go* against us. *Oh, yeah, we owe them a little payback. We don't care about their gold ball trophies because we're grinding for our first".*

Shorter added, *"It's a big matchup. It's two of the best teams in 4A and it's unfortunate we're playing in the third-round instead of a state championship. It's always a big game when Greenwood and Louisville play. We'd have to play them no matter what so we will have to take care of some business".*

Poor weather conditions moved the start time to roughly 10:45pm at Bulldogs Stadium. A scoreless first half of football led to a Bulldog tally in the 3rd quarter via a 55-yard DeAndre Smith pass to Daylin Metcalf. The two-pointer to Travlor Randle was good. Smith added their last score in the finale on a 4-yard run. Louisville, on the other hand, found the end zone only with 5:00 remaining after the Cats blocked a punt inside the Dog 5. Shumaker finally crossed for the last tally.

"This team had no quit in them. I'm proud of these seniors. They did everything that we asked them to do. I hate that they went out like this but I'm proud of this team. These kids fought. We expected to win the state championship. We fell short. This is a lesson that we teach these kids, that sometimes we fall but we don't quit".

All Division Awards went to Kristian Hopkins (Overall MVP), Jy'Kevious Hibbler (Defensive MVP), Drea Shumaker (Offensive MVP), Tyvoris Cooper (Most Valuable Defensive Lineman), Demarcus Eiland (Most Valuable Linebacker), Mike Foster (Most Valuable Running Back) and Kaleb Mosley (Receiver MVP). Hopkins and Shumaker played in the Bernard Blackwell North-South All-Star Game where Hopkins won the C-SPIRE Scholar Athlete Award.

Cats included in the 4-4A Super 22 were Niselbyion Kirk, Nasir Brown, Roper Stoots, Omauri Macon, Sammy Taylor, Jehmiah Hardin, Rankevious Johnson, Shontez Thames, Keandre Gill, Sacaro Goss, Jakeveion Miller, David Haynes, Joshua Nunn, Dantavius Triplett, Jaquayvius Hawthorne, Jaquez Thames and Fred Parker.

2020—2023

2020 (13-1)

After coming up just short in his inaugural season as Wildcat mentor, Tyrone Shorter felt good about their chances for his second stint. *"We feel good going into this season with this group of kids. We've been here. This is our second year here. I have the program exactly the way I want it. The guys are responding to us the way we want them to respond so we feel really good about where we are right now".*

Despite key losses due to graduation, the Wildcats did have one player (Ty Cooper) honored on <u>The Clarion-Ledger</u> Dandy Dozen list.

GAME 1:   LOUISVILLE (0-0) vs COLUMBUS (0-0)
                                  LOUISVILLE 13 COLUMBUS 0
                                  September 4, 2020

The Falcons dropped a 32-6 decision the previous season to Louisville but this encounter was a lot closer for the Wildcat opener at R.E. Hinze.

Scoring was complete after a half. An early Wildcat interception soon counted for the initial tally while, in the 2nd quarter, Jace Hudspeth dove in from a yard to finish it. Said Shorter, *"I thought our defense played really well. We did some really good things on that side of the ball. We still have to iron out a lot of mistakes that we're making and once we do, we'll be fine. We left about three touchdowns on the field. We've got to get a little better on that side of the ball".*

GAME 2:   LOUISVILLE (1-0) vs STARKVILLE (1-0)
                                  LOUISVILLE 14 STARKVILLE 24
                                  September 11, 2020

Hopes for another home win were somewhat dismal as the Yellow Jackets were not only 6A, but also the top-ranked team in Mississippi. *"They're a big time 6A program with a lot of Division 1 football players. We have to play mistake-free football to have a chance to win it. They have one of the best QBs in the nation and some really big receivers".*

Though Jason Triplett took the opening kick 83 yards to the Cat 10, it went for naught. Starkville went the other way for a touchdown, but Louisville retaliated with an 85-yard march and Emory James 7-yarder to tie it. In the 2nd quarter, Hudspeth hit Jarvis Rush from 47 yards and shocked fans saw their Cats up 14-7. Starkville added a FG before halftime to put the board 14-10.

The Jackets added two more scores in the second half to take the win back to Oktibbeha County. Jordan Mitchell dashed 65 yards for the first while Kobe Larkin tallied from 14 yards for the last. Louisville rushed for 163 with James accounting for 92 of those. Hudspeth passed for 190 with Dantavius Triplett grabbing 67.

"I'm really proud of them. We have a young offense and I'm so proud of those kids. I'm proud of our receiving crew. Those guys stepped up tonight. I told the team that if we continue to play like (that), everybody we play are 4A schools and this game let me know we have a championship football team. We just need to stay together, keep grinding, and see where it takes us".

GAME 3:   LOUISVILLE (1-1) @ SHANNON (1-1)
                                  LOUISVILLE 21 SHANNON 8
                                  September 18, 2020

Shannon, back on the schedule again, was an all-time 0-5 against the Cats. But the Cat coach thought they should not be overlooked. He noted that Shannon (and the following week opponent Yazoo City) were probably teams the Wildcats would face in the playoffs *"so we've got to make a statement in the next two weeks".*

The Cats scored all of their points before Shannon dotted the board later. James had a pair of touchdowns with Jacorey Coleman adding another. Jaden Triplett ran for 150 yards with James leading the way with 72. The defense held the Red Raiders under 100 yards of offense. Hudspeth was just 3-11-2 for 29 yards.

"I thought we came out and played really hard in the first half. We were really sharp and on top of our game but got off the gas in the second half. We had four turnovers and that concerned me a little. I think we're headed in the right direction. Like typical high

school kids, they think the game is over after getting a big lead. We got careless with the ball. It was a lack of focus but it's things we can correct".

GAME 4:   LOUISVILLE (2-1) @ YAZOO CITY (1-1)
                 LOUISVILLE 28 YAZOO CITY 0
                 September 25, 2020

The only two Yazoo City victories over Louisville came in 1954 and 1955. All other meetings ended in favor of the Cats. *"Watching them on film, they're huge and they're athletic. They've got a new coach this year so they're doing some things different. We're going on the road and have to play well. We have got to come out with a lot of intensity and get on the board early"*.

Like the previous week, the Wildcats held a 21-0 lead at halftime en-route to the 28-0 shutout. Louisville scored on their opening possession and added a defensive *"scoop and score"* for another. Two scores came from Hudspeth and another on a 4th quarter Chris Rush 17-yard reception. The others were unmentioned. James rushed for 83 of the 192 total ground yards, Hudspeth was 13-21 for 137, Keyarrion Jackson had 61 receiving and Keandre Gill led tacklers with 14.

"Yazoo City was a very surprising team. I knew they were big but when we saw them in person, they were a physical football team. Those guys came to play but I'm pleased with our kids. We came out and established the run and passed the ball off the run. Our game plan worked to perfection".

GAME 5:   LOUISVILLE (3-1) vs NORTHEAST LAUDERDALE (0-3)
                 LOUISVILLE 53 NORTHEAST LAUDERDALE 13
                 October 2, 2020: HOMECOMING

With only one victory (2005) and five defeats against Louisville, things did not look good for Northeast Lauderdale chances at Wildcat Homecoming. And that was not to mention the fact that they had yet to come out victorious in a contest thus far. This one marked the start of 4-4A competition.

"They play old-school football and have been catching some bad breaks in these first few games. It's a division game and anybody can get beat in any given game. They're going to be one of those teams that will be right there in the end. They're going to play us hard and have some really great looking athletes. We're going to take it one game at a time and not take anyone lightly".

Once again, The Winston County Journal does not provide specifics on game proceedings. It was 14-0 after the opening frame and 20-0 at halftime. Jones then tallied in the 3rd quarter for the next. Ty Cooper pitched in some on defense with a pair of fumble returns to fuel the attack. James (2), Coleman (1), Jaden Triplett (1) and Dakota Steele (1) had others. Hudspeth had one, as well.

Statistically, the Wildcats put up 413 total offensive yards. James rushed for 147 while Coleman had 116. Hudspeth was 6-17 for 88 yards. Gill paced tacklers with 11 while Cooper also had two fumble recoveries. *"I was pleased in all three phases of the game. Our offense took the field first and scored right away. That's what we wanted to do. I'm pleased with our offensive line. Those guys are playing great together and we're doing what we want to do on offense"*.

GAME 6:   LOUISVILLE (4-1) @ CHOCTAW CENTRAL (1-2)
                 LOUISVILLE 35 CHOCTAW CENTRAL 3
                 October 8, 2020

The COVID epidemic started to become apparent in the number of games played by opponents. By this meeting, their opponent apparently played only three games to date. *"They're a big football team with a lot of size. We don't take anybody lightly and we'll prepare for the next game like we do any game. They haven't won a game on the field yet, but this is district time. You can't afford to take anything lightly. They had a forfeit last week and got a district win so if they can steal one from us, they can get in the playoffs"*.

This runaway was held on Thursday night due to impending weather. The Warriors lone tally came early on a FG from the 10-yard line. It all went to Louisville after. James scored on runs of 11 and 8 yards while the defense added the next two touchdowns to make it 28-3 at intermission. Jaden Triplett added the next tally for the finale.

Hudspeth went 18-21 for 225 yards while the Wildcats added another 186 on the ground. *"I thought it started with the offensive line. It gave Jace time to throw the football and our coaching staff did a great job putting kids in the right position to be successful in the passing game. I want to be balanced and I think we're going to need that when we finish out the regular season and get into the playoffs".*

GAME 7:   LOUISVILLE (5-1) vs WEST LAUDERDALE (4-2)
                    LOUISVILLE 21 WEST LAUDERDALE 14
                    October 16, 2020

The Knights, 2-3 all-time against Louisville, started 0-2 before winning four-straight. *"West Lauderdale has a good defensive front and we know that teams are going to stack the box against us. It's important to show teams that we can pass the football. It makes our offense more of a threat and we can play against any defense we're given. The game is for the district championship. They are going to be fired up and we need to find a way to win".*

James opened scoring with a 50-yard dash to make it 7-0. West Lauderdale was able to tie it 7-7 at halftime. Hudspeth opened the 3rd quarter with a 41-yard strike to Jarvis Rush while Jaden Triplett added the last Wildcat touchdown later. The Knights put up their last in the finale. The Wildcat defense allowed 179 yards with 41 via the air. Meanwhile, the Cats had 315 yards with 201 passing.

"They're a very good football team, very well-coached and disciplined team. We knew (that) coming in and they were going to be tough to beat. We were able to pull it off and I'm proud of our kids and the way we played and handled the game. I think offensively it was our passing game. They had a good defensive front and that gave us some problems in the run game".

GAME 8:   LOUISVILLE (6-1) @ LEAKE CENTRAL (3-4)
                    LOUISVILLE 27 LEAKE CENTRAL 0
                    October 23, 2020

A win against the Gators at Leake Central give Louisville the 4-4A title. But Shorter was keeping a close eye on his opponent. *"They're very talented. I watched them on film and they have a good (team). Talent-wise, they match up with us and we have to control the line of scrimmage. We'll have to dominate the line to win the game. This is a game we will have to keep them off balance".*

James broke the ice in the 2nd quarter with a scoring run. The defense forced a turnover and Coleman rushed in to give Louisville a 14-0 lead. Dantavius Triplett and Swahili Earby pulled in catches to allow James a 4-yarder and 20-0 lead at the half. Coleman added the last midway through the final frame.

Hudspeth was 7-18-1 for 110 to move him over the 1,000-yard passing mark. On the ground, the Cats went for 200 with Coleman gathering 117 of those to go with two touchdowns. James, also with a pair of scores, had 70.

"I thought our defense played really well. Our backs were against the wall and they showed me something. Our defense has been playing well all year. We've just getting to a point where we can really shut down the running game. We're pretty balanced the way I want us to be. We run the ball really well and our backs and offensive line are doing a great job. We're passing as we need to be to keep the defense honest. I'm pleased with where we are right now".

GAME 9:   LOUISVILLE (7-1) vs KOSCIUSKO (3-5)
                    LOUISVILLE 29 KOSCIUSKO 9
                    October 30, 2020

The last regular season tilt was now at hand and against long-time foe Kosciusko. Their record was not particularly spectacular, but they provided tough competition against the Wildcats over their decades of meetings. Nothing could be taken for granted now.

"It feels really good to win the district title. I told our kids that we want to play in three championships: division, North State and state. We got one and we have two more to go. We want to finish this last game and go into the playoffs. We will be smart about playing players that are banged up but we want to win this game to take the momentum

into playoffs. We're going to take one game at a time and prepared these kids to get them ready to go".

Despite that, many starters sat as they prepared younger players for experience and avoided risking injuries for the title run. It put the game a tight one before the Cats pulled away in the finale. In fact, it was only 9-0 at the break and the Whippets tied the affair in the 3rd quarter. Aaryion Johnson dashed across the stripe in the last frame to give them back the lead while Jamarcus Eiland and Kaliyah Coburn took interceptions to the end zone.

The lone Kosy touchdown came on an Ethan Wood 9-yarder to Azikwe Mays in the 3rd quarter. They also added a safety in the same frame. Coleman rushed for 162 while Aaryion Johnson was 6-9-1 for 76. Other teams, like Shannon, were forced to end their season due to the virus outbreak.

Said Shorter, "We came out and played really well. They held the ball on us and ran the clock, which we expected them to do, but our defense played really well. We've been preaching all year that we've been blessed because COVID hasn't affected us this season. I hope we can continue to stay this way. Our guys have to sacrifice and stay away from crowds. That's all you can do. What we've done so far is working so we're trusting our kids and taking it one week at a time".

GAME 10:   LOUISVILLE (8-1) vs CALEDONIA (5-3)
                  LOUISVILLE 26 CALEDONIA 13
                  November 6, 2020

After six all-time wins over Caledonia in the series, Wildcat fans were accustomed to wins in this one. Shorter was not as sure. "Caledonia is not the Caledonia from the past. I haven't seen them in two years and this is the first time I've seen them on film. They're totally different... We've got to be a disciplined defense. I like our chances (in 4A North) and the way that we're playing. Anybody can get beat on any given Friday and you've got to play good, sound football".

Shorter was correct as this one sat 13-13 going into the final frame. Jaden Triplett opened with a quick 13-yard reception to make it 6-0 but the defenses took control. Later in the frame, Caledonia scored on a 46-yard Darrius Triplett run and the PAT put them ahead 7-6. Hudspeth then hit Rush and intermission was 13-7 Wildcats. In the 3rd quarter, Caledonia' Triplett scored again from 65 yards but a blocked kick by the Cats kept it even.

Louisville then came back with a 1-yard Hudspeth dive and Coleman added the dagger from 15 yards for the final tally. "That (Caledonia) offense is a tough offense to simulate but if you take out two plays in the game, they have less than 100 yards. I thought our defense played really well. I just thought we started slow offensively. They were better up front than I thought they were and gave us problems".

GAME 11:   LOUISVILLE (9-1) vs NEW ALBANY (5-3)
                  LOUISVILLE 28 NEW ALBANY 15
                  November 13, 2020

The two met only in 2012 when Louisville captured the win. The previous week, New Albany blew out Ripley 42-0 to win a trip to Hinze Stadium. "They're a very good football team with size. They're one of the biggest 4A schools in the state and could be 5A. We're going to have to come up with a great game plan and execute. This time of year, you've got to bring your A game every week. We can't have a bad game now".

Hudspeth broke the ice in the opening frame with a 1-yard dive and then hit Rush to make it 14-0 midway through the opening half. Midway through that frame, New Albany capitalized with a touchdown and two-point conversion to put halftime 14-8. Ty Cooper then added a Cat pick-six while Coleman dashed in from four yards in the last frame. New Albany added one more to the board after to close the gap somewhat.

Hudspeth was 8-15 for 158 yards with Rush 131 receiving 131 of those to go along with his touchdown. "Our defense played really well. We had big plays and they've been playing well all year. We did have a couple of touchdowns called back and it got our offense out of sync. Overall, having some key kids out, I thought we did pretty good. I give New Albany all the credit. They're a really good team".

GAME 12:   LOUISVILLE (10-1) @ PONTOTOC (10-1)
                  LOUISVILLE 28 PONTOTOC 7
                  November 20. 2020

Nobody remembered the tie game between the two in 1930, but many knew of the three other Cat wins since. *"They're really well-coached. They'll be solid defensively. We've got to play solid football. This time of year, everybody is good so we have to cut down on our mistakes. It's always tough to go on the road in the playoffs and it will be tough with the history they have. If you're going to win it all, you've got to take some of these games"*.

It started poorly for Wildcat fans as the Warriors hit the board first in the opening frame to make it 7-0. Triplett soon evened the board on his 30-yard run to keep the score the same until halftime. James opened the 3rd quarter from two yards, Josh Nunn picked off a pass to set up a 52-yard Rush reception *"going into the 4th quarter"*. Finally, James ended a march from four yards to ice the contest. Of the 212 total rushing yards, Coleman (130) and James (87) led the way. Hudspeth was 12-18-2 for 191 yards with Rush hauling in 105 of those.

"We prepared our kids and knew it would be a hostile environment. We prepared our kids that to win a state championship, you're going to win it on the road. It was a huge win for us and our guys came out and executed. They were mentally prepared for it. I wasn't pleased with the first half. We had three turnovers and it stopped our momentum and some opportunities that we had. We came out in the second half and played Wildcat football".

GAME 13:   LOUISVILLE (11-1) vs ITAWAMBA AHS (7-3)
       LOUISVILLE 18 ITAWAMA AHS 6
       November 27, 2020

Louisville was 3-0 since meetings began in 1989. Said Shorter the week prior to kickoff, *"It looks like it's going to be another rainy night, so we've got to prepare the kids the best we can and not let the elements stop us. They are a really good team that plays really hard. They've got great athletes. We've just got to be mentally sound to be ready to play"*.

Shorter was accurate as conditions *"were pretty rough"*. Coleman ended the opening drive from ten yards while a Shontez Thames pick set up a Hudspeth tally to Rush. Just seven minutes into the game, the Wildcats were up 12-0. Coleman added more to make it 18-0 at halftime. Of the 275 rushing yards, Jones (150) and Coleman (125) led the way. Hudspeth was 7-12 for 75 yards. Cooper was dominate on defense and stopped the last Pontotoc drive with a *"strip sack"*.

"Hats off to our coaches. They always do a good job. I'm a defensive minded coach and I think that defenses win championships. Our defense was stingy and that's what it's going to take. We have a very young offense with nine new starters that didn't go through a spring. I'm proud of those kids. It was ugly but with the weather we had, I'll take it every night".

GAME 14:   LOUISVILLE (12-1) vs POPLARVILLE (10-3)
       LOUISVILLE 15 POPLARVILLE 14
       December 5, 2020: Memorial Stadium; Jackson, MS

Poplarville played the Wildcats only two years before although coming up on a losing end of a 25-20 final that gave Louisville another state title. This year, they started 0-3 before ripping off ten consecutive victories to put them in Jackson. Said Coach Jay Beech of Louisville, *"They force you to make mistakes and make you pay for it when you (do)"*. Added Shorter, *"This is what I came here for. To be back in the state championship. We're going to come up with a great game plan. I expect this to go down to the wire"*.

Shorter was more accurate than he realized. The Hornets were first across the stripe via an 82-yard march ending on a 1-yarder. Hudspeth took the Cats back in response and finalized it with his matching 1-yard dive. On their next possession, Poplarville scored again with a 62-yard escape and 14-7 lead.

The Cats moved as far as the Hornet 6 as halftime approached and then marched to the Hornet 15 before failing once again. Now with 7:00 left at their 18-yard line, they drove steadily with passes to Jackson and Rush. With 1:00 remaining, they sat at the Poplarville 28 and, with :36 left, Hudspeth hit Rush on 4th down for the touchdown. Deciding to go for the win, Hudspeth gave it to Triplett who found paydirt for the two-pointer and tenth official state title.

Hudspeth, MVP of the game, went 23-39 for 276 with Rush catching 75 of those and Keyarrion Jackson grabbing 90. James rushed for 63 yards. *"We told them at halftime* that we would have to throw the ball to win the game and we did. This program has been here ten times and is 10-0. It feels good. For me to be a part of this program and follow along all of the legendary coaches that have been here, and to put my stamp on it, it's a great feeling".

Ty Cooper ended the season with a Dandy Dozen honor, Mr. 4A Football, and was voted "Best of the Best in Mississippi 4A". The Mississippi Association of Coaches awards went to Cooper (Overall and Defensive Player of the Year) and Shorter (Coach of the Year). First Team Cats included Jarvis Rush, Marcus Eiland, Omauri Macon, Keandre Gill, and Joshua Nunn. Jace Hudspeth was a Second Team vote.

2021 (10-3)

Even with the loss of key players to graduation, there were still valuable players back in Winston County. As usual, Louisville prepared for the season with a tough non-conference slate. Said Coach Tyrone Shorter, "Everybody that know me knows that I believe in playing a tough non-division schedule because you can measure where you are. We want to be able to compete in those games and I want to measure our team going into our division games".

As the season drew near, Shorter added, "It's all about continuing the tradition of this program. It's not about us. It's about our program and we have to continue that tradition. We want to finish the mission and that's what we're striving for right now. We're going for number eleven and we're going to work as hard as we can to get there".

GAME 1:   LOUISVILLE (0-0) vs GENTRY (0-0)
                      LOUISVILLE 31 GENTRY 12
                      August 27, 2021

The season was to open with powerful West Point, but their decision to move the school to virtual due to lingering COVID fears set up a game against the Indianola school. This marked their first meeting against one-another.

Though the Wildcats opened with an early touchdown, the visitors matched it quickly on a Troy Griffin run to cut it to 7-6. An LHS FG then made it 10-6. Emory James soon dove in from a yard but Gentry responded with a 55-yard Griffin pass to Pharheim Washington to put it 17-12. Jace Hudspeth added a 12-yard dash in the 3rd quarter while Jacorey Coleman iced it with his 14-yard effort.

Louisville had 290 offensive yards. Hudspeth was 11-18 for 106, Coleman rushed for 82, and Dakota led tacklers with 18. "I think we played pretty good. We just had a couple of days to prepare for a good Gentry team. We haven't seen them much and I thought they were big and athletic, but we played well for the first game. We've got a lot of work to do".

GAME 2:   LOUISVILLE (1-0) vs KEMPER COUNTY (1-0)
                      LOUISVILLE 41 KEMPER COUNTY 7
                      September 3, 2021

Kemper was a regular opponent for the Cats from 2011 to 2018 before a two-year hiatus. "It's going to be a big atmosphere game. It's a close school and will be another tough battle. (Coach Ray Westerfield) has got the guys headed in the right direction and they're playing with discipline and playing hard".

Early in the game, Hudspeth and Swahili Earby hooked up and it was a quick 7-0. James dashed in for the next in the 2nd quarter while Hudspeth followed it soon after with his own. James came back with another scoring dash to put halftime 27-0. James added his third tally in the 3rd quarter while Coleman did likewise from six yards. With reserves now in play, KCHS crossed in the 3rd quarter for their lone points.

"We wanted to be balanced on offense. Our guys did a great job. I think we had close to 300 yards rushing and I thought we played really well. The starters pitched a shutout and Kemper scored on our second team, so it was an all-round great game for us".

GAME 3:   LOUISVILLE (2-0) @ COLUMBUS (1-1)
                      LOUISVILLE 29 COLUMBUS 7
                      September 10, 2021

The Falcons were no strangers to Louisville with nine previous meetings resulting in only a pair of Cat defeats. *"It's going to be a tough one. Columbus is 1-1 right now and are big and physical on defense. They're not the Columbus of the past. They're a lot better and the coaching staff is doing a great job with them so we've got to be disciplined. Going over there, it's going to be tough to beat them".*

Louisville opened with a fumble captured by the Falcons to set up an 18-yard Omari Williams pass to Antonio O'Neal for a touchdown and 7-0 lead. Jackson then took the kickoff to the end zone and it was now tied. *"A string"* of Columbus turnovers soon led to a safety and 9-7 Cat advantage. Hudspeth finished the half with a touchdown run to put the board 16-7. Of two touchdowns thereafter, Kylan Tippett grabbed a second-half errant pass and raced it back for a touchdown to finish scoring.

Hudspeth was 13-22-2 for 228, Rush caught 129 yards and James led rushers with 55. *"We knew going into the game that Columbus' defense was really good. Their defensive front is big, physical and athletic and we they would give us problems. We made adjustments blocking scheme-wise and it started working for us. I've got to give credit to Columbus. They're the reason we started off slow".*

GAME 4:   LOUISVILLE (3-0) @ STARKVILLE (3-0)
                     LOUISVILLE 23 STARKVILLE 28
                     September 17, 2021

The regular 6A opponent Yellow Jackets were now ninth in The Clarion-Ledger Super 10. As such, that paper picked Starkville 42-31. *"We've got to prepare for two quarterbacks. It's going to make our job harder defensively. It's Starkville, so they're going to always have some guys. We've got to be ready to play".*

Lighting in the area forced the game into an hour and a half delay for their Homecoming. Once it got underway, Steele picked off a Jacket pass to set up Hudspeth's 11-yard strike to Jaden Triplett and 6-0 lead. Starkville came back with Trey Petty's 31-yarder to Jonathan Lampkin to put it 7-6.

Petty soon took it in from 15 yards but Hudspeth found Triplett from 56-yards to cut it to 14-13. Late in the half, Starkville tallied again on a 1-yard run. However, the Wildcats quickly put up more points on Ceidrick Hunt's 25-yard FG. In the finale, they went 92 yards ending on Triplett's 6-yard reception to put the Cats ahead 23-20. The Jackets came back with an 80-yard march and Jordan Mitchell 1-yard dive to re-take the lead.

Although Louisville had a couple of opportunities to snatch the road win, their last-gasp pass was intercepted in the final seconds to end hopes. Louisville led in yardage 301-284. They passed for 183 and rushed for 118. James' 61 yards led the ground, Triplett's 67 led the air, and Hudspeth was 14-27-1 for 183. Smith led tacklers with 8.

"It's an old rivalry and I know those kids. I knew it was going to be a good game. Our kids are not afraid of anybody and they'll go toe-to-toe with anybody that we face. No matter if they're 6A, 5A or whoever. We're going to come out and they're going to know that we've been on the field with them".

GAME 5:   LOUISVILLE (3-1) @ NOXUBEE COUNTY (2-1)
                     LOUISVILLE 42 NOXUBEE COUNTY 6
                     September 24, 2021

The absence of the Tigers on the 2020 calendar meant the end of a streak of meetings going back to 1981. Now they were back and the Wildcats could not afford to let the heartbreak of the Starkville loss creep into this contest. *"It's going to be a lot of emotions but I've got a job to do. I know a lot of those kids and a lot of those coaches but going back is always going to be fun. It's another big rivalry game for us and I can't wait".*

It was a quick 80-yard connection between Hudspeth and Earby to get it started. Then, he hit Triplett from 20 yards to set up his 1-yard dive. Up 21-0 at the break, James added more with a 50-yard dash and a 4th quarter Rush reception. In all, Louisville had nearly 600 offensive yards. James (172) and Hudspeth (96) led rushers while Hudspeth went 14-20 for 229. Gabriel Moore (72) and Triplett (70) led in receiving;

"They came out and really played well. I thought my coaches did a great job putting the game plan together and I was pleased with how they responded from last week. We were clicking in all three phases and that's where you want to be at this point in the season. I'm pleased with where we're at".

GAME 6:   LOUISVILLE (4-1) @ NORTHEAST LAUDERDALE (1-4)
                 LOUISVILLE 41 NORTHEAST LAUDERDALE 0
                 October 1, 2021

The 4-1 start with a slim loss to Starkville allowed the Wildcats to find their way to 10th in the AP High School Football Poll. *"My message to our guys is not to let this be a trap game. They're big and they're in just about every ball game. They just can't finish them. We can't afford for this to be a let-down game so it's my job to make sure that doesn't happen. We've got our work cut out for us"*.

Louisville made it a 20-0 lead after a frame with a pair of rushing tallies and one via the air. The Cat QB had a part in two of those. Hudspeth hit Earby late in the 2nd quarter to make it 27-0. Hudspeth and Rush hooked up from 24 yards in the 3rd quarter and Jy'kevious Goss added the last from two yards. *"I feel like we played really good. At this point, going into the first division game, we were where I expected us to be. Offensively we're balanced"*.

GAME 7:   LOUISVILLE (5-1) vs CHOCTAW CENTRAL (2-2)
                 LOUISVILLE 35 CHOCTAW CENTRAL 0
                 October 8, 2021: HOMECOMING

Louisville welcomed a Choctaw Central team to Winston County for Homecoming with two wins in their only meetings. *"They're going to fight hard. They're not going to quit. I'm really impressed with the QB. They've got a few formations that I'm concerned about and they play hard on the defensive side. It's got to definitely be a game that we can't overlook. I'm the type of person that I take one game at a time. Our next opponent is Choctaw Central and that's what I'm focused on"*.

Hudspeth and Rush hooked up for the first tally while Goss added a pick-six and Jackson hauled in a 14-yard pass to make it 21-0. In the 3rd quarter, Hudspeth and Rush connected again while Goss added a later 50-yard dash for the final score. The Cats put up 411 offensive yards on the night. Hudspeth was 18-29-1 for 243, Rush (120) and Jackson (82) led receivers, while Goss put up 118 of the 198 total ground yards.

GAME 8:   LOUISVILLE (6-1) @ WEST LAUDERDALE (6-1)
                 LOUISVILLE 35 WEST LAUDERDALE 36 (2 OT)
                 October 15, 2021

The Knights were also undefeated (2-0) in division play including wins over Meridian and Kosciusko. They were led by running back Ja'Karius Grant, already with 1,430 ground yards and 11 touchdowns. This one probably meant a division title. The Clarion-Ledger picked Louisville 42-35.

That score could have ended almost exactly, but it was not to be on this night in Lauderdale County. Hudspeth opened with a 20-yarder to Rush. Tied 7-7 before the half, Hudspeth ran in from 20 yards and the game sat 14-14. Now in the finale, West Lauderdale added a touchdown to make it 21-21 and send it to overtime. Hudspeth hit Jackson and the two points to make it 29-21. However, the Knights did the same to tie it again.

Now in the second overtime period, West Lauderdale added their touchdown and extra point. Hudspeth added a responding touchdown pass. Flashback to the game against Poplarville in 2020 when the Wildcats went for the win via the two-point play. This time, it didn't work and Louisville dropped the contest.

Hudspeth was 12-18 for 200 yards while Rush 188 had those receiving. *"The one thing about it is we can't worry about what happened. Our problem was that we had too many penalties (21) and they had eight. We kept their drives going with penalties and that was the difference in overtimes. We still had an opportunity to win the game and we couldn't put it away"*.

GAME 9:   LOUISVILLE (6-2) vs LEAKE CENTRAL (1-7)
                 LOUISVILLE 49 LEAKE CENTRAL 0
                 October 22, 2021

The Cats were an all-time 8-0 against Leake Central, but Shorter was more concerned about the Wildcat spirit. *"It's my job to get them back up to par and finish our goal. It's not the end of the world. We dug ourselves in a deeper trench (the previous week), but we've got to come out of it. It's how we handle adversity from here on out. We lost* homefield advantage, but we've got to win these last two ball games to finish second. We can't allow that game to define us".

Louisville did just that as they trounced the Gators at home for Senior Night. They put up 28 points in the opening quarter and 21 more before halftime. A Gator fumble recovered by the defense made it a 14-0 contest while another fumble by Travon McDonald allowed Smith to run it back to paydirt. Latterious Haynes then had a pick-six and gave Louisville the 28-0 lead.

Coleman recorded his second tally from 10 yards to start the 2nd quarter while Kylan Tippett added yet another pick-six. Hudspeth added the last on his toss to Goss to begin a running clock for the remainder. Rushing accounted for 221 of the total 279 yards with Coleman (46) and James (44) leading the way. Hudspeth was 5-7 for 58 yards.

"Our kids responded very well. We had our chances to win (West Lauderdale) and just didn't get the two-point conversion. We felt like we were the better team but penalties killed us. We came out and played really well against Leake in all three phases".

GAME 10:   LOUISVILLE (7-2) @ KOSCIUSKO (6-1)
                  LOUISVILLE 26 KOSCIUSKO 23
                  October 29, 2021

The Whippets were a long-time foe of the Wildcats, but this season they were at the top of their game. It would not be an easy Friday for the Cats. "The last ball games against them the last couple of years didn't matter. This year it matters. They are well-coached (and) they've got size. Everything is on the line for this game with the number two seed. It's important for you to play first round at home so there's a lot riding on this game".

James opened it up with his 6-yarder to make it 6-0 while Kosy came back to tie it in the 2nd quarter on an Ethan Wood sneak. Back came the Wildcats on a 30-yard Hudspeth pass to Rush to put it 13-7. In the 3rd quarter, the lead grew as Hudspeth and Rush connected from 60 yards while Hudspeth found paydirt later to put it 26-7.

In the finale, Kosy put it 26-10 on a Will Carter 39-yard FG and Jatavious Noel 3-yard run and then recorded a Jeremy Whitcomb pick-six. While the Whippets took it to the Cat 37, the Carter 54-yard FG with under 1:00 failed and gave Louisville the win. Hudspeth was 13-21-2 for 281, Rush had 147 receiving, and Tippett 18 tackles. There were only 77 Cat rushing yards.

"We started off really well and then we got careless. We had turnovers and they got back in it. I'm pleased with the team overall. We played well going into the fourth quarter. We're still have some pre-snap penalties that I'm not satisfied with. We've got to get more disciplined".

GAME 11:   LOUISVILLE (8-2) vs SHANNON (4-6)
                  LOUISVILLE 37 SHANNON 12
                  November 5, 2021

The win over Kosciusko meant a home meeting with a Red Raider team winless against Louisville in six attempts. "They are big and athletic. They match up with us well with their size and speed. We've got to play disciplined football. They easily could have been in second place in their district so we have to be focused and ready to play".

Thought the Wildcats opened with an 8-0 lead from Coleman's run, the Red Raiders came back with a touchdown to make it 8-6. James soon put the Cats ahead 15-12 after a trade of tallies. James then ran 70 yards for another midway through the 2nd quarter, Hudspeth followed with a 12-yard strike to Rush and then Jaden Triplett late to put the board 37-12.

A running clock soon took the air out of the game. "I thought our kids did a great job. We had seven total penalties and one pre-snap penalty. I was really proud of our kids on that. We're going to have some calls go against us, but it's the ones that we can control that we have to clean up".

He added, "The only thing that I was kind of disappointed in was that we turned the ball over three times. It's uncharacteristic of our backs because we haven't done that all year. It's not a big concern, but you can't do that in the playoffs. Besides that, our kids played a good game all around. We were focused and we played fairly well".

GAME 12:   LOUISVILLE (9-2) @ CLARKSDALE (8-1)
                  LOUISVILLE 16 CLARKSDALE 12
                  November 12, 2021

Clarksdale's other Wildcats had been on the Louisville schedule before and more than once stopped title dreams. In fact, they won five of six games between 1997 and 2006. They were not to be taken lightly this year in Coahoma County with a one-loss record. *"They're really good. They're big, physical and athletic. We have our work cut out for us. We're so young defensively and struggle against teams that can run the football and they can run the ball pretty good. They're big up front and have some big running backs. We've just got to buckle down".*

A Wildcat FG midway through the opening frame put them ahead 3-0. A turnover allowed Hudspeth to find Jackson from 40 yards and it was 10-0 at halftime. Clarksdale came back with a pair of touchdowns to put it 12-10. One came on a Kelly Jones rush while the next was on a DeMarlos Chapman reception. Hudspeth finally gave Louisville back the lead when he hit Triplett and the defense closed it out. Clarksdale did move inside the Wildcat 2 late but the defense stood tall.

Hudspeth went 15-22 for 138. The Cats put up 90 rushing yards while Jackson (69) and Triplett (45) led receivers. *"I was really concerned because our two losses were on the road. To go on the road and beat a Clarksdale team like that, it showed a lot of maturity and growth. We couldn't go in there and give them anything and we didn't. They had to go there and earn everything. I'm proud of our kids for being really disciplined".*

He added, *"I told our guys that if you're going to win one, you have to win it on the road. I'm proud of our kids in the way we responded; especially defensively. Clarksdale has a really good football team and we made some stops when we needed to. They were big up front and gave us some fits in the running game".*

The Clarksdale team had a different perspective on the ending as a picture showed 12 Louisville players on the fourth down effort from a yard. No flags were thrown and the game ended as called. Said Coach Henry Johnson, *"I've never seen anything like this in my career. It was heartbreaking for our kids. Our players and coaches worked so hard and came so far. This is a tough way to end the season".*

GAME 13:   LOUISVILLE (10-2) @ CALEDONIA (11-1)
                             LOUISVILLE 7 CALEDONIA 27
                             November 19, 2021

Despite Caledonia losing to Louisville in all seven previous affairs, Shorter was adamant to not let down their guard against a one-loss team. *"I'm trying to get our kids to understand that this isn't the Caledonia of old. Coach Kelly has this team going in the right direction. They have some really good players and have lost only gone game all year. I feel good about this team. They're a team that can get the job done on the road".*

When over, Coach Michael Kelly's Cavaliers had their first-ever trip to play for a state title. The home team held a 13-0 advantage with scores in the 1st and 2nd quarter. Kewon Wyatt took to the ball 70 yards to paydirt for the first and added a 75-yard Daniel Wilburn pass reception for the next. With under 8:00 remaining before halftime, the Cats tallied their last of the season via a 2-yard Coleman plunge. However, Caledonia tallied once in each of the final two frames for the runaway victory.

Wilburn garnered the first tally on his 1-yard dive while Wyatt added an interception to set up the next on a Johnson 2-yarder and Frady kick.

The Bernard Blackwell North-South All-Star Game included Jace Hudspeth, Jarvis Rush and Lanorris Hickman. District 4-4A honorees included Jace Hudspeth (Offensive MVP), Emory James (Most Valuable Running Back), Jarvis Rush (Most Valuable Receiver), and Kylan Tippett (Most Valuable Defensive Back). Super 22 players included Jaden Triplett, Lanorris Hickman, Ceidrick Hunt, Gabriel Moore and Shontez Thames.

First Team 4-4A was Key Jackson, Jaquavion Ivy, Chauncey Thames, Chistavious Savior, D.J. Miller, Jeff Smith, Caleb Hughes, and Jeremiah Kirk. Second Team included Jacorey Coleman, Randerous Leonard, Kenneth Hill, Jy'Kevious Goss, Swahili Earby, Tim Haskins and Victor Rush.

2022 (14-1)

Unfortunately, nothing was reported pre-season as to Louisville's prospects for the 2022 season under Coach Tyrone Shorter. One notation after the West Point game points to the team make-up. *"We're such a young group. We started seven sophomores (against WP). We try to coach them up and prepare them for everything..."*

GAME 1:   LOUISVILLE (0-0) @ WEST POINT (0-0)
           LOUISVILLE 24 WEST POINT 14
           August 26, 2022

The previous year, the Wildcats scheduled the Green Wave as the opener for the season. However, COVID protocols forced a replacement with Gentry. Now, Louisville traveled to West Point, a team picked seventh in The Clarion-Ledger Super 10. Additionally, they were the six-time defending 5A North State champions.

The defensive battle gave way with about a minute left in the first half when Kahnen Daniels hit paydirt for West Point. The Wildcats answered immediately with Xavier Hunt hitting Keyarrion Jackson for a TD and the PAT put them ahead 7-6 at intermission. The lead grew late in the 3rd quarter on Ceidrick Hunt's 36-yard FG. With 4:00 left, the Wave re-took the lead on a 24-yard run and a two-pointer. The 14-10 lead seemed as if it would hold.

However, with under 2:00 remaining, *"a key pass interference call"* allowed Hunt to find Jackson from 17 yards for the go-ahead 17-14 score. Laterrious Haynes iced it with a pick-six to steal the upset win. Hunt was 22-39 for 213, Jackson led receivers with 94 yards and Jaden Triplett led rushers with only 33 markers. Defensively, Semaj Knowles paced tacklers with 12 while Kendon Sanders added 11 more.

"Going into it, we knew it was going to be a battle, especially at their place. To get the win means a lot. It's a great start to the season and that win showed me a lot about my team".

GAME 2:   LOUISVILLE (1-0) @ KEMPER COUNTY (0-0)
           LOUISVILLE 54 KEMPER COUNTY 0
           September 2, 2022

This one marked the ninth meeting between the clubs and was held on the field of East Mississippi Community College in Scooba. *"We have to get better. I know that every week we're not going to play a team as good as West Point, but I still want to see improvement. We can't have a letdown. We can't overlook anybody. It's my job to make sure that doesn't happen".*

Louisville wasted no time in setting the tone. Triplett dashed in from 20 yards and then pulled in a Hunt pass to make it 14-0. Hunt then added a 2nd quarter dive from a yard, Christavious Savior took a punt 50 yards and Kenneth Hill recovered a fumble to put it 35-0. Hunt opened the 3rd with a 15-yarder, Savior took a punt 95 yards to paydirt, and Xzarion Haynes added the finale from 43 yards.

Hunt was 5-9 for 68, Triplett rushed for 53 and caught 36 more. The Cats had 192 ground yards in the game. TayQuan McKinney (14), Corxavier Coleman (11) and Sanders (10) led tacklers.

"I was worried about our kids coming out of a big game from week one to week two being flat. They weren't. They came out from the jump and started where we left off last Friday. We had a really good practice and I didn't have to keep them focused. I'm proud of our coaching staff for putting in a good game plan and keeping them focused".

GAME 3:   LOUISVILLE (2-0) vs COLUMBUS (0-2)
           LOUISVILLE 28 COLUMBUS 0
           September 9, 2022

The road was about to get rougher against a pair of 6A teams, starting with familiar foe Columbus. The Cats were 8-2 all-time since they first played in 1992. Said Shorter, *"They're really big and physical on defense. We have to be disciplined. On offense, they're real big up front. We just need to keep doing what we do and we'll be OK".*

Savior opened things with a fumble return to set up a Hunt scoring pass to Jackson. Goss was next via the ground and Triplett followed that with another to make it 21-0. Hunt and Goss hooked up in the 3rd quarter for the finale. Hunt was 13-19 for 171 with Triplett grabbing 81 of those.

Moore had 16 tackles and forced a fumble. Nigel Anderson, Sanders, Jacari Owens and Caden Thompkins reportedly had 17. Knowles had two interceptions while Hill added another. *"We were really fired up and clicking on all cylinders. We kind of had a* letdown and got comfortable in the second and third quarters but picked it back up in the fourth. The defense played really well and got another shutout".

GAME 4:   LOUISVILLE (3-0) vs STARKVILLE (3-0)
                     LOUISVILLE 20 STARKVILLE 21
                     September 16, 2022

Another 6A team was next and a Yellow Jacket squad ranked third in the state. The Wildcats sat 10th after their 3-0 start. The Clarion-Ledger thought Starkville just a bit better 31-28. Said Shorter, "I think it starts in the trenches. We've got to win the trenches on both sides. We match up with them well with our skill guys. I think the difference is going to be up front. They're a typical well-coached Starkville team. It's going to be a challenge for us, but it's a challenge that we like. I think the team that makes the least mistakes will have a good chance to win".

Trey Petty put the Jackets up 14-0 via a pair of running touchdowns in the 2nd quarter. Louisville responded with a 1-yard Jackson run to make halftime 14-7. Triplett took one ball 59 yards to paydirt but the missed PAT kept it 14-13. However, Haynes soon picked off a Petty throw for a 45-yard pick-six "to send R.E. Hinze Stadium into a frenzy". Up 20-14 in the 4th quarter, Courtland Cooper hit the end zone with under 2:00 left to put them back on top. An earlier Cat FG was unsuccessful to make it worse.

Moore and Sanders each led tacklers with 12. "I'm proud of the kids. We started kind of slow but they brought maximum effort and played their hearts out. We went toe-to-toe with a 6A powerhouse and should have won the game. We just had a couple of miscues. But I'm proud of the way they fought. They showed me a lot".

GAME 5:   LOUISVILLE (3-1) vs NOXUBEE COUNTY (2-2)
                     LOUISVILLE 21 NOXUBEE COUNTY 8
                     September 23, 2022

The rivalry everyone circled was now at hand against Shorter's former squad. "I look at it as a rivalry game and you can throw the records away. These kids know each other very well and we've got to be focused. We can't have a letdown because we had a big game the week before. We're coming in with a loss and they are, too. Knowing those kids over there, it's going to be a tough ball game, but I think we have a great game plan".

Eerily similar to the first time Shorter met NCHS, halftime sat 2-0. That came when the defense recorded a safety with the Tigers starting at their own 2-yard line after a failed Wildcat march. Noxubee punched back in the 3rd quarter with a touchdown and two-point conversion to put them on top 8-2. It was all Louisville afterwards.

Hunt later hit Swahili Earby from 25 yards while Sanders crossed from five yards to make it 15-8. In the last frame, Sanders dove in from a yard to finish scoring. Triplett rushed for 119 of the total 132 yards. Hunt was 7-17-1 for 126 and Earby pulled in 64 of those. Moore (13) and Coleman (12) led tacklers. Haynes had an interception.

GAME 6:   LOUISVILLE (4-1) vs NORTHEAST LAUDERDALE (3-2)
                     LOUISVILLE 42 NORTHEAST LAUDERDALE 0
                     September 30, 2022: HOMECOMING

It was Homecoming in Winston County and the guests of honor was a Northeast Lauderdale team that won only once in seven previous meetings. However, the Trojans were riding a three-game winning streak.

With Jackson in at QB to establish the running game, he broke away from midfield to make it an early 7-0. He then found Earby for another tally. A fumbled Trojan punt put the Cats at the six-yard line and Triplett easily crossed for the next. Knowles then picked off a pass and Triplett turned it into a 34-yard touchdown and 28-0 lead after a frame. Jackson's 2nd quarter scoring run made halftime a whopping 35-0.

The running clock kept scoring down with only a 4th quarter special teams tally to end things. Haynes led tacklers with nine while Savior and Knowles had interceptions. Jackson was 6-9 for 130 and rushed for 109 yards. Earby has 92 receiving yards.

"We just wanted to go into the game and establish the running game and I thought we did that. I thought our kids came out and played really hard and really fast from the start. There's so much distraction at Homecoming. We know that we're going to run the football when we get deep in our division so we need to work on that".

LOUISVILLE (5-1) @ CHOCTAW CENTRAL (3-2)
LOUISVILLE 50 CHOCTAW CENTRAL 18
October 7, 2022

The Wildcats were now eighth in The Super 10 after their shutout the previous week. *"The one thing after watching film is that they are big up front on both sides of the ball. I was kind of shocked at that. They have some kids that can really play. We can't go into that game with our guard down. We've got to play at their place and they do some things well, so we will have to (be ready)".*

No reporting on actual scoring came in The Winston County Journal aside from touchdowns from Jackson (5), Hunt (1), Goss (3), Triplett (2) and De'Areius Norton (1). Hunt and Jackson combined for 24-31-1 for 411 yards. Jackson was 18-22-1 for 344 while Hunt was 6-0 for 67 more. Goss had 174 receiving yards, Triplett 90, Haynes and Jacari Owens had interceptions while Savior had three deflections.

"I really thought we came out and really played well. Our offense is clicking on all cylinders. I thought our defense played really well. We played a lot of young kids in the second half and they scored a bit on us, but that's OK. That's how you build depth and get players experienced..."

GAME 8:   LOUISVILLE (6-1) vs WEST LAUDERDALE (6-0)
LOUISVILLE 40 WEST LAUDERDALE 15
October 14, 2022

Two undefeated teams met in Winston County and should have proved a measuring stick for the Wildcats. West Lauderdale was coming off a 27-0 shutout over Kosciusko. The Clarion-Ledger picked Louisville a slight 28-24 winner.

"They're a solid football team. They're well coached and disciplined and won't beat themselves. They can run the ball.... If you're going to win championships, you're going to have to win games like this. We have to treat this like it's a playoff game. It's going to be a big-time atmosphere and we have them at home so it's a huge game".

Jackson started with a 1-yarder before finding Earby from 40 yards to make it 13-0. The Knights cut it to 13-7 with a touchdown and conversion, but Triplett ran in from five and Jackson found Norton to put it 25-7 at halftime. West Lauderdale scored again and converted their two-pointer to make it 27-15, but it was all Louisville afterwards. Sanders got in from five yards, Moore forced a fumble scooped up by Thompkins for a 70-yard touchdown to end scoring on the evening.

The defense held the Knights to just 76 rushing yards. Sanders and Hill each had 18 tackles, Moore forced two fumbles to go along with 11 tackles and Savior had an interception. Haynes and Caden Thompkins recovered fumbles. Jackson was 12-18-1 for 152 while Triplett rushed for 99.

"The one thing is we treated that game like it was a playoff game. That's the mindset that our kids and coaches are trying to set. There's no tomorrow. Our guys came out and executed our plan as well as they could. Our coaches put our kids in the best situations possible. I thought we played all three phases of the game really well aside from a couple of miscues on extra points. We came out and set the tone. We knew they were a really good team and we had to play good football".

GAME 9:   LOUISVILLE (7-1) @ LEAKE CENTRAL (1-6)
LOUISVILLE 40 LEAKE CENTRAL 0
October 21, 2022

Louisville still sat eighth in The Super 10 poll despite a 7-1 record and a small margin loss to 6A Starkville. It seemed to be an easier week on the road against a one-win Gator squad. This meeting could be for the 4-4A title.

"They're very athletic and have size. This team can be dangerous because they have really good QBs and skill guys. We're going to have to dominate the game in the trenches because they can match up. We're going into the game preparing like we did last week. We've got to do us and continue to do our thing".

While a specific scoring recap is unmentioned, Jackson (2), Triplett (2) Goss, Earby ad Kamron Triplett had touchdowns. The Cats put up a pair of touchdowns in each of the last three quarters. Fourteen points came in the 2nd quarter and 13 each in the last two frames. The defense pitched another shutout for the fourth time. Jackson was 9-17-1 for

162, Triplett ran for 105, Sanders and Thompkins led tacklers with 10 each, Haynes and Hill again had interceptions and Travon McDonald recorded a fumble recovery;

"We dominated all three phases of the game every week. There's not a superstar on this team. It's more of a team this year other an individual play and that's one of the keys. These kids remember the feeling that we had last year in the playoffs when we came up short. We're doing what we need to do as coaches and they're doing what they need to do as players. They've bought in at what we need to do".

GAME 10:   LOUISVILLE (8-1) vs KOSCIUSKO (7-2)
                         LOUISVILLE 28 KOSCIUSKO 0
                         October 27, 2022

Former rival Kosciusko earned a playoff spot regardless of the outcome under Coach Casey Orr after a three-win campaign. *"They're a well-coached team. Coach Orr and his staff do a great job. They're big and have a lot of athletes. I know that they're going to come out and play hard and try to beat us on Senior Night. We'll be ready to play".*

Said Orr about the Wildcats, *"They are a good football team. Offensive they have gotten better since they changed quarterbacks. Defensively they are fast and they get after you. The defense has four shutouts".* The Cats made it their fifth on this Thursday affair.

Triplett dashed in from six yards to open scoring 7-0 but that lead held until the final frame. Jackson then hit Goss for a tally, Triplett broke free from 60 yards and a last-touchdown Earby reception ended it. Jackson threw for 91 yards with a pair of picks while Hunt was 2-2 for 80 more. Goss led receivers with 97 and Triplett ran for 76 of the 88 total yards. Corxavier Coleman led tacklers with 15 while Kendon Sanders and 14.

"I think we needed a game like that going into the playoffs. I told our guys that Kosciusko is a very good team and it was just like a playoff game to me. I've got to give Kosciusko credit. They gave us some problems on defense but we figured it out. Our defense is really playing well right now, too". He added, *"I'm proud of these guys. They worked their tails off. They come to practice every single day to get better. What I like about them is they're playing together and have one common goal: to win the state championship".*

GAME 11:   LOUISVILLE (9-1) vs GREENWOOD (5-4)
                         LOUISVILLE 35 GREENWOOD 0
                         November 4, 2022

Although the team began meeting in 1947, everyone remembered the competitions between 2017-2019. *"I told our coaches and kids that's a tough first-round matchup for us because of the history of the two teams in the past. Knowing coach (Clinton) Gatewood, he's going to have those kids ready to go. I remind our kids that a few years ago, some number one seeds went down in the first round. If you're not prepared, we can be in a battle. We've got a great game plan and I know they're going to be ready to play us".*

Again, no scoring specific are recapped. Jackson had a hand in three while Hunt and Goss had one each. Coleman led tacklers again with 14 and Haynes had an interception. In all, Louisville passed for 200 and ran for 150. Jackson was 9-14 for 145 and Hunt 3-5 for 47. Jackson led the ground with 37 yards and Goss the air with 74.

"Our guys came out and were really focused. It was how I expected them to come out in that first playoff game. We were really balanced on offense and were able to run and pass. I think we adjusted to whatever they gave us and our coaches put our kids in a great position. Defensively, we're still playing well".

GAME 12:   LOUISVILLE (10-1) vs RIPLEY (10-1)
                         LOUISVILLE 35 RIPLEY 0
                         November 11, 2022

The two met first in 2007 and followed that with meetings in both 2017 and 2018. All were Cat wins. For this one, Ripley also had just a lone loss to match that of the Wildcats. *"They're very talented and well-coached. They have a really good offensive line. They're a football team that's sound and disciplined so we have to be at our best on Friday".*

An early Hill interception set up a 35-yard Triplett touchdown reception. Jackson followed with a scoring run from midfield and then hit Earby from 40 yards to make it 20-0. Sanders opened the next frame with a scoring run to end the half. Hunt's later 13-yarder to Triplett ended any scoring with a running clock.

Jackson was 7-11-1 for 106 while Hunt was 5-10 for 56. Jackson ran for 79 of the total 191 rushing yards. Hill led tacklers with nine and a pair of interceptions while Jacari Owens added another.

"Once those kids came down to the complex, I saw in their eyes they were focused and ready to play. They came out from the beginning to the end and they just dominated. They are really starting to play some good football and we've been doing that since the Starkville game. The focus and maturity after last year is impressive. I've had some really good defenses over the years and this one is up there with some of the best".

GAME 13:	LOUISVILLE (11-1) @ CALEDONIA (6-6)
	LOUISVILLE 35 CALEDONIA 14
	November 18, 2022

Caledonia, despite a 6-6 season, just knocked off Clarksdale 26-0. Shorter knew the power of their next opponent. "Coach (Michael) Kelly and his coaches have done a great job. We played this team the last couple of years and I told people that they would be scary and here they are. They struggled at the beginning of the year but now they're playing their best football. We want to slow the ball game down because they know that we want to go fast. It takes us out of our rhythm, but I think our guys will respond".

The Cavaliers stuck first just a few minutes into the contest on a 5-yard run and Frady PAT to put them ahead 7-0 but the Wildcats were unbothered. Jackson soon added 16-yard escape to tie it 7-7. In the next frame, he found Triplett from 30 yards to put them ahead 14-7. Just before intermission, the Wildcats turned a fourth down play into an 18-yard Jackson strike to Earby to put it 21-7. After a fumble recovery, the Cats made it 28-7 though Caledonia responded with one of their own via an 11-yard Zack Gorum pass from Daniel Wilburn and Frady kick. Jackson put it away in the final seconds with a 1-yard dive.

GAME 14:	LOUISVILLE (12-1) vs HOUSTON (12-1)
	LOUISVILLE 31 HOUSTON 21
	November 25, 2022

Despite a string of victories and shutouts, the Wildcats were ninth in polling. That was better than the previous week where were 11th. The Clarion-Ledger picked Louisville to lose 31-24 after the Hilltoppers and Jamal Cooperwood (1,151 rushing yards) upset Itawamba AHS.

Late in the opening quarter, Houston found the end zone to take the lead but Hill took the ensuing kick 62 yards to the 10-yard line. Jackson finished it with his legs to tie it. Now tied 14-14 in the 2nd quarter, a Louisville FG put them ahead 17-14. In the final frame, Houston regained the advantage with their touchdown and PAT. But then, a forced fumble by Sanders allowed Thompkins to add a touchdown return to end scoring. Other tallies are not reported.

Jackson went 10-18-1 for 131 and led rushers with 36 of the total 52. Goss paced receivers with 52 yards while, on defense, Haynes, Thompkins and Owens had interceptions. Sanders forced a fumble while Moore led tacklers with 11.

"I feel good about how they performed. I don't think we played our best, but we played well enough to get the win. I don't know if our guys were too amped up or whatever, but we made some careless mistakes we haven't made all year. It's all about surviving and moving on the playoffs. You've got to win that tough, ugly one in the playoffs and we did that".

He added later, "I told them after the game that there were several times that we had to face adversity and we pulled through it. It showed me a lot of grit and they didn't hang their heads. We settled down and started playing football. We bounced back and that's what it takes".

GAME 15:	LOUISVILLE (13-1) vs MENDENHALL (13-1)
	LOUISVILLE 17 MENDENHALL 14
	December 3, 2022

Mendenhall earned their ticket with a 29-20 win over defending champ Columbia and a 26-14 win over Stone. The first meeting between the two came in 1962 with only three encounters since. The Clarion-Ledger picked Mendy 20-13 saying, "Mendenhall's defense holds up in a close matchup after allowing eight points per game this season".

Said Shorter, "*Coach (Chuckie) Allen and his staff have done a great job. They're just like us on film and you see a lot of athletes and a lot of speed. They kind of mirror us a little. We've got to go through this game and not allow the stage to be too big. Emotions are going to be high but emotions don't win ball games. As long as we execute and play our game, we are going to be in good shape*".

The Cats were first on the board with a 2-yard Sanders tally and a "*disputed*" 7-yarder from Nigel Anderson. Mendy came back with a "*one-handed touchdown grab*" by Walter Nono Owens from James to make it 14-6. In the final frame, Marcus Allen pulled in a 26-yard pass and the two-pointer tied it 14-14. Now the Tigers were looking strike again but Moore broke the ball away with under a minute remaining. Triplett ran for 19 yards to set up Ceidrick Hunt's 27-yard FG for the win with :04 left. Not only was the kick true, the Wildcats had their 11th official championship and the clock eventually ran out.

Jackson ran for 134 while Goss received 63 in the air. Mendenhall recorded 292 total yards. Sanders, however, was the Player of the Game. Moore recorded a forced fumble in the affair.

"*Our defense has been playing good all year and I told them that this was going to come down to a defensive battle. Watching them on film, they're really good with a really good offense. We knew we had to stop the QB and I thought our defense did a good job of stopping him all game. The only thing about it is that I didn't want to be the coach that came down here and lost it. I told our guys that it wasn't about us. It's about the tradition of the program. So, for me, to be part of all the Hall of Fame coaches that came through here, we wanted to continue to build the tradition*".

Post-season honors were numerous for Louisville. First Team All-State awards went to Gabriel Moore (Defensive Lineman), Keyarrion Jackson (Athlete), and Christavious Savior (Defensive Back). Second Team included Kendon Sanders (Linebacker) and Kenneth Hill (Defensive Back).

All 4-4A award were even more plentiful. Coaching Staff of the Year, Jackson (Offensive MVP), Moore (Defensive MVP), Jaden Triplett (Most Valuable Running Back), Savior (Most Valuable Defensive Back), and Ceidrick Hunt (Most Valuable Kicker). Super 22 awards included Xavier Hunt, Jy'kevious Goss, Swahili Earby, Dontae Cross, Dijaylen Miller, Sanders, Latterious Haynes, and Hill.

First Team All-District were Semaj Knowles, TayQuan McKinney, Corxavier Coleman, Caden Thompkins, Jeremiah Ash, Gregory Jernigan and Caleb Hughes. Second Team had Jayshunn Robbins, Christopher Hickman, Jacari Owens, Tristian Harrington, Dearrius Norton, Nigel Anderson, Cameron Skeen, Travon McDonald and Randerous Leonard.

2023 (15-0)

In just four years, Coach Tyrone Shorter had the Wildcats 48-8 including three 4-4A championships and two state championships. "*We've just been trying to get bigger and stronger. We have a lot of kids returning. Our biggest focus in the off-season was us and doing the little things to get better.*

The one thing that I do at the end of the season is self-scout. We just wanted to get better and work on us and that's what we did. We did a lot of camps and 7-on-7 and had great participation. Now it's here. Offensively we have seven returning starters and they're some really good players. Our strength is our offensive line with all five of those guys back and three more off the bench".

As for the continually-rugged schedule he added, "*There's no doubt that we should have a chance to win it again this year but we've got to do our job. I believe that the tough teams we play will prepare us for our district and the playoffs. Our district is tough and everybody that we played last year in the playoffs are in our district. But if you're going to compete for championships, you have to play tough. We're ready for the challenge*".

GAME 1:   LOUISVILLE (0-0) vs WEST POINT (0-0)
                 LOUISVILLE 35 WEST POINT 13
                 August 25, 2023

Though higher in division play, the Cats held a 2-0 mark against the Green Wave in their last two encounters. Of the last one, Shorter said, "*That win sparked our season and put us on the right track. The last two times we played West Point, we beat them and that's* our goal this time. The challenge is that we have to stop their run (with Dandy Dozen Kahnen Daniels). They have a big offensive line. That's going to be the key to win in the trenches on both sides of the ball". This one gave Louisville the first three consecutive wins over them since 2001.

The Wildcats took the early lead on a 40-yard Xavier Hunt strike to Jy'Kevious Goss. West Point responded with Kaleb Dyson's 20-yarder to Quinterion Tillman-Evans to tie it. A Cat fumble was later picked up for a touchdown to put the Wave ahead 13-7 at the half. Kendon Sanders opened the 3rd quarter with a 1-yard scoring dive, Xzarion Haynes ran in from 12 yards, and Tayquon McKinney took a West Point fumble back 26 yards to paydirt. In the finale, Sanders added the last points to ice the lid-lifter.

Louisville had 197 of their 385 yards rushing. Hunt was 13-19 for 188, Jaylin Jordan led rushers with 112, Goss grabbed 63 air yards, Jacari Owens (16) and Corxavier Coleman (15) paced tacklers, and McKinney and Travon McDonald recovered fumbles.

"I was really pleased. I told our kids at the beginning of this week that we had to dominate the trenches on both sides of the ball and I think our young men did a great job. We had so many guys returning that played in this game last year that we felt good about it. I have so much respect for Coach Chris Chambless and his program. They have a very good football team that will probably be playing for the state championship".

GAME 2:   LOUISVILLE (1-0) vs NESHOBA CENTRAL (0-1)
                       LOUISVILLE 31 NESHOBA CENTRAL 0
                       September 1, 2023

The Rockets held only five wins over Louisville since 1972 but now they moved to 6A. Unfortunately for them, they lost their opener to Pearl 35-10. "They're a very well-coached football team that's very disciplined. They have a lot of size. We've got to be very good offensively because they have one of the best defensive linemen in the state".

Unexpectedly, the game turned into a mud-bathed affair as "torrential rain" hit for the meeting. The lone notation of game specifics said the Wildcats led 10-0 at the half before adding 21 more in the second half. Hunt was 6-13 for 30 while throwing for two touchdowns (Aiden Coleman and Kellon Mann) and running in another. Sanders had two touchdowns. The offense ran for 122 yards, the defense had 11 sacks, Sanders recorded a fumble recovery and Coleman led tacklers with 13.

"It was kind of unexpected because we thought the rain was going to be out of there by six but stayed around for a while. Neshoba had a really good defense and they are coached well. Our game plan was to come in, spread them out and throw the ball. But the elements caused us to do something different. Once we got it going, we really got going".

GAME 3:   LOUISVILLE (2-0) @ COLUMBUS (0-2)
                       LOUISVILLE 45 COLUMBUS 20
                       September 8, 2023

The Falcons sat winless with losses to both Houston and Noxubee County. However, they were a familiar foe to the Wildcats and not to be taken lightly. "This past game is going to prepare us because they're very similar to Neshoba. Columbus is going to be big, physical and hungry. We're going to have to be ready to stop the run. We're going to take away what they do best".

Hunt started the first drive with a 3-yarder to Deniro Jackson and, later, Jordan scampered in from 59 yards to make it 17-0 after a Ceidrick Hunt 34-yard FG. The Falcons came back with a 59-yard TD pass and two-point play to make it 17-8, but Jamarion King added a pick-six and Hunt found Haynes from 28 yards. Just before intermission, he also hit Triplett from 32 yards to put it 38-8.

The reserves manned many spots in the second half with a running clock, Columbus hit two passing tallies. The last Wildcat touchdown is not reported. Hunt was 11-17 for 140, Jordan rushed for 133 with two touchdowns, Kamron Triplett had 58 receiving yards and a tally while Jackson was close behind with 53 yards.

"I thought the kids came out and did what we wanted to do in the first half. We came out with a lot of energy. I couldn't have asked more from our guys. We got to play a lot of players, especially in the end. I'm kind of disappointed with how the game ended because we gave up two touchdown passes, but want to give them experience and build for the future. We wanted the shutout, but sometimes that won't happen when you're playing young guys".

GAME 4:   LOUISVILLE (3-0) @ STARKVILLE (3-0)
                              LOUISVILLE 26 STARKVILLE 22
                              September 15, 2023

This one stretched back to at least 1920 and was one of the most-played series for Louisville. Now, after close Wildcat calls with victory, their opponent welcome Louisville ranked first in The Super 10 and featuring Dandy Dozen Braylen "Stonka" Burnside. The Clarion-Ledger called it the Game of the Week and picked the Yellow Jackets 35-34.

"Our guys remember last year. Even the last three years, we've had a chance to win going into the fourth quarter. We've got to make sure this year that we're ready for that final quarter and keeping our guys fresh because they wore us out the last three years with their depth. They've got more numbers and more kids and I think we've got to do a good job making sure that our guys can finish. They've got a good football team. It's going to be a tough task for us but we're excited".

The Jackets appeared to be on their way with an early interception and march to the Cat 1. However, Goss picked off Trey Petty in the end zone to kill the threat. They went the other way later and Hunt nailed a 24-yard FG to make it 3-0. Petty and Burnside turned the tide with a 1-yard Petty dive and 28-yard Burnside reception to put them ahead 14-3 at halftime.

The two connected again to open the 3rd quarter from 17 yards. The Wildcats then came alive early in the final frame. Hunt found Triplett from midfield to allow Hunt a later scoring run. Two Petty fumbles led to scores to start the comeback. The last was a 27-yard Hunt pass to Haynes. Ceidrick Hunt put it away with 2:20 left on his 32-yard FG.

"I told our team that I was going to coach them aggressively. I told our team that we were going to have a chance to win it at the end and that's what we did. We told our kids to keep fighting and keep believing. In the first half we shot ourselves in the foot. I'm proud of our guys for keeping fighting".

GAME 5:   LOUISVILLE (4-0) @ NOXUBEE COUNTY (2-2)
                              LOUISVILLE 7 NOXUBEE COUNTY 6
                              September 22, 2023

The Hattiesburg American called this "The Tyrone Shorter Bowl" and predicted that "the game will be close for three quarters before fatigue and the scoreboard impale": Louisville 42-28. Said Shorter, "You get the guys up so high for Starkville, but it's my job to make sure they don't play down (Friday). Now we have to come back with another rivalry game at their place". That same newspaper showed the Cats third in voting.

The previous year's lone loss came by one point to Starkville. This year, that one point favored the Wildcats. They tallied just before halftime when Hunt hit Jackson and Ceidrick Hunt added the crucial extra point. In the 3rd quarter, Kamario Taylor hit Jaylen King from 30 yards. Their two-point conversion to take the lead failed. Both defenses found a way to seal one-another for the remainder.

Louisville put up 316 offensive yards with Hunt 15-30-1 for 213. Kamron Triplett had 103 of those. They also ran for 100 yards with Jordan leading the way with 52. Dakota Steele led tacklers with 10.

"We knew coming in we were going to play them hard. I was trying my best to make sure that wasn't a trap game for us after a win against Starkville. I was disappointed in our offense because we didn't execute. Good teams find a way to win and I'd rather have an ugly win than an ugly loss. Defense has continued to play well. Our staff is doing a great job. We bend but don't break and that's our motto. We like to get shutouts, but that's a team averaging 27 points a game and they had to have a missed interception to score".

GAME 6:   LOUISVILLE (5-0) vs HOUSTON (5-0)
                              LOUISVILLE 50 HOUSTON 6
                              September 29, 2023

In 14 games since 1945, the Hilltoppers had yet to beat a Louisville squad. That included the 31-21 North State game the previous year. Said Shorter, "They've got a very good football team. Defensively (they) will come after us. It should be a good district game and we're battle-tested for it. We're pretty confident going into division play. It's the North State Championship game all over again. We're the two best teams in the North and there's a possibility that we play twice this year. We've got to go in and make a statement this week and I don't think there's anything I have to do to motivate our team. They know what is at stake. We've got be ready to play because it's going to be tough".

The Clarion-Ledger called Shorter "the original Riverboat Gambler and is not afraid to onside kick in the beginning of a football game. Houston has some great athletes who will provide a challenge for Louisville. Louisville 38, Houston 31". They were not close.

A quick opening kick return by Goss made it 6-0. They added another in the 2nd quarter on a Sanders two-yarder. While Houston added a late TD, the Cats answered with a Haynes kick return. Just before the half, Ceidrick Hunt nailed a 23-yard FG to put it 23-6. Hunt and Jackson opened the 3rd quarter from 60 yards while Sanders drove in from five yards. Hunt added a 20-yarder to Goss in the finale and Hoskins wrapped it up with his 23-yard escape.

Hunt was 9-14 for 182, Dinero Jackson had 89 receiving and a touchdown, and Goss had another score with a kick return. The Cats had 182 rushing yards of their total 365. Jayllun Hoskins rushed for 68 and a score while Sanders had a pair of touchdowns and led tacklers with 13.

GAME 7:   LOUISVILLE (6-0) vs KOSCIUSKO (4-1)
                       LOUISVILLE 41 KOSCIUSKO 0
                       October 6, 2023; HOMECOMING

The Clarion-Ledger thought Kosy may hold some surprises for Shorter in this one with his Wildcats "coming out flat and napping after an easy victory over Houston". Nevertheless, they picked Louisville 28-14.

Louisville jumped out with a fumble recovered in the end zone for a TD and a 20-yard Hunt pass to Goss to make it 14-0. Halftime sat 24-0 on a Ceidrick Hunt FG and yet another tally. In the 3rd quarter, Jordan ran in for a score, Hunt added a FG, and Hoskins hit paydirt from 25 yards. Hunt was 8-18 for 121, Goss had 56 receiving and Haynes had 48 of the total 133 rushing yards. The defense forced two fumbles, deflected five passes and had an interception. Owens (14) and Coleman (13) led tacklers. In all, they allowed the Whippets only 65 offensive markers.

"To be honest, we just take it one game at a time. We knew that we had a tough division and we had to take it one game at a time and come up with a good game plan. Houston and Kosciusko are good teams. I've got a mature bunch. What's so scary about this group of kids is we haven't reached our ceiling. We haven't played a complete game yet and we still have room to grow".

GAME 8:   LOUISVILLE (7-0) @ CALEDONIA (3-3)
                       LOUISVILLE 54 CALEDONIA 7
                       October 13, 2023

Louisville was 8-1 all-time against Caledonia but this year was in the Columbus area. "You cannot let their 3-3 record fool you. They're a very good football team and Coach Kelly turned their program around. They're going to be a playoff team and they're going to play tough. They're a scrappy bunch. We can't take these guys lightly".

The Cavaliers garnered their only points early after a kickoff return to make it a surprising 7-0 game. Louisville answered in bunches, first with a 50-yard Haynes dash. McKinney then forced a fumble and took it 17 yards to paydirt. Hunt found Triplett from 30 yards and then scored, threw another to Jackson and then Goss crossed to make it 38-7.

The clock began to run in the second half but Hunt passed for another while Sanders hit the end zone later. Ceidrick Hunt later nailed his second FG of the night. In all, the Cats put up 474 offensive yards with 242 coming on the ground. Hunt was 19-32 for 232, Triplett led receivers with 81, Haynes led rushers with 117. On defense, McDonald had 10 tackles and a forced fumble. Jayshunn Robbins had a fumble recovery and TD while Caden Thompkins added an interception.

"Besides the opening kickoff return, I thought we did a very good job in all three phases. Our defense played really well and didn't give them but one or two first downs the whole night. One thing I really like about the offense is that we have depth. Our special teams are playing really well and our kickers are doing good. So, we're pleased with where we are".

GAME 9:   LOUISVILLE (8-0) vs MENDENHALL (5-3)
                       LOUISVILLE 41 MENDENHALL 16
                       October 20, 2023

Though worse than their previous encounter for the state title, "*the talent and leadership is still on the squad*". Said Shorter, "*I don't think we have to get our kids' attention or motivate them to stay focused. Mendenhall is a team that we can possibly play down the road. It will be a great challenge for us. I want our guys to have that playoff mentality and stay sharp and on the edge. Stepping out of district play will be good for us*".

Now ranked first in The Clarion-Ledger Super 10, Haynes made a statement when he took the opening kick 88 yards for a score. Penalties allowed Mendy to tack on a touchdown and FG to take the 10-7 lead. Hunt's FG to tie the game led to a 5-yarder from Sanders to end the half.

Sanders picked up the 3rd quarter by forcing a fumble picked up and returned by Coleman for a touchdown. A later interception set up Hunt's 13-yard scoring toss to Aiden Coleman. In the finale, Hunt hit another FG. Mendy responded with a tally for good measure but the game was already decided.

Ceidrick Hunt had a pair of FGS and five extra points. The Cats put up 250 total offensive yards, Hunt was 14-23-1 for 178, Kamron Triplett led rushers with 45, and Haynes 44 receiving, McKinney had 16 tackles, a forced fumble and recovered a fumble. Sanders also forced a fumble while Khalin Macon had an interception.

"*I thought we handled it well. We played a very good football team and I felt like we needed a game like that in the middle of region play. I like the way our team came out and responded because we'll probably meet up with another team down the road as athletic as these guys were. Offensive, defensively and special teams, we matched up well against a very good team*".

GAME 10: LOUISVILLE (9-0) vs GREENWOOD (1-8)
LOUISVILLE 58 GREENWOOD 0
October 26, 2023

This was not a Greenwood team that Wildcat fans were accustomed to facing as they sat with just a lone victory. "*Greenwood is a young team. Watching them on film, they're very talented but they're missing something. They're not really playing for the playoffs. I'm quite sure they want to come in and beat us to look forward to next year*".

An early punt block by Ayden Coleman set up a Jordan touchdown early. He blocked another on the next possession and Macon took in to put it 14-0. The kickoff fumble recovery led to a Hunt strike to Triplett to end the frame. Zaiden Jernigan started the next frame with a 2-yarder, Goss took a punt deep to set up a 5-yard Hoskins dive and Dyjaylen Miller's safety put intermission 44-0.

The clock began to run in the second half again as reserves manned spots for the Wildcats. The last two tallies came from a Jernigan run and a 4-yarder by Sanders. Hunt was 4-8-1 for 72, Tristan Edwards also saw time at QB, Sanders had 35 yards rushing, and Triplett had 41 receiving. On defense, Kendon Sanders had 10 tackles; Macon forced two fumbles and a recovery taken for TD and Ayden Coleman blocked 2 punts and had an interception.

"*We came out of the game pretty healthy and at this time of the year, when you have just about everybody back, that's a plus. I thought our guys came out and played really well and we had a chance to see a lot of young guys play. You never know when you'll need them*".

GAME 11: LOUISVILLE (10-0) vs ITAWAMBA AHS (4-7)
LOUISVILLE 31 ITAWAMBA AHS 7
November 3, 2023

Louisville was 4-0 all-time against IAHS and was familiar with them in recent years. "*Itawamba is a well-coached football team. They have some talented skill guys with a big offensive line. Going into the playoffs, I tell our kids that It's more mental now. The weather is going to change and you don't know when it's going to be cold, rainy or snowy. You've got to be prepared. One bad night can end your season and we have to make sure that we have great practices and know our assignments*".

It looked to be a usual Wildcat offensive performance with Hunt and Triplett hooking up from 10 yards while Jordan ran in from six yards to make it 14-0. With under 3:00 left, the Indians tallied to slice the advantage. Hunt added a 32-yard FG to move it ahead a bit 17-7. The defense allowed nothing more from the visitors while the Cats garnered scoring runs from Jordan and Sanders in the finale.

IAHS had just 100 offensive yards but was held to a -21 rushing total. McDonald and McKinney each had three sacks and a combined 19 tackles. Sanders led with 15 and Goss added an interception. On the ground, the Cats put up 206 yards with Jordan leading the way with 63. Hunt was 14-26 for 114 and Triplett pulled in 48 more in the air.

"*The first two drives we came out and scored quickly and then penalties started hurting us. We had three or four holding calls that backed us up and killed drives. Our guys settled down and played much better in the second half. Itawamba came to play. They gave us a fight the first half. These are the playoffs and everyone wants to win so we had to make sure we took care of business*".

GAME 12:   LOUISVILLE (11-0) vs NEW ALBANY (8-2)
                                 LOUISVILLE 37 NEW ALBANY 0
                                 November 10, 2023

Their first meeting in 2012 and their last in 2020 ended in Wildcat wins over the Bulldogs. "*They're big on both sides of the ball. I think playing at home is our 12th man. Not going on the road and traveling out of your comfort zone is huge. Playing at home is very important and that's why you work so hard to get that number one seed*".

The lone opening-frame tally came late when Hoskins ran in from six yards and the two-pointer put them ahead 8-0. Haynes had the next late in the 2nd quarter while Triplett added the next to put intermission 20-0. Now in the finale, Ceidrick Hunt hit a 32-yard FG. Haynes added a 17-yard dash while Sanders found the end zone from six yards.

The offense had 400 yards with 336 coming on the ground. Hoskins led the way with 118. Hunt was 6-13 for 99 yards, Triplett had 94 yards receiving, McKinney led tacklers with 10 and forced a fumble while Corxavier Coleman also had 10 stops and three sacks.

"*I thought our kids came out and played really well in the (rainy) weather. I'm just proud of our kids the way they're playing right now in all three phases. For our kids to come out in that type of weather and play the way they did, it made me feel good no matter what the weather is in the playoffs. It's mostly mental*".

GAME 13:   LOUISVILLE (12-0) vs CALEDONIA (6-5)
                                 LOUISVILLE 39 CALEDONIA 0
                                 November 17, 2023

After beating Caledonia 54-7 back in October, the Wildcats had to do it again to advance. "*It is very scary to play a team twice. We went to their place and beat them and this is what I talk about when I tell them to be focused every week. Even though we played them a month ago and took care of business, it's a different ball game. If you don't win, your season is over. They're talented and have what it takes to win, but it's a focus. When you're dealing with teenagers, it's a hard job*".

Late in the opening frame, Jordan ran 97 yards to paydirt to make it 7-0. They increased that to 15-0 in the 2nd quarter and Ceidrick Hunt hit a 23-yard FG to make it 18-0. Haynes opened the 3rd quarter with a 4-yard run. Both Goss and Jordan added other scores in the game. The offense passed for 182 of the total 251 yards. Hunt was 6-13-1 for 182, Goss caught 116 of those, and both Jordan (123) and Hoskins (100) passed the century mark on the ground. Travon McKinney had 11 tackles, Sanders forced a fumble, and Kenneth Hill added an interception.

"*Our kids came out and they were focused. I thought we played good in all three phases again. Any concern I had ended after the game started*".

GAME 14:   LOUISVILLE (13-0) vs HOUSTON (11-1)
                                 LOUISVILLE 20 HOUSTON 7
                                 November 24, 2023

The only loss the Hilltoppers had this year came against Louisville 50-6 at the end of September. "*It's always a challenge when you play a team the second time in one year. This is a different ball game and it's for a trip to the state championship. When we played them the first time it was one of their worst games. They're going to come in and play us hard. All of our kids are excited. Continue to stay focused*".

Scoring was over late in the 2nd quarter starting with a D.J. Miller fumble recovery and score and Hunt's 37-yarder to Ayden Coleman. Houston found the board in the final minute but Hunt later dashed in from a yard to end it. The Cats rushed for 164 yards with Hoskins leading the charge with 71. Hunt was 2-6 for 46. The defense led the way with 12 tackles for loss with Tayquon McKinney's 13 tackles and a forced fumble.

"We knew that Houston was a good football team. We knew they were going to come in here and fight hard. They came in and fought and we knew they would. We beat a heck of a football team".

GAME 15:   LOUISVILLE (14-0) vs COLUMBIA (14-0)
                               LOUISVILLE 19 COLUMBIA 6
                               December 3, 2023: Vaught-Hemingway Stadium; Oxford, MS

Louisville was 3-1 all-time with games between 1946 and 1951 against the 4-7A Columbia squad. *"They're kind of similar to us. They've got a lot of athletes and a lot of speed. They have a good program and are a well-coached team. It should be a good game. They're just like some of the teams we've played on our schedule already. These kids know. There's pressure here that once you get to a state championship, you win it. Pressure is a privilege. I'm proud to be part of this and the kids are, too".*

Hunt grabbed the first two touchdowns, the first from a yard to make it 6-0 while the next came in the 2nd quarter on a sneak. Sanders dove in from a yard later to make it 19-0. Now in the finale, Columbia scored from 18 yards on a Collin Haney pass to Amarion Foxworth. With just under 6:00 left at the 21-yard line, Semaj Knowles killed the threat with an interception. One last effort late in the game at the 40-yard line also ended with a theft, this by Triplett.

The offense led yardage 255-186. Hunt was 6-8 for 109 and both Knowles and Owens led tacklers with seven each. *"Hard work and dedication. These guys come to work every single day. There are three other teams that play for a state championship this weekend. We played them in the first five weeks. And I told them that if we can survive, that you're going to in a state championship. Our defense has been playing great all year. You know, that's what we do in Louisville. We build our defenses".*

It marked the 12th state championship since 1985 while two other teams (1920 and 1944) could argue that they should be included. Either way, it proved that Louisville was strong for almost all of their 111 years of organized football and passed marks that many would never approach.

Year	Achievement	Year	Achievement
1920	State Champions	1991	District 2-4A Champions
1924	State Runner-Up	1991	4A State Champions
1930	East Central Regional Champs	1992	District 2-4A Champions
1933	Magnolia Bowl Champs	1992	4A North Runner Up
1939	East Central Regional Champs	1993	4A State Champions
1944	State Champions	1994	4A North Runner Up
1944	Magnolia Bowl Champs	1995	4A State Champions
1946	Lions Delta Bowl Champs	1996	4A North Runner Up
1948	Choctaw Conference Champs	1997	District 4-4A Champions
1948	Lions Delta Bowl	1997	4A North Runner Up
1950	Choctaw Conference Champs	1998	District 4-4A Champions
1951	Choctaw Conference Champs	1999	District 2-4A Champions
1957	Choctaw Conference Champs	1999	4A North Runner Up
1958	Choctaw Conference Champs	2000	District 2-4A Champions
1958	Lions Delta Bowl Champs	2007	District 2-3A Champions
1959	Choctaw Conference Champs	2007	3A State Champions
1962	Choctaw Conference Champs	2008	3A State Champions
1962	Mississippi Bowl Champs	2011	District 4-4A Champions
1969	Choctaw Conference Champs	2013	District 4-3A Champions
1971	Choctaw Conference Champs	2013	3A State Champions
1974	North MS Athletic Conf Champs	2014	District 4-3A Champions
1977	South Little Ten Conf Champs	2018	District 4-4A Champions
1981	Jaycee Bowl Champs	2018	4A State Champions
1984	District 4-4A Champions	2019	District 4-4A Champions
1985	District 4-4A Champions	2020	District 4-4A Champions
1985	4A State Champions	2020	4A State Champions
1986	District 4-4A Champions	2022	District 4-4A Champions
1986	4A State Champions	2022	4A State Champions
1987	4A North Runner Up	2023	District 4-3A Champions
1988	District 4-4A Champions	2023	4A State Champions
1989	District 2-4A Champions		

Perfect
1920
1944
1971
2013
2023

Undefeated
1920
1944
1950
1971
2013
2023

One Loss
1915
1916
1919
1923
1924
1929
1930
1932
1937
1939
1958
1959
1962
1966
1967
1969
1974
1975
1984
1993
2018
2020
2022

District Titles
1984
1985
1986
1988
1989
1991
1992
1997
1998
1999
2000
2007
2011
2013
2014
2018
2019
2020
2022
2023

LOUISVILLE WILDCAT COACHES

Unfortunately, some of those mentors went unmentioned. All best efforts were undertaken to find their names to give credit as best as possible.

1914	Unknown
1915	Coach Ross
1915	Reverend Stephens
1916	Cleave Jones
1917-1918	Unknown
1919	Carl Doss
1920-23	E. Bryan Smith
1924	Steve Bailey
1925-27	Unknown
1928-29	Roy Sheffield
1930	Unknown
1931-33	Harold Webb
1934	Unknown
1935-37	W.E. Strange
1938-39	Cohen Jenkins
1940-46	R. Elzie Hinze
1947-50	James "Obie" Brown
1951-53	H.C. Earhart
1954-55	Hugh Ellis Walker
1956-58	Ken Lawrence
1959-63	Fred Morris
1964-65	Jack Warner
1966-68	Charles Peets
1969	Matthew Turner
1970	Paul Wood
1971-74	A.J. Kilpatrick
1975-78	Art Nester
1979-83	Jack McAlpin
1984-89	Mike Justice
1990-92	Bobby Hall
1993-94	Lynn Moore
1995-02	Tony Stanford
2003	Joe Gant
2003-04	John Mullins
2005-09	Brad Peterson
2010-18	M.C. Miller
2019-23	Tyrone Shorter

LOUISVILLE WILDCAT HOMECOMING QUEENS

Unfortunately, some Queens went unknown. Even one year has simply pictures with no names. Another year is left off all together from reports and the yearbook remains missing. All best efforts were undertaken to find their names to give credit as incredibly required.

Year	Name	Year	Name
1935	Dorothy Kelly	1993	Wendi Watts
1954	Mary Ann Strong	1994	Lylanda Miller
1955	Lynn Cunningham	1994	Allison Parkes
1956	Jeanette Taylor	1995	Kamonica Craig
1957	Sandra Trest	1995	Dana Peterson
1958	Pat Wicker	1996	Corrin Chambliss
1959	Carol Cunningham	1996	Shana Coleman
1960	Janet Younger	1997	Andrea Buie
1961	Janice Small	1997	Jana Wylie
1962	Teddy McNeill	1998	Mia Eichelberger
1963	Sandra Gordon	1998	Holly Preston
1964	Cindy Chapman	1999	J.J. Misso
1965	Madalyn Cunningham	1999	April Smith
1966	Emily Ann Pearson	2000	Antinika Bender
1967	Carol Wright	2000	Cynthia Fleming
1968	Cindy Smith	2001	Amanda Loyd
1969	Janet Young	2001	Krystal Yarbrough
1981	Anita Hudson	2002	Erica Loving
1981	Christi Shumaker	2002	Ronda Stroud
1982	Beth Covington	2003	Kathy Smith
1982	Yolanda Hemphill	2003	Mallory Thompson
1983	Jackie Oglesby	2004	Jade Carter
1983	Annette Yarbrough	2004	Darneice Floyd
1984	Tara Powell	2005	Callista Coleman
1984	Sharon Yarbrough	2006	Audrey Hathorn
1985	Rita Jackson	2007	Yolanda Hudson
1985	Emy Nation	2008	Taiesha Young
1986	Crystal Pope	2009	Bethany Ball
1986	Tenela Rogers	2010	India Ball
1987	Stephanie Fulton	2011	Kaylin Hopkins
1987	Chevelle Hall	2012	Brianna Davis
1988	Cecilia Eiland	2013	Latesha Yarbrough
1988	Lisa Kennedy	2014	Diamond Love
1989	Kendralyn Crowder	2015	Jordan Sellers
1989	Amy Fussell	2016	Stephanie Hayes
1990	Natasha Rogers	2017	Imani Shell
1990	Salicia Jernigan	2018	Unknown
1991	Vanessa Anderson	2019	Dyshunte Bragg
1991	Terri Baker	2020	Erica Murry
1992	Wendy Parker	2021	Alyssia Joseph
1992	Kayla Rogers	2022	Trynitee Overstreet
1993	Monique Coleman	2023	Destinee Walker

LOUISVILLE WILDCAT CHEERLEADERS

Many who cheered for the Wildcats are unknown. If left off of newspaper reports and with some yearbooks not mentioning names, it is almost impossible to determine all who worked so hard to boost their school and team. All best efforts were undertaken to find their names to give credit as incredibly required.

Adams	Skylar	2015		Catledge	Pam	1960
Alford	Melanie	1994-95		Ceeter	Jada	2017
Allday	Christie	1987-89		Chambliss	Corrin	1994-96
Allday	Kim	1984		Chambliss	Klaye	1993-95
Allen	Amy	1953-55		Chapman	Cindy	1963-64
Ammons	Regan	2019-22		Charlton	Evelyn	1959
Anderson	Vanessa	1990-91		Childs	Carol	1962-64
Anthony	Cindy	1982-83		Childs	Marsha	1974
Atkinson	Mary	1988-90		Chiles	Jamie	1956-57
Avara	Donna	1971		Chiles	Jean	1967-68
Avara	Kim	1977		Cistrunk	Roberta	1974
Baker	Asia	2017		Clark	Jessica	2001
Ball	Bethany	2007-09		Clark	Samantha	1983-84
Barnett	Allix	2010		Clark	Tiffany	2002-03
Bates	Hayli	2019		Clay	Maya	2015-17
Bates	Tierra	2015-17		Clay	Willard	1935
Bearden	Marsha	1974-76		Cockrell	Carolyn	1949-50
Bennett	Asia	2009		Coleman	Gwen	1969-70
Bennett	Diane	1962-64		Coleman	Jocelyn	2007-08
Bennett	Frankie	1973		Coleman	Phoebie	1992
Berry	Jamilia	2022		Coleman	Shana	1994-96
Blackwell	Stacy	1996-98		Coleman	Tilda	1978-79
Boren	Julia	1955		Collier	Skyla	2023
Bouchillon	Stefanie	1998		Collins	Peggy Sue	1957
Bragg	Dyshante	2017-19		Cooper	Rhonda	1988; 1990
Brown	Darihana	2023		Cooper	Sonya	1998-00
Brown	Janet	1949-50		Cooper	Thonda	1987
Bruff	Angie	1976-77		Cornett	Misty	1988-89
Buie	Andrea	1995-97		Cotton	Melanie	1987
Bullock	Terralyn	2019		Covington	Beth	1982
Burchfield	Kim	1992		Craig	Faye	1958-60
Burt	Janice	1950-52		Cravens	Maggie	2003
Burton	Diamond	2015-16		Crawford	Beth	1975
Buskirk	Dorothy	1947		Creed	Bridgett	1987
Butler	Agnes	1929		Crowson	Beth	1968-70
Buzzerd	Meagan	2004		Crowson	Rachel	2000
Cade	Emily	1992		Crumpton	Gail	1966
Cade	Mary Ardath	1949		Cunningham	Faye	1959
Calvert	Kay	1967-69		Cunningham	Sherry	1958-59
Cannon	Mary Ann	1961-62		Curtis	Kathy	1988
Canty	Patty	1961-64		Daniel	Anna	2023
Caperton	Nora Gay	1986-87		Davenport	Erica	2003-04
Carothers	Betty	1957		Davis	Brianna	2009-11
Carr	Donna	1980-81		Davis	Mary	1953
Carter	Angie	1984-85		Davis	Sallye	1949-51
Carter	Lisa	1982-84		Dawkins	Kygeria	2016-17
Carter	Shanteeze	2009-11		Dempsey	Amanda	1995-96
Catledge	Marsha	1960-63		Dempsey	Norma	1977
Catledge	Mary Frances	1935		Dewberry	Kelsie	2022-23

Last Name	First Name	Years
Donald	Lindsey	2004-07
Donald	Whitney	2002
Edwards	Keyasha	2015-16
Edwards	Nathalie	1987-89
Edwards	Penni	1984
Edwards	Rickedra	2023
Eichelberger	Asia	2015-16
Eichelberger	Ebonee	2007-09
Eichelberger	Montana	2015
Eiland	Markiaa	2016
Eiland	Shacrecia	1999-01
Estes	Makaylan	2022
Etheridge	Mary Etta	1951-52
Fair	Davis	1929
Fair	De Vane	1960-61
Fair	Mary	1969
Fair	Stewart	1958-59
Faulkner	Jan	1969-71
Ferrell	Forest Jean	1947
Fleming	Cynthia	2000
Fleming	Gloria	1965-66
Ford	Miriah	2015
Forster	Kay	1963-65
Foster	Mary	1972
Foster	Rosie	1976-78
Fowler	Carol	1975
Francis	Blanche	1956
Frazier	Kaylee	2019
Frazier	Seretha	1996
Fulcher	Ellen	1969-70
Fulcher	Julie	1989-90
Fuller	Nora	2019
Fulton	Stephanie	1986-87
Fulton	Tammy	1979-81
Fussell	Amy	1987-89
Gale	Dana	2002-03
Gamble	Javrey	2022-23
Garrett	Leigh	1988-91
Gates	Jahayla	2023
Giffin	Yvonne	1951-53
Gladney	Netkianna	2015
Glenn	Bracina	2007-09
Glenn	Brookelyn	2004-06
Glenn	Cynthia	1979-1980
Glenn	Denitra	1999-01
Glenn	Lora	1987-88
Goldman	Courtney	2009
Goodin	Brittany	2000
Goodin	Destiny	2009-11
Gookin	Kathy	1969-70
Gordon	Sandra	1963
Goss	Jamaya	2022-23
Goss	Kaylee	2022-23
Goss	Kaylen	2022-23
Grady	Keesha	1991
Grant	Lindsey	2006
Greer	Jannell	1976-79
Greer	Mary	1982-83
Griffin	Audrey	2007-09
Grissom	Alicia	1993
Hailey	Kadie	2004-07
Hall	Judy	1959-61
Hamill	Patrice	1967-69
Hammond	Harold	1947
Hampton	Latashia	1991-93
Hampton	Leslie	1981
Hancock	Genia	1975
Hancock	Martha	1947
Hannah	Jamie	1976
Hannah	LaToya	1998-99
Hardin	Deterron	2009
Hardin	Jameela	2002-03
Harrell	Alex	2000
Harrington	Tiaa	1993
Hathorn	Audrey	2004-06
Hathorn	Claire	1973
Hathorn	Emily	2006-08
Hathorn	Erin	2007-09
Hathorn	Jalen	2019
Hawthorne	Cynthia	1973-75
Haynes	Catherine	1978
Haynes	Monifah	2015-16
Heath	Amanda	1991-92
Hemphill	Isis	2022
Hemphill	Katelyn	2017
Hickman	Arianna	2019
Hickman	Joni	2009, 2011
Hickman	Kenya	2008
Hickman	Na'Khia	2022-23
Hicks	Daneen	2009-11
Hicks	Danielle	2010
Hill	Allison	2003
Hill	Joelie	2011
Hill	Samantha	2009, 2011
Hill	Sharon	1971-72
Hindman	Bobbie	1978-80
Hisaw	Pam	1989-90
Holmes	Jasmine	2016; 2019
Holmes	LaQuetta	1994
Holmes	Latasha	1990-1992
Hopkins	Camera	2009, 2011
Hopkins	Kaylin	2011
Hopkins	Lindsay	2003-04
Hopkins	Tiara	2011
Hornesburger	Daralyn	1987-90
Hoskins	Delores	1995
Hoskins	Kaylin	2009-10
Houston	Dominique	2008-10
Houston	Erica	2002
Houston	Lanisha	2003
Hudson	Anita	1979-81
Hudson	Daphne	1967-68
Hudson	Sariyia	2022-23
Hughes	Ashley	2004
Hughes	Faith	2022-23
Hughes	Jackie	1960-62
Hughes	Jasmine	2011
Hull	Kaye	1973

Last	First	Years	Last	First	Years
Hull	Mary Joyce	1963-65	McNeill	Teddy	1960-62
Humes	Kierra	2023	Metts	Bobby	1935
Hunt	Lee	2004-06	Metts	Jackie	1968
Hunt	Mahayla	2023	Miller	Aries	2011
Hunt	Samara	2019	Miller	Brandi	2015-17
Hunt	Skyla	2023	Miller	Charleigh	2022-23
Huntley	Brenda	1965-66	Miller	Courtney	2004-06
Ingram	Hailey	2011	Miller	Jack "Bony"	1951
Ingram	LaShun	1990	Miller	Karen	1982-83
Isonhood	Any	1988	Miller	Meagan	2001-02
Ivy	Kim	1985-86	Miller	Mitzi	1947
Jackson	Ji'Maia	2016-17	Miller	Oricka	2017
Jackson	Kailey	2019	Ming	Marion	2016-17
Jackson	Mary	1947	Moore	Karl	1975
Jauch	Kathy	1972-73	Murry	Orica	2017
Jernigan	Gwen	1974-75	Myers	Audra	2000-01
Jernigan	Janet	2000-02	NcNeel	Jeanne	1966
Jernigan	Jennifer	1982-84	Nicholson	Brandi	1999-01
Johnson	Julie	1994-95	Nicholson	Tamika	1993
Johnson	Kourtney	2010	Nicholson	Zoria	2015
Johnson	Linda	1956-59	Nowell	Rachel	1998
Johnson	Marsha	1969-70	Older	McKenna	2017
Johnson	MyAasia	2022	Overstreet	Trynitee	2019; 22
Johnson	Shanika	1990	Owens	Rochelle	1985-86
Johnson	Simone	1996-97	Owens	Takiela	1994
Jolly	Mary Ann	1953	Pace	Bridgett	1991
Jones	Porcha	2017	Pace	Shawna	1989
Jones	Sybil	1949-50	Palmer	DeDe	1978-79
Jordan	Katelyn	2007-09	Parker	Zamiracle	2017
Jordan	Marla	1992-93	Parks	Makayla	2019
Joseph	Alyissia	2019	Patterson	Dianne	1972-74
Kelley	Brandi	1992	Paty	Sabrina	2006
Kennedy	Lisa	1988	Pearson	Nikki	1997-98
Kinard	Debbie	1985	Pease	Nevaeh	2022
King	Ciarria	2022	Perry	Rena	1995-96
Latham	Keeli	2022	Peterson	Carol	1957-58
Latham	Star	2015-17	Peterson	Dana	1993
Lewis	Destiny	2016	Peterson	Nancy	1953-54
Liddell	Judy	1974-75	Pham	Kayla	2022
Livingston	Leighanne	1991	Phillips	Carmen	2006-07
Long	Wendi	1994	Phillips	Jarhonda	2000
Love	Debbie	1982	Pickett	Adrienne	1993-94
Love	Tiara	2007-09	Porter	Beverly	1971-72
Lowery	Bessie	1971-73	Porter	Jaden	2019; 22
Loyd	Amanda	1999-00	Porter	Teresa	1977
Lucas	Katie	2017; 19	Preston	Holly	1996-98
Lucas	Lauren	2015	Price	LaKeisha	1990-92
Luke	Carol	1971-73	Reed	Amber	2003-04
Marsicek	Dianne	1962-63	Reed	Holly	1992-94
Marsicek	Gail	1964; 1966	Reed	Madelyn	2008
Mauldin	Martha	1935	Reel	Amanda	2002-03
Mays	Charlessia	2015-16	Roach	Callie	2015-17
McArthur	Brandi	1993	Roberson	Marshandra	1990-92
McCracken	Tracey	1999-01	Robertson	Carol	1958
McCully	Faye	1956-57	Robertson	Corinne	1955
McGraw	Mali	1965-67	Rodgers	Genela	1984
McKay	Ann Adelle	1952-53	Rogers	Natasha	1990
McNeel	Jean	1966-67	Rogers	Tenela	1984-86
McNeese	Khyla	1997	Rush	Victoria	2019

Rutherford	Jan	1988-90		Triplett	Lisa	1974-75
Sammons	Eric	1975		Triplett	Nicole	2000
Sammons	Tamara	1975-77		Triplett	Sarah	1997-99
Sangster	Breyonna	2015-17		Triplett	Schawn	1980
Scoggins	Angie	1987		Triplett	Sy'Keyria	2022-23
Sellers	Jordan	2015		Tullos	Martha	1953
Shanabruogh	Allison	2003-04		Turnipseed	Dacia	1990-91
Shelton	Diane	1968-70		Turnipseed	Juanita	1984-86
Sherwood	Jamie	1988		Tyler	Ariana	2015-17
Shinn	Sharon	1976		Tyler	Sheena	2000-02
Shumaker	Christi	1978-81		Unknown	Catherine	1981
Shumaker	Lori	1977-78		Unknown	Lorie	1983-84
Shumaker	Mary Lou	1976		Unknown	Pam	1981
Shumaker	Mary Nell	1956-58		Unknown	Penny	1984
Shurden	Jamie	1987		Unknown	Stephanie	1983
Simpson	Laura	2004-06		Vanlandingham	Christal	1993-95
Small	Janice	1959-61		Waldrip	Nataki	2009-10
Smith	Abbie	2009-11		Waldrip	Tatyana	2015-16
Smith	April	1997-99		Waldrip	Uminique	2016-17
Smith	Cindy	1966-68		Walker	Kim	2002-03
Smith	Melanie	1987-89		Ward	Delena	2022-23
Smith	Paige	1985		Ward	Lori	1984-85
Spann	Kaleah	2017		Warner	Babs	1969-71
Stallings	Ty	2019		Watts	Tisha	1997-98
Stevens	Chanda	1993-95		Watts	Wendy	1991-93
Stevens	Patty	1954-56		Webb	Sandra	1964-65
Stewart	Susan	1980		White	Carol	1965-67
Strong	Mary Ann	1951-52; 1954		White	Haley	2017
Sullivan	Jan	1972		White	Jeanne	1951
Tabor	Ashlyn	2022-23		White	Sissie	1969-70
Tabor	Debbie	1979-82		Whitfield	Amaya	2019; 22
Taylor	Jeanette	1954-56		Wilson	Lindsey	1993-94
Thames	Adria	2015-17		Windham	Brittany	2016-17
Thames	Shantwanna	2011		Winstead	Lois	1949-50
Thompson	Katy	1997-99		Woods	Leah	2015
Thompson	Mallory	2002		Wraggs	Bettie	1985-87
Thompson	Zahahyia	2019		Wraggs	Makayiah	2019; 22
Todd	Ginger	1996		Wright	Dale	1951-53
Tranue	Jamie	2000		Wright	Julie	1975
Tranum	Jan	1999-01		Wylie	Jana	1995-97
Tranum	Mary Claire	1996-98		Yarbrough	Erica	2008-10
Triplett	Ashley	2006-08		Yarbrough	Keoceania	2011
Triplett	Brenda	1992		Yarbrough	Latesha	2011
Triplett	Dynasty	2019		Yarbrough	Nancy	1953
Triplett	Jennifer	1991		Yarbrough	Saforina	1969-70
Triplett	LaKiaa	2015-17		Young	Ashley	2011
Triplett	Latiaa	2015-17		Young	Taiesha	2006-08

LOUISVILLE WILDCAT ASSISTANT COACHES

Like others noted previously, the assistants were rarely mentioned if not in yearbooks or newspaper recaps. Some years were non-existent for both. Also, some coaches moved down to JV or Junior High before coming back to Varsity. Others left before coming back to Winston County. This is what is found to date.

Anderson	Brady	Glenn	Allen	Moore	Ernie
Anderson	Brian	Goodin	Allen	Moore	Ray
Autry	Marcus	Hannah	Trent	Oswalt	Bryan
Baker	Preston	Harper	Ed	Peterson	Brad
Baker	Walter	Heard	Scott	Peterson	Tyler
Ballard	Bruce	Henderson	Wade	Porter	Crandall
Bane	Ricky	Hill	Clint	Powell	Andrew
Benton	Howard	Hill	Jerry	Ray	Jim
Black	David	Hill	Unknown	Reed	Justin
Boswell	Jimmy	Hodges	Terry	Reeves	Chris
Bounds	Mickey	Hopkins	Derek	Rhodes	Jim
Boykin	David	Horne	LaQuintis	Richardson	George
Boyles	Marcus	Hoskins	Markevius	Rogers	Berlin
Braddock	Keith	Hudson	Hilute	Rogers	Tyler
Brantley	Don	Hughes	Gary	Ryals	Torris
Brantley	Jess	Hunter	Justin	Sallis	John
Breland	Jeff	Ibrahim	Mustaffa	Sangster	Jaquavious
Bruce	Michael	Jackson	Haskell	Sangster	Jeremy
Buckhalter	Tony	Jackson	Marcus	Shorter	Tyrone
Byrd	Pat	Jenkins	Cohen	Smith	Bobby
Campbell	Ronald	Jones	Javancy	Smith	Charlie
Carlisle	Chris	Jones	Wayne	Smith	Drew
Catchot	Jim	Kemp	Jordan	Snow	Matt
Clay	Mantel	Killen	Paul	Square	Ed
Coleman	Elmer	King	Bill	Stanford	Tony
Coleman	Ronald	Lawrence	Ken	Stanley	Ed
Collums	Toby	Lee	Charles	Stephens	Royce
Conner	Omarr	Marshall	Eric	Taylor	M.C.
Duke	Buddy	McAdory	Buster	Thomas	Bryant
Duncan	Bill	McAlpin	Jack	Thompson	Rhyne
Duncan	Nick	McClelland	Unknown	Tippett	Kylan
Earhart	H.C.	McCool	Tommy	Turner	Matthew
Edwards	Corey	McCrory	Donald	Wade	Unknown
Edwards	Trenell	McCullough	Corey	Walker	Pete
Estes	Lawrence	McMullan	Ken	Walls	Jeff
Eubanks	Casey	Millen	Unknown	Westerfield	Charles
Fairley	Quentin	Miller	Dicenzo	Wilcutt	Jimmy
Fennell	Unknown	Miller	Jimmy	Wolf	Unknown
Finch	Robert	Miller	M.C.	Wood	Paul
Fleming	Jarred	Miller	Montez	Woods	Mickey
Garvin	Patrick	Miller	Tremond	Morris	Fred
Garvin	Patrick	Ming	Harold	Mullins	John
Gibson	Chad	Mitchell	Dillon	Murphy	Bill
Gibson	Chad	Montgomery	Randall	Oakley	Bob

LOUISVILLE WILDCAT PLAYERS

Perhaps the most difficult of all projects was to get the names of those who wore the jersey and attended practices to gain the recognition of the school. Reports vary from newspapers, the school, yearbooks, and more. You WILL notice names spelled correctly. You WILL notice missing names and missing years. This is the best that could be put together from reports found to date.

Adams	Patrick	2011		Baker	Unknown	1928
Adcock	Fred	1955-56		Ball	Bernard	1988-90
Adcox	Bubba	1976		Ball	Derrick	2007
Addkison	Donald	1946-49		Ball	Jarrad	2004-07
Addkison	Dwight	1943-47		Ball	Jerome	1988-89
Addkison	Homer	1930-32		Ball	Jevrick	2008
Addkison	Keaton	1955-57		Ball	Kendrick	1994-95
Addkison	Kenny	1951-54		Ball	Liderek	2015-17
Addkison	Larry	1968-70		Ball	Marcus	1991
Addkison	Roger	1936-38		Ball	Rufus	1995-97
Addkison	Truitt	1939-41		Ball	Tyrone	1987-89
Allen	Delver	1968		Ball	Unknown	1927
Allen	Jerry	1950		Ballard	Eddie	1969-70
Allen	Johnny	1949		Bane	Ricky	1973
Allen	Lowery	1937		Banks	Marcus	2012-15
Allen	Todd	1980		Banks	Melvin	1974
Allen	Wister	1951-53		Barnes	Harry	1960-62
Allman	Bobby	1960-63		Barnes	John	1955
Ammons	Joshua	2022-23		Bartlett	E.T.	1936-39
Anderson	Brady	2013-14		Baswell	Bruce	1967-69
Anderson	Devin	2013		Baswell	Bud	1969
Anderson	Jeffery	1992-94		Bates	C.J.	2009-11
Anderson	Lajordan	2013-16		Bates	Kendrick	2014-16
Anderson	Nigel	2019-22		Bates	Mark	2014
Anderson	Steve	1962		Batte	Bobby	1953-54
Anthony	Elijah	1999		Batte	Junior	1935-38
Arnett	Doug	1968		Battle	Sterling	1936
Ash	Jeremiah	2021-23		Beach	James	1952
Ashford	Broam	2007-09		Beasley	Daryl	1977
Ashford	Derrell	2000-02		Beeman	Tracy	1982-84
Ashford	Gary	1993-95		Bennett	B.	1933
Ashford	James	1970-72		Bennett	Brian	1997
Ashford	Mantrell	2000-02		Bennett	Dale	1950-51
Atkinson	Bradley	1989		Bennett	Gilbert	1938-39
Atkinson	Earl	1923		Bennett	Grafton	1916-17
Atkinson	Garland	1916		Bennett	Harry	1937
Atkinson	Leonard	1915-16		Bennett	Joe	1944
Atkinson	Unknown	1925-26; 28		Bennett	Percy	1930
Austin	Frank	1984-85		Berry	Joseph	2014-16
Austin	Mike	1978-80		Berry	Tyler	2011
Aycock	George	1959-61		Black	Barry	1978
Aycock	Kevin	1994		Black	David	2001
Aycock	Larry	1956-57		Black	Josh	2002-03
Aycock	Wayne	1956-57		Black	Mike	1965
Baker	Ced	1986-88		Black	Unknown	1927
Baker	Clyde	1972		Blair	Chris	2012-15
Baker	Demon	1994-97		Blue	Charlie	1944-46
Baker	Deserick	1998		Boler	Andre	1986
Baker	Rod	1984-86		Boler	Keyandre	2014
Baker	Roy	1951		Bond	Tommy	1951
Baker	Tony	1977-79		Bonney	Rob	1965

Last	First	Years	Last	First	Years
Boone	Justin	2003-05	Bryant	Paul	1966-67
Borland	Homer	Unknown	Burchfield	Brody	2014-15
Boswell	Bob	1969	Burchfield	Jason	1994-95
Boswell	David	1920	Burchfield	Larry	1959
Boswell	Jim	1961-63	Burns	Danny	1963-64
Boswell	Judd	1993-95	Burns	Jerry	1964
Boswell	Unknown	1916	Burns	Yancey	1988-90
Bouchillon	Charles	1947-48	Burnside	Dexter	1988-90
Bouchillon	Jimmie	1964	Burrage	Devonta	2004-05
Bourland	Shea	1989-90	Burrage	Zykueria	2016-17
Bowen	Jimmy	1982-84	Burrass	Orville	1921
Bowman	Bobby	1967-69	Burt	Hughes	1947-49
Boyd	"Siv"	1922-23	Burt	Jonathon	1994
Boyd	Alvin	1928-29	Burton	Bobby Joe	1966-68
Boyd	Cody	1986-87	Burton	Clyde	1936
Boyd	Eddie	1951-54	Burton	Damien	2008
Boyd	Henry	1950-52	Butler	Clinton	1926-27
Boyd	Lamar	1957	Butler	Robert	1915-16
Boyd	Sam	1991	Butts	Jimmy	1977-78
Boyd	Unknown	1925	Butts	Ken	1983
Boydstun	Herby	1962-64	Butts	Tim	1975-77
Boydstun	Unknown	1936	Butts	Will	2002-03
Boyet	Robert	1935	Cade	Adam	1992
Boykin	Richard	1940-42	Cagle	Nath	Unknown
Boyles	Mike	1963-65	Caldwell	Davian	2022-23
Boyles	Unknown	1936	Campbell	Brodrick	2000-02
Bradford	Brad	1993-95	Canty	Stewart	1968
Bradford	Unknown	1916	Caperton	Dickie	1956; 59
Bragg	Antwan	2007-08	Caperton	Eater	1947
Bragg	Ken	2001-02	Caperton	Hayes	2021
Bragg	Marques	1995-97	Caperton	James	1943
Braggs	Trey	2006	Caperton	Larry	1960-62
Brantley	"Ose"	1933	Caperton	Roger	1988-90
Brantley	Lamar	1923-24	Caperton	Tommy	1945-48
Brantley	Paul	1930	Carmichael	Sonny	1946-49
Brantley	Randolph	1920-21	Carr	Gerald	1982
Brantley	Trent	2011	Carr	Unknown	1946
Braxton	Bobby	1944-45	Carter	Brandon	2015-16
Braxton	Tommy	1944-49	Carter	Bryant	1983-85
Bray	Jack	1936-41	Carter	Charley	1943
Brazeale	Willie	1929-32	Carter	Chris	1991-93
Bridges	Gerald	1973	Carter	Darrel	1982-83
Brock	Cory	2023	Carter	Darren	1985
Brooks	Curtis	1998	Carter	Darryl	1985
Brooks	Demarcus	2011-14	Carter	Davis	1999
Brooks	James	1979-81	Carter	Davis	2000-01
Brooks	Jarron	2003	Carter	Earl	1971-72
Brown	Alex	2017	Carter	Elliot	1996-98
Brown	Anthony	1979-81	Carter	J.W.	1942
Brown	Bubba	1971-72	Carter	James	1975
Brown	Derrick	1992	Carter	Jerome	1994-95
Brown	Frank	2006-07	Carter	Kenneth	1985
Brown	Joel	2023	Carter	Kenny	1974-76
Brown	Kendrick	2012-14	Carter	Kevin	1998-00
Brown	Larry	1960-62	Carter	LaWilliam	2012-14
Brown	Lathomas	2011-12	Carter	Ollon	1989-91
Brown	Lee	1986-88	Carter	Pete	1985-87
Brown	Nasir	2016-19	Carter	Taradous	2008-09
Brown	Robert	1923	Carter	Ted	1958-59
Brown	Stefan	2010-12	Carter	Tivonney	2023
Brown	Timmy	1982-84	Carter	Tyrickious	2010-11
Brown	Trip	2013-15	Carter	Tyrique	2014-17
Brown	Tripp	2017	Carter	Unknown	1945
Bryant	James	1970	Carter	Unknown	1940-41

Last	First	Years
Carter	Vincent	1983-85
Carter	Willie	2011-14
Carter	Zamonte	2023
Carter	Zan	2008-10
Castle	Clarence	1939-40
Castle	Lee	1960-62
Castle	Orville	1935-38
Castle	Pete	1941
Castle	Richard	1936-40
Castle	Travis	1932-36
Catledge	Denny	1957-59
Catledge	Ennis	1932-33
Chambers	Kedarius	2014-15
Chambers	Tim	1997
Chandler	Donnie	1970-71
Chaney	Jaylen	2013-14
Chapman	Denton	1936-39
Chapman	Hunter	1929
Chapman	Joe	1929-33
Chapman	Johnny	1961-63
Chapman	Marshall	1929-30
Chappel	Michael	1994-95
Charlton	Leslie	1961-63
Cheatham	Chris	1988-89
Cheatham	David	1989-91
Cheney	Lowell	1930-32
Cherry	Benny	1967-69
Childress	Alfonso	1987-89
Childress	Chad	1996
Childress	Keneen	1996
Childress	Lamarrius	2004-05
Childress	Willie	1989-90
Childs	Noah	2022-23
Chiles	Cecil	1959-60
Chiles	Freddie	1956-58
Chiles	Randy	1960-62
Christion	Jacari	2009
Christion	Jordan	2006-09
Cistrunk	Ashanti	2015-18
Cistrunk	Bryceston	2021-22
Cistrunk	Henry	1995
Cistrunk	Kelvin	1994-96
Cistrunk	Lemarcus	2008-10
Cistrunk	Letrail	1992-94
Cistrunk	Morris	1978
Cistrunk	Reginald	1996-98
Cistrunk	Roderick	1994
Cistrunk	Rodney	1985-87
Cistrunk	William	1988-90
Cistrunk	Zedrick	1987-88
Clark	Anthony	1957-59
Clark	Anthony	1985-87
Clark	Ben	2000-01
Clark	Bob	1938-42
Clark	Bobby	1944-47
Clark	Bobby	1950-51
Clark	Brandon	2009-11
Clark	Cedric	2001
Clark	Charles	1951-53
Clark	Danny	1970-72
Clark	George	1951-53
Clark	Greg	1974-76
Clark	Gus	1915-16
Clark	Horace	1923
Clark	Howard	1938-40
Clark	James	2009-10
Clark	Jeremy	2001-02
Clark	Jerry	1972
Clark	Joe	1955-57
Clark	Jordan	2004-05
Clark	Justin	1998
Clark	Michael	1978
Clark	Mike	1972-74
Clark	Oliver	1928-29
Clark	R.E. "Bob"	1920-21
Clark	Ralph	1957
Clark	Ray	1940
Clark	Renardo	2003-05
Clark	Robert	1978-79
Clark	Rod	2008-09
Clark	Trey	2008-09
Clark	Unknown	1925-27
Clark	Walter	1915-16
Clark	William	1957
Clark	Willie	1980-82
Clay	Leroy	1944-46
Clay	Willard	1936-37
Clemons	Mark	1994-97
Coats	Travis	1991-93
Coburn	Charles	1987-89
Coburn	Cortez	2001-03
Coburn	Jamaal	2004-06
Coburn	Jatory	2008-10
Coburn	Jeremy	2004-06
Coburn	Juan	2001
Coburn	Juan	2003
Coburn	Kaliyah	2019-20
Coburn	Montreal	1997
Cockrell	Joel	1969-71
Cockrell	Lamar	1943-46
Cockrell	Wayne	1967-69
Cockrell	Wendell	1974-75
Coggin	Doug	1944-48
Cole	Patrick	1992-94
Coleman	Adrian	2000
Coleman	Albert	1977
Coleman	Alven	2000-02
Coleman	Alvin	2000-02
Coleman	Arthur	1970
Coleman	Ayden	2022-23
Coleman	Billy	1970-71
Coleman	Bryan	1972
Coleman	Clint	2004-06
Coleman	Corxavier	2021-23
Coleman	Courtney	2001-03
Coleman	Daryl	1971-73
Coleman	David	1987-89
Coleman	Derrick	1990-92
Coleman	Donnie	1981-82
Coleman	Earl	1972
Coleman	Greg	1984-86
Coleman	Grover	1976-78
Coleman	Henry	1983-85
Coleman	Jacorey	2019-21
Coleman	James	1943-44
Coleman	Jeff	1983-85
Coleman	Jerome	1978-79
Coleman	Johnathan	2009-11

Coleman	Ken	2002-04	Curtis	Kenneth	2006-07
Coleman	Kendrick	1987-89	Dailey	Denarious	2011-2014
Coleman	Keon	2012-15	Dailey	Evan	2007
Coleman	Lamon	1972	Dailey	Keith	1988-90
Coleman	Mavis	1975	Dailey	Orien	2010
Coleman	Pat	2003-05	Dale	Jim	1946-47
Coleman	Preston	1973	Dalton	Tommy	1936-39
Coleman	Ryan	1996	Daly	Mike	1962-64
Coleman	Sammy	1975-76	Daniel	Lakevias	2014-17
Coleman	Telvin	1990	Daniels	Albert	1990
Collier	Kenny	1969	Daniels	Horace	1997-99
Collins	Joe	2006	Daniels	Lakendrick	1994
Colter	Cornelius	2002-04	Daniels	Leon	1978
Colter	Daniel	1988-90	Daniels	Shun	1990-91
Colter	Howard	1992	Davenport	James	1987
Colter	Willie	1971	Davenport	John	1981-82
Combest	Jareel	1998	Davenport	Joshua	1993-95
Conn	Russell	1980	Davenport	Tommy	1972-73
Cooper	Delwin	1990	Davis	Anthony	2009-11
Cooper	Jerry	1975	Davis	Artis	1959
Cooper	Jimmy	1962	Davis	Bobby	1986
Cooper	Kelwin	1989	Davis	Brandon	2002-03
Cooper	Ralph	1937-38	Davis	Buddy	1946-49
Cooper	Shelton	2003	Davis	Charles	1955-56
Cooper	Tyvoris	2017-20	Davis	Clyde	1978
Cooper	Willie	1970-71	Davis	Howard	1986
Corcoran	Noah	2010	Davis	James	1920-21
Cotton	Andy	1996-98	Davis	Jennings	2002
Cox	George "Jeep"	1951	Davis	Jerome	1982
Cox	James	1951	Davis	Jim	1970-72
Cox	Ralph	1948-49	Davis	Jimmy	1958-61
Craig	Unknown	1917	Davis	John	1947-50
Cravens	Drew	2002	Davis	Jordan	2013
Crawford	Dewitt	1951-52	Davis	Junior	1972-74
Crawford	John Albert	1948-49	Davis	Maurice	1979
Crick	Buddy	1974	Davis	Steve	1965-67
Crosby	Chris	1993-95	Davis	Tim	1973
Crosby	Corey	1998-00	Davis	Tyjavian	2022
Crosby	Jaylin	2023	Davis	Walter	1985
Cross	Dontea	2021-23	Davis	Wyatt	1944-45
Cross	Nazyrion	2021	Dawkins	Darnell	1999-01
Crowder	Damion	2011	Dawkins	Ken	1998-00
Crowder	David	1992-94	Dempsey	Doyle	1944
Crowell	Bobby	1963-65	Dempsey	Dwight	1982-84
Crowell	Charles	1948-50	Dempsey	Fred	1920-23
Crowell	Johnny	1957	Dempsey	Houston	1932
Crowson	Herald	1946-49	Dempsey	Jack	2009
Crowson	Jimmy	1956-59	Dempsey	Jack	1944-47
Crumpton	David	1964-66	Dempsey	Jimmy	1969
Crumpton	Prentiss	1943	Dempsey	John	1976-77
Culberson	Jamrion	2020-22	Dempsey	Josh	2009
Cunningham	Anthony	1977-79	Dempsey	Kendall	1943
Cunningham	Blake	2008-10	Dempsey	L.	1926-28
Cunningham	Doug	1960-62	Dempsey	Unknown	1941
Cunningham	Jakob	2015-17	Dempsey	Unknown	1916-17
Cunningham	Ladarrious	2022-23	Depriest	Charles	1988-90
Cunningham	Lamont	1929-33	Dickerson	Wayren	1967
Cunningham	Larry	1960-62	Dismuke	Rodrick	1990-92
Cunningham	Phil	1935-37	Dixon	Ezra	1976-78
Cunningham	Scotty	2015	Dixon	Kedarius	2015-18
Cunningham	Stanley	1968-70	Dixon	Lee	1997-98
Curran	Ty	1988-89	Donald	Bobby	1943-46
Curtis	Chris	2006	Donald	Jerry	1953-55
Curtis	Clay	1989-90	Donald	Kyle	2004-07

Surname	First	Years	Surname	First	Years
Donald	Mark	1976-78	Eichelberger	Daniel	2003-05
Doolittle	James	1930-31	Eichelberger	David	1975
Dora	Darius	2010-13	Eichelberger	Demario	2007
Dora	Derrion	2015-17	Eichelberger	Dennis	1981-82
Doss	Barry	2003	Eichelberger	Ernest	1971-73
Doss	Brandon	2000-02	Eichelberger	James	1975-77
Dotson	Brandon	2001-03	Eichelberger	Javonte	2014
Dotson	Derian	1997-98	Eichelberger	Jimison	2000
Dotson	Luke	2003	Eichelberger	Levon	1971-72
Dubard	Marvin	1944-46	Eichelberger	Lou	1972-74
Duchaine	David	1967	Eichelberger	Malik	2013-15
Duff	Michael	1979-81	Eichelberger	Mario	2004-05; 08
Dunlap	Chuck	1991-93	Eichelberger	Mere	1985-86
Dupree	Dorian	2021	Eichelberger	Percy	1970-71
Duran	Clayton	2008	Eichelberger	Renaldo	1994-96
Durant	Henry	1951	Eichelberger	Ronnie	1971-72
Earby	Swahili	2019-22	Eichelberger	Tharin	1985-87
Earby	William	1970-71	Eichelberger	Troy	1973-75
Earhart	Buddy	1944-45	Eiland	Adrian	1998-00
Earhart	Dudley	1935	Eiland	Chris	1982-84
Earhart	H.C.	1936-39	Eiland	Craig	1986-88
Earhart	Hilas	1915-20	Eiland	Deonte	2010
Earhart	J.	1933	Eiland	Edward	1978
Earhart	J.T.	1922-24	Eiland	Grover	1987-89
Earhart	Jim	1916-21	Eiland	Jamarcus	2017-20
Earhart	John	1946-47	Eiland	Janell	2007
Earhart	Lowery	1920	Eiland	Jeremy	1993-95
Easley	Chris	1975-77	Eiland	Ken	1978-79
Easterwood	Billy	1944-45	Eiland	Kentay	1999-01
Easterwood	Larry	1955-57	Eiland	Kristian	2022-23
Eaves	Chris	1997-99	Eiland	Lentrell	2000-02
Eaves	Donnie	1965-67	Eiland	Medford	2002
Eaves	Freddie	1964	Eiland	Semaj	2014
Eaves	Gary	1961	Eiland	Shawn	1988
Eaves	Jack	1986	Eiland	Shemar	2015-18
Eaves	James	1941	Eiland	Thomas	1980
Eaves	Junior	1939-40	Eldridge	David	1990
Eaves	Kris	2017	Elgin	Kirk	1973
Eaves	Randy	1964-66	Ellington	Luke	2014
Eaves	Ricky	1972-73	Ellis	Bruce	1948
Eaves	Ronald	1959-63	Ellis	Charles	1948
Eaves	Ronnie	1964-65	Ellis	Emmit	1996-98
Eaves	Stanley	1968-70	Ellis	Mike	1951-53
Eaves	Thomas	1961-62	Ellis	Mike	1979-81
Eaves	Vance	1968-70	Ellis	Tim	1971-73
Edmond	Cornelius	1987-88	Ellis	Unknown	1946
Edmond	Howard	1979-81	Eskridge	Bobby	1955
Edmond	James	1989-91	Espinos	Santos	2016
Edmond	Markevious	2010	Estes	Bernard	1992
Edwards	Berlyn	1951-53	Estes	Craig	1976-78
Edwards	Billy	1955	Estes	Gene	1951-52
Edwards	Chester	1968	Estes	Gilbert	1944
Edwards	Daniel	1976	Estes	Hal	1979-81
Edwards	Dewayne	1985-87	Estes	John	1982-83
Edwards	Fielding	1947	Etheridge	Tommy	1948-50
Edwards	James	Unknown	Etua	Daniel	1994
Edwards	Joe	1965-67	Eubanks	Adam	2009
Edwards	Johnny	1968	Evans	Reggie	2012-13
Edwards	Makiley	2021	Ewing	Ellis	1953
Edwards	Ricky	1996-98	Ewing	Wynn	2022-23
Edwards	Tristan	2022-23	Ezell	George	1995
Eichelberger	Arthur	1970	Fair	Claude	1923
Eichelberger	Brian	2007	Fair	Dave	1962-63
Eichelberger	Cliff	1974-75	Fair	F.	1925

Surname	First	Years
Fair	Gene	1960-62
Fair	George	1964-66
Fair	Henry	1937-38
Fair	J.	1925
Fair	J.	1933
Fair	John	1962-64
Fair	Propst	1950-51
Fair	Unknown	1926; 28
Fairley	Chase	2020-22
Fairley	Seth	2021-23
Fancher	Homer	1937-41
Fancher	Homer	1966-68
Fancher	Slade	1990
Farmer	Donquarius	2004-07
Faulkner	Bobby	1944-49
Faulkner	James	1941-43
Faulkner	John	1947
Feigler	Ben	1947-48
Files	Harold	1952-54
Files	Therrell	1959-60
Finch	Robert	1994
Finch	Robert	1997-99
Fish	Mike	1974-75
Flake	Carl	1977
Flake	Jimmy	1978-79
Flake	Tim	1977-78
Fleming	Jarred	2006-07
Fleming	Jordan	2007-10
Fleming	Lamarcus	2014-17
Fondren	Unknown	1939
Ford	Tajh	2008-10
Forster	Mike	1956-59
Fortenberry	Jack	1967
Foster	Brandon	2015-17
Foster	Eddie	1961-63
Foster	Hendrick	2006-07
Foster	James	1980
Foster	Larry	1970
Foster	Michael	2016-19
Foster	Stanley	2007-09
Fowler	Robert	1992-94
Fox	Dan	1944-45
Frazier	Dave	2000-01
Frazier	Demarcus	2012-15
Frazier	Frankie	1979-81
Frazier	Gene	1951
Frazier	James	1970
Frazier	Michael	1986-88
Frazier	Michael	2012-15
Frazier	Mike	1959-61
Frazier	Nick	2000
Frazier	Percy Mac	1950-51
Frazier	Pervis	2014-17
Frazier	Ralph	1955-57
Frazier	Stanley	2004-06
Frazier	Willie	1984
Fulcher	Bobby	1961-63
Fulcher	Chad	1980-81
Fulcher	Damon	1990-92
Fulcher	Jerry	1960-62
Fulcher	John	1947
Fulcher	Shorty	1946
Fulcher	Todd	1985-87
Fulgham	Larry	1960-61
Fuller	Jerry	1966-68
Fuller	Mike	1968
Fulton	Bernard	1959-62
Fulton	Billy	1948-51
Fulton	Bradley	2000-01
Fulton	Brandon	2004-05
Fulton	Buddy	1978-80
Fulton	Donald	1952-55
Fulton	Gary	1965-67
Fulton	Greg	1983-85
Fulton	J.P.	1923-26
Fulton	Lamont	1944
Fulton	Lenny	1963-65
Fulton	Paul	1944
Fulton	Roy	1969-71
Fulton	Sam	1943-47
Fulton	Taylor	1930
Fulton	Tony	1982-83
Fulton	Unknown	1928
Fulton	Unknown	1948
Fulton	Walter	1948-50
Furr	Carl	1930-31
Furr	Unknown	1933
Gamblin	Larry	1970
Garnett	Jonteavis	2015-18
Garrigues	Joe	1930-31
Garrigues	Robert	1961-63
Garrigues	Unknown	1915
Germaine	Miller	2000
Geter	Clay	2006-07
Gibson	Keyshawn	2016-17
Gibson	Ronald	1994-96
Giffin	Billy	1940
Giffin	Bobby	1939-40
Giffin	Jackie	1952-55
Giffin	Keith	1967-69
Giffin	Larry	1964
Giffin	Unknown	1941
Gill	Daylen	2014-17
Gill	Donnie	1997
Gill	Jaron	2012-14
Gill	Jeremy	2002-04
Gill	Justin	2004-07
Gill	Keandre	2018-20
Gill	Levon	1971
Gill	Ray	1990
Gill	Rico	1993
Gipson	James	1935-37
Gipson	Keshawn	2019
Given	Garvid	1970
Gladney	Charlie	1970
Gladney	Dexter	1979
Gladney	Dwayne	1995-96
Gladney	Steve	1971-73
Glass	Foster	1974-76
Glass	Fred	2004-06
Glass	Jermaine	2003
Glass	Larry	1971-72
Glass	Tracy	1977-79
Glenn	Anthony	1991-93
Glenn	Antrous	2015-18
Glenn	David	1981-83
Glenn	Derrick	1987-89
Glenn	Devante	2012-15

Last	First	Year	Last	First	Year
Glenn	Donnie	1971-73	Green	Lee	1987
Glenn	Horace	1999	Green	Tim	1985
Glenn	Horace	2000-01	Green	Unknown	1940
Glenn	Kevin	1998-00	Greer	Ahmad	2003
Glenn	Kwas	2012-15	Greer	Kevin	1986-88
Glenn	Marcus	2015-18	Greer	Lance	1956
Glenn	Tykevius	2016-17	Greer	Lou	1975-77
Glenn	Tyler	2022-23	Greer	Sean	1988-89
Glenn	Undra	1990-92	Gregory	Boyd	1944
Glenn	Willie	1987-89	Gregory	Eric	1992-93
Glick	Sammy	1923-24	Gregory	Johnny	1943-44
Gooden	Earl	2008-10	Gregory	Unknown	1941
Goodin	Britt	1989-91	Griffin	Jim	Unknown
Goodin	Cory	2008	Griffin	Robert	1979
Goodin	John	1970-72	Griffin	Tyler	2007-08
Goodin	Mike	1971-73	Grody	Tony	1987
Goodin	Robert	1966-68	Grubbs	Corey	2003
Gookin	Brady	2009	Gully	David	1979
Gordon	Prentiss	1962-64	Gully	Frank	1916-17
Goss	Antonio	2011	Gully	Mark	1974-76
Goss	Cornelius	1995-97	Gund	Anderson	2011-13
Goss	Desmond	2010-13	Gund	Anthony	2011-13
Goss	Eddie	1977-79	Haaga	Bert	1970
Goss	Ellis	1970	Haaga	Rayford	1964-66
Goss	Emmanuel	2006-08	Halbert	Deqarius	2016-18
Goss	Jeremias	2018	Halbert	Troy	2016-17
Goss	Jim	2010	Hale	Buddy	1946
Goss	Josiah	2016-18	Hale	Earl	1944-45
Goss	Jykevious	2020-23	Hall	Don	1956-58
Goss	Keith	1985-87	Hall	Frank	1944
Goss	Kelvin	1993-97	Hall	Jadell	2012
Goss	Marlon	1989-91	Hall	Kevin	2003
Goss	Michael	1996-98	Hall	Stuart	2003
Goss	Montricus	2008-10	Hamill	Britt	1974-75
Goss	Nazyrion	2022	Hamill	Unknown	1946
Goss	Quinton	1972-73	Hammock	Harvey	1970
Goss	Sacario	2017-19	Hammond	Ham	1944-45
Goss	Stanley	1973-75	Hammond	Harold	1946-47
Goss	TaCorey	2002-03	Hampton	Cameron	2022
Goss	Ventrice	1986	Hampton	Chris	2007
Goss	Vincent	1988	Hampton	Dayton	2020-22
Goss	Willie	1970-72	Hampton	Dewayne	1978-79
Grace	Jacory	2016-17	Hampton	Frankie	1970
Grady	Tony	1986-88	Hampton	Freddy	1972
Grady	Zack	1994-96	Hampton	Karlton	1994-95
Graham	Donnie	1976-78	Hampton	Ronnie	1970-72
Graham	Dwight	1979-81	Hamric	John	1935
Graham	Kenneth	1992	Hancock	Bobby	1962-63
Graham	Matthew	2004-06	Hancock	Brad	1975-76
Graham	Obie	1970	Hancock	James	1944-45
Graham	Raquel	2010-12	Hancock	Joe	1951-55
Graham	Stephavon	1989-91	Hanna	Willie	1975-76
Graham	Travseon	2017-19	Hannah	James	1977-79
Graham	Walter	1986-87	Hannah	Marcus	1984-85
Grant	Gary	1986-87	Hannah	Michael	1981
Grant	James	1979	Hannah	Reginald	1972-74
Gray	J.E.	1955-56	Hannah	Rex	1972-73
Gray	Johnathan	2004-06	Hannah	Robert	2000
Gray	Lamar	2008-10	Hannah	Willie	1977
Gray	W.D.	1953	Hannah	Willie	2009
Green	Elliot	1935-38	Harden	Jehmiah	2017-19
Green	Elmer	1936	Hardin	A.J.	2018-20
Green	Harry	1947	Hardin	Antonio	2004-05
Green	Ken	2016-17	Hardin	Calvin	1993-94

Hardin	Chris	1997	Hathorn	Carl	1970-71
Hardin	Cory	1987	Hathorn	Cornelius	1999-00
Hardin	Derrick	1992-93	Hathorn	Greg	2001-03
Hardin	Deterron	2007	Hathorn	Hoy	1929
Hardin	James	1997-98	Hathorn	Jimmy	1951-53
Hardin	Jaymeis	2016-17	Hathorn	Martin	1994-96
Hardin	Josh	2008	Hathorn	Michael	1994-95
Hardin	Mario	1998	Hathorn	Stanley	1951-54
Hardin	Medford	1984-85	Hathorn	T.	1972
Hardin	Medford	2004-07	Hathorn	Ty	2011-13
Hardin	Michael	2004-07	Hathorn	Unknown	1941
Hardin	Orlando	1991-93	Hathorne	Kentill	2008
Hardin	Pierre	1993	Hawthorn	Jeffery	1988
Hardin	Sedrick	1991	Hawthorne	Deonta	2008-10
Hardin	Steve	1976	Hawthorne	Jaquayvius	2018-19
Hardin	Terrance	2006-08	Hawthorne	Jy'Kevious	2017
Hardin	Tevarius	2008	Hawthorne	Thomas	1991
Hardin	Troy	1972-74	Hayes	Andre	1987-90
Hardin	Unknown	1939	Hayes	Bernard	1977
Hardin	Ventric	1992	Hayes	Gerald	2003
Hardy	Corey	2010-11	Hayes	Gerald	1981-83
Hardy	Joey	1979-81	Hayes	Jatavious	2020
Harey	Henry	1989	Haynes	Alvius	2016-18
Harlan	Jack	1928-30	Haynes	Andrew	2003-05
Harmon	Darren	1992	Haynes	Anthony	1977-78
Harrington	Cam'ron	2013-16	Haynes	Chad	2000
Harrington	Dasaveon	2019	Haynes	Darius	2011-12
Harrington	Demester	2011-14	Haynes	David	2016-19
Harrington	Ellis	2016-17	Haynes	Demarco	2020
Harrington	Jerrell	2009-11	Haynes	Deontrist	2001
Harrington	Juan	2001-03	Haynes	Dequarius	2014-17
Harrington	Kirk	1983-85	Haynes	Dyron	2004-06
Harrington	Ray	2000-01	Haynes	Emmanuel	2012; 15
Harrington	Reed	1989-91	Haynes	Grunado	2001-03
Harrington	Ronny	1972	Haynes	Jamar	2018
Harrington	Tim	1989-91	Haynes	JaQuay	2021-22
Harrington	Trakevious	2013-14	Haynes	Laterrious	2019-22
Harrington	Travis	1973-75	Haynes	Tommy	1973
Harrington	Triston	2020-22	Haynes	Tony	1987
Harrington	Xzarion	2022-23	Haynes	Trophimus	2003
Harris	Avonte	2011-13	Hemphill	Larry	1983
Harris	Brock	2012-15	Hemphill	Tim	1975-77
Harris	Clifton	1999-00	Henderson	Arnold	2004-07
Harris	Dan	1939-41	Henderson	Mark	1978-80
Harris	Danny	1967-69	Hendricks	Joe	1952-54
Harris	Deangelo	2010	Hendricks	Unknown	1930
Harris	Dee	2007	Hendrix	Boo	1970-72
Harris	Kylan	2011-14	Hendrix	Brandon	2006-08
Harris	Unknown	1933	Hendrix	Brian	1994
Harrison	Bobby	1962-65	Hendrix	Bubba	1969-71
Harrison	Clarence	Unknown	Hendrix	Lance	2004-06
Harrison	Leland	1944-48	Henley	Cornelius	1998
Harrison	Paul	1995	Henley	Eddie	1977-78
Harsh	Eddie	1998-00	Henley	Steve	1993-95
Hart	Phil	1966	Henton	Charles	1992-94
Hartness	Casey	1995	Herring	Robert	1957
Harvey	Henry	1988	Herrington	Billy	1950-52
Hatcher	Harlan	1952	Herrington	Charles	1938
Hatcher	John	1992-93	Herrington	Checky	1972-73
Hathorn	Avonte	2010	Herrington	Chester	1944-47
Hathorn	Billy	1965-67	Herrington	Clyde	1984
Hathorn	Bobby	1947	Herrington	Gerald	1949-50
Hathorn	Booker	1972-73	Herrington	James	1939-41
Hathorn	Brad	1989-90	Herrington	Jim	1938

Last	First	Years	Last	First	Years
Herrington	Max	1939-42	Holmes	Marcus	2004-07
Herrington	R.	1941-42	Holmes	Markeye	1987-89
Hervey	Henry	1987	Holmes	Patrick	1994
Hester	Farrell	1987-89	Holmes	Pervis	1990-91
Hibbler	Jaquanes	2014-15	Holmes	Quentin	1993
Hibbler	Jy'Kevious	2016-19	Holman	Hykeem	2021
Hibbler	Marcus	1998-00	Holmon	Gerald	1987
Hickman	Christopher	2021-23	Holton	Dale	1987
Hickman	Dakendrick	2011-14	Hooker	Neal	1955-57
Hickman	Darrious	2020-21	Hooker	Unknown	1925-26
Hickman	David	1994-95	Hooks	Billy	1978
Hickman	Deon	2004-06	Hopkins	Christian	2017
Hickman	Happy	1968-69	Hopkins	Derek	1993-95
Hickman	Henry	1994	Hopkins	Derius	2015-18
Hickman	James	1929-30	Hopkins	Jerahme	2001-03
Hickman	Kendrick	1991-92	Hopkins	John	1920
Hickman	Kenneth	1976-77	Hopkins	Karl	2003
Hickman	Lanorris	2019-21	Hopkins	Kendrick	1995
Hickman	Mohammed	1990-92	Hopkins	Kristian	2018-19
Hickman	Moreno	1987	Hopkins	Kylon	2017
Hickman	Tyler	2011-13	Hopkins	Martez	1999-01
Hickmon	Lemoriss	1972	Hopkins	Najah	2013-16
Higgason	Frank	1955	Hopkins	Taylor	2014-15
Hight	"Baby"	1915-16	Hopkins	Tommy	1978-80
Hight	Bill	1920-23	Hopkins	Unknown	1916
Hight	Larry	1954-55	Horn	Orville	1920
Hight	Malcolm	1922-24	Hornesburger	Randy	2006-08
Hill	Bennie	1968; 71	Horton	Clark	1938-39
Hill	Danny	1969	Horton	Homer Lee	1937-38
Hill	David	1969	Horton	Jimmy	1981-83
Hill	G.	1941	Hoskins	Alvin	1999
Hill	Gerald	1928-30	Hoskins	Deaundray	1990
Hill	Grady	1929-33	Hoskins	Deunte	2012
Hill	Graham	1935-39	Hoskins	Eric	1979-81
Hill	Guy	1929-31	Hoskins	Fred	1985
Hill	Jerry	1964-66	Hoskins	Jayllun	2021-23
Hill	Kenneth	2020-23	Hoskins	Kendrick	1994-96
Hill	Mabron	1954	Hoskins	Lashun	1986
Hill	Price Edward	1936	Hoskins	Leon	1974-76
Hill	Unknown	1942	Hoskins	Markevius	2003-05
Hill	W.	1941	Hoskins	Sammie	1992-94
Hill	Wayne	1959-61	Hoskins	Sharod	2019-21
Hilton	Robert	2004-07	Hoskins	Timothy	2020-23
Hindman	Terry	1967-69	Houston	Billy	1985
Hisaw	Ray	1971-73	Houston	Billy	2017-19
Holdiness	Ellis	1955-56	Houston	Jaylon	2015
Hollingshed	Michael	2000	Houston	Lakendrick	1996
Hollingsworth	Joe	1931	Houston	Mon	1997-98
Hollingsworth	Unknown	1927	Houston	Osler	1981
Hollingsworth	Woodrow	1935-36	Houston	Terrence	1998
Holman	Bruce	1943-45	Howard	Kentareas	2004-06
Holman	Gerald	1986	Howell	Jimmy	1984
Holman	Hykeem	2020-22	Huber	Horace	1921
Holmens	LaDarron	1991	Hudson	Brandon	2001
Holmes	Chris	2000-01	Hudson	Cedric	1989
Holmes	KeDarius	2014-15	Hudson	Dennis	1959-60
Holmes	Kendrick	1992	Hudson	Fred	1940-42
Holmes	Kendrick	2014-16	Hudson	Henry	1935-36
Holmes	Kenneth	2017	Hudson	Hilute	1996-98
Holmes	Kris	2004-06	Hudson	Jeffery	1987-88
Holmes	LaWilliam	1994	Hudson	Michael	2006
Holmes	LaWilliam	2016-17	Hudson	Mike	1968
Holmes	Marcus	1991-93	Hudson	Nathan	1939-40
Holmes	Marcus	1996-98	Hudson	Patrick	1994-96

Hudson	Ryan	1991	Hunt	Melvin	1986-87
Hudson	Travian	2010-13	Hunt	Michael	1991-92
Hudson	William	1929-31	Hunt	Miguel	1986-87
Hudspeth	Dalton	2010-13	Hunt	Richard	1976
Hudspeth	Elkin "Doc"	1951-55	Hunt	Rodney	1992
Hudspeth	Henry	1953-55	Hunt	Rodney	2021
Hudspeth	Jace	2018-21	Hunt	Steven	2004-07
Hudspeth	Pat	1944-47	Hunt	Steven	2011-13
Hudspeth	Randy	1972-74	Hunt	Terry	1974
Huey	Griff	1976	Hunt	Xavier	2021-23
Hughes	Aiden	2019	Hunter	Stephen	1990-92
Hughes	Amos	1981	Huntley	Will	2016-18
Hughes	Andrew	2010	Hurst	Unknown	1927-28
Hughes	Anthony	2001	Hurt	James	1937-38
Hughes	Caleb	2020-22	Idom	Elvis	1998-99
Hughes	Cameron	2018	Idom	Ryan	2007-09
Hughes	Channing	2011-13	Ingram	Darryl	2000
Hughes	Charlie	1979-80	Ingram	Jackie	1978-79
Hughes	Daralyd	1988-90	Ingram	Kelsey	2015-17
Hughes	David	2000	Ingram	Mike	1967-69
Hughes	Donovan	2018-19	Ingram	Rod	2001-03
Hughes	Dra	2007	Ingram	Unknown	1932
Hughes	Drew	2007	Ivy	Chris	2003-05
Hughes	Harold	1973-75	Ivy	Jaquavion	2019-21
Hughes	Ivy	1974-76	Ivy	Ray	1993-94
Hughes	Jerry	1980-82	Ivy	Stanley	1950
Hughes	Kendrick	1990-92	Jackson	Deniro	2020-23
Hughes	Lee	1987-89	Jackson	Dexter	1985-87
Hughes	Lee	2008-09	Jackson	Harvey	1970
Hughes	Terry	1987-88	Jackson	Jeff	1967-69
Hughes	Thad	1977-78	Jackson	Jeremiah	2023
Hughes	Troy	1979-80	Jackson	Kameron	2014
Hughes	Tyrone	1987-88	Jackson	Kevon	2015-18
Hughes	Unknown	1941	Jackson	Keyarrion	2019-22
Hughes	Xavier	1994	Jackson	Lee	2020
Hull	Archie Reed	1920	Jackson	Lee Earl	1986-88
Hull	Billy	1960-62	Jackson	Leo	1968
Hull	Joe	1920-22	Jackson	Marquavion	2022-23
Hull	John B.	1922-23	Jackson	Marquez	2007
Hull	O.V.	1943-44	Jackson	Montrell	2007
Hull	Robert	1935-37	Jackson	Nicholas	2020-21
Hull	Unknown	1916-19	Jackson	Nick	2019
Humphrey	Lavon	1985-87	Jackson	Oriental	2011-12
Humphries	Evan	2006	Jackson	Rod	2014
Humphries	James	1958-61	Jackson	Rodquan	2016-18
Humphries	Roy	1956-58	Jackson	Sylvester	1979
Hunt	Anfernee	2015	Jackson	Tilmorris	1999-01
Hunt	Antonio	2020	Jackson	Tyren	2010-2011
Hunt	Bobby	1974	Jackson	Vent	1997-99
Hunt	Bre'Carlous	2004-07	James	Emory	2020-21
Hunt	Carl	1979-80	Jay	Boots	1939
Hunt	Ceidrick	2020-23	Jefferson	Clyde	1975-77
Hunt	Chuck	1989-91	Jennings	Davis	2004
Hunt	Delantric	2006-08	Jernigan	Anthony	1982-83
Hunt	Dickie	2014-17	Jernigan	Cliff	1972-74
Hunt	Dickie Ray	1984	Jernigan	Darrel	1987
Hunt	Eddie	1992	Jernigan	David	1977-79
Hunt	James	1964-66	Jernigan	Gregory	2021-23
Hunt	Jay	2010	Jernigan	Ken	1996-98
Hunt	Jonathan	2008-09	Jernigan	Melvin	1985
Hunt	Jordan	2023	Jernigan	Norris	1972-74
Hunt	Laudrick	2000	Jernigan	Tim	1984-85
Hunt	Lavon	1959	Jernigan	Zaiden	2023
Hunt	Marques	2000-02	Jimmerson	Anthony	1994-96

Last	First	Years
Jimmerson	Gary	1987-89
Jimmerson	Stacy	1985-87
Johns	Prentiss	1936-37
Johnson	Aaryion	2018-21
Johnson	Bill	1941-42
Johnson	Byron	1993-95
Johnson	Cecil	1999
Johnson	Cedric	1989-91
Johnson	Delande	2004-07
Johnson	Elijah	2011
Johnson	Eric	1995-97
Johnson	Jamarkus	2020-21
Johnson	Javonte	2004-06
Johnson	Jimmerdith	1990-92
Johnson	Jimmy	1969
Johnson	Jimmy	1964-65
Johnson	Lamar	1985-87
Johnson	Mario	2023
Johnson	Montravious	2014-17
Johnson	Napoleon	1970-72
Johnson	Rankevious	2017-19
Johnson	Scotty	1991
Johnson	Shykese	2017-19
Johnson	Stacey	1977-78
Johnson	Terrance	1996-98
Johnson	Willie	2000
Jones	B.	1942
Jones	Camrin	2023
Jones	Dontae	2011-14
Jones	Dorris	1941-42
Jones	Hermie	1947-48
Jones	James	1947-49
Jones	James	1951-53
Jones	Jonathan	1998-99
Jordan	Bernard	1976-78
Jordan	Desmond	2008-10
Jordan	Dyquan	2010-13
Jordan	Herky	1953-54
Jordan	James	1970
Jordan	Jaylin	2020-23
Jordan	Keith	1979-81
Joseph	Cameron	2019
Justice	Billy Charles	1962-64
Justice	Jerry	1963-65
Keene	Rufus	1949
Kelly	Caleb	2006-07
Kelly	Clarence	1962-64
Kelly	Davis	1968-70
Kelly	Gideon	1991-93
Kelly	Louie	1936
Kelly	Marquez	2003
Kelly	Nathan	2006-07
Kelly	Rod	1996-98
Kelly	Rodney	1994-96
Kelly	Terry	1977
Kelly	Thomas	1976
Kemp	Billy	1982-83
Kemp	Jordan	2000-02
Kennedy	James	1953-55
Kennedy	John	1951-52
Kerr	Butch	1944-48
Key	Rudon	1937
Kilpatrick	Jay	1974
Kimbrough	Barry	1946-47
Kimbrough	George	1943-46
Kimbrough	Unknown	1928
Kinard	Don	1963-64
Kinard	Edgar	1953-56
Kinard	Unknown	1941
Kincaid	Darren	1982-83
Kincaid	Malcolm	2007-08
Kincaid	Tyler	2013-16
King	Charles	1944
King	Jamarion	2023
King	Jaylan	2019
King	R.E.	1930
King	Unknown	1925-28
Kippett	K.J.	2020
Kirk	Jeremiah	2018-21
Kirk	Niselbyion	2016-19
Kirkpatrick	Tommy	1951-52
Kirkpatrick	William	1922-24
Kirksey	Mario	1999-00
Kirkwood	Arlando	2010-12
Kitchens	Jerry	1956-58
Kitchens	Rod	1990-92
Knight	Jeff	1956-58
Knobloch	James	1967
Knowles	Kenneth	2014-17
Knowles	Melvin	2020
Knowles	Semaj	2020-23
Kugle	Charles	1950-52
Kuhn	Kenny	1970-71
Kupis	Charles	1959
Laine	Donnie	1988-89
Land	Eddie	1946
Land	Hal	1985-86
Land	Harold	1953-55
Land	Mike	1974-75
Landers	Patrick	1989-90
Landrum	Dale	1950
Landrum	Howard	1960-61
Lane	Donnie	1987
Langford	Davin	1995
Langley	Grady	1943-44
Latham	Isaiah	2013-16
LeBlanc	Joseph	2000-02
Ledbetter	Mantrell	2003
Ledbetter	Marquess	1998-00
Ledbetter	Mentrell	2002
Lee	Arthur	1981-83
Lee	Bernard	1977-79
Lee	Dallas	2021-23
Lee	Devon	2013-16
Lee	Dewey	1987-89
Lee	Drew	2010-13
Lee	Gilbert	1952
Lee	James Eddie	1961-63
Lee	Jayden	2022-23
Lee	Joshua	2019
Lee	Marcus	1995
Lee	R.B.	1936
Lee	T.	1941-42
Lee	Unknown	1933-34
Legan	Marshall	1922-24
Legan	Unknown	1927
Leonard	Randerous	2019-22
Leone	Brian	1980

Letteri	Joe	1970-72
Lewis	Bo	1990-92
Lewis	Dontravious	2023
Lewis	Matthews	2008
Lewis	Michael	1977-79
Liddell	Frank	2003-05
Liddell	Orlando	1994-95
Liddell	Unknown	1915-16
Lightsey	Freeman	1933
Livingston	Bob	1966-68
Livingston	Larry	1966-68
Livingston	Randall	1964-66
Livingston	Scott	1994-95
Lockett	Alvin	1978
Lockett	Kavedrick	1994
Logan	Brent	2009-11
Long	Billy Joe	1962-64
Long	Donnie	1995-97
Long	Robert	2021-23
Long	Wyatt	2022-23
Love	Cass	2010-12
Love	Desmund	2014-17
Love	Freddie	1990-92
Love	Julius	2011-14
Love	Ken	1997-99
Love	Marcus	2006-07
Love	Scottie	1982-84
Love	Timothy	2004-07
Love	William	2001
Love	Willie	1970-71
Love	Willie	1986-88
Loving	Derrick	1989-91
Loving	Felix	1994-96
Lovorn	Rio	1994
Lovorn	Timmy	1983
Lowery	Adam	1994-96
Lowery	Phil	1966-68
Lowery	Reginald	1987
Lowery	Tommy	1975
Loyd	Sherrill	1936
Luckett	Ladarius	2014-17
Luckett	Terrance	2016-18
Luke	David	1963-65
Luke	Justin	2013
Luke	Phillip	1981-83
Lynch	Garvin	1935-36
Lynch	Harry	1929-33
Lynch	Unknown	1934
Lyon	Jonathon	1990-91
Lyons	Bardra	1981-82
Macon	Andre	2003
Macon	Khalin	2022-23
Macon	Larry	1994
Macon	Lee	1979
Macon	Omauri	2018-20
Majure	Harold	1929-30
Majure	Niles	1930
Majure	Tommy	1968-70
Majure	Unknown	1933-34
Malone	Justin	2005
Mann	Kellon	2021-23
Marlowe	Jimmy	1964
Marshall	Baron	1935-38
Marshall	Earnest	1984-85

Marshall	Harbert	1952-55
Marshall	Howard	1978
Marshall	Justin	2009-11
Marshall	Stanley	1976-78
Marshall	Terry	2003
Marshall	Willie	1981-83
Martin	Warren	1929
Mason	Willis	1997-99
Massey	Charlie	1974-76
Massey	Drew	1998-00
Massey	Josh	2002
Matheson	Jacob	1989
Mathews	Masud	2006
Mattern	Wesley	2000
Matthews	Danny	1999
Matthews	John	1986-87
Matthews	Josh	2011
Matthews	Masud	2004-05
Matthews	Musa	1993-94
Matthews	Trebenn	2016-17
Mauldin	Joe	1931
May	Unknown	1926
Mayo	Cal	1980-81
Mayo	James	1950-51
Mays	D.Q.	2007
McAdory	John	2010-13
McAdory	Paul	1980-82
McAllily	Alton	1929-30
McAllily	Hoyle	1934-35
McAllily	Wendell	1936-37
McBrayer	Andy	1962-64
McBrayer	Ray	1972-73
McCarter	Antonio	2002-03
McCay	Doug	1981
McCool	David	1935-36
McCool	Eddie	1996-97
McCool	Edward	1929-33
McCool	Tom	1931-34
McCorvey	Quinton	1984
McCoy	Kyle	1986-88
McCullough	Corey	2012-15
McCullough	Joe	1935-39
McCully	Kentrell	2008-10
McCully	MacArthur	1980
McCully	Robert	1943-44
McDaniels	Jack	1971
McDonald	Henry	1974-75
McDonald	Michael	1991
McDonald	Michael	2014-16
McDonald	Travon	2021-23
McGahee	Unknown	1930
McGahey	Ronald	1980
McGahey	Unknown	1916
McGarr	Zach	2007-09
McGee	Demetrious	1992-94
McGee	Henry	1948-50
McGee	James	1947
McGee	Lawrence	1921-23
McGil	Cedric	1990
McGough	Bubba	1967
McGough	H.G.	1939
McGraw	Dickie	1956-59
McGraw	Henry	1932
McGraw	Max	1924-28

McGraw	Robin	1961-63	Miller	Denarius	2014-15
McInnis	Cecil	1929	Miller	Dijaylen	2020-23
McKay	Danny	1969	Miller	Elon	1973
McKay	David	1950	Miller	Glendrell	2006-08
McKay	Donald	1951	Miller	Grover	1971
McKay	Douglas	1979-80	Miller	Hilton	1979-81
McKay	Raymond	1951-52	Miller	Jakerrios	2019
McKee	Clyde	1920	Miller	Jakode	2010-11
McKenzie	Will	2001-05	Miller	Jamie	1994-95
McKinney	TayQuon	2022-23	Miller	Jay	2017
McMillan	Arnell	1924	Miller	Jermaine	1998-99
McMillan	Burrass	1922	Miller	Jimmy	1982-84
McMillan	Carlton	1946	Miller	Kerry	2000-01
McMillin	Albert	1929-32	Miller	Keyairo	2004-07
McMillin	Arnell	1923	Miller	LaMarkus	2001-02
McMillin	Billy	1939-40	Miller	Larium	2023
McMillin	Boyd	1920	Miller	Lavell	1974-75
McMillin	Burrass	1920-23	Miller	Les	1995
McMillin	Carlton	1944-47	Miller	Malcolm	1993
McMillin	G.	1916	Miller	Michael	1982-84
McMillin	Jimmy	1941-43	Miller	Monquize	2003
McMillin	Unknown	1928	Miller	Paul	1967-69
McMullin	Michael	1986	Miller	Randall	2013-15
McNeal	Frank	2007-08	Miller	Randy	1990-92
McNeel	Harry	1930-31	Miller	Rico	2007
McNeel	Niles	1962-64	Miller	Romeo	2004-06
McNeese	Jeremy	2007	Miller	Roy	1971-73
McNeill	Josh	1996	Miller	Sammy	1973-76
McNeill	Unknown	1927	Miller	Sedric	1988-89
McQuirter	Sherrill	1958-59	Miller	Shalawn	1992-94
McWhirter	Bobby	1957	Miller	Warren	1983-84
Melton	B.	1929-31	Miller	Willie	1995-97
Melton	Oma	1927-29	Miller	Zack	2015-17
Metts	Albert	1916-21	Milling	Unknown	1915-16
Metts	Bobby	1937-38	Mills	Clinton	1973-75
Metts	Chad	2010-12	Mills	Danny	1980-81
Metts	D.D.	1943	Mills	James	1934-35
Metts	James	1944	Mills	Pete	1968-70
Metts	Jimmy	1977-79	Mills	Unknown	1934
Metts	John	1945	Ming	Charles	1966-67
Metts	John	1928-30	Ming	Kyle	2003
Metts	Lorando	1985-87	Ming	Scott	2006-08
Metts	Mark	2002	Mitchell	Anthony	1992-94
Metts	Phillip	1952-54	Mitchell	Bob	1948-50
Metts	Vic	1920-21	Mitchell	Chris	1994
Middleton	Darren	1991-93	Mitchell	David	1980-81
Middleton	Tommy	1969	Mitchell	H.C.	1951-53
Miles	E.L.	1960-61	Mitchell	Harvey	1982-83
Miles	Elliot	1939	Mitchell	Jack	1953-55
Miles	Elvin	1949	Mitchell	John	1956-57
Miles	John	1983	Mitchell	Johnny	1963-65
Miller	Bo	1956	Mitchell	Malik	2013-14
Miller	Bo	1991-93	Mitchell	Marshall	1951-52
Miller	Bobby	1975	Mitchell	Otis	1993
Miller	Bret	1993	Mitchell	Ronnie	1969
Miller	Butch	1968-70	Mitchell	Stacy	1973
Miller	Carey	2003-05	Mitchell	Stanley	1979-81
Miller	Coby	1992-94	Mitchell	Thomas	1960
Miller	Cornell	1991-93	Mize	J.R.	1953
Miller	Cortez	1994-95	Mobley	Richard	1964
Miller	Cottrell	2007-09	Moffett	James	1979-81
Miller	D.J.	2020-21	Moody	Charles	1951-53
Miller	Darius	2010-13	Moody	Marvin	1917-20
Miller	Dee	2009	Moody	Paul	1953-55

Surname	First	Years	Surname	First	Years
Moore	Aaron	2022	Odom	Brent	2009
Moore	Albert	1951-52	Odom	Marcus	2009-11
Moore	Billy	1975	Oliver	Kaleil	2019
Moore	Billy	1994-96	Overstreet	Keon	2000
Moore	Bobby	1974-76	Overstreet	Letron	1994-97
Moore	Brandon	1999-01	Owen	Romier	2006
Moore	Charles	2013-15	Owens	Harry	1979
Moore	Charles	2016-18	Owens	Jacari	2021-23
Moore	Clayton	2005-08	Owens	Jimmy	1972-74
Moore	Gabriel	2019-22	Owens	Jimmy	2007-09
Moore	Henry	1995	Owens	Leroy	1972
Moore	James	1930	Owens	Romier	2007
Moore	Jason	1994	Owens	Tracy	1978-79
Moore	Jeffery	2004-08	Pace	Benny	1974-76
Moore	Justin	2004-06	Pace	John	1974-75
Moore	L.C.	2007-08	Pace	Lakeives	2019-21
Moore	Mark	1992	Pace	Leon	1970-71
Moore	Michael	1990	Palmer	Bobby	1960
Moore	Myron	1987-89	Palmer	Grady	1954-55
Moore	Patrick	1992-94	Palmer	Lawrence	1967-69
Moore	Paul	1943	Palmieri	Rocco	1963-65
Moore	Ray	1990	Parker	Barry	1970
Moorehead	Freddie	1956	Parker	Bob	1929-32
Moorehead	Paul	1948	Parker	Charles	1967
Morgan	Willie	1972-74	Parker	Fred	2006-08
Mosely	Kaleb	2018-19	Parker	Frederick	2018-20
Mosley	Scott	1980	Parker	Immarion	2023
Mosley	Victor	2016-17	Parker	Jack	1952-53
Mullan	Deshun	2008-09	Parker	Jerome	1952
Mullendore	Maurice	1930	Parker	P.	1933
Mullins	Corie	1993-94	Parker	Pat	1923-24
Mullins	Dale	1984-86	Parker	Thomas	2004-06
Mullins	David	1975-77	Parker	Unknown	1927
Mullins	Phillip	1995	Parker	Unknown	1916-17
Munoz	Brayam	2020	Parker	William	1936
Murray	Dennis	1975-76	Parkes	Bobby	1943-44
Murray	John	1980-82	Parkes	Roger	1920-23
Murray	Jordan	2011	Parkes	Woody	1928-29
Murray	Riley	1975-77	Parks	Donald	1963
Myres	John	1953-55	Parks	Mario	2003
Nabers	Fred	1966-68	Parks	Quentarus	2009-10
Nabers	Scott	2004-05	Parks	Unknown	1925
Narahama	Makoto	1994	Partridge	Joe	1951
Nash	Ray'Sean	2004-06	Pate	Russ	2003
Neal	Travon	1981-83	Paten	Andrew	1988-89
Newsom	Calvin	1915-16	Paten	Anthony	1996-98
Nicholson	Dylan	2010-13	Paten	Willie	1989-91
Nicholson	Justin	2014-17	Patie	Tacorey	1997-99
Nicholson	L.J.	2011-14	Patterson	Ronnie	1969-71
Nicholson	Moine	1991-93	Pattie	Richard	1978
Nolen	Unknown	1939	Patty	Bobby	1952
Norton	Dalantae	2015	Patty	Devonte	2010-11
Norton	De'Areirus	2019-22	Patty	G.	1933
Norton	Michael	1984	Patty	Laderian	2011-13
Norton	Montez	1994	Patty	Raymel	1990
Norton	Randall	2006	Patty	Selento	1994
Norton	Robert	1970	Patty	Tyrune	2002
Norton	Tramon	1994	Patty	Unknown	1915-16
Nowell	Jimmy	1984	Patty	Walter	1921-24
Nowell	Russ	1987-89	Payne	Cady	2011
Nunn	Jerrick	1999-01	Payton	Andrew	1987
Nunn	Joshua	2017-20	Pearson	Jack	1948-50
Nunn	Reggie	2004-06	Pearson	Paul	1974
Oakley	Sean	1984-86	Pearson	Roy	1970

Last	First	Years	Last	First	Years
Pease	Chad	2013-16	Rhodes	Harold	1952
Peavey	Anthony	1988-89	Rhodes	Jack	1952-53
Perry	Chris	2001-03	Rhodes	Tully	1970
Perry	Henry	1974-76	Rhodes	Wylie	2003
Peters	Ned	1928-33	Richardson	D.A.	1959-60
Peters	Unknown	1916	Richardson	Dick	1948-49
Peterson	Brad	1990-92	Richardson	Howard	1936-38
Peterson	Chris	1987-89	Richardson	Spiva	1922-24
Peterson	Mike	1960-62	Richardson	Spiva	1951-52
Peterson	Ricky	1961-63	Richardson	Unknown	1928
Peterson	Tyler	1994-96	Riddle	Bernard	1993
Phillips	Deanquis	2016	Riddle	Carlos	1997
Phillips	Glenn	1976-78	Riddle	Cedric	2003
Phillips	Jay	2017	Riddle	Rotunda	1993
Pickett	Eddie	1964-66	Riggins	Isaiah	2013
Pickett	Mike	1980-82	Rives	Bill	1955-56
Pickett	Randy	1970-71	Roach	Kentay	2018-20
Pierce	Jared	1991	Roach	Raymond	1996
Pippen	Elijah	1997-99	Rob	Chad	1987
Pippen	Scottie	1984-86	Robbins	Darrell	1992-94
Pledge	Zytavious	2022-23	Robbins	Jayshunn	2021-23
Plummer	Tyler	2012-15	Robbins	Johnny	1990-92
Poe	Malik	2012	Roberson	Bobby	1971-72
Porter	Gary	1983-85	Roberson	Felix	1982
Porter	Troy	1999-01	Roberson	Steven	1984-85
Porter	Willie	1981	Roberts	C.	1941-42
Porter	Willie	1989-91	Roberts	D.	1941-42
Prisock	Davis	1971	Roberts	Frank	1939-41
Prisock	Jess	1916-20	Roberts	Naderion	2014
Prisock	Randy	1976	Roberts	Roderick	2011-13
Prisock	Travis	1976-77	Roberts	Ronnie	1969-70
Prisock	Unknown	1925-29	Roberts	Roy	1943-46
Puckett	Jimmy	1976	Roberts	Unknown	1929
Puckett	Johnny	1964-66	Roberts	Wyatt	2010-13
Puckett	Steve	1967-68	Robertson	Jamario	2011-13
Pudas	Donald	1973	Robertson	John	1976-77
Pugh	Allen	1937	Robertson	Myron	1986-87
Quinton	Steve	1960-61	Robertson	Unknown	1941
Rajevski	Martin	1995	Robinson	Chris	1998
Rasberry	Billy	1963-65	Robinson	Jimmy	1943
Rash	Jerome	1970	Robinson	Mark	1981
Ray	Jerry	1965-67	Robinson	Terrance	1980
Ray	Joey	1977-78	Rocker	Unknown	1924
Ray	Johnny	1959-60	Rocket	William	2017
Ray	Marcus	1978-80	Rodgers	Justin	1992-94
Ray	Scottie	1985	Rodgers	Leroy	1972
Ray	Unknown	1940	Rodgers	Tate	2007
Reaves	B.	1933-34	Rodgers	Vandrew	1972
Reaves	W.	1934	Rodgers	Xavier	2006-08
Reed	Caleb	2002-04	Rogers	Bubba	1970
Reed	Gene	1968-70	Rogers	Corey	1999-00
Reed	Justin	1996-98	Rogers	Johnny	1965
Reed	Kellis	1961	Rogers	Marvin	1986
Reed	Kellis	1957-58	Rogers	Roland	1968
Reed	Quinton	1956	Rogers	Sonny	1964
Reed	Scott	1987-89	Rogers	Tate	2006-09
Reeves	Victor	1933	Rogers	Tyler	1998-00
Reich	Frank	Unknown	Romedy	Randy	1967-68
Reich	Jerry	1966	Romedy	Vic	1975-77
Reynolds	Louie	1920	Romedy	Wallace	1938-40
Reynolds	Sam	1941-42	Ross	Quincey	2009
Reynolds	Unknown	1915	Rothe	Neil	1960-61
Rhodes	Bill	2003	Rowe	Irvin	1977
Rhodes	Byron	1946-49	Rucker	William	1978

Rush	Christian	2019-20		Shields	Nicholas	2010-13
Rush	Dantavious	2020		Shields	Perry	1978-80
Rush	Eric	1992-93		Shields	Preston	1983-85
Rush	Jarvis	2019-21		Shotts	Ryan	2007
Rush	Lorenzo	2004-05		Shumaker	Bryandrea	2017
Rush	Phillip	2023		Shumaker	Drea	2016-19
Rush	Scott	1990		Shumaker	Shaquille	2011-13
Rush	Victor	2020-22		Shurden	Henry	1958-59
Russ	David	1973-75		Shurden	Larry	1959-60
Russell	Harris	1957		Simmons	Adolphus	1976-78
Ruth	Scott	1988-89		Simmons	Neil	1970-71
Ruthven	Beamon	1938		Simpson	Randy	1972-73
Ryals	Howard	1956-59		Simpson	Steve	1976
Ryals	Torris	1954-57		Sims	Andre	1999
Sanders	Camden	2017-20		Sims	Bruce	1997-99
Sanders	Corey	1997-99		Sims	Michael	2002-04
Sanders	Jamie	2007-09		Sims	Unknown	1941
Sanders	Kendon	2021-23		Sisson	Kirk	2011-14
Sanders	Korben	2022-23		Skeen	Cameron	2022-23
Sanders	Menyon	2015-18		Skinner	Jerry	1960
Sanders	Rory	1998-00		Slaughter	Malik	2010-13
Sangster	Jalon	2011-14		Slaughter	Marcus	2003
Sangster	Jaquavious	2012-14		Slaughter	Maurice	1991-93
Sangster	Jeremiah	1982-84		Sligh	Demarcus	2010
Sangster	Jeremy	2021		Smith	Anfernee	2015
Sangster	Jeremy	2010-13		Smith	Ansel	1953
Sangster	Lawrence	1989-91		Smith	Antonio	1985-87
Sangster	Paul	1990-92		Smith	Billy	1952-55
Sangster	Willie	1975		Smith	Bobby	1947-48
Sangster	Willie	1980-82		Smith	Brett	1996-98
Saterfield	Tommy	1967		Smith	Bruce	1987-89
Savior	Christavious	2019-22		Smith	Burris	1935
Savior	Deanquis	2018		Smith	Clifton	1996-97
Savior	Remario	2001-02		Smith	Courtney	1999-01
Scaggs	David	1985		Smith	Darius	2014-16
Schaffer	Dava'is	2009-11		Smith	Darwin	1952-53
Schwanebeck	David	2000-01		Smith	Dra	2015
Schwanebeck	Jason	1997-99		Smith	Drew	2003-07
Schwartwolder	Jimmy	1935		Smith	Eddie	1994-97
Scoggins	Rick	1985		Smith	George	1943-44
Scott	Morris	1991-93		Smith	James	1961-64
Sharp	Berlin	1920		Smith	Jeff	1977-78
Sharp	Jimmy	1954-56		Smith	Jeffery	1983-85
Sharp	Johnny	1954		Smith	Jeffery	2019-21
Sharp	Unknown	1929		Smith	John	1929-30
Shaw	Billy	1952-54		Smith	Johnny Frank	1955-58
Shaw	Bo	1948		Smith	Keith	1989-91
Shaw	Bruce	1964-66		Smith	Kenyon	1993-95
Shaw	Davis	1955-57		Smith	Larry	1967-68
Shearer	Tony	1978-79		Smith	Lavagus	1976-77
Shedd	Leon	2006		Smith	Mario	1995-97
Sheets	Tony	1991		Smith	Mike	1996-97
Shell	Eddie	1990-92		Smith	Mitch	1970-71
Shell	LaKendrick	2015		Smith	Neil	2004-06
Shelton	Jason	1989		Smith	Patrick	2015-17
Shields	Bobby	1980-82		Smith	Pete	1952-53
Shields	D.D.	1965		Smith	Randall	1994-95
Shields	Danny	1966-69		Smith	Rico	1996
Shields	DeAngelo	2014		Smith	Rodneal	2010-13
Shields	Donald	1964		Smith	Rodney	1987-88
Shields	Jeff	1977		Smith	Shawncey	1998-00
Shields	Johnny	1976-78		Smith	Taboris	2010-11
Shields	Johnny	1981-82		Smith	Tony	1986-88
Shields	Ken	1999-01		Smith	Tyrekas	2015-17

Smith	Walter	1994-96	Taylor	Jerry	1957-59
Smyth	Charles	1959-61	Taylor	Jerry	1960-62
Snow	Gabe	1998-01	Taylor	Joe	2001
Snow	Johnny	1968	Taylor	Laquarrious	2018-20
Stallings	Tyrone	2012-15	Taylor	Larry	1944
Stanford	Anthony	1994	Taylor	Lee	1972
Stanford	Anthony	1998-99	Taylor	Michael	1982-84
Stanford	Anthony	2000-02	Taylor	Rex	1974
Steel	Tyler	2013	Taylor	Troy	1951-52
Steele	Arthur	2000-01	Taylor	Tyquan	1992-94
Steele	Chris	1996	Terry	Ronnie	1969
Steele	Dakota	2020-23	Thames	Anthony	1984-86
Steele	Josiah	2020-21	Thames	Chauncey	2019-21
Stembridge	Jerry	1965	Thames	Cornelius	1993-95
Stevens	Harold	1966-68	Thames	Darzine	1994
Stewart	Brad	1984-85	Thames	Dennis	2004-08
Stewart	Dale	1965-67	Thames	Deon	2006
Stewart	Dustin	2004-07	Thames	E.W.	1998-00
Stewart	Ellis	1964-66	Thames	Frederick	1988-89
Stokes	Billy	1953-55	Thames	Jaquez	2016-19
Stokes	Bob	1956	Thames	Marcus	1994
Stokes	Bryce	1967-69	Thames	Monty	1995
Stokes	Doug	1973-75	Thames	Petey	1995-96
Stokes	Jeff	1976-78	Thames	Shontez	2018-21
Stokes	Jerry	1974-76	Thames	Tyrell	2017-20
Stoots	J.R.	1992	Thames	Tyrese	2015
Stoots	Roper	2019	Thames	Willie	1983-85
Stovall	Brandon	2002	Thomas	Bryant	1998-00
Strahan	Jerry	1960-61	Thomas	Emmanuel	2004-07
Strickland	Buddy	1958-59	Thomas	Errieyon	2022-23
Strickland	Henry	1989	Thomas	Greg	1979
Stringer	Gene	1972-74	Thomas	Henry	2016-17
Stringfellow	Jonathon	1990-91	Thomas	Roderick	1995-97
Stroud	Allen	1996-98	Thomas	Walter	1971-72
Stroud	Marques	1997	Thompkins	Caden	2020-23
Suber	Horace	1920	Thompkins	Terrell	1989
Suber	Whitley	1923	Thompson	Bertram	1961
Sudduth	Eric	2014-17	Thompson	Davelle	1970
Sullivan	Billy	1951-53	Thompson	David	1961-62
Sullivan	Bobby	1948-49	Thompson	James	1949
Sullivan	Dan	1979-81	Thompson	Jermaine	1997-99
Sullivan	Doug	1952-54	Thompson	Jerrell	1994-96
Sullivan	Eric	1990-92	Thompson	Justin	1996-98
Sullivan	Paul	1950-52	Thompson	Rhyne	1999-01
Sullivan	Unknown	1948	Thompson	Rhyne	2013
Sullivan	William	2015-17	Thompson	Ronnie	1970
Swanigan	Leonard	1985	Thompson	Tony	1994
Swanigan	Lester	1995	Thompson	Torrence	1998
Swanigan	Terrell	1985-87	Thompson	TyKeena	2001
Sylvester	Jackie	1961-62	Thompson	Woodard	1936
Tabor	Jeremy	1986	Tiller	Jerry	1976-77
Tabor	Tommy	1957-59	Tippett	K.J.	2019
Talbert	Franklin	1948-51	Tippett	Kylan	2019-21
Talbert	Kenneth	1952-55	Tisdale	Devoris	2010
Talley	Calvin	2016-17	Tomlinson	Pat	1958-59
Tanner	Danny	1985-87	Towne	Bobby	1970
Tate	Tyler	2023	Towne	Carter	1962
Tatum	Anthony	2006	Towne	Fred	1976
Taylor	Antavious	2012	Towne	Mike	1968
Taylor	Bill	1945-48	Towne	Steve	1964
Taylor	Ester	1947	Trest	Warren	1944-48
Taylor	Frankie	1974-75	Triplett	Antoine	2001-03
Taylor	Fred	1968-70	Triplett	Armon	2022-23
Taylor	Frederick	2019	Triplett	Arrion	1998-00

Triplett	Barry	1989	Turnipseed	Terry	1978
Triplett	Bobby Joe	1970	Underwood	Derrick	2004-06
Triplett	Buddy	1943	Underwood	Desmond	2010-11
Triplett	Butch	1969	Underwood	Eddie	1994
Triplett	Chaffin	2009-11	Underwood	Kenneth	1937
Triplett	Channing	2002	Vance	David	1969-70
Triplett	Charles	1978-79	Varner	Travis	1950
Triplett	Chris	1993	Vasquez	Jose	2016
Triplett	Christon	2016-17	Vaughan	Jarrad	1998-99
Triplett	Claretavious	2016-18	Vaughn	Cecil	1996
Triplett	Coronda	1981	Vaughn	Ced	1996
Triplett	Damon	2007-09	Vaughn	Jarrad	2000
Triplett	Darius	2015	Vaughn	Lakendrick	2011-13
Triplett	Dontavious	2019-20	Vaughn	Markevious	2015-17
Triplett	Douglas	1979-81	Vaughn	Zack	2014-15
Triplett	Edward	1972-74	Veazey	Bill	1960-61
Triplett	Eric	2022	Veazey	Jamie	1962-65
Triplett	Eric	1987-89	Vernon	Mac	1976
Triplett	Ernie	2004-07	Vick	Britian	2010
Triplett	Faser	1948-50	Vickers	Unknown	1941-42
Triplett	Gail	1988	Vowell	Jack	2009-11
Triplett	Gary	1987	Vowell	Zach	2003-06
Triplett	Gary	1981-83	Waldrip	Isaiah	2010-11
Triplett	Gerald	1988-89	Waldrip	J.J.	2011-13
Triplett	Howard	1944	Walker	Chris	1991
Triplett	Isaac	2000-02	Walker	Jacob	2021-23
Triplett	Jaden	2019-22	Walker	Jerry	1960-61
Triplett	James	1976-77	Walker	Jirah	2023
Triplett	Jeff	1976-78	Walker	Oriental	2011-14
Triplett	Joel	1963-65	Walker	Renard	1971
Triplett	Johnny	1984-86	Walker	Terry	1973-75
Triplett	Kamron	2021-23	Walker	Unknown	1925
Triplett	Keafer	1987-89	Wallace	Jason	1993-95
Triplett	Kemale	2015-17	Wallace	Unknown	1945
Triplett	Kendrick	1998-01	Ward	Charles	1951-54
Triplett	Kerell	2008	Ward	D.	1934
Triplett	Kirkland	2020-22	Ward	James	1951-52
Triplett	Kyjhana	2006-08	Ward	Jay	1960
Triplett	LaCodi	2003	Ward	Jesse	1934
Triplett	Larry	1982-84	Ward	Joe	1970
Triplett	Levi	1976-78	Ward	Richard	1961-63
Triplett	Markese	2007-09	Ward	Ricky	1968-69
Triplett	Martez	1991-93	Ward	Roger	1930-34
Triplett	Orlando	1972-73	Ward	Roy	1928-31
Triplett	Ricky	1978-80	Ward	Unknown	1936
Triplett	Roland	1979	Warmack	Billy	1985
Triplett	Sam	1984-86	Warner	Billy	1944
Triplett	Stacy	1964-66	Warner	Jack	1941-44
Triplett	Telayevian	2017-18	Warner	Jim	1941
Triplett	Tony	1975-77	Warner	Robert	1967-69
Triplett	Tony	2007-09	Warren	Jerome	1981-82
Triplett	William	1978-80	Washington	Kevin	2008-10
Triplett	Willie	1972	Watson	Billy	1953-58
Triplett	Willie	1996	Watson	Darrion	2019-20
Trosper	John	1966-67	Watson	Devin	2014
Tucker	Hugh	1939	Watson	Glenn	1951-53
Tucker	Jeffery	2001	Watson	James	1924-25
Tucker	Taylor	1968	Watson	Pat	1929-30
Tucker	Unknown	1947	Watson	Unknown	1948
Turner	Cecil	1920	Watt	Terrance	1984-86
Turner	James	1926	Watt	William	1981-83
Turner	Kevulon	2023	Webb	Billy Joe	1979
Turner	Lenny	1981-82	Webb	Dwight	1944-46
Turner	Mitchell	2023	Webb	Harold	1948

Last	First	Years	Last	First	Years
Webb	Jay	1941	Willis	Markie	2000-02
Webb	Larry	1951-53	Willis	Sianquis	2009
Webb	Unknown	1933	Willis	Travis	1991-93
Webb	Unknown	1940	Wilson	Billy Ray	1964-65
Webb	Unknown	1933-34	Wilson	David	1932
Webb	Walter	1964-66	Wilson	David	1956-59
Webster	Ben	2001	Wilson	Donnie	1970-71
Webster	Gene	1944	Wilson	Irie	1923-25
Weems	Peyton	1991-93	Wilson	Junior	1970
Weil	Terry	1974	Wilson	Lamond	1988-90
Welch	Charles	1975-77	Wilson	Lashun	1984-85
Welch	James	1975-76	Wilson	Mike	1971-72
Welch	Jeffery	2012	Wilson	Travis	1921-22
Welch	Kris	2004-06	Wilson	Unknown	1926
Welch	Tavaris	2001-03	Wilson	Unknown	1915-17
Welch	Tim	1975-76	Wilson	Walker	1927-28
Wells	Dewitt	1939-40	Wood	Charles	1936
Wells	Floyd	1938-39	Wood	Charles	1998
Wells	Isaac	1936-37	Wood	David	1923-26
West	Al	Unknown	Wood	Harris	1953
West	Joe	1970	Wood	Henry	1935-37
West	Solon	1976	Wood	James	1945
Whatley	James	1937-39	Wood	Kenneth	1921-23
Whatley	Richard	1938	Wood	Paul	1955-56
White	Denny	1956-57	Wood	Robert	1923
White	Ernest	1960	Wood	Unknown	1928
White	Freddie	1958-61	Wood	Unknown	1941
White	Jack	1965-67	Woodard	Antonio	2007-08
White	Jay	2014-15	Woodard	Xavier	2009
White	Jerry	1959-60	Woodruff	Chris	1968
White	Joe	1952	Woodruff	David	1944
White	Justin	2013	Woodruff	Paul	1956-59
White	Mark	1980	Woodruff	Richard	1953
White	Shawn	1985-87	Woodruff	Unknown	1941
White	Steve	1962-64	Woods	Andy	1966-67
White	Terry	1949-50	Woods	C.	1942
White	Tucker	1956-57	Woods	H.	1926
Whitehead	Albert	1967-68	Woods	Isiah	2012
Whitehead	Eric	1994-96	Woods	Jemarcus	2010-13
Whitehead	Gary	1970	Woods	Ross	1943
Whitehead	Kenneth	1972-75	Woods	Roy	1979
Whites	Jack	1948-50	Woodward	Antoine	1999
Whitfield	Charles	1987	Woodward	Antonio	2007
Whitfield	Dan	1981	Woodward	Bobby	1929-30
Whitfield	Jakevious	2014-17	Woodward	Danny	1967-68
Whitfield	Kenneth	2003-05	Woodward	David	1946-48
Whitfield	Kenny	1976	Woodward	Davis	1984
Whitfield	Lawrence	1989	Woodward	Don	1960-61
Whitfield	Trukevious	2014	Woodward	Hank	1934-35
Whitmire	Eddie	1989	Woodward	Harry	1917-20
Whitmire	Steve	1969	Woodward	Jimmie	1935-36
Whitt	Butch	1963-64	Woodward	John	1978-80
Wicker	Charlie	Unknown	Woodward	John	1981-84
Wicker	Henry	Unknown	Woodward	Johnny	1956-58
Wicks	Brittian	2012	Woodward	Marcus	1993-95
Wicks	Vincent	2008-09	Woodward	Odie	1931-33; 36
Wilkes	Elijah	2016-18	Woodward	Richard	1974-76
Wilkes	Elijan	2015	Woodward	Roland	1951-52
Williamson	Lamar	1956-59	Wooley	Jackie	1986
Williamson	Unknown	1923	Wooten	Cedric	1984-86
Williamson	Wendell	1963-65	Worthy	Ralph	1970-71
Willis	Ben	1983-85	Wraggs	Charles	2004-06
Willis	Deangelo	2009	Wraggs	Chris	2007-09
Willis	Gary	1974	Wraggs	Christian	2012

Wraggs	Gregory	1981	Yarbrough	Jimmy	1956-58
Wraggs	Javonte	2023	Yarbrough	Joe	1970
Wraggs	Jeffery	1994-96	Yarbrough	Ken	1996
Wraggs	Johnny	1992-94	Yarbrough	Kenneth	1974-75
Wraggs	Kaken	1994	Yarbrough	Leron	2000-01
Wraggs	Lagarious	2023	Yarbrough	Moe	1960-62
Wraggs	Ricco	1995-97	Yarbrough	Steven	1985-87
Wraggs	Rodney	1992-94	Yarbrough	Stuart	1955-57
Wraggs	Tynarius	2022-23	Yarbrough	Terrance	1995-97
Wright	Charles	1969-70	Yarbrough	Tim	1996-98
Wright	Danny	1955-57	Yarbrough	Timothy	2016-2017
Wright	Jason	1987	Yarbrough	Tommy	1978-79
Wright	Lannie	1960	Yarbrough	Tyrone	1987-89
Wright	Thad	1968-70	Yarbrough	Unknown	1925; 28
Wylie	Doug	1974	Yarbrough	Vidashunn	2018-20
Wylie	Dwight	1963-64	Yates	Anthony	1994-95
Wylie	Lee	1991-93	Yates	Eric	1987
Wylie	Richard	1992	Yates	Tony	1979-81
Yarbrough	Bobby	1951-53	Young	Andre	1990
Yarbrough	Curtis	1973-75	Young	Edwin	1956-58
Yarbrough	Danny	1962	Young	Mark	1997
Yarbrough	Demon	2002	Young	Rion	2004-06
Yarbrough	Deonte	2015-18	Young	Terry	1985-86
Yarbrough	Deshun	2001-03	Young	Tony	1976
Yarbrough	Edward	1981-82	Young	Victor	1970
Yarbrough	Gene	1941	Younger	Mike	1968-70
Yarbrough	George	2003	Younger	Paul	1945-46
Yarbrough	Jakeveion	2019-21	Younger	Steve	1972-74

Made in the USA
Columbia, SC
14 December 2024

49225943R00215